Praise for *Abigail Adams*

"A captivating portrait of a reformer both inside and outside the home. . . . Tracing Adams's life from her childhood as the daughter of a poor parson to her long and sometimes uncertain courtship with John, her joys and sorrows as a mother and her life as the wife of a president, Holton's superb biography shows us a three-dimensional Adams as a forward-thinking woman with a mind of her own."

—*Publishers Weekly*, starred review

"Splendid. . . . What gives Holton's work fresh significance is that his perceptive scouring of the Adams Papers leads him to explore an aspect of Abigail's life that other biographers either have overlooked or chosen to ignore. . . . Every page is packed with detail about Abigail's career. Her story is all here. . . . A notable success and very much worth reading."

—*Boston Globe*

"A comprehensive yet highly readable account of Abigail's life. Unlike many previous biographies, Holton's depicts Abigail not as a forerunner of modern feminism but as an eighteenth-century woman making the best of a difficult situation. . . . In the best sections of the book, Holton provides a portrait of Abigail as something of an economic opportunist—in the best sense of the term. . . . Abigail used the proceeds not to underwrite a lavish lifestyle but to guarantee her family's economic future. . . . Holton suggests that Abigail's economic self-assertiveness represented far more than a pragmatic response to her financial situation. Her actions were part and parcel of her longstanding resistance to women's subjugated status, a 'tangible protest' against women's economic and political disenfranchisement. . . . In Holton's hands, Abigail Adams . . . emerges as a figure who, long before the 20th century, figured out the connection between economic power and legal rights."

—*The Washington Post*

"Holton's biography stands out for its treatment of Abigail's entrepreneurship, and if earlier biographers have discussed her proto-feminist opinions, he is often more thorough and nuanced than they were. His skillful use of primary sources, including Adams family correspondence, affords a fuller understanding of events in Abigail Adams's life than we have had. Holton's biography is required reading for anyone interested in the Adams family."

—*The Wilson Quarterly*

"[F]resh, entertaining, and exhaustive take on the life of one of the most independent and influential American women of her time. . . . Holton's considerable biographical talents shine through: Adams and members of her circle emerge as rounded characters, and Holton is an admirable guide to their intellectual and political concerns. . . . He gives his readers an unforgettable portrait of an American original."

—*Foreign Affairs*

"Richly detailed biography of Abigail Adams, sprightly with quotes from letters and chockfull of legendary names. . . . Compelling biography. . . . The "saucy" lady gets a generous treatment in this entertaining gambol through the founding era."

—*Kirkus Reviews*

"This eminently readable portrait. . . . portrays Adams as a model (for her time and place) feminist. . . . Although many writers have unrealistically idealized the Adamses' marriage, Holton paints a more balanced portrait of their relationship."

—*Booklist*

"Mr. Holton is to be congratulated in having produced an unforgettable picture of an unforgettable icon of our early history."

—*Telegram & Gazette*

"Biographies of Abigail Adams abound. Woody Holton has produced one as good as any and perhaps better than many."

—*Providence Journal*

"[B]egins irresistibly. . . . With so many accounts sentimentalizing the Adamses' marriage, Holton provides a refreshing and grittier account of the considerable tensions between this couple."

—Minneapolis *Star Tribune*

"This is not your father's Abigail Adams. Woody Holton has given us the gift of the most fully rounded picture of this most famous of Founding Mothers to date. Entrepreneur, politician, mother, wife—Abigail Adams emerges from Holton's burnished prose as the compelling, complicated person she was. The discoveries he has made, and the insights they have inspired, will shape how we think of revolutionary men and women and partnerships both political and personal."

—Catherine Allgor, Professor of History,
University of California Presidential Chair

"Insightful, sensitive, and original, Woody Holton's *Abigail Adams* presents the whole of this remarkable, slave-owning, financially savvy woman who lived, not just wrote, her constant concern for the rights of women. Here is a bounty of fine-grained social history as well as a feast of language, from the eye and the voice of a historian-poet."

—Nell Irvin Painter, Edwards Professor of
American History, Emerita, Princeton University
and author of *The History of White People*

"If you were intrigued by the glimpse of Abigail Adams in recent biographies and the HBO series about her husband, you will be fascinated by this new biography. Adams brought her quest for equality into the household, breaking barriers to a woman owning and managing property. Holton unfolds this virtually unknown story in fast-paced chapters that reach a climax in Adams's remarkable will. Jane Austen would have understood her contemporary across the sea. So will today's readers who appreciate that the personal is political."

—Alfred Young, author of *Masquerade: The Life and Times of Deborah Sampson, Continental Soldier*

"This is the Adams who deserves a mini-series! A woman who slides right into Twenty-first-Century sense and sensibilities. Abigail Adams is an American hero and Holton brings all the riches of her letters and legacy into literary technicolor."

—Ann Compton, White House Correspondent, ABC News

"A thorough and thoughtful portrait of a woman who deserves our attention as a heroine of both the American Revolution and the feminist one."

—Ira Stoll, author of *Samuel Adams: A Life*

"We always knew that Abigail Adams was feisty, but not until now did we realize how effective her feistiness was. She was a fair match for her husband—no prisoner of precedent himself—and a redoubtable foe of law and traditions that worked to keep women in their accustomed place. Woody Holton has written a book as lively as its subject, and one that will compel a reconsideration of this rambunctious icon of American history."

—H. W. Brands, author of *Traitor to His Class: The Privileged Life and Radical Presidency of Franklin Delano Roosevelt* and *The First American: The Life and Times of Benjamin Franklin f* **P**

Smith Family

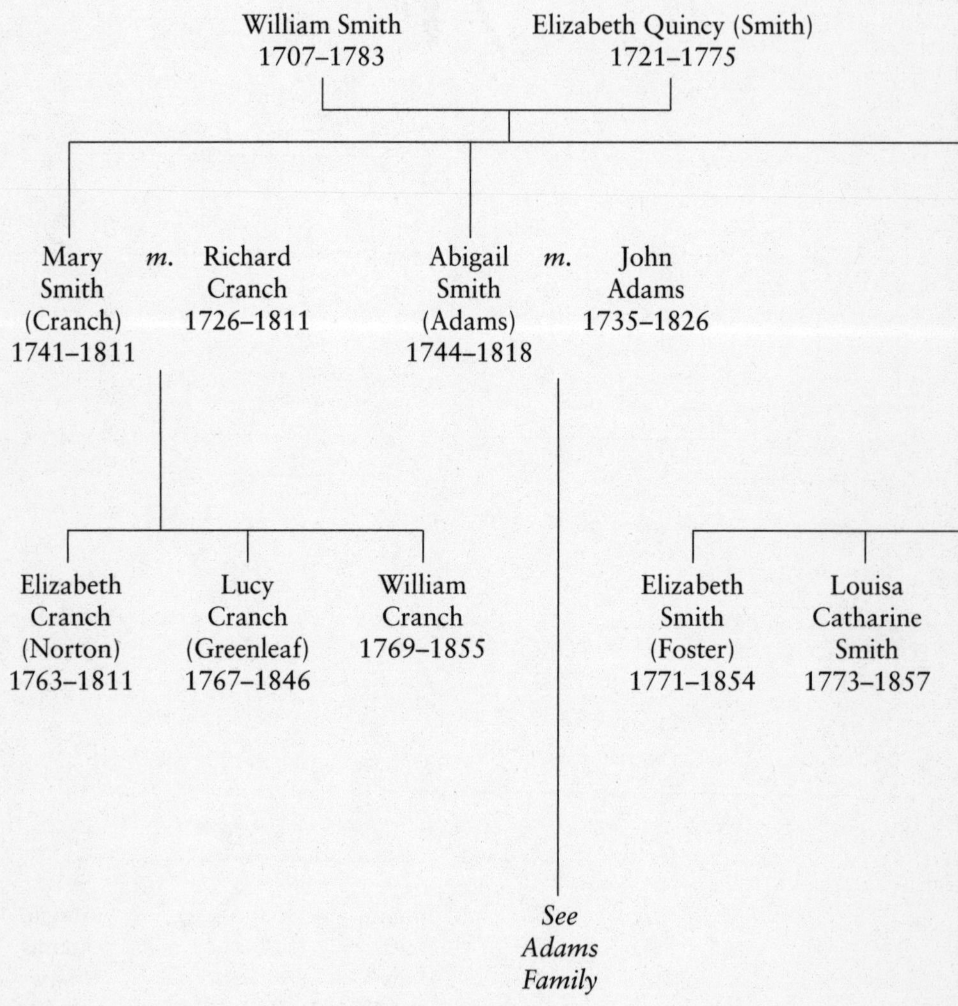

William Smith
1707–1783
Elizabeth Quincy (Smith)
1721–1775
Mary
Smith
(Cranch)
1741–1811
m.
Richard
Cranch
1726–1811
Abigail
Smith
(Adams)
1744–1818
m.
John
Adams
1735–1826
Elizabeth
Cranch
(Norton)
1763–1811
Lucy
Cranch
(Greenleaf)
1767–1846
William
Cranch
1769–1855
See
Adams
Family
Elizabeth
Smith
(Foster)
1771–1854
Louisa
Catharine
Smith
1773–1857

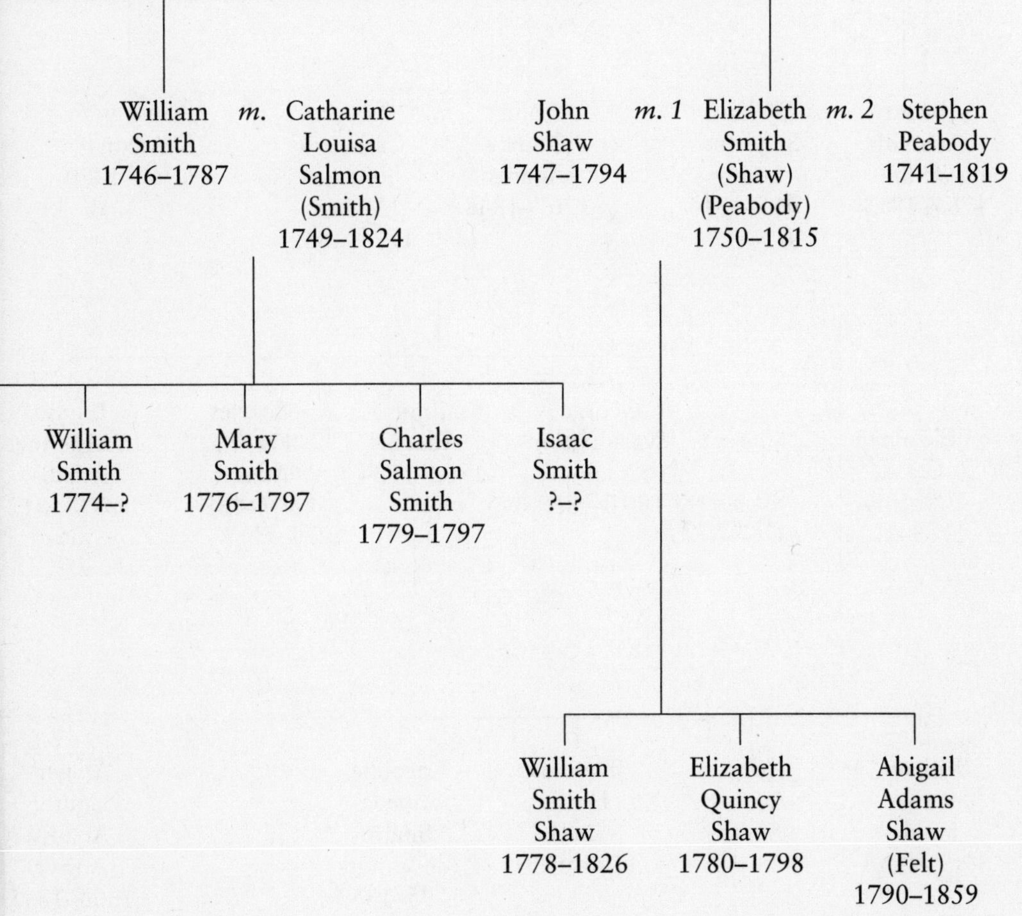

William Smith 1746–1787
m.
Catharine Louisa Salmon (Smith) 1749–1824
John Shaw 1747–1794
m. 1
Elizabeth Smith (Shaw) (Peabody) 1750–1815
m. 2
Stephen Peabody 1741–1819
William Smith 1774–?
Mary Smith 1776–1797
Charles Salmon Smith 1779–1797
Isaac Smith ?–?
William Smith Shaw 1778–1826
Elizabeth Quincy Shaw 1780–1798
Abigail Adams Shaw (Felt) 1790–1859

Adams Family

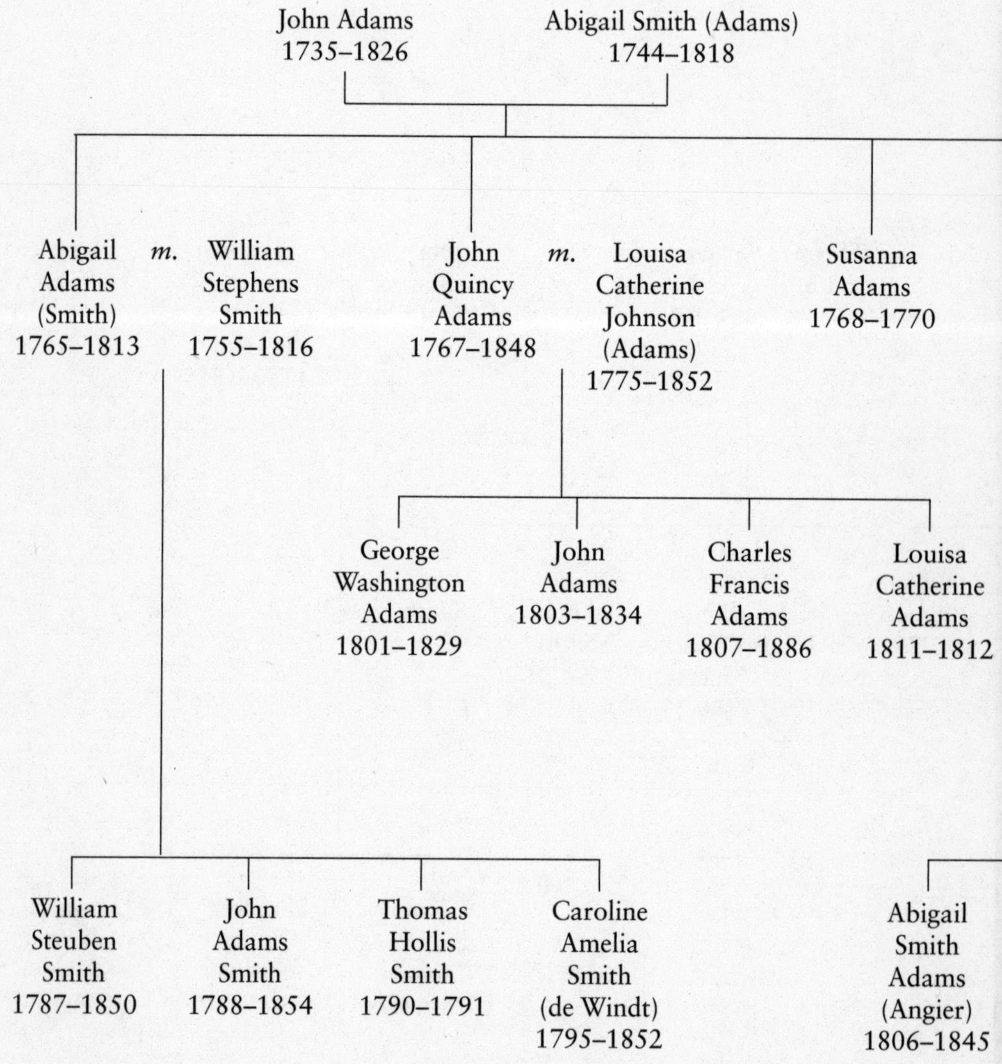
John Adams
1735–1826
Abigail Smith (Adams)
1744–1818
Abigail Adams (Smith) 1765–1813
m.
William Stephens Smith 1755–1816
John Quincy Adams 1767–1848
m.
Louisa Catherine Johnson (Adams) 1775–1852
Susanna Adams 1768–1770
George Washington Adams 1801–1829
John Adams 1803–1834
Charles Francis Adams 1807–1886
Louisa Catherine Adams 1811–1812
William Steuben Smith 1787–1850
John Adams Smith 1788–1854
Thomas Hollis Smith 1790–1791
Caroline Amelia Smith (de Windt) 1795–1852
Abigail Smith Adams (Angier) 1806–1845

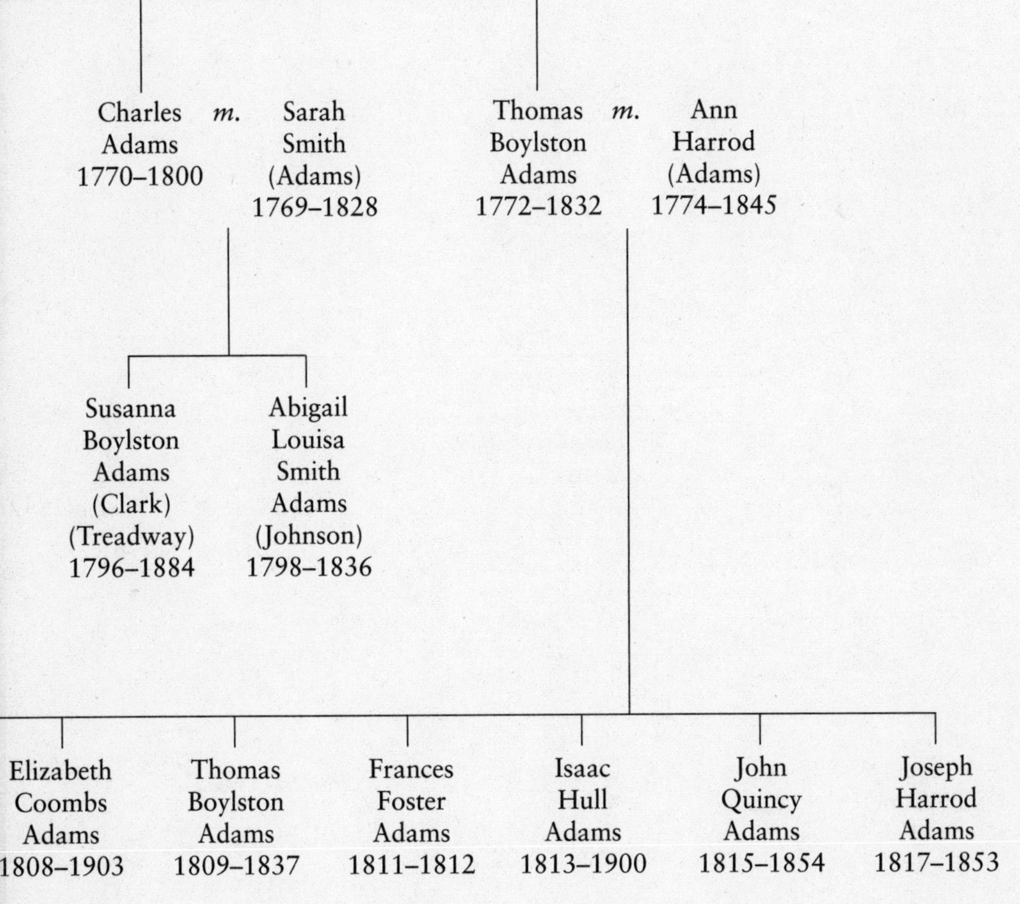
Charles Adams 1770–1800
m.
Sarah Smith (Adams) 1769–1828
Thomas Boylston Adams 1772–1832
m.
Ann Harrod (Adams) 1774–1845
Susanna Boylston Adams (Clark) (Treadway) 1796–1884
Abigail Louisa Smith Adams (Johnson) 1798–1836
Elizabeth Coombs Adams 1808–1903
Thomas Boylston Adams 1809–1837
Frances Foster Adams 1811–1812
Isaac Hull Adams 1813–1900
John Quincy Adams 1815–1854
Joseph Harrod Adams 1817–1853

ABIGAIL ADAMS

WOODY HOLTON

FREE PRESS

New York London Toronto Sydney

FREE PRESS
A Division of Simon & Schuster, Inc.
1230 Avenue of the Americas
New York, NY 10020

First Free Press trade paperback edition June 2010

For information about special discounts for bulk purchases, please contact Simon & Schuster Special Sales at 1-866-506-1949 or business@simonandschuster.com

The Simon & Schuster Speakers Bureau can bring authors to your live event. For more information or to book an event contact the Simon & Schuster Speakers Bureau at 1-866-248-3049 or visit our website at www.simonspeakers.com.

Manufactured in the United States of America

3 5 7 9 10 8 6 4 2

Library of Congress Cataloging-in-Publication Data

Holton, Woody.
Abigail Adams / Woody Holton.
p. cm.
Includes bibliographical references and index.
1. Adams, Abigail, 1744–1818. 2. Presidents' spouses—United States—Biography. 3. Adams, John, 1735–1826. I. Title.
E322.1.A38H65 2009
973.4'4'092—dc22
[B]
2009016288

ISBN 978-1-4165-4680-1
ISBN 978-1-4165-4681-8 (pbk)

For Beverly

CONTENTS

INTRODUCTION

On an unusually warm morning in the middle of January 1816, seventy-one-year-old Abigail Adams, wracked with pain and convinced she was dying, sat down to write her will. For Adams, scratching out this four-page document was, for one simple reason, an act of rebellion. The reason was that Adams's husband John, the former president, was still alive. Throughout Abigail's lifetime (which, despite her apprehensions that January morning, would continue into the fall of 1818), every wife in America was a *feme covert*—a covered woman. "The husband and wife are one person in law," the English legal theorist William Blackstone had explained back in 1765; "that is, the very being or legal existence of the woman is suspended during the marriage." The most tangible manifestation of this legal "coverture" was, as Adams complained to her husband in 1782, that married women's property was "subject to the controul and disposal of our partners, to whom the Laws have given a soverign Authority." Husbands assumed complete authority over their wives' real estate (land and buildings). And if a married woman brought to her marriage, or later acquired, personal property (which consisted of everything except real estate, be it cash or cattle), it, along with the income generated by her real estate, went to her husband, to dispose of as he pleased. Thousands of spinsters and widows left wills giving away their belongings, but married women were not permitted to distribute their real estate—it was divided equally among their children—and there was no reason for them to express their wishes regarding their personal property, for they had none to give.

Adams nonetheless decided to write a will. She began it by itemizing certain gifts she had previously made to her sons, explaining that she mentioned these so "that injustice may not be supposed to be done" to them. But the bulk of her will took care of her female relatives. They received gowns, watches, and rings—and also securities and cash. Adams's

Quincy Jany 18th 1816

I Abigail Adams wife to the Honble John Adams of Quincy
in the County of Norfolk, by and with his consent, do dispose
of the following property. First that injustice may not be supposed to be done to my sons. I have conveyd to John Q Adams by deed
all my right and title in the Farm given me by my uncle
Norton Quincy, valued at two thousand 2 hundred Dollars and to my
Son Thomas Boylstone Adams, all my part, being one half
of the Medford Farm given me by my honourd Father
William Smith of Weymouth which I consider of equal value
with what I have given to his brother -

Having in the hands of James H Foster
as trustee to me Bank Stock to the amount of four thousand
dollars, perhaps more as it was estimated by my late Trustee
the Honble Cotton Tufts Esqr lately deceasd. whether more or
less I direct that it be disposed of and divided as follows
1st my will is that my Granddaughter Caroline Amelia De
Wint, shall have seven hundred and fifty dollars exclusive
of a note of one hundred which I gave her at her marriage
and of my clothing a white sattin gown and coat trimd
with black velvet.

2dly I give to my Neice Louisa Catharine Smith a note
of hand given me by my son John Quincy Adams, part of
which has been paid. the remainder being over twelve hundred
dollars I give to her, and leave the note in her possession I
have written to him concerning it, I also give her the bed matrass
curtains pr Blankets counterpain looking Glass belonging to her
Chamber & 20 dollars to buy chairs - also 6 pr good Sheets &
pillow cases Also a purple sattin quilted gown and a [illegible]

First page of Abigail Adams's will, January 18, 1816.
Adams Family Papers, Topical Supplements (Wills, Deeds, Etc.),
Massachusetts Historical Society.

brother, brother-in-law, son-in-law, and one of her sons had all failed to provide adequately for their families. To make up for these male relatives' failures, she had spent the previous three decades giving money to several men and nearly a dozen women in her family circle, often concealing these payments from her husband. She now decided not to share her belongings—more precisely, the property she claimed to own—equally among her heirs, as her husband would do (with a few exceptions) in his own will three years later. Instead she sought to harmonize her benefactions with the recipients' needs. The residuary legatees—those receiving whatever, if anything, was left after all of her individual bequests had been carried out—were her six granddaughters.

In the vast trove of Adams Papers housed at the Massachusetts Historical Society in Boston, a copy of Adams's will, in her handwriting, is filed with the family's legal papers, but it was not actually a legal document that any court was bound to respect. Recognizing that hard truth, she did not begin it with the customary language about being of sound mind and body, instead writing, "I Abigail Adams wife to the Hon[ora]ble John Adams of Quincy in the County of Norfolk, by and with his consent, do dispose of the following property." *By and with his consent*. Although the document did not bear the signature of John Adams, Abigail insisted that she had persuaded her spouse to go along with her challenge to coverture. Over the course of their long lifetimes, John and Abigail Adams had worked together on a host of important projects that have earned them great renown, but this previously unreported collaboration—in which the wife, not the husband, took the leading role—may have been the most extraordinary of all.

Today Abigail Adams lives in the American memory as the most illustrious woman of the founding era. Yet the very existence of her will suggests that perhaps we do not know her quite as well as we think we do. What were the converging forces that prompted the wife of the second president to defy hundreds of years of statutes and legal precedents by writing a will? Given that married women of her era were not supposed to own personal property, how did she manage to acquire so much of it? When John discovered this document among his deceased wife's papers, he would have been well within his rights in throwing it in the fire, and that raises an additional question: what made her so sure he would carry out her wishes? The only way to solve these riddles is to trace two long-term developments. The first is the evolution of Abigail Adams's personality across the span of more than seventy years of revolution, war, and social upheaval. The second is the gradual working out, over the course of more than five decades, of her relationship with her husband. Abigail herself was never able to answer another question posed by her will, namely: Did John in fact carry out her instructions? But we can.

For generations, Abigail Adams's words—in particular her famous "Remember the Ladies" letter of March 31, 1776—have inspired women seeking equity in the workplace, before the law, and within their own families. Yet they have always been mere words, and skeptics have emphasized that the only place she ever dared to utter them was in confidential letters to her husband. But the skeptics are wrong. Adams actually shared her views on women's rights with numerous correspondents, male and female, inside and outside her family. She even published a brief critique of one particularly obnoxious misogynist in a Boston newspaper (albeit anonymously). Most important of all, she was not content merely to register her verbal objections to the subjugation of women. She turned her own household into a laboratory where she imagined what the emancipation of women might look like. In the fall of 1781, about the time of the British surrender at Yorktown, she had made the first of her own declarations of independence. She took some of the money she had earned as a wartime dealer in European finery (therein lies another tale, to be told in due course) and placed it "in the hands of a Friend," whose identity she conspicuously withheld from her husband. Later she invested this "money which I call mine" in ways that John considered unsavory. For instance, she speculated in government securities that Revolutionary War soldiers had been forced to part with for pennies on the dollar. Moreover, she sometimes devoted her mercantile and speculative profits to causes of which her husband did not approve, justifying the expenditures as coming out of what she variously called "my own pocket money" or "my pin money."

Adams's determination to enact some of her proto feminist ideals within her own household—to act as though the doctrine of coverture lost its force at her front door—is only one of the many surprises concealed within the pages of this woman's extraordinary life history. Given the sheer number of authors who have recounted her story, an astonishingly small portion of it has been told. Biographies of Abigail Adams generally portray her as agreeing with her husband on nearly everything—a depiction that is only accurate if you concentrate, as most of her biographers have, on her political views. On more personal matters, such as religion, the education of the Adams children, and—most of all—family finances, John and Abigail frequently clashed. The sparks that sometimes flew between them illuminate both personalities, and their disagreements can also bring some clarity to a range of broader issues, especially the complex question of what the American Revolution did for—or to—women.

Many of the Adamses' marital differences will resonate with modern couples. In fact, one astonishing aspect of Abigail's story is that much of it seems strikingly familiar. As a teenager, she bridled under her mother's overprotective gaze, and even as a young adult she continued to nurse the wounds she felt her mother had inflicted on her. She did not like the man who courted her little sister, Elizabeth, often called Betsy (primarily because he was too Calvinist). She was annoyed at the way her married friends prattled on about their children—until she became a mother herself. She wondered whether her infant daughter's first smiles were mirth or simply gas, borrowed baby gear from her older sister, Mary, and worried about whether the local school was doing her children more harm than good. Her husband irritated her by ignoring the family as he lost himself in his newspaper—and infuriated her by leaving her with a houseful of sick children and not even bothering to write. Her teenage daughter resisted her authority in ways that recalled her own adolescent rebellions.

One reason that many of the scenes of Adams's life have a modern resonance is that she prided herself on navigating the most important intellectual currents of her era. Long before her contemporary Thomas Paine christened their epoch the Age of Reason, Abigail and other educated men and women on both sides of the Atlantic had liberated themselves (as they saw it) from the bonds of blind faith, placing new emphasis on the thought processes of every individual. Letter writing and diary keeping both mushroomed during the Enlightenment. Abigail wrote more than two thousand surviving letters, and she devoted large portions of them to exploring her feelings. To an extent that does not seem unusual today but that would have astonished her grandmother, Abigail liked to think about her thoughts. A fortunate by-product of Adams's fondness for reflection and self-expression is that she is far and away the most richly documented woman of America's founding era. A matchless trove of personal information—primarily letters—makes it possible to trace the evolution of her personality in astonishing detail. John Adams constantly berated himself for vanity, and his enemies' accusation of arrogance sticks to him even today. Yet in many ways Abigail was even more self-possessed. To be sure, John's intellectual reach often intimidated her, but in all of her other relationships, she was surprisingly confident—"saucy," John called her. Adams's self assurance shown brightest in her approach to other people's offspring. Once it became clear that she had failed to dissuade her younger sister, Elizabeth, from marrying Reverend John Shaw, she urged the couple not to have any children. In 1809, her son John Quincy sailed to St. Petersburg, Russia, as the American minister (a diplomatic post below the rank of ambassador), leaving two of his boys behind with their grandmother. Adams periodically sent his mother explicit instructions about who should board and educate the boys, but she routinely overruled his decisions. At one point she placed George and John with Elizabeth (who by then had lost her first husband and taken another), but then she became dissatisfied with her sister's childraising technique and moved the boys yet again.

Having to give up John Quincy's sons was not only humiliating for Elizabeth but a serious financial blow. She and Mary had both taken husbands who were good men but poor providers (twice, in Elizabeth's case). Abigail and her sisters never lost sight of what happened when their brother's addiction to drink prevented him from providing for his family. William's children had to be sent away to be raised by various relatives, including Mary, Abigail, and Elizabeth, and his fate stood like a lighthouse on a rocky shoreline, a constant reminder that the worst consequence of poverty was not material deprivation. Coverture sharply limited Elizabeth's and Mary's ability to compensate for their husbands' financial failings, but they soldiered on, determined to accumulate and retain enough property to keep their families together.

Times were never as hard for Abigail as they often were for her sisters, but she too understood the connection between a family's economic status and its ability to stick together. She once offered to use some of the money she called her own to purchase an additional farm for her husband, but only if he would quit "running away to foreign courts" and return to Braintree. Two decades later she made a similar overture to her youngest son, Thomas, who had moved to Philadelphia to practice law. Abigail's wealth also allowed her to surround herself with other people's children. Louisa Smith, her brother's daughter, spent most of her life in the Adams household. And at various times Abigail's daughter and each of her three sons all felt the need to send their own children to live with "Grandmamma." For instance, her daughter Nabby's boys moved back to Massachusetts after their father spoiled them and then abandoned them (temporarily, as it turned out). Years later, Nabby's daughter Caroline joined the Adams household during her mother's last illness and remained there after her death. After Charles Adams replicated his Uncle William's failures, slowly drinking himself to death, his wife and daughters accepted Abigail's invitation to live with her. And for several years after John Adams's term as president, financial necessity forced his son Thomas's entire family, which included several rambunctious toddlers, to move into the mansion that John had once called "Peace Field."

The widening gap between the Adamses' growing wealth and Mary's and Elizabeth's continuing financial struggles strained Abigail's relationships with both of her sisters. Neither Mary nor Elizabeth could afford to refuse the help that Abigail pressed upon them, but their shared dependence on her embarrassed them terribly. Once in 1797, Mary gratefully acknowledged yet another round of her sister's gifts and then lamented that she and her children were "doom'd to always be the obliged." Abigail's effort to prevent her donations from fraying the sisterly bond called forth diplomatic skills rivaling those displayed on a grander scale by her husband.

Another recipient of Adams's charity was Phoebe Abdee, her father's former slave, who lived in the Adams home rent-free during Abigail's four-year sojourn in Europe. But this relationship was also put to the test when Abdee defied Adams's prohibition against sharing the house with others. Exhibiting a charitable instinct similar to Abigail's, Phoebe sheltered a variety of men and women, black and white, whose circumstances were even more desperate than her own. Whereas Abigail's sister Elizabeth once described Phoebe as "oderiferous," Abigail on at least one occasion referred to her as her "Parent." In 1797, Adams took a courageous stand on behalf of a black servant boy who was being driven from the town school because of the color of his skin. Yet she was by no means a consistent enemy of racial prejudice. After attending a London performance of *Othello*, she admitted her "disgust and horrour" at seeing the "Sooty" title character "touch the Gentle Desdemona."

If on the one hand Adams has the unnerving capacity to remind us of people we ourselves have known, on the other hand we would do well to remember that much of the apparent familiarity of her world is only a façade. The danger of misunderstanding is especially great in the area of language. While anachronistic terms such as *prog* and *ochlocracy* pose obvious challenges, other words sow even more confusion by seeming familiar when they actually are not. In John Adams's first diary reference to Abigail Smith, the parson's daughter who was destined to be his bride, he described her as "not candid." To modern eyes it might appear that he was saying she was dishonest, but his actual meaning was exactly the opposite of that, for he found her too blunt. In the eighteenth century, to be "candid" was to focus on other people's strengths and overlook their faults. Apparently John considered Abigail insufficiently candid because she could not resist teasing him about some of his foibles.

Visitors to Abigail Adams's era can count on finding a multitude of familiar faces, but they must nonetheless proceed with caution, for her world is also full of surprises.

A NOTE ON NAMES

This book inevitably contains nearly as many references to John Adams as to his wife, which raises the difficult question of what names to use for each of them. John Adams's biographers generally refer to him as *Adams* and her as *Abigail*, but in using his last name and her first, they perpetuate an ancient patriarchal practice that classified women with children. This book will use first names for both Adamses whenever there is any doubt about which one is meant. On the other hand, when it is obvious which of the two is under consideration, he or she will occasionally be called *Adams*. Abigail was generally known as *Nabby* in her youth. In this book, however, that name will be reserved for her daughter, who was also called both *Abigail* and *Nabby*. After Abigail Junior's marriage in 1786, she was referred to as *Mrs. Smith* in written communications and as *Nabby* in oral conversations within the family; both terms will be used here, especially the latter.

CHAPTER 1

"A Tender Twig"

1744–1761

First and last, she was a parson's daughter. Like nearly everyone who was born in the province of Massachusetts Bay in the year 1744, she greeted life in her father's home. For Abigail Smith, that meant the parsonage in Weymouth, Massachusetts, a farming community fourteen miles southeast of Boston. Weymouth fronts on Massachusetts Bay, and Abigail tasted the sea in her first breath. In colonial times the land along the Massachusetts coast alternated between cultivated farms and hills that were low but often steep. The heights were mostly wooded, but here and there granite outcroppings pierced through. Salt marshes covered the lowlands. But for the freshening easterly breezes blowing in from the bay, more people might have joined John Adams, who came into the world nine years before Abigail in the neighboring town of Braintree, in referring to these wetlands as swamps. Every storm coated the beaches with seaweed that was known to restore the vitality of the soil. For any farmer willing to take the trouble to cart it away, it was like manna from heaven.

On November 22, 1744 (November 11 under the old Julian calendar, used in the British Empire until 1752), when Abigail was born, her father was ten years into what would become the longest term that any minister had ever served the Weymouth church: a forty-eight-year stretch that would end only with his death in 1783. Six years before Abigail's birth, her father and mother, William and Elizabeth Smith, had convinced the members of the church to sell them the parsonage. In her youth, the Smiths made an addition to the house that was larger than the original structure and set at a right angle to it, giving the parsonage a distinctive L shape.

Reverend William Smith (1707–1783), Abigail Adams's father. *The "Chappel of Ease" and Church of Statesmen . . .* (Cambridge, Mass., 1890), facing page 81. *Courtesy Massachusetts Historical Society.*

The transaction that gave Parson Smith outright possession of his parsonage spoke volumes about both the region and the man. Since the mid-nineteenth century, the churches of colonial New England have been idealized as peaceable kingdoms, but the reality was that they were often scenes of constant bickering. In Weymouth, the primary contest was between the original church and the north parish, which seceded as the town grew. The parsonage was in the north parish, and both churches laid claim to it, a controversy that culminated in, but did not conclude with, the north parish's decision to sell the parsonage to their preacher. Parson Smith leapt at the opportunity, for he was not the type to follow the well-trodden path. An early indication of his restless ambition had been his marriage to Elizabeth Quincy of Braintree in 1740. The Quincys were among the Massachusetts Bay Colony's most prominent families, having arrived in 1633, only three years after the province was founded. In all but one subsequent generation, at least one man had attended Harvard. For many years, John Quincy, Abigail's grandfather, held the powerful position of Speaker in the provincial House of Representatives.

Quincy did not owe his political prominence to oratorical prowess. On the contrary, he was the first to acknowledge that the real secret to his success was his ability to keep his own counsel. Long after his death,

The parsonage in Weymouth, Massachusetts, where Abigail Adams was born and lived until her marriage in 1764. Watercolor, ca. 1800, *Smith-Townsend Family Papers, Massachusetts Historical Society.*

Abigail recalled that her grandfather "was remarkable for never praising any Body, He did not often speak evil, but he seldom spoke well," either.

Elizabeth Norton Quincy, Abigail's maternal grandmother, was in many ways her husband's polar opposite—as the maturing Abigail soon discovered. Abigail was a constant presence at her grandparents' mansion on the crest of Mount Wollaston, just north of the Weymouth Fore River, which separated Braintree from Weymouth. By her teenage years, she had walked the eight-mile round-trip between Weymouth parsonage and Mount Wollaston more times than she could count. Everyone knew which grandparent she had come to see—Elizabeth Quincy, whose most admired trait was undoubtedly her refusal to grow old. In a 1795 letter to her daughter, Abigail recalled that her grandmother's "lively, cheerful disposition animated all around her." It was with her "merry and chatty" Grandmother Quincy, she observed years later, that "I passed my early, wild, and giddy days." The tinge of rowdiness in the young Abigail's personality—she once acknowledged having a "volatile giddy disposition"—alarmed some members of her family, but Grandmother Quincy declared (quoting Plutarch) that "wild colts make the best Horses." Years later, Abigail described her grandmother as the person "with whom I chiefly lived during the early period of my life."

* * *

Abigail's wild side troubled her mother, who took after the sober-minded Speaker Quincy rather than his more mirthful consort. Elizabeth Quincy Smith was genial enough. But when she ventured out from the Weymouth parsonage—which she did nearly every day—it was seldom to make a purely social call, for she was usually on a mission of some sort. It was customary for ministers' wives to see to the needs of their husbands' less fortunate parishioners, but the relentlessness with which Mrs. Smith carried out these visits to the ill and impoverished astounded everyone who knew her.

Elizabeth's ministrations intensified just as her middle daughter reached the age where she could be a useful assistant. In the spring of 1751, when Abigail was six, an epidemic of diphtheria—known at the time as throat distemper—descended upon Weymouth. Over the next twelve months, it killed 150 of the town's 1,200 residents—one in eight. Most of those carried off by the epidemic were children and teenagers, but numerous heads of families died, too, leaving their wives and children to fend for themselves. Nor was the diphtheria outbreak the only disaster that filled Weymouth and other Massachusetts towns with widows and orphans during the 1750s. In 1755, Great Britain and its American colonies were drawn into renewed conflict against their ancient nemesis, the empire of France. For some British colonists, especially in coastal towns such as Weymouth, the conflict, which came to be known as the French and Indian War, was a godsend. Massachusetts ship captains who were skillful and lucky enough to outrun the French men-of-war prowling the waters of the North Atlantic and the Caribbean could take advantage of wartime shortages to extract astronomical markups from their customers. A still riskier venture was to set out as a privateer—a government-sanctioned pirate preying on French merchantmen. The surest way to profit from the war was to secure a contract for supplying the troops, but those were only available to the well-connected.

Yet like most wars, this one resembled the pulleys that colonists used to draw water from their wells: there were buckets on both ends, and as one rose, the other fell. The French never came near Boston, but British expeditions against forts in New France and along the frontier killed thousands of colonial militiamen as well as British regulars. In 1755, the ministry back in London set its sights on capturing Fort St. Frédéric on Lake Champlain—the primary corridor between French Canada and the British North American colonies. Out went the call for volunteers, and at least nine Weymouth boys—spoiling for the chance to test their mettle against the French papists and to bring home some booty—rushed to enlist. Several of the Weymouth recruits were killed in the unsuccessful expedition, and others died of disease. During the next two years, another three dozen or so farmers and laborers from Weymouth participated in other ill-fated British operations. The string of failures culminated in 1757 in the massacre of the garrison of Fort William Henry at the head of Lake George in upstate New York (the subject of James Fenimore Cooper's *Last of the Mohicans*). It would be another three years before the British finally conquered Canada.

Throughout the British colonies, but especially in eastern New England, the war's capacity to generate misery overwhelmed public officials' ability to relieve it. There were widows in Weymouth who might have died of hunger or cold had it not been for the assistance they received from Elizabeth Smith. Abigail often accompanied her mother on her charitable rounds. As the two of them rode from one house to the next, remaining with each widow only long enough to hand over their gifts and deflect the recipients' immoderate expressions of gratitude, it surely occurred to her that Elizabeth was able to do these good deeds only because her own financial situation was comfortable. But neither of them could have imagined that for Abigail to exhibit the sort of benevolence that was second nature for her mother, she would need all the ingenuity she could muster.

William Smith's comfortable financial situation had several sources. There was his income as parson—a scant resource, but a reliable one, since in those days taxpayers were required to support the Congregational (Puritan) church. Smith supplemented his salary by working his farm, but it seems likely that what really kept the family afloat was the property Elizabeth had received from her parents. One of William's investments may surprise many modern observers: he purchased at least four slaves. When Abigail Adams put her ruminations on race and slavery into writing, which she did on numerous occasions, she was not dealing in abstractions but speaking from intimate personal experience.

William Smith had something in common with his father-in-law: an iron-willed insistence on not making enemies. In pursuit of this goal, Smith resolved, as John Quincy had, "never to speak ill of any Body." He was more adventurous than his father-in-law, however. The advice he gave his daughter was not to keep her lips sealed (as her grandfather advised) but "To say all the handsome Things she could of Persons but no Evil." It was a maxim that Smith inculcated with a passion that approached fanaticism. As an adult, Abigail recalled that whenever she and her brother and sisters "were going abroad" (on visits), even "if it was but to spend an Afternoon," Parson Smith would detain them long enough to remind them to watch what they said. Whenever their friends' and cousins' conversations started to degenerate into gossip swaps, the Smith children were to steer the discussion back toward weightier matters—"to make Things rather than Persons the Subjects of Conversation."

Still, an entry in the diary of a young attorney from Braintree, John Adams, indicates that Parson Smith was not always as reticent as he admonished his children to be. Adams was twenty-three in the summer of 1759, when he first described his feelings about the minister of Weymouth's north parish. The young attorney's primary criticism of Smith was that he was too critical—even of fellow clerics such as Adams's own minister, Anthony Wibird. Smith "laughs at Parson Wibirds careless Air and Behaviour," Adams claimed. Smith's complaints about Wibird could be trivial indeed. For instance, he did not like the way Wibird chose to "Walk across the Room." Nor was the Braintree minister the only target of Smith's scorn. According to Adams, he criticized another man, a Mr. Macartney, for "his Conceit, his orthodoxy, his Ignorance." At the time Adams was unaware of Parson Smith's endeavors to prevent his children from ever speaking ill of others. Surely if he had known about those, his list of the preacher's vices would have included hypocrisy. As it was, Adams considered Smith a "crafty designing Man," and in his diary, he even leveled at the older man a charge that Puritans usually reserved for their archenemies, Catholic prelates. "Parson Smith," he wrote, "has no small share of Priest Craft."

So intense was Squire Adams's animus against William Smith that some of the vitriol spilled over onto the parson's two eldest daughters. Calling seventeen-year-old Mary and fourteen-year-old Abigail by their childhood names, Adams declared that "Polly and Nabby are Wits." For Adams, that was no compliment, especially when the subjects were women—and young ones at that. Later in the same diary entry, Adams asked himself whether the Smith girls were "either Frank or fond, or even candid." He already knew the answer: the two were "Not fond, not frank, not candid." That comment opens up the possibility that his ill will toward these two young women was not simply a by-product of his antipathy for their father. In the eighteenth century, the word *candid* did not mean, as it does today, "blunt." As Adams noted in the same diary entry, "Candor is a Disposition to palliate faults and Mistakes, to put the best Construction upon Words and Actions, and to forgive Injuries." Perhaps the closest modern synonym would be *nonjudgmental.* Apparently the Smith girls had shown Adams their lack of candor by wittily passing judgment on something he had done or said. They had made fun of him. For a man whose defining sin was vanity, there could scarcely have been an unkinder cut. It seems likely that Mary and Abigail had cut Squire Adams down for putting on airs, since both had imbibed their grandmother's contempt for all who did so. "It was a mercy to the World, some people were kept poor," ran one of Elizabeth Quincy's maxims, "since were they rich their haughtiness and insolence would be intollerable."

Aside from the disastrous decisions that three of Abigail's four children would make as adults, her greatest regret in life was her lack of education. Two distinct explanations for this deficit appeared in a letter she wrote one of her granddaughters a few years before her death. One of these focused on a flaw in the larger society; the other was much more personal. "I never was sent to any school," Adams recalled. "I was always sick. Female education in the best of families went no further than writing and arithmetic." Was the Smiths' predominant motive for keeping their daughter out of school her chronic illness or the traditional belief that girls did not need or deserve formal instruction? At different points in her life, Adams seemed to offer conflicting answers to that question. In the year of her marriage, she thanked her uncle Cotton Tufts, a physician, for nursing her through many a childhood illness. As an adult, however, Adams became more and more convinced that her lack of schooling was primarily a result of sex discrimination.

A small number of academies in colonial Massachusetts did admit girls. They were so rare, though, that Abigail could only have attended one if Elizabeth and William Smith had been willing to send her away to school, which they were not. Undoubtedly the couple had imbibed societal prejudices against female education, but the reason they gave Abigail for not letting her attend school in some distant town—concern for her health—made perfect sense. Amid the waves of epidemics that swept through Massachusetts during Abigail's childhood, the Smiths' decision to end her schooling at a rudimentary stage may well have saved her life.

Abigail's inability to obtain much in the way of formal instruction did not leave her uneducated. Fondly remembered amateur teachers showed her how to write well and think deeply. The first of these were her parents and, to an even greater extent, her grandmother, Elizabeth Quincy. "I have not forgotten the excellent lessons which I received from my grandmother, at a very early period of life," Abigail would tell her daughter in 1795. "I frequently think they made a more durable impression upon my mind, than those which I received from my own parents." One of Grandmother Quincy's secrets, Abigail recalled, was her "happy method of mixing instruction and amusement together." As Abigail matured, more and more of her education came from her peers, for she and her friends frequently read books and discussed them. They also exchanged numerous letters, not only trading gossip (although they did that, too) but making self-conscious efforts to teach and learn. Abigail cannot properly be described as self-taught, for she and her friends educated each other. The historian Laurel Ulrich has described the ministrations performed by early American women such as Martha Ballard, a midwife on the Maine frontier, as social medicine. Every community had its medical professionals such as Ballard, but numerous people, especially women, joined in the healing process. Something very similar happened in education. Networks of friends took responsibility for schooling each other. Even the well-to-do young men who benefited from the formal educational opportunities that were denied to Abigail often learned as much from their peers as from their teachers.

Only a small fraction of the teenaged Abigail's letters survive, but they clearly reveal her use of friendly correspondence for "instruction and edification." In an October 1761 missive to a recently married acquaintance named Hannah Lincoln, Abigail found a learned way to express affection. Hannah had previously extended an offer of friendship to Abigail, and her young friend responded by comparing Hannah's offer to a famous one in Esther—one of only two books of the Bible named for women. "What is thy request?" Ahasuerus, the king of Babylon, asks his wife, Esther. Whatever it is, "it shall be performed, even to the half of the kingdom." What Hannah had offered Abigail, the sixteen-year-old whimsically declared, was not half of her kingdom but half of her heart. Then a surprise: Abigail declined the offer, "lest your good man should find it out and challenge me." In this context, the verb *challenge* had a very specific meaning in the eighteenth century. Abigail was expressing concern that her friend's husband might challenge her to a duel.

She was joking, of course, but she persisted in portraying Bela Lincoln and herself as rivals. She wished for a place in Hannah's heart, but she urged that it be "well guarded and fortified." Otherwise, she wrote, "I shall fear being jostled out" by Hannah's husband.

Two letters that the teenaged Abigail wrote to a younger cousin, Isaac Smith, Jr., also reveal a mind eager not only to acquire knowledge but to experiment with new ideas. In the first, written in 1762, she accepted the twelve-year-old Isaac's invitation to correspond. Neither cousin disguised the fact that their intentions were as much educational as social, and Abigail reminded Isaac that this opportunity for mutual edification would not last forever. "In youth the mind is like a tender twig, which you may bend as you please," she wrote, "but in age like a sturdy oak and hard to move."

Another letter to Isaac Smith, written just a year later, showed how much Abigail had learned during that short period. She now possessed "some small acquaintance with the French tongue," an accomplishment that she proceeded to demonstrate by enclosing a document she had translated from French into English. It had not been selected at random, and in fact her choice supplied the earliest evidence of Abigail's lifelong preoccupation with the unique challenges faced by women. Back in 1703, Esther Wheelwright, a seven-year-old girl in the town of Wells in the district of Maine, then part of Massachusetts, was captured by Abenaki Indians and carried to the French province of Quebec. Some Indian captives were ceremonially tortured to death, others were ransomed by their friends and family or returned at the cessation of hostilities, and many were adopted as replacements for Indians who had recently died. Some, however, chose to join French colonial society, and Wheelwright was one of these. After living with the Abenakis for several years, she entered the Ursuline convent in Quebec City. In 1760, when the British conquered Canada, she was elected to the position of mother superior. It was a letter she had sent her nephew Joshua Moody back in Massachusetts that Abigail translated early in 1763.

Historians and biographers have long debated whether to describe Abigail Smith Adams as a feminist. Of course much depends on how that term, not invented until the late nineteenth century, is defined, but there is abundant evidence that throughout her adult life, Adams devoted a great deal of thought to women's status. Some of her positions were radical and others were highly conventional, even conservative, but her passion for analyzing sex roles never left her. Her choice of Esther Wheelwright—as opposed to any of a host of male French writers, from Descartes to Rousseau, that she could have found in the Boston bookshops—was not the only indication that she had already taken an interest in women as women. After closing her note to her "affectionat Friend" Isaac, Abigail added a postscript wondering why Wheelwright had ended her own letter with the phrase *votre serviteur* rather than *votre serveuse.* Both phrases translate into English as "your servant," but Abigail noted that *serviteur,* the term Wheelwright used, was "of the masculine Gender." Why not *serveuse*? She went on to conjecture that "like all other Ladies in a convent, she chose to make use of the Masculine Gender, rather than the Feminine." Actually, nuns did not use the masculine gender in referring to themselves, and we may never know why Adams thought they did.

Abigail's letter to Isaac Smith also contained another, still subtler, indication of her interest in women's status. The missive opened with praise for Smith's "great proficiончy" in the French language. By contrast, Abigail herself had to admit to being "ill qualified for such an undertaking" as translating French into English. The comparison was less self-deprecating than it might seem, for she went on to remind Isaac that he had been "taught the French language by one of the greatest masters." Taken in combination with her decision to translate a female author and the attention she devoted to Wheelwright's masculine self-depiction, the contrast that Abigail drew between male and female educational opportunities marks the March 1763 letter to Isaac Smith as the earliest surviving documentation of a curiosity about, and concern for, gender identity that would become one of the hallmarks of her life. It is significant, too, that Abigail complained (albeit in a very subtle way) about women's dearth of educational opportunities, for that was one specific aspect of women's status to which she would return again and again.

The friend who did the most to help Abigail make up for her lack of formal schooling was Richard Cranch, who was paying court to her sister Mary. Abigail never forgot that Cranch was the first person who "put proper Bookes into my hands, who taught me to love the Poets and to distinguish their Merrits." It was to him that she attributed "my early taste for letters; and for the nurture and cultivation of those qualities which have since afforded me much pleasure and satisfaction." Born in Devon in southwest England in 1726, Cranch immigrated to Massachusetts in 1746. Before sailing he had received training in the manufacture of cards—the metal combs used to prepare wool for the spinning wheel—and that was the first trade he practiced in New England. During the 1750s he and his brother-in-law opened a glassworks in Braintree, but it failed, as did the partners' later effort to manufacture candles from whale oil. When he met Mary, Richard was trying to earn his living making watches. That was not going well, either. Of all the people Abigail came to know closely, Cranch was probably the most inept at getting a living. At the end of December 1762, Richard's good friend John Adams made a long entry in his diary ridiculing his business acumen. Adams observed that Cranch had recently set his mind on buying a chaise (carriage) that was "old, the Leather damnifyed thro careless Usage, the Wheels almost ruined, the spokes being loose &c." Richard tried to get the seller to reduce his asking price but "could not beat him down." Still, Cranch could not walk away from the deal. In trying to justify his decision to meet the seller's price, he told John the man was "poor, and it would look like Ungenerosity or Narrowness of Purse to desire it for less." Richard had been "headstrong" enough to proceed with the purchase in the face of John's "repeated and enforced Advice" to give it up.

Adams reported that Cranch provided an even "worse Instance of his Tameness and Credulity" when buying a horse. The seller sang the animal's praises, and "Cranch believed every Word he said." The young watchmaker, John wrote, "was so secret about his Bargain, that he would not make it before me, who was then at his House but he must finish it, abroad, without Questioning the Horses Virtues or Abilities, or asking any Questions about the Price." Not only was Cranch "fairly cheated in jockey language out of 50" pounds, Adams noted, but "his Buying the Horse was a Piece of ridiculous Foppery, at this Time," since "he had no Occasion for one."

What Cranch lacked in business sense he made up for as an amateur scholar. Self-trained in Latin, Hebrew, and Greek, he possessed an intense desire to share what he knew. Abigail could not have chosen a better tutor.

One reason Abigail spent so much time tagging along with Richard and Mary was that she had reached the age of seventeen without acquiring a beau—at least none that she was willing to acknowledge in response to a sly inquiry from Hannah Lincoln (who had once been courted by John Adams). To read Lincoln's letter, Abigail replied, one would think that "sparks"—young men paying court—were "as plenty as herrings" around the Weymouth parsonage. Actually, there was "as great a scarcity of them as there is of justice, honesty, prudence, and many other virtues." The normally self-effacing Abigail did not blame the dearth of suitors on any shortcomings of her own. "Wealth, wealth is the only thing that is looked after now," Abigail wrote, and her parents would never be able to provide the sort of dowry that some of her friends would take to their marriages. Self-interest "governs the world," she lamented.

It was a theme that would resound through Abigail's life. Money did not buy happiness; she knew that. Yet nearly everyone around her acted as though it did. In order to accomplish what she wanted to do—even the little things, such as helping the poor, as her mother did—she was going to need a husband who was reasonably well-to-do. And that was just the problem, for most of the young men in her circle hoped to do what her own father had done: marry up.

On December 30, 1761, nearly fifteen years before serving on the committee that wrote the Declaration of Independence, John Adams wrote Mary Smith announcing that he planned to "foment Rebellion" against George III, the twenty-two-year-old who had just ascended to the British throne.

He was joking. By this time John was paying court to Mary's sister Abigail, and the socially awkward attorney thought it would be clever to express his affection in the language of politics. He asked Mary to convey a message to Abigail: "I hear she's about commencing a most loyal subject to young George—and altho my Allegiance has been hitherto inviolate I shall endeavour, all in my Power to foment Rebellion," all with a view to transferring Abigail's allegiance to himself. Adams's talk of foreswearing his loyalty to George III was, of course, more prophetic than he knew. By the fall of 1761, British officials had begun trying to clamp down on American smugglers, but no one could have imagined that Parliament was going to try to tax the colonists, provoking riots in the streets of North America and eventually a revolution.

Nearly as extraordinary as John's accidental prophecy was the complete reversal in his attitude toward seventeen-year-old Abigail. The disdain he expressed in the summer of 1759 had become, by the fall of 1761, an open avowal of affection. The process that changed his mind is somewhat mysterious, but not entirely so.

CHAPTER 2

"Miss Adorable"

1761–1764

Several factors conspired to transform John Adams's early aversion to Abigail Smith into its opposite. He was more or less forced to get to know her better, since Richard Cranch, one of his best friends, spent several years courting Abigail's sister Mary. Moreover, as John matured, he became increasingly aware that vanity was his potentially fatal flaw, and he began to see that he could use an intimate friend with both the capacity and the gumption to cut him down to size. That Abigail possessed both of these qualities had at first appeared unladylike, especially in one so young. Over time, however, her wit began to look more like "Saucyness"—the kind of spunk that a self-confident man like Adams could admire. Thus the very personality trait that had once alarmed him now proved a powerful attraction.

It did not hurt that Abigail Smith was becoming something of a beauty, with a "Dark complexion" and even darker hair and eyes. (Years later a British acquaintance joked that he had at first mistaken her for "an Egyptian.") She was somewhat taller and more slender than her peers. Also, as she grew into adulthood, she learned to temper her wit with more traditional feminine virtues. Indeed, even as John began to enjoy his jousts with Abigail, he described her, in wholly conventional terms, as "prudent, modest, delicate, soft, sensible, [and] obliging" (but also "active").

Abigail's growing affection for John is more difficult to explain. She kept no diary, and few letters from her teenage years survive. By contrast, the sources from this period describe John's personality in painstaking detail, and the portrait is not appealing. As his harsh assessment of Abigail's father indicated, John was something of a misanthrope.

And it was easy to see why. A modern social worker who worked up a file on the Adams family would assuredly conclude that it was dysfunctional. The parents often quarreled, and John and the other children were sometimes drawn into their disputes. In one such "conjugal Spat" (as John called it in his diary), the senior John Adams, who served on the governing board of the town of Braintree, decided duty compelled him to board two young women from broken homes who had become public charges.

"My Mamma was determined to know what my P[a] charged a Week for the Girls Board," John noted in his diary. "P. said he had not determined." The senior John Adams asked his wife what she thought would be a reasonable charge. "She absolutely refused to say," his son reported in his diary. Yet she was determined to find out how much money her husband was going to bill the town treasury for housing the girls. "I will know if I live and breath," she declared. In an apparent threat to scrutinize her husband's financial records, Susanna reminded him, "I can read yet." From there on the dispute was one-sided—at least as John reported it. "Why dont you tell me, what you charge?" Mrs. Adams demanded. "I wont have all the Towns Poor brought here, stark naked, for me to clothe for nothing. . . . [You] want to put your Girls over me, to make me a slave to your Wenches." All of this took place before the eyes of the new arrivals. In his diary, John recorded the inevitable result: "the 2 Girls cryed." At some point John's father "resolutely asserted his Right to govern," but it was clear that the nominal head of the household had long since lost control of it. In his diary John ruefully noted that "Passion, Accident, Freak, Humour, govern in this House."

It must have been a relief to enter Harvard in 1751. When John graduated, religious doubts prevented him from complying with his father's ambition for him to become a minister. He first tried his hand at school teaching, finding a position not in Braintree or even Boston but in Worcester, the seat of an agricultural county forty miles to the west. The boys made him more miserable than ever, so he read for the law and returned to Braintree to hang out his shingle. Given John's troubled history, it was difficult for Abigail's friends to discern what she saw in him. Only late in their long courtship did she begin to leave clues about how he had won her heart.

On November 25, 1762, Richard Cranch married Mary Smith in a ceremony presided over by William Smith. The groom was thirty-six, the bride twenty, an age gap that attracted less attention than it might today. After all, Parson Smith was fifteen years older than the bride's mother. After the solemn ceremony, the men and women retired to different rooms to celebrate, as was the custom. Cotton Tufts, Elizabeth Quincy's brother-in-law, regaled the men with one of his favorite "Matrimonial stories," which John Adams dutifully recorded in his diary. On her wedding night, "B. Bicknal's Wife . . . was very anxious, she feared, she trembled, she could not go to Bed. But she recollected she had put her Hand to the Plow and could not look back, so she mustered up her Spirits, committed her soul to G[od] and her Body to B. Bicknal and into Bed she leaped and in the Morning she was amazed, she could not think for her Life what it was that had scared her so."

Meanwhile John pursued Abigail. As "a Lover of Literature," Abigail recalled many years later, Adams "confirmd my taste, and gave me every indulgence that Books could afford." There may be no better explanation for her attachment to him. Although he would never overcome his tendency toward pomposity and never really try, she did not hesitate to tease him mercilessly about it, and his ability to withstand this playful abuse persuaded her that his legendary self-confidence was the genuine article and not simply a blustering cover for deep-seated insecurity. Let other people call John haughty. Abigail was increasingly willing to apply to him precisely the same adjective he had used on her: *saucy.*

The couple's earliest letters shed light not only on their developing love affair but on the principles and practices of eighteenth-century New England courtship. She and her friends had sometimes signed their letters with classical pen names, and the two lovers adopted the practice. Abigail was Diana, the goddess of the moon (and sometimes Jemima, one of Job's legendarily beautiful daughters). John was occasionally Jonathan (which did not seem to show much imagination) or Philander, which meant lover of mankind and was presumably intended to be sarcastic, but more often Lysander, a Spartan statesman. During the first two and a half years of their courtship, from late 1761 through early 1764, Abigail's letters expressed great affection, but usually in the modest terms that were appropriate for a young woman of her era. John's were at once more exuberant and more awkward. One Saturday morning in August 1763, he reported to Abigail that the previous night he had "dreamed, I saw a Lady, tripping it over the Hills, on Weymouth shore, and Spreading Light and Beauty and Glory, all around her. At first I thought it was Aurora, with her fair Complexion, her Crimson

Blushes and her million Charms and Graces. But I soon found it was Diana, a Lady infinitely dearer to me and more charming."

John also expressed his fondness for Abigail in less bombastic ways, for instance by referring to her sister Elizabeth, six years her junior, as "my Daughter Betcy." Only eight of the letters the two lovers exchanged before April 1764 survive, but it may be significant that among those, Abigail wrote two and John six.

One note John sent Abigail that spring contained language that, given the standards of the era and in particular the couple's social position, bordered upon the indecent. "Patience my Dear!" he wrote. "Learn to conquer your Appetites and Passions!" Never mind that John was kidding around or that his advice was really directed to himself; it was inappropriate for a young man to say anything about his sweetheart's capacity for lust. Trying both to express affection and to impress Abigail with his cleverness, John resorted to a variety of tropes and similes, some of which were a bit ham-fisted. He could not resist commercial metaphors. On October 4, 1762, he sent his love an "Order, or Requisition," modeled on the ones used by merchants. It required her to give John "as many Kisses, and as many Hours of your Company after 9 O'Clock as he shall please to Demand and charge them to my Account."

Other analogies that John drew were more conventional and less awkward. "Every experimental Phylosopher knows," he told Abigail in February 1763, "that the steel and the Magnet or the Glass and feather will not fly together with more Celerity, than somebody And somebody, when brought within the striking Distance." Although he had reached the age of twenty-six by the time they began courting and was nine years older than Abigail, John often displayed the painful self-awareness of a schoolboy pursuing a crush. In one three-page epistle, he repeatedly tripped over himself, interrupting his narrative of real-world events four times with references to the very letter he was in the process of writing.

Abigail rarely replied in kind to John's verbal effusions. More circumspect, she preferred to express her feelings for him by worrying about his health. And yet there was passion in her prose. At a time when her sweetheart sometimes addressed her as "Miss Adorable," she was more likely to begin her letters, "My Friend." Today that is the sort of salutation that might open a form letter, but in the eighteenth century, *friend* conveyed considerable intimacy.

* * *

If there was a certain boldness in Abigail's decision to proclaim herself John's "friend," it also appears that she was not above the occasional sexual tease. Once, after not spending the previous evening with John, she pretended to be glad they had been apart, since "we might, if we had been together, have been led into temptation." When John arrived at that place in Abigail's letter, he must have been astonished (and excited!) at her open avowal of passionate feelings for him—only to be deflated when she added, "I don't mean to commit any Evil, unless setting up late, and thereby injuring our Health, may be called so."

Some of the comments Abigail made to John conveyed obvious affection but were also meant to serve the subtler purpose of impressing him with the breadth of her reading. For instance, one Thursday afternoon in August 1763, she expressed her concern for his health using a classical reference. If the Roman orator Lucius Annaeus Seneca had only had himself to worry about, she said, he might not have tried to stay healthy. But Seneca was "careful and tender of his health" solely "for the sake of his Paulina" (his wife), and John ought to heed the example. For Abigail, the couple's correspondence was a continuation of the epistolary education she and her young friends had been providing each other for years. One issue that interested her throughout her entire life was a new cultural movement known as sensibility. It was a difficult term to pin down, because it had so many meanings, but Abigail was interested in all of them. Among the synonyms for *sensibility* were *taste* and *refinement*. It was the ability to appreciate the subtler pleasures of life—a glass of Madeira, a Gainsborough portrait, a Mozart sonata. But sensibility was primarily concerned with human relationships. A "man of feeling" (this was the title of an influential novel published in 1771 by Henry Mackenzie) was constitutionally incapable of hearing about another person's distress without being visibly affected.

In a sense the whole sensibility movement was a reaction against what John Locke had said about how human personalities form. In Locke's view, every newborn baby is a blank slate, and whether children become sinners or saints depends entirely upon how they are raised—which was why he devoted so much thought to enumerating the virtues that parents should cultivate in their children. But during the eighteenth century, numerous thinkers—the best-known of them was Adam Smith, the future author of *The Wealth of Nations*—disputed Locke's claims. They believed all human beings are born with an innate "moral sense" that all but forces them to sympathize with the joys as well as the sufferings of others. In his 1759 *Theory of Moral Sentiments,* Smith posited that everyone possesses "fellow feeling"—not just the ability to sympathize with other people's joys and pains but the compulsion to do so. Abigail's interest in sensibility was fueled by the sentimental novels of Samuel Richardson. She enjoyed his stories of women facing challenges to their virtue, for instance *Clarissa* and *Pamela,* but she actually learned the most from his *Charles Grandison,* published during her childhood. The title character of this seven-volume novel is an ideal man. Richardson's critics found Grandison so perfect as to be unrealistic and uninteresting, but Abigail appreciated the novelist's desire to create a model by which actual men could be judged. Near the end of her life, she pronounced Richardson a "master of the human heart" and affirmed that to him "was due whatever I possess[ed] of delicacy of sentiment or refinement of taste in my early and juvenile days."

A fascination with sensibility pervades the letters Abigail wrote John during their courtship. In August 1763, her concern that her spark might be ill (he had not written her recently) occasioned her first use of an image, borrowed from Ecclesiastes, that she would return to several times in later life: the "threefold cord." She and John were linked in three different ways, she said. Not only were they lovers and friends, but "Humanity obliges us to be affected with the distresses and Miserys of our fellow creatures"—even those with whom we are not personally acquainted. With this statement, Abigail placed herself squarely in the "moral sense" camp and in firm opposition to Locke's contention that humans will only sympathize with the distress of others if trained to do so. (John wisely demonstrated his appreciation for Abigail's trope by referring to it at the end of a letter he wrote her exactly eight months later, signing off as "your Admirer and Friend, and Lover.")

During the French Revolution, Thomas Paine pronounced the era in which he lived the "Age of Reason," and the term is often still applied. Yet the organ that sensibility celebrated was not the head but the heart. People were to be judged by whether they were hard-hearted—insensitive either to the pain or the joys of others—or impressionable. Exhorting men to be more soft hearted was asking them to be more feminine, for this was alleged to be one of women's signature traits. Yet that was precisely what sensibility required—and what Abigail required of John. In April 1763, she broached the topic with an affectionate affirmation that their hearts "were both cast in the same mould." There was one difference, however: John's heart "was made, with a harder mettle, and therefore is less liable to an impression" than Abigail's. When John read that his lover considered him more hard-hearted than herself, he may have considered this an entirely appropriate difference between a gentleman and a lady. Actually, though, Abigail was daring him to prove her wrong. Thus began a friendly contest that would last more than half a century.

There is a widespread modern misconception regarding the term *Puritan*. Today many people believe good Puritans abstained from all sensual pleasures, and certainly before marriage. Actually, the religious denomination now known as Congregationalist acquired the label "Puritan" for reasons that had nothing to do with moral purity in the modern sense. The movement arose in seventeenth-century England with the purpose of purifying the government-sanctioned Church of England of its Catholic vestiges; hence the name "Puritan." Without letting go of the myth of the Puritans as puritanical, we cannot comprehend why John Adams and Abigail Smith caused barely a ripple when, in the fall of 1763, more than a year before they married, they took a trip together—apparently alone. No one is certain where they went, though a good possibility is Worcester, where the superior court traveled every autumn on its circuit through the province. Abigail described the jaunt in a letter to her friend Hannah Storer Green, who had married the previous year. That letter unfortunately does not survive, but much of its contents may be inferred from Green's response.

Almost inevitably, traveling with John prompted Abigail to consider the similarities between a journey and a marriage. Green joked that she did not like Abigail's simile, because roads can be bumpy, and she did not like the idea of being "jumbled into Married Life." This was apparently a reference to couples who were forced to tie the knot when the woman became pregnant, and it led Green to more serious reflections on sexuality. In her letter Abigail had expressed irritation that her marriage to John had been so long postponed—apparently owing to Abigail's parents' doubts about John. Green sympathized with her frustration, since she and her husband had also been forced to delay their marriage. "I know of nothing more irksome than being just at the door of Bliss, and not being in a capacity to enter," she told Abigail. One of the great disadvantages of being stuck at the threshold was that "every ill natured person" felt fully entitled to subject the unhappy couple to "some rude unpolished joke." "They may call it wit, if they please," Green told Abigail, "but I think it bears the name of shocking indecency: I've experienced it, and it galls me every time I think of it; but I desire to be thankfull that it is over with me, and that I am now happily rewarded, for what I then suffer'd." Green was aware that the ribald stories did not stop when the couple finally set a wedding date. In fact, as John had noted in his report on the Smith-Cranch nuptials, the marriage celebration itself frequently proved a first-class opportunity for this particular form of torture. Green was probably being excessively optimistic when she told Abigail, "I hope your wedding-day will not be productive of such indelicacies."

And when would that day come? By the early months of 1764, Abigail's parents appear to have abandoned their objections to the match. But then two new obstacles arose. The first spoke volumes about the relationship Abigail and John had developed: they could not agree on a wedding date. Apparently John wanted to hold the ceremony in March, but Abigail favored May. Although the disagreement was genuine, both partners were prepared to treat it with levity. In fact, they resorted to the same device that neighbors often used to resolve property disputes, referring the matter to a third party, Hannah Green, for arbitration. Predictably, Green was not content just to help the couple set a date. First she asked the obvious question: why did John and Abigail not simply compromise on April? Was it "because you will neither of you condescend?" she asked. "If so, you are neither of you fit Subjects for Matrimony in my opinion."

Green threatened to "leave you to marry when you can agree, and to enjoy your blessed Prerogative when you can, in Love, determine whose right it is" to decide on the date. Finally she relented, pronouncing April "a very salutary month for the purpose." In the end Hannah's opinion did not matter. At about the time Abigail and John referred their dispute to her, Boston was hit with an epidemic of smallpox—far and away the worst of the contagious diseases that periodically swept through early America. The 1764 outbreak infected 699 people in Boston, killing 124 of them. Some of the survivors went blind; many were horribly disfigured. For Abigail the danger was not too great, since she rarely traveled to Boston, but John often had to go there on business. As soon as the magnitude of the epidemic became clear, he decided he would have to be inoculated. If the operation was successful, it would give him lifetime immunity to the disease. On the other hand, in 1 percent of cases, smallpox inoculation killed the patient.

CHAPTER 3

"For Saucyness No Mortal Can Match Him"

1764

In modern times, most people in the world are immunized against smallpox by receiving a harmless cowpox virus. The practice in colonial Boston—first suggested by an African slave who had witnessed it in routine use in his home country—was to insert into the patient's bloodstream a small quantity of the smallpox virus itself. The only way to obtain immunity to the disease was to deliberately contract a minor case of it. About one in every one hundred cases of self-inflicted infection proved fatal, but it was widely believed that inoculation patients could improve their odds by preparing themselves with a week of isolation, purgatives, and abstention from meat and dairy products. After a patient had been infected, he or she became a highly contagious carrier of the virus and therefore had to be quarantined for at least three weeks. This was the procedure that John Adams underwent in Boston in April 1764.

John's preparation, inoculation, and quarantine isolated him from Abigail for more than a month just at the point when the two had hoped to marry. Painful as it was for the two lovers, the prolonged separation was a boon for modern readers, since, if we may judge from surviving letters, it led the couple to exchange more of them in April and May 1764 than they had during the previous two and a half years.

Within hours of drinking the ipecac that cleansed his system by inducing intense vomiting, John penned a note to Abigail that was designed to allay her anxieties—and at the same time to flaunt his bravery. "For many Years past, I have not felt more serenely than I do this Evening," he wrote. Abigail was actually not as anxious for John as he expected. She knew there was a chance the operation could end up giving him a fatal dose of smallpox, but especially after a consultation with her uncle Cotton Tufts, a physician who was himself inoculated a few weeks ahead of John, she was convinced he was doing the right thing. In fact she wished she could have been inoculated, too. Unfortunately, though, her parents objected, and her mother was especially adamant. This imposition of parental authority on the nineteen-year-old Abigail was an irksome reminder that she was stuck in a sort of limbo. For a young woman in colonial America, marriage was anything but liberating, since it gave her husband nearly total power over her, but numerous girls in her situation were nonetheless impatient to escape their parents' yoke and choose their own masters. Even Cotton Tufts's decision to be inoculated created tension between his sister-in-law and his niece. In a letter to Tufts, Abigail reported a mother-daughter dispute about the danger he faced, concluding, "My Mother makes bugbears sometimes, and then seems uneasy because I will not be scared by them."

For Abigail, this was an old story. Time and again, Elizabeth Quincy Smith had exhibited excessive anxiety about her children's health. Once she had even prohibited Abigail from attending the biggest event on the Massachusetts social calendar, the commencement ceremony at Harvard, because she was suffering from a minor illness. On the other hand, Smith's anxiety regarding smallpox inoculation did produce one positive result for Abigail. It softened her mother's feelings toward John. In a letter to her sweetheart, Abigail described a brief exchange with Elizabeth. "My Mamma has just been up, and asks to whom I am writing," Abigail told John. "I answerd not very readily. Upon my hesitating—Send my Love say'd she to Mr. Adams, tell him he has my good wishes for his Safty."

Although Abigail did not worry too much about the danger John faced, she did show her concern for him by harrying him to follow the doctors' orders, which she feared he would fail to do. John was skeptical about some of the physicians' recommendations—especially their injunction to stop eating meat a week before the operation—and Abigail conspired with her uncle Tufts to conquer his resistance. On April 2, she was able to report to Tufts that John was saying, "if he was to follow his own judgment, he should not go into the method prescribed, but since his Friends advise other ways he will *Submit*." Abigail urged Tufts to press his advantage, advising John to show the same humility in other situations. By yielding to his friends' judgment on the matter of inoculation, John set "a good example," Tufts should tell him, "and if you value your own happiness you will in many cases follow it."

This is the sort of innocent plotting that is common enough within married couples, and it showed that John and Abigail were increasingly treating each other as spouses. Another indicator was that by this time they no longer had any compunction about opening each other's mail. When her uncle Tufts gave Abigail a sealed letter to pass on to John, she was happy to do so, but she confessed to Tufts that she "had the curiosity to unfold" it first. She felt justified in peeping into the note, since, as she told Tufts, "he serves me so sometimes." But in this case she wished she had resisted temptation, because the letter contained language that was "not very delicate"—perhaps gruesome details regarding Bostonians who were dying of smallpox. "The thought of it makes me Squemish," she told her uncle. Tufts could spare no sympathy for Abigail. "I never design'd that You should have open'd Pandora's Box, as such it seem'd to be to You," he told her. "All I can say upon the Affair is that if your *delicate* Stomach receiv'd a gentle Heave, You must comfort yourself with the trite saying 'Pay for Peeping.'"

On Friday, April 13, John traveled from Braintree to Boston. Scarcely had he settled in at his uncle's house, which was serving as a temporary smallpox hospital, when the doctor arrived. An incision was made in his arm, and then the surgeon placed a thread contaminated with smallpox in the wound. That was it. "The Doctors, having finished the Operation and left Us, their Directions and Medicines, took their Departure in infinite Haste, depend on't," John reported to Abigail later that day. For him it was all over but the waiting. If everything went according to plan, pustules would erupt on his skin in the next few days—but only a few of them.

The couple's long and unexpected separation during John's inoculation showed just how much the two of them had come to rely upon the labor of Tom, one of her father's three slaves. Tom transported letters between the two lovers, and when John asked to borrow some books from the Smith library to while away his hours of enforced leisure, it was Tom who carried those, too. Parson Smith also offered to have Tom bring John's horse, which would be useless to him while he was under quarantine, back to Braintree for him. Once John had received his inoculation, each of his letters had to be smoked twice—once before being sent and again upon arrival at the Smith parsonage—in order to prevent Abigail from being exposed to the virus. In Weymouth, Tom was given the responsibility of smoking the letters. Abigail was not altogether pleased with her slave's workmanship, and she urged John to enclose his "Letters in a cover, but seal only the out side, Tom makes bungling work opening them, and tares them sadly."

The records do not indicate whether Tom had already survived a bout with smallpox, which would have granted him lifetime immunity. It seems likely that he had, since even the most heartless slaveholder would not want his human chattel to contract a disease that could so easily be passed on to others.

John's extended quarantine drove his relationship with Abigail to an important milestone. In a series of three letters she sent him over the course of five days early in his confinement, Abigail revealed to John, as she already had to her cousin Isaac Smith the previous year, that she had an abiding interest in the status of women. She was intrigued by everything from men's attitudes toward women to the allegedly innate differences between the two sexes. On April 15, Abigail noted that John's doctors had told him that while recovering from his inoculation, he could participate in a variety of sedate activities, from card playing to checkers. Yet he had been admonished not to write letters, and this prohibition aroused Abigail's suspicions. Why would the doctors allow John to engage in idle amusements but not to write his sweetheart? "It may be [that] those who forbid you cannot conceive that writing to a Lady is any amusement," she wrote; "perhaps they rank it under the Head of drudgery, and hard Labour."

The reality, of course, was that John had been prohibited from sending mail to anyone, male or female. It seems likely that Abigail was picking a friendly fight simply for John's amusement. Even if that is the case, however, her whimsical complaint indicated that she also harbored more serious concerns about men's attitudes toward women. In the end John ignored the doctors' advice (which was probably intended for the protection not of the patients but of their correspondents) and continued writing Abigail—often every day—being careful to smoke the letters once himself and to enjoin her to have Tom smoke them again. "Did you never rob a Birds nest?" Abigail asked her fiancé one Friday evening after receiving one of these notes. "Do you remember how the poor Bird would fly round and round, fearful to come nigh, yet not know how to leave the place—just so they say I hover round Tom whilst he is smokeing my Letters."

The day after complaining about the doctors' ban on "writing to a Lady," Abigail again brought up her sex. "I wonder I write to you with so little restraint," she said, "for as a critick I fear you more than any other person on Earth." The big surprise for Abigail was that nothing about John other than his critical skills intimidated her. "Dont you think me a Courageous Being[?]" she asked him. "Courage is a laudable, a Glorious Virtue in your Sex, why not in mine?" Thus in the course of a two-day period in April 1764—twelve years before composing her famous "Remember the Ladies" letter—Abigail had (playfully, to be sure) denounced not only the men who claimed intellectual superiority over women but also those who saw intrepid women as unfeminine. It would be a mistake, however, to depict her as an unrelenting champion for women. Indeed, the same letter where she defended women's right to show valor took a turn toward the silly further down the same page, prompting Abigail to pronounce it "a right Girls Letter." And three days later, when John impatiently pressed Abigail for a morsel of gossip she had promised him, she replied, "Why my good Man, thou hast the curiosity of a Girl."

Some people have an uncanny ability to take a bird's-eye view of social situations—to see conversations and relationships from the perspective of a detached observer. Abigail Smith not only possessed that skill, she had something like a compulsion to use it. And the topic that most frequently called forth her observational abilities was the relationship not just between individual men and women but between the male and female genders.

Smith's growing awareness of women's inferior status did nothing to diminish her fondness for the man in her life, and during John's quarantine the gap between his effusively affectionate letters and her more restrained replies began to close. Yet Abigail continued to express her feelings for John using language that was designed in part to impress him with her learning. A week after he was inoculated and two weeks after their separation, Abigail emphasized her yearning for him with a reference to the prophet Muhammad's winged horse. At night, she said, "I no sooner close my Eyes than some invisible Being, swift as the Alborack of Mahomet, bears me to you." The letters that Abigail and John exchanged during his quarantine also brim with gossip. As the first comments that John Adams had written in his diary about Abigail's father back in 1759 had indicated, John had already, by the age of twenty-four, acquired a personality trait more commonly associated with much older men. He could be crotchety. He took much less pleasure from celebrating his neighbors' virtues than from painstakingly dissecting their faults. And he subjected himself to the same treatment. For instance, in an August 1762 diary entry he browbeat himself for neglecting his "Reading, Thinking [and] Writing." "Have I totally renounced all three?" he asked.

On the surface Abigail was just the opposite: cheerful and inclined to overlook people's flaws while highlighting their virtues. Yet even she was susceptible to the temptation to pass on the latest piece of mildly malicious gossip. The raft of letters that the couple exchanged during John's quarantine—all of them carried by the slave Tom or some other courier in whose discretion Abigail and John trusted implicitly—gave them an irresistible opportunity to poke fun at their friends without much danger of being discovered. Abigail enjoyed this exchange of rumors as much as John did—indeed, it was she who started it—but she limited herself to gentle pokes at her friends' most minor flaws. Anyone who tried to inflict deeper wounds risked throwing her into an aggressively defensive posture, as John would shortly discover to his great regret.

Abigail's long separation from John appears to have intensified her resentment against the parents who had done so much to prevent their marriage. In an April 16 letter to her sweetheart, she started to say something about her mother but then interrupted herself: "I have lately been thinking whether my Mamma—when I write again I will tell you Something." Four days later, John was at the peak of his contagiousness, yet she confessed that she was inclined to come visit him anyway. "But my own inclinations must not be followed—to Duty I sacrifice them," she wrote. She was talking not about her obligation to avoid infection but her filial duty to her overly cautious mother. Frustration at Elizabeth's rules caused Abigail to begin writing John an extremely cruel sentence about her, but she once again interrupted herself just in time: "O my Mamma forgive me if I say, you have forgot, or never knew—but hush." Recollecting herself, Abigail not only stifled this unkind reflection (although she knew John was smart enough to fill in the blank) but broke her earlier promise to disclose a piece of unflattering information about her mother. "Excuse me that something I promis'd you," she now wrote him, "since it was a Speach more undutifull than that which I Just now stop'd my self in."

By late April, it was clear that John was going to survive his inoculation. Indeed, on the twenty-sixth, he was able to tell Abigail (in a pun on his own surname), "None of the Race of Adam, ever passed the small Pox, with fewer Pains, Achs, Qualms, or with less smart than I have done." With his decision to be inoculated so thoroughly vindicated, he sent his lover his harshest-ever criticism of her parents. "I join with you sincerely in your Lamentation that you were not inoculated" as well, he wrote. "Parents must be lost in Avarice or Blindness, who restrain their Children" from receiving this lifelong blessing. Although he did not directly claim that Elizabeth and William Smith had denied their daughter the opportunity to undergo the operation because of the (admittedly high) cost, his use of the word *avarice* hearkened back to an accusation he had scratched into his diary five years earlier. "Parson Smith . . . conceals his own Wealth, from his Parish, that they may not be hindered by knowing it from sending him Presents," Adams had written during the summer of 1759. These two bits of evidence, fragmentary though they are, suggest that the real reason the Smiths did not want Abigail to marry John was that they were holding out hope that she would, like her father, marry money. Even if that was not the actual source of their objection to the match, John clearly thought it was.

Abigail's long separation from John during his smallpox quarantine got her thinking about their relationship, and on April 30, as he was about to be released, she shared some of her reflections. She began by describing a scene she had witnessed the previous day. "A Gentleman and his Lady"—most likely Abigail's aunt Lucy Tufts and her husband Cotton—were reunited after a long separation.

"How do ye," said the gentleman.

"How do ye," his wife replied.

The couple exchanged "a Smile, and a good naturd look." And that was it. Abigail was appalled that this "tender meeting" (as she derisively called it) provoked so little emotion from either partner. "Upon my word I believe they were glad to see each other," she wrote. Abigail was obviously thinking about her own impending reunion with John. Using their pen names, she wondered "whether Lysander, under like circumstances could thus coldly meet his Diana, and whether Diana could with no more Emotion receive Lysander." "I dare answer for a different meeting on her part," she concluded. No record of John and Abigail's reunion exists, but if John somehow failed to catch his fiancée's hints, he had only himself to blame.

Smith used the same letter to draw Adams's attention to some of his faults. To soften the blow she employed the conventional device of relating another person's analysis of him instead of her own. She did not identify her source or even state whether it was a he or a she, and this person was probably her own invention. The mystery person's commentary on John began with a compliment. It was not merely good luck that had prevented him from catching a more virulent case of smallpox during his inoculation. He had withstood the distemper "like an oak." Yet John's sturdiness, so advantageous to his health, was a shortcoming in social situations, according to the person whom Abigail quoted. "I did expect this purgation of Lysander would have set us on a level and have renderd him a Sociable creature," he or she declared during John's recovery. But that did not happen. Far from being reduced to whining misery, he persevered, remaining "as haughty as ever." According to Abigail's source, John's arrogance did not simply indicate a lack of sensibility (although that was bad enough). It was also intimidating. The source claimed Adams's "intolerable forbiding expecting Silence" made it "imposible for a Stranger to be tranquil in your presence." Contrasting John to Charles Grandison, the title character of the Samuel Richardson novel, he or she noted that whereas Grandison "call'd forth every one's excellencies," John's presence was so daunting that the people he conversed with could not even think straight. "Never was a thought born in Lysanders presence," her source claimed.

Abigail was careful to distance herself from the person she quoted. "As to the charge of Haughtiness," she told him, "I am certain that is a mistake, for if I know any thing of Lysander, he has as little of that in his disposition, as he has of Ill nature." The claim that John intimidated people was another matter, "for by experience I know it to be true." Indeed, she had always found him daunting, but she had "thought I had reasons by myself to account for it, and knew not that others were affected in the same manner." For Abigail, it was a relief to learn that she was not the only one John intimidated, but that did not solve the problem. "To this day I feel a greater restraint in your Company, than in that of allmost any other person on Earth," she told him. It was something about his physical presence, she said, because she felt no such trepidation about communicating her thoughts to him in writing. Sometimes admitting to a person that you find it difficult to speak intelligently in his or her presence only aggravates the discomfort. But for Abigail, clearing the air produced salutary results, enabling her to conclude her discussion of John's allegedly intimidating personality by demanding, in the boldest possible terms, "What say you to that charge?" Then she wrapped up the letter on a softer note, levying a new accusation that was much more whimsical. "I expect you [to] clear up these matters, without being in the least saucy," she wrote, adding that she knew this would be a tall order for John, since "for Saucyness no Mortal can match him, not even His Diana."

John retaliated in kind against his fiancée's enumeration of his faults, giving her a "Catalogue of your Faults, Imperfections, Defects, or whatever you please to call them." Nearly all the "Defects" he described were actually virtues. She had been "extreamly negligent" in failing to devote countless hours to playing cards, and she had a nasty "Habit of Reading, Writing and Thinking," which was particularly "inexcusable in a Lady." This last "Defect" was not only a compliment but an especially welcome one, since it reminded Abigail that John appreciated in her the very qualities that more conventional men considered unfeminine. Indeed, "Reading, Thinking [and] Writing" were the same three pursuits that, two years earlier, John had browbeat himself for neglecting. These blandishments disguised as disparagement made for a rather conventional love letter, but John considerably dampened the force of his compliments by interspersing them with what appeared to be genuine criticism. "You very often hang your Head like a Bulrush," he told Abigail, and "You do not sit, erected as you ought, by which Means, it happens that you appear too short for a Beauty, and the Company looses the sweet smiles of that Countenance and the bright sparkles of those Eyes." Abigail was also guilty of "sitting with the Leggs across. This ruins the figure and the Air, this injures the Health." Another of her faults was "walking, with the Toes bending inward." She was, in other words, "Parrot-toed."

In her reply, Abigail made it clear that she understood that much of her sweetheart's criticism was actually praise, and she declined to offer a point-by-point rebuttal. By contrast, each of his serious complaints, no matter how minor, received a specific reply. She promised to work on her singing, attributing her previous failure to cultivate this talent (which John had censured) to having "a voice harsh as the screech of a peacock." To John's assertion that she should not cross her legs, Abigail replied, "I think that a gentleman has no business to concern himself about the Leggs of a Lady."

For Smith as well as Adams, one of the more pleasurable aspects of the couple's conversations and correspondence was the verbal digs they took at their friends and acquaintances. It delighted John that this minister's daughter was not too prim to join in some of the rumormongering that was generally reserved to spouses or same-sex friends. Indeed, it pleased him a little too much, because on the last day of September 1764, scarcely a month before they were due to marry, he got carried away. He launched into a malicious verbal assault on one of their mutual friends. Adams did not name the man, but Smith knew who he was, because the criticism was painfully specific. "The other Evening," John reported while she was up in Boston visiting her aunt and uncle, "a certain Gentleman" (possibly his friend Richard Cranch, who was Abigail's brother-in-law) entertained a large company that apparently included ladies with his "Wit, Humour, smut [and] Filth." "Do you wonder, my Dear," he asked,

> why that Gentleman does not succeed in Business, when his whole study and Attention has so manifestly been engaged in the nobler Arts of smutt, Double Ententre, and Mimickry of Dutchmen and Negroes? I have heard that Imitators, tho they imitate well, Master Pieces in elegant and valuable Arts, are a servile Cattle. And that Mimicks are the lowest Species of Imitators, and I should think that Mimicks of Dutchmen and Negroes were the most sordid of Mimicks. If so, to what a Depth of the Profound have we plunged that Gentlemans Character.

Adams sensed that this diatribe had crossed the line, and he made a lame attempt to disarm Abigail's objections. Turning his critical blade back upon himself, he allowed that he was becoming "the most insufferable Cynick, in the World. I see nothing but Faults, Follies, Frailties and Defects in any Body, lately." He knew, why, too: it was his long separation from her during her sojourn in Boston. "My soul and Body have both been thrown into Disorder, by your Absence," he wrote. "But you who have always softened and warmed my Heart, shall restore my Benevolence as well as my Health and Tranquility of mind. You shall polish and refine my sentiments of Life and Manners, banish all the unsocial and ill natured Particles in my Composition." Thus had John artfully turned from abusing their mutual friend to criticizing himself to complimenting Abigail on possessing an abundance of one of her own favorite virtues: benevolence.

She did not fall for it, and the abuse that John heaped on their friend infuriated her. True, she had willingly joined him in good-natured lampoons of various acquaintances, but this time he had gone too far. She may have been offended by John's attempt to associate the unnamed gentleman with "Dutchmen" (Braintree had a large German population) and (even worse) "Negroes." More likely, it was the cruel pleasure he took in the man's failure in business. Your comments "really discomposed me," she informed him. Using a medical analogy, she said it distressed her to see "a corosive applied when a Lenitive"—a soothing ointment—"would have answerd the same good purpose." John's attempt to palliate his rant by mocking his own cynicism had just the opposite effect. It reminded Abigail that the man to whose authority she was about to commit herself had, along with his many harmless foibles, one great flaw. For all the abuse he heaped upon himself, he was a proud man, and he felt fully entitled to pass harsh judgment on other people. Replying to the diatribe as cheerfully as she could, she observed that "I have drawn a lesson from that which will be useful to me in futurity, viz. never to say a severe thing because to a feeling heart they wound to deeply to be easily cured."

Abigail was evidently thinking about her future in another sense as well. Breaking off their wedding engagement was the furthest thing from her mind, but she could not help wondering anew whether she would really be happy spending the rest of her life with a man who could be so arrogant and cruel. John had expected her to be flattered by his prediction that during their marriage she would restore his benevolence and polish his sentiments. Abigail was a great believer in the power of fellow feeling, and in almost any other context, being portrayed as a paragon of sensibility would have pleased her. But it was daunting to learn that her fiancé had invested her with the responsibility of keeping his cynicism at bay. Still, if this was the hand fate had dealt her, she would play it as well as she could, and she reminded John (as she would many times in the future) of the old saying that "the phylosopher who laught at the follies of mankind [passed] thro' life with more ease and pleasure, than he who weept at them, and perhaps did as much towards a reformation." She also told him how much his harsh comments had hurt her feelings, concluding, "I have only mentiond it, that when ever there is occasion a different method may be taken."

If John wrote a response to this letter, it does not survive, and the whole affair seems to have been forgotten as the couple prepared for a late October wedding. The hiring of servants might normally have fallen to Abigail's share, but John pitched in (probably because she was in Boston for so long), interviewing several local girls, even though his own preference was for a servant from farther away, who would not be tempted to make frequent trips home. In the end two servants were hired. One, Rachel Marsh, was described by John as "a clever Girl, and a neat one." The question of who the other servant would be was not so easily resolved. John named several possibilities but then mentioned an African American named Judah. She was one of the two young women from broken families who had boarded with the Adamses at public expense—despite the vehement initial objections of John's mother. Apparently Susanna Adams had changed her mind about Judah, retaining her as a servant even after the death of John's father in 1761. On the other hand, Susanna had no occasion for Judah's services during the winter of 1764–1765, so she proposed that the newlyweds take her on until the following spring, when John's mother would need her back. By then, surely, John and Abigail would find someone better.

Apparently no one thought to consult Judah on the matter. For her part, Abigail had spent enough time with Judah to know that she did not like her. Racial prejudice may have contributed to this attitude but could not have been its only source, since she had never had any compunction about being served by her father's slaves. Abigail did not want to cross the formidable Susanna Adams. After all, she was still living at the house where she had raised John—her second son, Peter Boylston Adams, had inherited the property from his father three years earlier—and it was right next to the home John had inherited at the same time, the one where Abigail and John would live after they married. Moreover, John had indicated that Judah could be had more cheaply than any of the respectable farmers' daughters he had interviewed. And as he told his fiancée in a September 30 letter, "Parcimony is a virtue that you and I must study." That settled the matter. Although John had offered to "submit to any Expence, for your Ease and Conveniency that I can possibly afford," Abigail knew better than to give any hint of extravagance right here at the start of the marriage. Replying to John's offer on October 4, she surrendered gracefully, using the same words he had chosen, only rearranging the order. "I am very willing to submit to some inconveniences in order to lessen your expences," she wrote, "tho you know I have no particuliar fancy for Judah yet considering all things, and that your Mamma and you seem to think it would be best to take her, I shall not at present look out any further." This was not an unconditional surrender, for with the qualifying phrase "at present," Abigail reserved the right to revisit the matter if she and Judah could not get along.

CHAPTER 4

"Mrs. Adams"

1764–1770

Abigail Smith and John Adams were married on October 25, 1764, in her father's parsonage in Weymouth. Three weeks shy of twenty, Abigail was nine years younger than the groom. By coincidence, the marriage took place on the fourth anniversary of George III's accession to the British throne. If someone had cornered the bride by the punch bowl and prophesied that within two decades she would be greeted by King George as the wife of the official envoy of the independent states of North America, she would surely have arranged for the reveler to be escorted home.

Parson Smith presided, as he had for Mary and would for her younger sister, Elizabeth, at the latter's marriage to Reverend John Shaw more than a decade later. At Mary's wedding two years earlier, her father had preached from Luke 10:42 ("Mary hath chosen that good part"). John 1:6, which William would select for his youngest daughter's nuptials, was equally upbeat: "There was a man sent from God, whose name was John." It is not known what verse he used at Abigail and John's wedding, but Charles Francis Adams, the couple's grandson and the family historian, claimed in 1840 that shortly after the wedding, Smith preached from Luke 7:33: "For John the Baptist came neither eating bread nor drinking wine; and ye say, He hath a devil." Smith's choice of that passage has been widely ascribed to his continuing discomfort with the man his daughter had chosen to marry, but that was not the explanation Charles Francis Adams heard. In the "Memoir" he published along with a selection of his grandmother's letters in 1840, Charles claimed that a large portion of the Weymouth congregation had objected to the match, both because of long-standing prejudices against lawyers and because "the family of Mr. Adams, the son of a small farmer of the middle class in Braintree, was thought scarcely good enough to match with the minister's daughter, descended from so many of the shining lights of the colony." Of course Charles may have felt the need to throw a veil over whatever tensions still existed between William Smith and his new son-in-law, but one indication that Parson Smith had more benign intentions is the context of the verse he chose. It was a quotation from Jesus Christ, who was not accusing John the Baptist of having a devil but saying that such an accusation had come from "the Pharisees and lawyers"—Jesus's arch-adversaries.

Coming from a man who had never liked Adams and who had managed to delay his marriage to Abigail for nearly three years, Smith's decision to call attention to a biblical figure who had been unfairly maligned certainly seems to have been an attempt at reconciliation. Adams eagerly accepted the olive branch, and from then on he and Parson Smith were friends. As a young father Adams would approvingly set down in his diary Abigail's childhood recollections of her father's maxims about the importance of not speaking ill of others. Apparently he had forgotten that, years earlier, he had written into the same journal a pair of derisive comments from Parson Smith that indisputably violated his motto. One factor making for good relations between Adams and his new father-in-law was that Smith was (at least according to "his Brother Clergymen") "the richest Clergyman in the Province." That meant that, despite Abigail's earlier anxiety that her father would not be able to provide her much of a dowry, Smith actually gave the couple a "very handsome sum of Money"—enough, John recalled years later, to purchase "an Orchard and a very fine Piece of Land near my Paternal House and Homestead."

The home where Abigail and John established themselves in the fall of 1764 was a clapboard-sheathed saltbox, with two stories in front, one in back, and a steep roof designed to prevent the accumulation of snow. There was a barn and forty acres of farmland. As Abigail took charge of the household, she knew that one of her first assignments would be to come to an understanding with her new next-door-neighbor, John's mother. Susanna Adams had often made life miserable for the senior John Adams, and there was real danger that she would take advantage of the newlyweds' close proximity to assert control over them. John and Abigail seem to have prevented her from doing that (it helped that Susanna remarried on December 3, 1766), but for the young bride, it must have been challenging to adapt not only to John but to his family.

The saltbox cottage where Abigail Adams delivered and raised her children (left). Her husband John had inherited the house from his father in 1761, three years before their marriage. Only seventy-five feet away was the home where John had grown up and where his widowed mother still lived (right). Unknown artist, 1849. *Courtesy Adams National Historical Park.*

Mrs. Adams (as even her closest friends now called her) wrote more than 2,000 letters, but not one of them describes her normal work routine during her years as a young wife. The reason her labor left such a scant trace in her writings was not that it was unimportant but that it was assumed. For her it would have made no more sense to report on accomplishments such as the preservation and preparation of food, the maintenance of the dairy, or the manufacture of clothing than it would have been to describe her breathing. So the only way to catch a glimpse of her daily routine is to be attentive to the little hints that she and other women dropped—usually without intending to do so—when the routine was disrupted. For instance, we know that Adams and the servants applied a heavy coating of spices to vegetables before putting them on the table, but only because Adams gave up vegetables altogether when the doctor who inoculated her against smallpox in 1776 imposed a temporary ban on condiments.

As often as she could, Abigail escaped to her sister Mary's home on the other side of Braintree. These halcyon days were too good to last, however. Early in 1766, only a year after Abigail became an Adams, the Cranches moved to Salem, fourteen miles north of Boston, ending the two women's casual visits. "O my Dear Sister I mourn every day more and more the great distance between us," Abigail wrote that fall. In July and then again in October, she wrote Mary to say that she often thought to herself, "if She was but there, I would run away and see her." These feelings were mutual. "I would give a great deal only to know I was within Ten Miles of you [even] if I could not see you," Mary told Abigail.

Abigail and John's first child, named Abigail but called Nabby within the family, was born on July 14, 1765. Adams went into labor only eight and a half months after her wedding day, which raises the possibility that Nabby had been conceived that very night. Or even sooner, for the reality of "Puritan" New England was that one-third of brides, including Paul Revere's first wife, Sarah, and Mary Adams, John's brother's wife, were pregnant on the day they married.

For Abigail, motherhood was exhausting but blissful. The baby was only a few weeks old when her mother exulted to an old friend that she had been "Bless'd with a charming Girl whose pretty Smiles already delight my Heart, who is the Dear Image of her still Dearer Pappa." Like parents everywhere, she caressed her child with endearing epithets (some of which sound strange in modern ears) and hated to see her suffer. "Poor Rogue," she wrote her sister a day after the baby's first birthday. "She has been very poorly these 3 or 4 Days, cutting teeth I believe. Her cough too is bad again." A short time later, little Nabby learned to give hugs. Abigail wrote her sister Mary in October 1766 saying how much she missed Mary's infant daughter Elizabeth. "What would I give to hear her prattle to her Cousin Nabby, to see them put their little arms round one an others necks, and hug each other," she wrote.

By this time Nabby was "fat as a porpouse." That was certain proof of good health, but it also heightened one of the traumas of childhood. The pudgy one-year-old "falls heavey," Abigail reported, and "Bruses her forehead sadly." Abigail asked Mary if she would be willing to lend Nabby the "quilted contrivance"—apparently a makeshift helmet—that a friend had fashioned for little Betsy Cranch. "How vex'd have I felt before now," Abigail wrote Mary two days before her daughter's eighteen-month birthday, "upon hearing parents relate the chitt chat of little Miss, and Master said or did such and such a queer thing." Abigail could "now more easily forgive" this foible, but she hoped that "in company I shall not fall into the same error."

On July 11, 1767, just three days before Nabby's second birthday, Abigail gave birth to a little boy. The next day she and John named him John Quincy after Abigail's grandfather, who was on his deathbed. Like his older sister, he brought the couple much joy and much anxiety. Whereas Abigail remained chiefly concerned about the children's health, John's greatest worries were financial. "What shall we do with this young Fry?" he asked his old friend Richard Cranch, also a father of two. "Johnny must go to Colledge, and Nabby must have fine Cloaths, aye, so must Betcy too and the other"—John had not yet learned the name of the Cranches' newborn daughter Lucy—"And there must be dancing Schools and Boarding Schools and all that, or else, you know, we shall not give them polite Educations, and they will better not have been born you know than not have polite Educations—These Inticipations are not very charming to me."

Richard's financial worries were considerably more pressing than John's. As it became clear that he was not going to succeed any better in Salem than he had in Braintree, Abigail tried to comfort Mary by shifting the blame to his suppliers and customers. The men and women who filled Cranch's orders and purchased his timepieces and wool cards all seemed to follow the motto "get what you can, and keep what you have got." Indeed, his troubles stemmed not from his own failings but from fundamental defects in human nature: "This is a selfish world you know. Interest governs it, there are but very few, who are moved by any other Spring." In the years before her marriage, Abigail had frequently celebrated eighteenth-century philosophers' discovery that humans are endowed with an instinctive feeling of benevolence toward one another. Her brother-in-law's travails seemed to belie that rosy affirmation. Humans are "Generous, Benevolent and Friendly when it is for their interest," she now told Mary; "when any thing is to be got by it, but touch that tender part, their Interest, and you will immediately find the reverse." Was Abigail just saying that to comfort her sister? Or had Richard's harsh experiences and her own maturing perception actually left her sadder but wiser about human nature? That involved the larger question of whether Abigail considered humanity innately good or evil, an issue she would never quite resolve.

Although neither John nor Abigail ever sat down to systematically describe their domestic life in their earliest years together, it is possible to catch glimpses of it. As a bachelor John had always left the shutters open all night during the summer in order to fill the house with the salty air of Massachusetts Bay, less than two miles to the east. Yet his "Squeamish" young wife pointed out that they lived right on the main road through Braintree, so an unshuttered home could not be a private one. The shutters remained closed until late morning, by which time everyone was dressed and doing their chores. John complained to his brother-in-law Richard Cranch that this policy encouraged him to sleep later than he ought.

Closing a letter to her sister Mary, Abigail aired an oddly modern grievance against her husband. Too often, he stuck his head in his newspaper, to the neglect of his consort. "My good Man would send his Love to you all only he sets by reading news paper politicks, and is so taken up with them," Abigail wrote, "that he cannot think of better matters." Abigail must have spoken these words out loud as she wrote them, for John, determined to vindicate himself, grabbed the letter before Abigail could seal it and added a postscript of his own. Insisting that Parliament's repeal of the Stamp Act—its attempt to tax American newspapers; college diplomas; deeds, lawsuits, and other legal documents; ships' papers; and even playing cards—had set his heart "at Ease," John denied being more interested in politics than his in-laws. "What care I for News Paper Politicks?" he demanded. The reality was that the imperial conflict was still very much on John's mind. He was in the thick of a newspaper battle against the royal governor, Francis Bernard. Even in his postscript to Mary Cranch, he could not help scoffing at the niceties of kin-keeping. He replaced the elaborate valediction that traditionally closed eighteenth-century letters with his own shorthand: "da da y[ou]rs, J.A."

As she had during her courtship, Abigail, ever attentive for negative as well as positive models, made a constant study of other couples. John's second cousin, Samuel Adams, and his wife, Elizabeth, visited Abigail and John for three days in July 1766. This was something of an honor, for Samuel had just achieved distinction as a principal organizer of the successful colonial resistance to the Stamp Act. Yet for Abigail, what was most remarkable about Sam Adams was his relationship with his wife. "They are a charming pair," she told her sister Mary. Whereas in 1764 the reunion of Cotton and Lucy Tufts had seemed devoid of affection, Sam and Betsy Adams appeared to have struck just the right balance between passion and public decorum. "In them is to be seen the tenderest affection towards each other, without any fulsome fondness," Abigail observed. Quoting one of her favorite poets, James Thomson, she rejoiced at witnessing the other Adamses' "Perfect Esteem, enliven'd by desire" and observed that in their relationship, "friendship full exerts her softest power." Soft power, founded not on brute force or even legal authority but on friendship: that was her idea of the proper bond between a husband and wife.

One indication that John and Abigail also came close to that ideal is that Abigail, who is best known (aside from being the wife and mother of presidents) for her denunciations of a legal system that treated women as little more than their husbands' slaves, saw her own marriage as liberating. She felt nothing but sympathy for her sister Betsy, still unmarried and living at home except when she could break away to visit Abigail or Mary. And those trips were rare, because all of Elizabeth Smith's overprotective instincts were now focused on the one daughter who remained under her roof. Betsy had planned to visit the Cranches during the summer of 1766, but her mother kept postponing the trip. "As to Sister Betsy, poor Girl her heart is with you, but when her Body will be, is uncertain," Abigail reported to Mary. Betsy had related to Abigail some of what she had been hearing from their mother. One of Elizabeth's objections to Betsy's going abroad was that her "cough is too bad," another that "it is too hot weather." Sympathizing with Betsy's travails reminded Abigail how grateful she was to be out from under her mother's protective glare. "O you know how it always was," Abigail wrote Mary. "Dont you remember the time when I wanted to go to Commencment—These matter[s] you know we always wish'd were otherways."

Throughout Abigail's lifetime married women were legally subsumed in the person of their husbands; a later generation would describe wives as civilly dead. Abigail's most famous utterance—her March 1776 "Remember the Ladies" letter to John—is also the best-known protofeminist statement of the American revolutionary era. And yet two years into her marriage, Abigail was feeling free. "I desire to be very thankful," she told Mary, "that I can do as *I* please now!!!"

Abigail's only major grievance against John was one that could not be helped: his legal business frequently required him to be out of town for days or even weeks at a time. He represented clients not only in his native Suffolk County but in county courts throughout central and eastern Massachusetts (including the district of Maine) and in the superior court, which rode circuit throughout the province. In October 1766, as Abigail approached her second wedding anniversary, she compared her husband to the wandering preachers who never set down roots. "He is such an Itinerant," she told her sister Mary, "that I have but little of his company." A decade later, at the end of John's first year of service to the American cause, Abigail would point out, "In the 12 years we have been married I believe we have not lived together more than six."

John's time away from home increased as his career advanced. "I may be compared to those climates which are deprived of the Sun half the Year," Abigail declared in September 1767. She reminded her husband of a commitment that he had almost never violated during their first few years of marriage: "upon a Sunday you commonly afforded us your benign influence." But not anymore. "When you are absent," she wrote, "Sunday seems a more Lonesome Day to me than any other." Two-year-old Nabby missed her father just as ardently. Abigail reported to John that the child had made up a little song to sing while she rocked her baby brother to sleep: "Come pappa come home to Brother Johnny."

John's frequent absences augmented Abigail's responsibilities. Historians of the colonial era have found that the many roles women had to fill included "deputy husband." No one considered it unfeminine for a wife to help out with the harvest, work the bellows in a blacksmith shop, or staff a store counter (as Benjamin Franklin's wife, Deborah, often did). Deputy husbands took on even more responsibility when their spouses went on lengthy trips, and John frequently wrote Abigail describing work he needed done. Only rarely did she have to perform these tasks herself; her duty was to make sure John's workers accomplished them. "Pray let the People take Care of the Caterpillars," John wrote in May 1772. "Let them go over and over, all the Trees, till there is not the appearance of a nest, or Worm left." Abigail also played a role in her husband's law office. On a June 1769 trip to the district of Maine, he informed her that he hoped to return to Boston in time to get all of his pending cases on the docket for the Suffolk County court that was to meet there the following month. But if he did not make it back in time, Abigail would have to "see that my Actions are entered."

Like John in his meadows and fields, Abigail in her kitchen and dairy was more of a supervisor than a laborer. By July 1767, when John Quincy was born, the family had four servants. Still, Abigail and John were both perfectly willing to soil their hands when the necessity arose. In John's absence Abigail looked upon herself as "left alone," even in a house full of servants, since none of them was her intellectual or social peer. Yet she felt she was on very good terms with her staff, as indicated by her description, in a January 1767 letter to Mary, of her return from an extended visit to the Smith parsonage. "It gives one a pleasing Sensation my Dear Sister, after haveing been absent a little while to see one's self gladly received upon a return, even by one's Servants," she wrote. "I do not know that I was ever more sensibly affected with it than I was to Day; I could behold joy sparkle in the Eyes of every one of them as I enterd the House."

"O Mam, I am glad to see you come home again," said one servant. "[H]ow do you do?"

Another held the returning Nabby and exclaimed, "Dear creature I was affraid she would forget me."

Still another addressed the eighteen-month-old directly: "Nab, do you know Polly, and will you come to her?" As tempting as it may be to accept Abigail's account of her homecoming at face value, it is possible that the servants had exaggerated their enthusiasm at the mistress's return in order to put her in a generous mood—or even that they would have told the same story differently.

By the winter of 1768 John was spending so much time away from his family, especially holding conferences with important clients in Boston, that he decided that the only way to see more of his wife and children was to move them to the provincial capital. At the end of April the family took up residence in a white house in Brattle Square overlooking the harbor. Abigail's feelings about the move were mixed: she would now be able to spend more time with John but much less with her parents, her sister Elizabeth (who had just turned eighteen and was still living at the parsonage), and her South Shore friends and kin. Betsy was distressed that both of her sisters would now be beyond the radius of casual visits and told a cousin, "I cannot bear the thought of their leaving Braintree."

The city to which John had moved his family boasted a population of sixteen thousand and a terrain that bore little resemblance to today's. Built on a peninsula named for the Shawmut Indians who had once inhabited it, Boston would have been an island but for a narrow neck of land connecting it to the mainland. There was not a single spot in the town that was more than half a mile from Boston Harbor. In sharp contrast to Philadelphia and New York, the two largest cities in the British North American colonies, Boston did not have an orderly street grid, and it would have been difficult to impose one on these hills. Legend had it that most of the roads followed old cow paths, but it is hard to imagine any sensible bovine devising such circuitous routes. Like nearly every city of that era, Boston was noisy from dawn to dusk, as horseshoes and carriage wheels clattered across cobblestones and peddlers cried their wares. It stank with garbage, offal, and dung. Cattle and sheep grazed freely on Boston Common, and many families kept chickens and pigs. The Adamses could scarcely have picked a worse time of year to move to Boston, since even in New England, the summers could be sultry, and the heat magnified the stench.

On the positive side, moving to Boston meant exchanging the "inanimate" Anthony Wibird, Braintree's minister, for Reverend Samuel Cooper, whose Brattle Street church was only two blocks from the Adamses' new home. When, eight years later, Abigail exclaimed, "I rejoice in a preacher who has some warmth, some energy, some feeling," she was thinking of Cooper.

Abigail and John were not the only new residents that Boston received in 1768. About this time, Thomas Gage, the commander in chief of His Majesty's forces in North America, decided to concentrate most of his nearly ten thousand troops in Boston and other coastal cities. This was partly a cost-cutting move. The soldiers had previously been stationed at British forts on the frontier, serving the dual missions of protecting the colonists from the Indians and trying to prevent unruly frontier settlers from provoking hostilities. Many of the forts were remote from navigable water, making them expensive to resupply. The British government was trying to balance its budget not only by taxing the colonists but by retrenching expenses. Yet most Bostonians, including the Adamses, suspected that Gage's other motive for moving the troops to the cities was the real one: he wanted to clamp down on the colonists. Urban "mobs" (as imperial officials called them) had nullified the Stamp Act, and the crown was not going to let the Townshend duties—taxes on paint, lead, glass, wine, and (most famously) tea imposed by Parliament in June 1767—suffer the same fate.

The sight of two regiments of soldiers camped on Boston Common and patrolling the town offended the city's pride, but the practical effects of the occupation were mixed. A small number of well-connected merchants won lucrative contracts to supply food and fuel to the soldiers, but working-class Bostonians faced competition from off-duty soldiers seeking to supplement their meager salaries by moonlighting. The troops, most of whom had nothing but contempt for these provincial bumpkins, were frequently accused of bullying the locals, and Patriot leaders repeatedly warned Gage that his use of soldiers to dampen civil conflict was going to have just the opposite effect.

The Adams family experienced the obnoxious British presence firsthand. Then as now, army sergeants liked to drill their men as often as possible, even during peacetime and even if the troops were hardened veterans, in order to keep them busy. In Boston, a highly favored location for these drills was Brattle Square, right outside the Adamses' window. As the officers called the cadences and the soldiers' boots struck the cobblestones, it must have been well nigh impossible for Abigail and her servants to get John Quincy, who had his first birthday on Monday, July 11, and Nabby, who turned three the following Thursday, down for their naps.

When the family moved to Boston, Abigail was pregnant again. Susanna, who was born on December 28, 1768, and baptized by Reverend Cooper on New Year's Day, was a frail child, and Abigail worried that the foul air of the third-largest city on the Atlantic seaboard was making her condition worse. So some time late in the spring of 1769 she made the agonizing decision to drop Susanna off in Braintree, where she was presumably cared for by servants and a relative (possibly John's mother, for whom she was named), Abigail returning to Boston to look after her two toddlers. By the end of June, John was in Falmouth, Maine (which then encompassed what is now the town of Portland), winning several big cases for his clients but pining for Abigail, Nabby, little Johnny, and Suky (as the infant was called). His homesickness is the only plausible explanation for the remarkably tactless comment he sent Abigail on June 29: "Cant you contrive to go to Braintree to kiss my little Suky, for me[?]" he asked.

By early autumn, Abigail was already pregnant with her fourth child. What more she tried to do to shore up Susanna's health is not known, but all her efforts proved unavailing. The girl died on February 4, 1770, at the age of thirteen months. Many years later, Abigail's sister Elizabeth would recall that the child had passed away "just as Reason was budding, & when her playful Innocence was most engaging."

* * *

A month after Abigail buried Susanna, while she was grieving one child and seven months pregnant with the next (Charles would be born at the end of May), the clash that every Bostonian had been expecting finally erupted. On March 2, workers at a ropewalk (where ships' rigging was made) taunted a British soldier seeking part-time work. One said he would only hire the man to "go and clean my shithouse." Three days later, on March 5, a Patriot barber contemptuously directed that a British officer have his hair dressed by an untrained apprentice. The officer refused to pay, and the boy ran after him and received a beating for his trouble. That night, furious colonists gathered outside the Customs House. The officer of the day, Captain Thomas Preston, feared the crowd intended to rush the guard and rob the king's revenue, so he hastened to the scene with a detachment of soldiers. As the crowd pressed against the troops, taunting them and pelting them first with snowballs and then with rocks, oyster shells, and shards of ice, someone—probably not Preston—shouted "fire," and the soldiers opened up. By the time Preston got control of his men, five of the townspeople were dead or mortally wounded.

There is no record of Abigail Adams's reaction to the so-called Boston Massacre. John was as angry as anyone at the imperial government's occupation of his adopted hometown, but he believed the crowd, which he described as a "motley rabble of saucy boys, negroes and molattoes, Irish teagues, and out landish Jack Tarrs," was in the wrong. When Preston was arrested for murder, Adams readily agreed to defend him. Part of his motivation was to disprove the widespread allegation that a British officer could never receive justice in an American court. If John could persuade the jury to acquit Preston, he would demonstrate that mobs like the one that had gathered outside the Customs House were not the true face of American resistance to imperial tyranny. The trials were scheduled for the following autumn.

Meanwhile Boston was rocked by another kind of disturbance: Reverend Whitefield came to town.

CHAPTER 5

"I Should Certainly Have Been a Rover"

1770–1774

Starting in the 1730s, a heavenly fire swept through New England. Evangelical revivals, sometimes led by the local minister but just as often targeting him, inflamed dozens of towns. A later generation would christen the movement the Great Awakening, which might suggest a discrete series of events. Actually, outbursts of religious passion flared up and died down throughout the rest of the eighteenth century, and the early 1800s brought a Second Great Awakening. One of the most passionate and persuasive voices of the revival belonged to George Whitefield. Although he never left the established Church of England, he had less in common with his fellow Anglicans than with religious dissenters, primarily Baptists, Presbyterians, and converted Congregationalists. Modern-day historians have compared Whitefield, who made a half-dozen tours through the North American colonies between 1740 and 1770, to a rock star, and the analogy is apt. As he traveled from town to town calling upon every individual to undertake a "new birth," his performances drew ever larger crowds.

A host of New England ministers were drawn into the fervor of the Great Awakening, but Abigail's father was not among them. Indeed, Smith stood with the sizable cadre of traditional ministers who saw the revival as worse than useless. In his eyes, religious "enthusiasm" (as opponents called passionate religious expression) was a form of delusion. People who had been born again often believed they had established direct communication with God, a conviction that qualified them to pass judgment on anyone who remained unconverted and to question all authority they considered impious. The revivalist Gilbert Tennent famously warned of the "danger of an unconverted ministry"—"Old Light" ministers like William Smith. Curiosity nonetheless propelled Abigail to several of the open-air revivals where Whitefield addressed Boston's saints and sinners in August and September 1770. Many of those who came to see and hear him that summer were profoundly moved. When, shortly after the Boston revivals, word spread that Whitefield had taken sick while preaching in Newburyport, Massachusetts, and died there on September 30, an enslaved Bostonian named Phillis Wheatley was moved to write a verse elegy. "Thou didst in strains of eloquence refin'd," Wheatley told the deceased preacher, "Inflame the heart, and captivate the mind." It was the first poem she ever published—and indeed the first time an African American woman ever appeared in print. (Three years later, Wheatley would become the first black American to publish a book of her poetry.)

Whitefield made much less of an impression on Abigail Adams. If anything, seeing his performances only confirmed her preference for her father's more sedate preaching style, which appealed more to the head than to the heart. Her only surviving reference to Whitefield can scarcely be described as religious. In a letter to her cousin Isaac Smith, who was traveling in Europe, she contended that North America, and especially New England, were better places to live than the British Isles. Americans were "more upon an Eaquality in point of knowledg and of circumstances," she noted, and they were also more sincere in their religious professions—as Whitefield had discovered. "The last Sermon I heard him preach," Adams told Smith, "he told us that he had been a very great traveller, yet he had never seen so much of the real appearence of Religion in any Country, as in America." Far from being persuaded by Whitefield that she needed to cast off her old life and be born again, Adams had mined his sermon for evidence of the superiority of her native land. Abigail's dispassionate reaction to Whitefield reflected a pattern of religious moderation she inherited from her father, confirmed during her teenage years—and shared with her husband.

It was not Abigail but John who in 1770 experienced the agony of self-doubt followed by an epiphany, and his travails were not religious but political. In a series of trials that took place in October and November 1770, Adams persuaded a Boston jury to acquit Thomas Preston on all counts. Most of his men were also cleared, although two who were determined to have fired fatal shots were convicted of manslaughter and branded on the thumb. But Preston's redemption had come at the expense of Adams's health, and the stress of the trial was not his only concern. The Boston town meeting elected him to the provincial House of Representatives on June 6, 1770, after he had agreed to defend Preston, which indicated that most of the townspeople approved of what he was doing. Others, however, believed he had betrayed the cause by enabling the man they considered the murderer of five good Americans to get off scot-free.

Early in 1771, John resolved to move his family back to their old house in Braintree. He was, he told Abigail's cousin Isaac Smith, Jr., "determined to shake off a little of that Load of public and private Care which has for some Time oppressed me." Had he not done so, he said, he might "soon have shaken off this mortal body" instead. It is clear enough what Adams meant by his load of public care. But what "private Care" did he hope to escape by returning to the place of his birth? Perhaps he was feeling crushed by the enormous expense of living in town. Selling his town house would allow him to pay off the debt he had incurred in purchasing it, and the Adams cottage in Braintree, a gift from his father, was his, free and clear. Apparently John had spent the spring of 1771 exactly as he had passed the spring of 1768, counting the days until the ice and snow would clear, allowing him to clear out—out of Braintree in 1768 and out of Boston in 1771. The Adamses left the provincial capital on April 13, three years after their arrival.

About the time they returned to Braintree, John and Abigail both received long letters from Isaac Smith, Jr., describing his travels through England. Smith's comments to Abigail provoked the most searching ruminations on the subjugation of women that she had ever yet put on paper. She began her April 20, 1771, reply by confessing that "from my Infancy I have always felt a great inclination to visit the Mother Country as tis call'd." Indeed, "Had nature formed me of the other Sex, I should certainly have been a rover." Abigail's desire to see England had been dampened by "the unnatural treatment which this our poor America has received" from the imperial government, but her wanderlust had not. Yet she would almost certainly never see Europe, because women never made the sort of educational tour Smith was now enjoying. One reason, she acknowledged, was their own frailty: "few are hardy eno' to venture abroad, and explore the amaizing variety of distant Lands." But still more onerous restrictions were imposed by men. "Women you know Sir are considerd as Domestick Beings," even though "they inherit an Eaquel Share of curiosity with the other Sex," Adams wrote.

At every stage of a woman's life, there was some insuperable obstacle to her traveling abroad. Before she married, she risked forming a compromising connection with some man—or being suspected of having done so, which was nearly as bad. Owing not only to women's weakness but to "the many Dangers we are subject too from your Sex," it was "almost imposible for a Single Lady to travel without injury to her character." It was nearly as difficult for married women to go abroad with their husbands. In this era before reliable birth control, most young wives, including Abigail, immediately began having babies, and the constant alternation of pregnancy and nursing, combined with the duty to care for older children—these were "obstacles sufficient to prevent their Roving."

There was still more evidence in Abigail's reply to Isaac Smith of her acute consciousness of gender differences. In his February 21, 1771, letter to John, Smith mentioned meeting Catharine Macaulay, England's renowned female historian. The compliment Smith paid Macaulay was backhanded at best. "She is not so much distinguished in company by the beauties of her person," he told John, "as the accomplishments of her mind." In the letter he wrote Abigail the same day, Smith did not mention Macaulay at all. But Abigail read her cousin's letter to John and mentioned it in her own note to the traveler. Passing over Smith's snide reference to Macaulay's physical appearance, Abigail expressed in effusive terms her own interest in learning more about the great female historian. "I have a great desire to be made acquainted with Mrs. Maccaulays own history," she wrote. "One of my own Sex so eminent in a tract so uncommon naturally raises my curiosity and all I could ever learn relative to her, is this that she is a widdow Lady and Sister to Mr. Sawbridge [an English radical]. I have a curiosity to know her Education, and what first prompted her to engage in a Study never before Exibited to the publick by one of her own Sex and Country, tho now to the honour of both so admirably performed by her."

Catharine Macaulay fascinated Adams for the same reason Esther Wheelwright had: she had confounded men's limited expectations of women. Whereas Wheelwright had begun her journey to nonconformity unwillingly—as an Indian captive—Adams suspected that Macaulay must have been set apart by her education. Like her interest in the great female historian, Abigail's seemingly offhand comment that women and men "inherit an Eaquel Share of curiosity" was a challenge to long-standing prejudices. At the time most men believed all of Eve's

CATHARINE MACAULAY
In the Character of a Roman Matron
lamenting the lost Liberties of Rome.
from an Original Painting of Miss Read.
Williams sculp.

Catharine Sawbridge Macaulay (1731–1791), English historian. Abigail Adams always idolized Macaulay but did not approve of her second marriage, in 1778, to William Graham, a ship surgeon's mate who was twenty-six years her junior. Engraving by Williams (after a painting by Catherine Read) in *London Magazine*, July 1770. *Courtesy Massachusetts Historical Society.*

daughters were by nature insatiably curious, and many women agreed. Adams herself had once kidded John about possessing the "curiosity of a Girl." Isaac Smith received his cousin's letter praising Catharine Macaulay and wishing she herself could travel abroad at about the same time he learned that John's personal and political burdens had persuaded him to move his family back to Braintree. Smith's response was to suggest that John Adams do what he himself had done: take a "voyage to Europe"—alone.

Within a year of the Adamses' return to Braintree, John's financial prospects had brightened, and in August 1772 he purchased a substantial brick house in Boston. The family could not move in right away, because Abigail was a month away from delivering her fifth child. Thomas Boylston Adams was born on September 15. Two months later, in November, Abigail and the children joined John in the provincial capital. The family's previous stay in Boston had lasted only three years, and this one was destined to be even shorter.

Two years after first expressing interest in Catharine Macaulay, Abigail began a long if uneven friendship with another woman of letters. In the summer of 1773, she accompanied her husband on a thirty-mile trip down the coast to the sessions of the Plymouth County court. The two lingered in Plymouth several days with John's friend James Warren and James's wife, Mercy, who had just begun what would become a long and distinguished literary career. The previous year, Mercy, the sister of Patriot firebrand James Otis, Jr., had published her first play, a satire based on the events surrounding the Boston Massacre entitled *The Adulateur*.

Warren's literary ambition was not all that set her apart from the typical middle-class woman of her era. At a time when one of the cardinal virtues that ladies were supposed to exhibit was cheerfulness, she could be quite unpleasant. For instance, when Abigail opened her first letter to Warren in the traditional way—with flattery—Warren wrote back lamenting that letter writers so often heaped praise on their correspondents, all "without any other design but to Convey an Idea of politeness as the Characteristick of the person the most Lavish therein." Warren of course went on to deny that she was accusing Adams of any such thing, assuring her that her compliments merely showed that she had a good heart. But even as Warren backtracked, she stumbled again, for she affirmed that Adams was generous to everyone who had not shown "any remarkable instance of depravity to Create disgust."

Disgust was the last word in Warren's first paragraph, and it seemed to hang there in a way that might have caused Adams to question her celebrated literary merit had she not been a published author. As it was, the Adamses were so impressed with Warren that they decided to leave Nabby, who turned eight that summer, with her for an extended visit.

For Abigail, Warren's willingness to look at the dark side of things paid immediate dividends. For more than a decade, Adams and her sisters, cousins, and friends had been exchanging correspondence with the explicit purpose of furthering each other's education. Since one of the principal subjects the correspondents discussed was the books they had been reading, the whole project was in some ways a precursor to the modern book group, with one important exception: thoroughly

Mercy Otis Warren (1728–1814). Abigail admired the acclaimed female poet, dramatist, pamphleteer, and historian, but their relationship, which began in 1773, was often troubled. John Singleton Copley, ca. 1763. *Photograph ©2009 Museum of Fine Arts, Boston.*

impressed with the authors they read and at the same time modest about their own powers of observation, the young letter writers rarely found anything to criticize in the books they discussed. Warren had no such compunction. When Adams sent her a copy of a pamphlet called *On the Management and Education of Children* (supposedly the work of a woman named Juliana-Susannah Seymour but actually written by a man named John Hill) and asked her opinion of it, Warren happily obliged. She did not like the author's assertion that the first thing a mother should teach her child was to be generous toward others. That precept was too general, she wrote. Moreover, honesty, not generosity, was the first thing a child must learn.

Warren's criticisms emboldened Adams. The following December, in a letter primarily devoted to British officials' attempts to land three shiploads of East India Company tea on the wharves of Boston, Abigail offered a review of a book of plays by the seventeenth-century French author Jean-Baptiste Poquelin (best known by his stage name, Molière). She hated it, and she listed half a dozen reasons why. The characters appeared to be "unfinished," "there seems to me to be a general Want of Spirit," and Molière had "ridiculed Vice without engageing us to Virtue," she wrote. "Tho he has drawn many pictures of real Life, yet all pictures of life are not fit to be exibited upon the Stage." To be sure, the mordantly sarcastic Molière made an easy target for Abigail, who was (as she well understood) "not Naturally of a gloomy temper." And she still felt the need to conclude her comments on an apologetic note, expressing fear that she would "incur the charge of vanity by thus criticising upon an Author who has met with so much applause." It was nonetheless a bold critique, and it cannot be a coincidence that Adams penned it only five months after reading Warren's harsh appraisal of Juliana-Susannah Seymour.

Adams's comments on Molière were addressed to Mercy Warren, who, once again showing her contrarian personality, immediately informed her that she disagreed with them.

Warren influenced Adams in other ways as well. In her very first letter to Abigail, Mercy observed that child raising "is of the utmost importance to society though for a Number of Years it is almost wholly left to our uninstructed sex." Warren's reference to women as the "uninstructed sex" was a more explicit denunciation of their paltry opportunity for formal education than anything Adams had written up to that time, and it would soon inspire her to lodge her own complaints. Moreover, Warren exhibited, in her own clumsy way, an acute consciousness of the ties of feminine solidarity that had fueled Adams's interest in Esther Wheelwright and Catharine Macaulay. After writing a patriotic poem, but before circulating it, she asked for John's opinion of it but not Abigail's, telling her, "I will not trust the partiallity of My own sex."

Warren was the first person outside the family with whom Abigail extensively discussed the conflict between Great Britain and its North American colonies. In 1770 Parliament had repealed all of the Townshend duties except the one on tea, retaining the tea tax as an assertion of its sovereignty. As expected, the repeal of all the other duties took the wind out of Patriot sails, and historians often refer to the subsequent three-year period as "the quiet years." Then in 1773 the government overplayed its hand.

By this time the British East India Company was near bankruptcy. Parliament decided in May 1773 to shore up the company's finances by removing an earlier requirement that its tea be sold only in the British Isles. Now, for the first time, the firm would be permitted to ship its product directly from India to the colonies. This concession was expected not only to refill the East India Company's coffers but to make British tea cheaper than the Dutch leaf that had been routinely smuggled into North America. Bargain-hunting colonists would feel compelled to switch to British tea—and to pay the parliamentary tax. Many Patriots believed their only chance to keep their countrymen from buying the tea, establishing a precedent of consumer consent to British taxation, was to prevent it from being landed. In reporting these efforts, Adams offered her first written discussion of imperial politics. "The Tea that bainfull weed is arrived," she told Mercy Warren on December 5. "Great and I hope Effectual opposition has been made to the landing of it. . . . The proceedings of our Citizens have been United, Spirited and firm." Indeed Patriot agitators were receiving new recruits at a brisk pace. "The flame is kindled and like Lightning it catches from Soul to Soul," Adams reported. She went on to predict that unless the crown backed down, which seemed unlikely, the empire would erupt in "civil War."

Patriots soon mounted the "Effectual opposition" to the landing of the tea for which Adams had hoped. She was home alone on the night of December 16, 1773, when a crowd of Patriots, famously dressed as Mohawk Indians, boarded three East India Company ships and emptied 340 chests of tea into the harbor.

The year 1773 held one more surprise for Abigail. In December, having made a rare solo visit to her parents in the neighboring town of Weymouth, she was trapped there by a blizzard. The roads were "impassible with any carriage," and she was apparently unwilling to brave the winter winds on horseback (indeed, there is no evidence that she ever in her life mounted a horse). Thus, for once, John had to take responsibility for the children while she was the one who yearned for home. "Alass!" she wrote him. "How many snow banks devide thee and me and my warmest wishes to see thee will not melt one of them." Adams had never "left so large a flock of little ones before," and she implored her husband to send a messenger informing her "how they all do." Also, "Our little Tommy you must kiss for Mamma." And John should let Johnny and three-year-old "Charlly" know that Grandmother Smith was sending them mittens. "I feel gratified with the imagination at the close of the Day," Abigail wrote John, "in seeing the little flock round you inquiring when Mamma will come home—as they often do for thee in thy absence."

* * *

As Abigail and others had predicted, the battle over the East India Company's tea brought the long-simmering dispute between crown and colony to a crisis. But before she could fully engage herself in the common cause, she had to deal with another calamity closer to home. Elizabeth, her younger sister, was, at twenty-three, still unmarried and living at home. Isaac Smith, Jr., Elizabeth and Abigail's first cousin, reportedly would have liked to have proposed to Parson Smith's youngest daughter, but he never mustered the courage to try to turn their longstanding friendship into something more. Elizabeth did show interest in one young man for a while, but they soon broke it off. Another suitor (unnamed in the records) also seemed entirely appropriate—to everyone but Betsy. "She knows the wishes of all her Friends and to them joins her own, but all will not avail," Abigail told Mary. "What pitty tis we cannot reason ourselves into love." Elizabeth noticed that she seemed to be spending more time with her parents' friends than with eligible bachelors, and she joked, "If I may judge by the Presents I have lately received," the only gentlemen among whom she was "growing a Favorite" were elderly. But the simple fact was that she enjoyed being single. "There seems to me to be at present a real aversion to change of state," Abigail reported.

Adams was becoming reconciled to her sister's determination to wait for a suitor she could truly love. "I really think she must take her own way and nobody say her Nay," she wrote. Betsy's other friends and family members were not so ready to give in gracefully (and indeed Abigail's sense of resignation was probably only temporary), for time was running out, and no one could believe that Betsy truly wanted to remain unmarried, an extremely unappealing prospect at the time. Unless a single woman came from a very wealthy family—and Betsy did not—she would spend her entire life shuttling from one relative to the next, never becoming the mistress of her own home. Once a colonial American woman married, her new husband could drop dead the very next day, and there would be no pressure on her to remarry. She could live out the rest of her life, even if she had decades to go, as a respectable widow. But women who never married at all earned no such esteem, as evidenced by the term *spinster,* which referred to their spinning thread in order to help defray the expenses incurred in their maintenance.

Finally a man came into Betsy's life. But her family saw no cause for celebration, because he was her father's boarder. By the middle of the eighteenth century, the young man who finds himself under the same roof as a ripe young maiden—whether a servant girl or the innkeeper's daughter—had already become a literary cliché. Word reached Abigail that Betsy was keeping company with the boarder, a schoolteacher named John Shaw, and alarm bells immediately went off.

Every young woman of the provincial middle class knew that her "character"—her reputation for chastity—was all she had. Even a sliver of suspicion that she had compromised herself with a man who had not pledged to marry her might doom her chances of ever finding a partner. Over the course of her lifetime, Abigail denounced a great many of the burdens that society placed on women, but she left it to future generations to question the sexual double standard. The moment she heard that her sister's reputation was threatened, she sprang into action. Early in 1774, she addressed a letter of warning that was veiled in euphemism (lest, God forbid, it should miscarry) but unmistakable nonetheless. Elizabeth must renounce the connection. The sooner the better, for spring was just around the corner, and everyone knew that was when young women's as well as young men's fancies turned to thoughts of love. "The Month of May," she warned, was "the most dangerous." Abigail thought it would be best if her sister decamped to Boston for the time being. That way she would no longer be living in the same house as the man with whom she had flirted. Moreover, she would find it easier to forget about Shaw if she met other men. "Boston," Abigail told Betsy, "is an excellent place to quench old Flames, and kindle new ones."

Abigail's warning did not have the desired effect. In fact, Betsy candidly told her, it "vexed me to be suspected"—so much so that she felt compelled to delay replying to her sister's letter until her initial "Bitterness," "Resentment," and "Acrimony" had abated.

CHAPTER 6

"Mrs. Delegate"

1774

When Elizabeth Smith was finally ready to respond to Abigail's admonition to stop seeing John Shaw, she emphasized the effort it had cost her to write with the "*gentle Treatment* due to a Sister"—the obvious implication being that she wished Abigail had done the same. Clever in her defense, Betsy suggested that the conversations she had been having with Shaw were no different from the dialogues (in-person as well as epistolary) that she and many of her kinswomen and female friends had used to compensate for their lack of formal education. It should be possible, she said, for a man and a woman to "be fond of conversing on what they have read, and on the different Opinions of various Authors, on particular Subjects, without exciting Suspicions in a Family that are dishonourary to both Parties." Or did Abigail really want her to "commence Prude" and distance herself from a man with whom she had never had any romantic connection?

Elizabeth hit upon a strikingly creative way to wrap up her response to Abigail's warning. The last page of her letter included a deposition declaring, "We John Shaw, and Elizabeth Smith have no such Purpose in Our Hearts, as has been unjustly surmised." She signed the document, and it was witnessed by both of her parents (although these were obvious forgeries). The deposition also bore the signature of John Shaw—which Betsy had cut out of one of his letters and clipped into place, presumably without his knowledge. Meanwhile she and Shaw continued their cordial conversations.

If there was a single moment when the American Revolution became inevitable, it was the day the British ministry headed by Frederick, Lord

North, determined its response to the Boston Tea Party. Only about fifty men had participated in the destruction of the tea (although hundreds of Boston radicals cheered from the docks). Yet North decided that the punishment for this outrage must be collective. Over a nine-week period in the spring of 1774, Parliament passed four measures that spread alarm not only in Boston, not just throughout Massachusetts, but all over British North America.

The first step was to suffocate Boston by closing its port. But the provincial capital would not suffer alone, for Parliament also adopted legislation overhauling the colonial government of Massachusetts. Up until this time juries had been chosen by the town meetings or by locally elected constables. Now they would be handpicked by the county sheriffs, who were selected by the governor. Since 1691 the provincial council, which had both executive and legislative duties, had been appointed by the lower house of the assembly (subject to the approval of the governor). Henceforth councilors would be chosen in London. The Massachusetts Government Act, adopted on May 20, 1774, attacked New England's bedrock political institution, the town meeting, restricting the towns to one meeting per year to elect local officials and provincial representatives.

Parliament was not yet finished. Thanks in large part to John Adams's vigorous advocacy, none of the British soldiers involved in the Boston Massacre had received more than token punishment. But North and his ministers worried that British officers accused of future crimes might not receive the same impartial consideration. So the Lords and Commons approved the Administration of Justice Act, affording special protection to any officer of the British government whose duties subjected him to prosecution for a capital crime in Massachusetts courts: he could opt to be tried in England, where he could count on facing a more sympathetic jury. All of these were aimed at a single province (and especially at its largest town), but two other laws that passed Parliament in the spring of 1774 had much wider application. Contrary to a widespread modern misconception, the infamous Quartering Act did not actually force colonists to board redcoats in their homes. It simply said that the owners of empty buildings could not refuse to house British troops in them. Although the proprietors would be compensated, the money was to come from the local legislature, so free Americans believed the Quartering Act posed the same threat to their property rights as parliamentary taxation.

Parliament was not trying to punish Americans when it adopted the Quebec Act, which received the royal assent on June 22, for it was simply a long-overdue effort to set up a permanent system of government in the vast northern territory wrested from France more than a decade earlier. Yet free subjects in other provinces viewed the Quebec Act as an attack on them, since it allowed the colony's Catholic majority to establish their faith as Quebec's official church. The law also extended the province's southern border all the way down to the Ohio River, denying settlers as well as land speculators in the older colonies access to the vast and fertile territory watered by the rivers that flowed into the Ohio from the north. Had the Quebec Act not been nullified by the American Revolution, the entire Midwest, from Ohio and Indiana to Minnesota and Wisconsin, would now be part of Canada.

Bostonians agreed that Parliament had launched a multipronged assault on their most basic liberties, but they differed on how to respond. Radicals wanted the whole colony immediately to halt all trade with Britain, punishing Parliament for closing the port of Boston by shutting down every other harbor in the province as well. Merchants and moderates did not think Massachusetts should act alone, and a final decision was deferred until the other colonies could be consulted. The twelve provinces stretching from New Hampshire to South Carolina agreed to send delegates to a continental congress, to be held in Philadelphia in September 1774. On June 17, the Massachusetts legislature elected John Adams as one of its five deputies.

This was the first in a series of honors that would eventually win Adams what he had always hoped for—lasting fame—but at great cost, both to him and to his family. Like many of Adams's later public assignments, this one required an extended separation from Abigail and their four children. Nothing new there, for John had spent his entire legal career traveling to distant county courts and following the superior court on its circuit. But this absence would be much harder on Abigail, and not only for its length. In the past, the couple had always been able to reach each other by mail within a few days, but that would not be the case while John was three hundred miles away in Philadelphia. Moreover, John had decided to move the family back to Braintree, and Abigail would be taking over the farm at a time when the Adamses' other principal source of income, John's legal fees, fell to a trickle owing to the judicial chaos resulting from Patriot refusal to comply with the Massachusetts Government Act. Nor would John be able to spend the rest of the summer putting the farm in order, because he felt compelled to accompany the superior court on its circuit through the northeastern corner of the state—even though he did not expect it to do much business.

As the judges and lawyers made their way north, John began sending Abigail instructions for the proper management of the farmhands. They must literally make hay while the sun shone, he exhorted her, for recent rains had imposed a delay that could prove disastrous. She should also consult with the hands "about a proper Time to get me a few freights of Marsh Mud" to fertilize the crops. A week later, John, having made it as far as the town of York in the district of Maine, asked Abigail to take on a task to which he himself had proved inadequate: she must get the farm tenants to pay their rent. The amounts due were nominally expressed in pounds, shilling, and pence, but the mutual understanding was that the tenants would pay with labor. "You must take Care my Dear, to get as much Work out of our Tenants as possible," John wrote Abigail on June 30. "Belcher is in Arrears. He must work. Hayden must work. Harry Field must work, and Jo. Curtis too must be made to settle. He owes something. Jo. Tirrell too, must do something—and Isaac. I cant loose such Sums as they owe me—and I will not." The next day John shifted his attention to the need to cut costs. "I must intreat you," he wrote Abigail, "to rouse your whole Attention to the Family, the stock, the Farm, the Dairy. Let every Article of Expence which can possibly be spared be retrench'd."

In urging Abigail to slash her expenditures, John sounded one of the major themes of the revolutionary era. The colonists needed to produce more and consume less if they hoped to sustain their boycott of British merchandise. This political imperative was accompanied by a quasi-religious feeling that excessive consumption of British luxuries had corrupted Americans. The only way they could purify themselves was to return to the simpler ways of the past.

Another of John's concerns as he made ready for his trip to Philadelphia was his sons' and daughter's education. "For God Sake," he wrote from Falmouth, Maine, on July 7, "make your Children, *hardy*, *active* and *industrious*, for Strength, Activity and Industry will be their only Resource and Dependance." John had confidence in Abigail's ability to keep the children's feet to the fire, but he was much less optimistic about the more practical matter of finding them decent instruction. The children would have no problem learning French, John wrote; their mother could take care of that. (Clearly he did not share his wife's low estimate of her proficiency in that tongue.) Other subjects, however, presented bigger challenges. "I am very thoughtfull and anxious about our Johnny," he told Abigail, specifically about "What School to send him to." He was appealing not so much for advice as for sympathy.

So little business came before the superior court that John was barely able to cover his considerable travel expenses. Even worse was the burden of involuntary idleness. Seething with a strange combination of anxiety and ennui, he sat down at a rough-hewn table at a tavern in York, Maine, on Wednesday, June 29, and wrote Abigail a letter. And then another. And then a third—all on the same day. On Thursday, still in York, he wrote her two more letters, and then one a day for the next three days. On Wednesday, July 6, he added to a missive he had started the previous day and then wrote her two more.

Not all of the grievances John expressed in the summer of 1774 could be laid at the feet of Lord North. During his idle hours in Maine he conversed with attorneys from all over New Hampshire as well as the northeastern counties of his own province. And he learned to his distress that many of them were immensely wealthy. "I find that the Country"—by which he meant everywhere except the Boston area, his home territory—"is the Situation to make Estates by the Law." Durham, New Hampshire, attorney John Sullivan was "younger, both in Years and Practice than I am," he wrote. "He began with nothing, but is now said to be worth Ten thousand Pounds, . . . consisting in Houses and Lands, Notes, Bonds, and Mortgages. He has a fine Stream of Water, with an excellent Corn Mill, Saw Mill, Fulling Mill, Scyth Mill and others, in all six Mills. . . . As he has earned Cash in his Business at the Bar, he has taken Opportunities, to purchase Farms of his Neighbours." As an inevitable consequence, "he is treated with great Respect in this Neighbourhood." The Adamses were by no means destitute, but John felt he was "poor in Comparison of others," and he could not escape the nagging feeling that he had missed his chance. And now, just when he was poised to join Sullivan and his brother James in the magic circle, Parliament's overreaction to the Boston Tea Party had virtually shut down the legal business.

Yet that was not the whole story. It was something of a relief for John to exchange his personal anxiety for something larger. "We live my dear Soul, in an Age of Tryal," he wrote Abigail on May 12, but she should not "imagine from all this that I am in the Dumps. Far otherwise." The standoff between Britain and its colonies posed a real threat to the family's finances, but it had restored John's fighting spirit.

The imperial crisis had a similar impact on John's old crony Richard Cranch and his wife, Mary, Abigail's sister. The Cranches were living in Boston in 1774, and all that summer, they agonized over whether to escape to Braintree, as the Adamses had. "I have been so long in an uncertainty what we ought to do," Mary wrote Abigail in August, what with "one Friend advising one way and one another . . . I feel rack'd. I think I cannot bear it much longer." In one way Richard's situation was just the opposite of John's. That summer, as Adams sat in taverns on the Maine coast fuming over his enforced idleness, Cranch was (as Mary reported) "so hurried with Work that he does not know how to spare time to see after any thing." And yet all this labor was not getting him anywhere. Richard's business instincts had not improved since the days when John had ridiculed his gullibility as a horse trader. For all the genuine sense of hurry he displayed as he repaired old clocks and watches and occasionally snatched time to make new ones, he was, like his timepieces, running in place. And Mary's distress was even worse. "I do not know what is the reason but I never felt so low spirit'd in my life," she confided to Abigail. "I am full of aprehentions of—I dont know what."

The Cranches' personal troubles, like those John complained about, were exacerbated by the imperial conflict. Early in the summer of 1774, it became clear that the colonies were going to halt all importations from Britain, which would prevent Richard from obtaining the spare parts he required. Moreover, the proposed ban on exports would deprive his would-be customers of the income they needed to purchase his wares. Already householders were resolving to forgo frivolous purchases (such as pocket watches). Yet for the Cranches, as for the Adamses, there was something liberating about merging their personal troubles with those that the North ministry had inflicted on the colonies. After complaining to her sister Abigail about being "rack'd" with depression and indecision, Mary exclaimed, "What unnumberd distresses has Lord North brought upon thousands of Innocent Creatures." Just as, eight years earlier, Abigail had tried to take the edge off her brother-in-law's failure to thrive in Salem by attributing it to the greed and parsimony of his customers and suppliers, Mary took some comfort in laying the family's continuing distress at the feet of the dominant party in Parliament.

* * *

On Tuesday, August 9, Abigail rode up to Boston with John. This was not a social call. The very next day he was to meet up with the other Massachusetts deputies to the intercolonial congress. On Wednesday morning, a huge crowd gave the congressmen a rousing sendoff, escorting them to the post road and the beginning of their three-hundred-mile trek to Philadelphia. Afterward, Abigail returned to Braintree, where, as she had predicted, she was soon pining for her husband. Less than a week after seeing him off, she assured him she would "rejoice at every Saturday evening," since that was when the mail came.

During some of the intervals Adams might normally have spent with her husband, she tried to console herself by contemplating the numerous parallels between the colonists' trials and those faced by the ancient Greeks and Romans. She predicted that the middle of September (when the First Continental Congress would get down to work) would be as ill-omened for Great Britain as the Ides of March had been for Julius Caesar. In an August 19 letter to John, she reported that seven-year-old John Quincy was reading to her from Charles Rollin's histories of ancient Greece and Rome. And she reminded him that the Greek historian Polybius had declared in his history of Sparta that "As there is nothing more desirable, or advantage[ou]s than peace, when founded in justice and honour, so there is nothing more shameful and at the same time more pernicious when attained by bad measures, and purchased at the price of liberty."

These classical comparisons inspired Abigail without assuaging her loneliness. In the same August 19 letter to John, written only nine days after his departure, she confessed that she was already miserable. "The great anxiety I feel for my Country, for you and for our family renders the day tedious, and the night unpleasant," she wrote. From this moment on, her mood would fluctuate wildly, partly in response to the good or bad news that reached her and partly according to whether she received or (more often) did not receive a letter from her husband. On September 2, Abigail wrote John pointing out that several other wives of Massachusetts congressional delegates had already heard from their husbands—a not-so-subtle reminder that he could have gotten a letter to her if he had really wanted to. Yet she was also feeling merry enough to make light of both a natural disaster (the extended drought Massachusetts was enduring) and the imperial conflict. Drawing a whimsical connection between the meteorological and man-made catastrophes, Abigail informed John that "My poor Cows will certainly prefer a petition to you, setting forth their Greavences and informing you that they have been deprived of their ancient privilages, whereby they are become great Sufferers, and desiring that they may be restored to them, more espicially as their living by reason of the drought is all taken from them."

Two weeks later Abigail was still feeling good. "I enjoy better Health than I have done these 2 years," she wrote John on September 14. Still she could not understand why she had not yet heard from him. "Five Weeks have past and not one line have I received," she complained. She suspected that her frugal husband was holding off on writing her until he could find a northbound traveler who would not charge anything for carrying his letters. Postage was expensive—and the burden of paying the post rider fell not on the author of the letter but on the recipient. But if the only way for her to receive mail without damaging the family's finances was by making personal sacrifices, she was prepared to make them. Do not wait for some traveler headed to Massachusetts, she told John: "I had rather give a dollar for a letter by the post, tho the consequence should be that I Eat but one meal a day for these 3 weeks to come."

As Abigail had predicted in December 1773, the conflict between the British imperial government and the rebel colonies soon became a "civil War." Although a host of New England farmers' sons traveled hundreds of miles to kill or be killed by people quite different from themselves—among them slaves and Indians who rallied, for their own reasons, to the king's standard—the imperial dispute also engendered conflicts among neighbors, friends, and cousins. In many places, these long-standing ties were dissolved even before the first shots were fired at Lexington and Concord.

One of the first issues to sever friendships in the Bay colony was the parliamentary mandate that the provincial council be chosen by the Privy Council in London instead of the House of Representatives in Boston. Reaction to the new legislation was swift and brutal. Crowds of Massachusetts farmers and tradesmen hounded the newly appointed councilors. Most soon concluded that they had no choice but to resign their positions or leave the colony. The remnant cowered on navy ships or in army camps. Then on September 1, British soldiers, acting under orders from General Gage (who by this time was governor of Massachusetts as well as commander of British forces in North America), seized a cache of gunpowder from the Quarry Hill arsenal in Cambridge. A rumor immediately spread that Gage was about to launch a much more wide-ranging attack. Nine days later, on Sunday, September 10, the crisis touched Braintree when a British soldier was spotted on the town common. The man was probably just a deserter, Abigail told John, but many townspeople feared he was actually a spy. Militia officers, fearful that Braintree's gunpowder cache might suffer the same fate as Cambridge's, called out their men and had them move the powder to a place of greater security.

The militiamen who rescued the gunpowder paraded right past the Adams home. "I opened the window upon there return," Abigail later wrote John. "They pass'd without any Noise, not a word among them till they came against this house, when some of them perceiveing me, askd me if I wanted any powder. I replied not since it was in so good hands." Shortly after securing the gunpowder, the Braintree Patriots happened to cross paths with a Suffolk County deputy sheriff who was in town trying to serve a pair of warrants. As far as the militiamen were concerned, the warrants were illegal, since Parliament's hated Massachusetts Government Act had empowered sheriffs, not local constables and town meetings, to select jurors. So they forced the deputy to deliver up the two documents, which they immediately burned. "They then call'd a vote whether they should huzza [cheer]," Abigail told John, "but it being Sunday evening it passd in the negative."

Even as the mustering of armed militiamen inspired Patriots like Adams, it terrified one segment of Braintree's population. For decades the town had tolerated its few residents who belonged to the established Church of England (known today as the Episcopalian or Anglican Church). By the middle of 1774, though, many of Braintree's "Church people" had ventured to endorse the punitive measures adopted by the imperial government in response to the Boston Tea Party, and they feared retribution. Abigail reported to John that when the town militia mustered to move Braintree's gunpowder, the Church of England "parson thought they were comeing after him." The frightened Anglican "run up garret they say, an other jumpt out of his window and hid among the corn whilst a third crept under his bord fence, and told his Beads." For Abigail the stories of the terrified Anglicans were a source of levity—and a chance to joke about Anglicans (crypto-Catholics in the eyes of many Puritans) praying with rosaries, which of course most of them did not do. But for the Church people and other Loyalists, the danger was all too real. "Not a Tory but hides his head," Adams affirmed.

Several of Braintree's Anglicans sought protection from town officials, who responded by calling a town meeting for October 3. This gathering (which was an illegal assembly, the Massachusetts Government Act having limited each town to a single annual meeting) derided the rumor about Church people being harassed, branding the accusation "malicious, false & injurious & calculated to defame the Town." The resolution was not designed to calm the Anglicans, and it did not.

The crisis split families as well as communities. Isaac Smith, Jr., had always been Abigail's favorite cousin. Like her he was a charter member of the little coterie of young people who educated each other through literary discussions. During Mary and Abigail's teenage years, Isaac was an especially welcome member of the group simply by virtue of being male. Until young ladies entered formal courtships, they could not with propriety form close emotional bonds with men their age, yet that rule did not apply to cousins, and both Abigail and Mary grew close to Isaac. Abigail's correspondence with her cousin had, for instance, provided the occasion for some of her first ruminations on the status of women. After his graduation from Harvard in 1767 and a tour of South Carolina, England, and France in 1770 and 1771, Isaac had returned to Massachusetts, eventually finding work as a tutor at Harvard. Trained for the ministry, he had already begun serving as a substitute pastor in several towns around Cambridge. For whatever reason (perhaps it was his long-standing friendship with Thomas Bernard, the ex-governor's son, or his extended visit to the mother country in 1771), Isaac increasingly found himself siding with Parliament in its dispute with the American colonies. He was certainly not one of the sycophants or government employees that Patriots such as Abigail and John imagined all Loyalists to be. He held no royal office, he agreed that Parliament had no right to tax the American colonists, and he told Abigail in 1771 that he was distressed to see Boston merchants violating their agreement not to import British tea bearing the odious parliamentary tax. But when Patriots destroyed the East India Company's tea, Smith believed, they became the aggressors, and Parliament had a right to punish them. And he had no compunction about expressing this viewpoint—even from the pulpit.

Abigail and Mary soon learned of their cousin's apostasy, and both felt betrayed. In a plaintive appeal to Isaac penned on October 15, Mary implored him to turn back. "Till very lately," she told him, he had been on his way to becoming "extencively useful" as a minister—"a good Sheepherd feeding his flock in the tenderest manner with the best and most wholesome food." Now, suddenly, it seemed possible that her "most sanguine expectations with regard to you would be dissappointed." "Tho you should preach like an angel," she warned her cousin, "if the People suppose you unfriendly to the country and constitution and a difender of the unjust, cruil and arbitary measures that have been taken by the ministry against us, you will be like to do very little good." In fact he would probably never find a job, for no parish would hire a minister who defended imperial tyranny. The same Massachusetts farmers who were violently forcing the royally appointed members of the provincial council to resign and harassing Anglicans and other Loyalists had also turned against Smith, Cranch warned her cousin. Indeed, "the very People who a Twelvemonth ago heard you with admiration and talk'd of you with applause, will now leave the meeting-house when you inter it to preach. . . . I have said every thing I could in your defence but cant remove the prejudice."

The imperial conflict had politicized every aspect of colonial life, Mary told Isaac—even the church. "Orthodoxy in Politicks is full as necessary a quallification for Settling a minister at the present Day as orthodoxy in divinity was formely," she candidly informed him. Even if Isaac did not believe that the Patriots were in the right, in the polarized atmosphere of Massachusetts Bay in the autumn of 1774, "while the spirit of the People runs so high," he had better act as though he did. "You have no doubt a right to enjoy you own oppinion," she wrote, "but I Query whether your Duty calls you to divulge your Sentiments curcomstanced as you are." Playing every card she held, Mary tried to persuade Isaac that he was not the only one his "imprudent" conduct threatened. Isaac's father was a prominent merchant in Boston. "You will not only hurt your self but you will injure your father in his business," she told him. Already people were saying, "If the son is a Tory the father is so to be sure." Moreover, she wrote, "You will grieve your mother beyond discription."

Women's rights were no part of the agenda of the American Revolution, but the imperial conflict often politicized women without anyone intending it to. Such was the case with Mary Cranch. In the middle of her passionate plea to Isaac, she acknowledged that "it is not my province to enter into politicks." Yet her desperate wish to reclaim a beloved cousin had led her to disregard the ancient taboo.

Occasionally the colonial conflict even threatened marriages. Husbands who tried to commit their households to the royal government were sometimes startled to find their wives adopting patriotic principles, and some Patriot husbands encountered similar defiance. These marital disputes often manifested themselves in awkward social situations, one of which Abigail witnessed. On Friday, September 16, she and Nabby were at a formal dinner with cousin Hannah Quincy, who did not share her husband Samuel's Loyalist views. "Mr. Sam's Wife said she thought it high time for her Husband to turn about," Abigail wrote John later that night; "he had not done half so clever since he left her advice." The following year, when Samuel Quincy took ship and headed into self-imposed exile in England, Hannah stayed behind.

Even many women who were of one mind with their husbands on the grand political questions sometimes found themselves driven to unprecedented acts of self-assertion. One of the first incidents that led Abigail (who sometimes whimsically referred to herself as Mrs. Delegate) to stand up to her husband involved the knotty question of what to do with his law office in Boston.

CHAPTER 7

"Portia"

1774–1775

By the fall of 1774, General Gage had turned Boston into an armed camp. Cannon appeared atop Beacon Hill, and soldiers dug trenches across the narrow neck that linked the provintial capital to the mainland. When word of these developments reached John Adams in Philadelphia, he decided to try to preserve as much as possible of his threatened property. By this time Adams was operating two law offices, one in Boston (where the family had been living until the previous summer), and one in Braintree. Several times in his letters, John hinted to Abigail that it was getting to be time to close the Boston office, and in October he sent her positive instructions. "I have advised you before to remove my Office from Boston to Braintree," he wrote. "It is now, I think absolutely necessary. Let the best Care be taken of all Books and Papers."

Abigail thought John's fears were overblown. She knew he was feeling terrible about having left his family in a far more vulnerable position than himself, and she was sure he was exaggerating the danger of a conflagration in eastern Massachusetts. Her husband's books and papers were actually fairly safe, she believed. There was also another reason not to consolidate the two offices. From John's vantage point in Philadelphia it might appear easy enough to load the contents of the Boston office into a cart and transport everything ten miles south to Braintree, but it was actually not that simple. Aside from the obvious challenge of finding storage space in the family's little cottage for all those client files and hefty legal tomes, there was the hardship the move would entail for Edward Hill and Jonathan Williams, John's clerks in Boston. If the office moved, they would have to follow it. Both of the unpaid legal apprentices were living with their families in Boston, and a transfer to Braintree would force them to come up with funds for their room and board. Moreover, it was not clear that accommodations in or near Braintree could be had at any price, thousands of other Bostonians having already exiled themselves to the surrounding towns.

So Abigail defied John's instruction. "You mention the removal of our Books &c. from Boston," she told him on October 16. "I believe they are safe there"—and so there they remained. Long before she wrote her famous "Remember the Ladies" letter, Abigail was asserting herself in a way she never had before. It was not revolutionary rhetoric that had bolstered her self-confidence; it was her belief that the great distance separating John from his household, farm, and law practice made him less capable than she was of deciding how the three enterprises could best be run.

Adams's newfound self-assurance was also evident in the decision she made regarding her son Johnny's education. Even if there had never been an American Revolution, John would probably not have had total authority over how and where the children received their schooling. In New England, education had always been a shared parental responsibility, and by the time of the revolution, it had begun to drift further into the wife's realm. Within the Adams household, this process was accelerated by John's prolonged absence.

Braintree's elementary school was improving in the fall of 1774. The town had just replaced its incompetent schoolmaster with one of John Adams's law clerks, Nathan Rice, who had made the move from Boston to Braintree in mid-August. Yet, Abigail informed her husband, "I have not sent Johnny." The problem was not the teacher but the students. "I have always thought it of very great importance that children should in the early part of life be unaccustomed to such examples as would tend to corrupt the purity of their words and actions," she wrote. Adams wanted John Quincy to "chill with horrour at the sound of an oath, and blush with indignation at an obscene expression," and he was unlikely to acquire that capacity for horror and indignation at the town school. So Abigail had him tutored by John Thaxter, Jr., another of John Adams's law clerks, who was also her cousin. Thaxter, she reported, "takes very good care of him," and the two "seem to have a likeing to each other." It was possible that the seven-year-old might "not get so much good" from this individual instruction as he would from going to a regular school, Abigail acknowledged, but he certainly received "less harm."

Adams emphasized that her decision to avoid the town school was subject to review. "When you return we can then consult what will be best," she told John. Yet even that statement showed how far the Adams marriage had diverged from the patriarchal ideal. Under the English common law, John enjoyed as complete control of the Adams children as he did of the family's property, but in actual practice, Abigail had no thought of deferring to her husband when it came to the children's education. Even more surprising than her nearly complete control over John Quincy during her husband's absence was her assumption that the boy's education would be a matter of spousal consultation even after her husband returned.

During the very weeks that free women such as Mary Cranch, Hannah Quincy, and Abigail Adams unexpectedly found themselves contradicting the men in their families, the American Revolution also began to offer new political possibilities to African Americans. On a visit to Boston in mid-September, Abigail learned that there had been "a conspiracy of the Negroes" in the provincial capital. The plot was unlike any of those that had periodically aroused free British colonists' fears—and their slaves' hopes—over the course of the previous century. Its primary instrument was a petition, an appeal to Governor Gage "telling him they would fight for him provided he would arm them and engage to liberate them if he conquerd." Gage was apparently giving the offer serious consideration. He discussed it with Hugh, Earl Percy, who commanded the redcoats stationed in Boston. A British officer named Small had been "very buisy and active" in the matter, but the proposal reached Patriot ears before it could be put into action. One of the men the conspirators tried to enlist objected to the plan and "endeavourd to diswaid them from it," whereupon he was "threatned with his life," Abigail reported. The man applied for protection to Edmund Quincy, a cousin of Abigail's who was a justice of the peace.

Boston was not the only town to be rocked by rumors of slave conspiracies in the fall of 1774. Down in Virginia, James Madison, fresh out of the College of New Jersey (Princeton) and living on his father's vast estate in Orange County, reported that "in one of our Counties lately, a few of those unhappy wretches met together & chose a leader who was to conduct them when the English Troops should arrive." In December, a group of slaves in St. Andrew's Parish, Georgia, killed four whites before being captured and executed. Everywhere the disorder that distressed white Patriots as well as Loyalists began to open up opportunities for the one-fifth of Americans who were enslaved.

As a child and teenager Abigail had benefited from unfree labor without giving much thought to its morality, but she and John apparently never considered purchasing a slave (Judah, the young African American woman who worked for the Adamses at the start of their marriage, was paid). At some unknown point the couple discussed their mutual opposition to slavery, a stance that seemed, in Abigail's eyes, to have been vindicated when Massachusetts bondmen offered to rally to the imperial standard. "I wish most sincerely there was not a Slave in the province," she told John on September 22. "It allways appear a most iniquitous Scheme to me—fight ourselfs for what we are daily robbing and plundering from those who have as good a right to freedom as we have."

One of the most popular sermon styles in colonial New England was the jeremiad, which took its name from the doomsaying biblical prophet Jeremiah and focused on the community's collective sin. Every Christian colonist, especially those who belonged to the Congregational church, understood that evil men could sometimes become the instruments of a righteous God, and the seemingly tyrannical legislation adopted by Parliament in the 1760s and 1770s led to a new wave of jeremiads. Not all of these were the work of ordained ministers, and in the fall of 1774, Abigail produced one of her own. "I greatly fear that the arm of treachery and voilence is lifted over us as a Scourge and heavy punishment from heaven for our numerous offences," she told John in an October 16 letter.

Pastors who preached jeremiads typically accused their congregations of a multitude of sins, but Adams focused on two offenses that in normal times might not have ranked very high on the list. Americans were being punished, she told her husband, for spending too much and for not working hard enough. "If we expect to inherit the blessings of our Fathers," she wrote, "we should return a little more to their primitive Simplicity of Manners, and not sink into inglorious ease." Abigail was especially worried about Bostonians, many of whom earned their livelihoods providing luxuries to their fellow colonists. Among "the Mercantile part," she told John, frugality was "considerd as throwing away their own Bread." It was "in the Country"—in little towns such as Braintree—that "you must look for that virtue, of which you find but small Glimerings in the Metropolis," she said. Although she herself had been living in Boston four months earlier, Abigail felt confident that she could navigate the path back to virtue. "As for me I will seek wool and flax and work willingly with my Hands," she wrote John in a close paraphrase of Proverbs 31:13.

Although she warned of impending "punishment from heaven," Abigail's jeremiad lacked the fire and brimstone of similar efforts written during these months, as the words *God, Lord,* and *Jehovah* were all absent from her letter. Elizabeth and William Smith had apparently taught her to shun ostentatious expressions of faith, a rule that applied even in a private letter to a spouse. This religious modesty was spreading fast, and Abigail's was not the only jeremiad penned during the era of the revolution that was surprisingly secular.

John's extended sojourn at the Continental Congress aggravated Abigail's long-standing irritation at women's limited opportunities for travel. In mid-October, when John's law clerk William Tudor headed to Philadelphia in hopes of being introduced to his mentor's illustrious colleagues, Abigail accepted his offer to carry letters to her husband but could not help adding, "I could wish to be a fellow Traveller with you." In a letter she wrote John the next day, Abigail said of Tudor, "I almost envy him, that he should see you, before I can." Only her desire to project a cheerful demeanor compelled her to say "almost."

The Continental Congress called for a boycott of trade with Britain, drew up a declaration of rights, and dispatched appeals to the king, the British populace, and even the people of Quebec, who had not sent delegates to Philadelphia. By November 9, John was back in Braintree. While Adams's public service had not yet given his wife the opportunity to venture out of Massachusetts—and she could not imagine that it ever would—it did expand her horizons in other ways. Back in 1771, Abigail had expressed keen interest in the author Catharine Macaulay, with whom John had subsequently opened a correspondence. Now that she was the wife of a congressman, Abigail worked up the gumption to write her own letter to the notoriously pro-American historian. Drawing upon the language of sensibility, she affirmed that few colonists were "unfealing or insensible to the general calimity." Unless Americans could "obtain a release from our present bondage by an ample redress of our Grieveances," she warned, they would have to obtain it "by the Sword." Adams introduced Macaulay to a slogan that Patrick Henry would popularize a few months later. "The only alternative which every american thinks of," she wrote, "is Liberty or Death."

In her eagerness to impress Macaulay, Adams dusted off one of her favorite images: the threefold cord. Back when she and John were courting, she bound herself to him by the threefold cord of common humanity, friendship, and a third "tye more binding." Now, writing Macaulay and daring to speak on behalf of all free Americans, Abigail wrote, "we earnestly wish that the three fold cord of Duty, interest and filial affection may not be snapped assunder."

The imperial conflict also provided the occasion for Abigail to become better acquainted with Mercy Warren, whose husband, James, was, like John, a leading Patriot agitator. The countless restraints that British colonial society placed on females had been a frequent theme of Mercy's letters to Abigail. In January 1774 Warren declined to join in Adams's dire prophecies about the probable consequences of the Boston Tea Party, since it seemed unwise to predict events she could not influence. "Our weak and timid sex" is "only the Echo of the other," she reminded her friend. In fact women were "like some pliant peace of Clock Work," Warren wrote. "[T]he springs of our souls move slow or more Rapidly . . . as hope, fear or Courage Gives motion to the Conducting Wiers [i.e., "wires"—men] that Govern all our movements." Warren joked about the limitations that men placed on women so frequently that it must have been clear to Adams that she took the matter very seriously. In May 1774 Mercy announced plans to be in Boston to watch the Massachusetts House of Representatives elect the provincial council, even though it was "not Absolutly necessary That Mrs. Warren should Attend on the Ensuing Election."

One of Warren's most extraordinary comments on men's and women's conflicting attitudes came in response to Adams's request to see the letters she had exchanged with their mutual hero, Catharine Macaulay. After agreeing to show Abigail her Macaulay correspondence (in return for a peek at Adams's), Warren launched into a discussion of the prevailing notion that Eve had bequeathed her infamous curiosity to all of her female descendants. She observed that inquisitiveness was "the one quality which the other sex so Generously Consigns over to us." The truth, however, was that women were not inherently any nosier than men, and their apparent hunger for forbidden secrets was actually a response to the limitations imposed upon them by the other sex. Men seemed less curious "for no other Reason but because they have the opportunities of indulging their inquisitive Humour to the utmost in the Great school of the World, while we are Confined to the Narrower Circle of Domestic Care."

Warren did not shrink from considering the larger implications of women's confinement to the private sphere. There might actually be one advantage in the restraints that men imposed, she wrote: "If the Mental Faculties of the Female are not improved it may be Concealed in the Obscure Retreats of the Bed Chamber or the kitchen which she is not often Necessitated to Leave." Men's failings were harder to cover up. "Man," she told Adams, "is Generally Called out to the full display of his Abilities but how often do they Exhibit the most Mortifying instances of Neglected Opportunities and their Minds appear Not with standing the Advantages of what is Called a Liberal Education, as Barren of Culture and as Void of Every useful acquirement as the most Triffling untutored Girl."

At the same time that Warren encouraged Adams to consider these issues, she also sought to inspire her with the examples of female Patriots, and one of Warren's Roman heroines would become especially important to her friend. Brutus, the lead assassin of his friend Julius Caesar and a revered figure among the American Patriots, had depended upon the unfailing support of his wife, Portia. It may seem strange that Warren, Adams, and other American women would take inspiration from the wife of an assassin. But in their eyes, everyone who had challenged the tyrant Caesar represented personal sacrifice to the cause of liberty, and Portia was an especially powerful symbol. Years after the assassination, Portia, hearing that Brutus had died in battle, made the ultimate sacrifice, killing herself. In a January 1775 letter to Adams, Warren speculated that Portia and Aria, another Roman heroine who committed suicide, would not have done so "had they Lived in the Days of Christianity." With her attempt at bolstering her friend's patriotism having somehow turned into a discussion of self-murder, Warren could only hope that neither of the two of them would ever "be Ever Called to such a Dreadful proof of Magnanimity." (Warren, at least, was in no danger of surrendering herself to the patriot cause: barely a year after this exchange, when the Continental Army left Massachusetts, she would help persuade her husband to resign his commission as paymaster general in order to remain in Plymouth.)

Back in 1764, when Abigail married, the idea of a pen name had begun to seem childish, and she had retired "Diana" and begun signing her letters with her own name. But on May 4, 1775, knowing that her correspondence might be captured by her husband's enemies, she once more resorted to a pseudonym, this time choosing one that expressed her values. The name she took was Portia.

Warren did not ignite Adams's fascination with women's status—that fire had been lit long before the two women met—but she certainly fueled it. For her part, Adams could sometimes go Warren one better. Early in 1775, when Warren solicited John Adams's help with a play she was writing, her big worry being that she had treated her villains a bit too harshly ("Candour and Charity," she knew, were supposed to be inherent in "the female Character"), Abigail reminded her that this was the second time that she had sought advice from John but not his wife. Anticipating that Warren would resurrect her earlier justification for this omission—"I will not trust the partiallity of My own sex"—Abigail pointed out that if women were incapable of judging each other's work objectively, then the same must be true of men.

By the spring of 1775, the one thing that British imperial officials and Americans of nearly every political stripe agreed on was that they did not want to go to war. Yet both sides expected to be attacked soon and devoted enormous energy to self-defense. Even in the absence of deliberate aggression on either side, these defensive preparations made a clash of some kind increasingly likely.

Since the fall of 1774, Patriots had been stockpiling gunpowder and other military supplies. Skeptical of the colonists' protestations that these arsenals were intended merely for defensive purposes, Lord North ordered the British governors and generals in America to find and seize Patriot munitions. On the evening of April 18, 1775, when British troops rowed across the Charles River to begin their long march to Concord, their primary mission was to capture a cache of arms and ammunition that Patriots had hidden there. Within a few hours the soldiers had crossed through the towns of Cambridge and Menotomy (present-day Arlington) and arrived at Lexington Green.

By this time General Gage knew that thousands of Patriot militiamen had mustered in towns throughout eastern Massachusetts, and he dispatched reinforcements. When these troops reached Cambridge, they were unsure which road would lead them to Concord. Dozens of Harvard professors and students milled about the campus and the Cambridge common. But when asked for directions, none of the scholars seemed to know how to get from Cambridge to Concord.

Finally the British officers found a tutor who would give them the information they needed, and the detachment's march into history resumed. The Loyalist tutor who came out to do his part for His Majesty's forces was Isaac Smith, Jr., the man who had been Abigail's favorite male cousin.

Meanwhile the first wave of British soldiers caught sight of Lexington's militiamen, who had gathered on the town green but not with the intention of engaging the troops or even blocking their path. The men were there merely to observe—and to shoot back if the redcoats fired first. There never would have been a Battle of Lexington if the British column had ignored the militiamen and continued along the road to Concord. But Jesse Adair, the young lieutenant at the head of the British column, mindful of the cardinal rule that an army must never leave an enemy on its flank, marched his men out onto the common to confront the militiamen. The colonists had begun to comply with a British officer's order to disperse when a shot rang out. Ralph Waldo Emerson later observed that the first shot fired at Concord on April 19 was "heard 'round the world"—but Lexington's first shot was not *seen* by anyone, so we will never know from which side it came. The front line of British soldiers took that first shot as a signal to fire, and their volley killed seven Americans, whereupon the detachment regrouped and marched on to Concord, where they fought the second in what turned out to be a long series of skirmishes that lasted the rest of the day.

Without anyone intending it to, the Revolutionary War had begun. "What a scene has opened upon us . . . !" Abigail wrote Mercy Warren. "Such a scene as we never before Experienced, and could scarcely form an Idea of." As important as Lexington and Concord were as the first battles of the Revolutionary War, their most significant result was to sever many colonists' last emotional ties to the mother country. "O Britain Britain," Abigail wrote, "how is thy glory vanished—how are thy Annals stained with the Blood of thy children." John had been elected to the Second Continental Congress, and on April 24, he again set off for Philadelphia. This separation would be even more painful than the previous one, since John was leaving Abigail and their four children in a war zone, and there was no way of knowing when he would be able to return.

* * *

One immediate result of the outbreak of hostilities at Lexington and Concord was to exacerbate acute shortages of most of the commodities that Americans customarily imported from the British isles. Among the essential items that were becoming increasingly scarce were pins. Abigail Adams's June 1775 request that her husband send her a shipment of pins featured prominently in a song in the Broadway play *1776,* which was later adapted for the screen. What does not come across in the Tony Award–winning musical comedy is that Abigail did not simply want pins for her own use. Her June 16, 1775, letter asking John to send her a bundle of six thousand pins marks her debut as a merchant.

CHAPTER 8

"My Pen Is Always Freer Than My Tongue"

1775

Abigail had noticed that, during the imperial crisis, the price of pins had nearly tripled. Along with nearly everyone else, she suffered from this wartime inflation, but she also spotted an opportunity to turn a profit. She was willing to spend as much as ten times more than pins cost before the war, because she was confident that the retail price was only going to rise. Thinking of everything, she even instructed John to ship the pins in a chest that would be conveyed home for him at government expense.

John managed to acquire "two great Heaps of Pins" and promised in a July 7 letter to bring them with him on his next trip home. By this time Abigail was unwilling to wait that long. On July 16, exactly a month after her first request for pins, she observed to her husband that in Boston, "Not one pin is to be purchased for love nor money," adding, "I wish you could convey me a thousand by any Friend travelling this way." Within days, John found a conveyance for the pins.

On June 17, at about three o'clock in the morning, Abigail Adams and her children were awakened by cannon fire coming from the north. Intermittent shelling was nothing new, but this day, it went on and on. The Adams cottage was at the foot of Penn's Hill, one of the highest of Braintree's many promontories. After the sun came up, the seven-year-old John Quincy and his mother climbed the hill to see what was going on. From there they witnessed the engagement that would become known as the Battle of Bunker Hill. At the distance of ten miles the two could have no idea of who was winning. But from the number of shots fired that day and the sheer volume of smoke filling the northern sky, they knew they were witnessing an epochal event.

By this time General Gage had heavily fortified Boston, and British warships had the run of Boston Harbor, but every land route out of the area was blocked by a crescent of Patriot troops, trenches, and breastworks. If the British had not had the option of escaping by sea, the rebels would have had them surrounded. On June 16, a detachment of Americans pushed their lines inward, throwing up rude fortifications atop Breed's Hill, just north of the Charles River and overlooking the abandoned village of Charlestown. Gage's years of military experience told him his position in Boston would become untenable if the rebels could place cannon on that hill, so the very next day—Saturday, June 17—he sent 2,500 troops to take it from them. First the soldiers burned Charlestown, and then they marched against the American positions on Breed's Hill.

By the end of the day the soldiers had accomplished their mission. Yet Gage and his officers were under no illusion that they had won a victory. The regiments that captured Breed's Hill (confused in early battlefield reports with nearby Bunker Hill) took heavy losses. Two hundred and twenty-eight British soldiers died; nearly nine hundred were wounded. For His Majesty's forces, this first major battle of the War of Independence turned out to be the bloodiest as well. Even more significant was the simple fact that the Americans guarding Breed's Hill had withstood two British assaults before finally retreating to higher ground. In holding out so long against what were widely considered the finest troops in the world, the rebels shocked nearly everyone in the opposing army, from the lowliest private on the front line right up to the commander in chief. Gage had fought alongside the American colonists in the war against France and its Indian allies back in the late 1750s, but the lessons he thought he had learned back then left him worse than ignorant on June 17, 1775. "These people," the stunned general observed after the battle, "shew a spirit and conduct against us they never shewed against the French."

The most prominent of the one hundred Americans who died on Breed's Hill was Dr. Joseph Warren, Mercy Otis Warren's brother-in-law. In his role as chairman of the Boston Committee of Safety, Dr. Warren had forged close friendships with Abigail as well as John. Decades later John Quincy Adams recalled that he had "witnessed the tears of my mother and mingled with them my own, at the fall of Warren." In her report to her husband, Abigail commemorated Dr. Warren with a quotation from William Collins's "Ode Written in the Beginning of Year 1746":

By fairy hands their knell is rung
By forms unseen their Dirge is sung
[There] Honour comes a pilgrim grey
To Bless the turf that wraps their Clay

About this time, Abigail taught her eldest son to recite Collins's verses every morning after saying the Lord's Prayer. The poem had been written to honor the English soldiers who died putting down the Jacobite rebellion of 1745 (a movement, centered in Scotland, aimed at restoring the Stuart monarchy in the person of "Bonnie Prince Charlie"). Note that Adams drew her inspiration from a memorial not to revolutionaries but to men who died suppressing a rebellion. Since she believed the threat to the social order came not from the colonists but from the North administration, she never considered herself an insurgent. Not only did she reject the term *rebels* for her fellow Patriots, she sometimes hurled it back at the colonists who had cast their lots with the Crown.

Although the British assault on Breed's Hill is renowned as the first major engagement of the Revolutionary War (the battles of Lexington and Concord having been a series of important skirmishes), it was also the last big battle of the seven-year conflict to take place in Massachusetts. But the failure of the province and then state of Massachusetts to produce another named battle did not mean that Abigail and her neighbors enjoyed peace and quiet for the rest of the war. In fact, the first in a string of smaller clashes had already erupted before the British assault of June 17, and some of the most meticulous reporting on these skirmishes came from Abigail's pen.

Boston Harbor is littered with islands in a variety of shapes and sizes. Many are large enough that colonial farmers had long planted them with hay and other crops. As the buildup of imperial soldiers, sailors, and livestock in the provincial capital increased the demand for everything edible, the cultivated islands became contested terrain. Even the immense British flotilla riding at anchor in the harbor was unable to guard all of the numerous islands against Patriot raids. Most of these

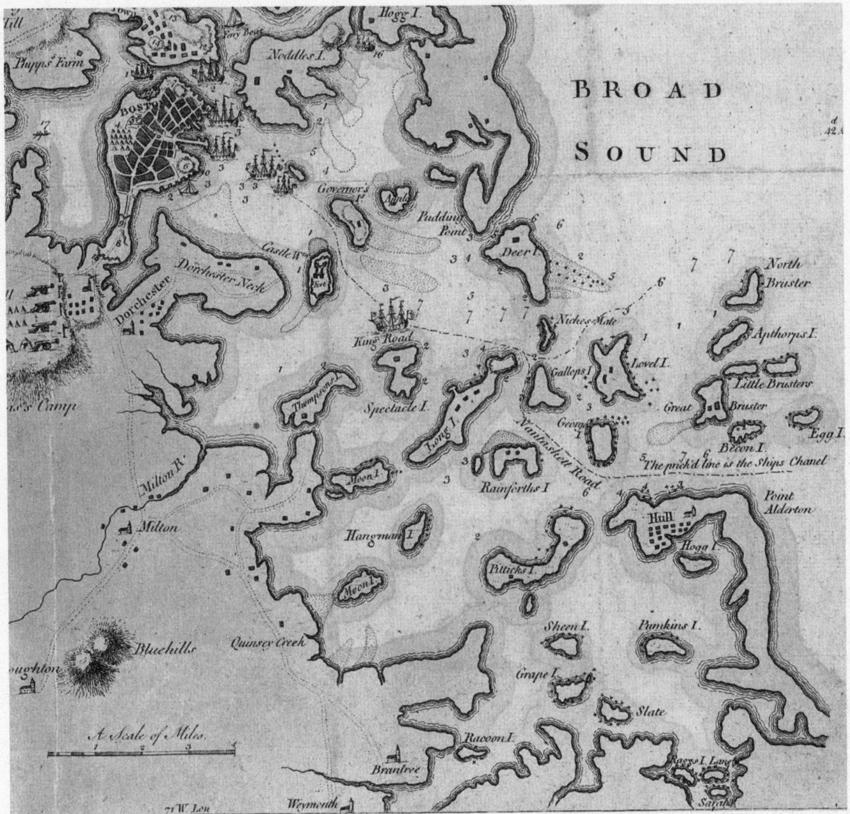

A Plan of the Town and Harbour of Boston, and the Country Adjacent. . . . J. De Costa, 1775 (detail). *Courtesy Library of Congress.*

attacks were launched from South Shore towns such as Braintree and Weymouth, so Abigail was often able to give John and her other correspondents moment-by-moment reports.

On Monday evening, July 11, three hundred volunteers in whaleboats pushed off from the Germantown section of Braintree. Their destination was the nearby Long Island (not to be confused with Long Island, New York, more than one hundred miles to the southwest). Slipping past three men-of-war, the Patriot volunteers landed unobserved. British officers, having grown desperate for animal fodder, had sent sixteen Loyalists and soldiers to Long Island to mow its hay. All were captured in their sleep. Adams reported that the Patriots also brought off "70 odd Sheep" and "15 head of cattle." The next day, another group landed on the island to burn a house and barn the British had been using, as well as several haystacks. The flames immediately caught the eyes of watchmen on board the men-of-war riding at anchor in the harbor. Adams described what happened next: "A number of armed cutters immediately Surrounded the Island, fired upon our Men. They came of[f] with a hot and continued fire upon them, the Bullets flying in every direction and the Men of Wars boats plying them with small arms." Standing on the shore, Braintree residents could hear the opposing forces shouting at each other. The Patriots were near enough to the British "to be calld to and damnd by their Enimies and orderd to surrender yet they all returnd in safty, not one Man even wounded," she announced. Reportedly an officer on one of the men-of-war commanded the captain of one of the Patriot whaleboats to "yield for he was his Prisoner," to which the Patriot captain replied, in the curt New England fashion, "Not yet." He hectored his oarsmen to strain every nerve, and the boat made it safely to shore.

Adams had only been reporting the activities of Patriot militiamen for a short time when she met their new commander in chief. On June 17, the very day that a group of informally organized militiamen forced the British to pay a heavy price for Breed's Hill, the Continental Congress, meeting down in Philadelphia, had chosen Virginia congressman George Washington to command the newly formed Continental Army. John Adams recognized that choosing a Virginian as commander in chief would rebut the widespread claim that New Englanders were the only colonists who were fighting mad at parliamentary tyranny, and so he took it upon himself to place Washington's name in nomination.

The new commander immediately set out for the Patriot military camp in Cambridge, arriving early in July. Soon afterward, Washington received a visit from the wife of the man who had nominated him. "I was struck with General Washington," Abigail wrote John on July 16. "You had prepaired me to entertain a favorable opinion of him, but I thought the one half was not told me. Dignity with ease, and complacency, the Gentleman and Soldier look agreably blended in him. Modesty marks every line and feture of his face." Adams was considerably less impressed with Charles Lee, the British general who had defected to the American side to become Washington's second in command. "General Lee looks like a careless hardy Veteran," she wrote. "The Elegance of his pen far exceeds that of his person."

As the summer wore on, Abigail continued to send John careful descriptions of military and political events in his home province. As a woman she was not allowed to attend the July 10 town meeting where Braintree chose its representative for the next session of the provincial legislature, but her detailed recounting of the hot contest for the town's legislative seat could easily have come from an eyewitness. When a man named Ebenezer Thayer challenged incumbent representative Joseph Palmer, the election quickly became something more than a contest of personalities. The rapid mobilization of many of the town's young men into the Patriot military forces raised the question of whether they gave up their right to vote when they donned their uniforms. Thinking the new soldiers had retained the franchise, Captain John Vinton marched his company to the meetinghouse with the express purpose of casting their ballots for Thayer.

Before the militiamen could vote, though, they had to watch as their fellow townsmen debated a motion by Thomas Newcomb that they should be excluded. "Newcomb insisted upon it that no man should vote who was in the army," Abigail reported. One of the Americans' most urgent grievances against the North ministry was its attempt to subordinate the civilian authorities to the military, he reminded the freeholders, and "he had no notion of being under the Military power." What might happen as the fighting intensified? "We might be so situated as to have the greater part of the people engaged in the Military," Newcomb warned, "and then all power would be wrested out of the hands of the civil Majestrate." Thayer "said all he could against" Newcomb's motion, but to no avail. The militiamen were not permitted to vote, and Palmer won another term.

Adams was forthright about the enjoyment she derived from reporting events such as these. "I know not whence it arises nor can I stop now to find it," she told John, "but I say there is a degree of pleasure in being able to tell new's." On the other hand, she was considerably less satisfied with some of the letters she received from John. For one thing, they were too short. "They let me know that you exist, but some of them contain scarcely six lines," she observed. Worse, the harried congressman wrote in such haste that he seldom exhibited anything like sensibility. "I want some sentimental Effusions of the Heart," she told him. The children were also feeling the strain of separation. In a July 16 letter to John, Abigail described how Nabby and the boys would "gather round mamma upon the reception of a letter to hear from pappa."

"What does par say[?]," five-year-old Charles demanded; "did not he write no more[?]"

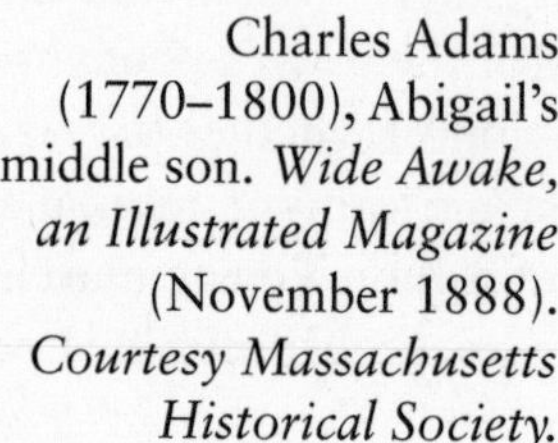

Charles Adams (1770–1800), Abigail's middle son. *Wide Awake, an Illustrated Magazine* (November 1888). *Courtesy Massachusetts Historical Society.*

"I wish I could see par," two-year-old Tommy affirmed.

Later in the month, Abigail reported on a conversation with Johnny, who had just turned eight. "Do you think Mamma pappa will write to me[?]," he asked his mother. Abigail promised he would, but the boy would not be comforted. "Has not he so many things to do that he will forget me[?]" he asked.

Even as Abigail tugged at John's heartstrings in hopes of bringing him home sooner, she became increasingly bold about advising him on matters of national policy. The moment she learned that Congress had determined that William Heath would outrank John Thomas (both were made generals), she warned her husband that he and his colleagues had made a grave mistake. "I fear General Thomas being overlooked and Heath placed over him will create much uneasiness," she wrote. "I know not who was to blame, but it is like to make a great and fatal Gap in the Army. If Thomas resigns all his officers resign; and Mr. Thomas cannot with honour hold under Heath." There could scarcely have been a more masculine realm than military preferment. Abigail knew she did not belong there, and after offering additional arguments in favor of Thomas, she stepped back from the brink. "But this is out of my Sphere," she wrote. Taking refuge in the journalistic role John had bestowed upon her and hiding behind unnamed others, Abigail closed her discussion of the whole affair by declaring, "I only say what others say and what the general disposition of the people is."

Less than a week after penning her defense of General Thomas (who would die of smallpox less than a year later, during the American invasion of Canada), Adams found herself in a situation that her husband had never experienced and never would. In the ongoing skirmishes over possession of the islands in Boston Harbor, Patriot forces had managed to capture several British marines, and Adams paid them a visit. In reporting the ensuing dialogue to John, she uncharacteristically portrayed herself as providing only the opening line. "I told them it was very unhappy that they should be obliged to fight their best Friends," she recalled.

The men's response was striking. "They said they were sorry," Adams reported; "they hoped in God an end would be speadily put to the unhappy contest." The men had not crossed the Atlantic bent on engaging with the rebellious colonists but simply because someone behind a desk had determined that it was time for the marines already stationed in Massachusetts to be rotated out. "When they came," they told Adams, "they came in the way of their Duty to releave Admiral Montague—with no thoughts of fighting."

The encounter with the prisoners left Abigail with conflicting emotions. It had been easy enough to hate the redcoats while they remained an anonymous mass, but now she was speaking with individuals. As prisoners they were anything but threatening. Several, in fact, had been wounded. Moreover, if their statements were to be believed, they had been animated not by a desire to reestablish British dominion in North America but by a straightforward sense of duty. The only real enmity the soldiers had felt toward their adversaries grew out of the mistaken notion that the Americans refused to give quarter to British prisoners. As Adams allowed herself to feel compassion for the prisoners, she grew angrier than ever at the British politicians and officers who had besmirched her province with lurid accounts of Patriots executing their prisoners. Adams's compassion for the soldiers and her anger at their imperial masters contended with yet another emotion: pride in the Americans' policy of trying to nurse their fallen enemies back to health. Concluding her report on the prisoners, she observed that her own uncle, Cotton Tufts, was among those who "Dress'd their wounds."

* * *

Not all of Adams's thoughts were on the military conflict. In keeping with her own inclinations as well as the laws of Massachusetts, she was a faithful churchgoer. Like John, she was not a fan of passionate preaching, but neither could she abide pastors who veered too far in the other direction. She did not think much, for instance, of Moses Taft, the minister of a neighboring Braintree parish. "I could forgive his weakness for the sake of his sincerity," she wrote her husband late in June, but "I want a person who has feeling and sensibility who can take one up with him." The still-unmarried Anthony Wibird, who had the care of her own parish, was no more inspiring than Reverend Taft, and one Sunday in July Abigail and her sister rode all the way to the church in Dedham, eleven miles away, for a break from the man she called "our inanimate old Batchelor." An additional reason for the jaunt to Dedham was to spend a day with Elizabeth Welles Adams (wife of Samuel), whom Abigail considered her "Sister Delegate," since both of their husbands were congressmen. Adams wondered what John would think of her claiming the title "delegate." "Why should we not assume your titles when we give you up our names[?]" she asked him.

On July 30, 1775, John finally sent Abigail the news she had been hoping for. The previous day, Congress had decided to call a brief recess, until September 5. One powerful reason to suspend the proceedings was to allow the delegates to escape Philadelphia until the summer heat broke. It was not just the discomfort of being confined to the stifling congressional chamber (where the windows were often closed tight to thwart eavesdropping). Big cities were widely viewed as dangerous places to endure the heat of summer—a judgment that has been confirmed by modern medical historians comparing urban and rural mortality rates (although the actual problem in cities like Philadelphia was not the heat but the mosquitoes who bred in standing water). John pointedly observed to Abigail that he himself had argued and voted against the recess, but he allowed that he was glad to be coming home for a few weeks—and even gladder to be getting out of the largest and seemingly hottest city in British North America. "In this exhausting debilitating Climate," he told Abigail, "Our Lives are more exposed than they would be in Camp."

John exaggerated. Only a few days after he wrote those words, his brother Elihu, who had spent the summer of 1775 commanding a militia company encamped in Cambridge, came down with dysentery. Abigail received the news in the midst of a letter to John. "He has been very bad for more than a week," she reported on August 10. By the time "I close this Letter I fear I shall write you that he is no more," she warned. That dark prediction proved accurate. Finishing her letter on August 11, Adams regretfully informed John that Elihu had died.

As soon as Congress recessed, John rushed home to Massachusetts—but not immediately to Braintree. First he stopped over in Watertown, just west of Boston, where the Massachusetts legislature had moved its sessions. For the next three weeks, Adams would spend most of his time at the provisional capital, visiting his family only on weekends. Not seeing enough of John, Abigail decided toward the end of the month to spend three days with him in Watertown. The two returned to Braintree for a long weekend at the end of August, but then on Monday, August 28, they bid their farewells, steeling themselves for what was certain to be another prolonged separation.

By the time John left Braintree, dysentery had invaded the Adams household. The first to come down with the disorder was a young farmhand named Isaac Copeland. Two days later, the disease struck Abigail herself. She felt a little better after three days, but a week further

Thomas Boylston Adams (1772–1832), Abigail's youngest son. Miniature watercolor on ivory by Parker, 1795. *Courtesy Massachusetts Historical Society.*

on, she observed to John that she seemed to "mend but very slowly." In rapid succession the bacteria spread to two servant girls, Susy and Patty, to two boarders, another servant, and, most ominously for Abigail, to little Tommy, who was a few days shy of his third birthday. "He lies very ill now," Abigail wrote her husband on September 8. "I hope he is not dangerous." There was no immediate reply to this letter, and in fact, just when Abigail most needed John's support, he went three weeks without writing a line. Even worse, it turned out that Adams had still been in Massachusetts when his wife contracted the disease, a stopover in Watertown having lengthened to three days. Had she known he was there, she would have sent for him. The reason she was unaware that John was at hand was that he did not bother to tell her. Nor did Adams leave a letter for his wife in Watertown when he finally set off for Philadelphia on September 1. "I was disapointed that you did not," she wrote.

Normally in such an emergency, a family like the Adamses could have counted on the aid of its neighbors, but in fact the dysentery epidemic had spread throughout eastern Massachusetts, and caregivers already had their hands full. "So sickly and so Mortal a time the oldest Man does not remember," Abigail wrote on September 8. By the time she resumed that letter two days later, she was "fearful of a return of my disorder," but still hopeful that she was simply feeling "fatigued with looking after Tommy," who was "unwilling any body but Mamma should do for him." Her son's fever had abated, but this normally "hale corn fed Boy" had turned "pale lean and wan." He had, Abigail said, been "intirely striped of the hardy robust countanance as well as of all the flesh he had, save what remains for to keep his bones together."

But the one who suffered worst was the servant girl Patty. "A general putrefaction seems to have taken place" within her intestines, Abigail reported to John on September 17. The stench was so overpowering that the family could "not bear the House" despite "constantly clensing it with hot vinegar." Susy and Isaac went home to their families, and Adams sent her sons Johnny and Charles to live with neighbors. It could not have been easy to find a home that was free of the disease, for in mid-September Abigail reported that eight Braintree residents had died of dysentery in the previous week alone. "The desolation of War is not so distressing as the Havock made by the pestilence," she declared in a September 25 letter to John. Adams's statement was accurate. Historians have shown that during the Revolutionary War, many more soldiers died from disease than from battlefield wounds and that pathogens spread by armies killed thousands of civilians as well.

Throughout the dysentery ordeal, there had been one constant in Abigail's life: she had always been able to count on a daily visit from her mother. Perhaps because she herself was so often sick, the fifty-three-year-old Elizabeth Smith had, throughout her adult life, frequently made the rounds of the distressed and infirm. Now the attention that she had so abundantly bestowed on her husband's parishioners flowed to her own daughter's household. In her youth, Abigail had chafed at Elizabeth's seemingly excessive anxiety about the illnesses threatening her children. Now that Abigail and one of her own infants had contracted a potentially fatal disease, she could view her mother's worries in a different light.

Dysentery cannot be communicated by simple skin-to-skin contact, but a disorder that most obviously manifests itself as diarrhea easily leaps from one human host to another. As the Adams household showed, children are among its likeliest targets. So are older people, and it was all but inevitable that the disease would spread to Abigail's mother. "Her kindness brought her to see me every day when I was ill and our little Tommy," Abigail wrote John. "She has taken the disorder and lies so bad that we have little hopes of her Recovery." Abigail was distraught. "In past years small has been my portion of the Bitter Cup in comparison with many others," she observed two weeks after her mother took sick. "But there is now prepairing for me I fear, a large draught thereof." Smith had never been an optimist in the face of illness. The moment she realized she had contracted dysentery, she became "possess'd with the Idea that she shall not recover," her daughter reported. "A solemnity possess'd her soul," Abigail wrote, "nor could you force a smile from her." Yet Smith was determined to discharge her maternal duties right to the end. With admiration, not annoyance, Abigail recalled weeks later that even "upon her dying Bed," her mother "gave counsel where she thought it most necessary."

Smith's illness forced Abigail to make impossible choices. Even as Isaac Copeland and Tommy recovered, little Patty's dysentery lingered on and on. The girl had lived with the Adamses for four years, and as the disease slowly consumed her, she could not bear to be separated from her mistress. So Abigail divided every day in half, spending twelve hours with her mother ("to give a respit to my sisters," she wrote) and twelve with Patty (who had "now become such a putrid mass as scarcely to be able for anyone to do their Duty towards her"). As she assisted at either of the two sickbeds, she constantly dreaded the arrival of a messenger bearing "fatal tidings" from the other.

Abigail did not fire off a letter to John the moment she learned of her mother's illness. John had taken no notice of Abigail's September 8 complaint about his not writing her, but when he realized she had waited ten days before clueing him to her mother's condition, it finally occurred to him that she had not rushed to tell him about his own family's affliction, either. He immediately conjectured that both delays were deliberate: retaliation for his not writing home at a time when Abigail most needed to hear from him. In an October 7 letter to his wife, he sheepishly admitted that he had failed to keep up his end of the correspondence. "I fear, that your not receiving so many Letters from me as usual may have been one Cause of Infelicity to you," he ventured. John insisted that he had perfectly good reasons for not writing. Letters he had sent James Warren (Mercy's husband) as well as Abigail shortly before the congressional recess—complete with snarky comments about "the Fidgets, the Whims, the Caprice, the Vanity, the Superstition, [and] the Irritability" of some of his colleagues—had been intercepted and published in a Loyalist newspaper, causing him no little embarrassment. Even while assuring his wife that this episode had not hurt the Patriot cause (John correctly conjectured that Abigail would blame herself for the interception of the letter intended for her, even though it had been captured in Connecticut), he pointed out that if the Loyalists got their hands on a more important message—for instance one reporting divisions within the Congress or previewing Patriot military plans—the results could be disastrous. So the prudent policy was to correspond with Abigail only when a safe conveyance offered.

This was, of course, a lame excuse. Although the threat of interception was real, it did not prevent John from writing Abigail on personal matters of no interest to the enemy. Adams may have been correct that his wife had made a deliberate decision to punish him by not immediately informing him of the family's illness. It seems even more likely that Abigail's growing pique at John's continuing silence led her to withhold the earth-shattering news of her mother's illness. On the other hand, her failure to take up her pen may have simply been the result of sheer exhaustion.

There were no good omens for Elizabeth Smith, so John tried to invent one. Reminding Abigail that her mother had been sick many times before, he surmised that she had acquired a unique ability to overcome illness. It was a forlorn hope, of course. On the morning of October 1, 1775, Abigail reported, "I rose and went into my Mothers room . . . with a cup of tea in my hand, raised her head to give it to her, she swallowed a few drops, gaspd and fell back upon her pillow, opend her Eyes with a look that pirced my Heart and which I never shall forget. It was the eagerness of a last look." Adams was convinced that her mother could not survive the day. October 1 was, however, a Sunday, and Parson Smith had a church service to conduct. Abigail had to go to church, too, because this was the communion Sunday on which twelve-year-old Betsy Cranch, Mary's daughter, was to be welcomed into the church. Abigail later described for John what her father had endured as he struggled through that day's service: "weeping children, weeping and mourning parishoners all round him, for every Eye streamed, his own heart allmost bursting as he spoke." After recounting the events of that day for her husband, Abigail observed that "My pen is always freer than my tongue. I have wrote many things to you that I suppose I never could have talk'd."

Undoubtedly attended by a servant, Elizabeth managed to hold on all through that Sunday morning and afternoon, but she finally succumbed at about 5 P.M., while her husband and daughter were both still at church. Eight days later, Patty, who had struggled against the disease and endured its torments for more than a month, also gave up the fight.

During her mother's final illness, Abigail had mentioned religion as a source of solace, but the biblical references in her letters were nearly as oblique and measured as those she customarily made. But when Elizabeth Smith died, her normally even-tempered daughter ran to the Bible, especially to the book of Job, for consolation. Twice in an October 9 letter, she referenced Job 16:14: "He breaketh me with breach upon breach." Once again rooting herself in the New England tradition of ascribing earthly calamities to divine retribution, Abigail in that and another letter paraphrased Job's desperate plea to Jehovah: "shew me wherefore thou contendest with me." She also sought comfort in the book of Psalms. John "rejoiced" in the solace that his wife derived from her Christian faith, but he himself seemed to take much more comfort from the secular tradition of stoicism. "It is our Duty to submit," he reminded Abigail on October 7, before he had learned of Smith's death. "If We live long ourselves We must bury our Parents," he wrote a week later.

John was simply unable to grasp the magnitude of his wife's loss. Always on the alert for opportunities to instruct his children, he tried to use Elizabeth Smith's death to teach Tommy, who turned three during his bout with dysentery, a lesson in gratitude. "Your excellent Grandmamma, it is to be feared, took the Distemper which proved fatal to her at our House when she was kindly assisting your Mamma in attending upon you and the rest of the sick Family," Adams wrote his son. The best way for Tommy to show his appreciation for those who had preserved his life at the risk of their own was to obey the foremost among them, his mother. John was by no means the first New Englander to use a relative's death as a training tool, but one wonders whether Abigail actually felt obliged to subject the boy to his father's guilt-laden message.

By the end of October, Abigail's life had begun to resume its normal rhythms. The servants Susy and Isaac had recovered and were once again sleeping under her roof. Tommy, having finally shaken off his dysentery, had become "so fat he can scarcly see out of his Eyes." Abigail returned to her war reporting, giving John a detailed account of the British destruction of the town of Falmouth, Massachusetts, on October 17. Angry as she was with Admiral Samuel Graves, who had ordered the shelling of the town, Adams ascribed Falmouth's calamity, like the dysentery epidemic, to God's wrath. "We have done Evil or our Enimies would be at peace with us," she told John. "The Sin of Slavery as well as many others is not washed away."

Within a month of her mother's death, Abigail was also ready to focus again on her little business retailing pins. Having received one shipment from John, she pressed for another. "I would not croud you with articles," she wrote, "but hope you will remember my other bundle of pins, the price of one paper now amounts to what we used to give for a whole Bundle." Yet Elizabeth Smith was never far from her thoughts. "My Evenings are spent with my departed parent," she told John in mid-November. "I then ruminate upon all her care and tenderness, and I am sometimes lost, and absorb'd in a flood of tenderness e'er I am aware of it, or can call to my aid, my only props and support"—her children.

Reverend Smith was still in shock. "It makes my heart ake to see him, and I know not how to go to the House," Abigail told John after one visit to Weymouth parsonage. "Child I see your Mother, go to what part of the house I will," the parson told his daughter. It seemed to Abigail that her father had "lost almost as much flesh as if he had been sick." Parson Smith took some comfort from having his unmarried daughter Elizabeth with him, but Abigail observed that Betsy herself seemed "broke and worne with Grief." Abigail sent Nabby, who had just turned ten, to the parsonage for several weeks in hopes she would provide her aunt and grandfather with a little distraction.

There was an extraordinary coda to the death of Abigail's mother. On October 29, less than a month after Elizabeth Smith's funeral, John—not Abigail—Adams expressed regret (in a letter to his wife) that her mother had never been permitted to display her talents beyond the domestic sphere. It was all well and good for "Benevolence, Charity, Capacity and Industry" to be "exerted in private Life," where they could "make a family, a Parish or a Town Happy," he wrote. But benevolent women as well as men also had a duty to act "upon a larger Scale," where they could support "the great Principles of Virtue and Freedom of political Regulations," possibly rescuing "whole Nations and Generations from Misery, Want and Contempt." John knew Abigail would welcome these reflections, for she had long since demonstrated acute consciousness of the restraints under which women operated. Yet her famous "Remember the Ladies" letter was still five months in the future, and in many ways, the ideas she expressed there would be less radical than those her husband had just committed to paper. Abigail never demanded that women be allowed to enter politics—not even on the frequent occasions when she herself took to the political stage. But here was John regretting that Elizabeth Smith's "Talents, and Virtues" had been "too much confined, to private, social and domestic Life."

Since John's meditation had begun as an obituary for Elizabeth Smith, there can be no question that he was talking about his daughter Nabby as well as his three sons when he emphasized in conclusion that "Public Virtues, and political Qualities therefore should be incessantly cherished in our Children." Where did *that* come from? John wrote Abigail three letters on October 29, so it is obvious that he was in a contemplative mood (and that he had time on his hands). Perhaps, too, he figured that flattering Abigail's mother and womankind in general would make up for his earlier failure to correspond with his wife. But there is also other evidence that John could sometimes leap ahead of his male contemporaries in his thinking about the status of women. At the end of September, as Abigail was shuttling back and forth between Patty and Elizabeth's sickbeds, John had written her a letter on the education of their children that showed surprisingly modern attitudes toward both his wife and their daughter. John wanted all four of their children, not just the boys, to be trained in two subjects that many schools reserved for their male students: geography and geometry. And Adams thought these lessons should come from Abigail herself. "I must intreat you, my dear, to teach the Elements of those Sciences to my little Girl and Boys," John wrote. "No doubt you are well qualified for a school Mistress in these Studies." Adams went on to report that his confidence in his wife's abilities had recently grown. An Englishman who visited Abigail in Braintree and then John in Philadelphia had told him she was "the most accomplished Lady, he had seen since he left England."

Nor was this all. "If I could write as well as you," Adams observed in response to one of the prose elegies Abigail penned for her mother, "my sorrows would be as eloquent as yours, but upon my Word I cannot." These were fine compliments, but if Abigail had been naïve enough to deduce that her husband was about to become an advocate for women, a letter he sent her on November 4 would have set her straight. In it, he praised John Hancock's new wife, Dorothy, who had accompanied him to Philadelphia, for her "Modesty, Decency, Dignity and Discretion." "She avoids talking upon Politicks," John added. "In large and mixed Companies she is totally silent, as a Lady ought to be." Abigail received her husband's none too subtle praise of apolitical women in the midst of a two-week bout with "jaundice, Rhumatism and a most voilent cold," and she made no reply.

During the fall of 1775, the Adamses' relationship exhibited the first signs of a pattern that would persist until Abigail's death forty-three years later. Whenever John took a stand on some political issue, Abigail invariably adopted a more extreme version of the same viewpoint. The previous summer, at a time when hardly anyone in the British colonies favored separating from the mother country, John had begun pushing his congressional colleagues to start acting as though independence had already been declared. In the July 24, 1775, letter to James Warren that unluckily had been intercepted by Loyalists, he contended that the Americans "ought to have had in our Hands a month ago the whole Legislative, executive and judicial of the whole Continent, and have completely modeled a Constitution; to have raised a naval power, and opened all our Ports wide." Four months later, in November, Abigail used considerably more radical language to express the same view. On the twelfth, a Sunday, she listened to Reverend Wibird praying for reconciliation between the colonists and the crown, then went home and wrote John that she could not join "in the petitions of our worthy parson, for a reconciliation between our, no longer parent State, but tyrant State, and these Colonies." "Let us seperate," she wrote.

CHAPTER 9

"Remember the Ladies"

1776

John's congressional service vastly expanded his social horizons, introducing him to a host of Europeans who had been drawn to Philadelphia by their curiosity and enthusiasm for the Patriot cause. Yet it would be wrong to imagine Abigail as his polar opposite, isolated in their Braintree farmhouse. As a congressional wife, she was often invited to dinners where the guests of honor were Continental Army officers hailing from all up and down the Atlantic seaboard and beyond. Adams's initial impression of Charles Lee, the British general who had defected to the Patriot side to become Washington's second in command, had not been favorable. Lee had every reason to dislike Abigail, too, since her husband's intercepted letter to James Warren had ridiculed Lee's infatuation with his ever-present hunting dogs. In December 1775, when Abigail received an invitation to a dinner party where she knew Lee would be present, she must have dreaded having to greet him for the first time since the publication of her husband's letter. But the evening went much better than she had expected, and she reported to her husband that Lee had been "determined that I should not only be acquainted with him, but with his companions"—those hunting dogs. Lee "placed a chair before me into which he orderd Mr. Sparder to mount and present his paw to me for a better acquaintance," she wrote. "I could not do otherways than accept it." Then Lee explained why he had been so eager to arrange this encounter. "That Madam," he said, "is the Dog"—the Pomeranian John Adams had "renderd famous."

Thomas Paine's incendiary *Common Sense* appeared in January 1776 and did more to advance the cause of independence than anything John

Adams or anyone else had written during the previous ten years. The publication of the pamphlet also provoked another rebellion—within the Adams household. John was ambivalent about *Common Sense*. On the one hand, he admired and envied Paine's ability to lay out the case for independence "in a clear, simple, concise and nervous [muscular] Style." Yet Paine had not been content to advocate separation from the mother country; he thought the thirteen states should invest sovereign power in democratically elected, single-house legislatures. Upon reading Paine's proposal, Adams had forthrightly told him it "was so democratical, without any restraint or even an Attempt at any Equilibrium or Counterpoise, that it must produce confusion and every Evil Work." Failing to persuade Paine, he quickly cranked out a pamphlet of his own, endorsing the call for independence but warning every state to create a strong senate, judiciary, and governor to rein in the lower house of assembly.

John expressed his distaste for the radically democratic politics of *Common Sense* in a March 19 letter to Abigail, telling her the pamphlet would prove much more effective at demolishing the British colonial establishment than at erecting a workable alternative. A month later John sent her a copy of his own effort, *Thoughts on Government*. Abigail simply ignored John's criticism of *Common Sense*. She shared his alarm at its radically democratic principles, but her assessment of its usefulness to the Patriot cause was not distorted by envy, as his obviously was. "Tis highly prized here and carries conviction whereever it is read," she told John on February 21. "I have spread it as much as it lay in my power." Even after receiving her husband's March 19 letter denouncing the pamphlet's "Sophisms," its "artfull Addresses to superstitious Notions," and its "keen attempts upon the Passions," Abigail continued to extol its virtues.

Although Adams's modesty was genuine, she seldom shrank from rendering judgment on the actions of others. One particularly negative assessment that she made in the spring of 1776—the subject was George Washington—quickly proved to be singularly unfortunate. On Saturday evening, March 2, she was in the middle of a leisurely letter to her husband, heaping yet more praise on *Common Sense*, when she suddenly interrupted herself. "But hark! the House this instant shakes with the roar of Cannon," she wrote. "I have been to the door and find tis a cannonade from our Army." She also learned that militiamen from all over eastern Massachusetts had suddenly been called up. "All the remaining Militia" were "to repair to the Lines a monday night by twelve o clock," she told John. Something was afoot. Was the Continental Army finally going to launch an assault on the British troops in Boston? An all-out attack might well result in the destruction of the Adams town house on Queen Street, but Abigail was perfectly ready to see it go, for she was thrilled by the prospect of at last driving the "Ministerial Army" from the provincial capital.

And then—frustration. It turned out that there was nothing more to the hullabaloo than some harebrained officer's scheme to establish a base atop Dorchester Heights, on a narrow peninsula just south of Boston. "I feel dissapointed," Abigail wrote John on Thursday, March 7. "This day our Militia are all returning, without effecting any thing more than taking possession of Dorchester Hill" and another promontory, Nook's Hill, just to the north of it. "I hope it is wise and just," she added, "but from all the Muster and Stir I hoped and expected more important and decisive Scenes; I would not have sufferd all I have for two such Hills." Adams's disappointment was understandable. Dorchester Heights had seemed so insignificant to General William Howe, who had replaced Thomas Gage as commander in chief of His Majesty's forces in North America after Gage's pyrrhic victory at Breed's Hill, that he had not even bothered to take it into the British lines. What Howe (who was of course supposed to be an expert in these matters) as well as Adams had somehow failed to recognize was that a Patriot gun battery atop Dorchester Heights would have a clear shot not only into the town of Boston but at the navy ships riding at anchor in the harbor. The purpose of the cannonade that commenced on the night of March 2 was to distract the British while Patriot troops dragged seventy artillery pieces to the summit of Dorchester Heights. The cannon were put in place on the night of March 4, and Howe quickly reached the conclusion that the hastily constructed fort protecting them was impervious to recapture.

By Saturday, March 16, Adams was ready to report that "the prevailing opinion of most people" was that the new American gun battery was going to force the British to evacuate Boston. For her own part, she was not "yet satisfied that they will leave it." But sure enough, the next day, eleven thousand British soldiers and more than a thousand civilian Loyalists were ferried out to the transports. For more than a week the fleet lingered in the outer harbor, but then the sails were raised once more, and the ships headed out into the Atlantic. Weeks later Bostonians learned that the fleet had put in at Halifax, Nova Scotia. The protracted British occupation of the provincial capital was over. Adams did not pause to scold herself for second-guessing George Washington and his generals on their greatest feat since the commencement of hostilities. She was elated. "I feel very differently at the approach of spring to what I did a month ago," she wrote John on March 31. In February she and her neighbors had still feared being "driven from the sea coasts to seek shelter in the wilderness." Now, she wrote (paraphrasing Micah 4:4), "we feel as if we might sit under our own vine and eat the good of the land." "I feel a gaieti de Coar [Coeur]"—a gaiety in the heart—"to which before I was a stranger," she told John. "I think the Sun looks brighter, the Birds sing more melodiously, and Nature puts on a more chearfull countanance."

The British evacuation of Boston filled Abigail with an intoxicating sense that almost anything was possible, and it inspired her to set down the words for which she is best known today. "I long to hear that you have declared an independency," she told her husband (and through him, his colleagues in Congress) on the last day of March, "and by the way in the new Code of Laws which I suppose it will be necessary for you to make I desire you would Remember the Ladies, and be more generous and favourable to them than your ancestors." Years later these words would transform Adams into a feminist icon, and it is easy to forget that she wrote them for an audience of one. Moreover, out of all the contexts in which men lorded it over women—politics, the courts, the workplace, education, and so on and on—she only called attention to one: marriage. "Do not put such unlimited power into the hands of the Husbands" as your ancestors did, she advised John and his fellow delegates. The wording of her plea was vague, but she seems to have been thinking of physical abuse, for her most specific request was that Congress "put it out of the power of the vicious and the Lawless to use us with cruelty and indignity with impunity." Although Adams chose to focus on only one of the myriad issues she might have raised, it was surely the most important of the lot. From the birth of the family in ancient times, the most significant relationship in a woman's life had been with her husband. Whether she was to be happy or miserable depended infinitely less on who ruled her colony or state than on who governed her household. And Abigail had intimate personal knowledge of spousal cruelty, for her alcoholic brother was known to have mistreated his wife.

Abigail did not simply ask John and his congressional colleagues to urge men to stop abusing their wives; she wanted a prohibition on spousal battery inserted in the new nation's "Code of Laws." Well aware that this was a radical demand, she did everything she could to soften the blow. For instance, she introduced the topic with the phrase "by the way," giving it the air of a casual aside. And she made the bold feminist statement that "your Sex are Naturally Tyrannical" only after paving the way by first paraphrasing the classical republican truism that "all Men would be tyrants if they could." John himself had used this phrase—without any thought of criticizing males' treatment of females—in an essay he had written (but had not published) more than a decade earlier, and Abigail knew her husband would be flattered, not furious, to see his own words used against him. Nor was this the only phrase she borrowed. The historian Elaine Forman Crane has shown that large swaths of this famous letter were lifted from other authors, mostly without any indication that they were in fact quotations. At the time, that would not have been considered plagiarism, even if this had been a published essay, since it was a widespread practice. Most of John's three-volume *Defence of the Constitutions of Government of the United States of America*, published in 1787 and 1788, was copied from other sources, often verbatim. But Abigail and John had different motives for relying so heavily upon quotation. Whereas John was mostly trying to save himself time, the passages his wife extracted from earlier writers were meant to serve at once as armor and sugarcoating. Although Adams often wove famous authors' words in with her own, she did so to a greater than usual extent whenever she skated near the limits of propriety.

In yet another effort to temper her plea, Adams injected an element of humor into it. "If perticuliar care and attention is not paid to the Laidies," she wrote, "we are determined to foment a Rebelion, and will not hold ourselves bound by any Laws in which we have no voice, or Representation." This threat to lead a revolt against the American revolutionaries was of course farcical, but it allowed Abigail to slip in the serious observation that male Patriots prohibited their wives from exercising the very right to self-government that now stood at the center of their own dispute with Parliament.

Adams also found other ways to wrap her barb in velvet. She concluded it with a wholly conventional appeal to Congress and men in general to "Regard us then as Beings placed by providence under your protection and in immitation of the Supreem Being make use of that power only for our happiness." Furthermore, she twice acknowledged that not all husbands exercised the sovereign power that the law assigned them. "Men of Sense in all Ages abhor those customs which treat us only as the vassals of your Sex," she wrote. Indeed, "Such of you as wish to be happy willingly give up the harsh title of Master for the more tender and endearing one of Friend." Since the most common salutation in John and Abigail's letters was "Dearest Friend," it would be easy enough for him to imagine that he was among the "Men of Sense" to whom his wife's complaint did not apply. But she did not grant him an explicit exemption, which left open the possibility that her assessment of him might well depend upon his response to her demands.

Adams's March 31, 1776, letter was noteworthy in other ways as well. The British evacuation of Boston provided the occasion for her to compare New England to the slaveholding South—a contrast she would draw many more times over the course of her lifetime. Was it not likely that the fleet that had just withdrawn from Boston would soon attack another American port—and with much greater success? The more southerly colonies had fallen behind New England in their military preparations, and the South's vulnerability was further exacerbated by its own corruption. Property was not evenly distributed as in New England. The southern "Gentery" had set themselves up as "Lords," and "the common people" were "vassals" (this was the very term Abigail used elsewhere in the same letter to describe the status of women under the English common law). Indeed, the oft-repeated British allegation that the rebelling American colonists were "uncivilized Natives"—as savage as the Indians—seemed, in Abigail's eyes, actually to be true of southern white colonists. The Virginia rifle companies that had marched north to aid in the defense of New England had failed to alter her unflattering ideas about white southerners. In fact the reports she had received about the riflemen—all of them apparently second- or third-hand—had only strengthened her preconceptions. "I hope their Riffel Men who have shewen themselves very savage and even Blood thirsty; are not a specimen of the Generality of the people," she wrote.

The Virginia riflemen were not the only intercolonial visitors who inflamed rather than dispelling Abigail's parochial prejudices. After attending a dinner party with several Continental Army officers and their wives, she expressed surprise that so many of the couples from Philadelphia were childless. "I beleive Phyladelphia is an unfertile soil, or it would not produce so many unfruitfull women," she had told John.

Of course the factor that most corrupted the South was not the maldistribution of wealth among whites but the pervasiveness of slavery. To be sure, Abigail's own father still owned slaves in 1776, but at least slavery had not sunk the same deep roots in New England that it had farther south. "I have sometimes been ready to think that the passion for Liberty cannot be Eaquelly Strong in the Breasts of those who have been accustomed to deprive their fellow Creatures of theirs," Adams wrote. "Of this I am certain that it is not founded upon that generous and christian principal of doing to others as we would that others should do unto us." Thus Adams's best-known letter, the one where she launched her harshest attack on the marital subjugation of women, also contained one of her most passionate denunciations of slavery.

Adams did not seal and send the "Remember the Ladies" letter until April 5, but it reached John in Philadelphia with uncharacteristic speed. His reply, dated April 14, seemed to be designed to tick her off. "I cannot but laugh" at your proposal, he told his wife. Abigail had tried to soften her appeal by expressing it humorously (for instance by threatening to "foment a rebellion"), and John followed suit. In fact his entire 250–word response was jocular. He noted, for instance, that Loyalists and conservatives had warned him and other white male Patriots not to disturb a social order from which they themselves had long benefited, and he joked that his wife's pleas seemed to confirm that dark prophecy. "We have been told that our Struggle has loosened the bands of Government every where. That Children and Apprentices were disobedient—that schools and Colledges were grown turbulent—that Indians slighted their Guardians and Negroes grew insolent to their Masters," he wrote. "But your Letter was the first Intimation that another Tribe more numerous and powerfull than all the rest were grown discontented." Nor had colonial officials simply stood by as Patriots reaped the whirlwind, John claimed. "After stirring up Tories, Landjobbers, Trimmers, Bigots, Canadians, Indians, Negroes, Hanoverians, Hessians, Russians, Irish Roman Catholicks, [and] Scotch Renegadoes," the British had now "stimulated" white women "to demand new Priviledges and threaten to rebell."

By April 1776, white male Patriots really were angry at the crown for hiring mercenaries from Hesse and other German states—and even angrier at the British policy of inciting Indians and slaves to attack them. Two months later John would serve on the committee that wrote the Declaration of Independence, where the capstone grievance would be that King George III had "excited domestic insurrections amongst us." The reality, of course, was that the natives and African Americans needed no such incitement; they were not so much Britain's pawns as its allies. Yet John was perfectly willing to associate Abigail and other white women with Indians and slaves. "This is rather too coarse a Compliment," he acknowledged, "but you are so saucy, I wont blot it out." Adams also offered another excuse for rejecting his wife's plea. In her March 31 letter, Abigail had acknowledged that the common-law practice of coverture—which gave the husband sovereign power within his household—did not actually operate in most families. John used this gap between legal theory and everyday practice to justify existing arrangements. "Our Masculine systems . . . are little more than Theory," he wrote. "We dare not exert our Power in its full Latitude. We are obliged to go fair, and softly." Adams would have been well advised to stop there, but he was having fun, and he could not restrain himself from adding, "In Practice you know We are the subjects." Thus did he defend an ancient system with an old myth: that males had "only the Name of Masters."

John's final defense of his male prerogatives echoed a claim he and other radicals had been using in their debates against colonists who favored accommodation with Britain. The reconcilers wanted Parliament and the thirteen colonial legislatures to work out some sort of power sharing arrangement, but independence advocates like John replied that sovereignty was indivisible—either Parliament had complete authority over the colonists or the assemblies did. He now contended that power sharing was equally impossible within a marriage. For men "to repeal our Masculine systems," he wrote, "would compleatly subject Us to the Despotism of the Peticoat." How could such a dismissive attitude toward women's rights come from the same pen that had, just the previous fall, lamented that Elizabeth Quincy Smith had only been permitted to exercise her talents within the borders of Weymouth? Like most people, John calibrated his observations on women's status to the context. In October 1775, when Abigail was in the throes of grief, he consoled her by singing her mother's praise. By the spring of 1776, on the other hand, Abigail had regained her strength and gone on the attack, thus awakening her husband's instinct for combat.

Which is not to say John actually felt threatened. He viewed the whole exchange as a continuation of the banter that, from the early days of his and Abigail's courtship, had provided them not only amusement but an opportunity to express their respect for each other's wit and resiliency. Yet the sarcasm of John's reply should not be read as evidence that he viewed the topic of masculine power lightly. During this period when he ribbed Abigail about the "Despotism of the Peticoat," he also beat back an actual, serious, challenge. Abigail wanted ten-year-old Nabby to learn Latin and Greek, and she directed John Thaxter, who was serving as the girl's tutor, to provide her the language instruction that her mother had been denied. Apparently suspecting that this decision would prove controversial, she found an offhand way to break the news to John. He had embellished a recent letter to her with a Latin passage, and she wrote back saying, "I smiled at your couplet of Lattin, your Daughter may be able in time to conster [construe] it as she has already made some considerable proficiency in her accidents, but her Mamma was obliged to get it translated." *Accidence* refers to the basics of Latin grammar.

Adams's effort to slip this information casually past her husband did not succeed. In his April 15 reply, John chose not to comment directly on Abigail's revelation, but he did remind her that Nabby required "a Different Education" from her brothers "by Reason of her sex." John also mentioned the matter directly to ten-year-old Nabby herself three days later. "I learned in a letter from your mamma, that you was learning the accidence," he wrote her. "This will do you no hurt, my dear, though you must not tell many people of it, for it is scarcely reputable for young ladies to understand Latin and Greek—French, my dear, French is the language, next to English—this I hope your mamma will teach you." By not expressly prohibiting Nabby from learning Latin, John hoped to show that he was one of the men Abigail had praised for choosing to "give up the harsh title of Master for the more tender and endearing one of Friend." For all his subtlety, though, he made his intentions clear, and there is no indication that Nabby's Latin or Greek lessons went beyond the rudimentary level.

About the same time, John also exerted his authority on a more trivial matter. Abigail asked him to send her a copy of Lord Chesterfield's letters of advice to his son, which had been widely circulated on both sides of the Atlantic. John demurred—Chesterfield's book was "stained with libertine Morals," he told her in an April 12 letter—and Abigail cheerfully submitted. Having concluded the "Remember the Ladies" letter by affirming that Providence had placed women under men's protection, she now deemed it prudent to let John protect her.

* * *

Abigail received John's facetious reply to her "Remember the Ladies" letter at the end of April and replied on May 7. "I can not say that I think you very generous to the Ladies," she wrote. Yet she went on to endorse her husband's view that women were able to compensate for their legal disability by exerting emotional power over their husbands, quoting Alexander Pope's advice to women: "Charm by accepting, by submitting sway / Yet have our Humour most when we obey." At the same time, though, she pointed out the inconsistency in John and his congressional colleagues on the one hand "proclaiming peace and good will to Men" and "Emancipating all Nations" while at the same time "retaining an absolute power over Wives."

"I have only been making trial of the Disintresstedness of his Virtue," Abigail wrote Mercy Warren at about this time, "and when weigh'd in the balance have found it wanting." Those words might seem harsh, yet the tone of Abigail's letter to Warren was as light as her exchange with her husband. By raising the issue with him "I have help'd the Sex abundantly," she told Warren. Since he had rebuffed her plea, she declared, "I think I will get you to join me in a petition to Congress."

Despite John's determination to preserve men's legal privileges and his willingness to assert his authority in matters ranging from Nabby's schooling to Abigail's reading, he was happy to grant his wife free rein in other areas, the most prominent of which was the management of the Adamses' farm and finances. Reveling in the patriotic sacrifices he was making for his country, John prided himself on not giving a moment's thought to his own personal profits and losses. In the coming years Abigail would alternate between shock at her husband's maddening disregard for his family's financial well-being and gratitude for the trust he placed in her, but the reality was that John expressed confidence in his wife's management of the farm long before she did anything to earn it. On April 11, 1776, Abigail confessed that she felt "uneaquil to the cares which fall upon me." When she expressed the hope that she would eventually "have the Reputation of being as good a *Farmeress* as my partner has of being a good Statesmen," it was less a boast than a prayer. John's reply was complimentary, falsely modest—and utterly predictable. "Your Reputation, as a Farmer, or any Thing else you undertake I dare answer for," he wrote. "Your Partners Character as a Statesman is much more problematical."

This lighthearted exchange concealed what was actually, for Abigail at least, a distressing situation. The Continental Army's voracious appetite for soldiers combined with the other unprecedented opportunities that were opening up for young men (among them potentially lucrative service on the privateers that preyed on British shipping) to create a dire shortage of labor. Early in 1776, soaring wages, added to the normal ebbs and flows of low-paid farm labor, left Abigail without a manager. "The Man upon whom I used to place dependance was taken sick last winter and left us," she reported to Mercy Warren. "I have not been able to supply his place—therefore am obliged to direct what I fear I do not properly understand." In combination with all the other demands on her time and the "Multiplicity of farming Business pouring in upon Us," Adams's ignorance of agriculture made her stint as her own farm manager untenable. In April, after only a few months of directly managing the farm, she capitulated, announcing to John that she had offered the job to one of his tenants. Even in normal times the expense of having a full-time manager could throw a small farm like the Adamses' into the red. Now, with wage rates soaring, it was almost certain to do so. But Abigail felt she had no choice.

A side benefit of giving up direct management of the farm was that it gave Abigail more time for what she called her "in door domestick affairs." Keeping a ten-, eight-, five-, and three-year-old clothed would have been challenging enough during peacetime, but the war had brought a virtual halt to the importation of textiles. Back before the revolution, the Adamses had purchased much of the family's clothing. But in December 1774, as Patriots initiated the last and most effective of their three boycotts of British merchandise, Abigail paraphrased Proverbs 31 in vowing to "seek wool and flax and work willingly with my Hands." There is no evidence that she meant this literally—no indication that she owned a spinning wheel or loom. But it was up to her and her servant girls to turn lengths of fabric into garments, and in the spring of 1776, she reported that it was "as much as I can do to manufacture cloathing for my family which would else be Naked."

The greatest challenge was procuring cloth. Abigail and Mercy Otis Warren had been friends since 1773, but by 1776 their relationship had taken on a commercial aspect, as they increasingly borrowed textiles from each other and relied upon each other for intelligence about the availability of additional fabric. Adams agreed to serve as Warren's conduit to the community of German artisans from whom the Germantown section of Braintree took its name. When Mercy needed to hire a weaver to turn a hundred pounds of woolen yarn into cloth, Abigail made all the arrangements—and she also assumed responsibility for pestering the weaver when he proved dilatory in completing the order. By the mid-1770s Abigail had established such close connections with one German weaver, a man named Hartwig or Hartwick, that on several occasions when he ran out of stocking needles, he came to her with a request that John procure needles in Philadelphia and enclose them in the letters he sent home to Braintree. On at least one occasion, John sent the needles—a real boon to Hartwick, since congressmen's letters paid no postage.

CHAPTER 10

"This Suspence Is Painfull"

1776

Although no one has ever written a full-length biography of either of Abigail's sisters, it could be done, since more than sufficient documentary evidence survives to follow the career of either Mary or Elizabeth. Abigail's brother, William, is a different matter. Although Adams and her family mentioned him periodically, he remains a shadowy figure, and the reason is clear. By his twenty-ninth birthday in 1775, William was in trouble. He had married Catharine Louisa Salmon several years earlier, but he was unable to provide for his family, and the couple had to send three of their daughters to live with his sisters. Abigail and John got Louisa, a toddler. Although she would return to her mother in 1784, when Abigail sailed to Europe, she moved back in with the Adamses upon their return four years later and remained a part of their household until both of them died.

In the spring of 1776, Abigail decided to try to share some of her own good fortune with her brother. John's election to Congress had given her both contacts and status, and she put both to work in an effort to get William commissioned as an officer in the Continental Army. First she spoke with several members of the Massachusetts legislature, which had the responsibility of recommending officers to Congress, and then she wrote to her husband. John was careful to make no promises. If the assembly were to recommend William, he assured Abigail, Congress would give him a commission. Then John would be willing to speak personally with George Washington about giving his brother-in-law a choice assignment. Meanwhile he suggested to Abigail that with the largest army ever seen in North America poised to attack New York, William, who had fought in the battle of Lexington and Concord, might want to reenlist as a common soldier for the time being. William ignored the suggestion.

Like many, perhaps most, of her fellow New Englanders, Abigail was intensely ambivalent about luxury. On the one hand she viewed extravagant spending as harmful not only to a family's and a nation's economy but to the spendthrift's morals. A series of patriotic boycotts against British merchandise during the 1760s and 1770s provided a new and still more powerful argument against extravagance. On the other hand, Adams, like most people, liked to indulge herself every once in a while. She had managed to comply with the Patriot boycotts of tea, but in April 1776, Congress allowed the sale and use of tea that had not been grown within the British empire. Many Americans nonetheless viewed tea drinking as a needless extravagance at a time of national political and economic crisis, so Abigail made sure to pen harsh denunciations of tea consumption at the beginning and end of a request she sent John in June 1776. The request was for tea.

Adams stressed that she had no plans to host tea parties. "I only wish it for a medicine," she told her husband, "as a relief to a nervious pain in my Head to which I am sometimes subject." John agreed to hunt up a canister of tea at a Philadelphia grocery shop, but he could not resist teasing his wife about her motive for wanting it. "I will endeavour to relieve your Head Ach if I can," he wrote. Abigail was used to her husband's ribbing, but her reluctance to acknowledge her fondness for tea would soon cause her additional grief.

Less than three months after the British fleet sailed out of Boston Harbor, the war came home to eastern Massachusetts in a more immediate way than ever before. During the British occupation of Boston, there had been occasional reports of people contracting smallpox, but army officers had rushed the victims into quarantine, preventing a general outbreak. But the departure of the British led to a vast movement of people. Colonists who had been cooped up in the town were finally able to leave, and Bostonians who had fled could now come home. The inevitable result of all this roaming was that by the beginning of June 1776, the town was in the grips of a major smallpox epidemic.

Massachusetts and other colonies had prohibited inhabitants from having themselves inoculated, since the operation involved exposure to the smallpox virus and made the patient highly contagious. But many people simply defied the law. Foremost among the illegal inoculators were recently recruited soldiers who were determined to protect themselves before joining the pox-ridden Continental Army. There were other vectors of smallpox infection as well. According to Abigail Adams, "The paper curency"—printed to fund the war against the mother country—"spread it everywhere," which may in fact have been the case. By June the Massachusetts legislature realized it had no choice but to suspend its prohibition against inoculation. Provision was made for the establishment of smallpox hospitals (actually private homes temporarily converted into inoculation centers) in every county in the province. The assemblymen also approved a far more radical proposal. For a limited time, they allowed inoculation anywhere within the limits of Boston—not just at designated smallpox hospitals. Patients undergoing inoculation would be allowed to roam the city freely, for the burden would be on those who chose not to be inoculated either to get out of town or to hole up in their homes. For ten days, the entire city of Boston would be turned into a giant smallpox hospital.

Abigail had been seeking an opportunity to have herself inoculated ever since 1764, when John underwent the operation. Even after their marriage later that year, Abigail's mother had continued to forbid her from deliberately contracting the virus. For a decade Adams had obeyed Elizabeth's wishes, but now that she was gone, Abigail was determined to protect herself and her children. Her wealthy uncle Isaac Smith offered to turn his Boston mansion over to the Adams party, which swelled to well over a dozen with the addition of Abigail's unmarried sister, Betsy; her older sister, Mary, and all her family; and several others. As the party rode up to Boston early in the morning of July 12, Abigail dared to hope that they would complete the whole ordeal as quickly as John had twelve years earlier—in three weeks—and that she and her children would be back in early August. At most they would be gone a month.

The Adamses were not the only country people who had decided to participate in the grand experiment in mass inoculation. Indeed, Abigail had never seen so many people in Boston. "Such a Spirit of innoculation never before took place," she wrote John; "the Town and every House in it, are as full as they can hold." Later she estimated that three thousand out-of-towners had come to Boston to be inoculated. Four thousand Bostonians underwent the operation.

At first it seemed likely that Abigail would be able to hold to her ambitious timeline. Like John in 1764, his wife and children had been inoculated within a few hours of their arrival in Boston. Borrowing the language of the battlefield, Abigail informed her husband that "Our Little ones"—even their daughter—"stood the opperation Manfully." Next came the wait. If the operation was a success, pockmarks would appear on the patients within ten days or so. Thankfully, their doctor, Thomas Bullfinch, was among a new breed of physicians who had dropped their elders' insistence on the ten days of preparation, complete with self-induced vomiting, that had tormented John twelve years earlier. But even Bullfinch prescribed medicines that caused "the Little folks" to "puke every morning." Abigail could not resist telling John that the whole experience would have been less of a trial if he had been more diligent about filling her order for tea. At the end of the July 14 letter in which she reported the family's inoculation, she added a postscript in which she betrayed her squeamishness about the topic by referring to it elliptically. "A little India herb would have been mighty agreable now," she wrote.

Abigail did not record her opinion of the unheard-of policy of allowing inoculated patients the run of the town, but less than a week after taking the virus, she had reason to be grateful for it. On July 18, she was able to join the crowd that stood on King Street outside the Massachusetts statehouse as the Declaration of Independence was read from the balcony. She described the scene for her husband:

> I went with the Multitude into Kings Street to hear the proclamation for independance read and proclamed. Some Field peices with the Train were brought there, the troops appeard under Arms and all the inhabitants assembled there (the small pox prevented many thousand from the Country). When Col. Crafts read from the Belcona [balcony] of the State House the Proclamation, great attention was given to every word. As soon as he ended, the cry from the Belcona, was God Save our American States and then 3 cheers which rended the air, the Bells rang, the privateers fired, the forts and Batteries, the cannon were discharged, the platoons followed and every face appeard joyfull. . . . The kings arms were taken down from the State House and every vestage of him from every place in which it appeard and burnt in King Street. Thus ends royall Authority in this State, and all the people shall say Amen.

Only two things prevented Abigail from taking full part in the celebration of Congress's decision to take the thirteen colonies out of the British Empire. One was John's absence. She also objected to the changes Congress had made to the rough draft of the Declaration of Independence, a copy of which she had received from her husband. "I cannot but feel sorry that some of the most Manly Sentiments in the Declaration are Expunged from the printed coppy," she told him. This comment may have been intended to salve John's wounded pride. The copy of the rough draft that Abigail received was in John's handwriting, and she apparently assumed that he was the author. Another reason that Abigail preferred the rough draft of the Declaration was that it contained a harsh denunciation of slavery.

Almost immediately, Abigail's joy at the adoption of the Declaration of Independence was submerged in private anguish. Inoculation only worked if the patient actually contracted the smallpox virus, which did not always happen on the first try. It took about ten days for the first symptoms of infection to appear. On July 22, eleven days after her inoculation, Abigail finally began to feel sick. But she was compelled to report to John that "The children are not yet broke out." Finally pockmarks began to appear on John Quincy and Nabby, and Abigail breathed a sigh of relief. But her two youngest children, Charles and Tommy, showed no sign of being infected, so she had to have them reinoculated. As of July 29, the two youngsters still betrayed no symptoms. Charles and Thomas were not alone. Citywide, doctors reported that their attempts to induce infection had failed in an alarmingly high percentage of their patients. "The small pox acts very odly this Season," Abigail wrote. Various explanations were offered. Some claimed that a new generation of doctors had imperiled their patients by neglecting the old practice of purging them before inoculating them. Also, doctors now made small punctures rather than large gashes in their patients' skin and inserted pus that was less virulent. John Adams, closely following events in the mail he received from Abigail and various friends and relatives, was furious at the physicians for taking on too many patients—some as many as a thousand. They could not possibly care for all of them properly, he claimed. The doctor themselves blamed the summer heat, which caused their patients to sweat out the infected pus before it could enter the bloodstream.

Of course no one really knew what had gone wrong. Paraphrasing Psalm 91, Adams observed to her husband that smallpox in its current incarnation was "a pestilence that walketh in Darkness." There seemed to be no pattern in whose inoculation succeeded and whose did not. Little Rebecca Peck, housed in the Smith mansion along with the Adamses but inoculated by a different doctor, Abigail reported, "has it to such a degree as to be blind with one Eye, swell'd prodigiously, I believe she has ten Thousand" pockmarks, Adams told her husband. "She is really an object to look at." In this extremity Abigail began to draw upon her own medical beliefs. It was standard practice to prohibit patients undergoing smallpox inoculation from consuming meat, seasoned vegetables, and other foods that could overheat their systems. Adams now began giving meat to her youngest sons in hopes of bringing on an infection. The greatest danger was not simply that inoculation would fail but that the boys would appear to have acquired immunity without actually doing so. Adams pointed out to her husband that many Bostonians had been inoculated the previous winter and had therefore felt safe remaining in town during the July 1776 mass inoculation. Some of them had now discovered their mistake, having "taken it in the natural way," which was more than ten times likelier than inoculation to prove fatal. "This Suspence is painfull," she wrote John on July 30.

Then, two days later, Abigail was finally able to report the appearance of twelve pustules on Tommy. To John she wondered aloud whether the meat she had insisted on giving him had made the difference. But Charley's skin remained smooth. "What to do with him I know not," she wrote John. "I cannot get the small pox to opperate upon him." She even offered the youngster wine along with his meat, but to no avail. Meanwhile Abigail was beginning to have doubts about whether Nabby really had caught the virus. The girl had shown some symptoms but not the telltale one: there were no pockmarks. The doctors assured Abigail that her daughter had acquired immunity, and at first she deferred to their expertise, but as she learned of more and more people whose apparently successful operations had in fact failed, she opted instead to obey her own instincts. She demanded a third inoculation. This time the operation was prodigiously successful, and the girl was eventually covered with more than a thousand pustules, each one, Abigail reported to John, "as larg as a great Green Pea." When John got the news, he shared in Abigail's relief. Through her he sent his "Speckeled Beauty" recommendations for keeping the pockmarks from turning into unsightly permanent scars, the most important being to stay out of the sun. And if that did not work, he wrote, she must content herself with inner beauty. Mercy Otis Warren offered similar advice.

By late August, John was feeling sufficiently lighthearted about his family's inoculation that he yielded to the temptation to remind Abigail of the delicious pun he had heard from Reverend Mather Biles back during his own inoculation twelve years earlier. Perhaps, Reverend Biles had said, we clergymen should be greeting smallpox patients with the Roman Catholic blessing, "*pax tecum*," which in the ears of the uneducated sounded like "*pox take 'em*."

At the end of July, Elbridge Gerry, one of John's colleagues in the Massachusetts congressional delegation and the man for whom the gerrymander would later be named, obtained leave for a visit to Boston. Abigail had never met him before, but when she spotted him in the pews at Brattle Street Church during a Wednesday prayer service, she "knew him . . . some how instinctively." A few days later Gerry paid Adams a visit. "I wanted to ask him many questions which I [could] not do as he was a stranger, and we had company," she told John.

For Abigail, the smallpox episode brought a scattering of compensations—most of which would undoubtedly have seemed trivial to a woman less accomplished at amplifying her blessings. Abandoning Braintree for an extended stay in Boston meant exchanging Anthony Wibird, the Adamses' lackluster hometown minister, for the electrifying Samuel Cooper, pastor of the Brattle Street Church. Despite the debilitating effects of inoculation, "I have attended publick worship constantly, except one day and a half ever since I have been in Town," Adams told her husband on August 5. "I rejoice in a preacher who has some warmth, some energy, some feeling." Since the quality that distinguished Cooper from Wibird was his sensibility, Abigail easily slid from (implicitly) complaining about the Braintree pastor to denouncing all such "cold phlegmatick Preachers, Politicians, Friends, Lovers and Husbands." "I thank Heaven I am not so constituted my-self and so connected," she told John. Abigail's celebration of her husband's lack of phlegm (the bodily humor associated with coldness, moisture, and impassivity) was intended as a compliment, of course, but also as a caution—a reminder to John that his greater-than-average sensibility was an essential ingredient in her affection for him.

Something—perhaps it was the grim suspense that hung over the Smith mansion as everyone awaited Charles's fate—kept Adams from merely reiterating her customary celebration of sensibility. For the first time in her surviving correspondence with John, she admitted that this admirable quality harbored inherent dangers. "May I ask if the same temperament and the same Sensibility which constitutes a poet and a painter will not be apt to make a Lover and a Debauchee?" she wrote John. Never mind that Abigail equated the "lover" with the "debauchee"—the man ruined by excessive drink or sexual promiscuity. What made her August 5 letter truly significant was its first-ever acknowledgment that too much sentiment could be as harmful as too little.

By coincidence John had, the previous day, sent Abigail his own report on a religious observance. He attended a Baptist church in Philadelphia, then reported to his wife that the minister's "Action was violent to a degree bordering on fury. His Gestures [were] unnatural, and distorted," and his "Voice was vociferous and boisterous." Sometime in mid-August, somewhere along the post road, Abigail's plea for "a preacher who has some warmth, some energy, some feeling" crossed paths with John's description of his Baptist host as excessively passionate.

The sojourn in Boston brought Abigail other compensations as well. She confessed that for all the anxiety she endured in the Smith mansion, it was nice to be able to spread out a little. "I have possession of my Aunts chamber in which you know is a very conveniant pretty closet with a window which looks into her flower Garden," she wrote John at the end of August. "In this closet are a number of Book Shelves, which are but poorly furnished, however I have a pretty little desk or cabinet here where I write all my Letters and keep my papers unmollested by any one. . . . I always had a fancy for a closet with a window which I could more peculiarly call my own." More than one twenty-first-century historian has noted the resemblance between Abigail's words and the title of Virginia Woolf's most famous book, *A Room of One's Own.*

As she lingered in her aunt's windowed closet, one issue that Adams paused to consider was education. Her thoughts were prompted by a letter from John lamenting New England's slow progress in the promotion of higher learning. Not only did the region lack anything resembling Philadelphia's American Philosophical Society, but there was also a more fundamental problem: "the little Intercourse We have had with strangers." Abigail began her reply by amplifying her husband's complaint about their fellow New Englanders' insularity and neglect of education. Unlike John, a graduate of Harvard, she also had criticism for that institution. But for Abigail, all of this was only a launching point for the topic she actually wanted to discuss. "If you complain of neglect of Education in sons," she asked, "What shall I say with regard to daughters, who every day experience the want of it[?]"

Adams provided two justifications for increasing women's educational opportunities. The first was traditional. "If much depends as is allowed upon the early Education of youth and the first principals which are instilld take the deepest root," she wrote, "great benifit must arise from litirary accomplishments in women." Abigail's other rationale was related to the first, but it would have been unthinkable before the American Revolution. In his August 4 letter, John had asserted that "New England must produce the Heroes, the statesmen, the Philosophers, or America will make no great Figure for some Time." "If we mean to have Heroes, Statesmen and Philosophers," Abigail declared in reply, "we should have learned women." With the advent of self-government in the former British colonies, John had said, virtuous soldiers, politicians, and scientists had become necessary to national survival. Abigail simply reminded him that the person who stood the best chance of steering a young man down the path of virtue was his mother. How could she educate her son if she herself was kept ignorant? Five months after writing the "Remember the Ladies" letter, Abigail was ready to talk not only about how some husbands tyrannized over their wives but about the restraints that men in general placed on women. And the demands she put forward in August 1776 were even more deeply rooted in the ideals of the American Revolution than those she had made the previous March. Without educated women, she claimed, the republic could not survive. It was a bold statement, so Abigail took the edge off it using a technique she often employed in such situations. "Excuse me my pen has run away with me," she wrote.

Four days later, Abigail's grand thoughts about women's education were driven from her mind by personal tragedy. After three inoculations, Charles Adams finally contracted the smallpox virus. However, it was not Dr. Bullfinch who transmitted the disease to the youngster but one of the boy's fellow patients. The six-year-old had been infected "in the natural way." Charles was "yet a very ill child," Adams wrote her husband on August 19. "I hope he is not dangerous, but we cannot tell the Event. Heaven grant it may be favorable." The stress that Abigail endured while caring for her son was aggravated by a minor annoyance: John had still not sent her any tea. Meanwhile the other Adams, his congressional colleague Samuel, had managed to get a canister of green tea to his wife, Elizabeth, who had served Abigail "a very fine Dish" of it earlier in the month. "The Scarcity of the article made me ask her Where she got it," Abigail later reported. "She replied her *Sweet Heart* sent it to her by Mr. Gerry. I said nothing, but thought my Sweet

Heart might have been eaquelly kind considering the disease I was visited with, and that [tea] was recommended as a Bracer." Abigail ended her August 19 letter on a cryptic note that carried a hint of menace. "Dont forget my Herbs for your own sake as well as mine," she wrote.

Actually, John *had* complied with his wife's request for tea, directing a Philadelphia grocer, Mrs. Yard, to send the canister to his home in Braintree. She agreed and readily found a courier—Elbridge Gerry—who somehow got it into his head that the tea was meant for the wife of Samuel, not John, Adams. A week later, when Elizabeth Adams received a visit from Abigail, the tea she drank was, unbeknownst either to her or to her host, her own. John's failure to supervise the dispatch of the tea canister was only one reason it went to the wrong Mrs. Adams. Abigail's insistence upon referring to the tea using opaque language prevented John from detecting the mistake. Ever since July 14, she had been reminding him of his promise to send "India herb," but John was either not astute enough or not engaged enough to discern her meaning.

Abigail spared her husband the worst of the details about Charles, but to his law clerk John Thaxter she was more forthcoming. "He has been exceeding ill, stupid and delirious for 48 hours," she told Thaxter on August 20. Charles was not the youngest of the Adams children, but in many ways he seemed even more fragile than four-year-old Tommy, who had barely survived the dysentery epidemic of the previous fall. In the same August 5 letter where she called little Tommy "Manly, firm and intrepid," Abigail described Charles as "soft, tender and pathetick." All of these were qualities associated with the man of feeling. The previous spring, she had related to John an anecdote about Charles that conveyed why both of them found him so endearing. Two months before his sixth birthday, Charles paid a visit to his father's mother and her second husband, John Hall. On Palm Sunday, Susanna and her grandson were walking to church when a horseman brought news that the British had evacuated Boston that morning. "Gone from Boston[?]" the incredulous child asked his grandmother, "gone away themselves[?]"

"Yes," Susanna replied.

"Then I say they are Cowards, for they have stood it but one year and we would have stood it 3," Charles told her.

As Abigail sat at her son's bedside, watching for any sign that his disorder had taken a turn for the better or worse, she recorded her own anecdote about him—and then put it to use in a dispute with her husband. John was planning to come home on leave soon, but he worried that he would not be able to hire a servant and horses in Philadelphia, so he asked Abigail to procure them for him in Massachusetts. But as she repeatedly reminded him, she was not exactly in the position to make his travel arrangements for him. For one thing, most of the horses and servants she knew about were in Braintree and Weymouth, and she was stuck in Boston until Charley got clear of the disease. Nor did she have time to stroll around town evaluating laborers and horseflesh. On the other hand, Abigail was obliged to obey her husband, so she eventually agreed to locate the servant and horses—which primarily consisted of dispatching letters that John could have just as easily written himself. Less than a week after reporting that their son had contracted smallpox in the natural way, she described a poignant scene: "I was talking of sending for you and trying to procure horses for you when little Charles who lay upon the couch coverd over with small Pox, and nobody knew that he heard or regarded any thing which was said, lifted up his head and says Mamma, take my Dollor and get a Horse for Pappa." The message was unmistakable: Abigail had more serious matters to attend to than hiring horses for her husband.

A week later Abigail once again used Charley to convey her own thoughts. The previous Saturday evening's post had, surprisingly enough, brought no letter from John. "Little Charles stands by and sends Duty to Pappa," Abigail reported to her husband. Then the sick child asked his mother a question: "Mamma did you get any Letters a Saturday?"

"No," Abigail replied.

"Then why do you write?" Charles asked.

Abigail's letter informing John that their most delicate child had contracted smallpox in the natural way reached her husband on August 27. Like her he was devastated. "Symptoms so terrible indicate the Utmost danger," he wrote her that same day. "Besides he will be more troublesome than the rest, if he recovers, because his exquisite Feelings make him more impatient." Three days later, John told Abigail, "My dear Charles is continually present to my Mind." Like his wife, Adams suspected that his middle son was not as hardy as the others. He feared the boy's infection would be "more than his delicate frame can support." Yet he remained hopeful. "Children of his Age," he reminded her, "are often seen to bear a great deal." As he read over Abigail's August 19 letter, John felt terrible about his earlier attempt to make light of the family's inoculation by recycling Mather Biles's "*pax tecum*" pun.

Before Adams could finish this letter, his servant returned from the post office with more recent intelligence from Abigail: Charles was still suffering, but he was doing better. The news "has given me fine Spirits," he told her. "I feel quite light. I did not know what fast Hold that little Pratler Charles had upon me before." John was especially pleased to read that, contrary to his expectations, Charley had been, as his mother put it, "as patient as a Lamb" in the face of all his suffering.

On September 2, Abigail and Charles were finally able to leave Boston. A sojourn that she had expected to last at most a month had stretched out to nearly two. Shortly after she returned to Braintree, she and John figured out, more or less simultaneously, what had happened to the tea he had tried to send her. Abigail sheepishly informed Elizabeth Adams that the shipment she had received from Elbridge Gerry had not been intended for her use. Elizabeth sent her what remained, but it was less than half the original canister. John also shipped Abigail some more tea—of far lower quality than the batch that had miscarried. The replacement reached her in fifteen days. If the original one had done so, she could have enjoyed its comforts throughout the inoculation ordeal.

Late August brought additional frustration on a much grander scale. Earlier in the month, thirty-four thousand British troops had landed on Long Island, just south of Brooklyn. On August 27, the imperial army managed to get around Washington's left flank, and thousands of Americans were wounded, captured, or killed in the ensuing rout. The surviving Continentals were lucky to escape across the East River to Manhattan two nights later. Like other Patriots, the Adamses were disheartened by the shattering defeat, and Abigail also had a personal reason to complain: the rout of the Continental Army dissolved John's determination to take a leave of absence. After all she had done, in the midst of all her travails, to procure her husband a servant and horses, he was not coming home after all. This news "damp't my Spirits," she acknowledged, but she put a brave face on things, telling her husband in a September 20 letter that if every man in eastern Massachusetts were to rush to New York to try to stop the British juggernaut, the women of the region would assume responsibility for its defense. If "we should be attacked," she assured her husband, "you would find a Race of Amazons in America."

By this time life on the Adams farm had returned to the wartime approximation of normal. There was nothing to distract Abigail from the anniversary of her mother's final illness a year earlier. "This Month twelve month was attended with so many melancholy Scenes, that my

Heart Bleeds afresh at the recollection," she wrote John on September 21. "The Image of my Dear Mother seems ever before me, and fresh to my memory." A recent visit to Weymouth parsonage had been especially painful. "I felt more than common depression of spirits the other day when I enterd the House," she wrote. None of Abigail's melancholy could be ascribed to anxiety about the seventy-year-old Parson Smith's physical condition. "My Father enjoys better Health than he has for many year," she told John. "He possesses a vigirous old age. He call'd here the other day comeing of a journey to dine with me having ride forty miles before dinner." Asked if the excursion had worn him out, he replied "No . . . thats a triffell for one so young as I am."

In mid-October, John, having finally decided that Congress could get along without him, obtained leave to return to Braintree. By early November he was home. Almost at once, he and Abigail conceived a child, and this pregnancy may in fact have been planned. Eighteenth-century women knew that they were more likely to conceive at some times than others, and many made use of this knowledge in limiting their reproduction. There was also a widespread belief that mothers who breastfed were less likely to become pregnant than those who did not, and many women prolonged nursing in order to postpone their next pregnancy. It is impossible to know for certain whether the Adamses used any of these birth control techniques, but there is tantalizing evidence that they did. In April 1777, about halfway through her pregnancy, Abigail reminded her absent husband of a promise he had made her. She did not specify what it was, but it involved his return to Braintree—possibly in time for the baby's birth. "Some perticuliar circumstances were really upon that condition," she wrote. The "perticuliar circumstances" to which Adams referred were her pregnancy, which appears to have been conditioned on John's promise to return the moment he could. If Abigail conceived this child only on certain conditions, her pregnancy must have been a matter of choice.

The Adamses had been together for all of Abigail's earlier pregnancies, so it was with an especially heavy heart that John headed south on January 9, 1777. Before he left, Abigail confided to him that she hoped the child, who would arrive around the middle of July, would be a girl. In February, as she silently commemorated the loss of thirteen-month-old Susanna seven years earlier, that hope must have intensified. Abigail later reported receiving a premonition that this sixth child would in fact be female.

CHAPTER 11

"To Bear What I Cannot Fly From"

1777

During John's absence from the Continental Congress, the British army had moved within striking distance of Philadelphia, forcing the delegates to reconvene in Baltimore. On his way back to Congress, John had to veer far to the west to avoid being captured. As he traveled, he learned that George Washington's Continental Army had, after retreating across the state of New Jersey and then the Delaware River, recrossed the Delaware on Christmas Night 1776 and won a pair of morale-boosting victories over British General William Howe at Trenton and Princeton.

John did not arrive in Baltimore until February 1, more than three weeks after leaving home. Shortly after returning to Congress, he found time to discuss a piece of family news the couple had received during their brief time together the previous winter: Abigail's sister Elizabeth Smith had gotten engaged. Betsy was twenty-six, and had she remained single much longer, she would have run a serious risk of slipping into spinsterhood, so her wedding announcement might have been expected to elicit relief as well as joy. But things were not quite that simple. It turned out that Abigail's suspicion of a romantic connection between Betsy and John Shaw, her father's boarder, was right on the mark, and he was the one who had proposed to her.

The seemingly inappropriate circumstances that brought the couple together were not the Adamses' only objection to the marriage. John Shaw was a dogmatic Calvinist who fiercely adhered to such bedrock Puritan beliefs as original sin and human depravity. He was absolutely convinced that most of humanity was doomed to spend eternity in Hell. By contrast, the Adamses' Congregationalism was much less doctrinaire. During the spring of 1777, John delighted in recounting for Abigail how a Portsmouth, New Hampshire, wit had ridiculed the concept of original sin—the notion that Adam had bequeathed his wickedness to all his descendants. Adam's iniquity had either been divided equally among all his billions of descendants, the man reasoned—and if so, each person's portion of it was infinitesimal—or it had descended intact to Adam's first son and then the first son in every subsequent generation, in which case everyone had only an infinitesimal chance of being Adam's heir. Either way, the matter could have been of no concern to anyone living in the eighteenth century. While Americans of the Adamses' mind-set found concepts such as original sin difficult to accept, the more serious problem was that people who held to such fundamentalist concepts tended to be unpleasantly judgmental. In February 1777, when John asked Abigail to tell Shaw that "he may be a Calvinist if he will, provided always that he preserves his Candour, Charity and Moderation," he was joking, because Calvinists like Shaw prided themselves on not possessing any of these three roughly synonymous qualities.

John's jest showed that, while he continued to harbor reservations about Shaw, he was willing to be a good sport about having him as a brother-in-law. Abigail was not so easily reconciled to her sister's choice, and she wrote John, "the mortification I endure at the mention of it is so great that I have never [ex]changd a word with her upon the subject." "I would not make an exchange with her for the mountains of Mexico and Peru," Abigail continued. "She has forfeited all her character with me and the world for taste &c. All her acquaintance stand amazd." To her it seemed clear that Elizabeth was marrying not for love but out of fear of becoming an old maid. At the time the majority of Massachusetts women had found husbands by the age of twenty-four. Betsy's thirtieth birthday was only three years away, and according to Abigail, the "Idea of 30 years and unmarried is sufficent to make people do very unacountable things." Not only did Shaw's judgmentalism annoy Abigail even more than it did John, she could feel what he could only imagine in the abstract: that once a woman took a husband, she had to submit to his will. Moreover, while John's affection for Betsy Smith was great, she was not, after all, his baby sister.

Abigail also received another piece of bad news late in the winter of 1777, albeit not of quite the same order as her sister's marriage plans. Charles Lee, the dashing if slovenly British general who had come over to the American side, had been captured by a British patrol during

General Howe's dash across New Jersey. In the confusion, Lee's closest companion—the Pomeranian whose paw Abigail had shaken a year earlier—had gone missing.

By early March, Abigail was well into her second trimester, but she was not feeling any better. None of her pregnancies had been easy, but this time, she assured John, her discomfort served as "a constant remembrancer of an absent Friend," one that excited "sensations of tenderness which are better felt than expressd." Barely a month later, on April 17, Adams received ominous news. A Boston acquaintance, "Mrs. Howard," who had delivered a child a week earlier, had suffered "a mortification in her Bowels" and died within a few days. "Every thing of this kind naturally shocks a person in similar circumstances," Adams told her husband.

Summer came early to New England in 1777, which ordinarily would have been cause for celebration in the Adams household, but not this year, because Abigail's pregnancy gave her insomnia, "which makes me more unable to bear the Heat of the day." John warned Abigail that at any point the British might return to Massachusetts. If they did, he advised, she should hasten to him in Philadelphia. "I should make a misirable hand of running now," Abigail gently reminded him in her reply. A week later her tone was more serious. "The thought of being driven from my own Habitation at this time is more distressing than ever," she wrote John. "I can but poorly walk about House." One of Abigail's few comforts was the care she received from Nabby, who was not yet twelve years old. "I am happy in a daughter who is both a companion and an assistant in my Family affairs and who I think has a prudence and steadiness beyond her years," she told her husband.

During the pregnancy, John was excitedly making plans. In early June he had magnanimously (as he must have viewed it) directed (he did not suggest) that the child be named Elizabeth after Abigail's mother if a girl and William after Abigail's father if a boy. And he hoped Richard Cranch would stand in for him at the christening. A month later, John's mood had darkened. For two days, Philadelphia had been pounded by a "cold, raw" thunderstorm that had come from the northeast—the direction of home. "It is unusual, to have a storm from that Point, in June and July," he observed to his wife. "It is an Omen no doubt. Pray what can it mean?" When he wrote Abigail on July 10, John knew his child would be born soon. Perhaps the baby had already come. He lamented that over the previous twenty-two months, his congressional service had kept him away from his wife during the dysentery epidemic that killed her mother, the family's inoculation against smallpox—and now this. "Three Times have I felt the most distressing Sympathy with my Partner, without being able to afford her any Kind of Solace, or Assistance," he wrote. "Now I think I feel as anxious as ever."

John's anxiety was justified. On the night of July 8, after a week of feeling sick, Abigail was "taken with a shaking fit," and she reported that she was "very apprehensive that a life was lost." By the next day, when she was able to write, the child had still given no sign of life. Adams could not ignore the danger that a miscarriage at this late stage of the pregnancy would pose to her own life. "I know not of any injury to myself," she told John, and "I would not Have you too much allarmd," yet there was that inescapable possibility. "I would have you prepaird for any Event that may happen," she wrote. The next night at nine o'clock, Abigail again sat down to write her husband. The doctor had visited. He "encourages me to Hope that my apprehensions are groundless respecting what I wrote you yesterday," she told John. She began to wonder whether she had caused John needless alarm with her letter of the previous day. Still, "I cannot say I have had any reason to allter my mind," she declared. If there should be good news to report, "you shall know it as soon as the post can convey it," she assured John. "I pray Heaven that it may be soon or it seems to me I shall be worn out." Just as she wrote those words, she began to experience a contraction. Even as the pain sharpened, she managed to write, "I must lay my pen down this moment, to bear what I cannot fly from."

"And now I have endured it I reassume my pen," she added after the pain had subsided, "and will lay by all my own feelings and thank you for your obligeing Letters." After writing those words, Adams set the letter aside until the next morning. It was July 11—John Quincy's birthday—and that fact alone seemed to renew her hopes. "This day ten years ago master John came into this world. May I have reason again to recollect it with peculiar gratitude," she wrote.

Later that day, Abigail delivered a little girl, but she was stillborn. "It appeard to be a very fine Babe," she told her husband on July 16, when she was able to resume her pen, "and as it never opened its Eyes in this world it lookd as tho they were only closed for sleep." Even amid her exhaustion and despair, she asked her husband to join her "in Gratitude to Heaven, that a life I know you value"—her own—"has been spaired and carried thro Distress and danger." Nor did her agony cause her to forget the ever-looming possibility that her letter would be intercepted by the enemy, and she was careful to withhold the cause of the child's death. "The circumstance which put an end to its existance, was evident upon its birth, but at this distance and in a Letter which may possibly fall into the Hands of some unfealing Ruffian I must omit particuliars," she declared. "Suffice it to say that it was not oweing to any injury which I had sustaind, nor could any care of mine have prevented it."

Adams also took some consolation from being vindicated in the medical judgment she had made three days before the delivery. "Tho my Friends would have fain perswaded me that the Spleen [or] the Vapours [depression] had taken hold of me," she told John, "I was as perfectly sensible of its discease as I ever before was of its existance." It was a month before Adams was ready to leave the farm. She witnessed the christening of her newest niece, Susanna, daughter of John's brother Peter, and the occasion inevitably stirred her thoughts about what might have been. "I wishd to have call'd ours had it lived after my own dear Mother, and was much gratified by your mentioning it and requesting it," she told John.

By the spring of 1777, the Revolutionary War had begun to wreak havoc on the American economy. The British navy's blockade of the Atlantic coast drastically reduced the number of vessels entering American harbors, and shortages inevitably ensued. At the same time, the financially strapped Continental Congress and the equally impecunious state legislatures (which retained the power of printing paper money until the adoption of the U.S. Constitution in 1788), flooded the economy with far more currency than it could absorb. The excess of money combined with the shortage of goods to drive prices ever higher. As if this were not enough, a band of criminals operating out of Londonderry, New Hampshire, further inflated the money supply with an infusion of counterfeit currency.

Abigail found laboring men as hard to come by as merchandise. Not only did the Continental Army draw in more and more recruits, but thousands of young men enlisted on privateers. When the "prizes" captured by privateersmen were auctioned off, the owners received most of the revenue, but some was customarily distributed to the crew. As more and more men beat their plowshares into swords, farms produced less and less food, flax, and wool. Often women stepped into this breach.

On his trip from Braintree to Baltimore in the winter of 1777, John was astonished to see women not merely supervising male farmworkers, as Abigail was doing, but actually performing the grueling task of "breaking and swingling" flax to free up its fibers, which were the basis for linen manufacture.

The economic turmoil of the late 1770s buffeted the Adamses from several different directions. John suffered worst in his role as a creditor. Numerous people all over eastern Massachusetts had owed him money for years. A few had received cash loans from him, but many more were in his debt because they had never gotten around to paying him for legal work or farm produce. Nothing extraordinary there; this was the everyday reality of colonial America's credit economy. In 1775, when Congress and the state legislatures began printing paper money, they required creditors to receive it at the value marked on its face. Over the course of the next two years, Massachusetts currency lost two-thirds of its value. Now that John's debtors could pay him off using money that was equal in value to only one-third of what they had obtained from him, the former procrastinators hastened to settle up. "Every fellow has his pockets full of money and chuses no doubt to pay his debts if he is a good Husband [money-manager]," Abigail wrote.

Abigail scrambled for ways to turn this rapidly-depreciating paper money into something valuable, and she finally found a solution. Back in October 1776, Congress had begun selling war bonds. As in subsequent military conflicts, investors were asked to supply the federal treasury with much-needed currency in return for interest-bearing securities. Initially the government only offered to pay 4 percent interest, but it got few takers, so in February 1777 the rate was raised to 6 percent. "I believe you will not find it difficult to procure Money since you have offerd 6 per cent," Abigail wrote John when she heard the news. "I was mentioning the other day to a certain Gentleman in this Town that Congress had agreed to give that," she continued. "An unusual pleasure lighted up his Countanance immediately, and he instantly replied, they shall have all mine immediately, I only waited for that."

Adams's unnamed friend was not alone; the offer of 6 percent turned the war bonds, called Loan Office certificates, into a hot commodity, and the purchasers included Adams herself. She quickly perceived that government securities were a highly effective hedge against inflation. No one knew for sure how Congress was going to come up with the wherewithal to pay interest on the certificates, so their actual market value steadily decayed—but at a much slower rate than paper money. So whenever people had depreciated currency thrust into their hands, as Adams did in 1777, wisdom dictated immediately converting it into federal bonds, and that is what she did. Adams was well aware of her husband's steadfast abhorrence of all forms of financial shenanigans, so she carefully explained this new investment—and only after introducing the topic, as she so often did when discussing controversial matters, with a joke. "This week I propose to send in to the continental Loan office a hundred pound[s]" worth of Massachusetts currency, she announced on June 1. "If I do not explain the matter I fear you will suspect me of being concerned with the [New] Hampshire money makers." After describing the superabundance of paper currency in Massachusetts, she declared that buying a Loan Office certificate was the only good way for her to dispose of the depreciated currency that John's debtors had foisted on her. "I have done the best in my power with what I received," she wrote.

In his reply, John acquiesced in Abigail's decision without specifically mentioning it. "I know not what would become of me, and mine, if I had not such a Friend to take Care of my Interests in my Absence," he told her.

By the summer of 1777 the economic crisis in Massachusetts and the other rebelling states had become acute. Two years into the war, the price of food and other basic commodities had more than tripled. With British privateers operating freely along the Atlantic coast, Caribbean commodities—primarily sugar, molasses, rum, and coffee—were often unavailable at any price. Inevitably, many consumers began to suspect that the shortage was artificial: that middlemen were deliberately holding commodities back from the market in order to drive the price still higher. Abigail was among those who believed the empty shelves were at least partly "occasiond by the merchants having secreted a large Quantity" of goods. So there was no sense of disapproval in her report that several groups of Bostonians had broken into shops—not exactly to steal the merchandise but to put it up for sale at a reasonable price, with the revenue going to the shopkeeper.

On July 24, Adams revealed that a group of women had joined the ranks of the rioters. Their quarry consisted of "Sugar and Coffe, articles which the Female part of the State are very loth to give up." It was "rumourd that an eminent, wealthy, stingy Merchant (who is a Batchelor) had a Hogshead of Coffe in his Store" that he refused to part with below the outrageous price of six shillings per pound. "A Number of Females some say a hundred, some say more assembled with a cart and trucks, marchd down to the Ware House and demanded the keys, which he refused to deliver, upon which one of them seazd him by his Neck and tossd him into the cart," Abigail told John. In short order the target of the women's ire—Boston merchant Thomas Boylston, who was in fact a bachelor—"deliverd the keys," whereupon the women "tipd up the cart and dischargd him, then opend the Warehouse, Hoisted out the Coffe themselves, put it into the trucks and drove off." People were saying "he had a Spanking among them, but this I believe was not true," Adams told her husband. "A large concourse of Men stood amazd silent Spectators of the whole transaction."

Abigail's description of the Boston coffee riot contained one glaring omission. The women who made up the mob were not simply caffeine addicts. As Boston selectman John Scollay insisted in his report on the same incident, they "kept Little shops to sell Necessarys for Poor People." Boylston had harmed these women not only by denying them their favorite hot beverage but by refusing to supply their retail establishments. Scollay's description of the riot offered what Adams's did not: a glimpse into the world of Boston's female shopkeepers.

The labor shortage also grew more acute in 1777—with disastrous consequences for Adams. Sometime during the previous year, she had found a new manager for her farm. We know only that he was a free black man, for Abigail did not tell John his name, and in fact she never mentioned him at all until late in August 1777, when, in the midst of hay-mowing season, he left her to join the army. Abigail entertained no illusions about the man's motivation for enlisting. "The High Bounty one hundred dollors, has tempted of[f] my Negro Head, and left me just in the midst of our Hay," she told John. No other reference to this man survives. On the one hand, racial prejudice did not prevent Abigail from putting him in charge of her white farmworkers. Yet when he left, the easiest way for her to identify him was not by name but by race.

A nearly simultaneous incident in Philadelphia revealed that John's attitude toward African Americans was equally ambivalent. During the summer of 1777, Adams decided to send home his servant John Turner. Part of the reason was simply that Adams did not have much need for him. Trained as a stocking weaver, Turner spent more time practicing his own trade than doing chores for his master. But John also worried about his character. He had a drinking problem, Adams alleged, and he was moreover a "low lived Fellow, playing Cards with Negroes, and behaving like a Rival with them for Wenches."

One obvious implication of Abigail's and John's nearly simultaneous references to African Americans is simply that blacks were (somewhat surprisingly, to many modern observers) ubiquitous in the eighteenth-century *North*. A month after Abigail complained about the defection of her "Negro Head" and John lamented his white servant's penchant for "playing Cards with Negroes," Abigail's uncle, Cotton Tufts, told John about the marriage of Phoebe, one of her father's slaves. "Phoebe is about to make the Leap—she takes the [Start?] with Mr. Bristol (a Freeman) of Boston, a Gentleman (to adopt the Language of News Papers in such Cases) *possessed of all the amiable Qualities necessary to render the married State happy.*" Although Tufts's reference to the presumably impoverished Bristol's ambition to seem a "Gentleman" of "amiable Qualities" carried the tinge of racial insult, it should be noted that New Englanders employed the same lightly ironic tone when reporting on betrothals between whites.

Early in September 1777, Abigail was handed a letter that, by her own reckoning, threw her into an "agitation and distress." Like the mail she regularly received from John, it had arrived postage free, since it was from a member of Congress. However, the man who had written his signature and the word *franked* on the outside of the letter was not John but James Lovell, a new member of the Massachusetts congressional delegation. No other delegate had ever written Abigail before, and at the sight of Lovell's signature, her heart and mind raced. She could think of only one reason to have received a letter from one of her husband's colleagues: he himself was unable to write. "The sickness or death of the dearest of Friends with ten thousand horrours seazd my immagination," she later reported. "I took up the Letter, then laid it down, then gave it out of my Hand unable to open it, then collected resolution enough to unseal it, but dared not read it, begun at the bottom, read a line, then attempted to begin it, but could not."

CHAPTER 12

"An Army of Women"

1777–1778

Abigail noticed an enclosure in the mysterious letter, ventured to take it up, and discovered that it was a map. A person sending condolences would not have enclosed a map, she thought, and she "recoverd enough to read the Letter." It turned out that Lovell had simply decided to send her a sketch of the terrain where the British and Continental armies were momentarily expected to meet, and the accompanying note was only a cover letter.

The reason Lovell gave for mailing the map directly to Abigail rather than having John forward it to her was a little strange. He explained that he "could not with delicacy have told him, *to his face*," that his admiration for Abigail was largely based on his high regard for her husband. Adams was also surprised to hear that she had inspired "affectionate esteem" in a man she had only met twice—both times briefly—and with whom she had never once corresponded. Indeed, Lovell himself acknowledged that his tone verged upon "Gallantry"—flirtatiousness. But Adams's surprise at the man's off-kilter comments was nothing compared to the relief she felt at discovering that her initial fears had been groundless. "It seems almost imposible that the Humane mind could take in, in so small a space of time, so many Ideas as rushd upon mine in the space of a moment," Abigail later wrote John. "I cannot describe to you what I felt."

Lovell's map had hardly been in Abigail's possession a month when it became extremely useful to her. General Howe's fleet had sailed out of New York Harbor on July 23 and then disappeared. For six weeks there were rumors of British landings from Massachusetts to South Carolina, but none proved true. Finally, on August 25, the imperial soldiers stepped ashore at the northern tip of Chesapeake Bay, on the west bank of the Elk River in Maryland. Everyone knew their destination: Philadelphia, where the Continental Congress met. Early in September, General Washington lined up his troops along Brandywine Creek in southeastern Pennsylvania, hoping the stream would aid him in halting the British advance. It did not. On September 11, Howe, who had managed to sneak around Washington's left flank on Long Island a year earlier, turned his right flank at the Battle of Brandywine. The Continentals suffered heavy losses and were forced to retreat toward Philadelphia.

Upon hearing of the disaster, one of Abigail's male neighbors panicked. He "was in the Horrours a few days ago upon hearing that General Washington had retreated within six miles of Phi[ladelph]ia," she told John in late September. "If How should get possession of that city," the man fretted, Congress "would immediately negotiate a peace." In that highly unlikely event, Abigail replied, "I hoped then that an Army of women would oppose him." A year and a day had passed since she had conjured up a "Race of Amazons" to defend Massachusetts in the absence of their menfolk.

Neither Washington nor Congress agreed to treat with the conquerors, but Philadelphia became untenable. The delegates moved their sessions to York, Pennsylvania, and the Continental Army headed west to Valley Forge, where the soldiers established their winter quarters. Much better news came from the north, where General John Burgoyne's entire six-thousand-man army was forced to surrender to the Continentals near Saratoga, New York, on October 17. Washington's defeat on the Brandywine barely a month earlier was among the worst he ever suffered, but Saratoga was the Continental Army's most important victory before Yorktown. The ambiguous disposition of the military conflict at the end of 1777 illustrated the challenge that the British government faced in battling a domestic insurgency: the only way to defeat the rebels was to do so everywhere at once, and that was well nigh impossible.

At the end of October, Abigail and her daughter rode up to Boston to participate in a public celebration of the capture of Burgoyne's army. Although like all Patriots she venerated the American heroes who had wrought the great victory, she also saw larger forces at work. Early on, Adams had viewed the war as an instance of divine wrath: God was punishing Americans for their many sins. At the end of 1777 she still detected the hand of Providence at work, but she had revised her understanding of the Creator's purpose. The spread of the military conflict to eastern Pennsylvania as well as upstate New York, she declared in an October 30 letter to her Loyalist cousin Isaac Smith, Jr., was a sign of God's grace. "Providence has permitted for wise ends that every one of the united States should feel the cruel depredations of the Enemy," she told Smith, so "that each one should be able to sympathize with the other"—a process that had "served to strengthen our bond of union."

Adams's understanding of the religious meaning of the war had also changed in another, more subtle and more significant way. In commenting on the surprisingly generous terms that Burgoyne and his soldiers received from Horatio Gates, the American commander at Saratoga, Adams observed that Gates had decided to "submit the punishment of their crimes" to God. For the first time ever, she described her fellow Americans not merely as the passive recipients of divine scourges and blessings but as active agents of their own destiny—so active, in fact, that they were able to task the Almighty himself with the punishment of their prisoners.

Although Abigail's morale was buoyed by the victory at Saratoga, she did have to confront one piece of very bad news in the fall of 1777. After failing to obtain a commission in the Continental Army, her brother, William, had decided to try his luck on a privateering vessel. He was as unsuccessful in this endeavor as he had been at everything else, and on July 12, 1777, after a drawn-out battle against a British merchantman, his ship was captured. Smith's solitary consolation was that for once the failure was not his fault. It took months for the news of the capture to reach eastern Massachusetts and even longer for Smith to make his way home.

On September 9, 1777, the Continental Congress took up a proposal that would have tremendous implications for the Adams family's finances. The measure's advocates believed that the interest on federal Loan Office certificates should no longer be paid with Continental paper money, which was losing its value at an accelerating pace. Instead the public creditors should receive their annual interest in bills of exchange (similar to modern bank checks), and these should be drawn on Congress's official envoys to King Louis XVI of France. Earlier that year, Benjamin Franklin and the other American representatives in Paris had persuaded the king to give their country a package of loans and subsidies. No doubt Louis expected his money to be used for weapons and other military supplies, and some was. However, numerous congressmen argued that none of these ingredients in military victory was as crucial as capital—and that the best way to sell more war bonds was for Congress to keep its current creditors happy, which meant paying interest on Loan Office certificates using French bills of exchange. John Adams opposed the plan. But every other member of the Massachusetts congressional delegation voted for it, and it sailed through Congress, nine states to one.

No doubt John's objections to the new arrangement arose partly from his long-standing suspicion of people who invested in government securities. He may also have felt ethically bound to vote against the proposal, since he knew it would yield immense benefits for his family. The Loan Office certificate that Abigail had purchased the previous summer had a face value of one hundred pounds (Massachusetts currency), but she had purchased it using paper money that had depreciated to about one-fourth of its face value, meaning that it would have bought only twenty-five pounds' worth of gold or silver. Under the new congressional decree, she would receive her 6 percent annual interest in a French bill of exchange that she could trade for gold or silver at its face value. The result was that she would earn an astronomical 24 percent return on her initial investment every year. By March 1782, when Congress finally stopped paying out French bills of exchange to the owners of Loan Office certificates, four and one half years had elapsed since Abigail's purchase, and she had collected about twenty-seven pounds in interest, earning back more than she had invested without touching the principal.

Shortly after casting his vote against this proposal, in November 1777, John obtained a leave of absence from Congress. He had business to attend to in New England, and his term was about to expire anyway. Lingering in Braintree only a few days—no description of his reunion with Abigail survives—he headed to Portsmouth, New Hampshire, for what would turn out to be his last big court case, a dispute over the ownership of a captured British merchant vessel. Before setting out for Portsmouth, he asked his wife to open any correspondence that arrived during his absence. Thus it was Abigail, not John, who first learned from his colleague James Lovell that Congress wanted him to go to France as part of the three-member delegation charged with negotiating a military alliance with Louis XVI.

Abigail was distraught. It was one thing for John to spend most of the year in Pennsylvania, where she could hear from him by each week's post. If he were now to travel to Paris, every letter he sent her would have to run a double gauntlet: a three-thousand-mile journey across an ocean that was swarming with British warships and privateers. Moreover, in order to take up his post, John would be forced to undertake his own midwinter Atlantic crossing in a vessel that might sink or be captured. Mercy Warren implored Abigail not to stand in John's way. "Why should you," wrote Warren, who was sixteen years her senior. "You are yet young." Yet even Warren could perceive the inconsistency in forbidding her own husband to travel out of the state while casually dispatching John across the Atlantic. "You will justly say we are very Ready to Give advice when we but Illy practice upon the principles we lay down," she wrote. "True—but we may profit by the advice Though we despise the Weakness of the Adviser." Warren's moment of self-awareness was transitory, for she immediately added, "Yet I have not so Ill an opinion of myself as to think were I just in your situation I shoud not strive for the Exertion of a Little Heroism upon such an Occasion."

In her distress at the idea of John's crossing the Atlantic, Abigail betrayed an uncharacteristic insensitivity to the plight of others. In a letter to Daniel Roberdeau, the Continental Army general with whom John had boarded during his sojourn in York, Pennsylvania, she observed that Roberdeau could appreciate the depth of her anguish, since he had learned "by melancholy experience, what it is to be seperated from one of the worthyest of women." This was a reference to the recent death of Roberdeau's wife. "Permit me to say your Subject will not bear a comparison," the general told Abigail as gently as he could. "You may go with or follow Mr. Adams, at a more agreeable season, or suffer only a temporary separation whereas time fixes no limits to my sufferings."

On one point Roberdeau was mistaken. Although Abigail pleaded with John to take her along, he resolutely refused to subject her to the hazards of the sea and the very real possibility of capture by the enemy. His son and namesake was another matter. John added to Abigail's anxiety by proposing to carry ten-year-old John Quincy with him to France. The logic of the idea was unassailable: the boy needed to spend more time with his father, and a voyage to the cultural capital of the world would be highly educational. Despite herself, Abigail consented to the arrangement.

The two John Adamses sailed out of Massachusetts Bay on an American frigate called the *Boston* on February 14, 1778. The ship had hardly

Locket that John Adams reportedly left with his wife, Abigail, when he sailed for Europe in February 1778. *Courtesy Adams National Historical Park.*

cleared the harbor when a shocking piece of news arrived in Braintree. Benjamin Franklin, already in France as an American envoy, had reportedly been the victim of an assassination attempt. Someone had entered his chamber late at night and repeatedly stabbed him. At the point when the ship bearing this fateful news had left France, no one knew whether Dr. Franklin was going to live or die.

The news about Franklin intensified Abigail's anxiety about the fate of her husband and son. Desperate for intelligence, she plausibly reasoned that information on the American diplomats might reach Philadelphia before Boston or Braintree, and a particularly valuable contact would be James Lovell, the Massachusetts congressman who had given her such a fright with his unexpected letter the previous fall, since he had reportedly confirmed the tragic story about Benjamin Franklin. Lovell was, moreover, one of the more active members of the congressional Committee for Foreign Affairs. So on March 1, Adams revived her correspondence with Lovell.

Abigail's urgent appeal for news of Johnny and John elicited an odd reply. Her anguish had "afforded me *Delight*," Lovell declared, since it

John Quincy Adams (1767–1848), Abigail's first-born son. Like Abigail's husband, John, John Quincy was elected to the presidency but was defeated after a single term. *Courtesy Adams National Historical Park.*

had provoked her to write with such eloquence. If you want your anxieties about your family to excite my sympathy instead of my admiration, he told her, "you must not send them to call upon me in the most elegant Dresses of Sentiment and Language." At the same time, Lovell informed Adams that the latest reports from France indicated that the alleged assassination attempt against Franklin had never actually happened. Over the next four years, Abigail and Lovell would exchange dozens of letters, and most of them followed the pattern laid down in the spring of 1778: Adams would write him because she needed something from him, and in his reply he would attempt to supply her wants but also to impress her with his wit. Lovell, who had spent sixteen years teaching school in Boston, sometimes seemed to confuse art and life, patterning himself on the title character of Laurence Sterne's satirical—and bawdy—novel, *Tristram Shandy*. As Abigail came to rely ever more heavily on the information that only he could provide, Lovell would take advantage of her desperate necessity, amusing himself by filling his letters to her with flirtatious comments that were designed to shock and often did.

Lovell was not, however, Adams's only correspondent in York. John Thaxter, who was her cousin, John's former law clerk, and John Quincy's former tutor, had traveled to the temporary capital to take up a position as a congressional clerk. He not only sent his cousin whatever tidbits of gossip he could gather about her husband but also other news items. One of these provoked the most passionate defense of women's rights she ever sent a man other than her husband. Thaxter was well aware of Abigail's interest in everything related to women, and he expected her to be excited about a clipping from the London *Public Ledger* that he mailed her in January 1778. The newspaper reported that Thomas Wilson, a minister in London, had placed a statue of Catharine Macaulay, the English historian and advocate for American rights, in his church.

Adams was, in fact, thrilled to learn that Macaulay had been honored with a statue, but the inscription engraved on it considerably diminished her delight. The great female historian was celebrated as "a Kind of Prodigy!" the *Public Ledger* reported. "Once in every Age I could wish such a Woman to appear," the inscription declared, "as a proof that Genius is not confined to Sex." Adams replied to Thaxter on February 15, the day after her husband and son sailed for France. Reverend Wilson "has sullied the glory of his deed by the narrow contracted Spirit which he discovers in the inscription," she told him. Startled that the minister could "wish that but one woman in an age might excell, and she only for the sake of a prodigy," Adams demanded, "What must be that Genious which cannot do justice to one Lady, but at the expence of the whole Sex?"

Adams's anger at Reverend Wilson's inscription launched her into a topic that the article in the *Public Ledger* had not even mentioned: "the difference of Education between the male and female Sex." "Every assistance and advantage which can be procured is afforded to the sons, whilst the daughters are totally neglected," she pointed out. "Why should children of the same parents be thus distinguished?" "It is really mortifying Sir," she wrote. Back in August 1776, when Adams had advocated women's education in a letter to John, she had emphasized that men who denied education to women harmed themselves as well as their wives and daughters. She now expanded on that theme. If the old saying about child raising—that the "first impressions are most durable"—was true, then surely it was "of great importance that those who are to instill the first principals should be suiteably qualified for the Trust." Educated women not only did a better job of nurturing their children but also made better spouses. Why, Adams asked Thaxter, "should your sex wish for such a disparity in those whom they one day intend for companions and associates"? Drawing upon her extensive knowledge of Roman emperors as well as modern European monarchs, Adams confessed to Thaxter that she could not "help sometimes suspecting that this Neglect arises in some measure from an ungenerous jealosy of rivals near the Throne."

Later in the letter Adams returned to the topic of woman's status, this time speaking in more personal terms. She asked her cousin to seek permission from James Lovell—who as a member of Congress was one of Thaxter's employers—to "communicate to me all the News and intelligence from your Quarter of the world which may be communicated to a *Woman*."

For Abigail the remainder of the winter of 1778 was a period of anxious suspense. The very best she could hope for was that the *Boston* might arrive in France in a month or so, and then it would take at least another month—until the middle of April—for her to receive word that father and son had landed safely. But the last two weeks of April came and went with no word from the travelers—and so did most of May. Only at the end of the month did she finally receive a report on the *Boston*. The news, which appeared in a royalist newspaper in occupied New York City, was that the ship had been captured by a British privateer.

"I have some faint hopes that she was not Captured till after she had landed my Best Friend," Abigail wrote John Thaxter. It was a thin reed to lean on, but it gave her sufficient hope to place letters for her husband and son on a ship bound for France. The note to John Quincy, who was a month shy of his eleventh birthday, reminded him of her high expectations for his good behavior. The boy was as affable as his two brothers, but the truth was that he was "not so manageable as either of the others." It was nonetheless surprising, given Abigail's anxiety about the two Johns' uncertain fate, that she underscored the importance of Johnny's proper comportment by telling him, "Dear as you are to me, I had much rather you should have found your Grave in the ocean you have crossd, or any untimely death crop you in your Infant years, rather than see you an immoral profligate or a Graceless child."

In mid-June, Adams finally learned that her hopeful suspicion about the *Boston* had been correct: the vessel had been captured only after discharging its cargo and passengers at Bordeaux, and John and John Quincy were safe. On the morning of June 30, four and a half months after their departure, Abigail finally received a letter from her husband. Upon disembarking in Bordeaux, Adams had discovered that Benjamin Franklin had already negotiated the Franco-American alliance that was the purpose of John's mission. Yet in the first of his letters to reach Abigail, his tone was lighthearted. "To tell you the Truth, I admire the Ladies here," he wrote from Paris. "Dont be jealous. They are handsome, and very well educated. Their Accomplishments are exceedingly brilliant. And their Knowledge of Letters and Arts, exceeds that of the English Ladies much, I believe." Even as Abigail had caught at the sound of every horse clopping down the post road, whispering a prayer that the rider was not bringing word that her husband and son had been captured by the British or killed at sea, John had been swanning around the salons, flirting with the Parisiennes and making invidious comparisons between Frenchwomen and their English-speaking counterparts.

If John's jovial report on his witty repartees with the women of Paris did in fact make Abigail jealous, she did not say so. In fact she played along with the joke, administering a droll rebuke for his failure to say more about his reception among the Parisiennes. One reason Adams did not express offense at her husband's comments was that they provided her an opening—a chance to return to one of her favorite themes. "I can hear of the Brilliant accomplishment[s] of any of my Sex with pleasure and rejoice in that Liberality of Sentiment which acknowledges them," she wrote. "At the same time I regret the trifling narrow contracted Education of the Females of my own country."

Having creatively interpreted her husband's boorish goading as willingness to acknowledge women's intelligence, Abigail gave John an earful on the topic. "I have entertaind a superiour opinion of the accomplishments of the French Ladies ever since I read the Letters of Dr. Sherbear, who professes that he had rather take the opinion of an accomplished Lady in matters of polite writing than the first wits of Itally," she wrote. John Shebbeare was an English physician and political writer whose *Letters on the English Nation*, published in 1755, was thinly disguised as an Italian Jesuit's observations on English society. Like John in his April 1778 letter to Abigail, the fictional priest, Father Batista Angeloni, had compared the women of Britain and France. In contrast to their English counterparts, Frenchmen exhibited profound respect for women's skill at literary analysis, Father Angeloni observed.

He went on to declare his own admiration for women's ability to assess literary merit, pointedly using the language of sensibility to do so. "Women have in general more delicate Sensations than men," Shebbeare had him say. "[W]hat touches them is, for the most part, true in nature; whereas men, warpt by education, judge amiss from previous prejudice, and referring all things to the model of the ancients, condemn that by comparison, where no true similitude ought to be expected."

In reporting these comments to John, Abigail omitted one important fact: Shebbeare had intended them to be sarcastic. Whereas the fictional Father Angeloni fretted that men had been "warpt by education," Shebbeare, his creator, venerated the educational attainments of Englishmen like himself, and he had nothing but contempt for the uninstructed women who presumed to analyze literature. Even Shebbeare's own fiction had felt the lash of female tongues and pens, which certainly helps to explain his hostility. Abigail was well aware that Shebbeare's book was satirical. On the same page where he launches into his extended praise of women's skills at literary analysis, he also says he is gratified that education has made the women of Paris "so artful in fact, and yet so artless in appearance," meaning that it has sharpened their native talent for deception. Yet Adams was willing to find her materials where she could. If the most eloquent praise of educated women she could unearth was a sarcastic comment by a misogynist, so be it. By changing the context she could reverse the meaning.

The other authority Abigail drew upon in her June 30, 1778, epistle on women's education was only a little less dubious than Shebbeare. She concluded her statement to John with a long quotation from a writer she did not name.

> If women says the writer are to be esteemed our Enemies, methinks it is an Ignoble Cowardice thus to disarm them and not allow them the same weapons we use ourselves, but if they deserve the title of our Friends tis an inhumane Tyranny to debar them of priviliges of ingenious Education which would also render their Friendship so much the more delightfull to themselves and us. Nature is seldom observed to be niggardly of her choisest Gifts to the [female] Sex, their Senses are generally as quick as ours, their Reason as nervious, their judgment as mature and solid. Add but to these natural perfections the advantages of acquired learning what polite and charming creatures would they prove whilst their external Beauty does the office of a Crystal to

> the Lamp not shrowding but discloseing their Brighter intellects. Nor need we fear to loose our Empire over them by thus improveing their native abilities since where there is most Learning, Sence and knowledge there is always observed to be the most modesty and Rectitude of manners.

Adams found this passage in a book titled *Letters Written by a Turkish Spy, Who Lived Five-and-Forty Years at Paris*. Like Shebbeare's work, it was actually a satire, apparently written by Giovanni Paolo Marana, a Genoese exile in Paris. Marana's case for female education seems sincere enough, yet on the previous page he had, like Shebbeare, ridiculed the educated women of France.

Given that these were the materials available to Adams, it should come as no surprise that her arguments in favor of women's education contained an element of contradiction. If women's judgment was superior to men's because they had not been "warpt by Education," how could they benefit from increased opportunities for formal instruction?

Back in 1776, when Adams wrote the "Remember the Ladies" letter, she had found several ways to take the edge off her radical demands, including flattery, humor, and a heavy reliance upon published authorities. Many of these sweeteners reappeared in her June 1778 statement. For example nearly all of her words were taken from Shebbeare and Marana. One of Adams's few original contributions was a statement that revived her 1776 strategy of granting her husband a flattering exemption from her sweeping criticism. "In this country," she wrote, "you need not be told how much female Education is neglected, nor how fashonable it has been to ridicule Female learning, tho I acknowled[ge] it my happiness to be connected with a person of a more generous mind and liberal Sentiments."

Like the most extraordinary men of her generation, Abigail somehow managed to entertain visionary thoughts even as more practical concerns threatened to overwhelm her. One domestic problem that especially vexed her during the spring and summer of 1778 was the cost of labor. Opportunities for unskilled workers expanded at the same time that the state and Continental governments pumped more and more paper money into the economy, pushing farmworkers' daily earnings to the previously unheard-of level of twenty-four shillings. Under Abigail's stewardship, the farm was losing money. In April she told John Thaxter that without a radical change for the better, she would soon face one of her greatest nightmares: an inability to pay her debts. In 1776, having given up on the idea of running the farm herself, she had brought in a full-time manager. But he had not lasted long, and neither had any of his successors. And who could blame them for seizing wartime opportunities that might never come around again? After Abigail's "Negro Head" quit to join the army, she resumed direct management of the farm.

In the spring of 1778, Adams responded to the twin challenges of taxation and inflation by doing just the opposite of what she had done two years earlier. Back then her strategy had been to hire a manager. Now she fired all of her employees except for two domestic servants. From now on the Adams acres would be worked by tenants "to the halves"—what later generations would call sharecroppers. Cotton Tufts helped her recruit two recently married brothers who would have the use of her land and livestock, splitting the harvest with her fifty-fifty.

Adams had first broached the idea of reorganizing the farm to her sister Betsy in March 1778 and, by early April, she had completed the changeover and announced it to Thaxter. But for some reason she did not inform John of her decision until mid-July. In fact, each of Abigail's family members received a different explanation for the change. To her husband, she spoke only of the scarcity of labor. Writing Thaxter, she gave just as much weight to her soaring tax bill, half of which would now be paid by her tenants. In explaining the reorganization of the farm to her sister, Abigail mentioned no specific motivation, and that omission was part of a pattern that was evident throughout her correspondence. Despite her numerous appeals to men to treat women more equally, she communicated with her male and female correspondents in different voices. With women she rarely discussed traditionally masculine subjects such as farming. Adams did share one aspect of the new arrangement with her sister: it would require much less of her time, permitting her to make longer and more frequent visits to Betsy and other relatives. In the eighteenth century, social calls were a stereotypically female avocation. Somewhat surprisingly, the one woman for whom Abigail described her switch to farming "to the halves" received an explanation that can only be described as feminine.

The most remarkable rationalizations for Adams's conversion to sharecropping were the ones she did not give. She never said she lacked the experience to keep the farm afloat or that she could not get the men to respect her authority or that the additional responsibility had worn her out. Her conclusion—that soaring wages and punishing taxes required her to convert to sharecropping—was one that John Adams might well have reached if he had still been in charge.

Abigail's reorganization of the family farm alleviated but did not eliminate her principal financial burden: her mounting tax bills. Congress and the state governments knew their only hope of shoring up the value of the tens of millions of dollars' worth of paper currency they had distributed to soldiers and suppliers lay in aggressively taxing the money back into the treasury. Free Americans soon found themselves in the ironic position of having rebelled against parliamentary "taxation without representation" only to elect representatives who levied taxes several times higher than those Parliament had tried to collect. When Abigail wrote John asking where she was going to get the money to pay her taxes, he instructed her to draw bills of exchange on him, then sell the bills, receiving in return gold and silver coins with which to satisfy the tax collector. But by the time John sent her this directive, Abigail had already discovered her own source of additional funds.

CHAPTER 13

"I Should Be a Gainer"

1778–1780

William and Elizabeth Smith had taught their daughters to accept misfortune with cheerful resignation. That all three sisters absorbed that lesson was evident from the language with which they responded to disasters such as the high prices and exorbitant taxes accompanying the Revolutionary War. But Abigail, unlike Mary and Elizabeth, was congenitally incapable of remaining idle in a crisis. "I have thought of this which I wish you to assent to," she wrote her husband in July 1778: "to order some saleable articles which I will mention to be sent to the care of my unkle"—Isaac Smith, Sr., a Boston businessman—"a small trunk at a time, containing ten or 15 pounds Sterling" worth of merchandise. From these trunks Abigail would extract the few items her family needed, then place the rest "in the hands of Dr. [Tufts's] Son who has lately come into Trade, and would sell them for me."

By the time Adams came up with the idea of going into trade, the entire North Atlantic was infested with British battleships and privateers. Yet if her husband was astonished by her proposal, he did not show it, and he immediately shipped her several small cargos. However, when John learned that at least two of the vessels carrying freight to Abigail had been captured by the British, he began to have second thoughts. "I have been so unlucky, that I feel averse to meddling in this Way," he wrote her in early November.

Abigail was not so easily discouraged. "There is no remittances you can make me which will turn to a better account than Goods," she told her husband. True, it was a "risk to send me any thing across the water" during wartime. But for that very reason, the New England shopkeepers' shelves were nearly empty, and the few importers whose merchandise managed to evade the blockade could name their own price. An importation business could remain profitable even if two-thirds of its cargoes ended up in the holds of enemy frigates and privateers or on the ocean floor. "If one in 3 arrives I should be a gainer," she wrote. Besides, there were ways to reduce the risks. Since most civilian vessels carried little or no armament, Adams reminded her husband, "A ship of war is the safest conveyance." John's shipments continued.

Abigail would have run another kind of risk if she had imported European goods and then retailed them herself. There were numerous female shopkeepers in eastern Massachusetts—among them the Boston merchants who had rioted against the coffee wholesaler in 1777—but it would have been undignified for the wife of a congressman to open a store. That was why Adams consigned the merchandise she received from John to Cotton Tufts, Jr., son of the physician. But since her cousin apparently worked on commission, the risks and rewards were hers.

Even as Adams expanded her importation business, she found other ways to prevent the war from devastating her family's finances. At his departure for France in February, John had left her nearly twelve hundred dollars of Massachusetts currency. Both Adamses understood that these funds were not a fixed asset, that the value of paper money eroded every day. Abigail shielded herself from this insidious process of depreciation using the same strategy she had employed with the currency foisted on her by John's creditors a year earlier: she bought another federal Loan Office certificate, this time in the amount of seven hundred dollars.

In October, Abigail was granted a short respite from her financial worries. The previous summer, a French fleet—one of the first fruits of the Franco-American alliance that Benjamin Franklin had negotiated as John Adams crossed the Atlantic—had put into Boston Harbor. The admiral, the Comte Charles-Henri Théodat d'Estaing, invited her to dine aboard his flagship, adding that she could bring along as many friends and family members as she liked. The party of thirteen was rowed out to the fleet on the admiral's barge and then treated to what Adams called "an entertainment fit for a princiss." The officers and their guests feasted on a succession of European and American dishes, and then "Musick and dancing for the young folks closed the day."

A short time after becoming acquainted with Comte D'Estaing, Abigail began sending John a series of bitter complaints about the length, frequency, and tone of his letters. She understood that he had written many more letters than she had received. The standard practice during wartime was for ship captains to keep correspondence and other important documents in a weighted pouch that could be thrown overboard moments before the vessel fell into enemy hands, and that was the fate of much of the mail sent across the Atlantic during the war. But Abigail also suspected that her husband was using enemy confiscations to cover up his own neglect of the pen. Nor was the rarity of his letters her only grievance. Most that did reach her were maddeningly short. "I determine very soon to coppy and adopt the *very concise* method of my Friend," read one especially sarcastic complaint, "and as I wish to do every thing agreable to him, send him Billits containing not more than a dozen lines at the utmost."

Worst of all, John's letters read like business correspondence, informing his wife only that he had shipped her various goods, that John Quincy sent his greetings, and so on. Suppose Nabby and I had been the ones who had braved the Atlantic during winter and wartime while you stayed home, she asked John on October 25, their fourteenth anniversary. "Could you after a thousand fears and anxieties, long expectation and painfull suspences be satisfied with my telling you that I was well, that I wished you were with me, that my daughter sent her duty, that I had orderd some articles for you which I hoped would arrive &c. &c. [?]" Sensibility, which favored the warm feelings of the heart over the cold calculations of the brain, gave Adams the perfect language in which to dress her complaint. She surmised that John must "have changed Hearts with some frozen Laplander or made a voyage to a region that has chilld every Drop of your Blood."

It is not entirely clear why Abigail chose to lodge her complaint at this particular time. Perhaps the first chilly nights of October reminded her that despite John's numerous absences over the previous four years, she had never yet spent "a whole winter" without her husband. And it was also true that John was so distracted by the twin challenges of navigating the French court and working around his colleague Benjamin Franklin's eccentricities that many of the letters he sent home in 1778 conveyed little more than a sense of duty discharged.

Abigail's plea did elicit passion from John, but not the kind she had hoped for. "This Moment I had, what shall I say? the Pleasure or the pain of your Letter of 25 of Octr.," he wrote her two months later. "As a

Letter from my dearest Freind it gave me a pleasure that it would be in vain to attempt to describe: but the Complaints in it gave me more pain than I can express." Nor was this the first time John had had to endure his wife's grousing—all of it unjustified, in his view. "Can Protestation of affection be necessary?" he demanded. "The very Idea of this sickens me." How could Abigail not see that her complaints exacerbated her husband's homesickness? "What Course shall I take to convince you that my Heart is warm?" he asked. "I beg you would never more write to me in such a strain." Indeed, if you keep grumbling, he told her, "I shall leave of writing intirely." John was so angry at the tone of Abigail's letters that he even borrowed a strategy she had used during his service in Congress, enlisting his son in his cause. Shortly after one of Abigail's harsher messages arrived in Paris, John Quincy described its impact on his father. "It really hurts him to receive such letters," the eleven-year-old declared in a letter to Abigail; "if all your letters are like this my Pappa will cease writing at all."

Alarmed by her husband's anger and even more by his threats, Abigail backed down, begging him in a February 1779 letter to attribute her harsh words to "an over anxious Solicitude to hear of your welfare, and an ill grounded fear least multiplicity of publick cares, and avocations might render you less attentive to your pen than I could wish." She begged him to "Bury my dear Sir, in oblivion every expression of complaint," and she never again reverted to the harsh tone that pervaded her fall 1778 and winter 1779 letters.

And then the course of political events opened up the possibility that the Adamses might never again be separated by the Atlantic Ocean. John's former congressional colleagues voted in September 1778 to replace their three-member delegation in Paris with a single envoy, Benjamin Franklin. For several months Congress left John in limbo as it debated whether to give him a different European assignment or call him home. Finally he got tired of waiting and packed his bags. Owing to a series of annoying delays on the French coast, Adams was not able to inform his wife that he and John Quincy were about to sail. So on August 2, 1779, when the *Sensible,* the French frigate that carried them across the ocean, dropped anchor in Nantasket Roads and the two were rowed to the Braintree shore, they caught Abigail completely by surprise.

John was home less than four months. In October he received word that Congress wanted him to return to Europe, this time to represent the United States in peace negotiations with Britain. Not that the North ministry had agreed to sit down with the rebel colonists, but the possibility of its soon doing so seemed great enough that Congress wanted to have a representative standing by in France. John could not resist this new challenge, and he immediately began making plans for another winter voyage across the Atlantic. It made sense, he determined, for John Quincy once again to accompany him. Johnny initially balked at returning to Europe so soon, but in time he yielded to his mother's advice and agreed to go. This time Adams also chose to bring along his middle son, Charles, who had turned nine at the end of May. As with the first mission to Europe twenty-one months earlier, there was no chance of Abigail coming along. John would not put her in that kind of danger. Besides, it was an old saying of his that "a Lady cannot help being an odious creature at sea."

Charley was proud to be considered mature enough for the voyage, but he could not hold back the tears when the time came, on the morning of November 12, to say good-bye to his mother, older sister, and younger brother. "The Tears my dear Charles shed at parting, have melted my Heart a thousand times," Abigail later wrote. John and his sons, accompanied by John Thaxter, who would serve as John's secretary and the boys' tutor, rode up to Boston, and the next day the whole party boarded the *Sensible*. The ensuing voyage was even more perilous than the one John and John Quincy had made two winters earlier. The ship sprang a leak and had to put into the nearest port, which turned out to be Ferrol, at the northwest tip of Spain. Workers would need several months to make the frigate seaworthy, and there were no other opportunities to reach France by sea, so John decided that the whole party would make the nearly thousand-mile trek by land. In early February, when the group finally reached Paris, Adams looked back in wonder at what he and his sons had endured: "The Mountains, the Cold, the Mules, the Houses without Chimneys or Windows—"

Meanwhile Abigail was once again left alone with her worries. "Why was I born with so much Sensibility," she wrote her husband the day after he left, and "Why possessing it have I so often been call'd to struggle with it?" She was especially worried about her middle son, who also abounded in sensibility. "My delicate Charles, how has he endured the fatigues of his voyage?" she asked John in December.

Abigail learned at the end of February that the Adams men had survived the ocean crossing, and a month later, she knew they had made it to Paris. She was especially gratified—and a little surprised—to receive John's response to her inquiry about Charles. "Your delicate Charles is as hardy as a flynt," he wrote. The boy was "a delightful little fellow," he added. "I love him too much." Despite John's insistence on Charles's sturdiness, he himself had described their second-youngest son in terms similar to Abigail's, and there may well have been a connection between Abigail and John's sense of young Charles's specialness and the problems he would endure later in life. Perhaps their shared sense that he was uniquely delicate discouraged them from pushing him to develop the emotional scar tissue that might have shielded him from the demons that would later beset him. Alternatively, it is possible that Charles gave in to those adult temptations because he really was as fragile as his parents thought he was. Certainly the Adamses were not alone in that perception. John Thaxter used the language of feeling to describe the youngster's reception in Paris. "Charles will be loved every where," Thaxter told Abigail in September 1780; "his delicacy and sensibility always charm."

Abigail did not allow her yearning for her absent husband and sons to distract her from the struggle to survive the war's financial ravages. She had sent John off with a list of trade goods she wanted, and he had promised to ship them to her the moment he reached France. He was better than his word, dispatching the first little cargo from Bilbao, the last major Spanish city on his overland trek from Ferrol to Paris. In his letter accompanying the merchandise, which traveled on a privateer called the *Phoenix,* John was careful to emphasize that he was only sending her "some necessaries for the family." John's descriptions of this shipment, along with other, similar statements by both Adamses, have led historians to underestimate the extent of their commercial operations. In the eighteenth century, when frigates and privateers seized enemy merchantmen and their cargoes, they often allowed officers, crewmen, and passengers to retain their "private articles." That apparently explains why John wrote that he had sent Abigail "necessaries for the family," even though 84 percent of the goods were linens and handkerchiefs that were actually intended for sale.

For a brief time in 1780, the word *family* became, in John's letters to his wife, a euphemism for its opposite: "family" goods were precisely those he expected her to sell. For instance, when he promised in June to "send you Things in the family Way which will defray your Expences," he meant that Abigail would be able to pay her bills using the money arising from the sale of the merchandise. In the spring of 1780 John further refined his effort to keep his wife's trade goods from being captured at sea. Henceforth he would stop sending conspicuous barrels and cases, as he had from Bilbao. Instead he would disperse his cargoes among multiple couriers. Writing from Paris, he announced that "every Gentleman who goes from here" to New England would be asked "to take a small present" to Abigail. Most of these gifts would actually be trade goods. The first man to serve as Adams's courier was the Marquis de Lafayette, who left Paris in March.

Meanwhile the *Phoenix* had successfully run the Atlantic gauntlet, putting into its home port of Beverly, Massachusetts, in March 1780. The ship could not have arrived at a more opportune time. Since John's previous trip to France, two of Abigail's greatest financial challenges—inflation and taxation—had both spiraled to new heights. Yet she anticipated earning enough on the 216 handkerchiefs and seven pieces of "Holland linen" she had received not only to meet her necessary expenses but to proceed with a purchase that had been a source of some anxiety in her household. For two years the couple had been debating whether to buy a new chaise. During John's first trip to France, when Abigail opened negotiations with Boston carriage maker Thomas Bumstead, she came away discouraged. "I inquired the price of a new carrage the other day and found it to be no *more* than 300 pounds Lawfull money," she told her husband; "at this rate I never will ask for a supply of this *light commodity* from any Body."

The arrival of the *Phoenix* revived Abigail's hopes of obtaining a new chaise. She reported to John that the handkerchiefs he had sent her would, by themselves, fetch enough money to pay for the vehicle. In the end she decided to retain some of her earnings for a possible real estate purchase. But she did put up 200 of the 300 dollars she needed to buy the carriage, so she only had to call on John for 100 dollars. Adams reported the purchase of the "you know what" (as she later called it) and the rosy prospects for the sale of the *Phoenix* shipment in the same April 15, 1780, letter to her husband. As she had anticipated, John was appalled that Bumstead had charged double his prewar price. "The Machine is horribly dear," he wrote her. However, she had supplied two-thirds of the purchase price out of the proceeds of her import business, so there was not much he could say.

As Richard Cranch, the Adamses' brother-in-law and one of John's oldest friends, witnessed Abigail's growing success as an import merchant, he decided to try to replicate it. Ever since the early 1750s, when his projected glassworks had failed and John Adams had secretly belittled his bargaining skills, Cranch had struggled financially. Like Abigail he understood that the war that had wreaked havoc on the Massachusetts economy also brought unprecedented opportunities. Shortly after Braintree elected him to the Massachusetts House of Representatives, he was appointed to the committee charged with selling off property confiscated from Loyalists. Few New Englanders had enough spare capital to bid on the Loyalist estates, but thousands of people in France did, and through his famous brother-in-law Cranch had excellent connections in the kingdom that had become America's most valuable ally. So in January 1780 he wrote John saying, "The great Number of Tory Estates that will be soon to be sold, makes me think that some Gentlemen among our worthy Allies might make Purchases of some of them on very advantageous Terms." Cranch was careful to note that he himself was "one of the Commitee of the G. Court for selling such Estates." Should any well-heeled Parisians be interested in making an investment, he told John, "I should be glad to transact the Business for them on Commission or otherwise."

Not much came of the scheme. John simply ignored it, and Cranch's reputation suffered when word leaked out that he was trying to profit from his legislative position. But Cranch always had another pot on the fire. In the spring of 1780, when his sister-in-law received her first shipment of handkerchiefs and linen from Bilbao, he predicted that the textiles "would fetch four Dollars in hard Money, for what cost one Dollar in Europe," which is to say her net profit would be 300 percent. Cranch was eager to share in the commercial harvest. "I would beg leave to mention to you that if any of your Mercantile Friends should be willing to become Adventurers to America," he wrote John, "I should be very glad to serve them in disposing of any Merchandize that might be consign'd to me." By proposing to receive goods on consignment, Cranch showed that he was unable to match either his sister-in-law's access to capital or her understanding of commerce. His plan was to market European merchants' goods for them in return for a percentage of each sale. Having assumed almost none of the risk, he would receive only a fraction of the rewards. Nor was it certain that Cranch's enterprise would even get off the ground, for John initially paid no more attention to this proposal than he had to his brother-in-law's scheme to profit from the sale of Loyalist estates.

Meanwhile the self-confidence Abigail derived from her successful trading venture was apparently one source of a noteworthy statement she made to her husband during the summer of 1780. Like John she had always expressed utter contempt for luxury—the purchase and display of clothing and other finery that served little purpose other than to assert one's social superiority. The two Adamses had rededicated themselves to frugality during the Patriot boycotts of British merchandise that preceded the Revolutionary War—and even more so after the fighting began. Yet in May 1780, Abigail took the extremely rare step of informing her husband that luxury was not always so bad.

The context of this extraordinary statement was a reminder she had received from John the previous spring. Both of us must "manage all our Affairs with the strictest Oeconomy" (frugality), he wrote. The problem for Abigail was that her fourteen-year-old daughter had just then been summoning the courage to ask John for some French gauze, lace, and ribbon—all of which were, by his definition, frippery. Abigail rushed to Nabby's defense. At the end of an order for trade goods, she told her husband, "And as a little of what you call frippery is very necessary towards looking like the rest of the world, Nabby would have me add, a few yard of Black or White Gauze, low priced black or white lace or a few yards of Ribbon." Nabby also raised the issue with her father, although she made a point of addressing him through her mother—an emotional rather than a practical necessity, since she had sent him a letter of her own by the same ship. John should rest assured that his daughter harbored "no passion for dress further than he would approve of," Nabby wrote. It was just that she wanted "to appear when she goes from home a little like those of her own age."

At the same time that she questioned her husband's infatuation with frugality, Abigail also challenged him in a different area. While thanking him for the trade goods he had sent her in Lafayette's trunk, she objected to his new strategy of dispersing his shipments among multiple couriers. John's system required him to stop buying merchandise wholesale. By instead paying the much higher price retailers charged, he had dramatically reduced the family's profits. She nonetheless reconciled herself to the new arrangement. "Your Letters are come safe to hand, as well as the presents you mention," she told him. "I find you can greatly benifit me in this way." In fact it occurred to her that many of the small items she ordered could be "contained in a Letter," which would confer an additional benefit. If John were to insert "Silk Gloves or mittins, black or white lace, Muslin or a Bandano hankerchief, and *even a few yard of Ribbon*" in the letters he sent home, they would travel freight free, since American diplomats' correspondence paid no postage.

By the time Abigail had accustomed herself to John's way of doing things, he had concluded that hers was superior. Although he continued to ask travelers to slip a "present" or two for Abigail in their trunks, for as long as the couple remained in business, she would receive the bulk of her merchandise directly from wholesalers.

In the fall of 1780, Adams expanded her operations, consigning merchandise not only to Cotton Tufts, Jr., but to her friend Mercy Otis Warren in Plymouth. Like Adams, Warren did not actually retail the goods herself (her teenaged son George handled that part of the business), but she was in charge of negotiations with Adams. These got off to a rocky start, since Warren believed the prices Adams set were too high. In December she reported to her principal that she had "not sold a single Article."

Even though Adams sold most of her merchandise through intermediaries, her business required constant attention. For one thing, she had to stay abreast of consumer taste. "Small articles," she had learned by the end of 1781, "have the best profit, Gauze, ribbons, feathers and flowers to make the Ladies Gay, have the best advance [markup]." In this trade, shortages gave way to gluts with astonishing rapidity. Although linen was "in great demand" in Massachusetts in mid-April 1780, ten weeks later Abigail was "well supplied" with that article. Linen handkerchiefs were unpopular in May 1780 but would "answer well" the following November. By contrast, the silken Barcelona handkerchiefs that Adams received from Bilbao in the spring of 1780 initially earned her lush profits, but by July her commercial rivals had also received shipments, and that market was glutted. Mercy Warren urged Adams to offer customers a discount on these handkerchiefs. But one type, the colored ones, were still selling briskly, so Adams only agreed to reduce the price of the black ones. Rather than offer a discount on colored handkerchiefs, Warren should simply return them to her. By January 1781, though, Adams had to acknowledge that there was "nothing from Bilboa that can be imported with advantage," not even colored handkerchiefs.

Adams knew her success required close attention not only to her customers but to her European suppliers. For John, dealing with the merchants of Spain, France, and the Netherlands was intensely frustrating. After dispatching two pieces of chintz (printed cotton cloth) to his partner in the spring of 1780, he lamented having to pay a "horrid" price for them. But if I do your procurement for you, he added, "you must expect to be cheated. I never bought any Thing in my Life, but at double Price." Adams was, in a sense, proud of his failure as a buyer, since it highlighted his unfamiliarity with the corrupt world of commerce. Abigail wrote back offering reassurance. Focus not on the price you pay for an item but on the difference between that figure and what the merchandise sells for in Massachusetts, she told him. By that measure, the chintz was "not dear as you Imagined," she wrote. Still, John continued to doubt his procurement skills, and he eventually suggested that Abigail send her orders directly to the European trading houses. From that point on, he financed his wife's purchases but otherwise stayed out of the business—to the relief of both of them.

When the merchandise that Abigail received did not meet her expectations, she did not hesitate to complain—first to John and later directly to her suppliers. "The Articles you were so kind as to send me were not all to my mind," she told John in a November 1780 letter. Having requested lead-colored silk, she instead received "clay coulour, not proper for the use I wanted it for" (a mourning dress). The ribbon John had shipped her should have been colored instead of black, and the accompanying tape was "of the coarsest kind." Regrettably the letter that Abigail fired off to the Amsterdam firm of John de Neufville & Son on January 15, 1781, does not survive, but we may infer something of its contents from the company's abject reply. We "deem ourselves peculiarly unfortunate, not to have been more happy in the choice of the Color of Silk we sent you," the company told her.

Adams apparently used most of her mercantile profits to pay the enormous taxes that the Massachusetts assembly had levied to fund the war. But she also bartered some of her European merchandise for the locally produced commodities her family required. Although taxes and other costs steadily increased over the course of the war, the self-assessment Abigail sent her husband in the spring of 1781—"I do not increase in wealth, nor yet diminish the capital"—was too modest, for she took in considerably more than she paid out. In fact by this time she had begun looking for profitable ways to reinvest her surplus funds. "I . . . have a desire to become a purchaser in the State of Vermont," she told John in April; "what do you think of a few thousand acres there?" John made no reply—an omission he would regret within a year, for by then she would interpret his silence as consent.

* * *

As the war dragged on, Abigail continued to cast about for ways to ensure her family's solvency. With John overseas, it was more important than ever to cultivate James Lovell, his former colleague in the Massachusetts congressional delegation. There were sentimental reasons to stay in touch with Lovell. As an active member of the congressional Committee for Foreign Affairs, he often received tidbits of information about John long before they reached Braintree. But Lovell also proved useful in more practical ways. In the early days of the republic, diplomats did not receive anything like a regular paycheck, and it often fell to Abigail to prod Congress to pay John his salary and reimburse his considerable expenses, a business in which Lovell proved extremely helpful. In September 1780, when Lovell was finally able to pry a payment out of his fellow delegates, Abigail thanked him for his troubles but also pointed out that her husband had apparently not received everything he was due. It seems unlikely that she would have mustered the nerve to question Congress's math if she had not cultivated an intimate intermediary like Lovell.

Lovell also possessed information that could help the Adams family survive the series of acute monetary crises that beset the new nation. Right before Congress voted to redeem the Continental currency at an assigned value that was much higher than its actual market price, Lovell sent Abigail a tip. "You will certainly do well to get all the *continental* you can just at this Time," he wrote her in May 1780. "It cannot fail to be a Benefit." Adams apparently did not follow Lovell's advice to speculate in the Continental currency, and it was a good thing she did not, because as it turned out, the value of the money eroded at a faster rate than ever that spring. Had she plowed her money into paper currency as Lovell advised, she would have lost nearly everything.

Abigail's epistolary relationship with Lovell also exposed her to another danger, infinitely greater than the loss of all her savings, for he quickly developed a crush on her.

CHAPTER 14

"A Queer Being"

1780–1781

There was no doubt about it—despite Abigail's best efforts to deny the fact, even to herself—James Lovell had conceived a powerful affection for her. Although both were married, he continued to flirt openly with her. In a September 1, 1778, letter, for instance, he quoted the Scottish poet Allan Ramsay: "gin ye were mine ain Thing how dearly I would *love* thee!" Lovell also tried to shock Adams with sexual innuendo about her marriage. During the winter of 1778–1779, when she lamented to him that John had been absent eleven months, he replied by offering congratulations that her partner had not, during his brief visit to Braintree the previous winter, displayed his *"rigid patriotism"* by getting her pregnant. "I will take pleasure in your *Escape*," he wrote. (Abigail replied to Lovell's crack about her *"Escape"* in a serious vein, noting that for women, the joy of presenting children to their husbands served to "mitigate the curse entailed upon us"—the birth pangs they suffered in punishment for the sins of Eve.) In a letter that Lovell wrote Abigail a year later, the first page concluded with the words "I shall covet to be in the Arms of Portia." Only upon turning the sheet over did she discover that the clause ended innocently: " 's Friend and Admirer," meaning his own wife, Mary. Lovell's technique of floating an innuendo across a page break was taken directly from Laurence Sterne.

The Adams-Lovell correspondence soon settled into a pattern. Abigail would tolerate Lovell's risqué writing up to a certain point, and then she would issue a reproof that caused him to mend his ways—but only briefly, whereupon his wit would once again get the better of him, setting the whole cycle in motion again. That Adams did not sever connections with Lovell is testament not only to her desperate need for the various services he was uniquely able to provide but also to her belief that he was only teasing her—that the compliments he lavished on a woman he hardly knew said less about his feelings for her than about the loneliness of a man who had lingered too long in a strange city without a single visit home.

And that, of course, was the one part of Lovell's story that troubled Adams. Why did he never return to Massachusetts during congressional recesses, as John always did? By the spring of 1781, four years had elapsed since he had last seen Mary. Adams may or may not have known that back during his Harvard days, Lovell had fathered a bastard child, but if she did, that could hardly have reassured her that his ribald rhetoric was just talk. It is possible, as several historians have suggested, that Abigail enjoyed her epistolary duels with Lovell—the challenge of deciphering his intricate innuendoes and of finding equally subtle ways to rein him in—but her real reason for stringing him along was that he was too valuable to cut loose. Much has been made of the fact that Lovell presumed to refer to Abigail as "Portia," the same pen name she used when writing John. But he would never have known her pseudonym if she had not inscribed it at the close of one of her earliest letters to him. Although Lovell's penchant for sweet talk led Adams to declare him "a very dangerous Man," she, too, knew how to flatter. Having discerned early on that her correspondent fancied himself a man of feeling, she assured him that "the Native Sensibility, tenderness and Benevolence of Mr. L[ovel]l . . . will ever attach the fair Sex to him and in a perticuliar manner Portia." One indication of the value that Adams placed on her relationship with Lovell is that she seems never to have mentioned his improper advances to her husband.

By the middle of 1780 the tide of military affairs seemed to have turned decidedly against the Americans. Two years earlier, when France entered the war on the U.S. side, the British had abandoned Philadelphia in order to focus their efforts on the South. Imperial officials in London viewed the southern colonies as the weak link in the American chain, both because of the prevalence of slaves and because many southern freemen were disaffected from the Patriot cause. A British army easily captured Savannah, Georgia, at the end of 1778 and defended it against a massive Franco-American assault early the next year. Then the redcoats moved north. On May 12, 1780, they captured Charleston, South Carolina—

the only southern city of any size—along with its defenders: more than eight hundred militiamen and nearly 2,600 Continental soldiers.

Abigail joined in the general outpouring of grief at the loss of Charleston, but at the same time, she was pleased to observe that a group of women in Philadelphia had taken the lead in seeking to rebuild the nation's morale. "Virtue exists, and publick spirit lives—lives in the Bosoms of the Fair Daughters of America," she declared in a July 21 letter to John Thaxter. The women had initiated a fund-raising campaign aimed at recognizing the efforts of the Continental soldiers by giving each of them a small sum of money—not paper currency but real silver and gold coins. "Blushing for the Languid Spirit, and halting Step" that they detected in too many of their husbands, fathers, and sons, the Philadelphia women had, Adams observed, resolved to "unite their Efforts to reward the patriotick, to stimulate the Brave, to alleviate the burden of war, and to shew that they are not dismayed by defeats or misfortunes." The Philadelphians' effort soon spread throughout the thirteen states. General Washington vetoed the idea of giving the soldiers gold and silver coins, out of concern that they would wonder why they never received their wages in hard money when it flowed so freely from the hands of these patriotic ladies. So instead the women sewed shirts for the soldiers, each of them embroidering her name into the back of the shirts she made.

Although she does not appear to have participated in the women's fund drive, Adams remained an active observer of politics in Congress and her own state assembly. In July 1780, she gave her husband a report on the recent Massachusetts representative elections and then exclaimed, "What a politician you have made me." In the eighteenth century, *politician* referred not to a candidate or legislator but to a person who followed politics closely. Yet in applying that term to herself, Adams expressed astonishment at the massive wartime expansion in her role.

The Adamses considered John Hancock a buffoon and a demagogue, and in the summer of 1780, they were distressed to learn that he was likely to become the first popularly elected governor of Massachusetts. In discussing the campaign, Abigail experienced brief regret that women could not vote—not because she felt entitled to the franchise but because she wanted to cast a ballot against Hancock. Her only consolation was that she could try to dissuade men from supporting him. "If I cannot be a voter upon this occasion," she told John, "I will be a writer of votes. I can do some thing in that way."

* * *

In January 1781, Abigail Adams passed a small but significant milestone: her first publication. It was a modest effort—an anonymous introduction to an essay of Mercy Warren's that she admired and wished to share with the readers of a Boston newspaper. But given that this was one of the very few occasions during Adams's lifetime on which she appeared in print, it is surprising that no historian has ever drawn attention to it.

Back in the spring of 1776, when John was serving in the Continental Congress, Abigail had asked him to find her a copy of a four-volume work called *Letters Written by the Late Right Honourable Philip Dormer Stanhope, Earl of Chesterfield, To His Son, Philip Stanhope*. Chesterfield's letters to his bastard son were famous in the English-speaking world not only for the author's thorough investigation of genteel comportment but for the polish of his prose. Adams had refused his wife's request for a copy of the book, but during the winter of 1780, she managed to procure an abridged version, and she found herself agreeing with her husband that Chesterfield, who died in 1773, had been "a Hypocritical, polished Libertine." She was especially appalled by the writer's "abuse upon our sex." Women, Chesterfield informed his son, "are only children of a larger growth; they have an entertaining tattle, and sometimes wit; but for solid, reasoning good sense, I never in my life knew one that had it, or who reasoned or acted consequentially for four-and-twenty hours together."

"I could prove to his Lordship were he living that there was one woman in the world who could act consequentially more than 24 hours," Abigail wrote Mercy Warren, "since I shall dispise to the end of my days that part of his character." Chesterfield's book admittedly displayed an intimate "knowledge of *Mankind*" (a word Adams underscored), but of womankind he was woefully ignorant. About the same time Adams first read Chesterfield's book, she learned that Warren had recently penned a rebuttal. Warren's essay, which took the form of a letter to her own son, had never been published. Adams requested and received Warren's consent to send it to Nathaniel Willis, the editor of the *Independent Chronicle,* who published the essay—and also Adams's letter introducing it. Neither woman's name appeared in the newspaper.

Both Warren's essay and Adams's introduction heaped invective not only on Chesterfield's loose morality but also on his unenlightened attitude toward women. "His Lordship has most certainly laid himself open to the utmost severity of Female pens," Adams wrote. Warren's essay exhibited the same "Elegance of Stile" for which Chesterfield was famous, she insisted, and her friend could also lay claim to a "discernment and penetration which would do honour to either Sex." After Warren's essay was published, Adams sent it to her husband in Europe, emphasizing that he should be sure to read the introduction—and leaving no doubt about who had written it.

By 1781, the Adams children had begun to cross a threshold in their parents' minds. Henceforth anxiety about their health would have to make room for concerns about their budding personalities. With her two eldest sons abroad and Tommy still a boy of eight, Abigail naturally devoted considerably more thought to the emerging character of Abigail Junior. Nabby, who had turned fifteen the previous summer, had developed an independent streak. Every winter she paid visits to her relatives in Boston, and these seemed to grow longer every year. She also lived in Boston for an entire summer while attending school there, and she spent more and more time with the Warrens. Nabby "longs to come to Plimouth," Abigail informed Mercy Warren in January 1781, "but I am jealous of trusting her there again least she should love it better than home." Adams was paying her friend a conventional compliment, but her anxiety was more justified than she knew. "I have a secret hope that Mamma does not intend to send for me," Nabby had told a cousin on an earlier visit to the Warrens, "yet tho I dearst not say so beceaus I know she must be very lonesome." It was not filial affection but a sense of duty that led Nabby to conclude that "When ever she command me to leive Plymouth I shall obey." In May 1781, James and Mercy moved to Milton Hill, just northwest of Braintree, making Nabby's visits more convenient for her and also easier on her mother.

Nabby showed just as little interest in the other members of her family. She rarely wrote her brothers in France. "Not a word in excuse will I say for her," Abigail told John Quincy and Charles in January 1781 as she once again took sole responsibility for bringing them up to speed on events in Massachusetts. "She ought to write to you and I call upon her too, but she is very neglegent." Although Abigail often worried that her daughter was simply lazy, at other times she toyed with the more charitable diagnosis that the girl's real problem was an unwillingness to put herself forward. "I cannot prevail with your Sister to write," she told her sons barely two weeks later. "I believe she is affraid you will shew her Letters," Abigail explained, and "she thinks she cannot write well enough." Even this possibility provided little consolation, however, for Adams suspected that her daughter's surface modesty actually concealed its opposite. In refusing to let her imperfections show, Nabby betrayed an excess of pride.

Perhaps Abigail's increased attention to her daughter's developing personality during the winter of 1781 helps explain why she once again addressed John Thaxter, her husband's secretary, on the topic of women's education. The complaints about educational inequity that Adams had conveyed to Thaxter three Februarys earlier had come in response to his news about Catharine Macaulay, but her only justification for returning to the subject on February 5, 1781, was her passion for it. Thaxter had recently moved to Amsterdam, where John was trying to get the Dutch government to recognize American independence, and Abigail's statement began with her usual request for a description of the town. But then she emphasized a point she had frequently made before: that travel was almost entirely a male prerogative. "It is not very probable that many of our American Ladies will ever become travellers," she wrote, "yet judgeing of others by myself, we could wish to obtain from those Gentlemen who have that priviledge . . . a recital of them." Reprising an assertion she had made to her cousin Isaac Smith, Jr., a decade earlier, Adams assured Thaxter that women were "Possess'd at least with an equal share of curiosity with the other sex." Yet men made few efforts to turn that famously acute female curiosity "into a channel of usefull knowledge, or literary endowments."

There was a crucial distinction between Adams's 1781 letter to Thaxter and the one she had written him three years earlier, for she now sensed that women's attitudes were changing. Traditionally "so few Ladies have [had] a taste for Historick knowledge, that even their own Country was not much known to them," she wrote. But women were becoming less complacent, and Adams was sure she knew why. "The present revolution," she wrote, had "become so interesting, that few I hope remain Ignorant of the principals which led our Ancestors to seek an asylum in the uncultivated wilds of America." Moreover, women understood as well as men that the war could not be won unless the new republic found friends among the nations of Europe, and "We therefore feel ourselves Interested in a knowledge of their customs, Manners, Laws, and Goverments."

* * *

Early in the summer of 1781, quite by accident, Abigail discovered a plot against her husband. The lead conspirator was not some nefarious British agent but John's own colleague in the American diplomatic corps, Benjamin Franklin. One reason Franklin had been so successful in persuading the French to form an alliance with the United States was that he was basically willing to give them a free hand in setting American foreign policy. The idea of the United States playing such a subservient role offended John's national pride, and his difference of opinion with Franklin on this issue ripened into bitter enmity. In 1780, Franklin made his move. In cooperation with the Comte de Vergennes, the French foreign minister—who of course agreed with him that Americans must defer to France on international matters—Franklin took the dispute to the Continental Congress. That body met in secret, and Abigail's contacts in Philadelphia were notably dilatory about informing her of the plot, so she might never have found out about it absent a postmaster's error. The Lees of Westmoreland County, Virginia, were long-standing enemies of Franklin's, and one brother, Arthur, had bitterly feuded with him during their service together as American commissioners in France. On the other hand, the Lee family had long been friendly with Samuel Adams and his wife, Elizabeth, so the letter that Alice Lee Shippen, Arthur's sister, sent Elizabeth Adams in June 1781 naturally contained blunt references to the Lee and Adams families' shared disdain for Franklin. Shippen mentioned in passing that the Philadelphian was trying to neutralize the other famous Adams, John. At the post office in Boston, someone inadvertently placed Shippen's letter with the mail destined for the wrong Mrs. Adams: Abigail.

The moment she broke open the letter, Adams knew she was not the intended recipient, but of course she could not resist reading through to the end. What she discovered was that Anne César, Chevalier de la Luzerne, the French envoy to the United States, was working with a group of pro-French congressmen to persuade their colleagues to revise Adams's commission. In all future negotiations with Great Britain, he was to defer to the wishes of the French. Moreover, he was no longer to be America's sole peace commissioner. Although John's fellow envoys were not immediately named, everyone suspected what turned out to be true, that one of them would be Benjamin Franklin, the man who had initiated the plot against him.

When Abigail learned what John's former congressional colleagues had done to him, she was furious at them for humiliating her husband

and worried about their subservience to France. "For myself I have little ambition or pride," she told James Lovell, "for my *Husband* I freely own I have much." Wasting no time in organizing John's defense, she lit a fire under Lovell and pleaded with his fellow Massachusetts delegate Elbridge Gerry, who had taken an extended leave of absence from Congress, to get himself back to Philadelphia. Prodding Gerry with spurs wrapped in velvet, she made fun of women like herself who trespassed on the political realm. "Will you suffer Female influence so far to operate upon you," she asked him, "as to step forth and lend your aid to rescue your Country and your Friend[?]" If Congress refused to retreat from its new position, she predicted, John would surely resign his commission.

For once Abigail had misread her husband. Although Adams was angry about his new instructions—and under her influence he would grow angrier—he was pleased with Congress's nearly simultaneous decision to give official sanction to the negotiations he had been conducting with the Dutch confederacy. He made it clear that he had no intention of quitting.

Meanwhile Abigail's relationship with Lovell arrived at a new crisis. In the three years since John's first departure for France, Lovell had continued to demonstrate his usefulness. For instance, when a shipment of merchandise intended for her arrived in Pennsylvania—in a warship commanded by John Paul Jones—he took charge of forwarding the goods to her. This proved a laborious task, as a substantial portion of the cargo had become waterlogged during the ocean crossing, and Lovell had to dry the fabrics out by his fire. Adams also suspected that some of her merchandise had been pilfered somewhere along the way, so she had Lovell draw up an inventory.

As Abigail waited for Lovell to forward her merchandise, a British vessel patrolling the Hudson River captured several of his letters, and one of these was printed in a royalist newspaper in New York City. Although relieved that it was not one of the innuendo-laden epistles he had been sending her, she was distressed to learn that it did contain statements that were extremely damaging to Lovell. In the letter, intended for Elbridge Gerry during his leave of absence in Massachusetts, Lovell declared that he himself had no interest in returning to his home state—even though he had not seen his wife, Mary, for four years. In Abigail's eyes, that statement was even more outrageous than the things Lovell had said directly to her. Combine his apparent disparagement of his own wife with all the compliments he had bestowed on Adams, and one of her darkest presentiments suddenly seemed dead-on accurate. Lovell had not just been joking around all this time. He really had fallen in love with her.

Abigail did not dare ask Lovell about his intentions toward herself, but she did give him an earful of her outrage at the comments he had allegedly made about his wife. Other women were even more ready to criticize Lovell, as demonstrated in a dialogue that Abigail reported to him. She identified her interlocutor only by the pseudonym Cornelia, but historians agree that it was probably Mercy Warren.

"Have you seen the intercepted Letter of your Friend L[ovel]ls to Gerry [?]," Cornelia had asked Abigail.

"No Madam," Adams replied, "but I have heard much of it, and some severe strictures about it."

"I have read it," Cornelia said, and "there are some things in it which for decency sake ought never to have been there. Were I his wife they would make me misirable, but I believe he cares little for her."

"O, Madam do not judge so hardly," Abigail pleaded.

Well, if Lovell loved his wife so much, how could he leave her for "3 or 4 years together[?]" Cornelia asked.

For Abigail, whose husband had spent most of the previous three years in France, that question hit too close to home. "Pray my dear Madam do not measure a Gentlemans regard for his wife by the last reason," she said. "Is it not misfortune enough to be seperated from our best Friends without the worlds judgeing hardly of us or them for it[?]"

John Adams's case was different, Cornelia pointed out. Diplomats could not cross the ocean to visit their families, but Lovell was only in Philadelphia, and his refusal to make the trek back to Boston once in a while spoke volumes about his marriage.

"I never heard his conjugal character aspersed," Abigail replied. "Did you[?]"

"No," Cornelia conceded, but "the world will naturally believe that a Gentleman possessing domestick attachments would visit his family in the course of 4 years, when only 3 hundred miles distant."

Abigail transcribed her conversation with "Cornelia" as nearly as she could remember it and sent it off to Lovell. Meanwhile he tried to refute the charges against him. Adopting, for the first time in his long epistolary exchange with Adams, a serious tone, he confessed that he had indeed avoided returning to his home state. But the reason was not a lack of affection for his wife. It was poverty. Congressmen earned no income while on leave, and Lovell, a schoolteacher in civilian life, simply could not afford to forgo his government salary.

Having admitted to something that was humiliating in his eyes but much less so than the marital indifference of which he stood accused, Lovell felt that a burden had been lifted, and some of his accustomed levity returned. In explaining to Abigail why he could not come home on leave, he wrote, "My Pay for Time and Service as a Delegate . . . ceases *the day I arrive in Boston,* though my Wife and Children will expect to dine the day after and peradventure they will be extravagant enough to expect it the third Day also."

Lovell also provided another financial reason why he could not visit his wife: he might get her pregnant. The couple already had half a dozen children, and they could not afford another. The "almost enevitable" prospect of another pregnancy, he told Adams, was the one "which I was afraid to name to you or to your Husband" until compelled to do so. Was it really Lovell's financial straits that kept him away from home all those years, or was he simply employing the shrewdness he gloried in to wriggle out of a trap? One indication that he really did fear another pregnancy is that he had already given the same explanation for not going home in a letter he had written Abigail two years earlier. She believed he was telling the truth, and she was touched by the vulnerability he displayed in owning up to his fears. Lovell's disclosure (if such it was) even elicited a stunning revelation from Adams about her own most recent pregnancy—the one that had ended in July 1777 in a stillbirth.

Coming at a time of war and at the start of another prolonged separation from her husband, the pregnancy had filled her with anxiety, she recalled. Then she told Lovell something she had apparently never revealed to anyone else, not even her husband: she now believed the psychological torment she had endured while carrying that child had caused the miscarriage. At the time she had taken some comfort from the conviction that the death of the fetus "was not oweing to any injury which I had sustaind, nor could any care of mine have prevented it." Over the course of the ensuing four years, however, she had changed her mind. The fetus had actually fallen victim to its mother's stress at John's absence and at the very real danger that he would be captured or killed. "Too great anxiety put a period to the existance of one at the very time you have hinted at," she told Lovell in a September 1781 letter. Moreover, carrying that dead fetus for several days before the final, fatal delivery had "c[o]me nigh finishing" Abigail herself. She believed she had escaped an even more serious threat to her health by not becoming pregnant right before John sailed for Europe. "Heaven only knows what might have been the concequences under a still greater degree of anxiety," she told Lovell.

A month later, in mid-September, Adams sent Lovell a letter marking their reconciliation. It began, "In truth Friend thou art a Queer Being." Confessing that Lovell remained something of an enigma for her, she nonetheless affirmed, "I shall find you out by and by." She only wished she had had more opportunity to see Lovell face-to-face before they began their correspondence. Adams had long dabbled in physiognomy (the art of reading a person's character in his or her face), and she assured Lovell that she had "tried not unsuccessfully to find out the Heart of many a one by the countanance." But with Lovell she had never had the opportunity to "study the Eye that best Index to the mind to find out how much of Rogury there was in the Heart, so here I have been these four years obtaining by peacemeal what I could have learnt in half an hour."

Shortly after patching up her relationship with Lovell, Abigail acquired a new and much greater burden. John informed her that their son Charles was headed home. Alone.

Adams would ultimately adduce a variety of explanations for sending his son back to Braintree. Like his wife, he was convinced that the low, flat Dutch terrain was unhealthy, and every Adams who visited the country suffered a serious bout of illness there, as did most of their servants. But it is clear that Charles's primary disorder was not physical. "He is a delightfull Child," John told Abigail in mid-July, "but has too exquisite sensibility for Europe." He held on well enough while he had his older brother to keep him company. But early in July 1781, John allowed John Quincy—still a few days shy of his fourteenth birthday but a master of French, the language of diplomacy—to sign on as secretary to Francis Dana, who was headed to St. Petersburg as America's first envoy to Russia. "After the departure of his brother," John recalled years later, Charles "found himself so much alone, that he grew uneasy, and importuned me so tenderly to let him return to America to his mother, that I consented."

Charles left Amsterdam on August 12 on an American frigate, the *South Carolina*. A fellow passenger, William Jackson, a major in the Continental Army, agreed to serve as his chaperone. When Abigail heard the news, she observed that Charles's homesickness "must have been great indeed to induce the poor fellow to cross the atlantick without Father or Brother." She wondered whether John would have put the boy on the ship if he had known that four British warships were cruising off the Massachusetts coast. "My Charles," she wrote, "O when shall I see him." Not for a long time, as it turned out. In those days fair winds could carry a ship across the Atlantic in as little as a month, sometimes even less. But Abigail had no word of her son's fate for the next four months. By November it was becoming more and more apparent that the *South Carolina* had either been lost at sea or captured.

During this anxious interval, Adams heard a new rumor about her friend James Lovell. It fit the picture his critics had painted, and it was much worse than anything that had come before. The story was that he and his landlady in Philadelphia were having an affair. Adams did not want to believe it, but she had to concede that the evidence against the man was piling up. He denied everything, which made it possible for her to maintain this immensely valuable contact without incurring a scandal of her own. But her friendship with Lovell was over. In short order the rumors about him became so rife that he felt obliged to give up his congressional seat and return to Massachusetts. There he had little contact with Abigail, who intensely regretted having lost her best conduit to Congress.

Around the middle of November, Abigail finally learned what had happened to her son. The *South Carolina* had not sailed directly across the Atlantic. Like many skippers of armed vessels operating in the North Atlantic during the war, the captain of the *South Carolina*, Commodore Alexander Gillon, was determined to capture some booty before proceeding across the ocean. When the vessel finally made port, it was in La Coruña, Spain, just across the Betanzos estuary from Ferrol, where Charles had landed with his father and brother nearly two years earlier. The eleven-year-old had come full circle without getting any closer to home.

By the time the ship put into La Coruña, a quarrel between Commodore Gillon and his passengers had grown so bitter that most of them decided to leave the ship. Among those who went ashore was Charles's chaperone, William Jackson, and the frightened boy clung to him as he made his way to Bilbao, where the two endured a seemingly interminable wait for passage home. At the end of October 1781, Charles was still in Bilbao. "He begs I will not by any means leave him," Jackson reported to the boy's father.

In December 1781, John Adams sent Abigail a rare criticism of her financial management. The previous January, the Massachusetts legislature had decreed that state and federal paper money would no longer have the status of legal tender, meaning that creditors would not be compelled to accept it from their debtors at its face value. Anyone who used paper currency, whether to pay a debt or to purchase merchandise, would have to plunk down enough of it to match its actual market value in gold and silver. Since by this time the old Continental money was trading at seventy-five for one, an item that could have been purchased with one paper dollar at the start of January 1781 rose to seventy-five dollars after the legislators acted. Abigail knew the assembly was going to devalue the paper money, but somehow, she confessed to John the following September, she had gotten stuck with "a sum of old and new paper which lies by me useless at present."

"I am sorry to learn you have a sum of Paper," John replied; "how could you be so imprudent?" It was a cruel comment, but in a way it also marked Abigail's progress. At the start of the Revolutionary War, John had viewed his wife as understandably ignorant of financial matters, but by the fall of 1781 he was holding her to a much higher standard.

Even as the devaluation of the paper money earned Abigail this rebuke from her husband, it also gave her the opportunity to turn some of the income from her import business into productive capital. Sometime in the fall of 1781, as she later reported, she placed a hundred pounds (sterling) "in the hands of a Friend" (undoubtedly her uncle Cotton Tufts) to invest for her. In this prebanking era, a person who had saved up money could set it aside—and earn interest on it—by lending it out. Often, as in Abigail's case, the lender agreed not to call for the money without giving several months' notice. It would not have made sense for Adams to invest her surplus funds before 1781, because she would have risked being repaid with paper money that was worth much less than what had she had invested. But after the Massachusetts assembly returned to the hard money standard, debtors had to repay their creditors with the same gold and silver coins they had received. It may seem strange that Adams decided to put her mercantile profits out at interest rather than plowing them back into the business. She could have easily sent some or all of this money to her husband to be used for the purchase of more merchandise. No doubt her primary motive for lending it out instead was to diversify her portfolio, placing some of her savings beyond the hazards of the ocean and the enemy.

John was nonetheless skittish about his wife's decision to lend out her money, for he had seen wartime inflation devastate his prerevolutionary savings. Even the Massachusetts legislature's recent decree prohibiting debtors from foisting paper currency on their creditors did not entirely reassure him, and he may have also been alarmed that his wife had placed the money with a "Friend" about whom she provided no identifying information. So he reacted to his wife's announcement with a curt instruction: "dont trust Money to any Body." Abigail could easily have implemented her husband's directive by calling in the loan, but she chose not to do so. And over time, the money that she had set aside would, by a process so gradual that even she seems not to have noticed it, metamorphose into something extraordinary: a challenge to the age-old assumption that married women could not own personal property.

Abigail had breathed a sigh of relief in the middle of November 1781, when she finally learned that Charles had landed safely in Spain two months earlier. But she knew better than to think her son was out of danger. Not only would he still have to cross the ocean, but his ship would have to evade an increasingly tight cordon of British frigates and privateers. The boy happened to arrive at Bilbao during a slack period, when few ships were setting out across the Atlantic, and each additional day of waiting nudged his crossing further into the winter, the most "disagreeable as well as dangerous" time to be on the high seas. Along with William Jackson, his chaperone and fellow passenger, Charles ended up having to cool his heels in Bilbao for nearly three months. Finally, in early December, the two embarked on the *Cicero,* headed for the little port of Beverly, thirty miles north of Boston.

Other ships that left Bilbao after the *Cicero* made it to the United States in early January, so Abigail knew in advance that her son was headed home. She was confident that she would hear word of his arrival at Beverly within a few days. But the message from the northward did not come and kept not coming, and Adams and her friends began to worry that the ship had been captured by the British or lost at sea. Then, at long last, an express rider brought word to Abigail that the *Cicero* had put into Beverly on January 21. The odyssey that had begun with the homesick youngster's departure from Amsterdam on August 12, 1781, finally ended in Braintree more than five months later, on January 29, in his mother's arms.

In the fall of 1781, John Adams finally managed to secure a consignment of merchandise for his brother-in-law. "I am much oblig'd to you for this beginning of Commission-Business," Richard Cranch wrote him when the cargo arrived in Boston. But the hapless Cranch's goods came to a market for European merchandise that had begun to cool off, for heavy taxation and currency devaluation—two policies that Cranch had championed in the state assembly—left would-be customers without the means to purchase. Additionally, the ship bringing his wares arrived toward the end of the season, after "the Market was supply'd" by his competitors. By this time even Abigail's business was suffering—at least in relative terms. "Goods will not double," she reported to John in December, meaning that for the first time her markup would fall below 100 percent. The following March, Abigail observed that the market for European manufactures was still "dull."

The downturn put Abigail in a reflective mood. Although she and John were inveterate enemies of all manner of luxury, she observed in July 1782, they had benefited immensely from the extravagant tastes of others, especially women's desires for "black and white Gauze and Gauze hankerchiefs." Despite the wartime spike in prices, which was especially acute for merchandise that had to run the British blockade, these items had continued to sell. "No articles are so vendible or yeald a greater profit," Adams told her husband, though their popularity "may not be to the Credit of my country." By this time Abigail had her sights on a new commercial venture. Acting on an inspiration she had first mentioned to John a year earlier, she set about purchasing a 1,650-acre tract in the projected town of Salem, Vermont, up by the Canadian border on Lake Memphremagog.

CHAPTER 15

"Nothing Venture Nothing Have"

1782

The parcel of Vermont land that Abigail wanted to buy was in the region that promotes itself today as the Northeast Kingdom, and it is almost in Canada. It would be a highly speculative investment, for while the syndicate with which she wished to deal had received a town charter from the Vermont legislature, New Yorkers believed their own colonial charter gave them a prior claim to this same region. Indeed, in their view, the state of Vermont had no right to exist. New Yorkers battled Vermonters such as Ethan Allen and his famed Green Mountain Boys even as both groups fought the British.

Yet Abigail's enthusiasm for her Vermont purchase was unbounded. I have "set my Heart upon it," she told John in April 1782. "I am loth to relinquish it." Yet she *did* give it up, at least for the time being, when doubts arose about whether Congress would ever recognize the legitimacy of the Vermonters' claims.

In mid-June, Abigail had the rare pleasure of receiving a letter her husband had written only six weeks earlier. John's mood was uncharacteristically buoyant. The French and American armies' great victory at Yorktown, Virginia, the previous October had the effect of vastly increasing Dutch interest in the United States and its envoy. Throughout the Netherlands, he exulted in a letter to Abigail, "Every City, and Province rings with De Heer Adams." In April, John finally obtained the prize that had first brought him to Holland two years earlier: formal recognition of the independence of the United States. That in turn paved the way for financial backing. The news from Britain was a little more ambiguous but also encouraging. The Yorktown surrender brought down the North ministry, and it was replaced by a new government that desperately wanted out of the American war. Yet even the newly ascendant Lord Shelburne was determined to find some sort of honorable exit, and he had unrealistic ideas about what the Americans could be brought to accept. Congress had set British recognition of the independence of the United States as a precondition for negotiations, a demand Shelburne found hard to swallow.

This expectant atmosphere provided the context for one of Abigail's most important ruminations on the political status of women. In many ways the statement that she sent her husband on June 17 was more radical than the "Remember the Ladies" letter she had written six years earlier. Back then she had only lamented husbands' sovereignty over their wives. Now, on the seventh anniversary of the Battle of Bunker Hill, she was also ready to complain that the female half of the population was "deprived of a voice in Legislation" and "obliged to submit to those Laws which are imposed upon us." Adams was by no means the only woman of her time who objected to her disfranchisement, but very few of her contemporaries had gone on to lament their banishment from public office. "Excluded from honours and from offices," she wrote, "we cannot attach ourselves to the State or Goverment from having held a place of Eminence."

Like the "Remember the Ladies" letter, which followed close upon the British evacuation of Boston, Adams's June 1782 declaration was written shortly after an important Continental Army victory, in this case at Yorktown. Both statements were fueled by an intense hopefulness about the American future. Yet for all its intensity, the optimism that Abigail expressed in 1782 was much more narrowly focused than what she had felt six years earlier. Back in 1776, it had seemed to both Adamses that anything was possible. With the colonies on the verge of declaring independence, the slate was about to be wiped clean, and no one could guess what would come next. Things were different now. Every state except New Hampshire had adopted a new constitution (Rhode Island and Connecticut had simply revised their colonial charters), and not one had extended the franchise to women. In this more subdued atmosphere, Adams lodged numerous complaints but did not make a single demand. She implored male Patriots to recognize women's contribution to the war effort, but she did not ask them to reward it. "Patriotism in the female Sex is the most disinterested of all virtues," she wrote. Subjugated to the will of their husbands and denied any say in matters of public policy, women had no expectation of ever benefiting from the nation's victories. Yet they were often the worst victims of national defeats. Men "can only die on the field of Battle," she wrote, while women "have the misfortune to survive those whom we Love most."

Bearing more than their share of the burdens of defeat and yet denied the fruits of victory, women had every right to be "indifferent to the publick Welfare," Adams observed. Still, far from being apathetic, they soldiered on. "All History and every age exhibit Instances of patriotick virtue in the female Sex; which considering our situation equals the most Heroick of yours," she told John. Back in 1776, Abigail had drawn upon the classical republican tradition in reminding her husband of the old adage that "all men would be Tyrants if they could." In 1782 she used republican rhetoric not to criticize one gender but to praise the other. Female patriots, she declared, possessed the one quality upon which the survival of the republic depended: they were "disinterested," meaning unselfish.

There was one more important difference between Adams's two best-known feminist statements. In the 1776 letter, Adams had made a point of stating that the reform she was seeking—a legal check on husbands who used their wives "with cruelty and indignity"—was one from which she herself would receive no benefit, since John had never mistreated her. The 1782 statement was more personal. Having shifted her attention to the suffering that women had endured on behalf of the war effort, Abigail made bold to "take praise to myself. I feel that it is my due, for having sacrificed so large a portion of my peace and happiness to promote the welfare of my country."

Adams's primary sacrifice, of course, was the companionship of her husband, whom she had not seen for almost three years. The news that John had finally succeeded in gaining Dutch recognition of American independence briefly gave her hope that he would be home soon, but then he informed her that he felt obligated to remain in Europe to try to carry out his earlier mission of negotiating a peace treaty with the former mother country. In addition to missing her husband, Adams felt increasingly intimidated by the challenge of single-handedly raising three of their four children. She worried most about Nabby, who turned seventeen on July 14. Abigail prided herself on rarely leaving home for social events, and in a letter to John she proudly contrasted herself to Elizabeth Dana, wife of one of his diplomatic colleagues, who, for her part, had not found it "necessary to domesticate herself." But Nabby took her mother's reclusiveness to an inappropriate extreme. For instance, she passed up numerous invitations to attend the 1782 commencement ceremony at Harvard. The Adamses had no close friends or relatives among the graduates, but every year hundreds of families in the same situation attended anyway (even though many of the orations were in Latin)—and hundreds more came to the parties. Nabby's brother Charles, who turned twelve during the summer of 1782, jumped at the chance to go to commencement, but she apparently feared that attending the grand event would make her feel even more awkward than usual, and she stayed home.

One prospect that did excite Nabby was unrealistic in the extreme: she wanted to sail over to Holland to live with her father, and she was willing to undertake the voyage alone. Despite her obvious discomfort in social situations, she imagined that if she were in Holland, she would be able to act as her father's "housekeeper," managing his household and servants and cohosting his parties and dinners. Abigail endorsed her daughter's proposal, even though it would deprive her of the company of all but her two youngest children. "What think you of your daughters comeing to keep House for you?" she wrote him. John need not worry that the girl would make an "ungracefull appearence at the Head of your table." More important, Nabby was "rather too silent," and a trip abroad might draw her out of her shell. And of course the very trait that Nabby needed to correct would endear her to father, Abigail predicted. Being taciturn, she observed, Nabby "would please you the better." But John refused to hear any talk of his daughter crossing the ocean in the middle of a war, especially unaccompanied by her mother. Indeed, it seems likely that Abigail had felt free to go along with the plan precisely because she knew John never would.

A short time later, John had to contend with a different and more perplexing request from his daughter. She wanted a piece of diamond jewelry. Since Nabby's letter to her father does not survive, it is impossible to know what exact item she asked for, but her request visibly astonished both parents. Nor was this the first time the girl had mounted a challenge to her father's beloved principle of frugality. The previous year, she had had the temerity to tell John she wished "to appear when she goes from home a little like those of her own age"—which meant wearing a little bit of finery. And she had persuaded Abigail to slip the odd request for fancy clothing into the merchandise invoices she sent her husband and business partner. In April 1781, for instance, Abigail had asked John to include in his next shipment "a small Box of flowers"—

artificial decorations for garments—emphasizing that she had ordered them "for Miss Nabby at her request."

But diamond jewelry! "I must confess," John wrote his daughter, "I should have been happier if you had asked me for Bell's British Poets." There was "more elegance and beauty" in that verse anthology, he declared, "than in all the diamonds which I ever saw about the Princess of Orange, or the Queen of France, in all their birth-day splendour." You must resolve upon "conquering your taste, (for taste is to be conquered, like unruly appetites and passions, or the mind is undone,)" he told her. Indeed, "there are more thorns sown in the path of human life by vanity, than by any other thing." In lieu of jewelry, John purchased a piece of "very Saucy"—and very expensive—scarlet fabric and shipped it to his wife with instructions to make herself and Nabby each "a Ridinghood in honour of the Manufactures of Haerlem." Disappointed though he was at his daughter's outrageous request, the ambassador stopped short of explicitly refusing it. But apparently neither of them ever broached the topic again.

In her mother's eyes, Nabby also suffered from another character flaw that was even more alarming than her self-seclusion and her expensive taste. "She has a Stat[l]iness in her manners which some misconstrue into pride and haughtyness," Abigail wrote. "Her sensibility is not yet sufficiently a wakend to give her Manners that pleasing softness which attracts whilst it is attracted. Her Manners rather forbid all kinds of Intimacy; and awe whilst they command." Abigail was even more troubled by her daughter's shortage of sensibility—after all, women were supposed to be the delicate sex—than she was by her son's surplus. In this important respect Nabby was very different from her mother, who by her own recollection had, like Charles, possessed "too much sensibility" when she was Nabby's age.

It annoyed Nabby that "some persons" (read: her mother) found her so wooden. But to her closest companions she acknowledged worrying that the accusation might be true. In the past the prospect of spending a few days or weeks with the Warren family had always excited her, she observed to her cousin Betsy Cranch during an April 1782 visit to the Warrens' new home in Milton. But no more. "My happiness is not greatly augmented by this visit neither will it be greatly decreased," she wrote. "I veryly believe I possess too large a share of that same indiference that some persons attribute to me." Seven months later she was still describing herself as "the same cold indifferent Girl" she had

Abigail Adams Smith (1765–1813), the only Adams daughter who lived to adulthood. Another daughter, Susanna, died in February 1770 at the age of thirteen months, and a third was stillborn in 1777. Abigail Junior was generally known as Nabby within the family until her marriage to Colonel William Stephens Smith in 1786. She died of breast cancer in 1813. Mather Brown, 1786. *Courtesy Adams National Historical Park.*

always been. "I have sometimes been at a loss to know whether I have a heart or not," she told Betsy, "but at last have made this conclusion, that in the days of my very youth I was deprived of it." Nabby did not indicate who had robbed her of her emotional side, but the strong indication was that her mother was at least partly to blame.

By this time Nabby and her female friends had established a correspondence network that in some ways resembled the one from which her mother had derived so much pleasure and instruction two decades earlier. For instance, in both cases, a girl might write to one of her friends even if she was in the same town. There was, however, at least one major difference between Nabby's and Abigail's writing clubs. Judging from Nabby's letters to Betsy Cranch, many of which survive, she and her friends almost never talked about books. Indeed it would appear that the only daughter of one of early America's most passionate advocates for female education was hardly reading anything at all. When her father asked what books she would like him to send her from Europe, she dutifully replied that she would be happy with "whatever" he sent her but provided no specific guidance beyond the confession that she had "not that taste for history which I wish."

The one topic that did excite Nabby was boys, and she often deflected her interest in them into curiosity about other people's relationships. Sometimes her observations could be sarcastic. In the spring of 1782, when a young widow, a cousin of her mother's, cut short her mourning period in order to remarry, Nabby told Betsy, "I must confess I can have no idea that a heart wounded by grief should be healed by aney one event in so short a space of time." "Perhaps," added the young woman who worried so much about her lack of sensibility, "my ideas may be romantick." The men who interested Nabby the most were those who seemed to orbit her cousins and other female friends. In general she prodded her peers to deepen the relationships that gave her so much vicarious pleasure, but she felt compelled to warn Betsy against one potential suitor who had just moved to Braintree. His name was Royall Tyler, and by his own admission, he had dissipated his youth—though he claimed to have subsequently reformed himself. Just as ominous as Tyler's shady past was the simple fact that he was a boarder in the Cranch home, which placed this Betsy in the same dangerous position her aunt Elizabeth Smith had faced seven years earlier.

Tyler "is practicing upon Chesterfeilds plan," Nabby warned her cousin in a June 1782 letter. He was a rake, the very "essence and quintessence of artfulness." The girls' mutual friends, she reported, worried that Tyler would "in some way or other ingratiate himself into the good opinion of your self." It made sense for Nabby to ascribe this fear to people other than herself, for to speculate openly that Tyler stood any chance of successfully seducing Elizabeth would have been a grave insult to her—at least in normal times. But Nabby feared that Elizabeth was especially vulnerable just at this moment. Her father, Richard, lay dangerously ill and was likely to die. "Your heart is at present uncommonly softened by affliction," Nabby reminded her friend. If Tyler were to "find a way to sooth your sorrows I will not answer for you, that you will not at least esteem him." As for myself, Nabby told Betsy, "I am determined to avoid the least degree of acquaintance" with Tyler. This was one resolution that she would soon find herself unable to keep.

In July, Abigail revisited the question of whether to invest in Vermont land. Colonel Jacob Davis of Worcester, the head of the syndicate promoting the Vermont town of Salem, paid her a visit and showed her a congressional committee report confirming that Vermont had met all the conditions that Congress had set for its admission as an independent state (chiefly that Vermont not impede neighboring states' territorial claims). Furthermore, Davis said, he was only selling plots in Salem to "persons of character and property"—and they were all from Massachusetts, too. As Abigail struggled with her decision, she "recollected the old adage Nothing venture nothing have," and she went ahead with the purchase. The town charter prohibited anyone from buying more than 330 acres, but Adams was able to obtain one grant for her husband and one each in the name of four straw men, who then deeded their tracts to the Adams children. The only member of the family who received no land was Abigail herself, since as a married woman she could not purchase real estate in her own name.

Abigail's initial cost estimate for the Vermont purchase proved unrealistic. She had expected to obtain 1,000 acres for at most £10, but the five lots she bought cost her £11 each, bringing the total price for the entire 1,650-acre parcel to £55. She was only able to come up with £44, so she paid Davis that sum and gave him a promissory note for the remaining £11. Adams was anxious to hear her husband's opinion of this transaction. Perhaps you will say "I have been Virmont Mad," she told him, but "If you approve of what I have done, and should like to purchase further I shall have more opportunities."

In the meantime Abigail continued her primary business of importing European textiles and other merchandise. During the winter of 1781–1782, she had worried that demand for her wares seemed to be slackening, but by the following summer prospects had brightened. In a September 5 letter to John, she marveled that not one of her cargoes had been captured or lost at sea. "My Luck is great," she wrote. "I know not that I have lost any adventure you have ever sent me." Actually, several of John's smaller shipments had in fact fallen prey to British privateers—and the following month, she would lose "some Small Bundles or packages" when the *General Greene* was captured.

Adams's upbeat entrepreneurial attitude dampened a little the following fall, when she received John's response to her Vermont proposal. Apparently he did not share her belief in the adage "Nothing venture nothing have," for he told her in no uncertain terms, "Dont meddle any more with Vermont." John probably assumed this would be the end of the matter. Abigail never bought another acre in Vermont, but the topic was far from closed.

Not all of the expenditures that Abigail undertook in the summer of 1782 could be considered investments. In an August 5 letter to John, she referred to Mercy Otis Warren's recent request for a set of fine European china. Then she added: "I should like to *prog* a little too if I thought you could afford it." *Prog,* a Dutch word that had made its way into vernacular English, meant "to beg." Given the Adamses' long-standing commitment to frugality, Abigail was embarrassed to be requesting "a compleat set of china for a dining table," and her jocular recourse to slang was aimed at putting John in the right mood. Apparently this strategy failed, for he did not send the china and in fact never made any response to his wife's request.

The same August 5, 1782, letter in which Abigail asked John for a set of china also contained an even bolder request. If, as seemed increasingly likely, John was determined to stay in Europe long enough to negotiate a peace treaty with Britain, she wanted to join him there. This was in fact the first of a series of appeals that all had the same object. What is most striking about these letters was how indirect they were. On August 5, Abigail mentioned hearing a rumor—possibly her own invention—that John had "sent for all your family." When she wrote him again a little less than a month later, she was even less explicit, telling him, "In my last Letter I made you a serious proposal. I will not repeat it at present." Then, two days later, she wrote, "In my other Letter I mention a serious proposal made in a former; but do not inform you of the Nature of it, fearing a rejection of my proposal and it is of so tender a Nature I could scarcly bear a refusal." Later in the same note, though, she finally ventured to give her wish forthright expression: it was "that I may come to you, with our daughter, in the Spring."

Abigail was finding life without her husband miserable. On November 13, the third anniversary of his second departure for Europe, she wrote him quoting Henry Mackenzie. "The social feelings grow callous from disuse," Mackenzie had written in a sequel to *The Man of Feeling,* and they "lose that pliancy of little affection, which sweetens the cup of life as we drink it." Later on in the same letter, Abigail told John she completely trusted him not to commit adultery during his time alone in Europe. "Such is my confidence in you," she wrote, "that if you was not withheld by the strongest of all obligations those of a moral Nature, your Honour would not suffer you to abuse my confidence." It must have saddened John to read that his wife rested her faith in him on his morality and honor rather than his affection for her. Moreover, this was the first time Abigail had ever raised the issue of his fidelity (except in jest), for she had always taken it for granted. It seems clear that in the depths of her loneliness, morbid subjects had begun to trouble her sleep.

It did not help that John had returned to his old pattern of writing excessively short letters. Abigail was wary of again provoking her husband on this topic, so she chose her words carefully. "I feel in my Heart a disposition to complain that when you write, you are so very concise," she told him. She wanted to upbraid him, she was saying, but dared not do so.

Adding to Abigail's sense of isolation was the paucity of correspondence she received from her eldest son. The few letters John Quincy did manage to send her often consisted almost entirely of descriptions of the cities on his itinerary that he had copied directly from guidebooks. After leaving Amsterdam for St. Petersburg, Johnny was only able to get one letter into his mother's hands, and she could not understand why. Finally she asked the boy a question that called to mind her supposition, four years earlier, that her husband must have "changed Hearts with some frozen Laplander." "Has the cold Northern Regions . . . chilled your affections," she wondered, "or obliterated the Remembrance of her who gave you Birth?" Abigail would have been even more upset if she had known that while in Russia, John Quincy maintained a lively correspondence with his father.

Adams continued to harbor similar anxieties about her daughter's "reserve and apparent coldness." Still, she had reason to think Nabby's emotional state was about to change. The source of her optimism could hardly have been more astonishing: Nabby was being courted by Royall Tyler, the (supposedly) reformed rake she had warned her cousin Betsy about only six months earlier.

And she seemed to like him. At least, wrote Abigail, using the cryptic language that was customary in such cases, "I do not think the Lady wholy indifferent." Abigail herself was thoroughly ambivalent. On the one hand, Tyler had, by his own admission, dissipated his youth. He had blown a substantial portion of the seventeen-thousand-pound fortune he had inherited from his father (and wartime inflation had wiped out much of the rest). It seems that he had also fathered a child with a cleaning lady at Harvard, though he apparently did not share that biographical detail with the Adamses. But in the spring of 1782, Tyler had opened a law office in Braintree, and in six short months he had begun to build a successful practice. Moreover, he was expected to receive another substantial inheritance when his mother died. But Tyler's most appealing quality was his sensibility. "I am not acquainted with any young Gentleman whose attainments in literature are equal to his, who judges with greater accuracy or discovers a more delicate and refined taste," she told her husband. He had won her over not only with his "obvious" affection for her daughter but also by recognizing Abigail's own surfeit of sensibility. "I can safely trust my dearest fondest wishes and persuits in the hands of a Friend that can feel," he told her in a December 1782 letter.

Despite her own favorable sentiments toward Tyler, Abigail labored to rein in Nabby's affection for him. If no maternal restraints had been applied, she believed, her daughter would have fallen head over heels for the man, for he was "possest with powerfull attractions." One reason Abigail tried to slow things down was that she knew her husband would want to weigh in on the matter. "I could have but one voice," she told Tyler, "and for that I held myself accountable" to John. Abigail's ambiguous statement accurately reflected the ongoing uncertainty about the governance of the Adams household. On the one hand, she asserted her right to a "voice"—a vote—in whether Tyler should marry her daughter. Few women of her time would have made such a claim. On the other hand, she held herself "accountable" to her husband in the matter, which seemed to indicate that as the couple considered what advice to give their daughter, he would have the final say.

Abigail clearly wanted her husband to like Royall, for the young attorney seemed to be just what their daughter needed. Nabby was not like other girls, Abigail explained to John, for "No air of levity ever accompanies either her words or actions." She was "a fine Majestick Girl," and she had "as much dignity as a princess." But there was still hope for her. "Should she be caught by a tender passion, sufficient to remove a little of her natural reserve and soften her form and manners," she would, according to her mother, "be a still more pleasing character." Already Tyler had fueled Nabby's dormant passion for the written word, Abigail reported: "She gathers new taste for literature perhaps for its appearing in a more pleasing form to her."

Royall had made his intentions clear, and Nabby's placid nature had, if anything, intensified his ardor. Even as Abigail lamented that the girl had not inherited "her Mothers sensibility," she detected in Tyler "a growing attachment" that was "stimulated by that very reserve." The big question was what John Adams would say.

CHAPTER 16

"I Will Run You in Debt"

1783–1784

On January 22, 1783, John began a series of letters in response to Abigail's report on the budding romance between their daughter and Royall Tyler. "I confess I dont like the Subject at all," he wrote. "I had flattered myself with the Hopes of a few Years of the society of this Daughter" before she found a husband and left him. Surely "my Child is too young for such Thoughts," he declared. In his surviving letters to Abigail, John had never once referred to his daughter as "my child," even when she actually was a child, but the word appeared two more times in his commentary on the seventeen-year-old's relationship with Tyler. Latching onto his wife's acknowledgment that the young man had once led a dissolute life, he insisted that "My Child is a Model" of probity "and is not to be the Prize, I hope of any, even reformed Rake." John did not share his wife's belief in Tyler's ability to rid himself of his decadent tendencies. "If they were ever in him they are not yet out," he declared.

The prospect of his daughter marrying such a man so infuriated Adams that he broached a topic that was as painful as anything he and his wife had ever discussed: her brother William's intemperance. Tyler had acquired habits that "your Family as well as mine have had too much Cause to rue," he wrote. Abigail's argument that Tyler had begun to refine Nabby's artistic taste did not impress the girl's father, who pointed out that he was "not looking out for a Poet, nor a Professor of belle Letters." A week later, addressing his wife but obviously speaking to his daughter, Adams urged Nabby not to be swept away by Tyler's "Gaiety and Superficial Accomplishments. . . . One may dance or sing, play or ride, without being good for much." Instead she should find a hearty fellow "who can ride 500 miles upon a trotting Horse and cross the Gulph stream with a steady Heart." Her future husband must be "a thinking Being, and one who thinks for others good"—in short, a man like her father.

John was even less impressed by his wife's claim that Tyler might be able to awaken the girl's sensibility. "In the Name of all that is tender dont criticise Your Daughter for those qualities which are her greatest Glory her Reserve, and her Prudence which I am amazed to hear you call Want of Sensibility," he wrote. "The more Silent She is in Company, the better for me in exact Proportion." Indeed, he added, "I would have this observed as a Rule by the Mother as well as the Daughter."

This thinly disguised dig at his wife's occasional sauciness was by no means the only criticism John leveled at her when he learned of the courtship. "You seem to me to have favoured this affair much too far," he wrote. In his eyes, Tyler had verbally seduced Abigail in order to secure her help in winning the main prize. "I dont like this method of Courting Mothers," he wrote. Tyler had engaged Mrs. Adams in his cause in part by praising her boundless capacity for feeling, and John, determined to meet his opponent on his own ground, implored Nabby not to fall for the simplistic version of sensibility that focused on artistic refinement. Instead she should find herself a man who "feels anothers Woe." Adams left only one door slightly ajar. Ironically enough, he did so in the midst of his most emphatic denunciation of Tyler's suit. "I positively forbid, any Connection between my Daughter and any Youth upon Earth, who does not totally eradicate every Taste for Gaiety and Expence," he wrote. That left open the possibility that Tyler might someday break the bad habits he had acquired in his youth.

When Abigail received the first of her husband's letters complaining about the courtship, she dutifully withdrew her support for Tyler, though she also reiterated her conviction that he really had reformed. "The former Beau, has been converted into the plain dressing Man," she wrote, "and the Gay volatile Youth, appears to become the studious Lawyer." Nabby chose not to address a letter to her father on the subject, but by the end of April, Abigail was able to report that she, too, had yielded to John's objections. She would suspend the courtship until his return to Braintree, when she hoped to change his mind. In the meantime, she would treat Tyler simply as a friend. When her mother suggested that perhaps she should not see him at all, the girl's reply was so spirited that Abigail copied it down for her husband:

> Why said she should I treat a Gentleman who has done nothing to forfeit my Esteem, with neglect or contempt, merely because the world have said, that he entertained a preferable regard for me? If his foibles are to be treated with more severity than the vices of others, and I submit my judgment and opinion to the disapprobation of others in a point which so nearly concerns me, I wish to be left at liberty to act in other respects with becomeing decency.

Although Nabby was her mother's primary source of domestic anxiety in the spring of 1783, Abigail was also vexed by the problem of her two youngest sons' education. Both boys' passion for learning was fueled by their sibling rivalry. While stuck in Bilbao, Charles had worried less about getting home safely than about the danger that his younger brother would overtake him during these months of enforced idleness. But who would prepare the boys for Harvard? For various reasons related to the wartime labor shortage, Braintree was not able to maintain a schoolmaster, none of the boarding schools had any openings, and Abigail had a devil of a time keeping tutors. Finally, in the spring of 1783, she surrendered. Although she had never liked John Shaw, the Calvinist minister who had married her little sister, she had to admit that he seemed to be achieving great success preparing boys for college. Through her sister, she wrote to ask how much he would charge for the two youngsters' tuition, room, and board. As if to confirm that he was as disagreeable as ever, the preacher became annoyed that she had not written him directly, and he pointedly retaliated by having his wife pen his reply. Despite this bad omen, in mid-April Abigail deposited Charles and Tommy at the Shaws' home in Haverhill. "I have done the best I could with them," she told John.

For the first time ever, the Braintree household to which Adams returned consisted entirely of females. Two servant girls did most of the cooking, cleaning, and milking and also helped make clothing, as did Abigail, Nabby, and little Louisa Smith, who had moved to Braintree about five years earlier. Although a veil of discretion obscures the particulars of life within the Smith household during the Revolutionary War, it had clearly become horrendous. Louisa's one nightmare, Abigail informed John that spring, was that he would "send her away" when he returned from Europe. As much as Abigail enjoyed the company of her daughter and her niece, her boys had been in Haverhill less than two weeks when she first commented that without them, "I feel quite dull."

At about the same time Adams sent her sons off to school, she also began another major transition: getting out of the business of importing European merchandise. The stupendous profits she had earned during the previous five years had been dependent upon the continuation of bloodshed. But now the war was over, for on January 20, 1783, her husband had signed an armistice with representatives of the former mother country. The French and Spanish had made similar agreements with the British that same day, enabling the vessels of all nations to sail the North Atlantic without fear of capture. The treaties also turned hundreds of British and American pirate ships back into run-of-the-mill merchantmen, greatly increasing the competition for Americans' pounds, shillings, and pence. Even as the volume of merchandise reaching the market soared, demand for it fell off, partly because would-be consumers had been picked clean by heavy taxation and partly because the armistice and the disappearance of the paper currency had dried up the money supply. Inevitably, prices plummeted. "My last adventure from Holland was most unfortunate," Abigail told John early in May. "The Length of the passage was such, that the News of peace arrived a few days before; Goods fell and are now sold much below the sterling coast; many are lower than ever I knew them." She ordered a few items for her own family but announced at the same time, "I expect to close my mercantle affairs with this Letter."

Nearly everyone who commented on the cessation of hostilities referred in some way to the Almighty, and so did Abigail, but she refused to ascribe the Patriots' triumph to direct divine intervention. Comparing the American victory to a flower, she declared that it was "raised and Nurtured, not by the gentle showers of Heaven, but by the hard Labour and indefatigable industery and firmness of her Sons, and water'd by the Blood of many of them."

On September 17, 1783, Abigail's father died after a "Short and accute" illness—a blockage of the urinary tract. Although she was of course saddened by her loss, she endured none of the anguish that had overcome her eight years earlier, when the dysentery epidemic had claimed the life of her mother. The reason for the difference was simple: Elizabeth Smith had gone before her time—at age fifty-three—and her husband had lived to seventy-seven.

Parson Smith's will did not divide his property equally among his children. Abigail's sisters received more than she did, not, presumably, because their father loved them more but because their husbands were less wealthy. Mary Cranch's inheritance included the Weymouth parsonage and its eighteen acres of farmland, and Elizabeth Shaw received forty-six acres in the neighboring town of Hingham. Shaw would also split a farm in Medford and a parcel of land in Malden with Abigail, and both sisters would hold on to this land for the rest of their lives.

In mentioning the Medford farm to her husband, Abigail once referred in passing to "my part of the Rent." Then she noticed what she had done: implied that the rent money was hers alone. She blamed the mistake, versions of which she had committed on several earlier occasions, on John's extended absence. "Forgive me if I sometimes use the singular instead of the plural," she told him; "alass I have been too much necessitated to it." Actually, in the eyes of the law, the Adamses's portion of the Medford rent did not belong either to Abigail alone (as she initially stated) or to her and her husband jointly (as she said in her correction). The doctrine of coverture required that all of the profits from a wife's real estate go to her husband to use as he pleased. By supplying two incorrect answers to the question of who was entitled to the Medford rental income, Abigail demonstrated just how far the reality of her household had diverged from legal theory over the course of the six years that she had managed her husband's property. Historians of the American Revolution have long debated its impact on women, and they may never reach a consensus, but one thing is certain: the prolonged absence of thousands of soldiers and statesmen led many of their wives to begin thinking of themselves in dramatically different ways.

The death of Parson Smith also had another impact on the Adamses that was not at all apparent from his will. Abigail's mother, Elizabeth, had owned several hundred acres of land. During her long marriage, authority over this parcel had passed to her husband, and even after she died, he continued to control it for the rest of his life. But at Reverend Smith's death his wife's real estate passed to her own heirs, including Abigail, who received "a Right in about [2?] hundred acers of land some where in Northburry"—possibly either Northborough, Massachusetts, or Northbury (now Plymouth), Connecticut. Adams apparently did not think this land had much potential—except as a bargaining chip. Her husband had blocked the one real estate development project that truly excited her—her speculation in Vermont land. Now she spotted a way to remove his opposition. She knew John would want to sell the Northbury tract in order to buy more land closer to home. But because this parcel belonged to her, it could not be sold without her permission. Abigail now offered to relinquish her right to the Northbury land in return for John's consent to an expanded investment in Vermont. "I will exchange with you," she wrote. John does not appear to have replied to this offer, but the mere fact that Abigail had made it showed her wide divergence from the ideal of the submissive wife. Historians have described Abigail's Vermont purchase as a mistake, but both of her eldest sons believed it had the potential to return a handsome profit. John Quincy would list his parcel among his assets in 1814.

The saddest and most embarrassing aspect of Parson Smith's will was the provision he made for the family of his son, William. By this time William Smith, Jr.'s wife and children were living on a farm in the town of Lincoln, Massachusetts (which adjoined Concord to the west), but William had abandoned the family. Years earlier Parson Smith had promised this property to his son, but in 1781 he had been forced to go back on his agreement, because William Junior had stopped paying taxes on the Lincoln farm, and it was nearly seized by the government. In his will, Parson Smith left this land not to William but to Cotton Tufts and Richard Cranch, who were to hold it in trust for the benefit of Catharine Smith and her children. Giving the property to Catharine herself was not an option, because under the doctrine of marital coverture, it would have fallen under the control of her husband. To his son Parson Smith bequeathed only his clothing and the cancellation of numerous loans. Even as the preacher had been "breathing out his last breath," Abigail reported, he had been "Labouring . . . for the reformation and salvation of the prodigal." In his will he was realistic enough to acknowledge that he had failed.

Smith also offered freedom to Phoebe, who was the last of his slaves. A recent ruling by the Supreme Judicial Court had abolished slavery in Massachusetts as inconsistent with the state's bill of rights, but slaves had to sue for their freedom, and Smith saved her the trouble and expense of doing so by emancipating her. He actually gave her the option of remaining the property of any of his three daughters, which would ensure her financial support when she could no longer work. Phoebe passed up that opportunity and claimed her freedom.

In November 1783, John Adams finally granted a request he had repeatedly received from his wife during the previous five and a half years. Abigail was now permitted—in fact directed—to join her husband in

Europe. John had just learned that Congress had renewed its earlier instruction that a commission—now consisting of Adams, Franklin, and Thomas Jefferson—negotiate commercial treaties with Great Britain and other European states. He predicted the negotiations would be over in less than a year, but that was long enough to justify Nabby and Abigail's crossing the Atlantic.

Unfortunately, now that John had finally acceded to Abigail's wishes, he had done so in a way that made it impossible for her to comply. It would take her at least a month to get her financial affairs in order, and by then winter would arrive, and that was the most dangerous and unpleasant time to cross the ocean. She reluctantly informed her husband that she would not be able to set sail until the following spring. One reason Adams was loth to drop everything and head to Europe was that she was busy implementing an earlier instruction from her husband. John had decided to begin buying up real estate. When his wife received his directive to be on the lookout for opportunities, she had already purchased eight acres of pasture and woods near their Braintree home. That purchase "gives me more Pleasure than you are aware," John told her in an August 14 letter. He went on to affirm that it was his "Intention when I come home to sell my House in Boston and to collect together all the Debts due to me and all other little Things that I can convert into Money and lay it out in Lands in the Neighbourhood of our Chaumiere [cottage]." Pleased to have John's approval, Abigail made several more small purchases. Then in December she announced to him that their neighbors William and Sarah Veasey had put their farm on the market. It was a tempting proposition, but it would also be much costlier than anything she had yet undertaken. How could she possibly pay for it?

Abigail had an answer to that question. "If my dear Friend you will promise to come home, take the Farm into your own hands and improve it, let me turn dairy woman, and assist you in getting our living this way; instead of running away to foreign courts and leaving me half my Life to mourn in widowhood," she told John, "then I will run you in debt for this Farm." Adams's proposal that her husband borrow money in order to purchase the Veasey place was so contrary to the couple's shared aversion to going into debt that it has caught the attention of nearly all of her biographers. Yet scholars have failed to identify the person from whom she wanted John to obtain the money. It was Abigail herself.

"I have a hundred pounds sterling which I could command" if you want to come home and develop the Veasey farm, she wrote. But only on that condition. If John decided to stay in Europe, Abigail's hundred pounds was "a deposit I do not chuse to touch." Under the English common law, which remained in effect wherever it had not been superseded by a Massachusetts statute, married women were not permitted to possess cash or other personal property. Abigail had nonetheless declared herself the owner of some of her husband's assets. Her sense of proprietorship over these funds was so strong that she even felt entitled to use them to try to lure John home. In the eyes of the law she was trying to bribe him with his own money—and this would only be a loan.

Less than a week later, Abigail wrote another letter to her husband that displayed a different kind of independence. She was beginning to have second thoughts about the couple's real estate buying spree. "There is a method of laying out money to more advantage than by the purchase of land's," she wrote, namely "State Notes." Back in 1781 the Massachusetts legislature had redeemed an earlier series of state government bonds by giving the owners a new security called the Consolidated Note. During the winter of 1783–1784, these state bonds were trading at about one-third of their face value. But the government multiplied the 6 percent interest rate by their face value, not the amount that had been paid for them, which meant that investors earned a lofty 18 percent interest on their bonds every year.

Abigail now proposed that the hundred pounds that she had put into "the hands of a Friend" be spent not on the Veasey farm but on Consolidated Notes. Then the annual interest could be used to pay Charley's and Thomas's tuition, room, and board while she was in Europe. At first glance Adams's proposition might not seem so radical, since she had been investing in government bonds ever since the summer of 1777. But purchasing depreciated government bonds from private individuals on the open market would transform her into a full-scale securities speculator.

By this time John Adams had also begun purchasing government securities. Having persuaded Dutch bankers to lend money to the U.S. government—a loan that was in turn financed by the sale of "obligations" in Amsterdam—he had resolved to place his own savings in these funds. But the resemblance between John's and Abigail's investments was actually only superficial. The credit-hungry Continental Congress preferred the Dutch bankers over all of its other creditors, and its punctual interest payments made John's bonds a low-risk—and low-yield—investment.

By contrast, Abigail's speculation in Consolidated Notes was risky, but the rewards were correspondingly high. Which raises a question: why did so few people purchase these extremely profitable securities?

Undoubtedly many backcountry farmers never learned of this opportunity. Other Americans knew about these high-yield bonds and would have leapt at the chance to buy them had they been able to. But as the shortage of gold and silver coin grew ever more acute, few owners of Consolidated Notes were willing to part with them for anything else. Abigail's access to cash—not only from John's government salary but from her own mercantile profits—placed her inside a narrow elite circle. At the end of 1783, when she briefed her husband on her purchase of a nine-acre woodlot belonging to William Adams, she quoted the seller as saying he had known John since his infancy. The reason he approached Abigail about the parcel before anyone else, he said, was "out of regard to you . . . whom he has carried about in his arms."

"An other reason . . . I fancyed weigh'd full as much," Mrs. Adams pointed out, first to William Adams and then to her husband. William "wanted the money down," and she was one of the few people in eastern Massachusetts who were able to pay for their purchases with cold, hard cash. Abigail's comment evinced the same self-assurance and hard-nosed pragmatism that had animated her earlier ventures into international trade and Vermont land titles.

By February, Abigail's thoughts were increasingly focused on her upcoming voyage to Europe. She was still not thrilled with the idea of crossing the Atlantic. Yet, as she told John in February, his "desires and requests" were "Law to me." And so she began her preparations. The couple had already decided that Uncle Tufts would succeed her in the management of John's property. No perfect tenant for the Braintree house appeared, but Abigail did not want to leave it empty. So she invited Phoebe, her father's former slave, to live there rent free along with William Abdee, her second husband (her first had apparently died). Abigail also had other affairs to put in order. The previous fall, she had discovered, somewhat to her surprise, that her brother-in-law John Shaw was turning out to be an "excellent preceptor" to Charles and Thomas. The boys' "Morals and Manners are strickly attended to," she told John. Coming from a woman who had never liked Shaw, it was a generous concession.

Nabby was a more perplexing challenge. Initially she and Royall Tyler had agreed to suspend their courtship in keeping with her father's wishes. But they had never stopped seeing each other, and they still intended to marry as soon as they could obtain John's blessing. In John's eyes, Abigail's impending voyage to Europe came at just the right time: Nabby would accompany her mother, and her prolonged separation from Royall would put their relationship to the test. If upon her return the two still wanted to marry, he would not stand in their way. John no doubt hoped that during their time apart at least one of the two would lose interest in the other. There was also the possibility that Tyler would fall back into his old pattern of dissipation, proving John's point that rakes never really reform.

Just like her mother, Nabby had repeatedly implored John to let her travel to Europe. Also like Abigail, when the opportunity finally arose, she had very good reasons for wanting to stay home. When Abigail wrote her daughter, who was on one of her frequent winter visits to Boston, asking if she was willing to undertake the voyage, Nabby called her bluff. "I presume you do not" ask that question "with an intention of being influenced by my reply," she wrote. Had she actually had a say in the matter, she declared, she might well have stayed home. The eighteen-year-old emphasized that while she was willing to accept the "sacrifice" of accompanying her mother to Europe, the journey would also entail sacrifice for Royall Tyler, so it was natural for her to wish that she really did have the option of remaining behind. In summarizing this mother-daughter discussion for John, Abigail stated only that Nabby was aware that her "duty and judgment" impelled her to make the trip, though her "passions" argued otherwise.

Ironically, John Adams had, by this time, withdrawn his objections to the match, granting Abigail full power to give or withhold parental consent. If she still approved of Tyler, he informed his wife in a January 25 letter, she should witness his marriage to their daughter and then place the newlyweds in the family's Braintree cottage before heading to Europe alone. John even raised the possibility that his son John Quincy and Tyler might someday become law partners. The fate of Adams's letter remains a mystery. It had plenty of time to cross the ocean before Abigail's departure, and the ship transporting it was not lost at sea, but she denied ever receiving it. Abigail's own theory was that the letter had simply miscarried. But she later confessed to her sister Mary that she was glad it had, because by this time she herself was once again having doubts about Tyler.

Abigail's children were not the only dependents she had to worry about as she planned her voyage. Following in her mother's footsteps, she had always given charity to her less fortunate neighbors, and she now set about making provision for them to receive support in her absence. In November, the Adamses' new business agent, Cotton Tufts, was to distribute a total of twelve dollars to eight of the family's impoverished neighbors. All of these "pensioners" (as Abigail called them) were women; the majority were widows. Adams knew her pensioners would worry about not having her around in case of emergency. In an April 12 letter to John, she was remarkably candid about the feelings that her beneficiaries' anxiety stirred in her. "I derive a pleasure from the regret of others," she wrote, "the blessing and regret of the poor and the needy, who bewail my going away."

On Friday, June 18, several dozen of Abigail's neighbors—"the Honest yeomanary, their wifes and daughters," she called them—came to see her and Nabby off. "I shook them by the hand mingling my tears with theirs, and left them," she later reported. On their way to Boston, she and Nabby stopped off at the Cranches' and then at John's mother's house. "Fatal day!" exclaimed Susanna Adams Hall, whose second husband had died four years earlier. "I take my last leave; I shall never see you again. Carry my last blessing to my son."

Mother and daughter spent Friday and Saturday nights in Boston. On Sunday they rode in a fellow passenger's carriage down to Rowe's wharf and went on board the *Active*, a merchantman bound for London, and the vessel immediately hoisted its sails and put out to sea. Since she was a child Abigail had dreamed of walking the streets of London. Now that her wish was about to be granted, she had to confront the accompanying anxieties. Could she win respect in a world of aristocrats and courtiers? How could she possibly compete with women who had spent their entire lives learning the social graces and whose wardrobe allowances were unlimited? Would she fall on her face? The only reason those questions did not entirely dominate her thoughts was that before they received definitive answers, she would first have to face down a different kind of fear. Abigail had never ventured out into the open ocean before, not even on a day trip. The thought of being beyond the sight of land for a month or more filled her with dismay.

CHAPTER 17

"A Lady at Sea"

1784

Adams's first ocean voyage was everything she had anticipated except terrifying. In the lengthy journal she kept during her month on board, she said almost nothing about being frightened. Still, this was no pleasure cruise. She was seasick for most of the first ten days. Old hands generally advise first-time sea travelers to stay on deck, but even in the middle of the summer, Adams found it too cold and damp to remain topside for long. Passengers were an afterthought on the *Active*. In those days, the only ships configured exclusively for hauling people were military transports and merchantmen refitted to carry immigrants (slaves traveled as cargo). The hold of the *Active* was filled with potash (ash residue used in making soap) and spermaceti oil (from sperm whales) for oil lamps. Both stank. The thoroughly caulked vessel trapped the odors belowdecks, and the stench would have been sufficient to induce nausea even if the seas had remained calm, which of course they did not.

Besides Abigail and her daughter, only two other women were on the boat: their servant Esther Field and a woman named Love Lawrence Adams (apparently not a close relation of John's). All were as sick as Abigail. "I have had frequent occasion since I came on Board, to recollect an observation of my best Friends," Abigail later reported to Mary. It was "that no Being in Nature was so dissagreable as a Lady at Sea." That Adams would endorse a comment that seems so sexist today is a reminder that despite her desires to reform the laws of coverture and increase women's educational opportunities, she never stopped believing that women and men were fundamentally different. Indeed, she even allowed that in some areas, men were not just more experienced than women but more robust. She was especially willing to concede the whole area of long-distance transportation—whether in a private vehicle or a stagecoach—to men. Above all, she was convinced that water was a male element. Back in 1771, while her cousin Isaac Smith was traveling in Europe, she had acknowledged to him that few women were "hardy eno' to venture abroad." Now, joining that elite corps gave her no pleasure. Given her tendency to cling to the rails of homely river ferries, it was a foregone conclusion that her weeks on the high seas would be miserable.

An additional source of Adams's discomfort was her never-abandoned conviction that decorum required strict separation of male and female bodies. The other women on the *Active* were so sick that none was able to nurse her through her nausea, a "disspiriting malady." She had made repeated efforts to add at least one male friend or family member to her party, but having failed, she was continually forced to choose between leaving basic needs unmet and allowing a strange man to meet them. Unable to take her shoes off or on, she ceded that task to Job Field, a young sailor from Braintree who was her servant Esther's brother. But of course she could not let him touch her clothes, so she wore the outfit in which she had embarked until she was well enough to change.

The ship was filthy. "No sooner was I able to move," she told Mary, "than I found it necessary to make a Bustle amongst the waiters, and demand a Cleaner abode." Having discovered that she could "reign mistress on Board without any offence," she orchestrated a massive cleaning operation. "I soon exerted my Authority with scrapers mops Brushes, infusions of viniger; &c.," she wrote, "and in a few hours you would have thought yourself in a different Ship."

Seldom does a group of strangers embark on an excursion without quickly discovering one of their number to be a constant source of irritation. The annoying passenger on the *Active* was a man named Green. He claimed to be English but Abigail suspected he was actually Scottish, because Scots were notorious for having supported the British crown in its struggle against the colonies, and Green was a "high perogative Man" who "plume[d] himself upon his country." The other passengers were affable enough, though. All were Americans. In assessing Captain Nathaniel Byfield Lyde, Adams had to acknowledge that for once her physiognomy had failed her. "This man has a kindness in his disposition which his countanance does not promise," she told Mary. There was "nothing cross or Dictatorial in his Manners."

The *Active* only had two staterooms, each of them eight feet square. Initially Abigail, Nabby, and the servant Esther Field were all packed into one of the two rooms. When Abigail balked at this arrangement, the teenaged boy who had planned to share the other cabin with his sister gave Nabby his berth, which meant that Abigail only had to share with Esther. The staterooms opened directly off the main cabin, which served as the ship's dining area and sitting room and as the sleeping quarters for the male passengers. Owing to the heat and the lack of fresh air, Abigail and Esther were only able to close their door to the main cabin while dressing. The rest of the time—for instance, all night—Adams was separated from those half-dozen males by nothing more than a thin curtain. She had never been forced to live with strange men on terms like these, and the indignities continued during the daytime, for the pitching of the ship prevented her from crossing the main cabin without a man holding her. Out on deck, it took two of them to brace her until she could be lashed into a chair. The only mitigating factor, Adams reported to her daughter's sweetheart, was that the male passengers were "all of them married Gentlemen except one, and he said to be engaged."

The voyage to Europe marked an important change in Abigail's thinking about race. Up until this time, her attitude toward the few black people she knew was often condescending but never hostile. She had repeatedly denounced slavery even as her parents continued to live off the labor of slaves. When John Adams was inoculated against smallpox, his correspondence had to be smoked by her father's slave Tom, and she groaned at the way he mangled the letters—but she made similar complaints about white servants. After another Smith family slave, Phoebe, obtained her freedom, Abigail added her to the ranks of her "pensioners"—the recipients of her charity. On the one hand, she trusted Phoebe and her husband, William Abdee, to look after the Adams cottage during her absence (and charged them no rent for it). But in describing this arrangement, she always referred to Phoebe as the head of the household, ignoring William in a way that she never did white men. Moreover, she emphasized in a letter to Cotton Tufts, who succeeded her in the management of the Adams properties, that Phoebe was "always to be under your direction and controul to be continued or displaced when ever you think proper."

Still, if there is such a thing as benign racism, this was it. Even when the "Negro head" who had briefly acted as Abigail's farm supervisor quit in the middle of the harvest, she expressed little hostility toward him. Not so the African American cook on board the *Active*. One of Adams's grievances against him—that he was unable to achieve "any kind of order in the distribution of his dishes"—could just as easily have been leveled against a white man. But in Adams's eyes, the cook was "a great dirty lazy Negro; with no more knowledge of cookery than a savage." She seems to have grown a little more comfortable around the man as the voyage progressed—otherwise she probably would not have "taught the cook to dress his victuals"—but her description of him as "dirty" and "lazy" marked the beginning of an erosion in her willingness to acknowledge the full humanity of African Americans. And worse was coming.

Around the first of July, ten days into the voyage, Abigail finally grew accustomed to the rocking of the boat. The next day she was able to report that she had "Hemd a hankerchief upon Deck." Then on July 14 she suffered an attack of rheumatism that she blamed on the dampness of the vessel. "I could not raise my Head, nor get out of bed without assistance," she told Mary. "I had a good deal of a fever and was very sick." Land was spotted four days later. Owing to contrary winds, the *Active* would probably need as much as a week to get up the English Channel and then the Thames River. So on the twentieth, when a pilot boat from the little coastal town of Deal (just north of Dover) came alongside and offered to run the passengers through the six-foot surf right up onto the beach, they all readily consented. That is how it came about that the most harrowing segment of Abigail's monthlong ocean crossing turned out to be the last hundred yards. "I could keep myself up no other way than as one of the Gentlemen stood braced up against the Boat, fast hold of me and I with both my Arms round him," she reported; "finally a Wave landed us with the utmost force upon the Beach; the Broad Side of the Boat right against the shore." She and the other passengers blamed "the bad management of the men" for bringing the boat in sideways. The roar of the waves "terrified us all," she wrote, "and we expected the next would fill our Boat." So they "all pressd upon the side next the Shore to get out as quick as possible."

It was only after joining in this mad scramble that Adams learned that the sailors had deliberately come in broadside, their plan being to "set still for a succession of waves to have carried us up higher." No matter, for she was now ashore, if not exactly on dry land. Abigail reported that "Mr. Green," the disagreeable man she suspected of being

Scottish, "set of[f] immediately for London—no body mourn'd." The other travelers made their way up the soggy beach to a tavern, where they dried off, changed clothes, had a hearty meal, and spent the night. The next morning at six, a pair of post chaises (carriages) were waiting to start them on their seventy-two-mile journey to London.

To an even greater extent than most other first-time international travelers, Adams analyzed everything she saw during her initial few days in England through the lens of comparison. Unlike in Massachusetts, there was nary a stone in the road. The fields were planted right up to the roadside. The oxen were smaller than back home, but the cattle and sheep were larger. The servants at public houses were surprisingly attentive ("But you must know that travelling in a post Chaise, is what intitles you to all this respect"), and the prices were not nearly as high as she had expected. One of the starkest contrasts was in religious architecture. Adams had spent nearly every Sunday of her life in simple Congregationalist meetinghouses. Although England had seceded from the Catholic Church more than two centuries earlier, many of its churches dated back to that earlier era, and showed it. When the group stopped in Canterbury, Abigail commented that the town's "old Gothick Cathedrals" were "all of stone very heavy, with but few windows which are grated with large Bars of Iron, and look more like jails for criminals, than places designd for the worship of the deity." The churches "have a most gloomy appearence and realy made me shudder," she wrote.

In Adams's eyes, even the one bit of real excitement her party experienced on the road to London provided the occasion for comparison. A man in another carriage passed the Americans, and a short time later they learned that he had been robbed. The thief was pursued and taken, and the travelers stopped to gawk at the captive. "We saw the poor wretch gastly and horible, brought along on foot," Abigail told her sister. "He looked like a youth of 20 only, attempted to lift his hat, and looked Dispair." "Aya," his captors were telling him, "you have but a short time, the assise [court] set next Month, and then my Lad you Swing." Abigail was appalled at the way the captors taunted their prisoner. "To exult over the wretched is what *our* Country is not accustomed to," she wrote Mary. "Long may it be free of such villianies and long may it preserve a commisiration for the wretched."

At eight o'clock in the evening of July 21—the same day they had left Deal—mother and daughter reached London and checked into Low's

Hotel in Covent Garden. The room charge being unconscionably high, they moved to cheaper quarters the very next day, and as soon as she was settled, Abigail wrote her husband. Back in May, John Quincy (who had rejoined his father in Amsterdam a year earlier, having returned from St. Petersburg by way of Scandanavia) had, at his father's behest, crossed the channel to greet his mother and sister. But after waiting around for more than a month, he had returned to Amsterdam. Since it would take at least six days for John or his son to reach London, Abigail and Nabby filled the time exchanging visits with well-wishers (numerous Britons had remained friends of America throughout eight long years of war, and others had reconciled themselves to the new order of things with astonishing rapidity) and seeing the sights. They went to several art exhibitions, and Abigail especially liked a portrait of her husband done by the American émigré John Singleton Copley. They visited the Tower of London, Westminster Abbey, St. Paul's Cathedral—and Patience Wright's wax museum. Wright was a Quaker from New Jersey, and she had moved to London before the war. During the imperial struggle, she had served as an American spy, passing information to Benjamin Franklin in France. Abigail reported that when her party entered the museum, Wright "ran to the Door, caught me by the Hand," and exclaimed, "Why is it realy and in truth Mrs. Adams, and that your daughter? Why you dear Soul you, how young you look!" Adams was intrigued by the wax figures, several of which she mistook for real people, but even more so by Mrs. Wright, whose eccentricity was at once annoying and endearing. In the journal that she had kept during her ocean voyage, Adams had shown pride in both her nation and her sex by asserting that Britain's three finest painters—Wright, Copley, and John Trumbull—had all been born in the colonies. At some point (presumably after her visit to Wright's museum) she edited her statement to say that Britain's *two* best painters, Copley and Trumbull, were both Americans.

On Sunday, July 25, Abigail and Nabby worshipped at the foundling hospital (for illegitimate children) in the morning and at the Magdalene Hospital (for reformed prostitutes) in the afternoon. During the afternoon service, she observed that the inmates were "screened from publick view" by a green curtain. "You can discern them through the canvas, but not enough to distinguish countenances," she told her sister Mary. "I admired the delicacy of this thought." Abigail was pleasantly surprised to discover that the service was "very full and crouded . . . In

Short I begin to hope that this people are more Serious and religious than I feard they were." There was a larger pattern here. "I assure you my dear sister I am better pleased with this city than I expected," Adams wrote Elizabeth. "The Buildings [are] more regular the streets much wider and more Sun shine than I thought to have found," she told Mary.

Adams was "agreeably dissapointed" in the people of England as well. Having expected to observe her hosts wallowing in luxury and conspicuous display, she was "not a Little surprized" to find that "the Gentlemen are very plainly dresst and the Ladies much less so than with us. . . . [A] common straw hat, no Cap, with only a ribbon upon the crown, is thought dress sufficient to go into company." The English entertained with greater moderation than their former colonists, too. She was informed that Americans were "extravagant to astonishment in entertainments compared with" their British counterparts. "You will not find at a Gentlemans table more than two dishes of meat tho invited several days before hand," she wrote. Scarcely a week after tumbling out of the pilot boat at Deal, Adams was wishing she did not have to leave England. "I have a partiality for this Country," she wrote.

The only Londoners who lived up to Adams's negative expectations were the women. Studying them seemed to fire her patriotism. "I have seen many Ladies; but not one Elegant one since I came," she told Mary on her second day in London. "The American Ladies are much admired here by the Gentlemen, I am told, and in truth I wonder not at it." In describing the women she met, Abigail contradicted her earlier statement about the surprising simplicity of English attire. "There is not to me that neatness in their appearence which you see in our Ladies," she wrote. Englishwomen also lacked their American sisters' delicacy. "The softness peculiarly characteristick of our sex and which is so pleasing to the Gentlemen, is Wholy laid asside here; for the Masculine attire and Manners of Amazonians," she claimed. This observation was not entirely the product of blind prejudice, for many English women did in fact make their morning social rounds in a riding habit, which included a waistcoat and a cocked hat or jockey cap. One woman with whom Abigail dined, an American expatriate, was "delicate as a lily, modest and diffident, not a London Lady by any means." As in Adams's earlier comments about women being less capable than men of surviving the rigors of the sea, so in her criticism of Englishwomen's "Masculine attire" and their lack of "softness": she repeatedly demonstrated that she was by no means a feminist in the modern sense.

Numerous aspects of metropolitan life astonished this American parson's daughter. After describing for her sister the elaborate process of paying and receiving visits—and of leaving and responding to cards—she observed that her "servant will frequently come and ask me if I am at home!" She marveled at London's indoor plumbing. There was no room for outhouses, because "there is not half an inch of Ground unoccupied." Instead, water was "conveyd by pipes" into "a closet by my chamber." Waste went into chamber pots, and "we have no occasion to go out of our rooms, from one week to an other." Although in private life Abigail was slow to forgive her enemies—witness her persistent grudge against her brother-in-law John Shaw—once in London, she demonstrated a surprising willingness to reconcile not only with the British but with Americans who had returned to the mother country rather than rally to the Patriot banner. Loyalists by the dozens called upon her in the little parlor at her hotel, and she returned as many of the visits as she could. On neither side was there any evidence of lingering resentment.

It had been nearly five years since Adams had seen John or John Quincy. She calculated that if one or both of them left Amsterdam as soon as they received her first letter from London, he would be with her by Thursday, July 29. When neither father nor son appeared on that day, she decided to spend Friday morning at home in case one of them arrived. The story of that morning is best told by herself.

"Whilst I am writing a servant in the family runs puffing in, as if he was realy interested in the matter," she later reported to Mary.

"Young Mr. Adams is come," the servant declared.

"Where is he?" Abigail demanded.

"In the other house Madam, he stoped to get his Hair dresst."

When John Quincy finally entered his mother's little parlor, she later told Mary, "I drew back not realy believing my Eyes." Back in November 1779, she had bid farewell to a twelve-year-old boy, and now she beheld a young man who had just turned seventeen. "Nothing but the Eyes at first Sight appeard what he once was," she wrote.

"Oh my Mamma! and my dear Sister," he exclaimed, and Abigail marveled that his voice, like "his Stature," was that of a grown man.

As she struggled to express her emotions to Mary, Abigail evoked the two sisters' ongoing debate (of which there is no earlier evidence) about Abigail's fascination with sensibility. "I think you do not approve the word *feelings*," she wrote, "but I know not what to Substitute in lieu, or even to discribe mine."

Abigail made no effort at all to depict her reunion with her husband a week later, but Nabby did. She noted in her journal that she spent the morning of Saturday, August 7, exploring London and returned at noon. "When I entered, I saw upon the table a hat with two books in it; every thing around appeared altered, without my knowing in what particular," she wrote.

"Has mamma received letters, that have determined her departure?" she asked the servant Esther Field. "When does she go?"

Esther could not resist the temptation to prolong the suspense: "No, ma'am, she has received no letter, but goes to-morrow morning."

Well, then, Nabby asked, "Why is all this appearance of strangeness? Whose hat is that in the other room?"

Then she answered her own question. "It is my father's. . . . Where is he?"

"In the room above."

Exhausted from his overnight journey, John had lain down for a nap. Nabby knocked softly and entered the chamber, she reported, and her father "received me with all the tenderness of an affectionate parent."

John remained in London for less than twenty-four hours. By the time Nabby returned to the hotel, Abigail and the servants had already begun packing trunks—thus the "appearance of strangeness" that she had observed—and the whole family set off for Paris the next morning. At John's direction, his son had purchased a used carriage for the reunited family—and also a copy of Samuel Johnson's *Lives of the Poets*, from which they all took turns reading aloud as they rode along. The servants followed in a rented post chaise, and on Monday afternoon, they all arrived at Dover and embarked on a channel boat for the overnight crossing to Calais. The next morning at dawn, Nabby and Abigail finally set foot on French soil, and later that day the group began the nearly two-hundred-mile journey to Paris, arriving on August 13.

France, like England, was a very different place from what Abigail had imagined, but in this case that was no compliment. She had had high hopes for the nation that was at once the cultural capital of the world and the knight in shining armor that had so recently rushed to the prostrate Americans' defense. Disappointment crept up on her slowly, because she went a long time without meeting the locals. Unlike the British, the French were not permitted to call upon new arrivals until first receiving a visit from them. Although Abigail had been reading and writing French since she was a teenager, she felt so uncomfortable with the spoken language that she paid no visits at all. After four days in the capital, John moved the family to Auteuil, the village four miles to the west where he had rented a "hôtel" (large house). As she arrived in Auteuil, Abigail was able to report that she had still not seen Paris. "One thing I know," she wrote her niece Lucy Cranch, "and that is, that I have smelt it."

The Adams carriage pulled up in front of the Hôtel Roualt in Auteuil on Tuesday, August 17. It was one of the largest private buildings Abigail had ever entered. The members of the family differed over how many rooms there were. Was it forty or fifty? Three weeks after moving in, Abigail had yet to enter all of them. The woman who had never complained about feeling cramped in her seven-room cottage estimated that her new home could accommodate as many as forty overnight guests. And the surroundings were magnificent, too: the house stood on a bluff overlooking the Seine, and there were five acres of formal gar-

The Adams house in Auteuil, France. Fernand Girard, *Maisons de Plaisances Francaises, Parcs et Jardins* (Paris, 1914). *Courtesy Massachusetts Historical Society.*

dens. Eight years earlier, as a guest in her wealthy uncle's Boston mansion, Abigail had staked out a little windowed "closet" overlooking the garden and daydreamed about someday having her own "closet with a window which I could more peculiarly call my own." And now she did. In one of her first letters from France, she described the setting for her niece Elizabeth. "I am situated at a small desk in an appartment about 2 thirds as large as your own little Chamber," she wrote. "This appartment opens into my lodging Chamber." In fact she took possession of *two* such rooms—one for writing and the other for reading and sewing.

Nearly everything else about the Hôtel Roualt appalled her. She was responsible for managing the servants, who preserved the medieval custom of craft separation, refusing to do any but their own tasks. "Your Coiffer de femme, will dress your Hair, and make your bed, but she will not Brush out your Chamber," she explained to her uncle Cotton Tufts. "Your cook will dress your vituals, but she will not wash a dish, or perform any other kind of business." As an employer, she was furious that her eight servants' rigid division of labor forced her to part with so much money for so little work. All this idleness also offended her Yankee faith in the redemptive qualities of strenuous exertion. Nor did she relish having to tell her sisters, both of whom customarily got by with two domestic servants, that she had four times that number. Adams would have been forced to hire even more help if her American servants, Esther Field and John Briesler, had not acted in a "double and trible Capacity." But she feared that seeing their "lazy" French counterparts "disdaining to perform what they do" would give Briesler and Field "heart burnings." She did eventually convince the hairdresser to do some sewing and the maitre d'hôtel (whose "Buisness," she reported, was "to purchase articles into the family and oversee that no body cheats but himself") to act as a footman as well, but these seemed like puny victories.

One reason Abigail objected to having to maintain eight servants was that Congress had recently reduced its European envoys' annual salaries from 11,000 dollars to 9,000, and she worried that her husband's expenses would exceed his income. "I have become Steward and Book keeper," she told her sister Mary, "determining to know with accuracy what our expences are, and to prevail with Mr. Adams to return to America if he finds himself straigtned as I think he must be." Although too few documents survive to re-create the family's budget, Adams's anxiety does not appear to have been warranted. As grand as the Hôtel Roualt was, the house, stable, and gardens rented for only 200 guineas a year, which was less than a tenth of John's salary, even after Congress cut it to 9,000 dollars (2,250 guineas). Abigail estimated that the family's living expenses (including rent and everything else she could think of) would add up to somewhere between 600 and 700 guineas per year—roughly a third of what her husband earned. To be sure, there would be other necessary expenditures. For instance, the Adamses would have to host at least a few "entertainments," which could cost up to 60 guineas each. But there was little real danger of his expenses exceeding his income.

As she had in England, Adams judged everything in Paris and Auteuil by the Massachusetts standard. Initially, at least, she could not find a single area where France excelled. Water would have ruined the Hôtel Roualt's tile floors, so instead they had to be waxed and polished—by a method that astonished and amused her. "A Man Servant with foot Brushes drives round Your room danceing here, and there," she wrote. The *frotteur* (polisher) was also responsible for emptying out the chamber pots found in nearly every room. Abigail had reconciled herself to the ubiquity of chamber pots in London, where there was no room for outhouses. Auteuil, on the other hand, boasted "plenty of land and places sufficiently convenient for Buildings," but "the fashion of the country" nonetheless required the use of chamber pots, "and against that neither reason convenience or any thing else can stand."

As Abigail slowly began to gather information—much of it secondhand—about the world beyond the Hôtel Roualt, she formed an impression of French society that was just as negative as her view of her servants. "Fashion is the Deity every one worships in this country," she told Mary, "and from the highest to the lowest you must submit." The two servants who had come over from Braintree with her initially refused to have their hair done, thus exposing themselves to constant ridicule from their French coworkers. "Ester had several Crying Spells," and eventually she and John Briesler gave in.

Whether Abigail compared France to England or Massachusetts, it nearly always came up short. The streets of Paris, like London's, were constantly bustling with people, but Londoners were out working, while in Paris "from the gayety of the Dress, and the Places they frequent I judge Pleasure is the Business of Life." The most decadent day of the week was the Sabbath, for "Paris upon that Day pours forth all her Citizens into the environs for the purposes of recreation." The nearby

Bois de Boulogne, Abigail reported, "resounds with Musick and Dancing, jollity and Mirth of every kind. In this Wood Booths are erected, where cake, fruit, and wine are sold."

Nor were all of the Parisians' pleasures so innocent. A friend of John's, an abbé (religious brother), informed Abigail that fifty-two thousand prostitutes had registered with the authorities. Marriages were often mere business arrangements, and in many, both partners routinely cheated. A proud Protestant despite her rejection of Calvinism, Adams explained the Parisians' loose morals by reference to their religion. "Whilst absolutions are held in estimation," she asked Mercy Otis Warren, "what restraint have mankind upon their Appetites and Passions?" To prove her point that the Catholic practice of granting indulgences encouraged the French to sin at will, she pointed to a counterexample. "In the family of Monsieur Grand, who is a Protestant I have seen a Decorum and Decency of Manners, a conjugal and family affection, which are rarely found," she wrote. But religion could not fully explain the differences between France and America, she realized, since Britain was also a Protestant country, and London, like Paris, was a cesspool of vice.

Adams was nonetheless intrigued by the different forms prostitution took in the two European capitals, and perhaps this was one arena where Paris was superior to London. "Which of the two Countries can you form the most favourable opinion of," she asked Mercy Otis Warren, "and which is the least pernicious to the morals?" Was it France, "where vice is Licenced," or Britain, "where it is suffered to walk at large soliciting the unwary, and unguarded as it is to a most astonishing height in the Streets of London and where virtuous females are frequently subject to insult[?] In Paris no such thing happens." Not only could virtuous women like herself avoid being propositioned on the streets of Paris, they also felt safer there. You can wander around the French capital with "perfect security to your Person, and property," she wrote, "but in London, at going in and coming out of the Theatre, you find yourself in a Mob: and are every Moment in Danger of being robbed." She was especially intrigued by the ubiquity of theft in England, where "Publick executions abound," as opposed to France, where both robberies and executions were rare. Perhaps, she surmised with no little cynicism, Parisians did not need to assault the propertied because they were so adept at cheating them. "With whomsoever you have to deal," she reported to Mercy Warren, "you may rely upon an attempt to over reach you." No one better demonstrated that truth than her own servants, who, as far as she was concerned, were all thieves.

As in London, the most negative impressions Adams formed in France were of women. Six years earlier, when John first arrived in Paris, he had been struck by the women's intelligence and wit. Not so Abigail. "The acquaintance I have had with several Gentlemen of this nation lead me to more favourable opinion of their exteriour, than what I have seen and heard respecting the other Sex," she told Royall Tyler in a September 5 letter. Much of Abigail's queasiness regarding Frenchwomen was summed up in the person of the Comtesse de Ligniville d'Autricourt, known as Madame Helvétius. She was a close friend of Benjamin Franklin, who had wanted to marry her. "She was once a handsome woman," Abigail had to acknowledge, but now "Her Hair was fangled, [and] over it she had a small straw hat with a dirty half gauze hankerchief round it, and a bit of dirtyer gauze than ever my maids wore was sewed on behind." Everything she did was appalling. At dinner, she was loud, she dominated the conversation, and her hands wandered from Franklin's neck to his hands to the backs of Franklin's and John's chairs. "After dinner she threw herself upon a settee where she shew more than her feet," sniffed Abigail. "She had a little Lap Dog who was next to the Dr. [Franklin] her favorite. This She kisst and when he wet the floor she wiped it up with her chimise." The only Frenchwoman of Abigail's own class whom she got to know during her first weeks in Auteuil, Madame Helvétius turned her against the whole tribe.

Nabby's initial assessments of France were as gloomy as her mother's. In Paris, she informed her cousin Elizabeth Cranch on September 4, "The people are I believe, the dirtiest creatures in the Human race." "If you wish to gain a higher relish for your own Country," she told Betsy, "I would advise you to visit Europe." Like her mother, she especially disliked the country's women. "I wish I could give you some idea of the French Ladies, but it is impossible to do it by letter, as I should absolutely be ashaimed to write, what I must if I tell you truths," she wrote. Increasingly, Nabby kept to herself, remaining at her writing desk for hours on end. When Abigail confessed to nineteen-year-old Pauline, her hairdresser, that she feared she would never master spoken French, Pauline replied that Madame would "soon speak French quite well, but Mademoiselle"—Nabby, whose hair she also dressed—"speaks neither French nor English," which is to say that she never spoke at all.

It was not just France that was bothering Nabby. Up until this time she had been careful not to acknowledge her affection for Royall Tyler in letters to third parties, even when corresponding with close friends such as her cousin Elizabeth. Upon reaching Auteuil, however, she wrote Betsy (in whose home Tyler boarded) pointedly asking her to "Remember me affectionately to your family—*all* of them." Try as she might to stifle it, Nabby's resentment at being separated from the man she loved came out in subtle ways. In a letter to Betsy's sister Lucy, she reported on the Adams women's efforts to conform to French fashions. Her mother had an elaborate new hairstyle, she wrote, and she herself was learning to squeeze into mantuas (gowns) that were, by design, too small for her. In reporting these makeovers, Nabby's pen failed her in a telling way. "My Mammas head is more Metamorphosed than any think elce about us," she wrote, "unless it is your Cousins [i.e., my own] waist which the mantuamakers have brought to a much less compass than you would believe it possible. The former, has not gained in point of beauty I assure you." It is highly unlikely that Nabby intended to inform Lucy that her mother had not "gained in point of beauty." Where she wrote *former,* she surely meant *latter,* which would have been an entirely conventional instance of self-deprecation. That she accidentally insulted her mother instead of herself may have reflected smoldering tensions. Nabby would have been even angrier had she known that she was the subject of three letters her father had sent her mother earlier in the year—and that her mother had suppressed all three of them.

CHAPTER 18

"This Money Which I Call Mine"

1784–1785

If Abigail was telling the truth when she claimed she never received the letter her husband sent her five months before she embarked for England—the one authorizing Nabby to marry Royall Tyler—then she did not learn of John's change of heart until John Quincy reached London and informed her that his father had placed two additional letters, also approving the match, on ships headed to Massachusetts. Abigail immediately dashed off a note to Mary Cranch instructing her not to forward this correspondence to her. Why revisit a decision that could not be unmade? Adams was eager to hear that her sister had complied with her wishes. But Nabby regularly read her mother's mail, so Abigail instructed Mary to place her note inside a cover that was addressed to some other person, then mark it with a secret symbol (□) before enclosing it in a letter to Abigail. Even if Nabby broke open the outer cover, she would have neither the inclination nor the nerve to peep into a letter that she thought was intended for someone else.

Meanwhile, Abigail's other sister reminded her of her own objection to separating the pair. Using Nabby's pen name, "Amelia," Elizabeth reflected in a letter to Mary on "the extatic feelings of a fond Lover, kept 18 months in fears, and doubts, and hopes and *dreams of fancied Happiness*," only "To be told—to be assured 'Amelia shall be thine. We shall return.' It was too much."

Unbeknownst to her aunt, Nabby's pain at being wrenched away from Royall had, by September 1784, acquired a different character. Three months after stepping aboard the *Active,* she had not received a single letter from her fiancé. Shortly after she sent him a "scolding Letter," she finally heard from him, but the floodgates had by no means opened. As more and more ships arrived with no letters from Royall, she began to fear that he had lost interest in her. Perhaps Abigail Junior's growing anxiety about her relationship may help explain why she began to speak favorably of the French. Indeed she became convinced that in many areas, they surpassed her friends and kinsmen back home. "I have often complained of a stiffness and reserve in our circles in America, that was disagreeable. . . . [A] little French ease adopted would be an improvement," she wrote in her journal at the end of November. Over time, Nabby even edged away from her mother's negative evaluation of Frenchwomen and toward her father's more generous view. "The women universally in this country, and the ladies of education in particular, have an ease and softness in their manners, that is not found in any other country perhaps in the world," she wrote.

Abigail, on the other hand, never really warmed to the female half of the French population. Lonely as she was, she quickly abandoned any hope of surmounting the linguistic and cultural barriers that separated her from potential companions of her own sex. She socialized with Paris's small community of American expatriates—including John Paul Jones (who was much shorter than she had expected) and her husband's diplomatic colleague Thomas Jefferson (whom she described as "one of the choice ones of the earth")—and with a few of John's French friends, all male. A virtual recluse, she bought a pet bird to keep her company. Like many another long-term traveler, she lived for letters from home. It solaced her to know that her sisters lamented their separation as intensely as she did. Elizabeth discovered one sense in which she and Abigail were still together. "I looked up," she wrote, "and considered the same Sun, as guiding your Course—the same azure Vault bespangled with Stars as spread over your Head—and with pleasure I beheld the Moon walking in brightness, and fancied *you* at the same moment contemplating its glory."

Abigail's mother-in-law missed her, too. One day Mary Cranch dropped by to read to her from one of Abigail's letters. Instead of thanking her for the news, Susanna Hall used a classic New England colloquialism to launch a bitter complaint. "Aya," she said, "I had rather hear that she is coming home." Susanna turned seventy-five in 1784, and the anxiety that had always haunted her increased with age. She had recently gained weight, Mary reported in October 1784, and "She told me she had been dreaming that she was so Fat that she could not move herself. She really seem'd concern'd about it." Upon learning that Abigail had instructed Cotton Tufts to provide Thanksgiving treats to her pensioners (the destitute neighbors on whom she focused her charitable giving), she told Elizabeth Cranch that she "took it very hard that She was not among the number," for "She was sure nobody was poorer than she was." Surely, Betsy replied, Mrs. Hall would have been offended to receive a charitable donation from her own son. But she insisted that she needed help.

When Betsy reported the exchange to her mother, Mary immediately went to see Susanna to remind her that the Adamses had said that if she needed anything, all she had to do was ask. Hall became agitated, Mary reported to Abigail, and "said she thought very hard of it that you did not leave her something when you went away that she could have commanded and done what she pleas'd with." Abigail had in fact sent her sister some money to be expended on a special gift for Susanna, but Mary worried that making a purchase on Mrs. Hall's behalf rather than just giving her the cash would imply that Abigail did not trust her to make good financial choices, so she handed it over to her. Abigail approved the measure, and she instructed Cotton Tufts to give her mother-in-law a quarterly cash allowance to spend as she wished.

The Adamses had permitted Phoebe Abdee, Parson Smith's former slave, and her husband, William, to take over their cottage during the family's absence in Europe, and Abigail frequently requested updates on her "sable Tennants." Every report she received was positive. "Pheebe has been exceeding attentive to the Preservation and cleanliness of Your House and Houshold Stuff," her uncle Tufts told her in December 1784. About the same time, Adams instructed Tufts to give Abdee seven pounds of sugar and a pound of tea. "Let her know that I am pleased with her care," she told her sister Mary, "and that I send my Love to her and Respects to her Husband." Adams's affection for Phoebe Abdee was genuine, though she never called her anything but "Phoebe," while she nearly always referred to married white women by "Mrs." and their last names.

Abigail informed her relatives in Massachusetts that she was prepared to continue her charitable support of the Abdees if necessary, but Mary replied that they were unlikely to require much help, since they were growing vegetables in her garden and "almost maintain[ed] themselves by selling the produce." Indeed, far from needing assistance, Phoebe and William learned to their surprise that they were expected to give it. Several destitute families that were accustomed to receiving charity at the Adamses' door insisted that Phoebe take over Abigail's role as almsgiver. "They impose upon her sadly," Mary Cranch reported. It must have amused Abdee, who had been a slave only a year earlier, that these people, many or most of whom were white, saw her as a potential benefactor. And if Cotton Tufts is to be believed, neither Phoebe's lowly origins nor her continuing status as an Adams family retainer had transformed her into a humble supplicant. "I have now and then a little Trouble to keep down the Spirit of the African and reduce it to a proper bearing," he informed his niece in the spring of 1785, "but upon the whole I generally succeed." Through the thin veil of Tufts's racially tinged quip, it is possible to perceive in Phoebe a woman who was prepared to stick up for herself.

The news Abigail was most eager to hear was, of course, about her sons, who were boarding with the Shaw family in Haverhill. Elizabeth reported that Charles and Thomas were studying diligently under her husband's care and that she had enrolled them in a dance class. They "both dance excellently," she reported, "but Mr. Charles exquisitely. You know what an Ear he has for Musick, and that has been of Great advantage to him in his movements." The dancing master had even accorded Charles and Sally White the honor of opening the quarterly ball, and Aunt Shaw observed that "the Misses all like to have him for a Partner." Charles had developed a special friendship with one girl, Nancy Hazen, another of his aunt's boarders. Elizabeth assured Abigail that it was all innocent enough, but she predicted that her sister would still be concerned, and she was right. Although at fourteen Charles was three years younger than John Quincy, he was the one whose relations with the opposite sex most worried their mother, since his "disposition, and sensibility will render him more liable to female attachments."

With the exception of occasional death notices (Cotton Tufts lost his wife, Lucy, in 1785), the most depressing Massachusetts news Abigail received was invariably about her brother, William. The information was often as vague as it was bleak, and surviving documents do not even establish his place of residence. "We have no very good accounts" of him, Mary Cranch reported in April 1785. "Some people from the place where he is say that he is out of business and does not behave well." New England religious belief required William's wife, as a victim of misfortune and recipient of family charity, to be resigned and cheerful, but Catharine fulfilled the role imperfectly. Elizabeth Shaw considered her "ungrateful." Smith complained to Abigail that she had to serve as her children's schoolteacher, since "I have no schools to send them to." When Catharine received Abigail's December 1784 letter informing her of the strides Frenchwomen had made toward intellectual independence, she referred to men in her reply as "the Lords of the Creation"—a phrase that women of the time frequently used to mock masculine pretentions to omnipotence. "I realy wish that those customs you speak of were indeed adopted here," she wrote. "I have more reason to wish it than many others, haveing been too much used to be considered as a Species apart from the Lords of the Creation. There are very few but what wishes it, yet have not resolution to bust those Magick fetters which that tyrant Custom has shackeled them with."

It would not, of course, do to compare Abigail's marriage to her brother's, but that union also remained contested terrain in the mid-1780s. One question that was still unsettled when Abigail arrived in Europe was what role, if any, she would continue to play in managing the family finances. Cotton Tufts, who replaced Abigail as her husband's agent in Massachusetts, was in the ticklish position of serving two masters whose priorities often clashed. On September 5, 1784, John wrote Tufts instructing him to buy two parcels of Braintree farmland, one belonging to William and Sarah Veasey (this was the property Abigail had offered to help John purchase a year earlier) and the other to James Verchild. Adams only had three hundred pounds (sterling) to spare, but if both tracts could be had at a reasonable price, he was willing to exceed that limit. Abigail wrote Tufts three days later. She had no objection to his purchasing from Verchild. On the other hand, "Veseys place is poverty," she wrote, "and I think we have enough of that already." Tufts sided with his niece, not with John, and did not make the purchase. Abigail may or may not have told her husband she had countermanded his instruction, but on April 24, 1785, John started a letter to Tufts by repeating his earlier directive to buy the Veasey farm. Later in the same letter, however, John wrote, "Shewing what I had written to Madam she has made me sick of purchasing Veseys Place. Instead of that therefore" Tufts was to purchase two hundred pounds' worth of "such Notes as you judge most for my Interest."

The "Notes" that Abigail had convinced John to purchase in lieu of the Veasey farm were depreciated government securities of the sort she had been accumulating for nearly eight years, and Tufts wasted no time in making the purchase. Astonishingly enough, Abigail's redirection of her husband's investment in the midst of his letter to Tufts was not the boldest financial move she made in the spring of 1785. Two weeks after persuading John to amend his instructions to her uncle, she sent Tufts a letter of her own. John Quincy was headed home to Massachusetts to prepare for the Harvard entrance examination. He was going to bring along his mother's letter—and also fifty pounds' worth of Massachusetts currency. "With this money which I call mine," she told her uncle, "I wish you to purchase the most advantageous Bills and keep them by themselves."

"Money which I call mine"—an extraordinary phrase. Abigail knew better than anyone that the common-law doctrine of coverture prevented married women like herself from owning personal property. In the fall of 1781 she had nonetheless put one hundred pounds "in the hands of a Friend," and these were the funds that she later used to try to lure her husband home from Europe. Adams was by no means the only married woman of her era who acted as though she owned personal property despite being prohibited from doing so. But it was quite rare for a wife to insist upon her ownership rights. The use to which Abigail now put these funds was also unusual, for she wanted to speculate in depreciated government securities. Tufts bought the bonds, and he carried out his niece's instruction to "keep them by themselves." In reporting the purchase to her, he used language that was vague enough—I "have followed your Directions [by?] your Son John," he wrote—to permit her, if she so desired, to conceal the purchase from her husband.

Meanwhile Abigail continued to play an ambiguous and contested role in the management of her husband's property. In January 1785, nearly two years into John's land-buying binge, Abigail announced that he had also decided to purchase his family a new home. Royall Tyler had informed the Adamses that Thomas Alleyne of Braintree wanted to sell his house and farm. "Mr. Adams requests You to see it," she told Tufts, and "if it falls within or about two thousand pounds Sterling, he empowers you to Close the Bargain for him." Abigail confessed that the purchase had been her own idea. "It is a bold Stroke for a Wife," she acknowledged, but how could she, after living in a mansion capable of sleeping forty, return to the family's "small Cottage" in Braintree? If the family could obtain the Alleyne estate, maybe she could convince John to give up public service and settle down as a gentleman farmer. "I am very desirous of having it," she wrote.

The previous fall, when John had instructed Tufts to purchase the Veasey farm, Abigail had countermanded his order. Now, in the spring of 1785, John returned the favor. He learned, presumably from Abigail herself, that she had told Tufts to buy the Alleyne mansion. Unable to complete the purchase "without running in debt, or Selling my Furniture, or both," he refused to go along with it. The couple differed not only about whether to purchase the Alleyne estate but also about who had said what on the way to the thwarted transaction. In January, Abigail told Tufts that if Alleyne would sell for two thousand pounds or less, then "Mr. Adams requests You . . . to Close the Bargain for him." When John wrote Tufts in March, he did not acknowledge ever having desired to acquire anything besides farmland. "Mrs. A. I believe has hinted a larger Purchase," he told Tufts, but he himself had not. To hear John tell the story, his initial enthusiasm for the Alleynes' mansion was a figment of his wife's imagination.

Did John's veto of a real estate purchase to which Abigail was wholly committed mean that the two of them had swapped sides in their ongoing debate over how to invest the family's assets? Was Abigail now to be the advocate for farmland? Not really. What interested her about the Alleyne place was not the acreage but the mansion house. She continued pushing her husband to invest his surplus funds in government securities rather than fields, meadows, and woodlands, and the episode actually revealed a larger truth about the couple's conflicting investment strategies. "I love to feel free," John told Cotton Tufts, and the Alleyne purchase would erode that freedom by putting him in debt. Abigail also hated the idea of borrowing money, but not to the same extent. As with the family's investments, so on the consumption side of its ledger: she was much more willing than John to take risks.

On March 8, Abigail sent Uncle Tufts some reflections on her relationship with her husband. "Mr. A has been so long a statesman that I cannot get him to think enough upon his domestick affairs," she wrote. "He chuses I should write and think about them and give directions. Tho I am very willing to releive him from every care in my power, yet I think it has too much the appearence of weilding instead of sharing the Scepter." Adams's statement is remarkable on more than one level. She envisioned only two models for the management of the family's finances. One has the couple "sharing the Scepter." In the other, Abigail (reluctantly) wields power alone. The option she did not mention was for her husband to take full possession of the scepter—even though that was how, for centuries, every other household in the English-speaking world had been run, at least in theory.

Yet it is impossible fully to appreciate Abigail's commentary on the management of the Adams family finances outside of the context in which she wrote them. John had just dashed her hopes of replacing the couple's cramped saltbox at the foot of Penn's Hill with an elegant mansion. And in doing so he had humiliated her, making it clear to Tufts that her instructions were subject to his review and reversal. If there was ever a time for Abigail to worry about wielding too much authority, this was not it. And that raises the possibility that the anxiety she professed in the spring of 1785 was precisely the opposite of what she actually felt. Her complaint to Tufts about having too much power can actually be read as an attempt to persuade him that, despite John's recent veto of the Alleyne purchase, she remained a force to be reckoned with. In her March 8 letter to Tufts, Abigail insisted that despite what her husband had written three days earlier, he and she had actually been in complete agreement, both in initially wanting to buy the Alleyne place ("I wrote you by his consent," she emphasized) and in later deciding that the purchase would be imprudent.

One of Adams's greatest burdens during her time in France was the absence of any demand for physical exertion. For all her complaints about her servants, they entirely freed her from bodily labor. "We rise in the morning," she told Royall Tyler, but "not quite so early as I used to when I provided the turkies and Geese we used to Feast upon." If Adams had had female friends or if the streets of Auteuil had been cleaner, she might have gone on long walks, as John did. As it was, she told her sister Elizabeth, "I cannot persuade my self to walk an hour in the day in a long entry which we have merely for exercise, and as to the Streets they are continually a Quagmire; no walking there without Boots or Wooden Shoes, neither of which are my feet calculated for." The result was inevitable: "I suffer through want of exersise, and grow too fat."

Adams acknowledged only one arena where Paris surpassed Boston: the opportunities to see stage shows were limitless. When she arrived in Europe, she had read numerous plays, but she had never seen one, and her earliest impression of the French theater was mixed at best. "I go into Paris sometimes to the plays of which I am very fond," she told sister Mary, "but I So severely pay for it, that I refrain many times upon account of my Health. It never fails giving me a severe Headack." The more crowded the theater, the more severe the headache. One reason theatergoing was so unhealthy for Adams was that, never having seen plays before (stage acting having been banned in Boston), she was too willing to mistake realism for reality. One show she saw in January 1785 depicted "a terrible sea-storm," she reported to Hannah Quincy Lincoln Storer, a distant cousin:

> The rolling of the sea, the mounting of the vessel upon the waves, in which I could discern a lady and little child in the utmost distress, the terrible claps of thunder and flashes of lightning, which flew from one side of the stage to the other, really worked me up to such a pitch, that I trembled with terror.

Plays and operas that involved dancing presented a special challenge to a person who had always prized decency as one of the great female virtues. "The first dance which I saw upon the Stage shoked me," Abigail admitted to Mary:

> The Dress'es and Beauty of the performers was enchanting, but no sooner did the Dance commence, than I felt my delicacy wounded, and I was ashamed to bee seen to look at them. Girls cloathd in the thinest Silk: and Gauze, with their peticoats short Springing two foot from the floor poising themselves in the air, with their feet flying, and as perfectly shewing their Garters and draws, as tho no peticoat had been worn, was a sight altogether new to me.

Abigail could not bear to contemplate "the passions" that these sensual dances "must excite, and the known Character, even to a proverb, which is attached to an opera Girl." Yet her scruples collapsed under the weight of the astonishing blend of sublime music, lithesome bodies, and sumptuous costumes and scenery. She labored to explain to Mary her growing affection for the French opera:

> Conceive a highly decorated building filled with Youth, Beauty, Grace, ease, clad in all the most pleasing and various ornaments of Dress which fancy can form; these objects Singing like Cherubs to the best tuned instruments most skilfully handled, the softest tenderest Strains, every attitude corresponding with the musick, full of the God or Goddess whom they celebrate, the female voices accompanied by an equal number of Adonises.

Adams told her sister that "Repeatedly seeing these Dances has worn of[f] that disgust which I first felt." Actually, she had not so much inured herself to the opera as been seduced by it. And by winter she was finding other aspects of France more appealing, too. Most significantly, she finally found a companion from among the ranks of the nation's women. In November, the Marquis de Lafayette and his wife made their annual move from their country house to Paris, and in time Abigail and the marquise became friends. Then, just as Abigail was beginning to appreciate Paris, John got his marching orders. All through the winter of 1784–1785, British diplomatic officials had been telling the members of the American trade commission that any negotiations would have to be carried out in England. On the evening of April 26, Adams received a still more definitive call to London: Congress had dissolved the commercial commission, naming him as its sole trade representative to Britain. The delegates had also designated John the nation's first minister (ambassador) to the Court of St. James's. He was to repair to London at once.

The task of supervising the servants as they packed the Adamses' belongings of course fell to Abigail. John Quincy left the Hôtel Roualt a week before his sister and parents and took a different route, for he was headed not to England but home to Massachusetts, where he would spend a year with his uncle Shaw preparing for Harvard. On the twentieth of May, Abigail had the household ready to move. Despite all the battles she had waged against her servants, she had warmed to them, and it was a painful farewell. There was one last hitch. When her pet bird was lifted into the carriage, it became frantic. Had she insisted on carrying it with her, she later told Thomas Jefferson, "the poor thing would have flutterd itself to death." So she handed its cage out to Pauline, the young Parisienne who had been her chambermaid, and they were off. Soon Adams would be recalling for Jefferson the common saying "that nobody ever leaves Paris but with a degree of tristeness." On the packet boat over to England, Abigail related the loss of her bird to a fellow passenger, and he felt so sorry for her that he insisted she accept a pair of songbirds he happened to have with him.

CHAPTER 19

"Honour, Honour, Is at Stake"

1785–1786

The Adamses arrived in London on May 28 and took rooms at a hotel in Westminster. Abigail immediately began the search for permanent lodgings, taking time out, however, to make and receive numerous social calls. A week after reaching England, she ventured out to Westminster Abbey for a benefit performance of Handel's *Messiah*. "It was Sublime beyond description," she told Jefferson. "I should have sometimes fancied myself amongst a higher order of Beings." During the Hallelujah chorus, she informed Betsy Cranch, the musicians and "the whole assembly rose. . . . Only conceive six hundred voices and instruments perfectly chording in one word and one sound!" Adams was, she declared, "one continued shudder from the beginning to the end of the performance." All that marred her pleasure was "a very troublesome female, who was unfortunately seated behind me; and whose volubility not all the powers of Musick could still."

Less than a month after their arrival in England, the Adamses were presented to King George III and Queen Charlotte. It was not a mere matter of John bringing his family to the throne room for an official welcome. Nabby and her parents were invited to a packed reception where they had to stand around for four hours waiting before the king and queen, circulating in opposite directions, finally reached them. The king arrived first. Somewhat to Abigail's disappointment, he was effusively polite to her and tried to make small talk. He "asked me if I had taken a walk to day," she later reported to Mary. "I could have told his Majesty that I had been all the morning prepareing to wait upon him, but I replied, no Sire."

"Why dont you love walking says he?" and Abigail "answerd that I was rather indolent in that respect. He then Bow'd and past on."

It was another two hours before Queen Charlotte and her retinue made their way around to the Adamses. She "was evidently embarrased when I was presented to her," Abigail told Mary, and "I had dissagreeable feelings too. She however said Mrs. Adams have you got into your house, pray how do you like the Situation of it?" Her daughters likewise spoke to the Adams women "with much affability, and the ease and freedom of old acquaintance." Abigail had to acknowledge that the queen and her daughters were "pretty." As for the other "Ladies of the Court," though, she found them "in general very plain ill shaped and ugly." Adams's great concern had been that she not embarrass herself at court, and she came away feeling that she had acquitted herself honorably enough, telling John Quincy, "tho I could not boast of making an appearence in point of person or richness of attire with many of them—the latter I carefully avoided the appearence of, yet I know I will not strike my coulours to many of them." English gowns of this era were often festooned with trimmings such as flowers, gauze, and gold and silver foil, but Abigail assured Mary that her own dress was "elegant but plain."

The Adamses got a much less cordial welcome from the London newspapers, which drove Abigail to distraction with nasty "squibs" about her husband. One even attacked her. Mocking the United States government's inability to equip its envoy to the Court of St. James's with a decent conveyance, the paper joked that "hearing the Honble. Mrs. Adams's Carriage call'd was a little better than going in an old chaise to market with a little fresh butter."

After her presentation to the royal family, Abigail focused in earnest on finding the family a permanent residence. It would have to be elegant enough to advertise the respectability of the nation it represented, but the rent must not prevent John from finishing the year in the black. Finally she found a place on the northeast corner of Grosvenor Square. Nabby noted that the neighborhood was said to be "the finest in this *Capitall*," and Abigail reported that one of her new neighbors would be the prime minister who had lost the American colonies. The Adams town house was "*opposite* . . . to Lord North," she wrote. They moved in on July 2, nine years to the day after the Continental Congress voted to take the thirteen colonies out of the British Empire. In numerous letters to colleagues and kinsmen, John Adams professed satisfaction with his new quarters without bothering to say who had found them for him. The ambassador's wife was only too happy to manage the search, and she made sure that she would have in her new home, as she had in Auteuil, her "own little writing room."

Shortly after the Adamses moved to Grosvenor Square, Abigail was blindsided by an extraordinary—and mortifying—case of mistaken identity. One day William Stephens Smith, her husband's new secretary, asked to see her. It seems he was being pursued for a debt he did not owe. Shortly after arriving in London to begin his work for John Adams, Colonel Smith had received a letter from a man named George Erving. Observing that Smith's new position was presumably a lucrative one, Erving rejoiced that the colonel would finally be able to pay off his creditors. Smith owed Erving a large sum as a result of a failed commercial endeavor, and since Erving stood in great need of the money, he hoped Smith would send it to him at once.

But Colonel Smith had never heard of George Erving. At the time of

Colonel William Stephens Smith (1755–1816), who married Abigail's daughter, Abigail Junior (known in her youth as Nabby), on June 11, 1786. Mather Brown, 1786. *Courtesy Adams National Historical Park.*

his alleged commercial failure, Smith had actually still been in college. Moreover, he had never owed anyone as much as one-fourth of the sum that Erving now demanded. Who was this man who accused him of failing in business and then shamefully dodging his creditors? Smith began reading Erving's letter out loud to Abigail. "The Col. had not gone half through his Letter before I was sensible who was meant," she told Mary, "and he would have seen my agitation if he had look up; I did not know what to say." Hardly anyone in London, and least of all her husband's new secretary, knew that Abigail had a brother whose first name was William, for none of the Adamses ever spoke of him. "When I had a little recoverd myself," Abigail recalled later, "I told him I could explain the matter to him." In order to give Smith the information he needed to get rid of George Erving, she was forced to tell him the whole story of her brother's descent into alcoholism and financial ruin.

What made Abigail's conversation with Colonel Smith all the more humiliating for her was that by this time, he had begun to figure in an even more dramatic narrative, one that held the potential to rescue her daughter from a disastrous marriage. Abigail Junior turned twenty on July 14, but she was in no mood to celebrate her birthday, for she was in an impossible position: honor bound to marry a man who seemed to take pleasure in the pain he inflicted by never writing her. Within a month, however, she would be free of Royall Tyler, and she would have a fair prospect of marrying a man who truly doted on her. Just how this transformation came about remains a mystery, for neither Nabby nor her father said anything about it in their letters home. For her part, Abigail described the departure of one fiancé and the arrival of another in great detail, but her story seemed to change every time she told it.

One day early in August 1785, Adams forced her congenitally tight-lipped daughter into a heart-to-heart talk. During the course of the conversation, Nabby asked her mother whether she thought a certain man—unnamed in Abigail's earliest reports—was honorable. She replied in the affirmative but went on to say, "I wisht I could say that of all her acquaintance." This was too direct a reference to Royall Tyler for even Nabby to ignore. Tyler had treated her shabbily, she acknowledged, but "a breach of honour in one party would not justify a want of it in the other," and for a woman to break off an engagement would be "committing an act of injustice." Abigail did not agree. "I said," she later told Mary Cranch, "if she was conscious of any want of honour on the part of the Gentleman, I and every Friend she had in the world, would rejoice if she could liberate herself."

Nabby could carry the conversation no further. "She retired to her Chamber" and returned two hours later, having put her thoughts on paper. She confessed that she had "too long" suffered from a combination of "fear, suspicion, doubt, dread and apprehension." The man to whom she had given her heart had made it abundantly clear that he no longer loved her—if he ever had. Abigail communicated the contents of the letter to her husband, who insisted on his own interview with Nabby, whereupon she confessed that Tyler's neglect of her was not her only grievance. She had sent him letters to forward to other people back home, and her friends and kin, acting under the incorrect presumption that Tyler wrote his fiancée frequently, had given him mail to forward to her. But he had detained both streams of correspondence, cutting Nabby off from her other friends even as he refused to communicate with her himself. Moreover, after being scolded for not writing more often, Royall had declared that he *had* sent Nabby numerous letters that must have miscarried. Initially that explanation was plausible and reassuring, but by August, Abigail and daughter were both convinced that it was a lie.

One reason Nabby had kept silent all these months was her conviction that her father, having gradually been won over to Royall, would now take his side. In that she erred. As a lawyer John knew better than anyone that a breach of contract by either party does in fact void the agreement. Passing over Tyler's failure to write—an infraction of which he himself had occasionally been guilty—he told his daughter that if she thought the man "capable of telling her that he had written Letters when he had not, he had rather follow her to her Grave, than see her united with him." That was all Abigail Junior needed, and within a few days a letter was on its way across the Atlantic:

> Sir
>
> Herewith you receive your letters and miniature with my desire that you would return mine to my Uncle Cranch, and my hopes that you are well satisfied with the affair as is
>
> A. A.

In later versions of this story, Abigail narrated a different set of events that, she insisted, just happened to coincide with Nabby's decision to break up with Royall. During the Revolutionary War, William Stephens Smith had served with great distinction, both in battle and as George Washington's aide-de-camp. In the spring of 1785, Congress named him secretary to the American legation in London. Abigail initially found Smith's appointment "not a little mortifying," since both he and his fellow secretary David Humphreys were members of the Society of the Cincinnati, an association of Revolutionary War officers that was alleged to have aristocratic pretentions. But then Colonel Smith endeared himself to her by refusing to wear the society's badge and by convincing Humphreys to follow suit. In June, when he welcomed the Adamses to London, Smith was almost immediately smitten with Nabby.

A single episode told the story. "Mamma and myself went to take a ride" in the family carriage, Nabby reported to her brother, and "Just as we were in the Carriage *Coln.* Smith came up in his Carriage with a General Stewart from America." The two men had come to visit John Adams. Abigail told Smith she had intended to ask him to accompany her daughter and herself on their jaunt, but she added that he was obviously unavailable, since "he had company." Whereupon Smith "ordered the Door opened and in jumpt telling his Companion that he would find Pappa at Home." Stewart went inside, "and we rode off." The amused Nabby had a pretty good idea why Smith had ditched his friend. "Perhaps you will say the Coln sacrifised politeness to Gallantry," she told her brother.

According to the senior Abigail, incidents like this one convinced her that Smith had developed a partiality for her daughter—and that he did not know about Royall Tyler. It was heartbreaking to watch William hover about Nabby, for, had she not already committed herself elsewhere, he would have been everything she could want in a husband. During the war, while Tyler was carousing his way through Harvard, Smith was (as Abigail reported to Uncle Tufts) exhibiting "his Bravery his intrepidity and his Humanity" on the battlefield. And unlike Tyler, Smith had a reputation for keeping his word. He was, moreover, "tall Slender and a good figure, a complextion naturally dark, but made still more so, by seven or 8 years service in the Field." Abigail took it upon herself to drop enough hints around Smith to provoke him to go ahead and ask Nabby her status. When she affirmed that she was, in fact, pledged to Royall Tyler, he was so disconsolate that he had to get out of London. He obtained leave from John to travel to Prussia to observe that nation's annual military exhibition. The former soldier felt terrible about abandoning a post he had only just taken up, but he affirmed (at least according to Abigail) that he "found it necessary for my own Peace." He promised Abigail that he would never again think of treating Nabby as anything other than a friend, and when he returned to London four months later, he was as good as his word. He did not even accompany the family on social outings. All this time Abigail was careful not to give him "the most distant hint" that the betrothal he so assiduously respected had actually been dissolved months earlier.

The story that Abigail told her relatives was not entirely true, for Smith did not actually flee to Prussia out of despair that Nabby was pledged to another. In fact throughout the trip he remained confident that she would one day be his, and a principal source of that confidence was the correspondence he received from her mother. "Time I dare say will extricate those I Love from any unapproved Step, into which inexperience and youth may have involved them," she told him in a September 18 letter. What, then, was the real reason for Colonel Smith's hasty departure? He needed to keep his distance from Nabby until an exchange of correspondence could put an end to her betrothal to Royall. "Untill that period may arrive," Abigail explained to the colonel, "Honour, Honour, is at Stake." One of the most dishonorable acts a young woman of that era could commit—nearly as grave as a sexual encounter with a man she did not intend to marry—was to break off an engagement in order to trade up. Such a transaction might earn her a reputation for "fickleness and perhaps infidility." If Smith were in London when Nabby broke up with Royall, everyone would suspect that she had severed the engagement not because Royall had mistreated her but because she had discovered that she could do better. So Colonel Smith had to be gotten out of the way. Despite what Abigail said in her letters home, he went to Prussia not to forget but to wait.

When Adams finally got around to admitting that Colonel Smith had fallen in love with her daughter, she repeatedly affirmed that his affection went unreciprocated until months after Nabby ended her engagement with Tyler. Not until July 1786 did Abigail Senior send Mary Cranch a more complete account. Shortly after meeting Nabby at the end of May 1785, Smith had noticed her "uncommon Sedateness." Without probing too deeply into the source of her melancholy, he had set about trying to cheer her up. A phenomenon best described by Samuel Richardson, that "the Grieved mind loves the Soother," operated almost immediately. Though Nabby could see no honorable exit from her engagement to Tyler, she began to view Smith's ministrations as "not unpleasing." This was the context in which Abigail forced her daughter into the series of conversations in which she learned that her parents would stand by her if she chose to break up with her fiancé. And those discussions in turn led Nabby to send Tyler his "final dismission." In the middle of September 1785—months before Abigail was willing to acknowledge that her daughter had any interest in Colonel Smith—Nabby sent John Quincy some philosophical reflections that she did explicitly link to her own situation. "No sooner than the Ilusion of one prospect vanishes," she wrote, "than we are building upon their ruin our future hopes."

During William Stephens Smith's long sojourn on the Continent (to John Adams's annoyance, he did not return until December 5), the ambassador's wife and daughter had time to enjoy London's cultural offerings. Abigail had just reached the conclusion that British plays were far inferior to those she had seen in France when she learned that Sarah Siddons was about to return to London from her annual exodus. Siddons, the foremost actress in the English-speaking world, was going to play Desdemona at the Drury Lane theater in Covent Garden. Her brother John Philip Kemble, heavily made up to appear African, would be Othello. Abigail noted that Kemble usually played opposite his sister, allowing the married woman to act in romantic situations without scandal.

Shakespeare's play breathes contempt for the characters who hate and fear the Moorish general because of the color of his skin, but those were the very characters upon whom Abigail patterned her own reaction to *Othello*. "I lost much of the pleasure of the play, from the Sooty appearence of the Moor," she told her sister Elizabeth. "I could not Seperate the affrican coulour from the man, nor prevent that disgust and horrour which filld my mind every time I saw him touch the Gentle Desdemona." In the play, Desdemona's father, Brabantio, conjectures that Othello must have used some magic potion to induce her to "fall in love with what she feared to look on," and in a letter to Colonel Smith, Adams said she thought maybe Brabantio was right. How could Abigail, a fervent opponent of slavery who repeatedly asked after Phoebe Abdee in her letters home, react so negatively to Shakespeare's interracial romance? The comments she sent Colonel Smith are all the more perplexing in light of the very next topic she broached in the same letter. Having heard that his traveling companion on his journey to the Conti-

Sarah Siddons (1755–1831) as Desdemona in her death scene from *Othello*. Abigail saw Shakespeare's play in London in 1785 and professed "disgust and horrour" at its focus on interracial romance. *Bell's Edition of Shakspere* (20 vols.; London, 1788), 19: between pages 126 and 127.

nent, a Spanish army officer named Francisco de Miranda, was bigoted against the French, she ventured to remind both men that "The liberal mind regards not . . . what *coulour* or *complexion* the Man is of." Adams was troubled by her feelings toward Othello, who had, after all, proven himself "Manly open generous and noble." Where her revulsion came from—"Whether it arises from the prejudices of Education or from a real natural antipathy"—she confessed she was unable to determine.

Nabby's relatives back in Massachusetts were astonished to learn that she had jilted Royall Tyler, but they were pleased, too. Mary Cranch, who had been one of the principal sources of the unflattering reports on Tyler's behavior, now revealed that she actually knew even more than she had told. It was only out of fear of "making mischief" that she had withheld some of the worst rumors. For instance, Royall had trumpeted his success at winning his fiancée's heart by showing her letters to other people—an unpardonable breach. And he had compounded his failure to write Nabby by bragging about it. She was crazy about him, he wanted people to know, but he could take her or leave her. Although the initial response to Nabby's decision to leave Royall was positive, her mother launched a campaign to stamp out any suggestion that she had been fickle. To anyone who would listen, she insisted that it was not her daughter but Tyler who had, through his actions, broken off the engagement.

By January 1786, five months after Nabby dismissed Royall, she and her mother were ready to disclose that there was a new man in her life. The young woman still could not bring herself to announce outright that she was once again being courted—not even to John Quincy, who was among her closest companions. So on January 22, she sent her brother a silhouette "of a friend of your sisters as an introduction to the Gentleman to your acquaintance and perhaps he may tell you the Whole Story."

The romantic machinations that agitated the house on Grosvenor Square in the summer and fall of 1785 did not prevent Abigail from carrying out her other duties. Before the year was out, she learned from her sister Mary that James and Mercy Warren were in financial trouble—they wanted to sell their house in Milton and move back to Plymouth, but they had not yet received an acceptable offer—and Mercy was unable to come up with a sum of money she owed Abigail. Mercy offered to pay the debt (which may have stemmed from her wartime labors as Abigail's commercial agent) with linen, and her old friend agreed to this arrangement. Learning about the Warrens' financial straits only amplified Adams's worries about her own family's situation. She was stunned by the high cost of living in London, and she compared notes with Thomas Jefferson, John's counterpart at the French court, regarding which of their expenses to try to recover from Congress. Abigail told Jefferson she planned to ask for house rent, and he wrote back saying he would also seek reimbursement for "court taxes"—the numerous tips that every diplomat had to fork over to the king's servants upon arrival at court and again every year at Christmastime.

On February 9, the Adams family was invited to St. James Palace for the queen's forty-second birthday. Charlotte had actually been born in May, but every year her birthday celebration was pushed back to February so as not to conflict with her husband's. Both Adams women wore satin gowns trimmed with crepe. Abigail's was bright green with gold fringe; Nabby's was pink with silver fringe. John's secretary David Humphreys escorted them—a violation of local mores, Nabby observed, for in England "the attendance of a Gentleman" was "Considered almost unpolite." Indeed, she told John Quincy, Englishwomen "assume all the Roughness, and Assureance necessary to support them upon every occasion, and in General I think they look like Giant apes." Scarcely had the two Abigails arrived in the king's drawing room when they noticed a crowd gathered around another of the guests. Nabby took him to be Joseph Brant, the Mohawk Indian chief against whom Colonel Smith had launched an expedition during the Revolutionary War. "It is a matter of speculation what can be his erand here at present," she wrote. Brant had in fact come to London to solicit British aid for a coalition of Indians that was endeavoring to resist United States encroachments on their land, but the turbaned diplomat standing before Nabby and Abigail was actually Tripoli's envoy to Great Britain. "I was absolutely frightened," Nabby wrote. By pushing their way through the great crush of well-wishers, she reported, she and her mother successfully "situated ourselvs, so that the King spoke to us very soon." It took them much longer to pay their respects to the queen, and they made for the exit as soon as they had, as custom required them to return after the midday meal for the queen's birthday ball. During a minuet, Nabby had the satisfaction of seeing the Prince of Wales (the future King George IV) stumble and fall "flat on his back."

Few of the social events to which the Adamses were invited proved any more entertaining than the queen's ball, and many were downright unpleasant. Abigail was appalled at the English ladies' addiction to card playing, invariably for money. At one card party, she reported to Mary, "I was Set down to a table with three perfect Strangers, and the Lady who was against me stated the Game at half a Guiney a peice. I told her I thought it full high, but I knew she designd to win, so I said no more, but expected to lose. It however happend otherways. I won four Games of her." This was no fluke, for despite her distaste for games of chance, she observed that when forced to gamble, she had "usually been fortunate as it is termd."

Each passing week of Abigail's sojourn in Britain further convinced her of the superiority of her own country. In America, she insisted, the absence of great extremes of wealth and poverty (obviously slaves were no part of her calculation), the lower population density, "the equal distribution of justice to the Poor as well as the rich," the widespread adherence to the Golden Rule, the impartiality of public officials, and the prevalence of public education (for boys, anyway) all had the effect of schooling the citizenry in virtue. Americans, especially the women, were healthier than their British and French counterparts, too. The daughters of the European aristocracy were living proof that wealth was not synonymous with beauty. "Not all their blaze of diamonds, Set of with Parissian Rouge, Can match the blooming Health, the Sparkling Eye and modest deportment of the dear Girls of my native land," she told one of those girls, her niece Lucy Cranch. Adams was so disappointed with London that she even adjudged it, in some areas, inferior to Paris. Certainly French plays were better. A person who has attended the theater in Paris, she informed Thomas Jefferson, "can have little realish for the cold, heavy action, and uncouth appearence of the English stage." To her surprise, Adams missed the French people as well. "I feel a much greater partiality for them than I did whilst I resided amongst them," she observed in a letter to her sister Elizabeth.

Every ship brought momentous news from Massachusetts and teased Abigail's sense that while she idled away at the center of the world's greatest empire, life in the only place that mattered to her was passing her by. "I seem as if I was living here to no purpose, I ought to be at home looking after my Boys," she told Mary. John Quincy passed his Harvard entrance examination on March 15. Having spent the previous five months working his way through his classmates' reading list, advancing one chapter further than they had into each of the Greek classics on the syllabus, he would enter Harvard Hall as a junior. Abigail's pride in her son's intellectual accomplishments was chastened by concern over his ability to get along in society. "He is a good youth only a little too possitive," she told his cousin Betsy Cranch. Elizabeth Shaw had to agree that the eighteen-year-old was "a little to decisive." When John Quincy sent his sister an assortment of sarcastic remarks about the people he encountered on his return to Massachusetts, she urged him not to be so grouchy. "I think my Brother that you do not discover Candor enough for the foibles, of others especially the Ladies," she wrote. "A Gentleman who is severe against the Ladies. . . . is soon established, for a Morose severe ill Natured Fellow." If John Quincy was more accomplished than his peers, his mother reminded him, it was because he had enjoyed vastly greater opportunities. Do not be "too tenacious of your own opinions," she implored him.

As pleased as Abigail was that none of her closest relatives believed Nabby had acted improperly in ending her engagement with Royall Tyler, she was alarmed to hear of Tyler's reaction to the breakup, which was becoming more and more bizarre.

CHAPTER 20

"The Grieved Mind Loves the Soother"

1786–1787

Upon terminating her relationship with Royall, Nabby had asked him to return the miniature portrait of herself that she had given him. Tyler not only refused to give up the miniature but went out of his way to let people know he still had it. From Mary Cranch, Abigail learned of his tendency to "leave it in the Bed when he is upon a journey and lodges in a gentleman or Ladys Family. This when found and with the rapturs he express's and the kisses he bestows upon it, are certain evidences that he has not been dismiss'd." When Tyler finally acknowledged that Nabby had sent him a letter of dismissal, he insisted that it was all a simple misunderstanding, the product of false reports by some of her "D——sh relations." He would soon visit her in England and straighten things out, he said.

Chief among those devilish relations were the Cranches. Officially Tyler was still boarding with them, but they rarely saw him, for he had also taken a room in Boston, where he spent most of his time. On May 19, Mary received a length of ribbon from Abigail, and her daughter Betsy noticed that it was wrapped around a card addressed to the Adamses and signed by "Mr and Mrs Smith." By this time the family knew Colonel Smith was courting Nabby, and Mary and her daughters immediately surmised that Abigail had chosen this unorthodox method of informing them that her daughter was married. On an unkind whim, Mary and the girls decided to leave the invitation on top of the clock—the family's *"post Office"*—where they knew their boarder would find it. As he did, he turned to eighteen-year-old Lucy and attempted to make small talk about the weather, declaring, "'tis a very changeable time Miss L——."

"Yes *Mr: T*," she replied, "these are changeable times indeed." Tyler walked away, reported a delighted Charles Storer, "without an other word."

As more and more reports of Tyler's self-inflicted humiliation reached Abigail, she speculated that he would eventually feel obliged to abandon Braintree. Never one to miss an opportunity, she set in motion the process of buying his house. Of course the Adamses would be the last family to which he would willingly sell, so she instructed Cotton Tufts to have someone else approach him. It turned out that Tyler actually had no immediate plans to leave town, and in fact he seemed to be sinking deeper and deeper roots. He had his house repaired, hired a housekeeper, and even built a windmill.

The Cranch family's surmise that Nabby had married William Stephens Smith proved premature, for the invitation around which Abigail had unthinkingly wrapped Mary's ribbon had actually come from a different couple who happened to be named Smith. But London was, in fact, about to acquire one more Mrs. Smith. Abigail had labored to postpone her daughter's nuptials, but the eager Colonel Smith would not be deterred, and the date was set for June 11. Since dissenting ministers were not allowed to conduct the marriage ceremony, John had to procure the services of his friend the bishop of Asaph. Adams did not have to give away his daughter in an Anglican church, however, for he obtained special permission from the archbishop of Canterbury to hold the wedding at Grosvenor Square. The couple did not want to make a big to-do, Abigail reported to Mary: "they were as timid as partrideges, and would gladly have had only the Bishop present." But Abigail insisted on inviting a few guests, including the painter John Singleton Copley and his wife, Susanna. Since Nabby was a month shy of her twenty-first birthday, a notary public came around beforehand to obtain John's "attestation of his consent."

The night before the wedding, "Some evil Spright" caused Abigail to have a dream about Royall Tyler. "I have felt for him I own," she wrote Mary. The wedding ceremony commenced at 8 P.M. on June 11. The official Anglican ritual, which had been among the grievances that provoked the Adamses' ancestors to leave the English church, was "quite Novel to us all," Abigail reported, but her daughter "past through it with a good deal of presence of Mind." When New England couples married, all they had to do was assent to the minister's statements, but Nabby and William were required to repeat them. Abigail admired her daughter for correctly intoning "I Abigail take the[e] William" and the rest of it, but she nonetheless observed to her sister that this procedure was "rather more embarrassing than the curtzy of assent in the dissenting form." Still, she was grateful to the bishop for omitting certain portions of the Anglican ceremony that were offensive to dissenting families like hers.

"Any agitation of mind, either painfull or pleasureable always drives slumber from my Eyes," Abigail affirmed at the start of a letter she wrote Mary at 4 A.M. on the morning after the wedding. "Such was my Situation last Night; when I gave my only daughter, and your Neice to *the man* of *her choice*." There was never any doubt that the Smiths would find their own residence, but like many couples of that era, they did not immediately move out. They finally "commenced House keepers" on nearby Wimpole Street on July 1. The very next morning, John was at the new couple's door before breakfast. "Mr A commonly takes his daily walk about one oclock, but by eleven he came into my room with his Hat and cane," an amused Abigail told her sister.

"Well I have been to See them," he said.

"What," his wife exclaimed, "could not you stay till your usual Hour[?]"

"No I could not," John replied. "I wanted to go before Breakfast."

John's worries about losing touch with his daughter were overblown. Every day, she and Colonel Smith took the midday meal (called "dinner" in those days) with Abigail and John in their home on Grosvenor Square. Still, in the weeks after the Smiths moved out, Abigail made a determined effort to expand her social circle. One notable prospect did not work out. Since she was a young woman, Adams had admired the author Catharine Macaulay, and during the summer of 1786 she finally got the chance to meet her. The noted female historian had taken a second husband, William Graham, and the couple came to Grosvenor Square for dinner along with Mrs. Graham's daughter by her first husband; the Copleys; and a few others. Abigail had absorbed a common preconception about Graham that she was now pleased to surrender. The historian's "manners are much more feminine than I expected to find them," she reported. Yet the two women were not destined to become friends, because Abigail could not reconcile herself to Graham's decision, eight years earlier, to marry a man who was a lowly surgeon's mate and, worse, twenty-six years her junior. "Why why did she tarnish her lawrels by so Youthfull a connection[?]," Abigail asked Mary

Cranch. "The Gentleman looks rather young to have been the Husband of her daughter." Adams thought she discerned in daughter Catherine Sophia Macaulay a "very sensible mortification . . . at her Mothers Marriage."

During the summer of 1786, with John Quincy at Harvard, Charles about to enter, and Thomas about to apply, Abigail was struck by the contrast between her sons' educational opportunities and those available to young women their age. In July, when she sent the boys some science books, she urged her Cranch nieces, who had shown themselves to be "eager for knowledge," to study them as well. Of course, she acknowledged to Elizabeth Cranch, "A course of experiments would do more"—science can only be learned in the laboratory—"but from thise our sex are almost wholy excluded." Nor was Abigail alone in lamenting that Elizabeth and her sister Lucy would not achieve their intellectual potential. The girls' mother observed to Abigail that Lucy seemed less equipped for traditional female pastimes such as playing the harpsichord (as her sister was learning to do) than for pursuits that were barred to her because of her sex. "Her Soul is not tuned to Harmony," Mary wrote, but "to Science. Had she been a Boy she would have been a Mathamatition."

Mary Cranch's comment was by no means out of character. Indeed, on at least one occasion, she proved even more eager than her better-known sister to see the female half of the population step forward. In May 1786, Abigail concluded a report to Mary on various political subjects by exclaiming, "These are droll subjects for one Lady to write to an other upon." Mary replied that the wives of public officials—her own husband was a state senator—actually had a duty to educate themselves about public affairs. "Ask no excuse my dear Sister for writing Politicks," she wrote. Indeed, she declared, the nation could not erase its trade deficit or escape the massive burden of private debt unless women returned to the frugal habits that had figured so prominently in the success of the American Revolution. "Let no one say that the Ladies are of no importance in the affairs of the nation," Cranch wrote. "Perswaide them to renounce all their Luxirys and it would be found that they are, and beleive me there is not a more affectual way to do it, than to make them acquainted with the causes of the distresses of thier country."

The imperative for women as well as men to renounce luxury only increased during the mid-1780s as Massachusetts and its twelve sister states slipped deeper and deeper into recession. When Abigail learned that a growing number of British merchants had resolved to extend no more credit to their American correspondents, she judged this a "fortunate circumstance" that would force Americans into the frugal habits they had failed to adopt on their own. For many Massachusetts citizens, the financial burden became unbearable in March 1786, when the state assembly adopted the heaviest tax any of them had ever seen. Abigail's correspondent Thomas Welsh rejoiced that the assembly had "taxed smartly," since there was no other way to pay down either the state government's enormous debt or Massachusetts's portion of federal obligations. Surely the state and Continental bondholders (including the Adamses) needed to be paid, but would farmers who were already staggering under the weight of accumulated back taxes as well as massive private debts be able to absorb this enormous new tax as well?

As Adams waited for these political issues to resolve themselves, she continued to pump her correspondents for reaction to her daughter's split with Royall Tyler. Although nearly everyone continued to side with Nabby, one prominent family did not. Tyler's Boston landlords were Joseph Palmer (who was Richard Cranch's nephew) and his wife, Elizabeth. As he passed more and more time with the Palmers, he won them to his way of thinking about the breakup. "When I was at a certain house in Boston the other day," Mary reported to Abigail at the end of September, "I was attack'd upon the Subject of my Niece's conduct. Many Slighty things were said" about her new husband, whom Elizabeth Palmer's brother and sister claimed to know. "I felt angry and spoke my mind very plainly," Mary wrote. She had no doubt that everything she said to her niece by marriage would immediately be communicated to Tyler himself, so she had no compunction about reconstructing her conversation with Elizabeth in a letter to Abigail. Mary's transcription provides a rare glimpse into the everyday exchanges of an era that predated the invention of recorded audio. Mary opened by criticizing Tyler's failure to correspond with his fiancée.

PALMER: If he was to blame for neglecting her so long he wrote her a long letter in vindication of himself.

CRANCH: And at my expence as well as that of others of her correspondence who never mention'd his name.

PALMER: Why he thought somebody must have been enjuring him so[.] She never would have treated him in such a manner only for not writing to her.

CRANCH: That was not all, and he knows it.

PALMER: Well he has Suffer'd for it I am sure, poor creature. He had nobody but me to open his mind too. . . . She has not better'd herself by what I can hear: my Brother and Sister know [William Stephens Smith], and say he is a man of no abilities and is of no profession.

Only a few weeks after Abigail learned of Elizabeth Palmer's unkind reflections on her daughter and son-in-law, she heard a devastating rumor about Palmer herself. Apparently Samuel Richardson's saying that "the Grieved mind loves the Soother" operated as effectively within the Palmer household as it did on Grosvenor Square. In the course of consoling Royall Tyler on the loss of his fiancée, the married Elizabeth had herself apparently fallen for him. Mary's suspicion that the relationship between the landlady and her boarder had exceeded the bounds of propriety was first aroused when, by some means or another, she saw a letter Elizabeth had written Royall. "What can we do[?]" she asked him. "I know you would help me if you could. Come to me immediately." Still more convincing proof followed in September, when Elizabeth was faced with the task of convincing her husband that the "large and Strong" child born to her on the second day of the month—five months after Joseph's return from a seven-month business trip—was in fact his.

The newborn was the subject "of So much Speculatin," Mary told Abigail, "that I was determin'd to see it. I went with trembling Steps, and could not tell whether I should have courage enough to see it till I had Knock'd at the Door." Joseph Palmer let her in and escorted her upstairs, where Elizabeth "was seting by the side of the Bed suckling her Infant." Nearby, "with one sliper off, and one foot just step'd into the other," sat Royall Tyler. "There appear'd the most perfect harmony between all three" of them, she wrote. It is possible that Mary's anger—at Royall for blaming his rupture with Nabby on her and at Elizabeth for siding with Royall—caused her to distort the events surrounding the birth of little Sophia Palmer. But it must be significant that years later, Sophia would be shipped off to Vermont to live with her big sister Mary and Mary's husband, Royall Tyler.

At about the same time that Abigail received her sister's update on the Royall Tyler saga, she also obtained an unsatisfactory report on Phoebe and William Abdee. Up until this time Mary's only complaint about the Abdees had been that they had allowed several rooms in the Adams cottage to become damp, which fostered mold and caused the wallpaper to peel. But they could hardly be blamed for that, since the only way to keep the house dry was to heat every room all winter long, and that required more firewood than they could afford. Nor did it bother Mary to see Phoebe "gaily dressd" at church on Sunday in a "larg'd figure'd callaco Gown" she had purchased secondhand. To be sure, Cranch was amused at the sight of her father's former slave "rig'd out in her French night cap," but how she spent her money (primarily earned by taking in washing) was her own concern. The source of Mary's anxiety was that the Abdees had offered refuge to successive waves of "Stragling Negros" who had been "lodging and staying in the House sometimes three or four days together." Dr. Tufts and "I have forbid her doing it," Mary reported to her sister, "but there have been poor objects who have work'd upon her compassion sometimes." Three years after receiving her freedom and becoming one of Abigail's pensioners, Phoebe had acquired pensioners of her own, and she had continued to help them even after being strictly forbidden to do so.

To Mary's astonishment, the guests admitted to the Adams cottage included a young black woman, apparently pregnant, who was a servant of Royall Tyler. Tyler had promised to supply the Abdees with food and firewood for his servant, but he made an unsuccessful effort to keep the arrangement secret. When Tufts and Cranch learned about the Abdees' newest boarder, they "forbid her sleeping again in the House." The servant "was not a good Girl," Mary told Abigail, "and I did not think, your things safe." When Phoebe reported this instruction to Tyler, he replied that the solution was simple: "keep her conceal'd." Phoebe faithfully relayed Tyler's directive to Mary. "This rais'd me," she later reported, "and I talk to mr T about sending such creatures thire, for this was not the first he had sent. He deny'd it, but look'd guilty enough. She went of[f] att last, and poor Pheby got nothing for all her trouble."

Abigail had not yet digested the news of all these domestic broils when she received distressing information of an altogether different order: the farmers of western Massachusetts had launched a rebellion. Unable to pay either their personal debts or the massive taxes adopted by the legislature in March 1786, farmers pleaded with the legislature to make both tasks easier by printing up paper money. Nearly everyone in the state's political establishment—including both Adamses—saw paper currency as nothing more than a ploy by which debtors could defraud their creditors. When the state assembly refused to print money, residents of central and western Massachusetts resorted to violence. Participants in "Shays's Rebellion" (Revolutionary War veteran Daniel Shays was actually only one of the movement's many leaders) surrounded the county courthouses and forced the justices to halt proceedings. Closing the courts protected debtors from being sued, and many of the protestors viewed the siege of the courthouses as "the only means to Convence" state assemblymen "that We Need Redress."

None of Abigail's correspondents in Massachusetts sided with the insurgent farmers, and her sister Elizabeth was typical in comparing them to unruly horses. The lesson of the rebellion, she informed Adams, was that "The reins of Government must e'er long be drawn closer." Abigail agreed that the fundamental problem was not economic, as the rebels claimed, but political. In liberating themselves from the oppression of the British monarchy, she believed, the residents of Massachusetts and the other states had swung too far toward the other extreme, creating governments that were too susceptible to popular pressure. "Our Liberty is become licentiousness," she wrote. The farmers' grievances—excessive taxation, the dearth of currency, high government salaries, and the rest—"have no existance but in their immaginations," she assured a skeptical Thomas Jefferson.

Many of the Adamses' friends and relatives suffered personally as a result of the rebellion. Richard Cranch was a judge and a state senator, and he also did occasional work in the state treasurer's office. By the summer of 1786 the government owed him three hundred pounds' worth of back salary that it was not able to disburse for the simple reason that tax collection was so far in arrears. "If the People will not pay their Tax how Shall we ever get it[?]" Mary asked Abigail. Richard might soon be forced to "come home and go to watch mending and Farming and leave the publick business to be transacted by those who can afford to do it without pay," she wrote. Mary cited her husband's inability to collect his government salary as the reason she was "oblig'd to do what gives me great pain": charge the Adams boys rent when they stayed with her during Harvard vacations. Up until this time, she had boarded John, Charles, and Thomas for free as a token of appreciation for the many gifts their mother had sent the Cranches from Europe. "The dissapointment" at having to abandon this arrangement "Sinks my spirits," Mary told her sister, "and has caus'd me not a few tears."

As the rebellion intensified, tax collection virtually ceased in many parts of the state. That prevented the treasurer from paying interest on Massachusetts government bonds, and their market value steadily eroded. The owners of federal securities received their interest in certificates called "indents," which were supposed to be taxed back into the treasury every year. But with taxpayers either unable or unwilling to purchase indents, their price plummeted as well, as did the market value of federal bonds. Cotton Tufts, who had always encouraged Abigail to buy more and more certificates, was worried. Perhaps, he suggested to her, it was time for the Adamses to get rid of some or all of their government paper, and he pointed out that federal securities could be exchanged for frontier real estate. In an effort to reduce Massachusetts's quota of the federal government's debt, state officials had begun accepting U.S. bonds—at their face value—as payment for tracts of land in the district of Maine. Tufts suggested that this might be a good way for the Adamses to unload some of their federal securities.

Abigail did not agree. If the price of government bonds was falling, she told Tufts, then this was hardly the time to sell them. On the contrary, she informed her uncle on January 24, 1787, that she and John wished to purchase another £210 (sterling) worth of "congress Paper." "Do not be affraid," she wrote. While it was true that the federal government's credit rating was at a low ebb, it was "not yet so low, but what Foreigners are eagerly tho Secretly buying up this paper." All that was needed was patience—and a little pluck. "The paper of America will be redeemed I have no doubt," Adams told Tufts in March, "but one must wait for interest, & run risks, but at all events it will fetch what is given for it."

On January 24, 1787, coincidentally the same day Abigail wrote her uncle, John Adams tendered his resignation as U.S. minister to the Court of St. James's. It would not be effective immediately, for Adams gave Congress a year to find a successor—that is, if the delegates chose to replace him. He was not sure they should. There was little for an American representative in London to do, because the British were not interested in negotiating a commercial treaty with their former colonists. Why should they, when the low price of Britain's manufactured goods and the easy access to credit there already compelled Americans to buy most of their merchandise from the former mother country? By the fall of 1786, Adams was feeling increasingly marginalized. If he had a political future, it was back home in the United States. Moreover, all of his sons were in America, and all three stood at the threshold of manhood. They needed his guidance.

As far as surviving records indicate, Abigail had not urged her husband to resign, but she was thrilled to be coming home. Even though the couple would not actually set sail for another year, she immediately began making preparations for their return. It soon became clear that she and John would not be returning to the modest home where all of their children had been born. Surely they could have made do there had necessity required, but it did not. Despite Abigail's frequent complaints about her husband's low salary, he was considerably wealthier than he had been when he embarked for Europe on his first diplomatic assignment a decade earlier. In a letter to her sister, Mary Cranch offered a reason for the Adamses needing a larger home, a reason that neither of them wished to discuss. Surely John would still be "imploy'd in publick business when he returns" to Massachusetts, she pointed out, and the governor of the state could not possibly entertain his official guests in the little cottage at the foot of Penn's Hill.

As it turned out, a stately mansion had just come on the market.

CHAPTER 21

"Wisdom Says Soloman Maketh the Face to Shine"

1787

At long last, Royall Tyler had faced facts: Abigail Junior was not going to marry him, and he was never going to be a well-connected Braintree attorney. So he simply walked out of his house, moved to New York City, and never looked back. Having purchased the mansion on credit, he felt no need to try to sell it, and it reverted to the previous owner. Tyler had undertaken a series of ambitious improvements on the property, also on credit, and as soon as he left, his creditors swooped in, armed with legal writs, to recover what they could. One even took his windmill. Mary and Richard Cranch had once made an attempt to acquire this property, but now that her own family's finances had deteriorated, Mary hoped her sister and brother-in-law would buy it. The place was not in good repair in the summer of 1787, but the seller, Leonard Borland, having burned his fingers in the aborted transaction with Tyler, was highly motivated. If Abigail understood anything, it was that a person with ready access to capital had a tremendous advantage in an economy suffering from an acute shortage of circulating currency. During the negotiations over the price of the house, she suggested to Dr. Tufts that Borland might be "induced to take less for the money in hand."

Once the Adamses had decided to return to Massachusetts, they resolved to spend their remaining year in Britain taking advantage of its unique opportunities. Early in 1787, for instance, Abigail purchased tickets to a series of science lectures. Illness prevented her from attending more than five of the twelve sessions—on electricity, magnetism, hydrostatics, optics, and pneumatics—but these gave her a rare thrill, and they also got her once again thinking about women's education. "It was like going into a Beautifull Country, which I never saw before, a Country which our American Females are not permitted to visit or inspect," she told her nineteen-year-old niece, Lucy Cranch. That the management of the household would always be the woman's "peculiar province" did not trouble her. "Yet surely as rational Beings, our reason might with propriety receive the highest possible cultivation," she wrote. As the lecturer took his audience through an often stunning exhibition of nature's hidden powers, Adams undertook an experiment of her own, enumerating the arguments against expanding women's access to instruction in order to rebut them. Opponents claimed that educated women made unpleasant companions. Actually, knowledge would make ladies "more amiable & usefull," she contended, and "In proportion as the mind is informed, the countanance would be improved & the face ennobled as the Heart is elevated, for wisdom says Soloman maketh the face to shine." True, Solomon had also pictured the virtuous matron "looking well to the ways of her household," and the critics of the educated woman contended that she was "less inclined to superintend the domestick oeconomy of her family." But that claim was also untrue, for sending a girl to school better equipped her, once she reached adulthood, to manage her household and to "form the minds of her children to virtue." Solomon offered support for this claim, too, one of his proverbs having affirmed that "The virtuous wife should open her mouth with wisdom."

Girls' schools had multiplied in the three decades since Adams's own youth, but their emphasis was often misdirected, she believed. There was too much attention to "the form of the Body" and "the Grace of motion" at the expense of intellectual development. Adams's grievance against "the present mode of fashionable education" was not that it trained young women to be meek. It seemed to be designed, in fact, to give them "a conscious air of superiority" that she found troubling. "A Boarding school miss" who displayed "the Blush of modesty, or diffidence . . . would be thought quite a novice," she wrote. Young women were developing a false and inflated self-assurance based upon the most trivial of accomplishments.

The same April 26 letter that described those five science lectures also reported exciting news of a different kind. "I am a *Grandmamma!*" Abigail told Lucy. Three weeks earlier, Nabby had given birth to her first child: William Steuben Smith, named for his father and for Baron Frederich von Steuben, the Continental Army's Prussian drillmaster. "I already feel as fond of him as if he was my own son," Abigail wrote: "nay I can hardly persuade myself that he is not." Adams's reflections on the sacrifices her daughter was making for the child mingled sympathy and admiration. The young mother was "so good a Nurse," she observed to her sister Elizabeth, that little William "keeps her rather feeble than otherways." By the age of three months the boy was eating solid food and nursing only twice a day. "His Mamma I think looks the better for being a Nurse," Abigail told Mary Cranch.

Billy Smith was not the only child Abigail helped take care of during the summer of 1787. Back in 1784, when Thomas Jefferson crossed the Atlantic—only a few weeks behind Abigail and Nabby—he had brought along his older daughter, Martha, but not her sister, Mary (known in her youth as Polly and later as Maria). Polly, who turned six that summer, had remained with one of her deceased mother's sisters—until Jefferson decided to send for her. Few ships traveled directly from Virginia to France, so she had to be routed through London, and Abigail was asked to look after her until her father could make the trip across the English Channel to pick her up. Wrenched from the only family she could remember, the traumatized eight-year-old attached herself to Andrew Ramsay, the captain of the vessel bringing her across the ocean, and endured another agonizing separation when the vessel docked in London on June 26. In fact, as Abigail reported to Jefferson, she had to be "decoyed from the Ship, which made her very angry."

Adams did her best to soothe the child, but it was evident that she was out of practice. "I tell her that I did not see her sister cry once," she reported. "She replies that her sister was older & ought to do better, besides she had her pappa with her." Nor could Abigail cheer Polly up by showing her a picture of her father. "She says she cannot know it," Adams told Jefferson, "how should she when she should not know you." When Abigail tried to get the girl excited about how much fun they were going to have at Sadler's Wells theater, Polly replied, "I had rather . . . See captain Ramsey one moment, than all the fun in the world." Adams wrote Jefferson again the very next day, assuring him that his daughter's agony had "lasted only a few Hours." She insisted that "miss is as contented to day as she was misirable yesterday."

Polly Jefferson did not travel to London alone. She was supposed to have been escorted by Isabel, one of her father's slaves. But Isabel had just given birth in April and was in no shape for ocean travel, so instead Polly was given a different traveling companion, an enslaved fourteen-year-old named Sally Hemings. She was "fond of the child and appears good Naturd," Abigail acknowledged, but she was barely more than a child herself. Hemings (who was actually five years older than Polly) would be useless to Jefferson, Adams and Captain Ramsey agreed, and both thought she ought to be sent straight home. Jefferson had previously promised Polly that he would come to London to pick her up, but being too absorbed in his work, he sent a servant, Adrian Petit. For the child, the prospect of parting with Abigail rivaled what she had endured upon her two previous separations, first from her aunt in Virginia and then from Captain Ramsey. When Petit, who spoke very little English, reached London, Polly "was thrown into all her former distresses" and could not help "bursting into Tears," Adams reported to her friend. "She has been so often deceived that she will not quit me a moment least She should be carried away." Polly felt she had been cheated, and judging from Abigail's paraphrase of what the child told her, she thoroughly agreed.

> She told me this morning, that as she had left all her Friends in virgina to come over the ocean to see you, she did think you would have taken the pains to have come here for her, & not have sent a man whom she cannot understand. I express her own words.

Abigail pleaded with Jefferson to allow his servant a few days in London to get to know Polly before dragging her off. "I have not the Heart to force her into a Carriage against her Will and send her from me, almost in a Frenzy; as I know will be the case, unless I can reconcile her to the thoughts of going," she wrote. In this case, to request a delay was to insist upon one, since Jefferson's reply to Adams's plea would not reach her for at least a week. Four days later, though, Abigail learned that Jefferson's servant had already booked two seats on a stagecoach bound for Paris. Finally consenting to Polly's departure, she struggled to reconcile the girl to the necessity of the separation. "If I must go I will," Polly told her, "but I cannot help crying, so pray dont ask me too."

Most of the news that Adams received from Massachusetts during the spring and summer of 1787 was bad. Governor James Bowdoin had no trouble suppressing Shays's Rebellion, but his harsh tactics shocked and angered the state's voters, and in the spring elections they defeated not only the governor but the majority of the state House of Representatives and numerous senators, including Richard Cranch. The new governor was John Hancock, for whom Abigail and John felt nothing but contempt. From her relatives Abigail learned that the infamous demagogue's return to the governor's chair had earned him a new ally: Mercy Warren's husband, James. Mary Cranch was sure she knew the reason for Warren's flirtation with Hancock: he was in financial trouble, and he needed a government job. That explanation made sense to Adams, who was still waiting for Mercy to repay a debt she had contracted several years earlier. With disgust, Mary told Abigail that James, who had turned down numerous public offices back during the war, when his services were really needed, was now whining about being neglected in the distribution of plum positions. At a recent dinner party, the Warrens had had an exchange that was obviously intended to be overheard.

> MERCY: I heard a gentleman say last night that the reason you was so neglected was because you was so honest that you would speak your mind let what would be the conseiquence.
>
> JAMES: It is very true my dear, I *once* had the affections of this People so much & was so popolar, that I tremble'd for my self.
>
> MERCY: Could you have trim'd like some others you might have retain'd them.

Mary's pen dripped with sarcasm as she asked her sister what she thought of this "modest conversation."

The Warrens' play for political preferment was not the only factor that alienated them from many of Abigail's set. According to Mary Cranch, Mercy was trying to force her sons on Abigail's three boys and Mary's son, William. The problem, Mary said, was that the Warren boys were nothing but trouble. Winslow had been jailed for debt the previous fall, and his brothers were no better. Mercy did not know that Mary had implored her son and nephews to avoid the Warrens, but she took it amiss that Billy Cranch and the Adams boys spent so little time with hers.

* * *

The single most important occasion that Abigail missed during her time in Europe was her eldest son's graduation from Harvard. Every graduate's family was expected to throw a lavish party, and the combined cost of these entertainments usually exceeded a thousand pounds. In view of the recession, the class of 1787 petitioned the university administration not to invite the public to graduation. When the request was denied, no one was more disappointed than John Quincy Adams, who had been chosen to present an oration. It was not that he had any doubt about his command of the subject (which, appropriately enough for the son of a bond speculator, was "The Importance and Necessity of Publick Faith to the Well-Being of a Community"), but he did not want to face such a large audience. John Quincy and his brothers stayed with the Cranches during the weeks leading up to graduation, and Mary, whose son, Billy, had also been asked to speak, could not help being amused by the young man's anxiety. "My Nephew walks about with his hands hung down crying 'oh Lord! oh Lord—I hope it will rain hard that all their white wigs may be wet who would not let us have a private commencment,'" she reported to Abigail. "Be compos'd said I, perform your Parts well & you will find that the Honour you will gain & the pleasure you will give your Freinds will over ballance all the anxietys you have experienc'd." John Quincy had already fallen into his father's pattern: although irresistibly drawn to politics, both Adamses were more comfortable around books than people. "I fear a little that my Eldest son will be so much of a Book worm & Scholar that he will grow too neglegent of those attentions which are due to the World," Abigail told Mary on the eve of his graduation.

Aunt Mary had her own anxieties about graduation day, since the Cranch and Adams families were going to host a joint graduation party, and Abigail's absence placed the entire responsibility for organizing the event, which involved serving a full dinner to a hundred people and cake and wine to another three hundred, on Mary's shoulders. Some sense of the magnitude of her task may be gained from her report to Abigail that twenty-eight pounds of flour went into her plum cake ("& fine Plumb cake it was," she told her sister afterward in a rare boast). To help with the cooking, serving, and cleanup, Mary enlisted the aid of the Adams tenants, and Boston relatives contributed two servants (both of them black). Phoebe Abdee, the former Smith family slave, helped, too. "She was exceeding useful to me after dinner in washing up the Dishes & clearing the Tables," Mary reported to Abigail. The youngest of the three Smith sisters, Elizabeth Shaw, noted that Phoebe's husband, William, also attended the event. Elizabeth's portrayal of the Abdees savored strongly of her sister Mary's sarcastic comment on the fancy clothes Phoebe wore to church:

> As I returned from Meeting, passing the Colledge Entry, there sate in state our sable Domestic, accompanied by her solemn faced Partner, with his sabbath Day Coat, & tie Wig full powdered, looking like a piece of mock majesty. I could not but be diverted after Dinner to see him devouring the delicious Fragments, now mouthing a sweet crumb of Bread—now a fat slice of Bacon, & Tongue—now a rich piece of alamode Beef—& now a fine spoonful of green Peas—Lettice—Pickles &cc clearing Plate by Plate & handing them, to his charming dewy, oderiferous Phebe, who was so kind as to wash them.

Like his Aunt Mary, John Quincy received praise for his performance on graduation day, but even his relatives had to acknowledge that his classmate Nathaniel Freeman's oration had outshone his. Most people would of course have been thrilled at being proclaimed the day's second-best speaker, but expectations for the statesman's son had been high—and none higher than his own. John Quincy was miffed at the coverage of commencement in the *Massachusetts Centinel,* which declared Freeman his "indisputable superiour, in style, elegance and oratory"—and especially at the newspaper's observation that Adams had been "the favourite of the officers of the College," which seemed to imply that he owed the honor of pronouncing a commencement oration not to his own merits but to his father's exalted position.

Guests at the Adams-Cranch graduation party could not help noticing that John Quincy's brother Charles had begun to achieve distinction in a different sphere. For years now, members of the family had been remarking upon Charles's extraordinary sensibility and predicting that he would someday break female hearts. By the summer of 1787, when he turned seventeen, those prophecies were being fulfilled. "The Misses think Charles a mere Adonis—a perfect Beauty," reported Elizabeth Shaw, who warned her nephew that his pleasing physical appearance would subject him to "dangers, & Temptations." "Do not forget it is a Gift of Nature," she said, "& as it is not your own acquisition, you can have no title to be vain." Shaw hoped her nephew would aspire to be "admired for the more lasting, & valuable Qualities of the Mind."

By this time Charles was in love with one of his female admirers, as his mother learned after Mary Cranch and her daughter Betsy accosted Mary's "cousin" (nephew) on the subject.

"Why charles who is this divine creature who has made you look so languid," Mary asked him one day.

"Oh aunt," he replied.

"Oh Cousin."

"It is a Neice of mrs Williams."

"She *is* a pretty Girl," Aunt Mary allowed.

"Well," said Charles, turning to his cousin Betsy, "did you ever see such *heavenly* Eye-brows—& she is as amiable as she is pretty."

Sweethearts in those days often exchanged locks of hair, which they carried in special rings. Mary noticed that Charles had not one but numerous rings, and she pressed him on whether all of them contained tresses from Mrs. Williams's niece. "My dear have you left her any hair upon her head[?]" she asked. Cranch actually knew the boy had numerous girlfriends, and she teased him about the "great variety of shades & colours" of hair in his rings. "I fancy you are a general admirer of the sex," she said: "if so—your heart is in no danger at present." She nevertheless worried that Charles's flirtations would interfere with his studies. "I am always a little affraid my dear Nephew when I find a schoolars Pockits so full of hair Rings that his head will not be as well Stor'd with Greek & Latten," she told him. John Quincy advised his aunt not to worry about his brother. "He will get it over soon," he said. "I was so two years but I would study out of spight." Far from reassuring Aunt Cranch about Charles, this comment no doubt renewed her concern that John Quincy's personality had swung too far to the opposite extreme.

On the investment front, Abigail and Uncle Tufts spent much of 1787 devising ways to thwart John's desire to buy William and Sarah Veasey's farm. Tufts felt obligated to report to Abigail in May that William was eager to sell the property—and that he would probably let it go for considerably less than the three hundred pounds he had once demanded. But he added that he could not recommend the purchase, and Abigail thoroughly agreed. "What shall I say to you respecting veseys place?" she wrote Tufts on July 1: "counteract my dears Frinds plan, by no means. It has always been his wish to Buy that place, and he would have done it long ago if I had not persuaded him to the contrary. 300 is certainly 50 pounds too much as money is so scarce & the place so poor." She estimated that even at £250, the farm would produce an annual return on investment of less than 4 percent. Three days later Abigail informed Tufts that John had "written to you to request you to Buy mr Veseys but between You & I dont be in a hurry about that."

Mary Cranch agreed with her sister and her uncle on this point—"mr veseys is miserable poor," she wrote—but John was adamant. "My View," he informed Tufts at the end of August,

> is to lay fast hold of the Town of Braintree and embrace it, with both my Arms and all my might. There to live—there to die—there to lay my Bones—and there to plant one of my Sons, in the Profession of the Law & the Practice of Agriculture, like his Father. To this End I wish to purchase as much Land there, as my Utmost forces will allow, that I may have Farm enough to amuse me and employ me, as long as I live[,] that I may not rust, alive. You will therefore oblige me very much if you will purchase that Piece of Land and every other, that adjoins upon me, which is offered to Sale, at what you shall judge an Advantagious Price.

Adams emphasized that he was not being naïve about the capacity of farmland to generate wealth. "I know very well, that I could employ my little Modicum of Means more profitably," he wrote. "But in no Way so much to my Taste and humour." Five months after receiving this letter, Tufts finally capitulated and bought the Veasey farm. The price was two hundred pounds—a third less than what John had been willing to pay.

By this time, Dr. Tufts had also made another, far more significant, purchase on the Adamses' behalf. After much dickering, he and Leonard Borland finally settled on a price for the mansion that Royall Tyler had recently abandoned: six hundred pounds. Even before she learned that the sale had been finalized, Adams began making plans for the family's new life in one of the finest houses in Braintree. She asked Tufts to send her the dimensions of the rooms so she could purchase English wallpaper, and she consulted with him about repairs and renovations. Early in October, she wrote her uncle and her sister proposing to hire Phoebe Abdee to run her dairy. "I think it may with safety be trusted to Pheby provided she will undertake it," she wrote Mary, "but then she must have an assisstant. The Question is, can she get one? or keep one after she has got her?" Certain that her uncle and sister would approve of hiring Abdee—after, all, she wrote, "I do not know a more trust worthy Hand"—Abigail sent her sister "a pamphlet upon darying" to share with their father's (obviously literate) former slave.

On July 4, 1787, Abigail sent Tufts a bold proposal. "What do you think Sir of selling our House in Boston & investing the money in [government] Notes?" she asked. Tufts's relish for bond speculation had once matched his niece's, but he now believed she was getting carried away. "You enquire, whether it would not be best to dispose of your House in Bostn," he wrote. "I think not." Knowing how much Abigail loved government securities, Tufts did not try to persuade her that they would be a much riskier investment than Boston real estate. Instead he compared the value of the Adamses' town house to that of the farmland that he and his niece both disdained. Keep the house, he advised her, since "at present it yields a clearer Income than all your Lands & Estate in Braintree" combined.

On October 20, Abigail sent her sister Mary another of her periodic requests for information on their brother, William. "Where is our Brother?" she asked. "Is he in any buisness[?] I hope he does not suffer for want of the necessaries of Life, tho he has been so underserving." As always, Adams's principal concern was for William's wife and children. She suggested to Mary that Catharine Smith, who had "a large family of Boys," might be able to use the clothing that their own sons had outgrown. It would be weeks before Abigail learned that Mary had written her the very next day, October 21, to say that William was dead. After contracting "black jandice," he had received good care from the people with whom he boarded, Mary reported, and "he was so well three days before his death as to be able to do considerable writing—but of what kind I do not know." Years of binge drinking had, however, weakened his defenses, and he passed away in early September at the age of forty.

It took a month for news of William's death to reach his wife, a sure sign that by this time his wanderings had carried him a great distance from home. And yet his location is not indicated anywhere in the Adams family's enormous collection of surviving documents, and the reason is clear: the Smith sisters were so ashamed of their brother that their references to him were always deliberately hazy. Indeed, when Abigail responded to Mary and Elizabeth's reports of their brother's death, she referred to him only as "an other Relative." William's demise did somewhat lessen his sisters' reserve. Elizabeth Shaw expressed astonishment that Parson Smith's son could have turned out so differently from his daughters, seeing as how "The same air, *we* breathed—the same cradle rocked us to rest—& the same Parental Arms folded us to their fond Bosoms." Elizabeth's comment implicitly absolved her parents of responsibility for William's downfall, but Abigail suggested, as gently as she could, that in the boy's upbringing, "Some very capital mistakes were very undesignedly made." Surely if she herself—or Mary or Elizabeth—had had a child with a disposition like William's, they would have adopted "a very different conduct," she told Mary. "I say this," she emphasized, not in order to cast aspersions on either of their parents "but only as a proof how much the best & worthyest may err, & as some mitigation for the conduct of our deceast Relative."

The same letters that informed Abigail of William's death also brought word that her uncle Isaac Smith had passed away, too. While living in Braintree, the Adamses had stayed in Uncle Smith's Boston mansion on nearly every trip to town, and Abigail and her children had lived there during their smallpox inoculation. Uncle Smith had helped Abigail get her wartime import business off the ground, and after she joined her husband in Europe, he had taken charge of forwarding her correspondence to and from other relatives. And now he had died—but under very different circumstances from Abigail's brother. Whereas William had abandoned his family a decade before his death, Isaac's wife died sixteen months before he did, throwing him into a persistent melancholy that was considered the primary cause of his own death. William had spent his last weeks living in poverty among strangers, but Isaac died in his mansion surrounded by his children. But if William died a pauper, it would not be quite correct to call Isaac a prince. When his executor, Cotton Tufts, opened his account books, he discovered an enormous debt, somewhere between £6,000 and £7,000, to Champion & Dickason, a British mercantile firm. Two of Smith's children, Elizabeth and William, moved back into the mansion where they had grown up, along with William's wife, Hannah. But Dr. Tufts worried that the house might have to be sold, along with the rest of Smith's belongings, to pay off his massive debt. The property that Smith left behind included public securities that were roughly equal in value to his debt—at least on paper. Tufts told Abigail "there would still remain on hand some Estate to be divided among the Children" if only Champion & Dickason would accept these government bonds at their "nominal

Value." Actually, no creditor in his right mind would agree to such an arrangement, because the actual market price of the bonds, unlike their face value, was vastly below what Champion & Dickason were owed.

Tufts believed much of the blame for the sorry state of Uncle Isaac's financial affairs could be laid at the feet of the state and federal officials who had allowed the market price of government securities to fall far below the amount printed on their face. If the dead man's bonds had actually traded at their ostensible price, Smith would have been as wealthy as he seemed. In ruminating about how much better off the Smith children would have been if the securities could have been sold at their face value, Tufts, a large-scale bondholder himself, forgot one crucial fact: Smith had not paid full price for these certificates. He had purchased them with paper money that had depreciated even more than the bonds had. Had the government mistreated Uncle Isaac, as Tufts implied? Only by not turning the slips of nearly worthless paper that he had purchased during the war into gold and silver coins.

Shortly after learning of the deaths of her uncle and brother, Abigail received more bad news from home. Thanksgiving dinner at the Harvard dining hall had turned into a riot—not just a food fight but a sufficiently serious affray to cause damage to the building—and her two youngest sons had both been involved. Just what role Charles and Thomas played in the riot was never entirely clear, for the same reason that Abigail's letters contained little specific information about her brother: the topic was too shameful to be committed to paper. Although both boys were fined ten shillings, Charles had apparently taken a considerably more active role than his brother. In fact he was suspected of being one of the ringleaders.

One reason John Adams planned to return to Massachusetts in the spring of 1788 was his conviction that he could have a greater impact on his nation's future at home than in Britain. The events that took place between January 1787, when he wrote his resignation letter, and the Adamses' arrival on American shores a year and a half later ratified that assessment. In the summer of 1787, fifty-five of the most prominent men in the country—Adams and Jefferson were arguably the two most prominent exceptions—gathered in Philadelphia and proposed a radical restructuring of the American government. At the time Massachusetts was a sovereign state, as separate from Pennsylvania and New York as the United States is from Mexico and Canada today. The constitution that was signed in Philadelphia on September 17, 1787, would, for the first time, turn thirteen autonomous states into a single nation. Under the Articles of Confederation, Congress had had no authority to levy taxes, but now it would be able to do so. That would permit the federal government to field an army capable of defending the United States against future attacks from European powers (the British were still in Canada, and the Spanish still had Florida and Louisiana) and of defeating the Indians who were resisting U.S. encroachment on their land.

Since the new national government would also be able to pay interest on federal bonds and eventually redeem them, bondholders supported the Constitution in greater numbers than perhaps any other segment of society. That raises the question of whether Abigail's support for the Constitution (her husband also favored it, with qualifications) was influenced by the near certainty that it would guarantee her an immense profit on her speculative investments. That Adams was one of the nation's more active bond speculators is evident from her proclivity for peppering her unofficial stockbroker, Cotton Tufts, with questions, suggestions, and instructions. But if economic motives fueled her enthusiasm for the Constitution, they did so on too unconscious a level to have left a trace in the written record. Adams knew that the proposed restructuring of the federal government would benefit the bondholders, but she sincerely believed that justice as well as prudence required the government to meet their demands.

That the Constitution would be adopted was by no means certain. The proposal won the support of most of the men who had led the nation through the Revolutionary War, but it was fervently opposed by Patrick Henry in Virginia, Elbridge Gerry (John's friend and onetime colleague in the Massachusetts congressional delegation), and many others. One of the most vocal critics of the Constitution was Mercy Otis Warren, who published a series of anonymous essays contending that the new frame of government would turn the thirteen American republics into a tyrannical empire. Warren's opposition to the Constitution hastened her alienation from Abigail's social set, but the fact was that many of the people Abigail admired most were Anti-Federalists (opponents of the Constitution) or at least skeptics. Although Cotton Tufts would benefit immensely from the establishment of the new national government, since he had, like his niece, speculated heavily in depreciated government securities, he had serious doubts about whether the Constitution should be ratified, as indicated by the series of leading questions he sent Abigail. "Does it not favour too much of Aristocracy for future Freedom Quiet & Duration?" he asked. "Does it provide for an adequate Representation? Is the Executive sufficiently independent?"

Tufts was eventually reconciled to the Constitution, but Abigail had other relatives who remained Anti-Federalists until long after the document had been ratified. One of them, surprisingly enough, was her son John Quincy.

CHAPTER 22

"I Design to Be Vastly Prudent"

1787–1789

In the fall of 1787, John Quincy Adams was studying law as a clerk to Newburyport, Massachusetts, attorney Theophilus Parsons. Having devoted his Harvard graduation speech to the problem of public credit, he understood the state and federal governments' financial woes as well as anyone. Yet in his view, the various economic maladies afflicting the United States during the 1780s were less lethal than the cure that had been proposed in Philadelphia. John Quincy was especially concerned about the ominous differences between the new national legislature that the Framers had devised and the old congress under the Articles of Confederation. The state assemblies elected confederation congressmen to one-year terms but could withdraw them at any time. By contrast, members of the new House of Representatives would serve for two years and could not be recalled. True, the Constitution instituted the direct election of congressmen, but their districts were so large that ordinary farmers would rarely if ever be chosen. The entire state of Massachusetts would have only eight representatives in the First Congress. "It is impossible that *eight* men should represent the people of this Commonwealth," John Quincy wrote. "They will infallibly be chosen from the aristocratic part of the community." Adams worked out his opposition to the Constitution in an exchange of letters with his cousin William Cranch (Mary's son), an ardent Federalist who was serving his legal apprenticeship in Boston. Braintree chose Billy's father, Richard, as one of its two delegates to the state ratifying convention, where he enthusiastically cast his vote in favor of the Constitution.

* * *

In the three years that had passed since Abigail sailed out of Boston Harbor, she had formed a close bond with Esther Field, the Braintree girl who was one of the two servants she brought with her (the other being John Briesler, also of Braintree). But from the early days of their voyage across the Atlantic, Abigail had worried about Esther's frail constitution. She was, for instance, the last passenger on the *Active* to overcome her seasickness, and she had suffered from a variety of disorders both in Auteuil and London. But none of these was as serious as the mysterious illness that struck Esther late in the summer of 1787. By the first day of 1788, when Abigail reported her servant's condition to Mary Cranch, she worried that Esther did not have long to live. The doctors did not know what to prescribe, because they could not figure out what was wrong with her. Nothing seemed to work, though the paralyzing effects of the disorder had been "kept of for some time by Elictrisity." Abigail thought it was time for Mary to warn Esther's family that she might not make it. She added that the Fields should also be told that Esther had "been a Good Girl untainted by the vile manners of the servants of this Country. . . . I shall feel her loss most severely."

Early in February, the mystery of Esther's illness was finally solved. "She came in the utmost distress to beg me to forgive her," Adams reported to her sister. It turned out that she was not sick but pregnant. Field swore to her mistress that she had only discerned the true nature of her affliction a few days earlier, and Abigail believed her. The child's father was Esther's fellow servant, John Briesler. "Tho I knew that it was their intention to marry when they should return to America," Abigail wrote, "so totally blinded was I, & my physician too, that we never once suspected her any more than she did herself." A wedding ceremony was hastily arranged, so the child would not be illegitimate, but it might well be born at sea, for it was due in mid-April, and by that time Abigail expected to embark for home. When Elizabeth Shaw heard Esther's news, she reminded Mary Cranch that the young woman's mother had also been pregnant on her wedding day. "I think if there is a family Sin, every Branch thereoff ought to be upon the watch, & place a double gaurd on that Vice," Shaw told Cranch. "Why did not the silly Girl read her Bible, & be married before?"

Growing up in colonial New England, Abigail had dreamed of one day visiting the mother country, though she felt certain she never would. Now, after more than three years in England, her wanderlust had been more than satisfied, and she was ready for home. Her one great regret was that leaving London also meant parting with her daughter. For much of the previous fourteen years, the Adams family had been widely dispersed, with John traveling as far south as Baltimore to attend the Continental Congress and John Quincy serving his country in St. Petersburg, Russia. But through it all, Abigail and Nabby had never been separated. Now that John was giving up his diplomatic position, Colonel Smith, his secretary, would also return to America, but not to Massachusetts. He and his wife and son would take a house in the town of Jamaica on Long Island in order to be near his family. When Abigail wrote Colonel Smith's mother, Margaret, expressing confidence in her ability to make Nabby feel at home, she also took the occasion to warn the senior Mrs. Smith that her daughter was "a very Silent Character." For the first time ever, she also tried to explain why. Having lost her only sister when she herself was but four years old, "the Relationship of sister, is a character She has no remembrance of," Adams wrote. That, she told Margaret (who had six daughters of her own), "must in some measure plead for her Native reserve." She noted that this was one area where Abigail Junior was "very unlike her mamma."

Nabby herself professed to be less anxious about her own future than about her father's. John was only fifty-two, and for all the nostalgia he expressed for his days as a farmer and country lawyer, she could not imagine him ever again contenting himself with drawing up writs and supervising the manure spreaders. Although by mid-February fewer than half of the states had ratified the proposed Constitution (the most recent vote in favor of ratification—by the narrowest of margins—had been in Massachusetts), the rumor was already going around that once the new government was organized, Adams would be chosen as vice president. Nabby hoped her father would in fact win the post. "He would not I am well Convinced be Happy in Private Life," she told her brother John Quincy. Mrs. Smith's insight applied with nearly equal force to her mother.

John and Abigail finally set sail from Cowes on April 20 on board the *Lucretia*. After a tedious voyage of nearly two months, the ship finally put into Boston Harbor on June 17. Governor Hancock, either unaware of both Adamses' contempt for him or willing to overlook it for one day, arranged a hero's welcome for the long-absent envoy. Cannon fired a salute, a crowd of several thousand came down to the wharf to give Adams three huzzahs, and the governor sent his carriage to transport the couple to his home, where he insisted that they spend the night. The

Home where Abigail and John Adams lived after their return from Europe in 1788 and again after John's single presidential term ended in 1801. John sometimes called the place Stonyfield but more often Peacefield. Abigail died here in 1818, John in 1826.
Courtesy Adams National Historical Park

next day, John slipped quietly out of Boston, and his wife followed several days later.

Having spent two decades in Braintree, Abigail knew the Borland mansion well. Yet she was in for a rude surprise, as she informed Nabby in early July. "We have come into a house not half repaired, and I own myself most sadly disappointed," she wrote. "Ever since I came, we have had such a swarm of carpenters, masons, farmers, as have almost distracted me." Even more bothersome than the condition of the house was its size. Although more than twice as large as the saltbox cottage she had vacated exactly four years earlier, it was considerably smaller than her London town house. And compared to her mansion in Auteuil, it was tiny. "In height and breadth, it feels like a wren's house," she told her daughter. When you visit Braintree, she advised, "be sure you wear no feathers, and let Col. Smith come without heels to his shoes, or he will not be able to walk upright." Almost at once, Abigail began planning additions. "We must build in the Spring an other kitchen a dairy room & a Libriary," she told Nabby. To add to Adams's woes, as she

Abigail's kitchen at Peacefield.
Courtesy Adams National Historical Park

supervised the unpacking of her furniture, china, and other belongings, she discovered that the long and stormy ocean crossing had done substantial damage. In time John would give the mansion he had bought from Leonard Borland the name "Peace Field."

Shortly after her return to Massachusetts, Abigail learned that her daughter was expecting another child, and she headed down to Long Island to help out. Her husband stayed home, because the first elections under the new federal constitution were being held that fall, and John worried that if he got anywhere near New York, the seat of the old government under the Articles of Confederation, people would think he was advertising his availability for the vice presidency. In those days electioneering was considered unethical, and he wished to avoid any appearance of impropriety. Before his wife ventured south of New England for the first time ever, he gave her some unsolicited advice: she should leave her window open at night, since fresh air would help maintain her health. With this suggestion, John continued a friendly quarrel that had erupted early in the Adams marriage, when the two had argued about what to do with their bedroom shutters every morning.

Abigail suspected that her husband would have liked to have given her another admonition as well. The federal election might well be decided while Abigail was in New York. She would be a lot closer than him to the best sources of political scuttlebut, but in pumping someone for information, she might say the wrong thing. "I design to be vastly prudent I assure you," she wrote him. She would follow the old adage "hear all, & say little." Of course it was still possible that John might learn his political fate before Abigail did. So she sent him a playful plea: "I shall want to know a little of politicks." "I suppose you will tell me I have no Buisness" with political matters, she told her husband, but she manifestly did not agree.

Nabby, unassuming as ever, did not want to trouble her mother, so she gave her no indication that the baby was coming soon, and John Adams Smith arrived before his grandmother did. Nabby had not even wanted to bother her sisters-in-law, most of whom lived nearby, with the result that she had no relatives and no professional midwife to assist with the delivery. "A Negro Woman whom she has was obliged to officiate for her," Abigail informed Mary Cranch after arriving at her daughter's bedside. "Happily she had on some former occasions assisted some of her own coulour, but all were teribly frightned." Today most people imagine eighteenth-century Americans to have been hardier than themselves, and perhaps they were. But one category of humanity, new mothers, were actually treated more tenderly then than they are now. Upper- and even middle-class mothers were instructed to "lie in" for up to a month after delivery. Nabby did not stay in bed that long, but she did take it easy after her son was born, giving Abigail ample opportunities to be useful, for instance by spending time with her grandson William, who was a year and a half old. Abigail told Mary Cranch the boy reminded her of his mother at the same age, "except that he has a great share of vivacity & sprightlyness [and] the merest little Trunchion [penis] that you ever saw."

Jamaica was only ten miles from Manhattan, and one day during Abigail's visit, New York congressman John Jay took the ferry over to Long Island for a conversation with his friend's wife. Abigail faithfully transmitted his comments to John. "You must not think of retireing from publick Life," he wanted Adams to know. "You had received your portion of the bitter things in politicks it was time you should have some of the sweets." When Abigail "askt him where he thought the sweets in the new Government were to grow," Jay "smild and said that he hoped for good things under it." Colonel Smith gave Abigail additional gossip to pass on to her husband: Alexander Hamilton had told him that Adams was likely to win the electoral votes of Virginia (at least according to James Madison) and Connecticut. On December 15, the very day that Abigail reported to her husband on her conversation with John Jay, the presidential electors gathered in their state capitals to cast their ballots for the two highest offices in the new national government. Everyone knew George Washington would win the presidency, so the only question was who would receive the second-highest number of votes and become his vice president. (The modern practice of a presidential and vice presidential candidate running together as an all-or-nothing ticket began only after the adoption of the Twelfth Amendment to the Constitution in 1804.) In February 1789, when the electors' ballots were finally counted, the nation learned that the number two spot had gone to Adams.

By mid-January, when Abigail set out for home, the outcome of the election was clear. In April, when John headed to New York to take up his duties as vice president, she remained in Braintree. One of her primary tasks was to find a tenant for the family farm. John's brother, Peter Boylston Adams, initially agreed to take it, but then he hesitated, fearing that the combination of state, local, and church taxes would eat up all his profits. Abigail explained her brother-in-law's dilemma to John Quincy. Uncle Peter "think[s] your Father has so much higher notions about his Farm than he can possibly answer, that he shall come under Blame," she wrote. Abigail sympathized with Peter's dilemma, for she was all too aware of John's tendency to set unrealistic goals—and to be disappointed when they were not met. After reporting her brother-in-law's fear that he would "come under Blame," she told John Quincy, "I know I shall"—no matter how hard she tried or how well she did. When Abigail told her son Thomas about her frustration at finding a suitable tenant for the farm, he replied that "if he was out of colledge he would come & live with Pheby & Abdee & improve it himself."

The Abdees were another of Abigail's challenges that spring. While she was in Europe, the Abdees had lived in the cottage at the foot of Penn's Hill rent free, but during the winter of 1788–1789, Abigail had moved them to another of her family's properties. Now, as she prepared to leave for New York, she believed it was time for the two of them (actually, she nearly always referred solely to Phoebe, as though she had no husband) to start paying rent, although the sum she demanded was a modest four dollars a year. Abigail also had the unenviable task of packing up her family's belongings, including much of the furniture she had brought back from London, for the trip to New York. Although she rarely complained to her husband, in this case she could not help it, telling him, "It is a very unpleasent Idea to me, to be obliged to pull down & pack furniture which has already sufferd so much by Removal just as I have got it well arranged."

A more painful responsibility for Abigail was dealing with her son Charles. Barely a year after participating in the Thanksgiving Day riot at Harvard, he had gotten into trouble again. As always, his relatives' written comments on his behavior were deliberately murky. "I have many anxious hours for Charles," Abigail told John Quincy at the end of May. "I have written to him upon some late reports which have been circulated concerning him." Johnny had heard the rumors, too, from his cousin Billy Cranch, among others. Earlier in the month, he told Cranch, he had sent his brother "a very serious Letter" and then "conversed with him at Haverhill upon the subject in such a manner as must I think lead him to be more cautious." Abigail and John hoped to break their son's pattern of misbehavior by removing him from the milieu that had spawned it. He was in his senior year at Harvard, and his parents decided that after graduation, he would move to New York with them and study law there in the office of Alexander Hamilton. Clearly the young man had fallen in with a bad crowd, and Abigail and John were so desperate "to take him intirely away from his acquaintance" that they eagerly caught at his offer to skip commencement and head to New York right after his last class.

Amid all her domestic duties, Abigail still found time to offer John her advice and opinions on political subjects. Although she liked his first formal speech to the U.S. Senate, she affirmed that "every one do not see the force of the first part of it" (which was her way of saying that she herself did not think the speech had opened well). She was appalled that the members of the House of Representative had decided to allow newspapers to publish rough transcripts of their debates. Even worse, they were insisting that their house stood on an equal footing with the upper chamber. "I had always supposed that in point of Rank the Senate were superiour to the Representitives," she wrote John. The House's claim to equal standing reminded her of an anecdote about the English writers Samuel Johnson and Catharine Macaulay:

> She was conversing upon her favorite topick of the Natural equality of Man. Johnson heard her very gravely, after some time he rose from table & bowing very respectfully to the servant who waited behind his chair, pray mr John, take my place & let me wait in my Turn. You hear what your mistress Says; that we are all equal.

On May 24, John wrote Abigail saying it was time for her to join him in New York. It would be another four months before Congress finally got around to voting the vice president a salary: five thousand dollars, which was one-fifth of what the president earned. Is it any wonder that Adams considered his post "the most insignificant Office that ever the Invention of Man contrived or his Imagination conceived"? In mid-June, Abigail left Braintree and travelled overland to Providence, Rhode Island, where she had dinner with the wealthy Quaker merchant John Brown (did she know Brown owned an immense portion of the federal debt?) and his wife, Sarah, before completing her trip by water.

None of Abigail's previous homes had charmed her like Richmond Hill, the place her husband had rented a month before her arrival in

Richmond Hill, Abigail and John Adams's home during their brief stay in New York City, 1789–1790. The house sat atop a hill overlooking the Hudson River, a mile and a half north of New York City in what is now Greenwich Village. Engraving by Cornelius Tiebout in *New York Magazine*, June 1790. Negative #47619. *Courtesy New-York Historical Society.*

New York. "I have a situation here, which, for natural beauty, may vie with the most delicious spot I ever saw," she told an English friend. The house sat atop a hill overlooking the Hudson River, a mile and a half north of New York City in what is now Greenwich Village. Richmond Hill is "most delightfully situated," the vice president's wife told her sister Mary; "the prospect all around is Beautifull in the highest degree, it is a mixture of the sublime & Beautifull." Abigail immediately received an invitation to visit Martha Washington, whom she had never met. "She is plain in her dress, but that plainness is the best of every article," she reported to her sister. "[H]er Hair is white, her Teeth Beautifull, her person rather short than otherways."

George Washington, who had met Abigail shortly after taking command of the Continental Army, was not able to come out to the first lady's drawing room to greet her guest. He was sick in bed with a mysterious lesion on his thigh that historians have identified as anthrax. But the second time Abigail called on Martha Washington, she was invited to pay the president a brief visit in his bedchamber. In her report to Mary, Adams noted the same quality that she had first discerned in Washington fourteen years earlier: "dignity." She observed that he possessed "a dignity which forbids Familiarity mixed with an easy affibility which creates Love and Reverence." The president asked Abigail how she "could realish the simple manners of America after having been accustomed to those of Europe." Abigail's reply was saucy. She said she "thought we approachd much nearer to the Luxery and manners of Europe according to our ability, than most persons were sensible of, and that we had our full share of taste and fondness for them." Washington returned Abigail's visit even before he was back on his feet. "The President has a Bed put into his Carriage and rides out in that way," she explained to her sister.

Adams enjoyed moving in such an exalted circle, but she worried that her friends and kin would think she was putting on airs, so she confronted the issue head-on. "I have a favour to request of all my near and intimate Friend's," she told Mary. "It is to desire them to watch over my conduct and if at any time they perceive any alteration in me with respect to them, arising as they may suppose from my situation in Life, I beg they would with the utmost freedom acquaint me with it." She did not think she was in any real danger of becoming proud, but she feared others might think she had, for "some are disposed to misconstrue the conduct of those whom they conceive placed above them."

John's elevation to the vice presidency did in fact introduce tension into some of his wife's relationships, but not in the way she had anticipated. In Abigail's day, as in ours, many Americans improved their fortunes through private enterprise (as she herself did during the Revolutionary War), while others (including her husband) did so by landing positions in the government. Indeed, during that preindustrial era, working for the public loomed even larger as a route out of financial embarrassment than it does today, and everyone assumed that John's influence could procure them plum positions. Job seekers descended upon him even before his election was official, and several also approached his wife.

During Abigail's four years in Europe, her old friend James Lovell had gone to great lengths to repair his reputation, returning to his wife every night and faithfully carrying out his official duties, first as a receiver of continental taxes and later as a Massachusetts customs collector, and his removal in 1787 was apparently the result of politics, not personal scandal. The Constitution transferred the right of levying import duties from the states to the federal government, opening up the possibility of Lovell returning to the customs service, which paid considerably more than he had ever earned teaching school. Toward that end, he ended the long hiatus in their correspondence. His tone was as jocular as ever, but he avoided the sexual innuendo that had gotten him in trouble before, and he shrewdly portrayed himself as acting on his wife's behalf as well as his own. Abigail indicated in her reply that she would be happy to help someone as deserving as Lovell. "Mr & Mrs L may be assured that an old friend so well qualified for the office he holds will not be forgotten," she wrote.

Another job seeker caused Abigail and her husband considerably more discomfort. Over the years the Adamses had become increasingly alienated from Mercy Otis Warren, for personal reasons (their desire to shield their sons from the corrupting influence of the Warren boys) as well as public (James and Mercy Warren had cast their lot with the hated John Hancock, and then Mercy had vocally opposed the adoption of the U.S. Constitution). That did not stop Mercy from rejoicing that the first federal election had placed John "in a situation to do eminent service to your country, to establish your family and to assist most *essentially* your friends." Although she kept her request vague, Warren clearly wanted the vice president to find positions for one or more of her ne'er-do-well sons. Abigail reported that John had responded to his old friend in high style, declaring "that he has no patronage but if he had, neither her children or his own could be sure of it beyond his own clear conviction of the publick good."

One other request for patronage put Abigail in an even more awkward position, because it came from her sister Mary. The Cranches were experiencing serious financial difficulties in the late 1780s, and one source of these was the Massachusetts state government's failure to compensate Richard for his service as a treasury office employee and state senator with actual gold and silver. Instead he had received securities that were only worth a fraction of the amount printed on their face. Since Cranch's distress could be blamed in part on a weak state government, it only made sense in Mary's eyes for him to make himself whole with an appointment in the new national administration. Abigail had long admired Richard Cranch, a linguist and biblical scholar as well as an armchair philosopher, but neither she nor her husband had ever thought much of his suitability for more practical tasks. He was, moreover, sixty-two years old in 1789, and Abigail could not imagine the federal job to which he would bring credit. On the other hand, Mary Cranch was not only her sister but her best friend. Now that she was in need, how could Abigail refuse to help her?

CHAPTER 23

"Much More Productive"

1789–1792

Abigail knew she would never be able to convince her husband to procure a federal job for Richard Cranch. So she let Mary down as gently as she could. First she informed her of Mercy Otis Warren's brazen appeal for patronage positions for her sons. The implication was clear: no matter how desperate her family's situation, Mary must not follow Warren's unappealing example. Then Adams announced that while she was wholly incapable of obtaining a job for Richard, she could help him in another way. Over the years Mary had run up a series of small debts, totaling about ten pounds, to her sister. For instance, she had asked Abigail to purchase numerous items for her in London. Knowing her sister's situation, Adams had never pressed her for payment, and she now offered to wipe the slate clean. Mary's debt to Abigail was partly offset by a small sum that John owed Richard, and Abigail now instructed the Cranches to sit down together, calculate the net amount they owed the Adamses, then transmit this figure to Abigail. As soon as I know the amount, she told Mary, "I will send you a Receit in full." Despite being under legal coverture, Adams believed she was "at full liberty" to write off this debt without obtaining her husband's permission, since "the little sum Lent you was my own pocket money." It came from the personal funds that she had been socking away for nearly ten years.

Even though Abigail believed she had full authority over these funds, she decided not to tell her husband what she had done. Keeping him in the dark would not be easy, since John had the annoying habit of opening her mail. So she instructed Mary to enclose her letter in one addressed to Nabby. "It will then fall into no hands but my own," she explained. The frugal Abigail still hoped to avoid paying postage on the letter, so Mary's cover letter to Nabby should itself be enclosed in one to John Adams, who as a high federal official could avoid paying postage by "franking" (signing) his incoming as well as his outgoing mail. Thus John would receive a packet, sign for it, tear off the outside cover, and see that it was actually intended for his daughter Nabby, who would then remove another cover, find the enclosed receipt, and give it to her mother. Abigail would be able to expunge Mary's debt without incurring an additional expense for postage and without tipping off her husband.

Mary Cranch was offended that Abigail had implicitly compared her talented husband to Mercy Warren's miscreant sons. And she was extremely reluctant to accept her sister's charity. In the end, though, she had no choice.

The Adamses had to endure another temporary separation during the fall of 1789. A congressional recess that began at the end of September permitted John to return to Braintree, but Abigail remained at Richmond Hill. He went in hopes of improving his health (he was not ill but "close & unremitting attention to Buisness" had exhausted him), and she stayed put out of fear of endangering hers. Congress was due to reconvene in January, and reluctant as Abigail was to part with her husband even for a few months, she did not wish to accompany him on a midwinter trek back to New York. It was certainly not the attractions of Manhattan that kept her there, for in truth they seemed to be far outnumbered by the annoyances. As in London and Paris, her servants were a constant source of irritation. Although she realized that her financially straitened sisters could derive no pleasure from reading her grievances against the help, she could not stop herself. "I hate to hear people for ever complaining of servants," she told Mary in October, "but I never had so much occasion as since I came here." Her New York servants surpassed everyone who had ever worked for her in only one area: the consumption of alcohol. "I cannot find a cook in the whole city but what will get drunk," she lamented to Mary. "It is next to imposible here to get a servant from the highest to the lowest grade that does not drink male or Female," she wrote eight months later. When she finally found a sober footman, she was quick to point out that "he was Born in Boston."

Now that her husband held the second-highest office in the land, Abigail had more extensive social obligations than ever before, and most were onerous. Richmond Hill was so far from town that she could not decently pretend to be away when guests came calling—a maneuver that otherwise would have been perfectly acceptable. Custom obliged Adams to return every visit she received, but she gamed the system as well as she could. She was required to try to call on everyone who had come to see her, but not necessarily to see them. So she refused to attempt any social calls in the morning, when her would-be hosts might actually be home, instead making her rounds in the afternoon, when they were likely to be gone. "In an afternoon after six oclock I can return 15 or 20 [visits] & very seldom find any Lady to receive me," she bragged to Mary. That still left the problem of her own guests, who seldom waited for invitations, but she soon copied Martha Washington's strategy of getting most of her entertaining out of the way on a single day by holding a levee (open house) once a week.

The ratification of the Constitution in 1788 had given the nation a new governing class that needed time to work out its rules of social etiquette. At Martha Washington's levees, "My station is always at the right hand of Mrs W.," Abigail explained to her sister. Some of the women in her social circle did not realize at first that this favored position next to the first lady was reserved for the vice president's wife. "I find it some times occupied," she told Mary, "but on such an occasion the President never fails of Seeing that it is relinquishd for me, and having removed Ladies Several times, they have now learnt to rise & give it me, but this between our selves, as *all distinction* you know is unpopular."

She was by no means miserable at Richmond Hill. Nabby and her growing family had taken up residence there at about the same time as Abigail, making it easier than ever for her to treat her daughter's children as her own. Charles also lived with his parents (for the first time in five years), and to all appearances he had left his dissolute tendencies behind him in Massachusetts. John had to find his son a new mentor after Alexander Hamilton became the nation's first secretary of the treasury, but the snag did not slow him down. "There is no fault to be found with his conduct," the young man's relieved mother reported to Mary Cranch as the year 1790 opened. "He has no company or companions but known & approved ones." If the nineteen-year-old had a vice, it was one that ran in the family. "Charls is quite fat," Abigail observed.

The vice president returned to New York in time for the resumption of congressional business early in January 1790. One of the first items on the representatives' agenda was the extensive report on public credit that Secretary Hamilton had prepared for them during the recess. Abigail was convinced that Congress was going to "fund" the enormous federal debt, which Hamilton estimated at $54 million. That meant calling in all outstanding federal certificates, including the indents that had been paid out as interest on U.S. bonds, and replacing them with new securities. Then the interest on these new notes would be faithfully and regularly paid using the ample revenue streams accorded to Congress in the Constitution. Hamilton knew from his extensive investigation of the British financial system that punctual interest payments would boost the market price of the securities to parity with their face value. Indeed, his appointment as secretary of the treasury the previous September had increased the price of one series of bonds from 25 percent of par to 40 percent.

Abigail did not doubt that the "General Good" required the adoption of Hamilton's plan or something like it. If the United States did not pay what it owed, it would never be able to borrow in the future. The funding bill was also a simple matter of justice. The government had received tangible benefits from its creditors—war materiel, cash loans, and (most importantly) soldiers' service—and the effect of the precipitous decline in the market price of the bonds had been to defraud the public creditors of their just compensation. During the war, Adams reminded her sister Mary, Americans had been "Robbed by our Enemies." Now, seven years after the cessation of hostilities, if Congress refused to fund the federal debt, a significant portion of the population would also be "cheated by our Friends." The owners of government securities, she insisted, were "sufferers by the instability of Government." Now that the federal union had a broader and deeper foundation, they must be made whole.

But not everyone agreed. During the 1780s, James Madison had been a strong advocate for the public creditors. Yet as a member of the House of Representatives, he pointed out that most of the federal debt was no longer owed to the people who had lent money to the government, fought in the Continental Army, and supplied it with food and fuel, for speculators had bought up most of the war bonds at a fraction of their face value. Most of the state governments had disbursed tens of thousands of dollars' worth of interest to the holders of federal as well as state bonds. Since the interest rate on these notes was multiplied times the face value rather than the actual amount that had been paid for them, the annual return on the speculators' investment had been enormous, and by 1789 most of them had not only recouped their initial outlays but amassed tremendous profits. (This was certainly the case with Abigail's earliest bond purchases.) Men such as Madison agreed with Hamilton that Congress must fund the federal debt, but they thought the current holders of federal securities should be forced to share the government's bounty, on a fifty-fifty basis, with the original recipients of their bonds—the people who had received them in exchange for merchandise, cash, or service in the army.

The final vote on Madison's proposal was scheduled for February 22, and it was no coincidence that the vice president's wife chose this very day to ride down to Federal Hall for her first-ever visit to the gallery of the House of Representatives. It is unlikely that anyone else in that hall knew that she was among the speculators who would lose half the money they felt they deserved if Madison's amendment passed. House clerk John Beckley called the roll, and the vote was thirteen for, thirty-six against.

Back in 1785, when Cotton Tufts's wife, Lucy, had died, Abigail and her sisters had waited only a few months before urging him to find a new wife. Four years later, on October 22, 1789, he finally obliged them, marrying Susannah Warner. But Warner was not exactly what the Smith sisters had had in mind. At forty-five, she was twelve years younger than Tufts, and Abigail and her sisters were apparently under the mistaken impression that she was even younger than that. "I wish the dr much happiness with his *Young wife,* is she not young for him?" Abigail asked Mary a week after the wedding. It may seem strange that Adams and Cranch could view their uncle's choice of a mature woman like Warner as robbing the cradle, but four months after the marriage was solemnized, Abigail revealed her real reason for questioning it: she feared the doctor and his new bride would have children. That would cut into his son's inheritance, and the ensuing conflicts "would be like to distroy the Harmony between the two Families."

During this period Abigail also offered strong opinions about other mothers, actual as well as potential. Nabby was having children way too fast, she told Mary Cranch at the start of 1790. John, her second, had arrived a mere nineteen months after William, and a third child was due before John reached the age of two. Judging those intervals too short, Abigail expressed the hope that Mary's daughter Elizabeth, who had married a preacher named Jacob Norton, would wean her first child before bringing another one into the world. The same January 5 letter that contained this advice also expressed astonishment that Adams's thirty-nine-year old sister, Elizabeth Shaw, was pregnant. "It is really a foolish Buisness to begin after so many years, a Second crop," Abigail told Mary in March, after the child was born. Adams's commentaries on her daughter's and sister's pregnancies and on Tufts's and Norton's potential pregnancies showed that she was as willing as ever to give her opinions on the most intimate of matters. (Recall that years earlier she had advised the Shaws not to have any children at all.) Her advice also cast light on the society in which she lived, for the obvious implication was that women had children when and if they chose to do so, reinforcing the scholarly consensus that the females of this era were aware of methods, however imperfect, of limiting their reproduction.

In the spring of 1790, George Washington contracted a severe case of influenza, raising the distinct possibility that John Adams might have to assume the presidency. It was only after Washington was on the mend that Abigail was able to discuss her feelings about the crisis. While the president's prognosis remained uncertain, she wrote her sister Mary, "I feard a thousand things which I pray, I never may be calld to experience," adding, "most assuredly I do not wish for the highest Post."

One of Abigail's greatest regrets about living in New York was the lack of good preaching. In London she and her husband had not balked at spending a good portion of their Sundays traveling to and from the nearby town of Hackney to hear Reverend Richard Price, a supporter of the American Revolution who was also a well-regarded moral philosopher. Price had been a marked improvement over the plodding Anthony Wibird, who still presided over their home church in Braintree, but the Adamses were not so lucky in New York. "Alass," Abigail wrote Mary shortly after her arrival in the largest city north of the Rio Grande, "I do not find a dr Price." Two months later, the situation was no better. "I can tell you something which may well excite your surprize," she told her sister in October. "It is that I have cause every Sunday to regreet the loss of Parson Wibird, and that I should realy think it an entertainment to hear a discourse from him." Not only did New York's dissenting ministers lack Price's intellectual reach, they were far too Calvinist for Abigail's taste—and the Adamses were not about to join the Anglican Church. All of the preachers she had heard were "predestinarians . . . whose Noise & vehemence is to compensate for every other difficency," she wrote. Adams did not identify the church she and her husband attended as part of an ecumenical Fourth of July celebration, but she reported to Mary that "the oratary of a Clergyman here consists in foaming loud speaking Working themselves up in such an enthusiam as to cry." New England had its share of evangelical preachers as well, but there Abigail had been able to avoid them. In New York it seemed she could not.

Although Abigail had no use for New York Calvinists, she showed during the summer of 1790 that she was surprisingly willing to bridge a different cultural divide. In July, a group of Creek Indians journeyed north from present-day Georgia and Alabama to negotiate a peace treaty with the United States—the first treaty of any kind ever ratified by the U.S. Senate. The delegation stayed at an inn near Richmond Hill, and the leading men paid a daily visit to the vice president and his wife. "We entertain them kindly, and they behave with much civility," Abigail told Mary Cranch. The treaty was ratified on August 7, and that afternoon, one of the Indian diplomats, Mico Maco, dined with the Adamses and gave Abigail a Creek name: "Mammea." That night, to celebrate their successful negotiations, the Creeks "had a great Bond fire dancing round it like so many spirits hooping, singing, yelling, and expressing their pleasure and Satisfaction in the true Savage Stile." Adams was impressed with the men's physical conditioning. "They are very fine looking Men placid contanances & fine shape," she wrote. The painter John Trumbull told her they would make "perfect Models." One of the Creek leaders was a man named Alexander McGillivray, who had Scottish, French, and Creek ancestors. He "dresses in our own fashion," Abigail observed, "speaks English like a Native, & I should never suspect him to be of [the Creek] Nation, as he is not very dark." Despite his mixed ancestry, McGillivray had taken a leading role in the Creeks' violent resistance to white Georgians' encroachments on their land, but a secret provision of the Treaty of New York put him in the pay of the U.S. Army.

For Abigail and many others, the ratification of the Creek treaty was only the second most important political event of August 1790, for this was also the month during which Congress finally adopted legislation funding the federal debt. On three separate occasions, Vice President Adams cast the tiebreaking vote against amendments unfavorable to the bondholders. The funding act obliged the federal government to use the taxing authority it had received at the Constitutional Convention to pay interest to the public creditors every quarter, and its adoption had a predictable effect. The price of federal and state securities, which had been on the rise ever since the ratification of the Constitution two years earlier, now received yet another boost. Soon the old bonds would be replaced with new ones that were expected to command an even higher price. That meant enormous profits for speculators like Abigail, who had purchased her securities for as little as 12 percent of their face value.

Even before the legislation received its final passage, Adams began the process of exchanging her old bonds for new ones, instructing Uncle Tufts to compile an inventory of all her bonds. She also asked him to find out whether he could sign for the new securities in his own name in order to conceal her speculation from public view. John Adams made no such effort to keep his status as a public creditor secret, indicating that the information that Abigail wished to hide was not that her family was profiting from the funding legislation but that she owned personal property, which wives were not supposed to do. She advised Tufts to veil her bond ownership by claiming her federal bonds "as a trustee for an other," without naming that other person. Tufts regretfully informed his niece that he would not be able to "conceal the Name" of the actual owner of the bonds, and he signed a receipt for them as "Trustee to Mrs. Abigl. Adams."

The designation of Tufts as Abigail's "trustee" gave the redemption of her bonds a significance that even she probably did not immediately discern. The only way a married woman of that era could own personal property was by obtaining her husband's permission to place her holdings in a so-called separate estate. There is no evidence that the Adamses ever signed such a contract, but couples that did so typically put the money in the hands of a trustee. The financial relationship that Abigail established with her uncle in 1781, when she first asked him to invest money for her, had been informal. But now, a decade letter, her decision to have Tufts identify himself as her "Trustee," though only applied to this one transaction, moved her one step closer to asserting ownership of personal property in defiance of the doctrine of coverture.

Despite Adams's excitement at the adoption of the funding act, she found several aspects of the legislation disappointing. Congress had not given the bondholders everything Secretary Hamilton had wanted them to have. For instance, the representatives devised a complex for-

Cotton Tufts (1732–1815), Abigail's uncle and financial "Trustee." Benjamin Greenleaf, 1804. *Courtesy Boston Medical Library in the Francis A. Countway Library of Medicine.*

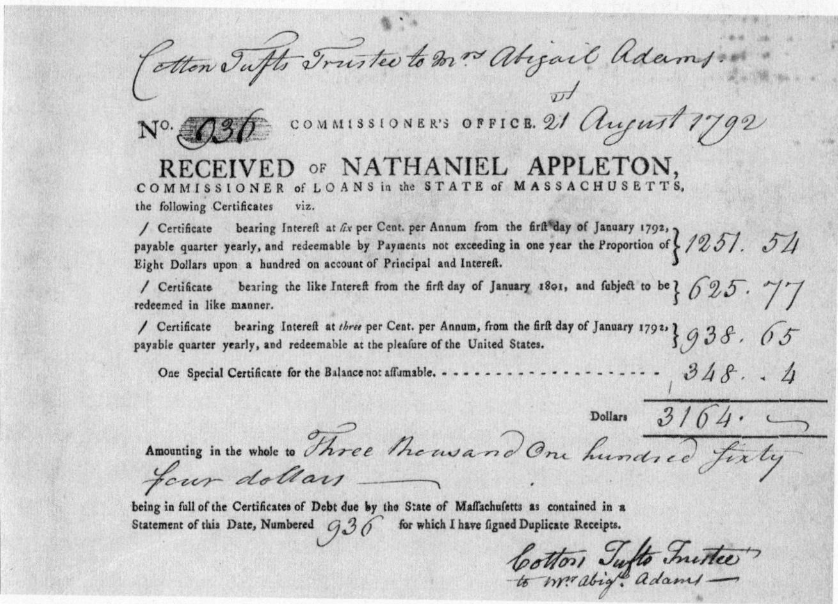

Cotton Tufts Trustee to Mrs Abigail Adams.

No. 936 COMMISSIONER'S OFFICE. 21st August 1792

RECEIVED OF NATHANIEL APPLETON,
COMMISSIONER of LOANS in the STATE of MASSACHUSETTS,
the following Certificates viz.

1 Certificate bearing Intereſt at *ſix* per Cent. per Annum from the firſt day of January 1792, payable quarter yearly, and redeemable by Payments not exceeding in one year the Proportion of Eight Dollars upon a hundred on account of Principal and Intereſt.	1251. 54
1 Certificate bearing the like Intereſt from the firſt day of January 1801, and ſubject to be redeemed in like manner.	625. 77
1 Certificate bearing Intereſt at *three* per Cent. per Annum, from the firſt day of January 1792, payable quarter yearly, and redeemable at the pleaſure of the United States.	938. 65
One Special Certificate for the Balance not aſſumable.	348. . 4
Dollars	3164.

Amounting in the whole to Three thousand One hundred sixty four dollars

being in full of the Certificates of Debt due by the State of Maſſachuſetts as contained in a Statement of this Date, Numbered 936 for which I have ſigned Duplicate Receipts.

Cotton Tufts Trustee
to Mrs Abigl. Adams

Receipt signed by Cotton Tufts (as "Trustee to Mrs. Abigail Adams") for $3,164 in U.S. Government securities, August 21, 1792. Jeremiah Colburn autograph collection, 7243. *Courtesy Bostonian Society, on deposit with the Massachusetts Historical Society.*

mula by which each bondholder would receive three new types of bonds, one of which would not begin paying interest until the year 1800. Moreover, a heavy price had been paid for southern support for the federal government's assumption of responsibility for paying off the states' debts. Most of the states below the Mason-Dixon Line carried smaller loads of debt than those above it, and southern taxpayers were unwilling to fork over the money the federal government would need to redeem the northern states' bonds. Assumption could not pass without the support of at least a few southern congressmen, and its champions were able to obtain those votes only by yielding to a southern demand that the nation's capital be moved to the banks of the Potomac River in 1800. During the intervening decade, Congress would meet in Philadelphia, which meant that Abigail would have to abandon Richmond Hill. "Do you not pitty me my dear sister to be so soon all in a Bustle?" she asked Mary early in October. Before her lay "as much Boxing and casing, as if we were removing to Europe. . . . I feel low spirited and Heartless."

As the price of federal and state securities steadily climbed, Abigail's greatest disappointment was that she had failed to persuade her husband to purchase more of them while the price was low. In October 1790, her reflections on this missed opportunity provoked her to criticize John to a third person—something she hardly ever did. Adams told her sister Mary that if she and Uncle Tufts "had been left to the sole management of our affairs, they would have been upon a more profitable footing. In the first place I never desired so much Land unless we could have lived upon it. The Money paid for useless land I would have purchased publick Securities with." Abigail lamented that "in these Ideas I have always been so unfortunate as to differ from my partner," for John believed he "never saved any thing but what he vested in Land," and her regretful tone has led some historians to the mistaken conclusion that her efforts to persuade him to purchase government securities had proved unavailing. Her actual grievance was simply that John had not put even more money into the bond market.

There is no indication that John shared his wife's regret, even after the market value of government paper began to rise. In tallying up his property holdings, the vice president did not rate government securities and Vermont land titles much higher than another notorious form of paper property in which his wife had also invested, lottery tickets. One reason for the couple's disagreement, Abigail well knew, was that John considered land safer for the nation as well as the man. His dedication to republican values bred in him a deep suspicion of bond speculators, a narrow faction that possessed the motivation and clout to manipulate the government in its favor. Like other adherents to this Real Whig or country ideology (also known as classical republicanism), Adams sometimes lapsed into anti-Semitism. Bond traders, he told Thomas Jefferson in June 1786, were nothing but "Jews and Judaizing Christians" who were "Scheeming to buy up all our Continental Notes at two or three shillings in a Pound, in order to oblige us to pay them at twenty shillings a Pound." The ideal Adams constantly held before himself was the virtuous Roman senator whose vote was not for sale. Such rectitude, he knew, required economic independence, the surest source of which was "A solid Income from a landed Estate in the Country."

Like many of his contemporaries, even Alexander Hamilton, Adams also believed stockjobbing inhibited economic growth. Speculators, he believed, diverted capital away from ventures such as shipbuilding and livestock raising that added to the nation's wealth rather than simply redistributing it. "While a Bit of Paper can be bought for five shillings that is worth twenty," he wrote Jefferson in July 1786, "all Capitals will be employed in that Trade, for it is certain there is no other that will yeild four hundred Per Cent Profit."

For Abigail, that was just the point: depreciated government securities were a "much more productive" investment than land. As she saw it, John had given the United States the best years of his life, forgoing a lucrative legal career, and the Adamses were entitled to more than his paltry government salary. One way Abigail nudged her family's compensation in the direction of what a more grateful nation would have cheerfully granted was by having John frank her friends' and relatives', mail for them—a practice she followed right up until the year of her death. A much more significant form of compensation was her speculation in government securities. Like Abigail, John resented his fellow citizens' apparent ingratitude, but he differed from his wife in one important respect. As a man he could take pride in the political independence that his ownership of farmland guaranteed him. Abigail, on the other hand, would not be able to control her real estate or acquire more of it until her husband died (and as it turned out, he outlived her). Entitled to use and charged with managing property that she could never actually possess, she cared less about what form the family's assets took than about the rate of return.

Historians have long been mystified by the stark contrast between John Adams's financial trajectory and those of his two immediate successors in the White House, Thomas Jefferson and James Madison. The two Virginians both died deep in debt, and their beloved estates—Jefferson's Monticello and Madison's Montpelier—had to be sold to satisfy their creditors. One reason Adams finished his days wealthy and debt free was that he embodied the frugal Yankee. But great wealth also requires substantial income, and attorney Adams tried his last case in 1777, a half century before his death. Of the numerous public offices that Adams held, several paid quite well, but it may well be that if his financial records had survived the ravages of time as well as his correspondence did, they would show his wife making a larger contribution to the family's wealth than he did. Certainly John was much more carefree about money than Abigail was—though deep down he knew that the reason he was able to take a casual approach to his family's financial situation was that Abigail never did.

Abigail also had one more cause for regret in the summer of 1790. In order to complete work on the funding act, Congress had stayed in session until August 12—something it would not do again until 1841. As president of the Senate, John had no choice but to remain in steamy, unsanitary New York City, and Abigail elected to stay with him. During this summer—one of the few to catch Abigail south of New England—she contracted an illness she called "intermitting Fever." On the evening of October 10, within hours of informing her sister of her disappointment in her husband's investment decisions, Abigail "was taken with a shaking fit which held me 2 Hours and was succeeded by a fever which lasted till near morning," as she later reported. Based on Adams's symptoms, historians believe she had contracted malaria. It would periodically flare up throughout the rest of her life.

Early in November, Abigail undertook the journey to Philadelphia that Congress had imposed on her. John had already arrived and rented them a house that was even farther from the center of town than Richmond Hill was from New York. The place was called "Bush Hill," but Abigail pointedly observed that "there remains neither bush nor shrub upon it, and very few trees, except the pine grove behind it." In a letter to her daughter, she granted that this was "a very beautiful place," but she added that "the grand and sublime I left at Richmond Hill." The area around the house had "too much of the level to be in my style," she told Elizabeth Shaw. "The appearance of uniformity wearies the eye, and confines the imagination." Other burdens also awaited. Philadelphians, she knew, would subject her to the same ostentatious welcome she had endured a year and a half earlier in New York. Once again she would have "to make and receive a hundred ceremonious visits." Even worse, she had to bid farewell to Nabby and Charles, to both of whom she was "much attached." And then there was that other issue that, as she told Mary, "I cannot communicate by Letter"—undoubtedly a reference to the danger that without his mother's supervision, Charles would once again stray from the straight and narrow.

Less than two weeks after Abigail reached Bush Hill, she received word that Nabby's husband had suddenly decided to sail to England. The Adamses had long worried about their son-in-law's financial situation. Convinced that he was entitled to a lucrative government position that kept not coming (his job as federal marshal for the state of New York paid far too little), Colonel Smith showed little interest in securing private employment, and Elizabeth Palmer's description of him as a man "of no profession" was starting to seem apt. But now he had found a way to establish his fortune without soiling his hands, for he had joined a partnership to speculate in government securities. The plan was to purchase bonds using money borrowed in Europe. The steadily rising price of government paper would allow the partners to repay their creditors with interest and still pocket a handsome profit. It was William's task to sail to London to obtain the loan.

Smith's timing could scarcely have been worse. Immediately after his ship left New York Harbor, the price of federal securities rallied. By the end of the year, one series of bonds, those that would begin paying 6 percent interest in 1791, were already trading at their face value. Smith and his partners had been correct in their prediction that government paper would soon become more valuable, but they had not been able to act quickly enough. The price increase from which they had expected to profit occurred before William even reached England.

Abigail was also worried about John Quincy. Toward the end of his legal apprenticeship, he fell in love with Mary Frazier, the sixteen-year-old daughter of a Newburyport merchant, and the two were soon talking about marriage. Without meeting Mary, both of John Quincy's parents opposed the match for the simple reason that their son had not yet established himself financially. "Common Fame reports that you are attachd to a young Lady," Abigail told John Quincy shortly after he finished his clerkship and established a law office in the front room of his father's house on Court Street in Boston. "Believe me my dear son a too early marriage will involve you in troubles that may render you & yours unhappy the remainder of Your Life." Given that he was in no position to marry, she wrote, "an entanglement of this kind will only tend to depress your spirits"—not to mention the damage it would do to Mary's reputation. As Abigail had predicted, Johnny insisted that he was "perfectly free" of any romantic commitments. She did not believe him, but eventually he broke off with Frazier altogether. "I was never in less danger of any entanglement, which can give you pain than at present," he told his mother in December 1790.

If John Quincy was going to remain faithful to his parents' injunction against starting a family until he could support one, he might have a long bachelorhood, for his financial prospects were not bright. Boston already had too many lawyers, and he spent many idle hours waiting for his first client. When he finally got one, he had the humiliation of losing his first case, which of course did nothing to boost either his client base or his morale. Although more pragmatic than his brother-in-law, John Quincy was not immune to the speculative fever that gripped much of the country after Congress passed the funding act. He solicited and received a detailed report on bond prices from his brother Charles, and he wrote his mother echoing (perhaps unknowingly) a proposal that she had made three years earlier. The family should sell its Boston house—he thought it would fetch as much as five hundred pounds—and invest the proceeds in government bonds. Johnny realized his proposal would probably go nowhere. "I am aware of my father's predilection in favour of real Estate," he told his mother as he sat at his desk in Court Street. "But as it respects this house it seems to me, the only question must be how to make the property the most profitable." Abigail could not have agreed more, but she knew her husband would never sell the Boston house, and in fact it remained in the family for another century.

The young attorney was so desperate to achieve financial independence that he sent his father a request that he must have known was inappropriate. John Quincy had heard that the U.S. government was about to solicit a large loan in Europe. If the money could be obtained, one effect would be to raise the price of government securities, so anyone who purchased bonds before the loan was secured would make a handsome profit. No one could know better than the vice president, who had negotiated several loans from Dutch bankers back during the Revolutionary War, whether the United States would be able to obtain the requested funds, so John Quincy asked his mother to solicit the vice president's insight on the subject. John appears to have ignored his son's query.

Abigail's youngest son was also a source of anxiety—and of dispute—in the fall of 1790. John had always assumed that Thomas, who had graduated from Harvard in July, would follow his father and brothers into the legal profession, but Abigail made a desultory effort to give him some additional options. For Thomas to practice law, she told John Quincy (who fully agreed with her), "will be a force to his inclinations." He would be much happier as a merchant in Philadelphia or even Amsterdam, she believed. It was a futile gesture. In the fall of 1790, when John and Abigail headed to Philadelphia, Thomas went with them and began his apprenticeship in a law office there.

All three of the Adams boys received financial help from both of their parents during these years. Abigail's contributions came from the interest she received on the new federal securities issued to her after Congress adopted the funding act. These interest payments also paid for gifts to Abigail's pensioners. Prominent among the recipients of her largesse were the Cranches, whose financial situation continued to deteriorate. "I wish you would send mrs Cranch 5 cords of wood on my account, but do not let even her know from what quarter it comes," Abigail wrote Cotton Tufts at the end of 1791. Mary was not the only person from whom Adams hoped to conceal her benefactions. Aware of her husband's penchant for opening her letters, she asked Tufts not to send her an explicit report on the distribution of her gifts. Instead he should convey that information surreptitiously: "‡ a mark of that kind in your Letter will inform me that what I request will be Complied with," she wrote.

A decade earlier, when Abigail had purchased her first depreciated government securities, Tufts had served as her mentor. But during the 1790s, their roles were reversed—partly because Adams spent so much time in the nation's capital but also because her uncle recognized her growing financial savvy. "Will it [be] best to sell or best to buy[?]" he asked her at the end of September 1790. Five months later, Tufts learned that Congress was going to create a national bank and allow public creditors to purchase stock in it using their federal bonds. "Will there be an advantage in becoming a Sharer in the national Bank[?]" he asked his niece; "if so How is a Share to be obtaind[?]" Abigail's replies to these queries do not survive.

Adams's extensive travels had made her a more flexible person, and she adapted quickly to life in Philadelphia. She held a levee every Monday, then used Tuesday to prepare for the dinner she hosted for sixteen to eighteen people every Wednesday, leaving her much "Replacing & restoring to order" to do on Thursday. In between these regularly scheduled chores and events she found time to return visits, sometimes "dinning abroad" with her husband. This routine left her "very few hours to myself," she complained to Mary, but she had to admit that she was having fun getting to know the prominent women of Philadelphia. "The ladies here are well-educated, well-bred, and well-dressed," she observed to Betsy late in March 1791.

During Abigail's initial months in Philadelphia, her servants caused her even more grief than their counterparts in New York had. "Such a vile low tribe, you never was tormented with & I hope never will be," she wrote Mary; "not a virtuous woman amongst them all; the most of them drunkards." In a year and a half, Adams went through seven cooks, and she blamed her problems partly on the ethnic diversity of the urban workforce. "We know little of vileness in our state when compared to those cities who have Such Numbers of Foreigners [immigrants] as N york and Philadelphia," she told Mary at the start of 1791. Although she had grown up around slaves, Adams was initially repelled by the greater proportion of African Americans in New York and Pennsylvania than in New England. "As to the Negroes," she wrote shortly after her arrival in New York City, "I am most sincerely sick of them." By April 1790, though, her opinion had changed. "The chief of the Servants here who are good for any thing are Negroes who are slaves," she told Mary; "the white ones are all Foreigners & chiefly vagabonds." In the spring of 1791, as she planned her annual summer sojourn in Braintree, Adams declared to her sister, "I had rather have black than white help, as they will be more like to agree with those I bring," most of whom were African American. By overcoming her reluctance to hire black laborers, Adams was finally able to find a good cook. "I have a cleaver sober honest & Neat black woman as my daily cook," she exulted to Mary at the end of 1791. "In this respect I am happier than formerly."

Another black woman, Phoebe Abdee, did cause Abigail some grief early in 1791, but Adams could not help approving her good intentions.

A year and a half earlier, during the summer of 1789, Abdee had revived a long-simmering controversy by requesting permission to board a black family. As he had in the past, Dr. Tufts "utterly refused," but that did not end the matter, for in January 1791, Mary Cranch reported to her sister that a black couple ("The man came from Guinea when a child," she noted) had been staying with the Abdees for the previous nine months. At Mary's suggestion, Abigail hired the pair as servants during her summer sojourn in Braintree.

When the Adamses returned to Philadelphia in October 1791, they passed up the opportunity to reoccupy Bush Hill, their rural estate, instead settling at the corner of Fourth and Arch streets. The new house was smaller and more expensive than Bush Hill, but John would no longer have to commute two miles every day, and Abigail and her servants would be able to get the marketing done much more quickly. The central location of the new house also made it easier than ever for Abigail to follow politics. At the end of 1791, Philadelphians learned that an American military expedition against a coalition of Indians in the present-day Midwest had been soundly defeated. Hundreds of soldiers had lost their lives. In a letter to Mary Cranch, Abigail toyed with the heretical view that right might not actually have been on the army's side. "The justice the policy the wisdom of this cruel enterprize lies with higher powers to investigate than mine," she wrote.

The spring of 1792 brought disaster of a different kind. The funding act of 1790, which had been designed in part to raise the market price of federal securities, worked too well, and the bonds became targets of intense speculation. The fever intensified in 1791, when Congress enacted Hamilton's related proposal to create a national bank. The buying and selling (mostly buying) of securities and bank stock inflated the price of both forms of paper wealth to unsustainable levels, and early in 1792, the bubble burst. "Terrible is the distress in N[ew] York, from the failure of many of the richest people there, and from the Spirit of Speculation which has prevaild & brought to Ruin many industerous Families who lent their Money in hopes of Gain," Abigail reported to Mary Cranch in April. In the coming years, Adams would watch paper speculation ruin several of the people she loved most in the world, and her anger at the practice would grow increasingly bitter over time. Never once, in all of these denunciations of speculation, did she show any consciousness of the simple fact that by buying depreciated government bonds, she herself had made a fortune.

Although Colonel Smith's 1790–1791 voyage to England had proved a bust, some of his other projects turned out much better. By December 1791, Nabby was able to boast to her mother that "Lands which he purchased of the State last summer for 3/3 [3 shillings, 3 pence] pr acre he can now dispose of to people who wish to settle upon them for 10 shillings." Inspired by this success and angry at President Washington and Secretary of State Jefferson for not giving him a sufficiently lucrative government job, Smith decided to return to England in the spring of 1792 on a new venture, the details of which were shrouded in mystery (where they mostly remain today). This time he took Nabby and their two sons with him.

Barely three weeks after the Smiths sailed out of New York Harbor, John and Abigail left Philadelphia for their annual summer vacation at home. In their absence the north parish of Braintree had seceded, taking the name of Abigail's grandfather, John Quincy. As the Adams carriage was ferried across the Delaware River on the first leg of the couple's journey to Quincy, Abigail could hardly have guessed that she would not see Philadelphia again for another five years.

CHAPTER 24

"With All the Ardour of Youth"

1792–1795

In November 1792, when John set out on his annual autumn trek from Massachusetts to Pennsylvania, Abigail did not accompany him. Though it pained both of them to be separated, they had agreed that she should spend the winter in Quincy. Abigail's malaria and rheumatism had both acted up in Philadelphia, and she had been especially miserable the previous spring. The malaria "still hangs about me & prevents my intire recovery," she reported to her sister Mary in April, and "a critical period of Life"—menopause—"Augments my complaints." Although Abigail's rheumatism would surely trouble her to a greater extent in Quincy than in the more temperate climate of Philadelphia, she was convinced that the bracing New England air was ultimately healthier. Moreover, long carriage rides aggravated her complaints, and she would skip two of these by remaining in Quincy until her husband returned in the spring.

It appears, however, that Abigail's health was not the principal reason she stayed home during the winter of 1792–1793. For nearly a decade, she had worried that John's considerable expenses would exceed his inadequate government salary. During the previous three years, that dire prophecy had finally been fulfilled. John informed his wife at the end of 1792 that during his term as vice president, he had run up a debt of two thousand dollars. The couple were determined to retrench their expenses, and if Abigail remained in Massachusetts, that would cut their costs by more than half. Politicians who brought their wives to the capital were expected to host numerous social events (recall that Abigail's practice had been to serve a sumptuous meal to sixteen to eighteen people every single Wednesday), but those who came alone were not. If the vice president were to leave Mrs. Adams in Quincy, freeing himself from the obligation to entertain, he would also be able to rent a much smaller place. Indeed, many federal officials stayed at boardinghouses, which reduced not only their rent but their need for servants.

In some ways, America's second national election in 1792 resembled the first one four years earlier. Once again George Washington was unopposed for the presidency. Yet it was much less certain that the vice president would win a second term, for the country was much more divided than it had been in 1788. John and Abigail described the two parties that contended for control of Congress and the state legislatures as "Federal" and "Anti-Federal," as though they were continuations of the two factions that had clashed over the ratification of the Constitution. Actually, a multitude of new points of contention had arisen. The Federalist party was becoming increasingly northern—sympathetic to business and hostile to slavery—while most of the leading Republicans were southern slaveholders.

One of the most prominent issues in 1792 had not even existed four years earlier. The French Revolution initially inspired enthusiasm throughout the United States, but as it grew more violent, Federalists turned against it, and their skepticism was reinforced by the leading role that the party's natural allies in Great Britain took in trying to restore the French monarchy. Jefferson and other Republicans were excited to see American revolutionary fervor spreading to France, and the last thing they wanted the United States to do was enlist in the former mother country's counterrevolutionary crusade. "I firmly believe if I live Ten years longer, I shall see a devision of the Southern & Northern states, unless more candour & less intrigue, of which I have no hopes, should prevail," Abigail wrote Mary Cranch in April 1792.

The nascent conflict between Federalists and Republicans nearly derailed John's bid for reelection. One of the keys to his success in 1788 had been the dispersion of the anti-Adams vote among several other candidates. He would not have that advantage this time around, for the Republicans settled on a single opponent. Afraid to nominate Jefferson, since the president was also a Virginian, they chose George Clinton, the populist governor of New York. The incumbent vice president's wife viewed the election in apocalyptic terms. On December 5, the day before the presidential electors were to meet in their state capitals to cast their votes, Abigail told John that while Americans might not realize it, "Tomorrow will determine whether their Government shall stand four years longer or Not." Seldom has anyone placed so much weight on the selection of a vice president.

John beat Clinton, 77 electoral votes to 50, but it hurt his feelings to have come so close to giving up his post to a man he considered a demagogue. The entire House of Representatives was also up for reelection in 1792, but the new congressmen would not take their seats until the fall of 1793. The lame-duck session did not linger in the capital long, and the vice president was back in Quincy by the middle of March 1793. This turned out to be a good year to get out of Philadelphia before the warm weather set in, because during the summer, the city was hit by the worst yellow fever epidemic in the history of North America. About 3,000 people out of a total population of 30,000 died. Once the extent of the catastrophe became clear, two-thirds of the residents of Philadelphia got out of town. The only ones who stayed were those who were too poor to support themselves elsewhere and a few brave medical professionals, including John's friend Benjamin Rush. The Adamses' son Thomas, nearing the end of his legal apprenticeship, joined in the mass exodus and spent the summer in Woodbury, New Jersey.

No one at the time knew that yellow fever was caused by the mosquitoes that flourished wherever water was left to stand, but it was widely understood that the epidemics were almost entirely confined to the summer months. The 1793 outbreak was so severe that Philadelphians were especially wary about returning to their homes, and when John entered the city on November 30—the anniversary, he observed in a letter to Abigail, of his signing the preliminary peace treaty with Great Britain in 1782—he was one of the first to do so. Most Americans would have joined in the vice president's hope that the disaster would "convince Philadelphia that all has not been well." But he was not among those who saw in the epidemic a divine scourge calling sinners to repent. "Moral and religious Reflections I shall leave to their own Thoughts," he told Abigail, "but The Cleanness of the Streets I shall preach in Season & out of Season."

Like many other Americans who wrote about politics during the summer and fall of 1793, Adams could not resist the temptation to employ the yellow fever epidemic as a figure of speech. Two years earlier, Thomas Paine, whose pamphlet *Common Sense* had played such a critical role in advancing the American Revolution, had endorsed the French Revolution in a book called *The Rights of Man*. "Paines Yellow

Fever," John told his wife at the end of 1793, was "a putrid, malignant mortal fatal Epidemic." This was the year that Louis XVI and Marie Antoinette were beheaded and a coalition of monarchies declared war against the French republic. Inevitably the flames engulfing Europe cast a long and menacing shadow over American politics. In 1793 mere differences of opinion between men like Adams and Thomas Jefferson, a supporter of the French Revolution, began to ripen into intense personal enmity. Abigail endorsed and amplified her husband's alarm at Jefferson's apostasy, but the two expressed their growing distrust of their old friend differently. John's interpretation of Jefferson's affection for the French Jacobins and hostility toward Britain was essentially economic: he owed a reported seven thousand pounds to British merchants from before the Revolutionary War, and his was the expected animus of the desperate debtor against an importunate creditor. On the other hand, Abigail's analysis of Jefferson focused on his religious views. She liked him, but she was convinced from their conversations in Paris that he was essentially an atheist (a term Jefferson never used for himself). "I know Mr. Jefferson to be deficient in the only sure and certain security, which binds Man to Man & renders him responsible to his Maker," she told her husband.

Abigail had never stopped expressing her political opinions to her husband and other family members, but she did so with increasing intensity and frequency as she was swept up in the rising tide of political passion that accompanied the French Revolution. On the last day of 1793, she addressed her husband, who had once again traveled to Philadelphia without her. "If as a Female I may be calld an Idle, I never can be an uninterested Spectator of what is transacting upon the great Theater," she declared. Adams's horror at the events in France caused her political views to take a more conservative turn. Two months later, she told John that she now believed humans were "unfit for freedom." The simple, sad fact, she wrote, was that "Some were made for Rule others for submission."

Abigail did not confine her political expression to the letters she sent her husband. John Quincy had begun writing newspaper essays lambasting the French Jacobins and their American supporters, and his mother often offered him advice. One of his series, published over the pseudonym "Barnevelt," had gone on long enough and ought to be concluded as soon as possible, she told him. When John Quincy's comments about one of his opponents, Massachusetts attorney general James Sullivan, took a nasty turn, his mother admonished him that the man's age and status entitled him "to a respecctfull language." Upon receiving this reproof, she reported to John, their son "instantly stood corrected." One of the primary purposes of John Quincy's essays was to defend George Washington against the relentless abuse that had been heaped upon him for refusing to commit the United States to the defense of the French Revolution, and in May 1794, the president rewarded the young attorney's loyalty by making him the official U.S. envoy to the Netherlands. As "minister resident," he would only be paid half the salary of a full-fledged minister, but even that amount, $4,500, was much more than he could expect to earn anytime soon practicing law. Indeed it was only $500 less than what his father earned as vice president. In the Netherlands, John Quincy would be following in John's footsteps, since one of the senior Adams's assignments during the Revolutionary War had been to represent the United States at the Hague. John Quincy sailed from Boston in September, with his brother Thomas accompanying him as his secretary.

Although the new ambassador seemed to be well on his way to a distinguished political career, the Adamses continued to worry about their other children. John informed Abigail in a January 1794 letter that he wrote Charles more often than his brothers in hopes he could thereby "fix his Attention and excite his Ambition." Charles surprised the family by initiating a courtship with Sally Smith, younger sister of Nabby's husband, William. Although Abigail at first viewed Sally through the same skeptical lens that she had trained on Royall Tyler and Mary Frazier, the young woman soon proved considerably more stable than her brother William, and the family became convinced that she might be just the safe harbor Charles so desperately needed. The two were married at the end of August 1795 with the approval of the entire Adams family. "After all the Hair Breadth scapes and iminent dangers he has run, He is at last Safe landed," Nabby wrote.

The Smiths had returned from England in February 1793, and William's speculative enterprises seemed to be flourishing. With decidedly mixed emotions, John described Nabby's "Adventurer of an Husband" as "proud of his Wealth." The following month, as the vice president prepared to head home from Philadelphia in a stagecoach, he mused that his son-in-law would probably not allow Nabby to travel in anything shabbier than "a Coach and four," which he himself regarded as "Monarchical Trumpery." John had cautioned Smith "against his disposition to boasting," but he had to acknowledge, at least to his wife, that William had proved himself "very clever and agreable." Nor could Adams suppress a wish "that my Boys had a little more of his Activity." Further complicating John's and Abigail's feelings about Colonel Smith was his announcement that, while in England, he had made a side trip to Paris, where he had been chosen as an official French representative to the U.S. government. His primary mission was to persuade his home country to immediately pay back all the money it owed France.

John spent the summer of 1794 in Quincy with Abigail and then headed back to Philadelphia alone for the third year in a row. This pattern—Abigail living full-time at Quincy, John spending most of the year in Philadelphia—would continue until 1797. Although the two saw much less of each other than they had in England and during John's first three years as vice president, this was an easier separation than the one they had endured between 1779 and 1784, when the Atlantic Ocean had rolled between them. The rhythm the couple established in the mid-1790s resembled the one they had followed twenty years earlier, when John was a member of the Continental Congress. The vice president returned to his wife every summer, and all through the winter months, each wrote the other at least once a week.

Less than a month after his arrival in Philadelphia, John told Abigail he was "as impatient to see you as I used to be twenty year ago." The expression charmed her. "Years subdue the ardour of passion," she wrote, "but in lieu thereof a Friendship and affection deep Rooted subsists which defies the Ravages of Time, and will survive whilst the vital Flame exists." Unwilling to concur even in the minor concession with which his wife had prefaced her affectionate comment, John concluded his next letter, "I am, with all the Ardour of Youth yours[,] J.A." Three years later, Abigail complained of the separation that the nation had imposed on the Adamses by not paying John enough to bring his wife with him to Philadelphia. "No Man even if he is sixty years of Age ought to live more than three Months at a Time from his Family," she wrote. Once again the vice president's reply was saucy. "How dare you hint or Lisp a Word about Sixty Years of Age," he declared. "If I were near, I would soon convince you that I am not above forty."

Several times, Abigail noticed that she and her husband had written down very similar thoughts on the same subject, with their letters crossing on the post road somewhere between Philadelphia and Quincy. For instance, on November 10, 1794, Abigail, who had become more involved in the management of the family farm than ever before, started sending John a daily report on her activities. That letter reached John on the seventeenth—right after he mailed his wife a request for "A Journal, or diurnal Register of farming." Coincidences like this one put Abigail in mind of the chains of signaling stations European military commanders were starting to use to convey important information over long distances quickly. They proved, she declared to her husband, that the two of them were linked by the "Tellegraph of the mind."

By the mid-1790s, the French Revolution had degenerated into a bloodbath, the struggle between American Federalists and Republicans had grown increasingly passionate, and politics consumed more and more of the Adamses' correspondence. Abigail's horror at the atrocities of the French Jacobins, and her fear that their domestic followers planned to import revolutionary violence into the United States, combined to transform her into something of a reactionary. The woman who had exhibited remarkable audacity as a bond speculator, who had outdone her husband in voicing opposition to British measures (albeit only privately), and who had disparaged religious conservatives now declared, "Speculation in Property, in politicks and in Religion have gone very far in depraving the morals of the higher classes of the people of our Country."

To an even greater extent than other Federalists, Adams persuaded herself that the southern slaveholders who dominated the Republican party ("a packe of Negro drivers," she called them) had been irretrievably corrupted by their sexual access to the women they claimed to own. When Virginia senator John Taylor published a pamphlet denouncing Treasury Secretary Hamilton's partiality toward bankers and bond speculators, Abigail archly observed his recourse to prostitution as a figure of speech. He could not help himself, she declared in a February 1794 letter to her husband, for "his uncloathd Negroes had blackned his mind." This was, of course, a partisan comment, but Abigail worried that even President Washington's family had been tainted by interracial sex. When John informed her that Elizabeth Custis, Martha Washington's granddaughter, had married an "English East India Nabob" who was reportedly more than twice her age, Abigail replied that Custis could not have done much better, since in Virginia, "Black are so plenty and manners so licentious" that no white woman—not even the president's step-granddaughter—stood any chance of "marrying one of her own States Men, without some progeny" by his slaves. "You must not tell the good Lady"—Martha Washington—"all this story," she added. "Tell her that I hope Her connextion will be productive of much satisfaction to her."

Abigail had not forgotten that during the Revolutionary War, thousands of enslaved Americans had cast their lots with the British. Now that slavery had been abolished in Massachusetts, she contemplated a second Anglo-black alliance with equanimity. Indeed, she told John, if the southern Republicans should drag the United States into renewed warfare against the British, "I hope their Negroes will fight our Battles, and pay these real and haughty Aristocrats all the Service due to them, from the Real and true Republicans" of New England.

During the 1790s, Abigail, who had always assumed the superiority of her own region, became nearly as suspicious of European immigrants as she was of white southerners. In Philadelphia, she regretted the necessity of hiring "foreigners," as she called them, as servants. And in the fall of 1796, when a series of devastating fires struck Savannah, Georgia; Wilmington, North Carolina; and Baltimore, she claimed not only that the blazes were the work of arsonists but that the culprits must be immigrants. "I fear America will be the harbour and assilum of the dissolute and abandoned of the Nations of Europe, unless more vigilence is adopted with respect to foreigners," she told John. Abigail's newfound conservatism even extended into the religious realm. While her husband was vice president, the woman who had so often denounced biblical literalists affirmed that she was still "no friend of bigotry." On the other hand, she declared, "I think the freedom of inquiry, and the general toleration of religious sentiments, have been, like all other good things, perverted, and, under that shelter, deism, and even atheism, have found refuge."

Adams's mid-1790s lurch to the right did nothing to diminish her conviction that women were men's equals. Indeed, the battles between Federalists and Republicans gave her numerous opportunities to challenge timeworn myths of male superiority. In 1794, when Samuel Adams, who was serving as governor of Massachusetts, gave an address that exhibited his Republican leanings, Abigail reported to John that many Federalists were calling it "an old woman's speach."

Actually, she said, "I would deny my sex, if any old woman in the Country would have made a speach so little to the purpose." And when the authors of a pair of Republican pamphlets pursued their partisan agenda by exposing confidential information, she reminded John of the common prejudice that women were unable to keep secrets. The two writers had "taken of[f] the reproach from the Female Character," she declared. In raising this issue, Abigail mockingly referred to men as "Lords of the creation."

As historian Rosemarie Zagarri has shown, the phrase *female politician* did not initially carry any pejorative connotation. It simply referred to a woman who exhibited an interest in policy making. Charles Adams meant no criticism of his mother when he applied that term to her in a February 1795 letter (and in fact Abigail sometimes described herself as a "politician"). But by this time, many men were starting to wield the phrase as an epithet, and Abigail protested this trend, observing in a letter to George Cabot, a U.S. senator from Massachusetts, that men had fixed "a sutle Stigma upon the character of a Female politician to deter us from entering too far" into the political realm. Telling women not to follow politics was not only unjust but absurd, she claimed. "At such an Aeon as the present who can be an unconcern'd Spectator?" she asked.

In keeping with these convictions, Abigail's interest in female education was, if anything, more intense than ever. In December 1794, the vice president informed his wife that he planned to attend commencement exercises at Philadelphia's seven-year-old Young Ladies Academy. She was eager to hear how the day had gone. "You promised me an account of the Female Commencment," she wrote him early in January. "Was you dissapointed, either in your expectations or in your attendance?" In the same letter, Abigail commented on a book John had previously sent her at her request, Reverend John Bennett's *Strictures on Female Education*. "You may be sure Bennet is a favorite writer with me for two reasons," she wrote. "The first is; that he is ingenious enough, to acknowledg & point out the more than Egyptian Bondage, to which the Female Sex, have been subjugated, from the earliest ages, and in the Second place; that he has added his Mite, to the cultivation, and improvement of the Female Mind." Women's education had made more progress in America during the previous fifteen years than it had throughout the entire previous century, Adams averred. Still, "Much yet remains to be done."

Given the harsh reality of women's educational deprivation, Adams was willing to concede, in a letter to her sister Elizabeth, that she enjoyed "the Society (but do not you betray me) of the gentlemen more than the Ladies," adding, "I have mixt more with them, and I find their conversation more to my taste." Here Abigail was of course referring to traditional women—not to those (including Elizabeth and Mary) who had managed to educate themselves despite the odds against them. Abigail had always been a voracious consumer of books by female authors, and in the mid-1790s, she avidly acquired, read, and circulated women's reflections on the French Revolution, including the work of Anne-Louise-Germaine Necker (known as Madame de Staël), Helen Maria Williams, and Marie-Jeanne Roland.

As Abigail aged, she seemed to make peace with the plain fact that women were not going to share in the fruits of independence anytime soon. In a May 1796 letter to John Quincy, she once again mocked men as the "Lords of the Creation," but she also seemed to withdraw her 1782 complaint about women not being able to hold elective office, conceding to men the "Government of States and Kingdoms." Still, she was resolute in observing that male rulers were often incompetent, and she noted that on the rare occasions when the reins of power had fallen into female hands, they had generally been well managed. "Of the few Queens who have reigned for any length of Time as absolute Sovereigns," she informed John, using an extract from the *Universal Magazine*,

> the greatest part of them have been celebrated for excellent Govenours. Pliny, tells us that in Meroe, women rained for many successive ages. Among the Lacedemonians [Spartans], the woman had a great share in the political Government; and that it was agreeable to the Laws given them by Licurg[u]s. In Borneo, the women Reign alone, and their Husbands enjoy no other privilege than that of being their most dignified Subjects.

Abigail and John had been debating male-female relations for so long that she could joke about the subject without any danger of him thinking that she no longer took it seriously. When one of the vice president's friends, New York attorney Egbert Benson, declared that Abigail ought to be named "Autocratrix of the United States," she feigned indignation. "Tell Benson I do not know what he means by abusing me so, I was always for Equality as my Husband can witness," she wrote.

Like her sister, Elizabeth Shaw continued to follow developments in women's struggle against male domination. "I wish you would be so kind as to lend me the Rights of Women—the first opportunity," Shaw wrote Adams at the end of 1793. She was referring to Mary Wollstonecraft's *Vindication of the Rights of Woman*, published in London the previous year. As for the other Adams, John, even the enormous respect he came to feel for his wife's intellectual gifts failed to eradicate his scorn for most other women. In a January 1794 letter to Abigail, he lamented that their son Thomas seemed to be wasting his time. "I fear he makes too many Visits in Families where there are young Ladies," he wrote. "Time is Spent and nothing learn'd." At this point in the letter Adams realized what he had just said—and to whom he had said it. He did not blot out those words, but he tried to recover with a jocular reference to the leading feminist of the era. "Pardon me! Disciple of Woolstoncroft," he pleaded. Then John clarified: "I never relished Conversations with Ladies excepting with one at a time and alone rather than in Company." Abigail replied that she was not a disciple but a "*Pupil* of Woolsoncraft."

At the end of September 1794, Abigail received shocking news from Haverhill. Elizabeth reported that at 9:30 P.M. on Sunday the twenty-eighth, her husband "said he was weary & would go to Bed." Reverend Shaw "went up Chamber, came part of the way down, & called for his Cap," which she retrieved for him. "It was after eleven" when his wife finally climbed into bed. "I thought he breathed hard," she later told Abigail, "but as he so frequently did, I was not apprehensive of Danger." Around six the next morning, Elizabeth said to her husband, "Is it not time for us to get up? have you not slept enough?" Reverend Shaw made no reply. His wife's attempts to rouse him attracted the attention of the couple's two daughters, who came running into their parents' chamber.

"Pappa—Pappa—do wake him, Mamma," the four-year-old cried.

"It is not in my power my dear little Abby, do you not see how much your Sister, & I try," her mother replied. Shaw never regained consciousness and died at about nine-thirty that morning. Elizabeth grieved for her husband—and for herself and her children too. The Adamses took responsibility for paying her son William's Harvard tuition, but where would she and her two daughters go? The house the Shaws had lived in for two decades did not belong to them but to the town, and as soon as Haverhill settled on a new minister, she and her two girls would have to leave. (At one point she was accused—falsely, she insisted—of trying to postpone her eviction by talking a promising candidate out of applying for her husband's job.) "If we owned an house we could do very well, & [I] only had my Health we could take Boarders in this Town which would enable me to keep my Family together," Elizabeth wrote Abigail. As it was, she herself might be forced to board out, which could mean sending one or both of her daughters to live with relatives. William Smith's family had dissolved as a result of his addiction to drink. His sister could not be arraigned for any such vice, yet now her family might also have to be dispersed.

Nabby's prospects, by contrast, continued to improve. By the spring of 1795, Colonel Smith's speculation in government securities and western land had proved so successful that he decided to build a monument to his success. In March he agreed to pay five thousand pounds (roughly triple his father-in-law's annual salary as vice president) for a twenty-three-acre tract along the East River just north of New York City—on East Sixty-First Street on modern maps. There was already a house on this land, but Smith announced plans to replace it with a replica of Mount Vernon.

As speculators like the colonel created immense fortunes with almost no work, they set an example that impressionable young men like Abigail's sons found irresistible. Unsurprisingly, Charles, at once charming and easily charmed, was the first Adams to take the bait. The only irony was that the money with which Charles bought into the speculation game had been advanced by his financially conservative father. Painfully recalling the sacrifices he had endured while building up a client base, the vice president had given each of his sons two thousand dollars to help them through this rough patch. The money came in the form of U.S. government certificates issued by a Dutch bank. John strongly advised his sons to leave their securities, which paid 5 percent annual interest, in Holland, withdrawing the interest to supplement their income while preserving the principal. But he left the final decision up to them, and Charles immediately rejected his father's advice. Money could earn at least 7 percent in America, he pointed out in a letter to his brother John Quincy. While a difference of two percentage points might not seem large, seven is 40 percent more than five, and Charles was convinced that he could obtain this higher rate of return without undue risk. He assured John Quincy that he would be able to obtain solid collateral—mortgages on real estate—for the money he lent out. Charles made such a convincing case that his elder brother agreed to unload his own federal bonds as well, and he asked Charles to invest his two thousand dollars in New York. A short time later John Quincy, who had evidently pared his personal expenses to the bone, managed to free up an additional two thousand dollars for his brother to invest.

In the fall of 1795, less than a year after burying her first husband, Elizabeth Shaw received a marriage proposal from Stephen Peabody, the minister in the neighboring town of Atkinson, New Hampshire. The preacher's financial situation was scarcely better than hers, but he did have a house, and Elizabeth freely, if painfully, acknowledged to her sisters that her consideration of Peabody's offer would be influenced by "pecuniary motives." "I must change my place of abode, & retire into a room, if I do not go to Atkinson," she wrote. Renting a room might mean living apart from her daughters, an unthinkable prospect. Elizabeth also had other reasons to marry Stephen. She had "never heard anything amiss" about him, and he was "one of the warmest advocates for female education." Indeed, he had admitted several girls, including a daughter from his first marriage, to the academy he ran in Atkinson, making the school, which is still in operation, the nation's oldest coeducational institution of its kind.

In the end Elizabeth decided to accept Stephen's offer on one condition: he must allow her to have a separate estate. At her first husband's death, Betsy had finally gained control of her half of the Medford farm that she and Abigail had inherited from their father more than a decade earlier. Puritan New Englanders frowned on separate estates, which flew in the face of their conviction that man and wife were one person. But money problems might tempt a man to save himself and his own offspring using assets intended for his stepchildren. By continuing to control her half of the Medford farm, Elizabeth could retain some of the financial autonomy she had enjoyed during her brief widowhood and give her children a measure of economic security. In a letter to Abigail, she explained that she "wanted the interest for my own use, & Childrens, & the principal secured to them, when I am gone, & they stand in the greatest need of it."

Even at the end of the eighteenth century, separate estates remained rare in New England, for the simple reason that they required the husband's consent. But Reverend Peabody agreed to "sign any obligation which is reasonable." The instrument was drawn up, the signatures were affixed, and the couple married on December 8, 1795. Elizabeth moved across the state line to Atkinson, where she wasted no time in enrolling her oldest daughter in her husband's academy.

CHAPTER 25

"Presidante"

1796–1797

It is nearly impossible to exaggerate the anxiety that Americans experienced on March 4, 1797, when John Adams succeeded George Washington as president of the United States. The nearly universal sense of unease—to which Abigail and John were by no means immune—had roots deep in the American character. As soon as a politician lays his hands on even the smallest quantum of power, Americans of the founding era believed, he inevitably uses it as a tool or weapon with which to obtain more. Even if historians are correct in describing the politically aware Americans of the eighteenth century as excessively suspicious, theirs was a uniquely productive form of paranoia, for it was a principal ingredient in their decision to wrench thirteen colonies out of the British Empire. All of the taxes Parliament tried to levy in the 1760s—on molasses, tea, stamps, and the rest—would collectively have given Americans a lighter fiscal burden than that borne by their fellow British subjects on the other side of the Atlantic. The tyranny that sparked the rebellion was not actual but potential. If the Parliament in which Americans were not represented could tax them at all, it could take everything they had.

One of the ironies of the ensuing Revolutionary War was that in the course of preventing a group of men on the other side of the Atlantic from "enslaving" them (as they repeatedly phrased it), free Americans put themselves at the mercy of another set of would-be despots at home. Educated colonists continually ransacked the pages of history in search of the rules that govern human relations, and one of the axioms they found was that men who achieve success on the battlefield invariably ride the wave of military fame into political power. Julius Caesar would never have become an emperor if he had not been a victorious general first. Knowing that, free Americans who lived through the Revolutionary War wavered between gratitude toward the men who commanded their armies and fear that today's generals would become tomorrow's tyrants. Yet the man Americans might have naturally feared most, George Washington, managed to persuade them that the old maxim about commanders in chief grasping at political power did not always apply. He did it through a series of renunciations, and it was these, more than anything Washington accomplished on the battlefield, that won him a place in the hearts of his fellow citizens.

As a young man Washington had hardly seemed destined to become the embodiment of political virtue. In 1754, when France and Great Britain were at peace, he led a detachment of Virginia soldiers into the frontier region near present-day Pittsburgh and attacked a French reconnaissance party. A third of the Frenchmen were killed. Barely a month later, Washington was forced to surrender his little army—and to confess in writing that he had "assassinated" Ensign Joseph Coulon de Jumonville, the commander of the French detachment. The ensuing conflict, variously known today as the French and Indian War, the Seven Years' War, the Great War for Empire, and (in Canada) as the War of the Conquest, is generally recognized as the first world war.

The extended conflict gave Washington plenty of time to restore his military reputation, but he was still a long way from becoming an exemplar of political virtue. He acquired fabulous wealth in 1759, when he married Martha Dandridge Custis, but he was determined to improve his fortunes by fair means or foul. In defiance of royal edicts aimed at keeping peace with the Indians by allowing them to hold on to their hunting territories, he aggressively speculated in frontier land, not even scrupling at inveigling land bounties from the soldiers he had once commanded. By 1774 Washington had acquired rights to nearly thirty thousand acres. When, during the course of that year, imperial authorities adopted a series of decrees affirming their determination to halt the American colonies' westward expansion, they did more to fuel Washington's anti-British sentiment than Parliament could ever do by levying taxes on him.

Today many Americans believe Washington used the Indian-fighting skills he had honed during the French and Indian War to fight and win an asymmetrical conflict against the waves of redcoats thrown against him by the British military establishment. Some scholarly provocateurs even suggest that his unconventional tactics made him, by the standards of the time, a terrorist. The truth is that Washington fought conventional battles—and lost most of them. Until the last year of the war, all of the great American victories—the grandest of them at Saratoga, New York, in October 1777 and Cowpens, South Carolina, nearly three years later—occurred when Washington was hundreds of miles away. During the entire course of the Revolutionary War, the troops under his direct command won all of three major engagements, and the word *engagements* is carefully chosen here, because not one of the three could properly be called a battle. The cannon that Continental Army soldiers stealthily dragged to the top of Dorchester Heights on the foggy evening of March 4, 1776, did not sink even one of the British men-of-war riding at anchor in Boston Harbor. Nor did they do much damage to the imperial troops quartered in the town. The British evacuated Boston on March 17 essentially without a fight. Likewise the Hessian troops quartered in Trenton, New Jersey, nine months later—on December 26—were so completely surprised by Washington's decision to cross the Delaware River and attack them that the ensuing events can hardly be described as a battle.

And then there was Yorktown. It is true that the two vast armies lobbed shells at each other for more than a week, but the actual fighting was confined to the American capture of a pair of redoubts, one of the assault parties being led by a young army colonel named Alexander Hamilton. Those two raids and the steady advance of the American trench diggers were sufficient to persuade General Cornwallis to surrender on October 17, 1781. So it was not really on the battlefield that Washington won his fellow citizens' affection. It was by keeping his army together, by avoiding bigger mistakes than the ones he made at Long Island (where he failed to secure his left flank) and Brandywine Creek (where he was outflanked from the right), and, more than anything, by what he chose not to do, which was to grasp at political power. Even before the war ended, Washington had convinced most Americans that his model was not Caesar but Cincinnatus, the Roman general whose claim to fame was that he had successfully fought his nation's battles and then returned to his plow. The confidence Americans had placed in Washington was confirmed on an unseasonably warm afternoon in December 1783. As Washington took leave of his officers in the long room at Fraunces Tavern (near the southern tip of

Manhattan Island), and as a picked crew rowed him across the Hudson River on the first leg of his journey home to Mount Vernon, his Virginia plantation, nearly everyone present believed they were seeing him for the last time.

In May 1787, when Washington was asked to chair the convention that had gathered in Philadelphia to write the Constitution, and eighteenth months later, when he was elected president, he accepted both posts against his will, and that very reluctance persuaded Americans they had the right man. Many of the people who followed politics assumed that President Washington would remain in office until he died. Sure, he would have to stand for reelection every four years, but the outcome would never be in doubt. He would thereby establish a precedent of chief executives serving for life. His successors would be able to exploit their incumbency to continue this pattern, and the executive magistracy would become in practice what Hamilton had wanted all along—an elective monarchy. The men who formed those expectations somehow forgot about the process that had made the president so popular, but he himself remembered. In the words of a noted historian, Washington had "perfected the art of getting power by giving it away." In September 1796, he committed one last, grand act of renunciation. He announced that he would not seek a third term.

Some Jeffersonian Republicans, especially in the South, were so worried about Hamilton's campaign to strengthen the federal government—and about his apparent ability to bring the president around to his way of thinking—that they were glad to see the old man go. On the other hand, to many Americans it seemed the president was guilty of "leaving others to hold the bag," as Jefferson put it. At the moment when Washington chose to give up the helm, the United States faced a host of foreign threats and, much more ominously, the prospect of civil war. France had erupted in revolution three months after he took office, leading to renewed hostilities against its neighbors, including Great Britain. In the 1778 Franco-American treaty that had supplied the blue coated soldiers who guaranteed Washington's victory at Yorktown, the United States and France had sworn to defend each other against all enemies. In 1793, Washington essentially tore up the treaty, proclaiming the United States neutral in the war that had engulfed the Old World. An Anglo-American treaty negotiated by John Jay, the chief justice of the Supreme Court, and ratified in 1795 was viewed in France as violating Washington's neutrality pledge, and French privateers stepped up their depredations on American shipping. As Washington left office, the two revolutionary republics were on the brink of war. The much greater threat, however, was internal, for the Republicans who supported France and the Federalists who favored Great Britain were at each other's throats.

There was no heir apparent, so the election of 1796 would be the first contested presidential race in American history. Not only the candidates but the republic itself would be put to the test. The modern procedure by which party conventions choose presidential candidates was decades in the future, but everyone knew the Federalists in Congress would put forward the name of John Adams. But would he agree to run? On the one hand, neither he nor his wife had learned to tolerate the personal attacks that were constantly hurled at him. On the other hand, John was nothing if not ambitious, and Abigail was ambitious for him. From his vantage point as vice president, he could tell that the top post commanded infinitely greater prestige, as symbolized by the salary, which was five times higher than his own. An even more important factor was the Adamses' wish to avoid the "Humiliation"—and even "Mortifications" and "Disgrace"—of electoral defeat.

Although they shared these feelings, Abigail was more prepared than John to return to private life. As soon as Washington began talking about retiring, raising the possibility that her husband would succeed him, Abigail wrote John lamenting that becoming first lady would mean having to "look at every word before I utter it, and to impose a silence upon my self, when I long to talk." She repeated that concern again and again throughout the election season and during John's first months in office. John did not share Abigail's regret at the prospect of her displaying greater "taciturnity," archly reminding her, "A Woman *can* be silent, when she will." And he wondered whether service as president, for all its stresses and dangers, might be the lesser of two evils. Like Abigail, he had frequently waxed eloquent upon the ennobling qualities of the simple rural lifestyle. Yet in the fall of 1796, he was uncharacteristically honest with himself about the drawbacks of the village routine. Imagining defeat in a December 16 letter to Abigail, John wrote that it was "rather a dull prospict to see nothing but ones Ploughshare between one and the Grave."

The Republican caucus in Congress nominated Thomas Jefferson, and the two men's rivalry for the presidency further frayed the bonds of friendship. John and Abigail encompassed Jefferson in the same suspicion they harbored about a host of other politicians: that he had sacrificed his principles in order to gain the favor of the electorate. Even before Washington announced his retirement, John wrote Abigail saying he did not like his chances of defeating the popular Jefferson. That prompted her to remind him that the Constitutional Convention had been careful not to leave the selection of the president to ordinary Americans. The chief executive would be chosen by the electoral college, and in about half the states, voters did not even pick the presidential electors, since state assemblymen had retained the choice in their own hands. Abigail ventured that John's unpopularity—arguably his greatest source of personal pride—would not keep him out of the presidency. No matter what ordinary citizens thought, she wrote, "the chief of the Electors will do their duty."

In the end Jefferson proved less of a threat to John's candidacy than a group of extreme Federalists who worried that he was not sufficiently anti-French. Hamilton spearheaded an effort to push John's running mate, the fervently pro-British Thomas Pinckney of South Carolina, ahead of him. Abigail was not surprised. She had never trusted Hamilton, whom she considered "a man ambitious as Julius Ceasar, a subtle intriguer." His evil was apparent, she told her husband, even in his eyes. "The very devil is in them," she wrote. "They are laciviousness it self, or I have no Skill in Physiognomy."

The election was not Abigail's only source of anxiety in 1796. Earlier in the year, she had learned that Colonel Smith was having financial problems. At first she had managed to convince herself that he had been an innocent victim of the "Mountabank Swindler" Felix de St. Hilaire, the dancing-school master and covert arms dealer who, a year earlier, had married the colonel's sister Margaret in a joint wedding that also united his sister Sally to Charles Adams. But by September, she knew that Smith's problems were largely of his own making. He and his brothers had purchased tens of thousands of acres of frontier real estate on loan, and they could not sell the land fast enough to pay their debts. "Whether on the winding up he will have any thing left is what I believe neither he or any one else knows," Charles told his mother. Unfavorably comparing his brother-in-law to one of the great speculators of the age, Charles declared that Smith "acted on a very large scale and whatever he may think you and I know he is not a Robert Morris." The colonel was forced to sell "Mount Vernon," his unfinished estate on the East River, and his family retreated to the inexpensive backwater town of

East Chester, in Westchester County, twenty miles north of New York City. As her daughter dealt with this stunning setback, Adams was able to take comfort from the fact that her middle son seemed to have found his footing. "Charles increases in buisness and in reputation," a relieved Abigail told his elder brother. She could scarcely have imagined that as Smith sank further into the quicksand, he would drag Charles and even John Quincy down with him.

On February 7, 1797, when Congress gathered to hear how each state's electors had voted, it fell to John Adams, as the sitting vice president, to break open the sixteen sealed packages and announce the totals. The extreme Federalists' efforts to push Pinckney ahead of Adams had fizzled like a damp fuse, and John edged out Jefferson (who would now become vice president) by a margin of three votes. Adams's victory elicited an ambivalent response from the future first lady. By New Year's Day 1797, Abigail felt certain John was going to win, and she described a "singular" dream she had had the night before. "I was riding in my Coach, where I know not, but all at once I perceived flying in the Air a Number of large black Balls of the Size of a 24 pounder," she wrote. The cannon balls "appeard to be all directed at me. All of them however burst and fell before they reach'd me tho I continud going immediatly towards them." "How would the Sooth Sayers interpret this Dream?" Abigail asked John. It was clear that she had already settled upon her own interpretation: the dream revealed her anxiety as she and John headed into the line of fire.

As first lady, Abigail would no longer be able to avoid living in Philadelphia. But before taking up her new post, she still had some battles to fight in Quincy. In reporting one of these to John, she showed how her attitude toward African Americans had evolved since her return to the United States less than ten years earlier. As recently as 1785, shortly after her arrival in London, Abigail had been shocked by a performance of *Othello,* unprepared as she was for her own repugnance at Othello's "sooty appearance" and the "disgust and horrour" that, as she told her sister Elizabeth, "filld my mind every time I saw him touch the Gentle Desdemona." Yet in January 1797, when one of the Adamses' black servants, a young man named James who worked in the family stables, approached her with an unusual request, she showed that she had changed. A night school had recently opened in Quincy. The instructor's specific mission was to teach basic math and accounting to the town's apprentices, and Abigail had enrolled James at his request. About a week later, a man named Faxon, the father of two of James's fellow students, paid Abigail a visit. He informed her that if her servant continued attending the classes, "it would break up the School for the other Lads refused to go." Abigail reported the ensuing exchange in a letter to John.

"Pray mr Faxon has the Boy misbehaved?" she asked. "If he has let the Master turn him out of school."

"O no," Faxon replied, "there was no complaint of that kind, but they did not chuse to go to school with a Black Boy."

Adams pointed out that blacks and whites in Quincy worshipped together every Sunday. "Why not object to going to meeting because he does mr Faxon?" she asked.

For years James had earned pocket money by providing music at local dances, and that gave Abigail another opening. "Did these Lads ever object to James's playing for them when at a dance[?]" she asked. "How can they bear to have a Black in the Room with them then?"

"O it is not I that object, or my Boys," Faxon replied. "It is some others."

"Pray who are they? Why did not they come themselves?"

Faxon had no ready answer, and so Adams pressed her case. "Merely because his Face is Black," she asked, "Is he to be denied instruction[?] How is he to be qualified to procure a livelihood? Is this the Christian Principle of doing to others, as we would have others do to us?"

"O Mam, you are quite right," Faxon replied. "I hope you wont take any offence."

"None at all mr Faxon, only be so good as to send the young men to me. I think I can convince them that they are wrong. I have not thought it any disgrace to myself to take him into my parlour and teach him both to read & write. Tell them mr Faxon that I hope we shall all go to Heaven together."

How did the woman who in 1785 had spoken to her sister of her "disgust and horrour" at seeing Othello touch Desdemona become, by 1797, a champion of school integration? The fact that the Moorish general was only a fictional character (and that the man who played him was white) makes her transformation seem all the more mysterious. Perhaps the difference between Adams's two comments can be explained partly by the different contexts. Although James's exact age is not recorded, he was young, and he was a member of Abigail's family as the term was used in the eighteenth century. His vulnerability and victimhood appealed to the nurturing instincts that had been central to Abigail's character ever since she accompanied her mother on her charitable rounds. Othello, on the other hand, was a stranger and a warrior—and it was easy enough for Adams to suspend her awareness that he was a product of Shakespeare's imagination, because *Othello* was one of the first English-language plays she ever saw. Perhaps the most important difference between Adams's servant and Shakespeare's general was that Othello was part of an interracial sexual union—a sensitive subject not only for Abigail but for many of her contemporaries. At about the time she protested the Moor's marriage to Desdemona, her friend Thomas Jefferson was preparing to publish a book called *Notes on the State of Virginia*, in which he ascribed to African men a decided "preference" for white women.

Abigail's contrasting responses to James's expulsion and Shakespeare's play may also be explained by differences of place and time. When she saw *Othello*, she was the wife of the official American envoy to Great Britain. She took her role as a representative of the United States seriously, and while she was a consistent opponent of slavery, the play's implicit criticism of racial hierarchy may have offended her national pride. In addition, the interracial sex in *Othello* may have seemed like an extreme form of the licentiousness that this proper New England lady had reported to her sisters throughout her European travels. A lot happened during the ensuing twelve years. By 1797, the United States was sharply polarized along regional lines ("oil & water are not more contrary in their natures, than North and South," Abigail believed), and she stood squarely in the northern camp. There was still slavery in the North (though not in Massachusetts) in 1797, but it was not the region's defining characteristic as it was below the Mason-Dixon Line. In the same way that Adams might have watched *Othello* through the lens of offended American morality and patriotism, Mr. Faxon's racism seems to have posed a threat to her regional pride.

Which is not to say that Abigail's attitudes pervaded New England—or even her own family. Less than a month after receiving his wife's report on her conversation with Mr. Faxon, John wrote her about his search for servants for their new house in Philadelphia. "I am peremptorily for excluding all blacks and Molattoes," he wrote. Two weeks later, worried that his Philadelphia servants would be "ruined by them turbulent blacks," he instructed Abigail to fire James and another black servant named Prince. "Give them their Cloaths handsomely and dismiss them," he insisted. Abigail did not bring James to Philadelphia, but she did not fire him, either, and he remained a part of the household for several more years.

On New Year's Day 1797, even as Abigail was writing John about the cannonball dream she had had the night before, he penned his own letter urging her to arrive in Philadelphia in time for his inauguration on March 4. Abigail demurred. Despite her eagerness to reunite with her husband, she was in no hurry to take up residence in Philadelphia. She had already had her fill of the capital during John's first term as vice president. Although the Republican party that had formed around prominent national figures such as Jefferson and James Madison was primarily a southern and rural phenomenon, Philadelphia was the one great exception to that rule. Federalists such as Abigail and John suspected that artisans and laborers flocked to the party in the hope that it would transform American equality from a political status and promise of shared opportunity to an actual fact of daily life. The Adamses could see little difference between the urban Republicans and the French revolutionaries, and Abigail often referred to Philadelphia's Republicans as "Jacobins," the name that had attached to the most powerful and radical of the artisan clubs terrorizing Paris. In her eyes, Philadelphia was not the city of brotherly love but "the city of Sedition, the Hot bed of France." To hear her describe them, the city's poor might at any moment erect their guillotine in the middle of Market Street.

Nor was this all. Abigail had discovered during John's first term as vice president that Philadelphia, for all its vaunted religious diversity and toleration, harbored no church that fit her spiritual tastes. She would not worship with the Quakers, any more than she was going to attend the city's sole Roman Catholic church. Most Pennsylvanians were dissenters from the established Church of England, as were Abigail and John. Yet the Adamses were liberal Congregationalists, while by this time the majority of Pennsylvanians were Presbyterians. Like Abigail and John's Puritan ancestors, most Presbyterians believed that man is inherently evil and destined for damnation. When worshipping in Philadelphia, Abigail once complained to her sister, "I must sit under as strong Calvinism as I can possibly swallow."

For all these reasons, Abigail did not choose to move to the capital in time to hold the Bible as John was sworn in as president. In fact not one member of his family was present in Congress Hall that Saturday morning to share in his moment of triumph. "It would have given me great Pleasure to have had Some of my Family present, at my Inauguration which was the most affecting and over powering Scene I ever acted in," the new president confessed to his wife. John was, moreover, disappointed to have to start his term without the new first lady by his side—and not just because he missed her company. "I never wanted your Advice and assistance more in my Life," he told her in a letter written two weeks after his inauguration. Of course distance had never stopped Abigail from offering John her counsel, and by the time she became "Presidante" (as John sometimes called her), she had overcome her last scruples about advising him on matters of public policy. She sent him an extended critique of his farewell address to the U.S. Senate, over which he had presided as vice president. And shortly before the inauguration, she told him the impending naval conflict against France should be funded with a land tax instead of levies on windows, stamps, or houses, all of which would be "very unpopular" in New England. John later had reason to wish he had heeded this suggestion, for the house tax that Congress adopted at his behest provoked a tax revolt.

Abigail thought the question of whether she would have to be by her husband's side during his first months as president had been resolved in favor of her remaining in Quincy. But at the end of the March, when it became clear that he would not be able to leave Philadelphia for his summer vacation until the end of July, the president changed his mind. "I must intreat you," he told Mrs. Adams. "Loose not a moments time in preparing to come on that you may take off from me every Care of Life but that of my public Duty, assist me with your Councils, and console me with your Conversation." Abigail initially demurred at the renewed summons. "O I had got a going so cleverly," she wrote. "I expected to have got all things in order for your reception" in July. But three days later, when she received another entreaty from John (several more followed), she reluctantly informed him that she would head south as soon as she could get ready, a process that would take about two weeks.

CHAPTER 26

"I Did Get an Alteration in It"

1797–1798

The journey from Quincy to Philadelphia that Abigail undertook at the end of April 1797 was one of the saddest of her life—and not only because she knew she was venturing into enemy territory. Just before she left, on April 21, John's eighty-eight-year-old mother, who for all her grumpiness had become one of her closest companions, died in her arms. Two days later, as Abigail headed west, she learned of another, sadder, death in Quincy. Her late brother William's twenty-one-year-old daughter, Mary, who had been living with the Cranches, lost a long and painful struggle with tuberculosis. After Mary's death, her mother, Catharine, took her agony out on her relatives. "She was very cross," Mary Cranch reported to Abigail. Insisting that she "had no body to take any care of her," she told Cranch, who nursed her as well as she could, that she "wishd she could be among people who had some feeling."

On the way to Philadelphia, Adams stopped off at East Chester, New York, to visit Nabby and her family on their isolated farm. Her daughter had distressing news for her: Colonel Smith's financial situation was even worse than she had apprehended. "My reflections upon prospects there, took from me all appetite to food, and depresst my spirits, before too low," Abigail told her sister Mary. Smith somehow managed to avoid debtors' prison, but many of his fellow speculators, including Robert Morris (known as the financier of the revolution) and James Wilson (a Supreme Court justice), two signers of both the Declaration of Independence and the Constitution, did not. Another victim of the financial panic was James Greenleaf, whose brother and sister had both married children of Richard and Mary Cranch. Greenleaf had "drawn into his Vortex the whole of the Family, not a connection I fear has escaped," Abigail's sister Elizabeth Peabody informed her in July. Under the terms of his father's will, Greenleaf had set up an annuity for his brother John (Lucy Cranch's husband), but Mary reported that James's bankruptcy would prevent John from receiving the money he was owed. She lamented that Lucy had not required her brother-in-law to back the annuity with collateral. William Cranch, Mary's only son, was even more deeply involved in Greenleaf's collapse. Leaving behind a promising legal business in Haverhill, he had moved to Washington, D.C., to serve as a lawyer for the North American Land Company, a speculative firm Greenleaf had formed with Robert Morris and others. In 1797, when the company failed, Billy became personally liable for numerous debts that he had contracted in his official capacity.

With the benefit of hindsight, the roots of the disaster are clear enough. The windfall profits that Congress had disbursed to war-bond speculators had had an unintended consequence. Throughout the 1790s, young men (and a few young women) dreamed of matching the previous generation's fabulous returns, and their wheeling and dealing created a speculative bubble. As Abigail surveyed the wreckage of the Smith and Greenleaf families' finances, she was moved to exclaim, "Such is the folly and madness of speculation and extravagance." Despite this denunciation of securities traders (and many more like it), whenever she could scrape a few hundred dollars together, the first lady continued to purchase more bonds.

Colonel Smith's and James Greenleaf's misfortunes intensified John Adams's already intense disapproval of speculation. Early in his presidency, acutely aware that his wife disapproved of his investing the family's savings in land instead of government securities, Adams tried to complete the purchase of a farm without her knowing about it. She soon discovered the scheme and scolded him for it. He ought to have known better than to try to keep a secret from her. During his term as president, John grew more suspicious than ever of bondholders' influence on government policy. While dining with his old friend Benjamin Rush, the Philadelphia physician, scientist, and signer of the Declaration of Independence, Adams learned that one Republican, a Dr. Edwards, had recently returned from France imbued with Jacobin principles. John asked Rush whether Dr. Edwards's support for France might be the result of his "Speculating in french revolutionary funds." ("Oh no" came the rapid reply.)

After just two days in East Chester, Abigail paid a quick visit to

Charles in New York City, where she was pleasantly surprised to discover that he was living "prettily but frugally." Although she had met his wife, Sally, she did not know her well and was relieved to find her "a discreet woman . . . quite different" from other members of the Smith family. The couple had a year-old daughter, Susanna. On Monday, May 10, when Abigail was still twenty-five miles outside Philadelphia, she was surprised at the approach of a carriage she recognized: the president had come out to greet her. The pair dined in the riverside town of Bristol, Pennsylvania, and arrived in Philadelphia just as the sun was setting. Pennsylvania's gentry class was also waiting to greet the first lady, and her first few days in the capital were wholly absorbed in receiving company. The only way to have any time to herself, she quickly discovered, was to rise at 5 A.M. That gave her three hours to write letters and complete other tasks before breakfasting with the family at eight and then taking up her duties as head of the household. She was required to receive company from noon until two—"sometimes untill 3." Dinner was at three, and after that she usually went for a long carriage ride until about sundown. The most expensive and crowded social event she had to endure was the president's Fourth of July reception. Every congressman and prominent public official had to be invited, along with the leading citizens of Philadelphia. George Washington had started this tradition, and in doing so he incurred a rare criticism from Abigail (expressed only to her sister Mary, of course). The well-heeled Virginian ought not to have imposed this costly precedent on his less wealthy successors, she declared.

The first scene of Abigail's ordeal as first lady lasted less than three months, for at the end of July she and the president were on their way home for a summer holiday. Like everyone else in Philadelphia with the means to do so, they fled the pestilential capital during each summer of John's administration. By this time Colonel Smith had abandoned East Chester to pursue another of what Abigail called his "Ideal Schemes." This time his penchant for land speculation had carried him all the way out to Detroit, prompting his abandoned wife to tell her mother that "existance was a burden to her." In a letter to Mary Cranch, Abigail confessed to being "more distresst for her than I have been ready to own," for Nabby had "always kept every thing to herself that she could." In the first lady's eyes, her son-in-law's disappearance had a silver lining, in that it enabled her and John to stop off in East Chester and carry Nabby and her children with them to Quincy, where they arrived on

August 5. Abigail persuaded her daughter to enroll William and John in Stephen Peabody's academy in Atkinson. They would board with their great-aunt Elizabeth as all three of their uncles had done. Had the colonel's good fortune continued, he would not have been willing to give up his sons. "The Fathers misfortunes will prove the Salvation of the Children," the president observed.

The Peabodys were appalled at the pair of wild colts who raced across their threshold early in the fall of 1797. The younger boy, John, who turned nine on November 9, was especially rambunctious. He "hears, & is faulty the next moment," Elizabeth reported. Her husband was "very kind to them," she added, "but is resolute in exacting proper obedience." It was all Mrs. Peabody could do to persuade the parson, who had never met Nabby, that their mother was a "woman of Breeding & politeness," Abigail learned from Mary. Nabby's relatives of course blamed her sons' bad behavior on Colonel Smith. Nor was he the only bad influence. "I was fully sensible that the Boys must be taken from all their connections to break them of habits which they had imbibed," Mary wrote. Abigail agreed, noting that in New York there had been a whole "train of uncles and Aunts and servants to spoil them," and adding, "I dread their Fathers return least he should take it into his Head to take them away." Barely two months after William and John arrived in Atkinson, their great-aunt was able to report that both had become "much more respectful than they were," though she still had to "add precept, to precept, and line upon line."

Late in the summer of 1797, while the Adamses were enjoying their respite at Quincy, they received word that their son John Quincy was a married man. Since the winter of 1795–1796, he had been courting a young Londoner named Louisa Catherine Johnson. She was the daughter of Joshua Johnson, a wealthy merchant, originally from Maryland, who was serving as the American consul in London, and his British-born wife, the former Catherine Nuth. The two had been betrothed for more than a year, but John Quincy worried about his ability to support a family, and he did not set a wedding date until more or less compelled to by his fiancée. They were married on July 26, 1797, at All Hallows Barking, an Anglican church near the Tower of London. Joshua Johnson promised Adams a five-hundred-pound dowry, but it was never paid, for by the time of the wedding feast, the bridegroom learned that his father-in-law's fortune was gone. A short time later, Johnson would move his family back to Maryland in a vain attempt to recover his for-

Louisa Catherine Adams (1775–1852), wife of John Quincy Adams. Edward Savage, 1791–1794. *Courtesy Adams National Historical Park.*

tune. John Quincy had managed the same feat as his big sister: he had found a marriage partner whose financial prospects were considerably dimmer than they seemed.

It would later emerge that the groom's economic position was not quite what it appeared to be, either, which came as a surprise not only to Louisa Catherine but to John Quincy himself. He had authorized his brother Charles to invest four thousand dollars for him, emphasizing that the funds should only be trusted to people who offered "unexceptionable" security. Initially Charles had complied with these instructions. He lent two thousand dollars of his brother's funds to Justus Bosch Smith, Nabby's brother-in-law, receiving in return not only a handsome interest rate of 7 percent but also a mortgage on a lot in New York City worth twice the amount of the loan. But about a year later, Smith had come to Charles and asked him to return the mortgage—while continuing to lend him John Quincy's money. The Smith brothers had desperately needed cash, and Justus could not sell his land (or use it as collateral for a new loan) while it had a mortgage on it. Charles agreed to exchange the mortgage for a simple promissory note. Later, when the details of the transaction were finally revealed, Charles claimed that he had acted out of sympathy: unless the Smiths could raise a great deal of money in a short time, William's creditors would send him to debtors' prison. It seems likely that the Smiths also offered Charles some additional financial incentive that left no trace in the historical record. In any event, he did not think his decision to give up the mortgage posed much of a risk, because the Smiths were in the process of selling tens of thousands of acres of land, recently acquired from the Six Nations of the Iroquois, in upstate New York.

And then came the crash. By 1796 the bursting of yet another speculative bubble had scared off investors and sent real estate prices plummeting. The Smiths' landjobbing business fizzled, and Justus could not even come up with the interest on John Quincy's note, much less the principal. Nor would Charles be able to force Smith to pay his brother back (at least not without a long, costly, and mutually-embarrassing lawsuit), because he no longer held a mortgage on Smith's land.

Abigail was informed of Charles's mismanagement of his brother's funds during an October 1797 visit to New York City. Her source was not Charles but his wife Sally, who worried that he had invested his own money in the Smiths' operations along with his brother's. Abigail immediately wrote John Quincy suggesting that he ask Cotton Tufts to take Charles's place as his commercial agent. She provided no specific reasons for her recommendation but hoped her son would take the hint. The ambassador did not immediately fire his brother, but he stepped up his efforts to get Charles, who had not sent him a financial report since September 1796, to tell him what was happening with his money. His letters nonetheless continued to go unanswered. By the end of 1798 Abigail looked upon her eldest son's entire four thousand-dollar investment as "sunk."

Not all of the financial news that John Quincy received in 1797 was discouraging. Early in the year he learned that President Washington had promoted him from minister resident to minister plenipotentiary, which doubled his salary to nine thousand dollars a year, at the same time transferring him to the Portuguese court in Lisbon. By the time he left the Netherlands, word had arrived that his father, who had assumed the presidency, had decided to send him to Prussia instead. The ambassador and his brother went ahead with a planned stopover in London, during which John Quincy wed Louisa. The three Adamses spent several months in England awaiting congressional funding for the Prussian mission, finally embarking for Hamburg on October 18. During the rough overland journey from that port city to Berlin, the Prussian capital, both of John Quincy's traveling companions became gravely ill, and Louisa suffered a miscarriage—the first of many.

The yellow fever epidemic that struck Philadelphia during the summer of 1797 was second only in virulence to that of 1793, and Abigail initially expected her husband to keep his family in Quincy until the first frost, which always ended the dying. But the president felt the need to station himself closer to the capital, and he insisted on Abigail accompanying him. Early in October, the couple headed south, but they got no farther than their daughter's house in New York. Philadelphia remaining lethal, John and Abigail stayed on and on at East Chester before finally completing their journey at the end of the month.

During the president's absence, relations between the United States and France had reached a new low. John had sent three representatives to try to negotiate with the Directory, the committee that now ruled the French republic. For a long time nothing was heard from the three emissaries, and in the hyperpartisan atmosphere of the 1790s, rumor rushed in to fill the void. In February 1798, an anonymous essay appearing in the Boston *Independent Chronicle,* a Republican newspaper, asserted that the president had "received Dispatches from France a month ago, notwithstanding which, the most profound secrecy has been maintained on this subject." Abigail's cousin William Smith lived in Boston, and he knew that the statement he read in the *Chronicle* was false, for he had just opened a letter from the first lady stating that there had been "Not a word yet from our Envoys." He took his cousin's letter to a Federalist newspaper, the *Columbian Centinel*, which printed the relevant passage almost verbatim but without identifying the source.

Even as the *Centinel* was publishing this extract from Abigail's letter, the emissaries' first report finally reached Philadelphia. The story it told was almost beyond belief. Three French representatives, known in official dispatches only by the code names X, Y, and Z, had presented their American counterparts with three demands. The U.S. government must lend France $12 million, President Adams must apologize for the allegedly anti-French speech he had made upon assuming office—and the

American government must give French prime minister Charles Maurice de Talleyrand-Périgord and his cronies $250,000.

Even the most fervently pro-French members of Congress were, as Abigail reported to Mary Cranch, "struck dumb" by Talleyrand's demands. "Millions for defense," the Federalists cried, "*not a cent* for tribute." Now it was the Francophobes' turn to spread rumors, a process in which Abigail eagerly joined. "We have felt no small share of the balefull influence of the Age of Reason," she told her older sister in May. The French Jacobins were not content simply to overhaul the government of their own country. Their real goal was "To destroy and undermine Religion" throughout the Western world. "To have a thorough Idea of the deep laid system," she informed Mary, "you must read a work lately publishd calld proofs of a conspiracy against all the Religions and Governments of Europe." This volume, written by John Robison, claimed to expose a French scheme to send secret agents throughout Europe and the United States with orders to foment sedition and attack Christianity. Today Robison's suspicions seem paranoid, but in Adams's eyes, they were fully confirmed when a host of artisans, newspaper editors, and even congressmen rallied to the *tricouleur*. Pro-French crowds marched in the streets of Philadelphia and other major American cities, and President Adams received death threats. "I really have been allarmd for his Personal safety," Abigail wrote.

The XYZ affair and the apparent surge of Jacobinism on the streets of the United States terrified many Americans, who counterdemonstrated in favor of their country and its chief executive. Independent militia companies sprang up with the openly avowed purpose of defending the administration against domestic as well as foreign enemies. In dozens of towns, citizens held special meetings that sent formal addresses to President Adams praising his handling of the crisis and vowing to stand by him. Adams was determined to craft an individual response to every single town that addressed him, a task that strained his creative powers. The statement he sent the town of Boston was, by all accounts, awkwardly phrased; some people even read it as hostile. When Mary Cranch gently criticized John's language in a letter to her sister, Abigail confided that she, too, had "objected to the answer to the Boston address upon the same principle you mention." "I did get an alteration in it," she confided, though obviously not a big enough one. Abigail's affirmation that she had persuaded her husband to revise his address to the Bostonians is the only surviving evidence of what may in fact have been a fairly common practice. We will never know for certain just how many of President Adams's public statements were edited by the first lady.

Abigail participated in the debate over the perceived French threat in other ways as well. Early in May, she added her voice to a growing chorus of demands for a legal crackdown on the American Jacobins. If they are "not surpressd," she told Mary, "we shall come to a civil war." Later in the month she endorsed a congressional effort "to punish the Stirer up of Sedition, the writer and printer of base and unfounded calumny." Her only concern about "the Alien Bill" was that it might be "curtaild & clipt untill it is made nearly useless." Adams was referring to what would become the most controversial legislation of her husband's presidential term, the Alien and Sedition Acts, adopted in June and July 1798. Frequently cited as the most egregious assaults on (white people's) civil liberties ever to emerge from the halls of Congress, this new legislation made it much harder for immigrants to become U.S. citizens—and much easier for federal officials to deport them. In addition, the administration would now be able to throw its critics into prison. Several Republican newspaper editors—and even one congressman—were in fact jailed. John and Abigail Adams both endorsed the Alien and Sedition Acts, with one important difference: Abigail complained to John Quincy that, just as she had feared, the legislation had been "shaved and pared, to almost nothing." The only justification that can be offered for Adams's enthusiasm for the Alien and Sedition Acts is that she sincerely believed that the French government had placed secret agents, men bent on destroying her husband, the American republic, and Christianity, throughout the United States.

In addition to favoring a harsher approach to sedition than the legislation her husband signed during the summer of 1798, Abigail also disagreed with his military response to the Gallic threat. A formal "declaration of war ought undoubtedly to have been made" against France, she told John Quincy. This was a stronger line than even Hamilton took, and the president was fully satisfied with having persuaded the Senate and House of Representatives to create a new military establishment that would be ready to defend the nation should the French strike the first blow.

As horrified as Abigail was by the gruesome excesses of the French Revolution, she continued to favor radical changes in the relationship between American men and women. "If man is Lord," she told her sister Elizabeth, "woman is Lordess—that is what I contend for." She had never expected women to obtain men's permission to hold office or even to vote, she had never demanded either right, and by the time she became first lady, she had even ceased to complain about these two injustices. But she held fast to her insistence upon women's right to be politicians as her era defined that term: active participants in the conversation about America's future. "If a woman does not hold the Reigns of Government," she wrote, "I see no reason for her not judging how they are conducted." This was, of course, a very personal matter for her. "My mind has ever been interested in publick affairs," she told her husband.

Some of Adams's musings on women and politics during her years as first lady can only be described as whimsical. In 1797, New Jersey assemblymen allowed propertied women to vote (a gift that they would take back ten years later). Although the enfranchisement clause did not extend to married women (who by definition controlled no property and thus could not meet the property qualification for voting), for Abigail it conjured up interesting possibilities. Reverend Kilbon Whitman had been her favored candidate for the office of assistant pastor of Quincy, but the all-male town meeting had turned him down. "Present my compliment[s] to Mr. Whitman," she wrote her sister Mary after learning of his defeat, "& tell him if our State constitution had been equally liberal with that of New Jersey and admitted the females to a vote, I should certainly have exercised it in his behalf."

Despite Abigail's passionate engagement in the pitched battles that roiled American politics during her husband's presidency, she did not neglect her domestic concerns. Throughout the winter of 1797–1798, William Abdee was laid up with what would turn out to be his final illness. His months as an invalid were agonizing for him and exhausting and expensive for his wife, Phoebe, who frequently had to stay up all night monitoring him. December 1797 was cold even by New England standards. Abigail sent the Abdees some food and several loads of firewood, and the town of Quincy helped out as well, but Phoebe depleted her meager savings, drawn mostly from washing clothes, in hiring watchers to sit with her husband so that she could get a little rest.

William Abdee finally died on New Year's Day 1798, but his death only complicated relations between his widow and the first lady. Now that Phoebe's husband was gone, Abigail believed, it was a waste of space for her to have an entire house to herself. But where else could she go? There was nothing keeping Abigail from forcing Abdee to share the house with tenants paying market rent, but, as she observed to Mary, "no other person will occupy it, who will give any thing for it, whilst she resides there." And the truth was that Abdee did *not* have the Adams cottage all to herself. Although for more than a decade Abigail, Cotton Tufts, and Mary Cranch had sternly instructed her not to provide refuge to homeless people, she had continued to do so. Adams had initially been informed that all of Phoebe's pensioners were black, but during the 1790s, she received a growing number of reports like the one Mary Cranch sent her a week after William Abdee's death. "I am concern'd about Phebe," she wrote. "She is very unwell and unable to do much towards her support. She seems to have a house full of Blacks and white about her." Cranch was not sure whether any of the people who stayed with Abdee paid her any rent. It seems likely that they helped with expenses as they were able—but also that they were a net drain on her meager resources. Still she could not turn them away. "Pheby will be surrounded as long as there is any thing to eat or drink," an annoyed Adams told her sister. "[T]ho I am willing to assist towards her mantanance, I do not like to support all she may keep with her."

Mary Cranch thoroughly agreed. "All the black that passes thro the town smell her out," she told her sister, "I talk'd to her yesterday and charg'd her to bolt her door against them for we would not nor could not furnish her with intertainment for them." The people who stayed with Abdee were not the only ones who took advantage of her, Cranch claimed. A Quincy resident named Jonathan Rawson had committed a "cruel" outrage similar to what Royall Tyler had done a decade earlier, foisting on Phoebe a servant who was no longer useful to him, in this case "a sick negro woman." "He took her out of Bed and sent her in a Sleigh with a Boy in a storm to be left with her," Mary reported to Abigail in February 1798. Rawson promised to have the servant transported to Bridgewater, but the bad weather prevented that. Indeed, Mary wrote, the woman was "so ill Phebe could not send her back in the storm."

CHAPTER 27

"They Wisht the Old Woman Had Been There"

1798–1800

Another of Abigail's domestic concerns caused her even more grief. By the end of January 1798, she was convinced that her son-in-law, William Smith, having avoided debtors' prison by heading out into Indian country (allegedly to broker a new land deal), was never coming back. Prophecy was never Adams's gift, for just then Colonel Smith reappeared in East Chester and "notified his Credittors to meet him in order to adjust with them his affairs." He still held out hope that he would be able to pay all his debts once his real estate ventures began to pay dividends. Nabby as usual said nothing. "I know her silent manner of receiving both good and evil," observed Mary Cranch.

John Quincy, the most cautious of Abigail's sons, also suffered serious financial setbacks during his father's presidential term, and not only because of his brother Charles's unwise financial decisions. The minister's agent in Boston was physician Thomas Welsh, a cousin by marriage of Abigail's. Dr. Welsh used the money that John Quincy and numerous other people had entrusted to him for risky speculations that proved disastrous, and it appeared in 1798 that much of the money John Quincy had left with Dr. Welsh was lost. As Abigail watched "one bubble bursting after an other," she was moved to send her sister Mary a remarkable piece of financial advice. The Cranches had recently sold John Adams a farm in Quincy, and they were trying to decide where the proceeds should go. All three of Richard and Mary's children were in need, two having suffered at the hands of James Greenleaf and the third having married a preacher. All were raising small children. Abigail understood her own maternal instincts well enough to know that the Cranches would be tempted to give their children at least some of the money arising from the sale of the farm, and she now urged Mary to resist that impulse. "I have seen too many instances of parents dependant upon Children," she wrote. "Tho there are instances which do honour to humane nature, there are more which disgrace it." Hold on to the money, Adams advised her sister, and invest it in public securities. Even though the price of government paper had stabilized, denying investors the sort of windfall profits that early purchasers such as Abigail had earned, bonds would still "yeald you more real profit than the Land."

Abigail herself was still in a position to exercise the benevolent instinct that she urged her sister to suppress. She was able to provide help to pensioners like Phoebe Abdee as well as to Mary's children (when William Cranch returned to the practice of law after his partnership with James Greenleaf ended in disaster, Abigail stepped in to buy him the necessary legal books) as well as her own (she paid Nabby's sons' tuition at Atkinson Academy). Even these expenditures did not unduly strain her budget, so in October 1797, as she was returning to Philadelphia, she decided to expand Peacefield, resolving to keep the renovations secret from her husband until their return to Quincy the following summer. Why add to his worries, she reasoned, and it would be fun to surprise him. (She may also have feared he would object to the project.) Cotton Tufts agreed to supervise the construction and to keep it secret from John. The president sometimes opened Tufts's letters to Abigail, so she arranged for them to be enclosed in the mail sent to her by her sister. In recent years John had even fallen into the habit of peeking into the mail his wife received from Mary, but he had recently been "scolded" for doing so, and he seemed unlikely to repeat the offense.

If the Adamses had managed to get home to Quincy in June 1798, as Abigail had hoped, she might have pulled off her surprise. As it was, the French crisis kept John at his post all through June and into July. During this interval, a Quincy neighbor who knew about the renovations but not about the secrecy surrounding them visited Philadelphia, stopped in to see the president, and inadvertently spoiled the surprise. "The President had a hearty laugh & says he is sorry it was not carried clear along," Abigail told Mary.

The Adamses did not get out of Philadelphia until the end of July. By then the heat inside their carriage was stifling. "I never sufferd so much in travelling before," the first lady reported to Mary during a stopover in East Chester. The rest of the journey to Quincy was even worse, and by the time the couple pulled into the driveway at Peacefield, Abigail had contracted an illness that lingered all through the fall. For a long time she thought she was going to die. It was November before John learned that Philadelphia had had its first frost (meaning the danger of yellow fever had passed), and by then winter had come to New England, making the journey back to the capital too cold and wet for the still-weak Abigail, so he left without her. The first lady was distressed at once again being separated from her husband, but there were advantages to lingering in Quincy. For one thing, the couple had decided to make additional improvements to their estate—a new barn and a carriage house—and Abigail was able to supervise the construction. She and her husband clashed over how large and fancy the barn should be. It "must not be a monument of Foppery," John told her when he learned that she envisioned twenty-foot vertical beams. "I should be content to have it 16 foot Post." With a large family and scant resources, with numerous grandchildren and "shiftless Children," John was determined to "Spin an even thread of Plainness thro Life." By the time the president received his wife's reply—she thought the barn must be twenty feet high if the adjoining stables were—he had already conceded that twenty feet was the correct height.

Abigail was also glad to be in Quincy in mid-December, when a pair of town officials came by to assess Peacefield for the new federal tax that John had obtained from Congress in order to help fund his military buildup. She managed to remain "a silen[t] hearer" until one of the assessors announced that he was "loth that it should appear that the president had not the best House in Town." Unless Peacefield really was Quincy's most expensive address, she replied, she would just as soon decline the honor, since a higher valuation of course meant a higher tax. In determining the value of a home, "Did the Law say, that the owner of the House was to be taken into consideration[?]" she asked. In the end the assessors valued Peacefield at two thousand dollars—a thousand less than Captain Beale's place down the road.

Even with the imposition of this new tax, the federal government would be unable to finance President Adams's military mobilization without borrowing, so Congress voted in March 1798 to issue a new series of federal securities. The nation was still in the grips of a credit contraction, so Congress decided that in order to obtain the needed funds, it would have to offer investors a high interest rate: 8 percent. Abigail urged her husband to buy some of the new bonds. The president balked at the idea, and it is not clear what he eventually decided, but by the end of 1799, the first lady bought more than a thousand dollars' worth of the new certificates on her own "particular Account." She also continued pushing John to purchase the securities that the government had issued back in 1790 and 1791 in exchange for the certificates left over from the Revolutionary War, and she was especially interested in a series of bonds that would not start paying interest until 1800. The deferral of the interest set a limit to the market price of these notes, making them a real bargain, but the price was sure to rise as soon as interest payments began, so anyone who was able and willing to buy and hold them could make a tidy profit. The president initially showed no interest in these "deferred" securities (he wanted to save his money for additional improvements to Peacefield), and surviving records do not indicate whether he ever purchased any, but Abigail bought several hundred dollars' worth on her own private account.

Abigail ended up spending the entire winter of 1798–1799 in Quincy, and it was, for the most part, a lonely time. There were only three guests for Thanksgiving (at that time a New England regional holiday): the Porters (a married couple who were serving as her farm managers) and the ex-slave Phoebe Abdee, whom she described as "the only surviving Parent I have." As for the president, he regretted not having his wife's "Society, Advice and Assistance," but the pair resumed the lively correspondence that had sustained them through the years of John's earlier public service. Among the topics they debated was John's admitted mania for buying Quincy farmland. In January, Abigail reported that Solomon Thayer had two parcels for sale, adding that she mentioned them not because she thought her husband ought to buy them but only to avoid incurring "blame for delinquincy" in failing to report such an opportunity (as she apparently had in the past). She also joked that when it came to real estate purchases, John seemed to be susceptible to reverse psychology. "I always observe your inclination to abate for Land, in proportion as I bring it forward before you," she told him.

Meanwhile Abigail continued to advocate for her own favored investment, federal securities. On February 1, when she wrote her husband suggesting an additional purchase, she characteristically portrayed herself as a mere messenger. Cotton Tufts, she reported, wanted to know whether John wished to buy more government paper. John agreed to the purchase. By this time the couple had also begun to expand their share of the federal debt by a process that was essentially automatic: with Abigail's consent, Tufts used the interest he collected on the Adamses' securities to buy more bonds.

The president and his wife wrangled over public as well as private matters. George Washington agreed to come out of retirement to command the troops that were being raised for a possible war against France, but everyone understood that he would not actually lead them into battle. That duty would fall to his second in command, and the president shocked many Americans, including his own wife, by offering the job to Alexander Hamilton. Letting others speak for her, as she often did, the first lady declared that the appointment "ill suits the N[ew] England stomack." Surely John had not forgotten about the scandal that had marred Hamilton's service in Washington's cabinet. Caught making a series of payments to a man named James Reynolds, the secretary of the treasury was accused of using Reynolds as an intermediary to engage in insider trading in government securities. In order to refute this accusation, the secretary had been forced to confess to a lesser offense. Yes, he admitted, he had given money to Reynolds, but not for the purpose of investment. The married Hamilton had had an affair with Reynolds's wife, and Reynolds had blackmailed him.

Hamilton had resigned his cabinet position halfway through George Washington's second term. His return to public life revived the prospect of new scandals, the president's wife told him. Evoking the image of an Old Testament cuckold and the wife who cheated on him, she warned that with Hamilton back on the scene, "Every Uriah must tremble for his Bathsheba." And she wondered how a man who had confessed to "breaking the most solemn private engagement" could be counted on to "not betray a public trust." John defended his appointment, but he agreed with Abigail about Hamilton's personal life. Indeed he could see little difference between the former treasury secretary and another of the Adamses' old nemeses. Hamilton, he told his wife, had "as debauched Morals as old Franklin."

John and Abigail agreed about another of his appointments to the officer corps, but it nonetheless provoked a sharp exchange between them. The president named his son-in-law William Stephens Smith as adjutant general of the new force, placing him third in command. But the nomination had to be confirmed by the Senate, where Adams's enemies exposed Smith's bankruptcy and voted him down. The rejection was a humiliation for both men. The largest force the senators could see Smith commanding was a regiment, which John duly offered him. The commission ought to have been declined, the president and first lady agreed, but Smith's financial desperation left him no choice but to accept. "His Pay will not feed his Dogs," a contemptuous John wrote Abigail early in 1799, "and his Dogs must be fed if his Children starve." William's financial travails and the few hints the president received from his wife about Charles's entanglement in them prompted him to painful reflections. "Happy Washington!" he declared, "happy to be Childless! My Children give me more Pain than all my Ennemies." This was too much for Abigail. "I do not consider G W. at all a happier man because he has not Children," she replied. "If he has none to give him pain, he has none to give him pleasure."

The Adamses disagreed about other issues during the winter of 1798–1799 as well. In January the president received an adulatory address from the members of the Maryland legislature, who worried that the French revolutionaries aimed at "the destruction of religion." In his reply, Adams assured the assemblymen of his conviction that moral and religious values were essential foundations of civic life. But he prefaced his comments on religion with an admission that he was "not fond of introducing this sacred topic into political disquisitions." Why not? Abigail wanted to know when she read her husband's statement. Ignoring the president's extended praise of religious belief and focusing on his prefatory confession that he was (as she paraphrased him) "not fond of mixing Religion with politicks," the first lady declared that "When religion has been equally attackyd with the Liberty and Government of the Country, it is proper to manifest a due Respect for that upon which both the other[s] Rest." John's confidential reply to his wife differed from his public statement to the Maryland legislators in one crucial respect: he praised Christianity in particular rather than religion in general. But he went on to remind Abigail that the vast majority of his fellow Christians would be aghast at his own religious system, since "It excludes superstition."

At least in principle, Abigail shared her husband's aversion to religious enthusiasm. "I do not believe that a people are ever made better by always hearing of the terrors of the Lord," she told her sister Mary at about this time. "Gloom is no part of my Religion." But the dialogue she had initiated by criticizing her husband's address to the Maryland assemblymen revealed an important difference in their belief systems. Abigail and her sisters, especially Elizabeth, often responded to the deaths of friends and relatives and the other tragedies of life by assuring each other that God inflicted these scourges on his creatures for the benevolent purpose of keeping them from becoming too attached to an earthly existence that they must one day forfeit. John did not agree. In a February 25 letter to his wife, he lamented that his three married children had been so "Blind thoughtless, [and] Stupid" as to find their marriage partners in families no wealthier than their own. He could not go along with those who insisted that "Nature contrives these Things with others to reconcile Men to the thought of quitting the World." He himself was able to "acquiesce in what is unpleasant" for a different reason: his expectation that eventually, "it will work out a greater degree of good." Uncharacteristically, Abigail let the matter rest there.

In February 1799 the president announced a measure that stunned his enemies but also his staunchest supporters, including the first lady. Even as he prepared the nation to do battle with France, he made one last attempt at negotiation. Although Talleyrand had treated the Americans' most recent diplomatic overture with contempt, demanding loans, a presidential apology, and a bribe, Adams decided to have William Vans Murray, the American minister to the Netherlands, travel to Paris with a renewed offer to negotiate. When the Federalists, who for years had been calling for war with France, learned that the president they had elected had made what they considered a humiliating peace overture, they were furious. And many of them thought they knew why Adams had suddenly gone soft. Almost simultaneously, Abigail and John observed to each other that (in Abigail's words) "Some of the Feds who did not like being taken so by surprize, said they wisht the old woman had been there" in Philadelphia when her husband conceived the idea of sending Murray to Paris, since she surely would have shot it down. John noticed the same reaction in the capital. "Oh how they lament Mrs Adams's Absence!" he reported to her. The Federalists were convinced that "If she had been here, Murray would never have been named nor his Mission instituted."

The truth was that Abigail instantly overcame her astonishment at her husband's decision to revive negotiations with France and persuaded herself that this was "a master stroke of policy." And even if she had disagreed with the president's move, Abigail affirmed, she could not have prevented him from making it, for "I never pretended to the weight they asscribe to me." But neither the first lady nor the president was surprised that people perceived her as being more bellicose than her husband when it came to France, because she really was.

Abigail had originally planned to join her husband in Philadelphia as early in the spring of 1799 as soon as the roads dried up enough for travel, but she ended up not having to go at all. Congress began its summer recess on March 3, and John was soon on his way to Quincy. The first lady was glad to have not only his companionship but his advice, because the couple had decided to undertake a major expansion of the mansion house at Peacefield. The third addition in as many years was to be, by far, the most ambitious yet, for it would double the size of the house. The first floor would have a cavernous drawing room, and directly above that, equally large, would be John's new office. At a time of crisis both for the nation and for the Adams family, with war against France seemingly imminent, Nabby's and Charles's families in financial turmoil and their other two children far from safe, the Adamses were determined to transform Peacefield into a Gibraltar where any and all of their tempest-tossed progeny could find asylum. Only then would the house be a genuine refuge for Abigail and John.

The president and first lady headed south again in October 1799, John a few days ahead of Abigail. Both stopped off at East Chester and were shocked to learn that Sally Adams, Charles's wife, had retreated to Nabby's house with her two children. Charles's struggle against alcoholism and depression, it soon emerged, had entered a new and more serious stage. "Sally opened her Mind to me for the first time," an anguished John reported to his wife after continuing his southward journey. "I pitied her, I grieved, I mourned but could do no more." Charles himself was virtually unrecognizable. He was "A Madman possessed of the Devil . . . a mere Rake, Buck, Blood and Beast." "I renounce him," the president declared. When Abigail visited with Charles's daughters a short time later, she was astonished at the progress they had made despite their traumatic home life. Susanna, who was only three, "would stand all day to hear you read stories, which she will catch at a few times repeating," and she had memorized all of Mother Goose. Her year-old sister, Abbe, seemed to be doing well, too.

During the winter Abigail closely monitored events in Massachusetts as well as New York. She must have been astonished to learn that the ex-slave Phoebe was still arousing controversy with her determination to harbor vagrants who paid her little or no rent. By this time she had taken a third husband named William (although Adams and her correspondents referred to him frequently, they never gave his last name), and Mary Cranch told her sister that the old couple got along well, except that Phoebe insisted on taking in boarders, and her husband balked at admitting "such creatures into the house, & threatens to inform you when you return." The man had told Cranch he was "willing to work & do any thing for Pheby, but not for such a vile crew." For her part, Mary reported, "Pheby thinks he has no compassion."

In the spring of 1800, as the first lady made her annual trip from Philadelphia to Quincy, she again stopped off in New York, this time persuading Sally to allow Susanna to travel to Massachusetts with her. Later in the summer, Sally and Abbe hastened there as well. Both Adamses spent the summer of 1800 nervously monitoring the presidential election while pretending not to care about the outcome. The chance that the electors might release John from his burdens was high, for he faced enemies on every front. To no one's surprise, the Republicans in Congress nominated Vice President Jefferson for the top post. The Federalist and Republican congressional caucuses both balanced their tickets with vice presidential candidates who hailed from the opposite side of the Mason-Dixon Line from the standard-bearer: New Yorker Aaron Burr for the Republicans and South Carolinian Charles Pinckney for the Federalists. Adams was amenable to running with Pinckney, but early in the summer, he learned that a group of Federalists, upset with his refusal to go to war against France, planned to try to push Pinckney ahead of him when the electors cast their votes. It came as no surprise that the chief conspirator was Alexander Hamilton.

Since the prevailing custom militated against candidates soliciting votes, there was little that John could do to affect the outcome, and for both Adamses, the election of 1800 was primarily a matter of waiting. To be sure, they had plenty of intermediate challenges to occupy them. Congress had voted back in 1790 to move the capital from Philadelphia to the new city of Washington, D.C., in the fall of 1800, and Abigail would have the dubious honor of being the first mistress of the new home (not yet called the White House) that was still being constructed for the president's family.

CHAPTER 28

"A Day of Darkness"

1800–1804

Abigail's arrival in the brand-new capital early in December 1800 carried with it none of the sense of limitless possibility that might normally be associated with such an occasion. A month earlier, her customary stop-off in New York had led to one of the saddest episodes of her life, for Charles's condition had further deteriorated. When she arrived in Manhattan early in November, she found her son "upon a Bed of sickness, destitute of a home." His wife and children had left him, he had been evicted from his house, and he would have been literally homeless if a charitable friend had not taken him in. When Abigail left New York, she feared she would never see her son again. "A distressing cough, an [affliction] of the liver and a dropsy will soon terminate a Life, which might have been made valuable to himself and others," she told her sister Mary.

John had gone on a few weeks ahead of his wife, and upon arriving in Washington, he had reported that the executive mansion was "habitable" but still very much under construction. Abigail's journey from Philadelphia to Washington went well enough as far as Baltimore. From there she planned to travel another thirty-six miles and then stop at an inn before completing the trip the next day. But her driver took a wrong turn, and the party wandered aimlessly for two hours before "a solitary black fellow with a horse and cart" led them back to the post road. By then darkness was coming on, and the inn was still miles away. A man named Thomas Snowden had offered to accommodate the first lady and her entourage, but she had declined to impose on him "with ten Horses and nine persons." Now she had no choice, and in fact Snowden rode out to repeat the invitation. She and her companions were received with "true English Hospitality," and they completed their journey without incident the following day.

For Adams, the sight of the city of Washington was as discouraging as the final leg of the trip that had brought her there. On paper the District of Columbia was a model capital for an enlightened republic, with wide avenues laid out in a symmetric grid, but in reality it was little more than a swamp, and most of its structures were mere shanties—with a few unfinished public buildings scattered among them. Abigail suspected that a primary reason the creation of the federal city was so far behind schedule was that it relied so heavily upon slave labor. Unlike free New Englanders, she observed to her friends back home, southern slaves had no incentive to work without physical compulsion.

Admittedly a little daunted, Abigail set about trying to turn one of the town's construction sites, the President's House, into a home. Scarcely had she unpacked her trunks when she learned that the dire prediction she had made in New York had been tragically correct: her son Charles was dead. Abigail expressed no regret about having abandoned her dying child, since there was nothing she could have done for him. Now that he was gone, her one consolation was that, outside

Washington, D.C., in 1800. *Courtesy Library of Congress.*

his two families, he had caused little harm to others. "He was no mans Enemy but his own," she wrote. For his "near connections," his death had actually been "a dispensation of Heaven in Mercy." One result of Charles's passing, imperceptible to Abigail but of interest to the student of her ideas, was to diminish her faith in the power of sentiment. John Adams had always associated sensibility with weakness (even when he applied the term to himself), and Abigail herself had long understood that men and women of feeling were doomed to suffer pains that their callous neighbors would never know. Watching the decay and dissolution of this "soft," "tender," "delicate," young man, whose "exquisite Feelings" and "sensibility" had attracted notice ever since he was a child, nudged Abigail still closer to her husband's less positive view of sensibility.

Less than a week after learning of her son's death, Adams received bad news of a different sort. South Carolina had always been a Federalist stronghold, but in 1800, that state's electors gave their votes to the Republicans. Without South Carolina, there was no way John could retain the presidency. It was some consolation to the Adamses to learn that Hamilton's effort on behalf of Charles Pinckney had failed. But Jefferson and Burr both pushed ahead of Adams, and he was not going to have a second term. For a man who had always acknowledged, if only to his wife, that vanity was his greatest vice, nothing could have been more humiliating than electoral repudiation. As John's most passionate champion, Abigail suffered nearly as much as he did.

Adams's defeat also had practical consequences. For all the complaints Abigail had made over the years about the paltriness of her husband's salary, the reality was that the family had finished nearly every year of his public service in the black (the one exception being his first term as vice president), and the surpluses had been especially large during the presidential years. Abigail had invested much of this money in shrewd ways that had greatly magnified it. Now she at the age of fifty-six and John at sixty-five would be thrown back on their own resources, for in those days presidents received no pension. All the same, Abigail was convinced that the loss was her country's, not her husband's—and certainly not her own. "At my age, and with my bodily infirmities, I shall be happier at Quincy," she told her son Thomas in mid-December. The question was whether the United States could survive four years of Republican leadership. "If ever we saw a day of darkness," she wrote her sister Mary after learning that John had been defeated, "I fear this is one."

After the states had chosen their electors, word arrived that William Vans Murray (along with the additional peace commissioners that the Senate had burdened him with) had successfully negotiated a treaty with France. Napoleon Bonaparte had made the team's work considerably easier by overthrowing the Directory just before the Americans arrived in Paris. Entanglement with the United States was, in Napoleon's view, a diversion from France's true destiny on the European continent and in North Africa, and he was only too happy to reach an accommodation with the Americans. When the treaty arrived in Washington, John and Abigail tasted that special flavor of satisfaction that comes with being vindicated too late.

As the year 1800 ended, no one knew for sure which of Adams's two Republican challengers was going to succeed him, for Aaron Burr had managed an electoral-college tie, at 73 votes, with his running mate Thomas Jefferson. That threw the election into the House of Representatives, where Federalists launched an effort to deny the top spot to Jefferson. Abigail struggled to reconcile her horror at the prospect of a Republican administration with her long-standing affection for the vice president, and all she could do was compartmentalize the two conflicting emotions. In January the Adamses invited Jefferson to a farewell dinner. As she often had during their sojourn together in Europe back in 1784 and 1785, Abigail went into dinner on the widowed Jefferson's arm. And yet on January 15, she shared with her uncle her anxiety that the new Republican ascendancy reflected "an increasing infidelity in Religion, an allarming corruption of manners from the highest to the lowest ranks of Society, a wrestless Spirit of discontent and turbulence," and "an unchecked spirit of calumny."

The worst of the Republicans' crimes was their irreligiosity. Jefferson "makes no pretentions to the belief of an all wise and suprem Governour of the World," Adams observed in a February 7 letter to her sister Mary. He "believes Religion only usefull as it may be made a political Engine, and that the outward forms are only, as I once heard him express himself—mere Mummery." The rise of the Republicans had a subtle but significant impact on Abigail's beliefs about human nature. She had participated as avidly as anyone in the eighteenth-century cult of sensibility, and her interest in that impulse would remain strong throughout her life. But her belief in the power of sentiment had already been chastened by the loss of her son Charles, by the emotional excesses of the French Revolution, and by what she viewed as the passionate extremism of the American Jacobins. When the reins of federal power were snatched from her husband's hands by men who elevated their faith in the human capacity for sympathy over their belief in God—the Republicans' "only religion is benevolence," she told Dr. Tufts—Abigail's fondness for sensibility suffered another blow. Unlike many other Federalists, she never went so far as to describe it as pernicious, and indeed she would always see herself as a woman of feeling, but for the rest of her life she would view sensibility less as a beneficent force that linked humans together than as a lamentable weakness.

In mid-December, Martha Washington, who had lost her husband a year earlier, invited Abigail to Mount Vernon for a final visit. The first lady had only just put on mourning for Charles, and had it not been for her predecessor's "pressing invitation," she would not have made the trip. Abigail's first impression of Mount Vernon was similar to what she had written a short time earlier about the executive mansion. The location was magnificent: from the piazza one had "a fine view of the River Potomac at the bottom of the Lawn." But the building itself was underwhelming. "The Rooms are small and low, as well as the Chambers," she wrote. Nor did the gardens impress her. She allowed that "the grounds are disposed in some taste," but she pointed out to Mary that "it required the ready money of large funds to beautify and cultivate the grounds so as to make them highly ornamental," and apparently President Washington had lacked those funds. For Adams, what was most striking about Mount Vernon was the three hundred slaves who labored there. In his will, the former president had ordered that those Mount Vernon slaves whom he owned be freed at his wife's death. (He lacked full legal discretion over about half of the slaves, since they belonged to the estate of Martha's first husband, Daniel Parke Custis; at Martha's death, they would go to the heirs Custis had designated.) Martha had subsequently decided not to make the slaves to whom her husband had promised freedom wait for her death to taste it. In providing for their immediate emancipation, she laid no claim to humanitarian motives, Abigail observed: "She did not feel as tho her Life was safe in their Hands, many of whom would be told that it was there interest to get rid of her." Martha Washington's emancipation deed took effect on New Year's Day 1801, less than two weeks after Adams's visit to Mount Vernon.

On February 13, Abigail set out on what she knew would be a slow winter's trek to Quincy. She had only spent three months in the new capital and knew she would never return. Her greatest challenge came early: the ice on the nearly mile-wide Susquehanna River north of Baltimore had been melting rapidly, and carriage drivers had stopped trying to drive on it. But it would be weeks before the Susquehanna would be sufficiently free of ice for a ferry to cross. Abigail and the other stagecoach passengers had no choice but to put up at an inn on the south bank of the river while they considered their options. The next morning, one of the passengers, a Mr. Parker, noticed that the ice had thickened during the night, and he decided to try to get the coach and its cargo over the river piecemeal. Workmen led the horses across the ice, then pushed and tugged the carriage itself over, and then finally loaded the passengers onto a little boat, which was dragged across. The boat had nearly reached the opposite bank when it broke through the ice, dropping the workers knee-deep into the frigid water. They scurried ashore with their cargo, the horses were reharnessed to the stagecoach, and the northward journey continued.

Abigail's decision to return to Quincy a few weeks before John turned out to be the last of the couple's countless separations, and it produced the last of the more than twelve-hundred letters they exchanged. John's fondness for levity had not slackened over the years. "I sleep the better for having the Shutters open," he informed the first lady three days after she headed north, "and all goes on well." Thus continued a lighthearted debate that went back at least to 1766, when the couple had had their first friendly quarrel over whether and when to close the bedroom shutters in the cottage at the foot of Penn's Hill. The dispute crops up in the written record just often enough to remind us that as abundant as the Adams correspondence was, its volume is insignificant in comparison to the oral exchanges that we can only imagine.

By the time Abigail reached Philadelphia, word arrived that the scheme to elect Burr instead of Jefferson had suffered the same fate as the earlier effort to push Pinckney ahead of her husband. On February 17, the House of Representatives awarded the presidency to her old friend. By this time John was less than three weeks from the end of his term, but he did not idle away his final hours staring into the fire. Worried that the Republicans would fill the judicial and executive branches with incompetent hangers-on, Adams worked feverishly to staff as many as possible of the vacant posts with his own men. Some of the appointments inevitably led to charges of nepotism. Abigail's nephew William Cranch, who had wasted some of the best years of his life on James Greenleaf's speculative schemes and then failed to prosper as a private lawyer, became a federal judge, and Joshua Johnson, who had declared bankruptcy, received a much-needed job as revenue collector. There can be little doubt that the first lady had encouraged her husband to make these appointments: at the end of her last surviving letter to her husband, written from Philadelphia on February 21, she told him, "I want to see the list of judges." Yet there is no reason to question Adams's claim that he considered his nephew and his son's father-in-law the best men for the positions he gave them. In common with the vast majority of his politically inclined contemporaries, including his wife, the outgoing president suffered from a chronic inability to perceive that his judgment could be clouded by self-interest.

In June 1800, President Adams had given Colonel Smith a post in the customs office for the port of New York. If, as seems likely, the first lady had something to do with that appointment as well, she soon had reason to regret her intervention. The government salary allowed Smith to assume the burden of financing his sons' education—which also gave him the right to choose their teachers. Before the year was out, he pulled them out of Atkinson Academy and brought them to New York. According to Elizabeth Peabody, Colonel Smith implored her and her husband not to view the removal of William and John as a slight. It was just that he wished to have his boys near him, he declared, and he did not want them to "imbibe sentiments foreign *to his domestic Circle*."

Some of President Adams's last-minute appointments, especially his elevation of John Marshall to the post of chief justice of the Supreme Court, were destined to change the course of American history. All of them infuriated the Republicans, who derided them as "midnight appointments." Jefferson could do nothing about Adams's judicial nominations, since judges served for life, but he fired many of the men his predecessor had appointed to the executive branch and to low-level judicial posts. One of the appointees, William Marbury, whom Adams had named as a justice of the peace for the District of Columbia, sued, leading to the famous case of *Marbury v. Madison*, in which Chief Justice Marshall and the Supreme Court majority upheld Jefferson's power to choose his own men, at the same time establishing the Court's authority to review executive decisions.

The midnight appointments finally accomplished what Adams's electoral defeat had not: they ended his friendship with the man who had turned him out of office. Jefferson viewed Adams's attempt to salt the judicial and executive branches with his loyalists as the final proof that the Federalist party was trying to create a permanent government impervious to electoral defeat. After March 1801, cordial occasions like the executive mansion dinner party where the Adamses had entertained Jefferson the previous December became unthinkable. In fact, for the next three years neither Abigail nor John sent the president a single letter, and neither received one from him, either.

John left Washington early on the morning of his successor's inauguration, and by the end of March, both Adamses were back in Quincy. For the first nine months after their return, Peacefield lived up to its name, for the only other family members living with them were Louisa Smith and Charles's daughter Susanna. But then John Quincy, whose father had called him home from Berlin in order to save him the humiliation of being dismissed by Jefferson, returned to Massachusetts with his wife, Louisa. The Adamses did not travel alone. After suffering through three miscarriages, Louisa had finally, the previous April, given birth to a healthy little boy. His parents named him George Washington Adams—a decision that Abigail considered "ill-judged" and "wrong." "I am sure your Brother had not any intention of wounding the feelings of his Father, but I see he has done it," she told her other son, Thomas (who was still single). "Children do not know how much their parents are gratified by the continuation of their Name in their Grandchildren." Although she did not say so, it seems likely that John Adams was also miffed to discover that the popular rage for crediting the recently deceased President Washington with fighting the American Revolution more or less single-handedly had even infected his own son.

Before sailing, little George's parents took advantage of an opportunity that had not been available during their own youth. Just five years earlier, in 1796, Edward Jenner had demonstrated that humans could be inoculated against smallpox using the cowpox virus, which was infinitely less lethal. By taking nearly all of the risk out of inoculation, Jenner's method dissolved objections like those Abigail's mother had lodged more than three decades earlier. The new technique spread across Europe nearly as fast as the contagion against which it offered lifetime protection. In time cowpox inoculation against smallpox would sweep the dreaded disease from the face of the earth. Already by 1801, doctors had recognized the superiority of Jenner's method with a new term, based on the Latin word for cow: *vaccination.* "Master George is going through the process of vaccine inoculation," John Quincy informed his brother Thomas in June, on the eve of the family's embarkation. He and Louisa were not entirely confident that Jenner's method would work, he acknowledged, "But we think it some security, and have not time to carry through the other sort of inoculation."

Disembarking in New York in September, John Quincy and Louisa could not agree on which of their families to visit first, so he went to his while she went to hers (in the Potomac River village of Georgetown, Maryland, which by this time had become part of Washington, D.C.), then he joined her in Georgetown before they both headed to Quincy.

Abigail Adams mentally divided the women of the world into two broad categories. The first group worked hard all of every day, constantly found ways to scrimp and save, and almost never indulged in luxuries. More than anything else, they were cheerful. They might suffer from a host of chronic illnesses, as she did, but they rarely complained about their aches and pains—least of all to their husbands. Then there were the spoiled and weak women, nearly all of them wealthy. They were accustomed to idleness and to wasting their fathers' and husbands' money on "baubles," and they constantly complained about their physical ailments. Although it would have been immodest to place herself in the first group, in her heart she knew she belonged there, and she was sure the second category was much more prevalent in Europe, especially in England, even though during her four-year sojourn in that part of the world, she identified very few women who fit the bill (and some of these were American expatriates). As she waited to greet Louisa Catherine, the woman her son had married nearly four years earlier, Adams feared that her daughter-in-law must belong to the second category. Recently her family had fallen on hard times (this, indeed, seemed to be the fate of every family into which Abigail's children married) and moved to America, but in Louisa's youth the Johnsons had been wealthy Londoners, and Abigail could not conquer the suspicion that she had been spoiled. As for the first lady, she had, of course, filled her letters to her daughter-in-law with effusive expressions of affection, but Louisa somehow sensed her skepticism long before the two actually met. Years later, she would confess that as the stagecoach carried her little family north toward Quincy, her sense of dread approximated that of a prisoner headed to the gallows.

The two women's first weeks together did not dispel either one's suspicions about the other. Abigail was unfailingly kind to Louisa, who nonetheless could not overcome a sense of terrible inadequacy in her presence. Almost immediately, she confirmed one of Abigail's prejudices against her by becoming sick. She was confined to her bed for the better part of her monthlong stay with the senior Adamses. In letters to other relatives, Abigail expressed sympathy for her daughter-in-law but added that with a "constitution so delicate," it was little wonder that Louisa was so often bedridden. Decades later, when Louisa penned (but did not publish) her memoirs, her comment on her first encounter with her husband's parents was arch. "The old gentleman took a fancy," she wrote, "and he was the only one." Abigail, by contrast, seemed to consider her daughter-in-law a "fine Lady"—which in her mind was no compliment, as Louisa well knew. Although custom required Abigail to refer to all of her daughters-in-law as *Mrs. Adams,* she had no compunction about flouting the rules when mentioning Charles's and Thomas's wives, who often showed up in her letters as *Sally* and *Nancy*. But John Quincy's wife was never anything but *Mrs. Adams*.

One result of Louisa's sense of rejection and inadequacy, she later recalled, was that while at Peacefield, she "seldom spoke at all which was deemed pride." She was immensely relieved when, a week before Christmas 1801, John Quincy drove her and their infant son to the house he had purchased on Hanover Street in Boston. With John Quincy settled in Massachusetts, where he immediately resumed the practice of law, Abigail focused on persuading her only other surviving son to move home as well. No doubt about it, Thomas's struggle to prosper on his own in Philadelphia had so far come to nothing. In February 1802 he joined the ranks of his mother's pensioners. Years earlier Abigail had informed her son of the funds she referred to as "my pin money," but he must have been astonished to learn that she had managed to salt away several thousand dollars. She never touched the principal, and she was usually able to reinvest the two interest payments of one hundred dollars each that she received every year. But half of her 1801 dividend went to Thomas.

"I have but one injunction to make you," she told her son in the note accompanying this gift. "It is that you make no mention of it; further than to say you received my Letter safe." There can be little doubt that the person from whom Abigail wished to conceal the remittance was her husband, but the reason for her secrecy is more perplexing. Did she fear he would think she was mollycoddling their thirty-year-old son? Or did she not want him to know how large the stash of money she called her own had grown? In any event, Thomas complied with his mother's desire for confidentiality. In his next letter to her, he lamented that the complaints of financial stringency that frequently appeared in his letters to his parents had "produced so much uneasiness and anxiety, not to say more, on my account." And he quietly accepted at least one more cash gift from his mother later in the year. For the moment, however, he rebuffed her plea that he give up on Philadelphia and move back to Massachusetts.

Meanwhile Thomas's elder brother was making no effort to feign interest in drawing up writs and collecting delinquent debts. No one was surprised when, in April 1802, only five months after returning to Massachusetts, John Quincy advertised his interest in a seat in the state senate, which he easily won. In the fall he ran for the U.S. House of Representatives and lost, but he barely had time to feel sorry for himself, for in 1803 the Massachusetts legislature elevated him to the U.S. Senate. (It would be another century before a constitutional amendment mandated the direct election of senators.)

John Quincy's political success occurred against a backdrop of personal disaster. His mother's uncle, Norton Quincy, had died two years earlier, in 1801. The childless Uncle Quincy had inherited his parents' enormous Mount Wollaston estate, which he in turn bequeathed to his nieces and nephews, including Abigail, her sisters, and Cotton Tufts, Jr. The Adamses were determined to buy out the other heirs and claim the entire estate, and Abigail's impoverished sisters were only too happy to receive the former president's cash—$2,251 each—instead of their late uncle's land.

Normally when married women sold land for cash, the money went to their husbands. But Abigail informed Reverend Peabody that she did not believe he had any right to his wife's share of the proceeds from the sale, and Elizabeth thanked her sister for expressing herself so freely on this sensitive subject. "It might be received better from you, than from me," she wrote. Elizabeth wanted to put the money into a trust for William, her son by her first marriage, and Reverend Peabody apparently agreed to this arrangement. Mary Cranch also placed the $2,251 that she received from her brother-in-law in a trust, so now both of Abigail's sisters had separate estates. Adams herself never acquired one, but her sisters' actions may help explain why, around this time, she began referring to Dr. Tufts, who had managed her money for more than two decades, as her "trustee." Using that term (and not just for a single transaction, as she had in 1790) moved Abigail a little closer to claiming ownership of a portion of the property that, by law, belonged to her husband.

Uncle Tufts's son and namesake, who had inherited one-third of Uncle Quincy's estate, was initially reluctant to sell it to the former president, but he finally relented in the fall of 1802. To come up with the money he needed to buy out his wife's relatives, Adams planned to use some of the securities he had purchased years earlier from a bank in Amsterdam. (These had been issued on behalf of the U.S. government.) The former president asked his eldest son to take charge of selling about sixteen thousand dollars' worth of the certificates and transferring the money to Massachusetts. In order to take advantage of the favorable exchange rate between the British pound and the U.S. dollar, John Quincy routed the money through Bird, Savage, & Bird, a mercantile and banking firm in London. It was a seemingly safe transaction, but it proved catastrophic, for in the middle of it, the company collapsed, later declaring bankruptcy.

For John Adams, the stoppage of Bird, Savage, & Bird could not have come at a worse time. John redeemed his bank stock and his other government securities, but that still left him seven thousand dollars short of what he owed. One way to raise the necessary funds would be for Adams to dispose of some of his land, but he hated the very idea. Moreover, if he was forced to sell in a hurry, the only bids would come from bargain hunters. As Abigail and John struggled with this quandary, their son came to their rescue. Although, as Abigail hastened to acknowledge, John Quincy had handled his parents' money "with as much circumspection as possible," he still felt terrible about leaving them in the lurch. Honor, he believed, required him to help them complete the purchase of Mount Wollaston. He had recently bought an investment property in Boston, and urban real estate was much more negotiable than farmland, so he was able to re-sell his Boston house for ready money and still obtain the exact amount—seven thousand dollars—that his parents still owed. Instead of simply offering them the cash, which they undoubtedly would have refused, he used these funds to buy seven thousand dollars' worth of their farmland—including the little saltbox cottage where he and his siblings had been born as well as his father's birthplace next door (which John Adams had purchased from his brother back in 1774). For the senior Adams, this complex transaction had important advantages over simply selling farmland on the open market. His son paid him much more cash than he would have received from any other buyer, and, more important, he kept his beloved farmland in the family.

Abigail avidly supported her husband's effort to obtain title to all of Mount Wollaston. She had warm memories of visiting her grandparents there, and she also knew the acquisition would bolster her ongoing campaign to lure her youngest son back to Quincy. With John's permission, she announced to Thomas that if he would come live with his parents, they would give him one of their farms to manage for his own profit. The offer bore a striking resemblance to one Abigail had made twenty years earlier, when she had tried to lure her husband home from Europe with a proposal to lend him sufficient money to buy an additional farm. In both cases, Abigail aggressively used hard-won property to draw her loved ones closer to her.

Thomas finally surrendered in the fall of 1803. He would be back in Quincy as soon as he could wrap up his affairs in Philadelphia. John Quincy implored his mother not to press her victory too far. Thomas should be "left entirely, and in the most unqualified manner, to his own choice and humour in his mode of life and his pursuits," he lectured Abigail. "I would even wish that no *advice* upon these subjects be given him unless at his own desire." Abigail accepted the reproof with good cheer, assuring John Quincy, "as far as depends upon me, he will be left to follow the bent of his own inclinations."

The "Lord of Mount W[ollasto]n" (as his wife christened her husband in May 1803) still had to confront the loss of sixteen thousand dollars in the collapse of Bird, Savage, & Bird. Given the magnitude of the "Catastrophe," it was perhaps natural for Abigail to make dire (and ultimately incorrect) predictions about its impact on her family's standard of living. Putting on a brave face, she told Thomas, "If I cannot keep a carriage, I will ride in a chaise."

On April 17, 1804, President Jefferson's daughter, the twenty-five-year-old Mary Jefferson Eppes, died after childbirth. Seventeen years earlier, when "Polly" was eight, she had traveled from Virginia to Paris with her father's slave Sally Hemings, and Abigail had cared for her during her traumatic layover in London. During that short period the two had forged a bond more powerful than politics, and in the wake of Eppes's death, Abigail became more irritated at the wall that had arisen between the Adamses and Jefferson than she had ever been at her husband's successor. "The powerfull feelings of my heart, have burst through the restraint, and called upon me to shed the tear of sorrow over the departed remains, of your beloved and deserving daughter," she told the president in a May 20 letter—the first she had written him in sixteen years. Newspaper accounts of Eppes's death put her in mind of "the tender scene of her seperation from me . . . when she clung around my neck and wet my Bosom with her tears, saying, 'O! now I have learnt to Love you, why will they tear me from you,'" she wrote. Adams knew what Jefferson was going through, she noted, for she herself had lost two children, Charles less than four years earlier and the infant Susanna thirty years before that. "I have tasted the bitter cup," she wrote.

The president's reply was warm and full of gratitude. The nurturing care that Abigail had bestowed on Polly "had made an indelible impression on her mind," he observed, and during the ensuing years, she had frequently asked "whether I had heard lately of you, and how you did." If only Jefferson had stopped there. But he could not resist trying to explain the dissolution of his and John's long-standing friendship. "One act of Mr. Adams's life, and one only, ever gave me a moment's personal displeasure," he wrote, and that was his decision to make the midnight appointments. By filling the executive branch with Jefferson's "most ardent political enemies," Adams had put him in an impossible position. If he did not want to entrust his initiatives to men bent on thwarting them, he had "to encounter the odium of putting others in their places."

Perhaps the widowed Jefferson's ongoing shock at the loss of his daughter clouded his memory of his correspondent, for he should have known that Abigail would be unable to leave such serious charges against her husband unanswered. Adams not only refuted Jefferson's accusation but made two of her own. The first was that the president had pardoned James Callender, who had been duly convicted, under the Sedition Act, of libeling John Adams. In reminding Jefferson how richly Callender had deserved his prison term, she alluded indirectly to the newspaperman's later break with the president and his ensuing accusation that Jefferson kept Hemings as a concubine. "The serpent you cherished and warmed, bit the hand that nourished him," she pointed out. Adams's other grievance was that the president had removed her son John Quincy Adams from a minor post as a federal bankruptcy commissioner, an action she viewed as a deliberate insult to her husband. Jefferson defended himself from both charges without making fresh accusations against his predecessor, but it was already too late. Over the course of the next five months, he and Adams exchanged a total of eight letters—none of which, after the first two, even mentioned the young woman whose death had provoked their resumption of correspondence. Yet any chance of a permanent reconciliation had disappeared the moment Jefferson broached the subject of the midnight appointments. He thought he deserved an apology, Abigail thought John did, and she had the additional motivation of believing that she could make Jefferson a better president if she could only get him to confront his failings. "Faithfull are the wounds of a Friend," she reminded him.

Soon enough, however, Adams accepted the futility of trying to reform her old friend, and on October 25, she announced to the president that she had decided to "close this correspondence." She had never said anything about the affair to her busband, but a month after writing Jefferson for the last time, she showed John the entire exchange—her letters as well as Jefferson's. At the foot of his wife's draft of her final letter to the president, John wrote, "The whole of this Correspondence was begun and conducted without my Knowledge or Suspicion. Last Evening and this Morning at the desire of Mrs. Adams I read the whole. I have no remarks to make upon it at this time and in this place."

During his last year as president, John had provided a decent sinecure to his son-in-law William Stephens Smith, naming him customs surveyor for the port of New York. But there was little chance that the flamboyant war hero would be content to live out his days as a lowly government functionary. In November 1805, Smith joined an enterprise that strained many observers' credulity. Even worse, he enlisted his son and namesake in the project as well.

CHAPTER 29

"Your Mothers Legacy"

1805–1809

Back in the fall of 1785, when Colonel Smith had bolted London to disguise his complicity in Nabby Adams's dismissal of Royall Tyler, his traveling companion across the English Channel had been Francisco de Miranda, a native of the Spanish colony of Caracas (in present-day Venezuela) who was at the time an officer in the army of Spain. In the ensuing decades, Miranda, who became Smith's "intimate friend," dedicated himself to the liberation of the Spanish colonies in Central and South America. Failing to find effective backing during his extensive travels through Europe, he decided to try his luck among the New World's first successful rebels against colonial authority. He landed in New York City in November 1805 and persuaded Colonel Smith to help him prepare an attack against Caracas. It would be, in part, a filibustering expedition: an attempt to grab booty. But Miranda also hoped to ignite a rebellion that would free the colony of Caracas—and perhaps others—from the Spanish yoke. The scheme appealed to Smith's self-perception as a freedom fighter, and it also held out the possibility of instantly restoring his fortune. The colonel helped fit out Miranda's little navy and assisted in the recruitment of his soldiers, one of whom was his own eighteen-year-old son, William Steuben Smith, who dropped out of Columbia College in New York City and enlisted.

Nabby and the colonel chose not to tell her parents about the adventure, informing them only that William Junior had found a way to fulfill his longtime dream of going to sea. But Abigail immediately suspected that her son-in-law and grandson were somehow mixed up in Miranda's scheme. She had been suspicious of Miranda from the moment of his arrival on American shores. "We shall hear more of that man," she predicted in a letter to John Quincy and Louisa Catherine; "he is capable of troubling the waters, and fishing in them too." Abigail surmised that Miranda was "one of Tallyrands agents"—a secret representative of the French government. Although inaccurate, that conjecture was not unreasonable, since Miranda had, in fact, spent time as a general in the French revolutionary army.

When the expedition sailed out of New York Harbor on February 2, 1806, the colonel's official duties prevented him from being on board. But his son was stationed on the flagship, the *Leander* (named after Miranda's eldest son), as Miranda's aide. On March 15, the *Leander* put into the little port of Jacmel, on the southern coast of Haiti, the site fifteen years earlier of the world's first successful slave revolt. Miranda took on water and other provisions, but his primary purpose in landing in Haiti, at least according to newspapers in the United States, was to enlist large numbers of mixed-race Haitians for his army of liberation. William Smith was in the party that traveled overland to Port-au-Prince, the Haitian capital, to recruit soldiers. The *Leander* next stopped at the little island of Aruba, just off the coast of South America, for a rendezvous with two schooners, the *Bacchus* and the *Bee*. On April 16, the three vessels set sail for Caracas.

The slow pace of Miranda's preparations had given Spanish officials plenty of time to learn of his intentions and to send a pair of privateers out to meet him. In a two-hour naval battle fought on April 28, 1806, the schooners were captured, and the *Leander* narrowly escaped. The first reports of the action to reach the United States brought devastating news for the family of William Smith: he had been aboard one of the schooners, and he was now a prisoner. In Spanish eyes, everyone involved in Miranda's expedition was a pirate, and throughout the Atlantic world during this era, the sole punishment for piracy was death. Carlos Yrujo, the Spanish minister to the United States, tried to exploit Colonel Smith's anxiety about his son's fate to obtain information from him. John Quincy Adams reported to his mother that Yrujo had offered to "intercede for William, *on condition*, that Coll. Smith would discover to him every thing that he knew of Miranda's plans, and *the names of the Spaniards* with him; and in short every thing that could be confess'd by a criminal under sentence of death, to save himself."

Smith "returned a very spirited, indignant, and proper answer." John Quincy thoroughly approved of his brother-in-law's decision not to save his son's life by betraying his comrades in arms. "I had rather weep for my friends than *blush* for them," he told Abigail. It helped that by this time, Colonel Smith seems to have known that his son was not actually in Spanish hands. He had remained on board the *Leander* and escaped with Miranda—who was not finished yet. A complement of his soldiers landed at the little town of La Vela de Coro, two hundred miles west of Caracas, and captured its small fort. To Miranda's chagrin, the population of the region was not interested in being liberated, and two weeks later, the expedition was once again afloat. No one in his family knew for sure how long William remained with Miranda, but at the end of February 1807—more than a year after he sailed out of New York Harbor—he was still on the Caribbean island of Trinidad. In the end, the Miranda episode created fewer problems for the youthful William than for his father. On March 1, 1806—before the *Leander* even reached Haiti—Colonel Smith was arrested. By this time the newspapers were reporting (accurately) that Miranda had met with both Secretary of State Madison and President Jefferson, and Smith claimed that they had countenanced the expedition. The administration believed its only hope of refuting this accusation lay in dealing harshly with Miranda's co-conspirators. Ultimately the U.S. Supreme Court acquitted Smith, but the president removed him from his post as customs surveyor. The Smith family was once again without a reliable source of income.

One of the minor mysteries that every biography of John or Abigail Adams must confront is why it took the two of them so long to express outrage at Mercy Otis Warren's *History of the Rise, Progress, and Termination of the American Revolution*. When it appeared in 1805, Warren's three-volume work won her much praise. Yet the author's determination to tell the whole truth as she saw it led her to paint a portrait of John Adams that was unflattering in the extreme. She claimed his "passions and prejudices were some times too strong for his sagacity and judgment," that he had accomplished nothing as the American minister in London, and that he had had an unsuccessful presidency. Worst of all, she asserted that when Adams returned from England in 1788, "a large portion of his countrymen" believed he had "forgotten the Principles of the American Revolution."

For the next two years, neither Adams said a word about the book to Warren or to anyone else. At the end of 1806, Mercy wrote Abigail an affectionate letter apologizing for not having written in such a long time and attributing her neglect to her deteriorating eyesight. The following March, she received a cordial reply. Then in July, John Adams finally sent Warren a response to her published characterization of him. He itemized a host of statements he considered erroneous, emphasizing that "the most exceptionable passage" was Warren's claim that during his time in London, he had become "so enamoured with the British Constitution and the Government, manners and laws of the nation, that a partiality for monarchy appeared." As aggrieved as he felt, Adams tried to express his criticism constructively. Surely these were mere "mistakes," he suggested, and it would be easy enough for his "ancient friend" to "correct them for any future edition of the work."

Warren refused to acknowledge having mischaracterized the former president. She had meant what she said, she told him, and she was proud that she had not let her continuing affection for both Adamses cause her to forget "the moral obligation of truth." Warren's intransigence provoked a similar reaction from Adams, and over the next two months, the two former friends sent each other a total of sixteen increasingly vituperative letters. At one point John suggested that the real reason for Mercy's animus was that as president he had refused her requests for federal jobs for her sons, an assertion that may well have been true, for he had indignantly refused to bestow patronage appointments on her sons while hiring several of his and Abigail's relatives. On August 27, Mercy closed the correspondence, telling John she was astonished at his "rancor and [in]decency and vulgarism." "Yet," she concluded, "as an old friend, I pity you, as a Historian I forgive you." Years later, John would tell Elbridge Gerry, who maintained cordial relations with Warren, "History is not the Province of the Ladies."

Abigail wisely stayed out of this exchange, but there could be no question about where her loyalties lay. Warren joined Thomas Jefferson on the list of old friends with whom she no longer communicated. There had always been a stiffness about the relationship between the two women—for instance, each constantly tried to dazzle the other with her literary skills, producing some jarringly awkward constructions, especially on Warren's side—but Adams needed all the friends she could get in the fall of 1807, and one reason was that her daughter was about to be transported to the wilderness. Over the years, Nabby's husband had proved himself wholly incapable of succeeding at anything besides waging war. Having failed miserably as a securities and land speculator, armchair pirate, and customs official, Colonel Smith resolved to become a tiller of the soil. Years earlier, he and his brothers had speculated in land in the Chenango Valley in upstate New York. If all had gone according to plan, the sale of backcountry farmsteads would have financed the construction of "Mount Vernon," the colonel's mansion on the East River north of New York City. Now, however, circumstances had turned Smith into one of those backcountry farmers. He began building a house in the little town of Lebanon, New York. Two of his brothers had already moved to the region, which was becoming known as Smith's Valley.

With John Quincy and Louisa spending summers in Boston with their three sons, the Adamses had the satisfaction of seeing their family more concentrated than it had been since the two Johns had embarked for France thirty years earlier. While Colonel Smith was building his frontier farmhouse in upstate New York, he permitted Nabby and two of her children, William (who had finally made it home from Trinidad) and Caroline, to live at Peacefield. Both of Charles Adams's daughters were there, too, as was their mother. In 1805, Thomas had married Ann Harrod of Haverhill, and they and their growing brood of children lived with Abigail and John as well. One evening in the summer of 1807, Abigail marveled at having all but one of her surviving grandchildren (the exception being Nabby's younger son John, who was studying law in New York City) with her at the dinner table.

It was a fine moment, but a brief one. In the middle of the winter of 1807–1808, Colonel Smith announced that he had completed work on the family's new farmhouse. He came as far east as Albany and instructed his wife to catch the next stage and meet him there. Abigail rebelled at the idea of her daughter taking a 140-mile stagecoach ride in the dead of winter, and she finally persuaded Nabby to suggest to her husband that it might be better for her to spend the winter at Peacefield and join him in the spring. But Colonel Smith knew his mother-in-law and called her bluff. If Nabby did not want to ride out in the stagecoach, he would come get her. When he arrived in Quincy in January 1808 in his own sleigh, Abigail had to acknowledge that her daughter's duty was to clamber aboard. Caroline went along, too, though William Junior was permitted to stay behind to teach school in Quincy and receive advanced mathematics instruction from his grandfather.

Back in 1787, John Quincy Adams had expressed skepticism for the U.S. Constitution, but he had subsequently become as ardent a Federalist as any of the Adamses, and in 1803, when the Massachusetts legislature elected him to the U.S. Senate, his party loyalty had been a prerequisite. Yet he had inherited from his father the contrarian streak that had prevented President Adams from going to war against France at the behest of the High Federalists. The new senator was determined to demonstrate his political independence, and he often did so in quirky ways. For instance, he joined the Republicans in supporting the Louisiana Purchase but then insisted that Congress could not adopt legislation for this vast territory until the Constitution had been amended to provide the proper authority. In 1807, when President Jefferson decided that the only way to keep the United States from going to war with either France or Great Britain was to sever all trade ties with Europe, most members of John Quincy's family, including his mother, were appalled at the idea. But John Quincy agreed with the Republicans that Jefferson's embargo was the only way to preserve peace, and he infuriated his fellow Federalists by voting for it.

Abigail came around to her son's position that the embargo was a necessary evil—though she repeatedly stressed that it ruined not only the merchant but the farmer, who watched helplessly as the price of his produce plummeted. But in 1808, when Jefferson announced his unwillingness to stand for a third term, she was appalled to learn that her son had helped choose the Republican candidate to succeed him. There were no nominating conventions in those days, and in theory the presidential electors had the right to vote for whomever they pleased. But as voters began to divide into two major political parties, members of Congress of both persuasions quickly recognized that they could dramatically improve their chances of electing like-minded men to the presidency and vice presidency if they could agree on a pair of candidates to put before the public. Thus was born the party caucus system of presidential nominations, which would survive into the middle of the nineteenth century. Early in 1808, Senator Adams scandalized partisan Federalists by participating in the congressional Republicans' caucus to choose presidential and vice presidential candidates. And Abigail, who had supported her son's earlier departures from Federalist dogma as tokens of political independence, was appalled to see him forgo allegiance to his father's party only to align himself with its inveterate foe. "I have considerd it as inconsistant both with your principles, and your judgment, to have countananced such a meeting by your presence," she told him.

Abigail's husband did not agree with her criticism—and neither, of course, did their son. He pointed out that the parties had been caucusing since 1792—which meant that John Adams had been selected to stand for the vice presidency and presidency by Federalist caucuses. Contrary to media reports, he had not initiated contact with the Republicans but merely accepted their invitation. At a time when the nation stood on the brink of war with Great Britain, he considered it his duty to state whom he believed most capable of filling the nation's highest office, whether or not that made him popular in the country at large or even within his own family. "I could wish to please my Country. I could wish to please my Parents," he told Abigail. "But my duty, I *must* do. It is a Law far above that of my mere wishes." Nothing else that the senator could have said to his mother could have been better calculated to reconcile her to his decision. It always thrilled Abigail to see her son stand up to political bullying—even if, in this case, she was one of the bullies. She even accepted John Quincy's ironic contention that caucusing with the Republican party was, in fact, the nonpartisan thing to do.

Adams's latest demonstration of political independence did not inspire equivalent enthusiasm from the Massachusetts legislators who had given him his U.S. Senate seat, and they now moved to take it away from him. Senators could not be recalled, but they could be humiliated, and Bay State Federalists set about shaming John Quincy out of office. The two houses formally instructed him to vote against the embargo—a vote that could not bind him but could and did embarrass him. Worse, they resolved in the spring of 1808 to replace him when his term expired in 1809. The timing of the vote was a deliberate insult, occurring as it did a full year before he was scheduled to finish his term. These actions had the desired effect, and Adams immediately resigned his seat. Abigail approved his decision. "I . . . pride myself more in being the Mother of such a son, than in all the honours and titles which Monarch could bestow," she told Nabby in August.

Abigail was proud of Nabby, too, for she had demonstrated a different kind of courage. Not only had she stuck with her husband through all his financial travails—everyone knew she would do that—she had done so cheerfully. Nabby's plight elicited sympathy and admiration from Abigail's sisters, too. Elizabeth, recalling their mother's declaration that her granddaughter "was born to exhibit great Vertues," observed that Nabby "has had an unusual call for there Exercise." Abigail poured her heart into the letters she regularly dispatched to her only daughter. In one of these, she described for Nabby "the pleasing interview I had with you" and several other family members—in a dream, that is.

> Your Father accompanied me, and we came rather unexpectedly upon you, but were not the less joyfully received. I was quite delighted with your situation, and found you so cheerfull and happy that it augmented the pleasure of my visit which was only interrupted by the strikeing of the clock at the morning hour when I usually rise.

Nabby was the only correspondent to whom Abigail confessed her pain at not being able to respond appropriately to James Warren's death on November 28, 1808. Of course she ought to have sent Mercy a letter of condolence. "But after the injustice she had done your Fathers Character in her History," she wrote, "I thought a Letter of the kind would appear insincere."

At the close of 1808, Abigail's eldest son was almost unique among her close relatives in never having required her to make a deduction from her pocket money. In January 1809, he finally did solicit her help—not because he was in desperate straits, like the other family members Abigail had assisted over the years, but because he had spotted an opportunity. Just what he wanted to buy remains unclear. By 1814 he owned numerous lots in the town of Boston and several parcels of farmland, but none of his deeds was executed in 1809, so the greater likelihood was that he wanted to buy stock in a canal, toll bridge, or insurance company, for by 1814 he had invested in a variety of firms. For whatever the reason, John Quincy made the largest-ever deduction from his mother's personal funds: $1,700. But this was only a loan, and Abigail received regular interest payments at the rate of 6 percent per year. Indeed, the transaction should perhaps be viewed not as an instance of maternal assistance but simply as Abigail's latest business deal.

The money that Adams lent her son came from the sale of what appears to have been her last set of federal bonds. Congress had issued them ten years earlier, at President Adams's behest, to prepare the nation's military for possible war with France. The notes had been issued during a credit contraction—the one that ruined men such as William Stephens Smith and James Greenleaf—and the government had been forced to offer investors 8 percent interest. Congress was eager to call in these high-yield certificates, and it essentially forced the public creditors to redeem them in January 1809. Otherwise shrewd investors like Adams would have held on to them.

In February 1809, John Quincy Adams was in Washington arguing (unsuccessfully) a case before the U.S. Supreme Court, so it was Louisa's mother-in-law, not her husband, who comforted her on yet another miscarriage. This time her doctors gave her the agonizing news that the death of the fetus had not been inevitable, for she had fatally injured it in a fall.

John Quincy Adams was no doubt being honest when he asserted that his principles compelled him to abandon the Federalist party that had sent him to the Senate. Yet the plain fact was that his conversion to the Republican party also put him in line for public offices that would have been closed to him had he remained a Federalist. On June 29, 1809, a year and a half after Adams participated in the Republican caucus that nominated James Madison for the presidency, Madison chose Adams as the American minister to St. Petersburg. It was not exactly a plum assignment, since Russia was still in the second rank of European powers, and in addition to being bitterly cold for half the year, its capital was cut off from the rest of the world every winter due to the freezing of the River Neva. But it was an opportunity to serve, and at nine thousand dollars the salary was very good. Moreover, this post might well lead to higher ones, and Adams accepted.

Louisa Catherine pleaded with her husband to let their sons accompany them, but he only agreed to take the youngest, Charles Francis, who was not yet two. Eight-year-old George, and John, who had just turned six, would board with their fathers' relatives in New England and attend school there. Louisa Catherine would at least have the companionship of her sister Catherine (known as Kitty), who agreed to accompany the Adamses to Russia. John Quincy received a letter from Nabby's son William, candidly acknowledging his failure "in the mercantile line" and asking to come along to St. Petersburg as the minister's secretary. In keeping with the Adams tradition of hiring relatives, John Quincy agreed.

Abigail was distressed at the prospect of her eldest son embarking for Europe for a fourth time. On August 5, the day of his departure, she could not bring herself to ride up to Charlestown (across the Charles River from Boston), the point of embarkation, to bid him farewell. If

I were to come, "I should only add to yours and my own agony," she wrote John Quincy that morning. "My heart is with you, my prayers and blessing attend you." A week earlier she had sent him a bit of verse from her favorite poet, James Thomson, labeling it "Your Mothers legacy," and adding, "May a blessing accompany it." As "far as I am now going from you," John Quincy replied from sea four days after his departure, "I still indulge and will enjoy the hope that we shall yet have the happiness of meeting together again." Abigail was not so sure. She told her granddaughter Caroline that for herself and her husband, parting from John Quincy at this time of life—John was seventy-three, and she would turn sixty-five in November—was "like taking our last leave of him."

CHAPTER 30

"Rather Positive"

1810–1811

Abigail Adams's biographers sometimes claim that she mellowed during her final years back home in Quincy. It is a beguiling image of an increasingly frail great-grandmother (as of 1814) gradually releasing her grip on her household and family as she prepares for her journey to the other world. But it is a myth. The truth is that in old age Adams tried harder than ever to manage the world around her. Her "incontrollable attachment to the superintendence of every part of her household" worried her husband, but John ought to have realized that the domestic labors that exhausted her body refreshed her mind. What seemed to him like an inability to let go appeared in her eyes as a simple expression of self-confidence. She confessed her tendency to micromanage her household in a December 1811 letter to her sister Betsy, concluding, "I am really so self sufficient as to believe that I can do it better than any of my family—so I am punished for my self conceit & vanity." And besides, even as John rallied his wife on her inability to slacken the reins, he leaned more heavily upon her judgment than he ever had before. In fact, Abigail told John Quincy, your father "usually submits his Letters to the inspection of the old Lady, for her approbation, or dissent" before posting them. (She noted, however, that he sometimes failed to make the alterations she suggested.)

As a young wife back in the 1760s, Abigail had grieved at seeing John's legal business carry him farther and farther from home for lengthening periods. The family separations had multiplied in the ensuing decades, and they had never gotten any easier for her. She had always been ambitious for her kinsmen, but in old age she became less and less willing to give them up to public service, and as an example, she simply could not

Abigail Adams (1744–1818) at around fifty-five years old. Jane Stuart after Gilbert Stuart, ca. 1800. *Courtesy Adams National Historical Park.*

John Adams (1735–1826) at around sixty-four years old. Jane Stuart after Gilbert Stuart, ca. 1800. *Courtesy Adams National Historical Park.*

abide her eldest son's posting to St. Petersburg, Russia. The first reports John Quincy and Louisa sent home were grim. Their punishing eighty-day voyage across the Atlantic and Baltic Oceans had thrown them on the shore of the River Neva at the end of October 1809—just at the start of the interminable Russian winter. Even more dispiriting than the arctic air was watching the sun set at three o'clock in the afternoon. The ambassador and his lady both managed to post several letters before the river froze up for the winter, and every one of these told a tale of unremitting woe. The locals—especially the women, Louisa claimed—were "haughtily repulsive." Given the high cost of living (the obligatory excess of servants cost even more here than in other European capitals), John predicted that he would have to dip into his savings just to make ends meet. Abigail did not fail to notice that these were the very grievances that had filled her own European dispatches a generation earlier.

Although on the surface John Quincy's and Louisa's complaints were nearly identical, Abigail could have detected a subtle difference had it served her purposes to do so. Louisa really did want to come home, but John was simply doing what his mother and father had done three decades earlier: enumerating his sacrifices in hopes of having them recognized. And since it was the wife who truly wanted out of St. Petersburg and the husband who wished to stay, the outcome was never in doubt. Abigail nonetheless chose to detect in John Quincy and Louisa a mutual desire to return to Quincy. On her own authority—without even informing her son—she wrote President Madison to say that Ambassador Adams wished to be recalled from St. Petersburg. The president replied promptly, but his letter indicated that he was no stranger to Adams family dynamics, because he indicated that he would approve his minister's request for a recall—as soon as he himself filed it. When John Quincy learned what his mother had done, he responded with remarkable indulgence, thanking her for her pains but also informing her that the couple's living conditions had improved and that they had found a way to live within their means. He was not coming home.

Like Adams's efforts to keep her family near her, her engagement in politics remained intense throughout her final years. She continued to read every word of the congressional debates printed in the *National Intelligencer*. "I cannot wean myself from the subjects of politicks," she told Louisa Catherine's mother in 1810. Early the next year, when she learned that John Quincy had been maligned in the London press and in several pro-British newspapers in her own country, she corrected the record. America's Russian representative had been accused of trying to keep his own country's merchant vessels out of St. Petersburg, but he had actually been straining every nerve to convince Alexander I, the Russian emperor, to favor American commerce. And he had largely succeeded. The only basis for the newspaper attacks was that several British ship captains had tried to evade their own government's ban on trade with St. Petersburg—Britain and Russia were at war—by disguising their vessels as American owned. When Abigail received her son's letter explaining all this, she had the relevant excerpts published in a Boston newspaper, and they were reprinted throughout the United States and in several European ports, including St. Petersburg.

Abigail presumably expected her son to be grateful for her intervention, but he actually felt humiliated. Spread before the public, his claim that he had obtained imperial favor for his own nation's trade looked like "vainglorious boasting which mortified me," he explained to his father. Furthermore, while Alexander had indeed given American ships preferential treatment, John Quincy feared he was "not pleased" at seeing his favoritism "publicly stated under the authority of my name." Abigail's motivation in having her son's letter printed was "entitled to all my gratitude," he told her in a June 1811 letter, and she had in fact helped to refute "an infamous calumny" against him. But in the future, she should not publish any of his correspondence without being asked.

Abigail's abiding confidence in herself extended, albeit in somewhat attenuated fashion, to her entire generation, and she worried that her children and their spouses were less capable than their parents of getting on in life. This prejudice against the rising generation had been stoked by the manifest failures of Abigail's son Charles, but if it was fair to use one person to tar the entire age bracket, why not reproach Abigail's generation with her brother William? Adams appears never to have confronted that question, and she continued to act on the assumption that even in their old age, she and her sisters were more competent than their children at nearly everything. That attitude may explain why, at the end of June 1810, Ann and Thomas Adams, who had lived with Abigail and John at Peacefield since their marriage four years earlier, finally moved out with their three children. The family took up residence in the little cottage on the other side of Quincy where John Adams had been born and raised. Thomas was still not a homeowner—

he rented the place from his brother John Quincy—but he was finally master of his own house. Almost immediately, he and Ann offered to assume responsibility for raising the two sons Louisa and John Quincy had left behind when they sailed for Russia—provided, of course, that the boys' great-aunt Mary Cranch and her husband, Richard, with whom they were boarding, were willing to give them up.

John Quincy liked the idea. He had carried his copy of Adam Smith's *Theory of Moral Sentiments* with him to Russia, and he had recently come upon a passage that, as he put it, "smote me to the heart." Smith had written, "A father is apt to be less attached to a child, who, by some accident, has been separated from him in its infancy, and who does not return to him till it is grown up to manhood. The father is apt to feel less paternal tenderness for the child; the child, less filial reverence for the father." From his arrival in St. Petersburg, the ambassador had worried that time and distance would dissolve the boys' attachment to their parents, and he was distressed to see his fears confirmed by the respected author who had popularized the term "fellow feeling." "As it has pleased Providence to make it impossible for me at present to superintend the education of my boys," he told his mother when he learned of Thomas's and Ann's offer to take them, "it is a great consolation to me to have them entrusted to those who next to ourselves will feel the deepest and tenderest interest in their welfare."

Living with Thomas's family would be especially salutary for George, the older boy. At nine, he was "coming now to an age, when he must learn much for which there are no schools," John Quincy observed in a September 1810 letter to his mother, and Thomas was just the man to give him those informal lessons. Although proud that his son shared his love for books, John Quincy suspected that he was actually in danger of becoming too studious. Upon receiving his brother's offer to superintend the boys' education, the ambassador wrote back urging Thomas to introduce his eldest son to manly pursuits. "As you are a sportsman, I beg you occasionally from this time to take George out with you in your shooting excursions," he wrote. Indeed both boys needed to learn how to maintain and fire a gun, and their father observed with concern that it was "customary among us, particularly when children are under the direction of ladies, to withhold" these skills "too much and too long." These comments reflected John Quincy's assumption that Mary Cranch, not her eighty-three-year-old husband Richard, was the one actually raising his sons. Now that they would be moving in with the much younger couple, the ambassador wanted his eldest son to develop "hardihood" by learning to swim, skate, fence, and ride horseback. If he wished to travel to Boston, he must make the twenty-four-mile round-trip on foot, not in a carriage. "Let him be encouraged in nothing delicate or effeminate," the anxious father wrote.

The Cranches were apparently amenable to having George and John move to the cottage at the foot of Penn's Hill, but Abigail raised several objections. Like John Quincy, she was especially concerned about George. Unlike him, she feared that living with the younger couple would actually do him and his brother harm. At the Adamses', she explained in an April 1811 letter to her son, the boys would receive less adult supervision, since Thomas's judicial work often required him to be out of town for days on end. Thomas and Ann lived farther away from George's school than the Cranches did. Moreover, they had three young children whose raucous play would prevent their cousins from concentrating on their homework. The last of these objections was so specious as to call the others into question. In January 1811, Elizabeth Norton—who as Betsy Cranch had been young Nabby's most frequent correspondent—died of a pulmonary fever. She left eight children, and the four youngest—three girls and a boy—piled in with Mary and Richard Cranch, who were also raising another grandchild. Counting John Quincy's two boys, the Cranches had eight children under their roof. The oldest was twelve.

Abigail may have had other reasons for wanting to keep the boys at the Cranches'. During his years abroad, John Quincy paid his sons' room and board, and she may have concluded that her sister and brother-in-law stood in greater need of this supplemental income than did her youngest son. But it appears that her most pressing reason for not wanting the boys to move to their father's birthplace was that Thomas and Ann might spoil them. Back in May 1810, she had alerted Louisa Catherine to her concern about George's "positiveness." Excessive self-confidence "was an error I endeavourd to correct in his Father in early life," she wrote, "but the Boy inherits it, by regular descent, as his Father did before him." Surely "Age, a knowledge of the world, and experience will correct it and modify it." In the meantime, though, she had noticed that George was willing to "yield to the decisive Authority of his Aunt" Mary, since "Her Age and the respect which the other children pay to her orders, are an example to him." Would Thomas and Ann command the same deference? Abigail could see no reason to put that question to the test.

Mary Cranch agreed with her sister that certain aspects of George's "manner & temper" still needed "to be corrected," although she described the situation with more tact. "There is no one can make more good resolutions than he does," she told the boy's mother, "As his reason ripens they will I doubt not be executed." For his part, John Quincy was not so sure his son's stubborn self-assurance was such a bad thing. In deference to his mother, he allowed that he hoped "George will be taught to controul his disposition to be overpositive," and he addressed some of her concerns in a December 17, 1810, letter. By a remarkable coincidence, he quoted the same authority Abigail would quote to him a month later—long before hearing from her son. In an April 19, 1774, speech applauding tax resisters in the American colonies, the British statesman Edmund Burke had affirmed "that obstinacy is a vice nearly allied to great virtues." John Quincy agreed. "A determined *will,* is one of those things without which no man can be good for much in the world," he told his mother.

At about the same time, Abigail was also consulting Burke's reflections on obstinacy. In the August 1810 edition of the *Edinburgh Review,* she read a long review of the works of the painter James Barry. The reviewer quoted Burke as recommending to Barry "a great deal of distrust of ourselves," a phrase that Abigail approvingly quoted to John Quincy. If the ambassador was startled that his mother had derived the opposite message from the same author that he had quoted in support of his son's stubbornness, he did not say so. Rather, he insisted that she had taken Burke's statement out of context. Barry suffered from an overwhelming excess of vanity, and if he was going to get along with the arts community in Rome, where he was then living, he would have to show a little humility, Burke believed. Although this advice "was precisely that of which Barry stood most in need," John Quincy wrote, it was by no means a universal rule. In fact Adams thought he himself had erred in the opposite direction. "My own experience of life and self observation has often led me to the conclusion that one of my failings was too much distrust of myself," he wrote. Adams's condemnation of his upbringing was subtle but unmistakable. Abigail had once criticized her own mother's child-raising skills, but as she confronted the manifold challenges of raising children of her own, she had become less critical of Elizabeth Smith's techniques. John Quincy's attitude toward Abigail's methods went through no such mellowing process, and on the crucial question of what to do about his son's stubbornness, he himself remained at least as inflexible as his mother.

On the other hand, John Quincy was more than four thousand miles away. When Abigail received his letter enthusiastically endorsing the idea of moving George and John to his brother's house, she wrote back saying George was "a fine Boy," but "as I have mentiond rather positive." He required his great-aunt's discipline, so he and John would remain with the Cranches. On the same day that Abigail wrote her son, Thomas also sent him a letter asserting that he was the one who had decided not to move the boys into his household. But Thomas also noted that he had made that decision only after his wife received a letter from Mary Cranch that had in turn been prompted by correspondence from Abigail.

In January 1811, Abigail received an anguished letter from her daughter-in-law. That Louisa was miserable in St. Petersburg was not news. What alarmed Abigail was that her misery had gotten her thinking about her marriage. I have pleaded with John Quincy to take us home to Massachusetts, she wrote, but "It is perfectly unnecessary for me to say how little influence *I have*." Up until this time, Abigail had sympathized with Louisa's plight, which inevitably reminded her of her own sojourn in Europe a quarter century earlier. But when Louisa crossed the line from complaining about her situation to accusing her husband of ignoring her, her mother-in-law's sympathies began to shift. And she was even more disturbed to read Louisa's explanation for why she held so little sway over John Quincy. It had, she wrote, "been an invariable rule with me as I had no fortune never to object or decline any thing which he thinks can tend to promote his ambition his fame or his ease."

The phrase that stuck in Abigail's craw was "as I had no fortune." It was true, of course. Shortly after Louisa married John Quincy, her father had declared bankruptcy, and her family had not been able to provide her a dowry. That was not what disturbed Abigail. The Johnson family's financial straits were "well known to Mr Adams before he was connected with you," she wrote her daughter-in-law. "Nor was you ever reminded of it by any of his connections." Yet Louisa herself had "repeatedly mentiond" it, leaving the impression that she thought the Adamses held it against her. Given that no Adams had ever supplied any fuel for this suspicion, Louisa's persistence in it was manifestly unfair.

Abigail was also troubled by her daughter-in-law's belief that she would have had more power within the marriage if she had brought more property to it. No dowry, no matter how large, would have diminished Louisa's duty to promote her husband's "honour and his reputation." A marriage was not, after all, a joint-stock company.

In one respect, Abigail's anger at Louisa Catherine is perplexing. Had she not spent the previous thirty years amassing her own independent property—the very thing she now condemned her daughter-in-law for coveting? Two factors may have prevented her from pitying Louisa's plight. The first was a sense of loyalty to her son that was powerful enough to trump her commitment to the principle that wives needed greater access to property. Louisa had also alienated her mother-in-law with her gloomy tone. For Abigail, one of the paramount duties of all women was, even in the worst of circumstances, to remain cheerful. Louisa had violated that commandment in the worst of ways—by criticizing her husband to his mother.

Abigail also rebutted another of Louisa's claims: that John Quincy had elicited the anger of his fellow Federalists by accepting a professorship at Harvard—a career move that his wife had opposed. "I think you are entirely mistaken with respect to your opinion of the professorship," Abigail wrote. John Quincy had lost favor with the Federalists not by taking that job but by voting for Jefferson's embargo and supporting Madison for the presidency, she said. Adams's irritation at her daughter-in-law was too intense to be confined within the paragraphs replying to her reflections on her marriage. As she nearly always did, Abigail updated the ambassador's wife on the sons she had left behind in Quincy. But this time the tone of her report was bitter. "I should not be forgiven if I did not say the Boys were well," she wrote. And when she acknowledged that she had not written her daughter-in-law many letters in recent months, she did not apologize, as was the custom, but pointed out that Louisa had received plenty of mail from her relatives in Washington, so she ought "not complain that I do not write often enough to you."

The context in which Abigail wrote her January 21 letter made its hostile tone all the more surprising, for she knew that Louisa Catherine was about to receive devastating news. On Christmas Day 1810, her sister, Nancy Hellen, who was in an advanced stage of pregnancy, had "taken ill." As Abigail later reported, the illness intensified over the next three days, and "it was found necessary from her situation to force a delivery upon the 28th." The child was stillborn, and Nancy's own body was so traumatized by the forced delivery that "she fainted under it and never recoverd." She was buried on New Year's Day. It was not until mid-February that Abigail provided these details to her daughter-in-law. In fact, her January 21 letter contained no mention of Nancy's death, even though she had known about it for at least two days. Abigail had decided that it was best for Louisa to hear the bad news from her husband, so she and other members of the family sent it to John Quincy Adams instead of Louisa. Yet Abigail's sympathy for her daughter-in-law's plight apparently did not cause her either to delay sending her January 21 letter or to soften its tone.

Louisa's comments on her marriage were the sort of thing Abigail could not imagine anyone in her own generation committing to paper, and as she aged, she increasingly marveled at how much the average woman's experience had changed since she was a girl. By far the most significant transformations, she noted in a February 26, 1811, letter to her sister Elizabeth Peabody, were in the area of education. Betsy had apologized for the infelicity of her prose, and Abigail replied,

> You well know what our early Education was. Neither grammerr or orthography were taught us. It was not then the fashion for females to know more than writing and a little arithmetic. No Books upon female Education were then in vogue. No Academies for Female instruction were then establishd.

Elizabeth was also impressed with the remarkable progress women had made. Like Abigail, her dominant feeling was one of regret at having been born just a few years too soon. "Every day I feel more sensibly my own deficiencies & the want of early Initiation in those Branches of Learning for which my longing Soul panted, & with which our more favoured Daughters are blessed," she told her sister.

Perhaps one reason Peabody's and Adams's attitudes toward female education were more bittersweet than optimistic is that in the still more important arena of marital relations, they had not witnessed any progress at all. In an undated letter apparently written around 1812, Abigail warned a young friend (whose name was not recorded) not to marry a man who lacked her sensibility, since the mistake would be much costlier to her than to her husband (whom Abigail euphemistically called "an other"). "A woman of refined sensibility," she pointed out, may "feel herself hurt & wounded and disgusted, and yet be unable to complain or even to receive any redress for wrongs which an other is not sensible of having committed or thinks them of too trifling a nature to merit attention." Such a wife, she said, must "bear in silent agony what an other has not sensibility enough to feel." Adams's continuing concern about the subjugation of wives helps explain her persistent admiration for Samuel Richardson's novel *Sir Charles Grandison*. She recognized that some critics considered Grandison too perfect to be believed, but she thought Richardson had done right in creating an ideal type to which actual men could aspire. Abigail gave more weight to the criticism that Hester Chapone, an English writer, had made of Grandison, albeit in jest. Chapone "was only affraid that the character of Sir Charles would occasion the Kingdoms being over run with old Maids."

Despite her progressive ideas on topics such as female education, it should never be forgotten that there were many more areas where Abigail was wholly traditional. She believed women were weaker than men in some areas (for instance in their inability to endure ocean voyages), and she considered many women (especially in England) too masculine. She accepted—and frequently joked about—her contemporaries' belief that women were more curious than men (in the negative sense that Eve was). With the significant exceptions that have been noted, she was even a traditionalist on the subject of marriage. During the War of 1812, she lamented that two of Benjamin and Julia Rush's daughters had moved to Canada and married local men, since that placed them on the British side of the conflict. But she never doubted where the two women's loyalties must lie. "What ever their feeling may and must be as respects their Country," she told Julia Rush, "it is there duty to follow the destinys of their Husbands."

Abigail's response to Louisa Catherine Adams's reflections on the marital bond arrived in St. Petersburg at the end of May 1811. Louisa chose not to continue the exchange, one reason perhaps being that by this time she was nearly seven months pregnant. The ambassador's wife had previously suffered several miscarriages, and she and her husband worried that the depression she inevitably suffered upon learning of her sister's death in childbirth would kill this fetus as well. It was, as her husband put it, "in the dispensations of a merciful Providence to determine to what extent she has been or may yet be a sufferer by the consequences of this heavy calamity." Actually, by the time John Quincy wrote those words, Louisa was starting to speak of her "anticipation of a premature confinement"—a possible miscarriage—in the past tense. She emphasized, however, that it had been a very near thing.

Louisa and John were by no means the first Adamses to worry that a fetus might be harmed by its mother's anxiety. Three decades earlier, as Abigail had struggled to understand why her last pregnancy had ended in stillbirth, she had reached the conclusion that the child had fallen victim to her own distress at being deprived of John's companionship at this critical time. In describing John Quincy and Louisa's fears to Louisa's mother, Catherine Johnson, Abigail observed that her son had reported receiving the news of Nancy Hellen's death "at a most unfortunate period for his wife," adding that the news "came very near producing an event she has so often experienced."

The baby was due in August, and Louisa's pregnancy foreclosed the possibility of the couple's coming home before the spring of 1812, since it would be folly for either an expectant mother or a newborn to cross the Atlantic, and by the time the child gained strength, St. Petersburg would be trapped in ice. As soon as John Quincy concluded that his wife's pregnancy was going to keep him in Russia another year, he declined an appointment that both of his parents had expected him to accept. President Madison had named him to the Supreme Court, and he had been confirmed by the Senate. Abigail was gleeful, and she suspected that the letter she had written the president the previous August had played some role in his decision. John Quincy should establish his primary residence in Quincy instead of Washington, where most of the other judges lived, his mother had advised him. She was dismayed to learn that he had declined the appointment, though even she had to acknowledge that he had no choice, since he could not ask Madison to hold the place open for an entire year.

In the winter of 1811, Abigail's only daughter informed her of an ominous swelling in her right breast. Although cancer was not diagnosed as often in those days as it is now, physicians and educated laypeople such as the Adamses had a basic understanding of how it worked. They knew, too, that not all lumps were tumors and that not all tumors were malignant. The question that Abigail Adams Smith would now have to confront was whether the possibility of the lump being cancerous was great enough to have a mastectomy.

CHAPTER 31

"The 'Threefold Silken Cord is Broken'"

1811–1812

In May 1810, as Abigail Adams Smith would later recount to Dr. Benjamin Rush, "I first perceived a hardness in my right Breast just above the nipple." The swollen area gave her "an uneasy sensation—like a burning sometimes an itching—& at times a deep darting pain through the Breast." For several months, Smith held out hope that the lump was a harmless cyst. She refused to treat it or to mention it to anyone other than her husband. All through the ensuing fall and winter, William "pressed her" to travel to Boston, where she could consult expert physicians and receive her mother's comfort. But, as he later told Abigail, "I was not able to induce the movement." In January, Nabby was finally prevailed upon to disclose her condition to her family in Quincy. Abigail was distressed, of course, and she promptly swung into action. She elicited general advice from two eastern Massachusetts doctors, Thomas Welsh and Amos Holbrook. But both men balked at further long-distance diagnosis, Abigail told her daughter, and they "agreed you had better be present that they could judge better & advise to more effect."

Still Nabby refused to budge, one reason being that her husband was also ill that winter, and she could not bring herself to travel to Boston without him. Abigail told her daughter-in-law Louisa Catherine that she suspected the real reason Nabby resisted making the trip was apprehension that "the physicians would urge the knife, which she says, the very thoughts of would be death to her." At this distance it is difficult to say what combination of the terrors associated with mastectomy prevailed in Smith's mind. Any of them—the pain of being operated on with no stronger anesthetic than opium, the possibility of dying on the operating table, or the permanent disfigurement—was more than sufficient to explain her dread. Even as Abigail struggled to change her daughter's mind, she did what she could from a distance of three hundred miles. From her friend Hannah Cushing, the Scituate, Massachusetts, widow of a Supreme Court justice, she learned of a man in Connecticut whose cancer had reportedly been cured by a root concoction, and she set about obtaining the recipe.

By June, the tumor was causing Nabby so much pain that she felt she had no choice but to consult the experts. Her husband was still sick, so she traveled to Quincy with two of her children, arriving in mid-July. John and Abigail had not seen them for three and a half years. The doctor who examined Smith initially told her she was only suffering from an "obstructed Gland." "I am exceeding glad to hear that the Drs. do not think Mrs Smiths Breast in so dangerous a state as we feard," Abigail's sister Elizabeth told her. Hannah Cushing went so far as to say her friend Abigail's "fears respecting Mrs. Smiths tumour were in a great measure removed" by the diagnosis. But then the doctors backtracked, acknowledging that they really could not tell whether the tumor was malignant. One prescribed hemlock pills. These caused "a heaviness in my head," Nabby reported, and she stopped taking them.

Nabby and her mother sent Colonel Smith regular reports on her examinations and treatment. After comparing these accounts to the information he had gleaned from popular medical tracts, William sent his mother-in-law a sarcastic denunciation of his wife's doctors. They should stop waffling about whether the lump was cancerous, he declared. In order to make a clear determination, they should bring it to the surface. When they did, he predicted, they would discover that it was not malignant, and they would be able to get rid of it without removing the breast. Frustrated at being a distant observer of events in Quincy, he proposed to rent a house near Peacefield and join his wife there.

Abigail did not like that idea, and she batted it down as delicately as she could. She was considerably less tactful about her son-in-law's presuming to second-guess the doctor's decision not to try to bring the lump to the surface, "Would it not be best having advised with physicians to follow their advice?" she asked. The moment Abigail's August 28 letter arrived in Lebanon, Smith immediately retreated on both fronts. I have "given my opinion too decidedly in opposition to that of professional men," he acknowledged, especially given that "I am totally ignorant of the case." He gave his mother-in-law a promise: "I shall never hazard an opinion on the subject again." And he agreed that it was probably best that he remain in Smith's Valley.

If Abigail had a closer companion than Nabby, it was her sister Mary. Late in May 1811, she, too, became dangerously ill with pleurisy. Her condition rapidly deteriorated, and by the middle of June her chances of survival seemed slim. Abigail wrote her nephew William Cranch, a federal judge in Virginia, to warn him that the next letter he received from Quincy would probably report his mother's death. Yet she wished her sister's life would be preserved, she told John Quincy—not for Mary's sake, since death would surely carry her to a better place, but "for the sake of her motherless grandchildren" (the family of her deceased daughter Elizabeth) and of Richard Cranch, "who could not many days survive her." Mary slipped down to the very "brink of the Grave," Abigail reported, but then rallied in early July. By the end of the month she was again thought to be at death's door. "A most distressing cough and loss of appetite, with a very sour mouth, have succeeded her other complaints," Abigail told Catherine Johnson, and "exhausted Nature appears sinking under the accumulated Burden."

Meanwhile Nabby's doctors had become increasingly convinced that the lump on her breast was a malignant tumor and that her only hope lay in a mastectomy. Members of her family joined in pressing her to make this fateful choice. About this time, Abigail learned that the root remedy in which she had placed so much hope was not to be her daughter's salvation. The Connecticut man whose cancer initially "seemed entirely healed by the use of dock root" had recently suffered a relapse and was not expected to last long. Nabby found a paper on cancer by Dr. Benjamin Rush. A Pennsylvania signer of the Declaration of Independence and a friend of her father's, Rush was the best-known physician in the country. Surviving documents do not reveal which of his many writings on cancer she read, but it may have been an essay called "An Account of the Use of Arsenic, in the Cure of Cancers," which appeared in Rush's four-volume *Medical Inquiries and Observations*, which was in the library at Peacefield. Rush's paper fed Nabby's hope of ridding herself of the tumor without resorting to surgery. So she decided to communicate with him directly.

Smith sent Rush a detailed description of her case and of the various treatments that had been recommended. The lump now seemed to be loose, she reported, and it was apparently "becoming harder." She had observed "a little redness at times on the skin," which she knew to be a sign that the tumor might soon erupt onto the surface. What Smith really wanted from Rush was some way to avoid breast-removal surgery, which was "a remedy that I don't know in any Event I could consent to submit to." Rush did not reply directly to Nabby. Instead he sent his recommendation to her father in hopes (as he told John) that "You and Mrs. Adams may communicate it gradually and in such a manner as will be least apt to distress and alarm her." The reason Rush adopted this method was that his advice was precisely what Smith had prayed it would not be. Notwithstanding what he had written in *Medical Inquiries and Observations*, he believed his fifty years of medical practice had taught him that in cases like hers, "local applications and internal medicines" would not suffice. "In 19 cases out of 20 in tumors in the *breast*," he told the former president, pills and plasters served only to "suspend the disease until it passes beyond that time in which the only radical remedy is ineffectual." The breast must be removed. "Let there be no delay in flying to the knife," he declared. Although sympathetic to Nabby's dread of having her flesh cut open (and certain in his own mind that this was her only objection to a mastectomy), Rush assured her parents that "the pain of the operation is much less than her fears represent it to be."

John could not bear to take any part in breaking the news to Nabby, as Rush had advised, so he ignored his friend's suggestion that he and his wife confront their daughter together. "Your Letter of the 20th. of September I communicated to Mrs. Adams as you advised. Mrs. Adams to her daughter," he wrote his friend. Nabby's doctors unanimously endorsed the venerable Rush's recommendation, and finally she gave in. Abigail, who had previously rebuffed William Smith's offer to come to Quincy, now summoned him to her bedside. He left at once, but Nabby "chose to save him the pain" of watching her suffer, as Abigail later reported. She scheduled the operation for Tuesday, October 8, before he could possibly reach her.

Meanwhile the family received more bad news from a different quarter. For nearly four months Mary Cranch had oscillated between periods of strength that appeared to herald a full recovery and episodes that seemed likely to kill her at any moment. "When dr Tufts gave her his opinion that her complaint tended rapidly to dissolution," Adams later reported, "she thought he was mistaken and seemd offended with him." But Abigail knew the doctor was right, and she later regretted not saying so to Mary. "I now blame myself that I never said to her, I think you in a situation very hazardous," she would soon recall. "Yet knowing how earnest she appeard to be to live for the sake of her Husband and Mrs Norton's Motherless children I did not love to damp the ardour of her spirit by saying you cannot live."

One day early in October, Abigail was caring for her sister when Peter Whitney, their minister, came by to see Mary. "She calld him to her and thanked him," Abigail later reported; she "conversed with him upon religion, said she thought frequently that she was not an inhabitant of this world [and] if she could but write down her thoughts we should find that she held converse with superior Beings." Her husband, Richard, came in from the garden and spoke to Reverend Whitney about the couple's "trouble." Abigail reported the exchange that ensued:

"Trouble sayd she. Why what troubles you?"

"Your [illness] my dear."

"O said she be like me. There is not any thing troubles me."

For months Richard Cranch had been saying he could not bear to outlive his wife, and it now appeared that he would soon have to face that test. Then on Saturday, October 5, Richard was "seized with a lethargy which deprived him of his speech," as Abigail informed John Quincy. Elizabeth Peabody, less inclined than Abigail to mince words, later reported that both "his reason, & speech failed." The eighty-four-year-old went down fast. "He did not appear to be sensible except a few times for a few moments," Abigail wrote. The only question now was which of the Cranches would die first.

Three days after Richard took sick, on October 8, the eminent surgeon John Warren and his son, who was also a physician, rode out from Boston to operate on Nabby. Three other doctors came along as observers. Nabby's only anesthetic was a dose of laudanum (liquid opium). The lead surgeon, the senior Dr. Warren, removed the entire breast. "The operation was twenty five Minutes in performing, and the dressing an hour longer," John Adams reported. In separate letters, he and Abigail both described their daughter as a "Heroine." With enormous relief, John informed Rush that the doctors all agreed "that the morbid substance is totally eradicated and nothing left but Flesh perfectly sound." The physicians also concurred that "the Probability of compleat and ultimate success is as great as in any instance that has fallen under their experience." Abigail was equally elated with the apparent success of the operation. "Every affected part was removed," she told

John Quincy, "so that we have every prospect of her perfect recovery to Health and usefullness again."

Two days after Nabby's operation, on Thursday, October 10, Richard Cranch died. He was two weeks shy of his eighty-fifth birthday. In a letter to her son, Abigail reported Mary's response to her husband's death, "O he has only stept behind the scene," she said. "I shall know where to find him." Hannah Cushing recalled that one of the last things her friend said to her was "*We shall meet again.*" As usual, Elizabeth Peabody painted a darker portrait. By the last hours of Richard's life, she wrote, Mary's mind was, like his, "unstable, & deranged." Abigail was at her sister's bedside again on the morning after Richard's death, later reporting, "We were all in tears but herself, she shed none." Adams rushed home for the midday meal and returned to find that her sister had died at noon. "If I had known or suspected her change would have been so sudden, painfull as the scene would have been I should have endured it," she later wrote. But "I was not permitted to witness it or to see her dear living face again."

Everyone who commented on the death of Richard and Mary rejoiced that after a half century of marriage, they had departed life together. "In Death we may say, they were not divided," Elizabeth Peabody wrote, "Together freed, their gentle spirits flew, to scenes of immortal Bliss." Yet for their survivors it was a time of great sadness. "My dearly beloved & only Sister," Peabody observed to Abigail, "the 'threefold silken cord is broken,'" and Abigail repeated that phrase to her son. The worst victims of Mary Cranch's death—potentially, at least—were the children of her deceased daughter Elizabeth. As Hannah Cushing put it in a letter to Abigail, Betsy Norton's children had "in a few months been deprived of two Mothers." There were also John Quincy's two sons, who had been living with the Cranches, to worry about. For the moment all of the children moved in with John and Abigail.

A week after the Cranches died, William Stephens Smith joined the crowded household at Peacefield. Abigail believed Nabby and her children—but not William—should remain in Quincy for the winter. He acquiesced in that verdict, heading back to Lebanon a month later. Meanwhile John Quincy's sons were bundled off to Atkinson Academy, run by their great aunt Elizabeth's husband, Stephen Peabody. Along with three Cranch grandchildren, they would board with Elizabeth, as their uncles and cousins had previously done. By this time, Abigail had additional reasons for not placing the boys with the family of Thomas and Ann Adams. Thomas's judicial duties had expanded, and he had also been elected to the governor's council. Judge Adams was "so much from home," she explained to John Quincy, "that it was impossible for him to attend to them." Having once given the proximity of the Cranch place to Peter Whitney's school as a reason for boarding them there instead of with Thomas and Ann, Abigail now declared that Reverend Whitney allowed his students too many days off. "It was concluded upon, both by your father and by me, that the Academy at Atkinson . . . was the best place," she wrote. When John Quincy learned of the new arrangement, he raised a concern that was reminiscent of the explanation Abigail had given a year earlier for not letting the boys board with Thomas's family. I have no doubt of the Peabodys' kindness, he wrote, but "where there are such numbers at once to whom it must be extended, I cannot altogether avoid the apprehension of accidents which may be unavoidable."

Abigail had long worried about ten-year-old George's stubbornness, but an incident that occurred on the day the boys left for New Hampshire convinced her that John suffered from the same vice. John, who was eight, picked up a ceramic jug, and Abigail warned him that it was too heavy for him.

"O No Grandmamma it is not," he replied.

"You will break it child," she said.

"O No I shall not."

Finally Abigail relented, and sure enough, John dropped the jug, shattering it. At the time, Abigail recalled in the first letter she wrote her grandson after he and George had settled in at the Peabodys', "you looked so mortified that I had not the Heart to find fault with you. I only chid myself for yielding to importunity against my better knowledge." But she thought the incident might prove instructive to the boy as he began this new phase of his education. "Never be positive," she wrote. "Remember the broken jug the day you went away. . . . [T]hose who have lived longer in the world than you have; and have more experience ought to be minded, and their judgment submitted to without murmuring." Elizabeth Peabody reported that when she read Abigail's account of the jug incident aloud to her household, most of her boarders were "much diverted," but "the dear conscious little fellow, put up both his hands to cover his Face." "I fancy the fate of it, will be impressed upon his young mind," she told her sister.

Atkinson is just across the state line from Haverhill, Massachusetts, where Aunt Elizabeth had lived with her first husband. The boys' removal to Atkinson Academy meant that they would not be making any more Sunday visits to their grandmother, but Abigail's one consolation was that she would now receive regular letters from them. To a voracious consumer of correspondence, this was no small advantage. Adams would also be able to monitor the boys' handwriting, spelling, and grammar. On reading her first letter from John, she was astonished to find that his handwriting far surpassed his older brother's. Although alarmed about George's lack of progress, Adams allowed herself a measure of feminine pride in John's having, as she told him, "learnt more good hand writing under the female instructors you had been taught by than your brother with all the masters he had been to."

By November 17, when Abigail finally found the strength to send John Quincy a long report on Nabby's mastectomy and the deaths of her sister and brother-in-law, there was additional bad news to convey. "A malignant billious fever has prevaild in Washington," she wrote, and on September 29, it took the life of Catherine Johnson, Louisa Catherine's mother. The following Wednesday, one of Louisa's sisters lost her husband. Abigail observed that the young woman had been "deprived both of Husband and Mother at the same time, with an infant Babe, and I fear, without any means of support." Adams further lamented that Louisa's relatives in Washington had chosen her, of all people, to inform her daughter-in-law of the two deaths.

There was one bright spot in Abigail's letter to her son. She had received word of the arrival of John Quincy and Louisa's first daughter, born in St. Petersburg on August 12. The child was named after her mother and baptized at an Anglican church. The wives of two of John Quincy's fellow expatriates—the Portuguese minister and a merchant who belonged to the Society of Friends—served as little Louisa Catherine's godmothers. "That a Quaker and a Portuguese Roman Catholic should join with a Church [of England] Clergyman to baptize the child of a New-England Congregationalist at St. Petersburg the capital of Russia," John Quincy told his mother, "is an incident rather extraordinary in the annals of the World."

One of John Adams's comforts during the gloomy summer and fall of 1811 was the epistolary conversation that he and Benjamin Rush had initiated several years earlier. Adams, who turned seventy-six at the end of October, and Rush, who was sixty-five, reminisced about their service in the Second Continental Congress, where both had advocated for, and later signed, the Declaration of Independence. In a July 20 letter, Rush reminded Adams that as the delegates were preparing to sign the document that many feared would be their death warrant, Virginia congressman Benjamin Harrison livened the mood with some gallows humor. "I shall have a great advantage over you, Mr. Gerry, when we are all hung for what we are now doing," he told the diminutive Massachusetts representative. "From the size and weight of my body I shall die in a few minutes, but from the lightness of your body you will dance in the air an hour or two before you are dead."

Rush and Adams agreed that in the thirty-five years since the Declaration of Independence, historians and Fourth of July orators had thoroughly distorted the epic events in which both had played such significant roles. Neither disguised his bitterness at America's infatuation with George Washington. It sometimes seemed that an ungrateful nation was determined to forget the sacrifices of lesser-known Patriots such as themselves. To document his own sacrifice for the common cause, Adams sent his friend a financial autobiography. It listed a lifetime's worth of income sources, starting with the grammar school and Harvard tuition his father had paid for him and concluding with the canal stocks currently in his portfolio. In between he itemized the property he had inherited from his father and father-in-law, touted the profitability of the law practice he had given up during the Revolutionary War, and totted up his other investments—all with a view to showing how much wealthier he would have been had he not heeded the call to public service.

Adams mentioned the first Loan Office certificate his wife had purchased for him back in 1777, claiming that he had "advised" her to take this step. Did John forget that the files in his office contained Abigail's June 1, 1777, letter explaining the whole idea to him? Or did he deliberately conceal her financial initiative in anticipation that his letter might someday appear in print? One indication that Adams did not simply suffer a memory lapse is that as he continued his narrative, he did not mention any of the other government securities his wife had purchased for him, much less those she bought on her own behalf. Nor did he say anything about the income she had earned importing European finery during the Revolutionary War. John had benefited immensely from Abigail's entrepreneurial activities, but he had no desire to see them broadcast to the wider world.

It is impossible to say whether John showed his financial autobiography to his wife, but if he did, she probably did not resent her exclusion from it. After all, Abigail herself had tried to conceal her ownership of government securities. Indeed, if she did see her husband's letters to Rush, her dominant feeling must have been one of vindication, for John acknowledged that the farms he had insisted on purchasing (despite his wife's repeated entreaties to buy more bonds instead) had never returned more than 2 percent a year.

CHAPTER 32

"God Loves a Cheerfull Christian"

1812–1814

Abigail always believed that good could come out of evil, and that notion appeared to have been borne out in the case of her daughter's cancer. As a teenager, Nabby had frequently visited James and Mercy Warren for weeks at a time, and she had stayed in touch with them until Mercy's break with her parents. Two months after the operation, Warren wrote Abigail to ask how her daughter was faring. As with Mary Jefferson's death seven years earlier, a family tragedy provided the occasion for former friends to contemplate reconciliation. Adams replied warmly to Warren's overture, and the two women set about repairing their friendship. At about the same time, John Adams undertook a reconciliation of his own. Through the energetic mediation of Benjamin Rush, he was moved, on New Year's Day 1812, to write a holiday letter to Thomas Jefferson. Jefferson sent him a cordial reply, and the two began a renewed correspondence that would end only with their deaths in 1826.

By the spring of 1812, Abigail had recovered from the shock of losing her sister and brother-in-law, and Nabby felt increasingly certain that her doctors had removed her cancer before it could spread. Finally Abigail was able to focus her cares on her grandchildren. Ann Adams presented newborns to her husband, Thomas, at regular intervals: three girls and a boy arrived during the first six years of their marriage. Abigail also delighted in the reports she received on the second Louisa Catherine Adams. "Louisa is ten months old and has 6 teeth and 1 more nearlly through," the infant's mother bragged in a June 1812 letter from St. Petersburg. Your sister "almost begins to [say?] Papa and Mama," John Quincy told his son George at about the same time—and Louisa

Catherine insisted that her namesake had already passed that milestone six weeks earlier.

As grateful as she was to finally have a daughter, the ambassador's wife freely confessed to her mother-in-law that her maternal duties could be taxing. In the spring of 1812, erysipelas, a nasty skin disease, invaded her ears, and in June she told Abigail she did not expect to shake it until she weaned the child, which she expected to do well before little Louisa's first birthday. After closing this letter, Louisa Catherine wrote on the cover, "I am ashamed to send this scrawl[.] Louisa will suck and Charles will talk I am almost bewilder'd." John Quincy's other two sons, George and John, were not too busy at Atkinson Academy to keep Abigail apprised of their progress, and nearly every school vacation found them at their grandparents' mansion in Quincy. Abigail rejoiced to see the older boy maturing as she had predicted. "George has improved in all respects," she told her daughter-in-law. "He has conquerd much of that overbearing disposition, which too easily beset him, and is mild, and ready to listen to advice, and to profit by it." His eight-year-old brother was a different matter. John was "too *quick*, & rash in resenting a supposed insult," Elizabeth Peabody told Abigail.

Although confident that she and her sister were giving the boys a good upbringing, Abigail worried about the family's prolonged separation. "A Father and a Mother may be too long absent from their Children," she reminded Louisa Catherine in a February 24 letter; "parents cannot forget their Children, but may not the Children upon whose youthfull minds impressions are deeply engraven, by long absence feel less sensibly the stamp?" Abigail may have been using the boys to lure her son home—a tactic she had employed against her husband a half century earlier—but there is no evidence that she meant to cause her daughter-in-law pain. That was, however, the effect. "What can I say to you dear Madam[?]" she wrote; "your Letter distress'd me beyond conception." Abigail's warnings about the boys forgetting their parents had "cut me to the heart," Louisa declared.

Abigail's absorption in her own grandchildren did not prevent her from taking an interest in those left behind by her deceased sister. Ever since Elizabeth Cranch Norton's death a year earlier, Abigail and her kinswomen had been asking each other whether it would ever be possible to find her widower a wife who would also be a mother to his eight children. "Who could he get," Abigail asked her New Hampshire sister shortly after Reverend Norton's wife died, "who would be spent for his family to the last spark of existence like the departed and deceased sufferer[?]" Elizabeth could think of only one candidate for the position, and she feared the lady in question would choose to remain single "rather than be accountable to any man." The eldest Norton child, Richard, had turned twenty-one the previous year, and Abigail persuaded John to ask Benjamin Rush to recommend him to the attention of his son, who as comptroller of the federal government had numerous patronage appointments to bestow. Abigail reviewed what her husband had written to Rush in favor of their grand-nephew—that he was "an amiable and ingenious young Gentleman of education"—and was not satisfied. On the back of the letter, John added, "P.S. My Rib says I have not been particular enough." He explained that Richard was his great-nephew, a man of "Modesty, Civility, and Ingenuity"—and the first American to discover the comet that passed the earth in May 1811.

All in all, the Adams grandchildren were about as healthy as any of their contemporaries, but of course this was an era when childhood illnesses were frequent, severe, and sometimes fatal. In early February, Thomas and Ann's daughter Francis, who was seven months old, contracted whooping cough. Ann had lost a brother to the same disease, and she could not help dreading the worst. It turned out that her fears were justified, too, for the child struggled for a month and died on March 5. "Oh what a sight for a parent to behold!" Thomas told his brother. "To be intimate with Death he must be introduced into your own family." Ann was distraught, of course, and she became physically ill as well. More than a month after the child died, Abigail reported that her daughter-in-law had been "sick with a fever since the loss of her Dear Babe."

By the spring of 1812, John Quincy and Louisa Catherine knew they had no prospect of coming home to Massachusetts anytime soon. If the family was to be reunited, it would have to be in St. Petersburg. Louisa Catherine not only missed her sons but felt she was neglecting them. Her husband did not relish the idea of summoning George and John to cross the Atlantic and Baltic Oceans, but in March he finally gave in. It is possible that Abigail's obstinacy in boarding the boys first with one of her sisters and then with the other—rather than with his brother Thomas, as John Quincy desired—convinced him that his wife was right. Adams could only imagine one circumstance that might prevent his mother from dispatching John and George to Europe, and that was a war between the United States and Great Britain—which was, in fact, a real possibility. Even as neutrals, American merchantmen had faced constant harassment from the Royal Navy. A congressional declaration of war would sever the last restraints, and the boys would stand little chance of completing the lengthy voyage to St. Petersburg.

Louisa should have stood her ground sooner. American grievances against the former mother country had been piling up for more than five years. In its determination to starve out the emperor Napoleon, the British Privy Council had ordered the captains of frigates and privateers to seize neutral vessels bound for France or any of its puppets, allies, or colonies. By the terms of a series of "orders in council," even American ships that did not try to trade with France were frequently stopped and stripped of crewmen by Royal Navy captains in need of replacements for sailors lost to enemy fire or (more commonly) disease. White Americans also blamed the British for the resistance they encountered from the Indians. The reality, of course, was that Native Americans attacked settlers for their own reasons. They wished to keep their land and to avenge white raids against their own villages. Many native cultures also had a custom of replacing deceased kinsmen with enemy captives. In the early years of the nineteenth century, a cadre of extraordinarily talented Indian leaders—the most famous of whom were a pair of Shawnee brothers named Tecumseh and Tenskwatawa (better known as the Shawnee Prophet)—fomented spiritual revivals that inspired Native Americans to resist white encroachments and to unite with other native nations in doing so. The material assistance these Indian rebels received from British officers in Canada was, in their eyes, pitifully inadequate. But white Americans convinced themselves that the whole impetus for the Indian attacks was Canadian instigation. "The SCALPING KNIFE and TOMAHAWK of *British savages, is now, again devastating our frontiers*," a Kentucky newspaper declared.

By the spring of 1812, President Madison could see no way to stop British depredations on American shipping and British-supported Indian attacks short of declaring war, and Congress adopted the official resolution on June 17. William Stephens Smith heard the news shortly before heading to Quincy to bring home his wife and daughter. When he arrived, he asked Abigail—he dared not approach John—to intercede with the powers that be in Washington to get him a commission in the army that was being raised to fight the British. The former first lady was only too happy to write a letter on her son-in-law's behalf, since leading troops was the one form of gainful employment for which he had demonstrated real aptitude. Unfortunately, no one in the capital had forgotten about Smith's involvement in the Miranda disaster, and the commission never came.

Even before Congress declared war, Abigail worried that the Americans' resistance to British provocations was being undermined by their own internal conflicts. The commercial boycotts adopted at the behest of Presidents Jefferson and Madison during the half decade leading up to the war crippled New England shipping and revived the previously moribund Federalist party. John and Abigail's former allies declared that the United Kingdom was justified in preventing the United States from trading with its mortal enemies and in drafting British-born sailors from American ships. The Americans, not the British, were responsible for deteriorating relations between the two countries, they claimed. Abigail reacted to these seemingly treasonous statements the same way she had to Republican criticism of her husband back during the late 1790s: she believed they must be suppressed. In January 1812 she celebrated the news that one anti-administration printer had been fined and imprisoned, and she told her son, "If the spirit rises a little higher, *our writers* must not be tolerated, nor he who dares assume the name of rebel."

A British blockade of American ports drove up the prices New Englanders had to pay, even for grain coming from other American states, since the only safe way to transport it was overland. But the war by no means dominated Abigail's thinking during the summer of 1812. In July she journeyed to Plymouth to mark her reconciliation with Mercy Otis Warren. Elizabeth Peabody exulted that her sister and Warren had decided to "to bury the Hatchet," but the reunion was marred by John Adams's refusal to participate. Shortly after returning to Quincy, Abigail received a letter from Mercy asking for John's copies of all his letters criticizing her history of the revolution. Warren knew as well as anyone that historians are the servants of their sources, and she wished to deprive future authors of John's "wounding and grievous" commentaries on her work. Having previously destroyed her own copies of these letters, she hoped to burn John's originals as well. Abigail does not appear to have responded to her friend's request—every page of John's invective survives—but she was nonetheless determined to continue the reconciliation. So she conveyed her affection for Mercy using a standard device of the era, sending her a ring with lockets of her and her husband's hair.

During the summer of 1812, Abigail had to devote more and more time to the care of her father's former slave Phoebe. For more than a year, she had been unable to work. Parson Smith had set up a small trust fund for her, but in recent years the annual interest had proved insufficient and Dr. Tufts, her trustee, had been forced to deplete the capital. "She has lived to an Age when she has out lived not only her own personal comforts, but the means our dear parent left to support her," Abigail told her sister Elizabeth. The servant girl who lived with her (her wages apparently paid by the town of Quincy) was "young and heedless." Knowing her patient was "too infirm to compel her," she was frequently "neglectfull," even about providing meals. Abigail's efforts to find a replacement for the girl had proved unavailing. "We have not any Blacks in town," she explained to Betsy, "& white people who are good for any thing do not like to live in a negro house." Actually, she wrote two months later, there was "one black woman in Town . . . she has a family to take care of, but we get her as often as we can." On the frequent occasions when Phoebe's illness took a turn for the worse, Abigail marshaled her female relatives—especially her nieces Lucy Cranch Greenleaf (her late sister's daughter) and Betsy Smith (her late brother's daughter) and her daughter-in-law Ann Adams—to attend her through the night. "It requires two of a night to look after her as she has frequent need to be got out of Bed," she wrote. Abigail herself made "daily" visits, on each of which Phoebe would grasp her hand and ask, "when shall I see you again . . . ?"

Despite her infirmity, Phoebe seemed (at least in her lead caregiver's eyes) as willful as ever, a trait that Adams explained in racial terms. "The high affrican Blood runs in her veins," she told Elizabeth Peabody, "and she has much of the sovereign yet." Although the two women's decades together had failed to dissolve the racial barrier between them, both had managed to reach across it. "I love and respect and venerate her," Abigail wrote. Even Betsy, who had once described Phoebe as "oderiferous," now spoke of her in respectful, albeit still racialized, tones, urging her father's former slave to "trust in Him, who has made of one blood all the Nations of the Earth." Phoebe apparently died in the fall of 1812 or soon thereafter, for a September 11, 1812, report that she was "sick and dying" was the last reference to her in Abigail's correspondence.

In September, Thomas and Ann Adams's young family again faced affliction. While Ann was visiting her family in Haverhill with her children—but without Thomas, who could not escape his judicial duties—four-year-old Elizabeth fell gravely ill. When the news reached Thomas, he set off at once for Haverhill, stopping in Braintree only long enough to convey the ominous tidings to his parents. The first leg of the journey had exhausted him, Abigail later reported to Ann. He "came in, took his Father and me by the hand without speaking & got as far as the door when the agony burst forth in such a manner as intirely overcame him." The sun had set, and as Abigail informed her daughter-in-law, she pleaded with him "not to ride all night as I feard he would get sick and add to your troubles, instead of diminishing them." But "his heart [was] torn with the anguish of seeing his darling child no more," and "No persuasion could prevail upon him to defer one hour; sitting out to be with you," she wrote.

The child was still living when Thomas reached her, and after her father's arrival she began to gain strength. By September 19, Elizabeth was on her way to a full recovery, and in fact she ended up living to 1903, when she died at the age of ninety-five.

During the same weeks when Elizabeth was giving her parents such a fright, John Quincy and Louisa were undergoing a similar ordeal. Even as Napoleon's army stormed toward Moscow, little Louisa, who had always been "the strongest and healthiest" of the ambassador's children, contracted a mysterious illness. The child had "sickened . . . soon after being weaned," John Quincy reported to his mother. So soon, in fact, that "on the appearance of her illness she was by the advice of the physicians taken back to the Breast." The return to nursing did not arrest Louisa's decline. What had started as a violent fever turned into a nervous fever. Then the child began having convulsions. "The sufferings of the Child were protracted through nearly four weeks," John Quincy later told Abigail. "They were so severe that the sight of them would have wrung with compassion a heart of marble." At 1:30 P.M. on Tuesday, September 15—the very day that the retreating Russian army abandoned Moscow, setting forts and palaces ablaze in order to deny Napoleon the use of them—Louisa died.

John Quincy had devoted a portion of his ample spare time in St. Petersburg to a detailed exploration of the Bible, but now he could find no comfort there. On the contrary, he noted in a letter to his mother, the little girl's agonizing death shortly after her first birthday had introduced into his thinking, for the first time ever, a "distrust of the goodness of Providence." He observed, "There are passages in the Scriptures, which seem to imply, if they do not directly assert that the death of infant children is sometimes inflicted as chastisement for the transgressions of their Parents." What horrible sin had he and his wife committed?

Louisa Catherine suffered even worse than her husband. Although her child's death was self-evidently a result of disease, she convinced herself, as she told Abigail, that she had "lost my darling owing to a fall which I had with her in my arms"—a fall like the one that had in fact killed her fetus in 1809. "My heart is almost broken my health is gone and my peace of mind is I fear for ever destroy'd," she wrote six months later. With the exception of Charles Adams, who had died young, all of Abigail's children had now experienced the agony of losing an infant. There is no evidence for the widespread modern belief (based in part on the common eighteenth-century practice of referring to babies as "it") that early Americans inured themselves to these afflictions by deliberately choosing not to become too attached to their children until they had survived infancy. Eighteenth-century parents did not love less than their twenty-first-century counterparts; they simply suffered more.

By the time George and John Adams learned of their sister's death, they were no longer boarding with their great aunt Elizabeth in New Hampshire. Abigail had once again relocated them, pulling them out of Atkinson Academy, run by her brother-in-law Stephen Peabody, and enrolling them in Hingham Academy near her home. The letter in which she explained the move to the boys' father was ambiguous in the extreme. At first she laid the decision on her husband and youngest son, but later she referred to "my object in removing them" from her sister's home. And she never quite defined that objective. Perhaps a minor leg injury that John suffered while chasing a rabbit finally convinced her that John Quincy might have been justified in his "apprehension of accidents" in a houseful of youthful boarders too numerous to be properly supervised. Another possibility is that Abigail discerned the inadequacy of the boys' progress in George's still-sloppy handwriting. That, at least, was Elizabeth Peabody's suspicion as she protested the move in a letter to Abigail. George and John "*well know* if they did not improve, it was their *own* Fault," she told her sister on the last day of 1812. "I did all I could to encourage George to write well. I have ruled his paper. I have guided his hand times, & times. We have suggested *every motive* to stimulate their progress in Learning, which was likely to have any effect upon a manly, ingeneuous mind, & it was *grievous* to find, & be convinced that nothing but *Time,* would complete our ardent wishes." She noted that other parents were perfectly satisfied with Mr. Vose, the boys' teacher at Atkinson Academy, and she warned that the Hingham family now boarding them might "not take the pains with them, that others before them have done." The "others" to whom she referred were herself and her husband.

On January 15, 1813, Abigail learned of little Louisa Adams's death the previous fall. "Early in life I was called to taste the bitter cup," she told her daughter-in-law, and all the intervening years had "not obliterated from my mind the anguish of my soul upon the occasion." She nonetheless informed Louisa Catherine that it was selfish to mourn for the infant, since she was in heaven, and she went on to remind her of the Christian imperative to be "cheerfull submissive and resignd," since "God loves a cheerfull Christian." (Anticipating this reaction, Louisa had implored her mother-in-law "not to condemn a grief which is beyond my reason to subdue," affirming, "Had you witnessed the horrid circumstances of my Angels death you would pity and forgive me.") On the very day the sad news reached Quincy, Abigail set it all down in a letter to her grandsons. Then she and John decided to take a sleigh ride to Hingham to visit the boys, arriving well before the letter. George and John's joy at seeing their grandparents "was so full and so great," Abigail later admitted to John Quincy, "that I could not damp it, whilst I stayed by the melancholy tydings. I referred them to a letter which they had not then received."

At Hingham, George and John were once again within walking distance of Peacefield, and Abigail was thrilled to be able to spend more time with them. At eleven George was increasingly ready for adult conversation, and Abigail began raising serious issues in her letters to him. In a January 1813 letter that began with praise for the improvements the boy had made to his handwriting at Hingham Academy ("I shall not now be ashamed to have you write to your parents," she declared), Abigail went on to acknowledge that her own script had never achieved the graceful ideal. The reason was clear: "When I was young I was brought up in a Town where it was not at that time, customary for Girls to attend schools for writing, and female education was much less attended to than at the present day." Thus did Abigail transmit to a new generation of Adams men her conviction that women of her generation had suffered a grave injustice.

* * *

Nabby had returned to Lebanon, New York, with her husband and daughter in the summer of 1812. Shortly after the cold weather set in, she began to experience intermittent pains that her doctors diagnosed as rheumatism, a disorder that had attacked all of Parson Smith's descendants, though none so severely as this. Nabby was confined to her bed for days at a time, and her spirits were not lifted, to say the least, by a letter from St. Petersburg informing her that her son William had amassed a thousand-dollar debt to John Quincy Adams. William's uncle needed his money, and Louisa Catherine, knowing William did not have it, pressured her husband to try to collect it from the young man's father. Colonel Smith was not able to cover the debt, either, and all Nabby could do was lament to Abigail that her husband's financial ineptitude had apparently passed intact to his son. Even the compliment that Colonel Smith's fellow backcountry New Yorkers paid him in the fall of 1812 by electing him to the U.S. House of Representatives added to his invalid wife's burden, since it would deprive her of his companionship. Abigail suggested that when Colonel Smith went to Washington, Nabby should travel to Massachusetts. Why should she linger in Smith's Valley to superintend a household that consisted only of herself and her daughter, who could just as easily accompany her to Quincy?

William Smith saw things differently. Nabby had spent nearly a year at Peacefield recuperating from her mastectomy, and she by no means owed her parents another visit. She should remain in Lebanon during her husband's absence. The colonel's pronouncement infuriated his mother-in-law, who fired off a smoking protest to Mrs. Peabody. Elizabeth was of course sympathetic, though she also tried to make Abigail see reason. "My dear sister, we can travel but a little longer in this Wilderness," she wrote, "& it seems a *Duty* to keep your Daughter with you all in your power—to cheer you on your way." No matter how "kind & good" a woman's male relatives might be, to them she could never "communicate so unreservedly, as to a Daughter." On the other hand, Abigail had to face facts. "In a Family so heterogeneous as yours, there will be opposing Interests, & offences must be expected," she wrote. "But I should be grieved if anything took place, to interrupt your Tranquility, or the Peace of your excellent Daughter."

In April the Adamses learned that Nabby's disorder had grown so severe that she could not conveniently travel to Quincy even if Colonel Smith were now to change his mind. Abigail was furious, of course, but a month later her anger gave way to despair as she learned that the pains that had left her daughter "almost a cripple" were not rheumatic after all. Her cancer had returned in the form of a new tumor on her other breast. "Not willing to give pain to her Friends," she had, as Abigail later informed John Quincy, "kept the source of all her complaints to herself." By the time Nabby faced the necessity of informing her mother of her real condition, she feared she did not have long to live. "With increased virulence," Abigail reported, the cancer had "rapidly diffused itself through her whole frame, destroyd her constitution and renderd her a perfect cripple." In her agony, incapable of writing, Nabby instructed her daughter Caroline to ask her aged parents to undertake the grueling journey to the Chenango Valley to be with her one last time. It was Abigail's painful duty to inform Nabby that she was herself "too infirm" to make the trip. Colonel Smith had just gone to Congress, which convened on May 24, and he was too absorbed in his legislative duties to persuade himself that his wife's condition was terminal. Only Caroline—and possibly Nabby's younger son John, if the final summons reached him in time—would be there to bless her on her way.

Nabby could imagine nothing worse than dying without taking proper leave of her parents. Since they could not come to her, she resolved to go to them. In order to make the three-hundred-mile trip, she would have to entrust her pain-wracked body to a crude carriage with little capacity for absorbing the lurches and jolts common enough on any of the era's roads—and all the more so in the backwoods region through which she would have to pass. Nabby's one desire was actually more of a forlorn hope, and that was simply, as Abigail put it, "to come and die in her native place with her parents." Two of her children, John and Caroline, accompanied her on the trek, as did Colonel Smith's sister Nancy. They set out in early July and made frequent stops, prolonging Nabby's agony but also, the wayfarers hoped, increasing her chances of surviving the journey. Abigail described the recurrence of Nabby's cancer as "the most trying affliction of all I have ever been caled to endure."

As she waited, Abigail wrestled with a moral dilemma. Since the middle of June she had been party to a devastating secret about Nabby's family. Without any warning, Nabby's oldest son, William Steuben Smith, had gotten married. For three years, the young man had been in St. Petersburg serving as his uncle John Quincy Adams's secretary. Another member of the ambassador's household was Catherine "Kitty" Johnson, Louisa Catherine's sister. At the end of his January 30, 1813, letter to Abigail, John Quincy added an abrupt postscript: William and Kitty were engaged and would soon be married.

Abigail liked Kitty well enough, though she had known her only casually during her short stint in Washington, D.C. And she was not bothered, apparently, that the connection had developed while the two unmarried adults were living in the same household, a circumstance that had been among her foremost objections to John Shaw's courtship of her little sister forty years earlier. The problem was financial. Kitty's father had declared bankruptcy, and so had Colonel Smith. At twenty-five William Junior had shown no greater aptitude than his father for getting and keeping money. Three years earlier Abigail had celebrated when another of Louisa Catherine's sisters, Eliza, had broken off with her "deserving" but destitute fiancé—a preacher who earned only seven hundred dollars a year—in order to marry a man with better prospects, John Pope (to her daughter-in-law, Abigail joked that in marrying Pope, Eliza had "got absolution without doing penance, which she must have done if the former connection had taken place"). Now Kitty and William had given her "much uneasiness" by shunning that pragmatic path. These two ought to have married up instead of each other.

Abigail was hardly alone, for nearly everyone who heard the news had the same reaction. In a letter to his mother-in-law, Colonel Smith confessed his difficulty at "burying all disappointment" regarding the match. The only member of William Steuben's family who was not devastated by his decision was his mother, for the simple reason that her relatives decided not to tell her about it. On July 26, Nabby and her caretakers finally entered her parents' gate, and she was immediately carried in to bed. The trip had of course intensified her pain. "Opium was the only paliative, the only releif she could obtain, to relieve the spasms which as she described it, cased her up in armour," Abigail reported. Congress adjourned on August 2, allowing Colonel Smith to reach Quincy two weeks after his wife. Knowing that the end was near, Nabby decided to select a hymn for her funeral. She was too weak to hold the hymnal or even to turn the pages, so Abigail slowly paged through the book for her. Finally she found the song she wanted: "Longing for Heaven."

Having made it to her parents' house and held on until the arrival of her husband, Nabby had but one regret. "I shall never see my dear William again!" she exclaimed. These were very nearly her last words.

She died on August 15, 1813—"in the Arms," her father informed Thomas Jefferson, "of Her Husband her Son, her Daughter, her Father and Mother, her Husbands two Sisters and two of her Nieces, in the 49th. Year of her Age, 46 of which She was the healthiest and firmest of Us all: Since which, She has been a monument to Suffering and to Patience." For her part, Abigail tried to take comfort in the fact that her daughter had been, as she told John Quincy's sons, "permitted and enabled to encounter a most hazardous journey in her weak state, and allowd to see her parents & friends again and to live until [Colonel Smith] returnd from Congress, when as tho all her wishes were fulfilled, she cheerfully resignd her life into the hands of her maker."

Abigail's sister Elizabeth understood what she was going through, for she, too, had lost an adult child (Elizabeth Quincy Shaw, who was was eighteen) back in 1798. "I fully know, what a fond Parent suffers, at beholding a beloved child, fatally arrested, smiling in anguish, & secretly suppressing a groan, lest it should wound her Mothers Heart," she wrote. "It makes Nature bleed at every pore." In a December 1813 letter to Louisa Catherine Adams, Abigail went so far as to contend that her own loss was more devastating than the one Louisa had suffered a year earlier, when her daughter and namesake died shortly after her first birthday. "Bitter is the loss of a sweet infant," Abigail wrote, "but how much increased are the pangs which rend the Heart of a Mother, when caled to part with the Head of a Family, in the midst of her days, and usefulness? Endeared by a thousand strong ties?"

The afflictions that Abigail had endured over the course of the previous two years—especially the deaths of the Cranches, of two of her grandchildren, and now of her only daughter—aged her in a way that time alone could not. Late in the summer of 1813, when the Adamses' old friend François Adriaan van der Kemp made a visit to Quincy, he encountered Abigail amid a large concourse of people and did not even recognize her. After his arrival back home in New York, he made the second mistake of admitting in a letter to John that until they were introduced, he could not imagine that this "elderly lady" was his friend Mrs. Adams. "I was thunderstruck," he wrote. John of course relayed the comment to his wife, who was not offended, only saddened to be reminded of the troubles that had furrowed her countenance. "Be assured," she told Van der Kemp, "I took no exception to your expression of surprize at the vast change time had wrought upon the face of your Friend, my faithfull mirror had told me the same serious truth long before."

Despite her many losses, Abigail still had numerous ties to life. John grew ever more reliant upon her as he himself became more feeble and as more and more of his friends faded away. She also supervised the education of John Quincy's sons, though she only saw them on the weekend. With a mixture of pride and alarm, she reported to the boys' mother that George "devote[d] himself to reading without any inclination to mix with his schoolmates in play." John was "much more active," "like a Top always spinning." He was "ardent and quick as lightning," not only as he galloped around the lawn at Peacefield or charged up the hill just outside the front gate but in another sense as well: he was easily provoked. Abigail's other grandchildren gave John the nickname "Hot Spur," after Shakespeare's impetuous soldier-hero, but she herself was not too worried about him. "Reason and time will correct this disposition, as the qualities of the Heart are good," she told his mother. After her husband, Abigail's most cherished companion was Nabby's daughter Caroline, who was happy to accept her grandmother's invitation to take up permanent residence at Peacefield. Abigail entertained no illusions about Caroline's physical beauty—in fact she seemed strangely compelled to inform nearly all of her correspondents that Nabby's daughter was "not handsome"—but she was an agreeable companion, possessing a sweetness of temper that was "than beauty dearer."

Abigail's concern about Caroline's appearance was by no means universally shared. "You think Caroline *has* not personal attractions," Adams's friend and distant relative Harriet Welsh told her in the spring of 1814. "We Bostonians think differently." More to the point, Peter de Windt, a young New Yorker who had known Caroline's brother John in college, had met her the previous February, and, only a month later, asked her to marry him. The proposal caught Abigail completely off guard. She had had no time to get to know Peter or "to learn something respecting the Mother of this gentleman and of his whole family." On the other hand, if the courtship could only be carried out with more deliberation, Abigail was thoroughly excited about it. As the only son of a well-to-do Fishkill, New York, widow, De Windt stood to inherit a comfortable fortune. And the very fact that he had chosen Caroline spoke volumes about his character. Clearly he was not given to "fashionable pleasure," Abigail told Harriet Welsh, since he had been "captivated, with Caroline; whose Beauty could not attract and to whose fortune, or expectations he could be no stranger to."

Adams also admired Peter's decision to propose to Caroline before soliciting her father's approval of the match. On the other hand, Colonel Smith scolded the young man for not putting the "previous question" to himself. Smith could scarcely have chosen a more effective strategy for endearing De Windt to Abigail. "I cannot condemn the foresight of the gentleman who feeling the full force of an attraction took care to have as few repellants as possible," she told Smith. "I shall maintain the supremicy of the ladies in this matter." Thirty-eight years after threatening to "foment a Rebellion" if the Continental Congress did not "Remember the Ladies" in its new legal code, Adams remained a spirited advocate for her sex. Recounting the whole episode for Harriet Welsh, she boasted that she had "rebelled against" Colonel Smith's policy of being approached ahead of his daughter "as encroaching upon the Sovereign rights of the ladies." Smith easily conceded the point. "I bow with respect to your declaration of rights to maintain the supremacy of the Ladies," he wrote.

After some negotiation, Colonel Smith agreed to allow De Windt to pay Caroline a series of visits at Peacefield. He arrived for the last of these on Friday, September 9, and proposed that the wedding take place the very next day. Abigail was shocked at the idea of losing her closest female companion on such short notice and flatly vetoed De Windt's plan. But she was persuaded to allow the ceremony to go forward the next evening, Sunday, September 11. The morning after their wedding, Caroline and Peter climbed aboard their carriage for the journey to Fishkill, leaving Abigail happy for her granddaughter but distressed at losing her. "She was the prop of my Age, my solace, my comfort," she lamented to her sister Elizabeth.

Now only two of Abigail's granddaughters were approaching the age of marriage: Susanna and Abigail Adams. Their deceased father, Charles, had left them even more financially vulnerable than Caroline Smith had been before becoming Mrs. De Windt. The former first lady was especially worried about her namesake, Charles's daughter Abbe, because she had recently adopted extreme religious views, and it was hard to imagine anyone other than a fellow zealot enjoying her company. "The rejection of every amusement, however innocent in it self and congenial to youth, is no part of my Religion," the senior Abigail told her sister Elizabeth, "for I read in the Scriptures there is a time to dance & to sing."

CHAPTER 33

"I Was Thunder Struck"

1814–1815

Adams need not have worried about Abbe. In 1814 the sixteen-year-old was living with one of her mother Sally's unmarried sisters in Utica, New York. On the way to and from school every day, she passed the home of Alexander B. Johnson, a twenty-seven-year-old wine merchant. The senior Abigail reported that Johnson "was smitten with the young Lady as she was going to school with her Books under her Arms and got an introduction into the Family." He began calling at Abbe's aunt's house. That Johnson had romantic intentions was clear enough, but Abbe assumed they were directed at her aunt. Finally the wine merchant had his mother "break the ice as it is said" to Abbe's mother, who encouraged him to make his feelings known. Abbe was astonished to discover that she was the object of Alexander's affection, but she was pleased, too, and they were married on October 23, just two weeks after he proposed.

Abbe's marriage was a godsend for her entire family. Six years earlier, her widowed mother had herself been engaged to a man named Minchin. But then she had discovered that Minchin had either lost his fortune or greatly exaggerated it, and she called it off. Johnson, on the other hand, was in sufficiently comfortable circumstances to provide not only for Abbe but also for Sally, who moved in with the newlyweds. In addition to running his retired father's wine import business, Alexander had an independent income of five thousand dollars a year. He was, moreover, an only child, so he stood to inherit all of his parents' property. And he was "well Bred self possesst very conversable—and a man of breeding & knowledge of the world." The bride's paternal grandmother was amused to report that Johnson had "published some pamphlets upon Finnnance and banking." Surely she and he would have plenty to talk about.

The senior Abigail was thrilled about her namesake's highly advantageous marriage. Owing to their fathers' failings, all three of her granddaughters of marriageable age were poor—and now, within the space of six weeks, two of the three had found wealthy husbands! On the other hand, Adams was appalled not to have learned of Abbe's courtship until after her wedding. She suspected that Abbe—or, more likely, her mother—had decided to take revenge on John and Abigail for not telling them about Caroline's marriage to Peter de Windt until after the ceremony. "I presume family pride was touchd, by Carolines not writing herself to them," Abigail surmised in a letter to her friend Harriet Welsh. Abigail acknowledged the omission but insisted that it was unavoidable: Caroline had demanded that her impending marriage be kept a secret. And even if, as she suspected, Sally was offended at not hearing in advance about her niece's nuptials, that did not justify her in withholding her own good news from the Adamses. After all, Abbe's sister Susanna was living at Peacefield, so leaving them in the dark meant subjecting her to the same shabby treatment. "It was really a want of that sisterly confidence and affection that ought to exist between sisters," Abigail Senior declared.

Sally Adams had not yet finished exacting her revenge. Shortly after her daughter married Alexander Johnson, the couple, accompanied by the bride's mother, made the customary bridal tour. The three showed up unannounced at Peacefield and proclaimed that they had already booked rooms at a nearby inn. This preemptive refusal of Abigail's and John's hospitality was a deliberate and severe snub. "I was thunder struck," Abigail told Harriet Welsh. When the visitors announced that it was time to retire to their rented quarters, John exclaimed, "You shall not go," but Sally replied, "it must be so." In an insular community like Quincy, everyone was bound to find out that Sally and the Johnsons had not stayed at Peacefield. As the three headed off to the inn to rest, Abigail knew they would "set the world and the whole Town astaring." She had no doubt about who had hatched the idea of humiliating her. "Abbe [was] quite passive," she reported to Welsh. "Mrs A[dams] was spokeswoman." Abigail absorbed the insult as well as she could. Over her long lifetime, she had made few enemies, and the vast majority of her resentments—against Benjamin Franklin, Thomas Jefferson, Mercy Otis Warren, and many others—were vicarious, in that these people were John's adversaries before they were hers. It seems significant that both of the people who expressed hostility toward Abigail for her own sake—Catharine Louisa Salmon Smith, her brother's wife, and Sally Adams, her son's widow—were financially straitened women whom she had tried to help. Given Adams's abiding compulsion to exercise her charitable instincts, one wonders whether she ever reflected on the frequent tendency of philanthropy to create bitterness instead of gratitude.

Elizabeth Peabody's only daughter, Abbe Shaw, also found a husband at about this time. Since her mother and grandmother had married preachers, she knew better than anyone that doing so was nearly equivalent to taking a vow of poverty. Yet she received a proposal and accepted it. Shortly after Abbe announced her engagement, her stepfather was hit by a series of financial "Embarrasments" that were attributable partly to the British blockade of the American coast and partly to his overly ambitious borrowing to rebuild Atkinson Academy after a fire. At about the same time, both of Abbe's parents contracted illnesses so severe that their lives were despaired of. Elizabeth worried that her husband might die so deep in debt that the family home would have to be sold to satisfy his creditors. At the height of her own disorder, she later reported to her sister, her "lungs were so oppressed, that I could not speak a word, & I could convey my thoughts only by warming a slate, & taking it into bed, & writing with a pencil, for I could not sit up to hold a pen." On the slate, she scratched out her "thoughts & wishes upon the subject." Reverend Peabody should pay off his creditors using money borrowed from William Shaw (Elizabeth's son by her first marriage), mortgaging the family home to him as collateral. That way, if Peabody died insolvent, the first claimant to his house would be his stepson. "In his hands," she believed, "the House would be an asylum for us all."

That still left Abbe Shaw to be provided for, and another development in 1814 caused Elizabeth additional worries on her account. The Adamses had decided to build a new barn on the Medford, Massachusetts, farm that they co-owned with the Peabodys. Expenses like these were customarily shared among the owners. William Shaw, who anticipated inheriting half of his family's share of the farm, agreed to help finance the construction of the new building, but Elizabeth knew what would happen if her son contributed to the cost of the barn and her daughter did not. When Elizabeth died and the two siblings came into

Elizabeth Smith Shaw Peabody (1750–1815), Abigail Adams's younger sister. Gilbert Stuart, *Mrs. Stephen Peabody*, 1809. Oil on wood panel, 26¾ x 21¼." *Collection of the Arizona State University Art Museum; Gift of Oliver B. James, 1953.132.000.*

their inheritance, William would have the right to demand that Abbe match the payments he had made toward the upkeep of the farm. She would probably be unable to do so, leaving her no choice but to sell her portion of the inheritance, thus exchanging real estate for personal property in the form of cash.

Elizabeth was desperate to avoid that outcome. When Abbe married, all of her personal property would pass into the hands of her husband. "Womens personal property we know flys with the wind," Peabody reminded her sister. "But real estate, is heavier, & not so easy blown away." Whatever real estate Abbe brought to her marriage would remain hers (although her husband would control it and receive the profits from it). In order to maintain her daughter's full stake in the Medford farm, Elizabeth decided to try to finance her family's half of the construction project out of her own limited funds. For some unknown reason, Abigail advised against the scheme, and Elizabeth abandoned it, but her attempt was yet more evidence, along with her demand for a separate estate nearly twenty years earlier, that she shared her sister's conviction that women needed to search aggressively for the financial security that the male-dominated society tried to deny them. Still another of Elizabeth Peabody's strategies for protecting herself and her children was to conceal assets from her husband. "We all have duties, & calls, when it might not be proper for the right hand, to know that the left doth," she told Abigail in March 1814, "& therefore, I like to have some property subject to no enquiry." ("Burn this," Elizabeth wrote in the margin of her letter.)

All of these domestic travails took place against the backdrop of renewed warfare against the British. For citizens of the United States, the worst day of the so-called War of 1812 was August 25, 1814, when the British burned the capitol building, the president's house, and other public buildings in Washington, D.C. On the one hand, Abigail told her eldest son, she could not find the "language to describe my feelings at the Torpor which blinded the government to a sense of their danger." By this time President Madison had appointed John Quincy as one of the American representatives at peace talks with the United Kingdom—just as Congress had chosen his father to negotiate with the British three decades earlier. Mindful that the men sitting across the negotiating table from her son in the town of Ghent (in present-day Belgium) would try to use their army's capture of Washington to extract additional concessions from their American counterparts, the former first lady strained to minimize the loss. Washington "is but a city in name," she said—which in fact had been true during her brief sojourn there thirteen years earlier. She also wanted the British representatives at Ghent to know that the ease with which their countrymen had overrun the American capital had been something of a fluke. The redcoats would encounter much stiffer resistance in Philadelphia, New York, or Boston, she affirmed. For one thing, the regions around these cities were more thickly settled, so many more men were available for militia duty. Washington also differed from the nation's three largest cities in being "inhabited by slaves who were as much feared by the inhabitants as the enemy who attacked them."

The war against the British led Adams to offer yet another defense of women such as herself who took an interest in public affairs. After describing the Massachusetts political scene for her husband's old friend Van der Kemp, she observed, "I would ask an excuse for thus treading upon ground which some suppose exclusively belongs to your sex. But are we not bone of your bone & flesh of your flesh and what must that heart be which at such a period as the present with a youthfull progeny rising up to share in the future destiny of their Country can be an indifferent spectator as to its fate?" Van der Kemp enthusiastically endorsed Adams's efforts "to guide and instruct the youth, and those of riper years." Reviving a justification for female political engagement that had flourished during the Revolutionary War, Van der Kemp wrote, "When mothers, sisters, daughters cease to be Patriots, adieu then with our liberty."

In New England, one important way in which the War of 1812 differed from the Revolutionary War was that the proportion of the population who opposed the conflict dramatically increased. Hardly any Congregational clerics remained loyal to the British in 1776 (Abigail's cousin Isaac Smith, Jr., was a rare exception), but many of them criticized the War of 1812. To Abigail's disgust, the dissenters even included her own minister in Quincy, and she protested his opposition to the war by skipping church. "I have so often heard from the desk [pulpit], this war calld a wicked and unnecessary war and our rulers abused for declaring it," she told John Quincy, "that I have determined not to give countanance to such sentiments."

Another New England minister who opposed the War of 1812 was

Abigail Adams ca. 19th century. Engraving by Oliver Pelton after a pastel by Benjamin Blythe, Waterson Autographs, vol. 4, *Massachusetts Historical Society.*

Stephen Peabody, husband of Abigail's sister Elizabeth. Mrs. Peabody was of course loyal to her husband's viewpoint, and neither she nor her sister could resist the temptation to try to convert the other. When Elizabeth offered a mild criticism of President Madison, Abigail replied, "I could not agree with you in your politics. You seem to have imbibed an undue prejudice against the chief majistrate from the papers stiled Federal." Peabody had the additional challenge of managing a disagreement about the war within her own blended family, for her husband's children generally opposed President Madison, while her own son and her future son-in-law (Abbe's fiancé, Joseph Barlow Felt) supported him. "Our own House, is nearly equally divided," she told Abigail.

Like the American Revolution (albeit to a lesser extent), the War of 1812 strained the government's finances, making public securities a fertile field for speculation. In the fall of 1814, Abigail's friend Harriet Welsh wrote her, apparently at her brother's behest, proposing that the three of them make a joint purchase of depreciated federal bonds. The Welshes had good reason to think Adams would jump at this opportunity, since they apparently knew she had earned handsome profits as a securities speculator during the previous war. Their reason for wishing to form a partnership with her was presumably to benefit from her expertise—and they may have also been hoping for access to John Quincy's analysis of the prospects for a successful treaty, which would drive up the price of government paper. Adams acknowledged to Harriet that she "might have been tempted to have acceeded" to the proposal. But there was a problem. "I see every thing in so shaking and hazardous a situation that no one can see what public credit is falling to," she wrote. Why did Adams hold back? Although as she noted, the government's credit rating was shaky in 1814, it was much stronger than it had been back during the Revolutionary War. Moreover, Adams was much wealthier than she had been thirty-seven years earlier, when she purchased her first war bond, so she could have absorbed even substantial losses without jeopardizing her family's quality of life. Perhaps she was simply waiting to see how low public credit would go. The best time to buy securities, she well knew, was not while their price was falling but just before it began to rise.

While it is possible that Adams was simply biding her time, it appears that she was actually becoming a more conservative investor. Certainly she had good reason to be wary, having seen Colonel Smith wipe out his wife's and children's financial security through unwise speculation, which had also contributed to her son Charles's self-destruction and ruined the families of two of Mary Cranch's children. Even John Quincy had suffered as a result of the speculative activities both of his brother Charles and of Harriet's father. Although the advice that Abigail gave Harriet was expressed in insider slang that exhibited her familiarity with the business of speculation, her recommendation was caution. "Tell your Brother not to run any great risks," she advised. "If he specks keep nothing long upon hand. We stand upon such sandy ground that it is easy to slip."

During the twelve months that followed Nabby's death, Abigail enjoyed an unexpected respite: none of her close friends or relatives passed away. But the mortality resumed in the fall of 1814 with the death of Mercy Otis Warren on October 19. (Her son Henry later reported to Abigail that one of the last things she was able to say was, "Tell my dear Mrs. Adams to write me or see me very soon, else we only meet in Heaven.") Adams knew that she, too, was fading. "I who am in my seventyth year find my memory, like a sieve," she told her son John Quincy. She compared her most recent memories to the copy that could be made of a page of text by pressing a fresh sheet of paper onto it while the ink was still wet. "Like a press coppy," her recollection of events that had just occurred was "faint, difficult to retrace, and often escapes me."

On March 19, 1814, Catherine Johnson Smith, the wife of Nabby's son William Steuben Smith, gave birth in St. Petersburg to a little girl, making Abigail a great-grandmother for the first time. The Smiths returned to the United States the following year, but Louisa and John Quincy Adams were not with them. After months of negotiations, Adams and his fellow American commissioners signed a peace treaty with their British counterparts on Christmas Eve 1814 that left relations between the two countries exactly where they had stood before the war. By that time the European winter was far advanced, but Adams instructed Louisa Catherine to pack up the family's belongings, sell the furniture, and meet him in Paris. Since the sea route from St. Petersburg was choked with ice, Louisa and seven-year-old Charles made the trek by land. It took them forty days. They reached Paris in the midst of the general rejoicing at Napoleon Bonaparte's return from exile on the island of Elba. The reunited couple and their son spent the next two months enjoying the capital, marveling at Napoleon's resumption of the reins of power, and waiting for the commission that John Quincy had long since anticipated. Like father, like son: his next task after negotiating peace with the British was to represent the Court of St. James's.

The cessation of hostilities and John's new assignment at last permitted him to bring his two oldest sons over to Europe, finally fulfilling a promise he had made to Louisa more than two years earlier. When Abigail received her son's instructions, she knew there was no longer any rational basis for keeping George and John in Massachusetts, but it still saddened her to give them up. Although her niece Louisa Smith and granddaughter Susanna (Charles's daughter) still lived at Peacefield, Abigail predicted that with the loss of John Quincy's rambunctious youngsters, she and her husband would be like "a tree in the midst of a plain striped of our branches." She repeatedly predicted that she would never see them again. They left Boston on April 18, 1815—thirty-seven years and two months after John and John Quincy had embarked on their first voyage to Europe. "The parting with them is another trial added to the many of the kind, which I have had to encounter through life," Abigail told her son.

In her determination to sustain her relationship with the two boys, she sent them some of the most whimsical letters to emerge from her pen since the senior John Adams courted her a half century earlier. She began a July 1815 note to George and John by quoting the opening of the nursery rhyme "This is the House That Jack Built," attributing the flourish to her giddiness at learning that they had arrived safely in London. A month later she told John that Americans had recently celebrated his twelfth birthday "with the ringing of Bells public orations, military parade and social festivals"—which was true, in a sense, because the boy had been born on the Fourth of July. Upon learning that John had become enthralled with navy ships, she used an extended naval analogy to inform him that his aunt Susanna Adams was being courted by a lieutenant in the American navy. She "had enterd on Board the United States Ship Independence, as mate to a Lieut." Cupid, "in revenge for his having escaped powder and Ball from the cannons mouth, undertook to try the force of an arrow, and shot him to the Heart."

John Quincy's sojourn in England differed from his father's in some important ways (for instance, he had his entire family with him), but there were numerous similarities as well. Like his father, he was denied the privilege of naming his secretary of legation. William Steuben Smith, who sailed into New York Harbor with his wife and infant daughter on May 2, asserted that Adams had offered him the job but that he had turned it down. The truth was that Smith's service as John Quincy's secretary in St. Petersburg had been a disaster, for his successful handling of the simple clerical tasks assigned to him had been overshadowed by his personal failings. In particular, Louisa Catherine observed in a November 1814 letter to her husband, a "large gaming debt" had led William "to behave very shabbily." He had borrowed more than a thousand dollars from John Quincy, who had little hope of ever seeing his money again.

Smith's brother John now wrote their uncle seeking the position. John Quincy adamantly refused to give the job to his nephew. "I have too sorely felt the evil of nepotism in that political relation, ever to incur it again with my own consent," he told his mother at the end of June. Unfortunately for John Quincy, Abigail herself had already begun advancing the young man's candidacy. She wrote letters on his behalf to Attorney General Richard Rush and first lady Dolley Madison, and these recommendations were undoubtedly part of the reason that John Quincy learned, to his astonishment and great annoyance, that John Adams Smith was coming over to be his secretary. By this time Abigail knew of her son's vehement opposition to the appointment, and she strained to justify her intervention in the decision. She claimed that the recommendations she had written for her grandson "were mere letters of introduction," and she added, with considerably more sincerity, that "Johns tender affection and assiduous attention to his mother, in her last sickness, endeard him to me."

John Quincy seems to have quickly forgiven his mother's interference with his public duties (it certainly helped that Nabby's younger son was much more responsible than his brother) and it must have pleased him to see that his appointment to London had begun to strengthen his mother's relationship with his wife. As Louisa reprised the role Abigail had played three decades earlier, both of them enjoyed comparing notes. Abigail's introduction to Queen Charlotte had been a highlight of her sojourn in the former mother country, and she knew it would be for her daughter-in-law as well. "I should like an account of your reception and presentation to Court, and the appearance of the Queen at this Age," she wrote Louisa Catherine in May. "She was not esteemed a Beauty thirty years ago, when I was presented to her." Abigail herself shuddered at the thought of being exhibited to public view at the advanced age of seventy-one, and she had heard that Charlotte was three years her elder. (Actually the wives of New England's last king and its most illustrious

Abigail Adams. Engraving by John Sartain (after painting by Christian Schussele) in Rufus Wilmot Griswold, *The Republican Court* (New York, 1854), facing p. 169. *Courtesy Massachusetts Historical Society.*

Patriot were born in the same year, and they would die in the same year, too.) On the other hand, she had to acknowledge that "the Germans" (Charlotte had begun life in the duchy of Mecklenburg-Strelitz) "bear their Age better than the Americans, or the English." Louisa undoubtedly delighted her mother-in-law with the report that "Her Majesty is grown fat," but she had to admit that "the Queen received me . . . in the most gracious manner." Charlotte had disappointed Louisa, as she had Abigail three decades earlier, by exhibiting no bitterness toward her husband's erstwhile enemies.

On the other hand, members of her court and assorted London aristocrats fulfilled Louisa's unsavory expectations. Although she had been born in London, she described that city's courtiers and aristocratic leeches with the same contempt Abigail had expressed thirty years earlier. The minister's wife also echoed her mother-in-law's complaints about her husband's low salary, which did not permit her to put on the sort of entertainments that might have impressed those contemptible aristocrats. Abigail of course agreed with Louisa that John Quincy was underpaid, and she attributed Congress's parsimony to a misunderstanding of the spirit of '76. Egalitarianism, she insisted in a letter to Attorney General Rush, was a product of the French, not the American, revolution, and her fellow citizens ought never to have imported it. "That pretty french doctrine of liberty and equality poisoned the minds of this people, as much as it dazild the french populace," she believed. It was "a doctrine contrary to nature to scripture and all civilized nations." Even a casual survey of her own farm revealed that to "talk of equality is absurd," she wrote. "Not a goose in the yard who erects his head and struts before the flock, but feels his preeminence. Not a bee in the hive but acknowledges its sovereign."

Adams's persistent attachment to social hierarchy was not the only evidence that she remained, in many ways, an archconservative in her final years. The denunciations of bawdy and cynical literature that she penned in 1810s were virtually indistinguishable from the critique of Moliére she had written back in 1773. Of Jonathan Swift, the author of *Gulliver's Travels,* she wrote, "I like those writers who dignify & exalt humane Nature, not those who represent Beings created a little lower than the Angles, as upon a level with the Brutes." His writings were, moreover, "unfit for a Ladies library," and she was not sure she should admit having read him. She was even more appalled by one of her contemporaries, Lord Byron. "He has a wild excentrick imagination" and possesses "some touching & pathetic strokes of Nature & genius," she acknowledged in a letter to Louisa Adams, "but he is sarcistic gloomy malicious envious & unprincipled a man neither capable of love or friendship. His genius is abortive and his tallents misapplied."

Adams never detected any inconsistency between her conservatism in some areas—including her persistent contempt for egalitarianism and her distaste for racy literature—and her desire for a radical transformation in relations between the sexes. And she continued to advise women to exploit every loophole in the doctrine of coverture. Louisa Catherine Adams's sister Adelaide had married Walter Hellen, the widower of another Johnson sister, Nancy. Shortly after Walter's death in the fall of 1815, Adelaide wrote Abigail seeking advice on a sensitive subject. The law required husbands to leave their widows the profits from one-third of their real estate, but Walter Hellen's will had only bequeathed his wife the sum of four hundred dollars a year. She believed she was legally entitled to much more, but she did not want to disgrace her family, herself, and her husband's memory by going to court to demand her due. *"You are the first person I have applied to for advice,"* she wrote Abigail. Adams did not hesitate in recommending that Adelaide challenge her husband's will, and she also had advice on a topic that her correspondent had not raised. If Adelaide should ever remarry, she must demand a marriage settlement guaranteeing that her children would inherit her property. Hellen promised to follow Adams's advice.

Abigail made a similar suggestion to her sister Elizabeth, who was in serious danger of being dragged into the financial abyss unwittingly dug by her second husband. Unable to ignore Reverend Peabody's desperation, she had lent him five hundred dollars from the funds in her separate estate. It was an interest-free loan (between spouses nothing else would do), and, worse, he had given her no collateral. Early in 1815, Betsy began receiving her share of the proceeds from the sale of a woodlot that her mother had jointly inherited with her siblings. Stephen had an urgent need for that money, but his wife felt that by giving it to him she would be committing an injustice against her children, who stood to inherit it from her. "My good friend does not know that I have this," she reasoned in a letter to Abigail, "& therefore will not think it unpleasant or unkind that he does not have it." Abigail agreed and advised her sister to place the money in government securities. "I wou'd direct Mr. S"—Elizabeth's son, William Shaw—"to [in]vest in stocks in your name as trustee for you," she wrote. "I think the stocks will rise in value."

In another area, religion, a schism within the Congregational church provoked Abigail to reaffirm her beliefs, even though it meant disagreeing with her son. For several years a group of New England ministers had been mounting an increasingly vocal challenge to some of the fundamental tenets of Calvinism. Among these were the idea that all humans were sinners doomed to spend eternity in Hell (with only an elect few predestined for salvation) and "trinitarianism"—the notion that God consisted of three separate persons: the Father, Son, and Holy Spirit. In 1815, William Ellery Channing, pastor of Federal Street Church in Boston, wrote a public letter denouncing the Calvinists, and a pamphlet war ensued. Abigail did not hesitate to stake out her position in the controversy. "I profess myself a unitarian in Mr Channings sense," she told her son John Quincy. "The soil of N England will not cultivate nor cherish clerical biggotry or intolerance altho, there is a struggle to introduce it." When John Quincy expressed skepticism of the

Unitarian position, which he associated with the liberal political views that he and his mother both abhorred, Abigail stood her ground. "There is not any reasoning which can convince me, contrary to my senses, that three, is one, and one three," she told him in a May 4, 1816, letter. The next day, informing Harriet Welsh that her husband agreed with her, she claimed that he had pronounced his son an "Excellent politician, but no Theologian."

Adams's religious dispute with her son was something of an anomaly, for it is clear that, opinionated though she was, she was determined to not let her religious creed endanger the personal relationships that were the real center of her existence. Indeed, she often adapted the language of her letters to the spiritual beliefs of her correspondent, a strategy that was especially evident in the ways she edited her prose. In an April 1815 letter to her niece Abigail Adams Shaw, Adams initially referred to the creator as "Our Maker," then crossed these words out, replacing them with "Heaven." A year later, however, while writing the presumably more religious Harriet Welsh, she replaced "heaven" with "god." Abigail was a woman of firm religious and political beliefs, yet for her, relationships trumped ideology.

CHAPTER 34

"Dr Tufts Has Always Been My Trustee"

1815–1818

Elizabeth Peabody had always had "a delicate constitution and feeble frame," yet she had hung on through the years, outliving a daughter as well as her first husband. During the winter of 1814–1815 she had complained of weakness in her lungs, but Abigail occasionally suffered from the same affliction, and both sisters had learned to live with it. On the evening of Saturday, April 7, she read two sermons, then went to sleep with no other complaint than "a slight soar throat." She woke up at midnight "in distress." A servant rushed out to get the doctor while Reverend Peabody and Abbe sat with Elizabeth, who fell back to sleep. When the physician arrived, he shocked the preacher and his stepdaughter by informing them that Elizabeth had died at least twenty minutes earlier. As she had so often in the past, Abigail used the language of the forest to express her feelings, calling herself, in a letter to Harriet Welsh, "the only surviving branch of the Ancient stock." She also found words to express her sentiments in Smith's *Theory of Moral Sentiments*, telling Harriet "I know your feeling and sympathizing heart can weep with those who weep as well as enter into their joys."

Three weeks after her mother's death, Abigail Adams Shaw informed the aunt for whom she was named that she and her brother William planned to make a magnanimous gesture. They wanted to divide Elizabeth Peabody's clothing and furniture equally with Elizabeth Smith Foster, who had been reared in their household in Haverhill while Abigail Adams was raising her sister, Louisa. (Both were daughters of the Smith sisters' ne'er-do-well brother, William.) The children of married women did not normally inherit their furniture, since wive's beds and tables, along with all of their other personal property, passed into the hands of their husbands. But Elizabeth Peabody's children knew that she had placed her moveables, along with her half of the farm in Medford, in a separate estate before remarrying. Replying to her namesake, Adams warned that she and her brother should not count on obtaining the dead woman's furniture, for Reverend Peabody's creditors would surely attempt to claim it for themselves. It was Abigail's sad duty to inform her niece and nephew that the only way to secure title to this portion of their mother's legacy was to sue their stepfather for it. "You certainly have the best right to have it secured to you & your Brother," she wrote. The idea of suing a family member was even more odious then than it is now, but Adams insisted that William and Abbe had no choice. "Altho it will feel to you a subject you know not how to touch," she wrote, "would it not be the better for you to be the owner, who will not remove it, at present than to see it in the possession of any other person to the still greater embarrassment of Mr Peabody[?]"

On Wednesday, December 6, Abigail and John rode down to Weymouth for a visit with Cotton Tufts, who was now in his eighty-fourth year. He was able to hold a conversation with them, but as they were leaving, Abigail whispered to John, "He is going." Her prophecy was fulfilled sooner than she anticipated, for he died just after midnight the next night. Despite Tufts's advanced age, his death, which was "not preceded by any sickness or alarming symptoms," hit Abigail like "an electric stroke." It also reminded her of her own mortality, and she decided that now—"while my reason is sound, and my mind tranquil"—was the time to put her own affairs in order. Her greatest anxiety was for Louisa Smith, to whom she decided to leave a substantial legacy. In recent years, John Quincy had earned sufficient income from his diplomatic posts and his investments to repay the entire $1,700 loan he had received from his mother more than a decade earlier. But Abigail had only permitted Thomas, who served as his brother's agent, to pay her $500, and she now revealed one reason for her reluctance to clear the loan. In a Christmas Eve letter to John Quincy, she expressed her desire to give the outstanding balance of $1,200 to Louisa. No one in the world seemed likelier than Abigail's eldest son to have both the means and the desire to disburse these funds as she directed. So placing John Quincy in Louisa's debt was the safest thing to do for her. Abigail's observations on the arrangements she had made for Louisa naturally led her into a discussion of the assets that, as she asserted, "I have your

Fathers consent to dispose of as I please." But she downplayed her role in acquiring and managing this money. "There was some property left me by my fathers will," she noted. "After I went abroad," she told John Quincy, these funds were "converted into publick stock" by her uncle Tufts. Adams did not inform her son that she had considerably augmented her inheritance by her own action—for instance by investing in depreciated government securities, which Dr. Tufts had purchased for her not on his own initiative but at her direction. "Dr Tufts has always been my trustee," she wrote.

During the winter of 1815–1816, Abigail suffered through her usual cold-weather ailments, especially rheumatism. But the sickness that struck her just after Christmas was something new. She suspected it might be her last, and that focused her attention even more intently on the years that would follow her death. On January 18, 1816, she drew up a will. She began by observing that she had already given her son Thomas her half of the Medford farm that she and Elizabeth had jointly inherited from their father. She also noted that her other surviving son, John Quincy, had received "all my right and title in the Farm given me by my uncle Norton Quincy." But her primary purpose was to distribute the personal property she had been accumulating since the early 1780s. One imperative was that none of her impoverished female relatives or servants incur any expense in mourning her death. So she gave each of these women enough money to purchase the traditional mourning ring, and several were allocated additional funds with which to obtain material for mourning dresses. Most of the women mentioned in the will also received one of Adams's gowns. In addition to these bequests, Abigail distributed more than $4,000 worth of bank stock, John Quincy's $1,200 debt instrument, and a total of seven shares of stock in the companies managing the Weymouth and Haverhill toll bridges. Although Adams had markedly enhanced her personal wealth by investing in depreciated public securities, all of these had subsequently been redeemed or sold.

Unlike the will her husband would draw up three years later, Adams's "Disposition of Her Property" took into consideration the tremendous variation in her heirs' material circumstances. She began with gifts to her granddaughters. In addition to clothing and jewelry, each received a cash payment of anywhere from $400 to $750, depending on how wealthy she was. Caroline de Windt, Abigail's oldest and apparently favorite granddaughter, and Charles Adams's daughter Susanna, who remained single in 1816, each received $750. Susanna also got a gold watch, several gowns, "the upper part of my pearl Earings," and a share in the Haverhill toll-bridge company. The smallest bequests, $400 each, went to Thomas's daughters, both of whom were still children.

The cluster of granddaughters that headed off Abigail's roster of heirs contained one anomaly: Adams included Louisa Smith in this list, even though she was actually a niece. Louisa had lived with John and Abigail for most of the previous four decades, ever since her father, Abigail's brother, William, abandoned her family back in the mid-1770s. She had never married, and she had become her aunt's steadiest companion—and, in her frequent illnesses, her most faithful nurse. In the process she had become an honorary granddaughter, so it made sense in Abigail's eyes to list her with the other five. Louisa received no cash from her aunt, but her inheritance was actually the largest of all. In addition to transferring John Quincy's $1,200 promissory note to Louisa, Abigail gave her a share in the company managing the Haverhill toll bridge. Adams's one great concern was that Louisa's outsized bequest would cause friction within the family. "I hope no unkind or hard thought will be entertaind that I have given to Louisa more than the rest," she wrote, "her case is peculiar, having no relative upon her Mothers side but a sister—I commend her to the kindness of my children."

Additional bequests went to Adams's other nieces, her sister-in-law Catharine Smith, a pair of distant cousins who were sisters, and two female servants. One aspect of the will that must have jumped out at everyone who read it—though it has not been noticed by her biographers—is the provision she made for her grandsons, nephews, and male servants. They received nothing at all. Adams listed only two male heirs: her sons John Quincy and Thomas, each of whom received, in addition to the real estate that Adams had already given them, a tankard and a share in the Weymouth toll bridge. Nabby's son William Steuben Smith was one of the poorest of the Adams grandchildren. In the winter of 1816, he was living with his wife and children in a run-down boardinghouse. But no member of his family was listed as an heir. Nor was William's brother John or any of John Quincy's three boys or Thomas's three sons. Unlike their female counterparts, none of Abigail's nephews or male servants received anything, either.

There is no indication that Adams had any animus against her male relatives. So why did she exclude all but two of them from her will? She knew that custom as well as law put women in a much more precarious position than men, and she had lived long enough to see this vulnerability increase in an important way. In 1816, most American women, especially slaves and servants, still worked with their hands. But there was a growing sense among the nation's (mostly, but not entirely, male) opinion leaders that women should not be producers. Women who sold their skills on the open market were well on the way to losing any claim to middle-class respectability. So Adams may have believed that the need to provide for her female relatives was greater than ever.

There is, however, a simpler explanation for the virtual exclusion of men from Adams's will. Throughout her adult life, she had denounced men's subjugation of women, and one of her most pressing grievances had always been the prohibition against married women owning personal property. Far from simply denouncing wives' legal disability, she had lived most of her adult life as a tangible protest against it, insisting that a portion of the property that the law accorded to her husband was actually hers. This decades-long remonstrance culminated in Adams's will. Having spent the previous three decades asserting control over land and ownership of personal property despite being married, Adams now bequeathed her estate to her granddaughters, nieces, daughters-in-law, and female servants in order to enable them, as far as lay in her power, to make the same claim.

Several resemblances between the senior and junior John Adams's years representing the United States in Great Britain were noted above. There was one other similarity between the two men's ministerial terms: they were both short. John Adams had spent three years in London, and his son did not even last that long—for a very good reason. When Madison's secretary of state, his fellow Virginian James Monroe, succeeded to the presidency in March 1817, he asked Adams to take over his old job. John Quincy and the family sailed into New York Harbor on August 6, 1817, and almost immediately headed to Quincy for a visit. Abigail described the arrival of their rented carriage twelve days later. The travelers who were most openly excited about returning to Abigail's arms were the two she had most recently embraced: George and John. "I ran to the door," she later wrote. "The first who sprang out was John, who with his former ardour was round my neck in a moment. George followed half crazy calling out o Grandmother—o Grandmother."

Abigail and her eldest son took the occasion of this visit to try to quash any doubts Louisa Smith might have about someday receiving the

$1,200 her aunt had promised her. John Quincy took back the promissory note he had given Abigail years earlier, replacing it with a new bond in which he agreed to pay $1,200 to "John Adams . . . on account of Mrs. Abigail Adams." By adding his father's name to the bond, he turned an informal promise that could have no legal standing—since Abigail was not actually permitted to own personal property—into a legal instrument that, if worse came to worst, Cousin Louisa could produce in a lawsuit against him. In mid-September, John Quincy finally left Peacefield to take up his post in Washington. Louisa Catherine accompanied him, but the couple once again left their boys—all three of them, this time—in Massachusetts. George was ready to enter Harvard, and John and Charles would board in Boston and attend school there. Three months after her son became secretary of state, Abigail was able to report that she had enjoyed a "Pleasant Thanksgiving day" with nine of her fourteen grandchildren.

John Quincy was so busy in his new post that he and Louisa Catherine almost did not get away from Washington during the summer of 1818. As it was, they did not make it to Quincy until early September, and they were only able to remain there a month. Shortly after returning to the capital, the couple received word that Abigail had contracted typhus fever. John Quincy did not immediately sit down to write his mother—or anyone else in Quincy, for that matter. "In the agitation of my own heart," he later explained to his father, "I knew not how to order my speech."

With the possible exceptions of Harriet Welsh and the servant Rebecca Dexter, all of the numerous women who watched over the ailing Adams—her son Charles's daughter Susanna, her niece Lucy Cranch Greenleaf, her daughter-in-law Ann Adams, and faithful to the last, her brother William's daughter Louisa Smith—had previously benefited from her ministrations. Abigail was especially grateful for the care she received from Lucy Greenleaf, the daughter of her deceased sister Mary Cranch, who had been her closest female companion. Lucy, Adams told her husband, has been "a Mother to me." Over the years, Abigail had endured her share of emetics, purges, blisters, and bloodlettings. Now her doctor, convinced that the least movement would aggravate his patient's fever, forbade her "to speak or be spoken to" (as her husband reported to Thomas Jefferson on October 20). For a woman who had spent her entire life struggling against silence, there could be no harsher sentence. Abigail held her tongue for a few days, but she was soon declaring to her husband that "she was going and if it was the will of heaven she was willing." According to Harriet Welsh, Abigail told John "she had no wish to live but for his sake."

When Harriet tried to offer Abigail some encouragement, she found that her battle against the disease had worn her out. "Dear Soul," she declared, "I am very weak." But she retained traces of her sense of humor. When Harriet's father, Dr. Thomas Welsh, the man whose reckless speculations had proved so costly to John Quincy Adams, ordered the use of blisters (irritating ointments that raised blisters in order to reduce inflammation), "she called them a present from Dr. Welsh," Harriet later reported. Nor was Harriet surprised that despite her condition, Adams "attended to some business at intervals."

John was distraught—not so much that she was dying but that she was in such pain. Perhaps, he wondered aloud, he should be praying that a "stroke of Lightning" or "an appoplectic fit may put an end to her sufferings." Convinced that even if she survived, she would be a miserable invalid, John told some of her attendants, "I know not whether I ought to ask that her life may be spared, for to her it must be after such an illness but labour & sorrow." Harriet reported that after another session with his wife, Adams "came down and said in his energetic manner, 'I wish I could lay down beside her and die too . . . I cannot bear to see her in this state.[']"

Abigail died at about 1 P.M. on October 28, three days after her fifty-fourth wedding anniversary (as John observed to Harriet Welsh) and a few weeks shy of her seventy-fourth birthday. She only had one regret, Harriet informed the Adamses' granddaughter Caroline de Windt in New York: "she said. . . . she should like to have the family together once more."

John's grief for his wife was surprisingly muted. He placed this separation in the context of the many others the couple had endured over the previous four decades. Infirm himself, he expected to be reunited with Abigail sooner than any of his European missions had permitted. Less than two weeks after she died, the former president told John Quincy, "The Pangs and the Anguish have not been so great as when you and I embarked for France in 1778."

In her will, Abigail had assigned Thomas the responsibility of supervising the distribution of her property. She had not used the term *executor,* since she was aware that her list of bequests was not actually an official document. Some of Thomas's kinsmen may have worried that he would abuse the trust his mother had placed in him, for by this time he was struggling with the alcoholism that had killed his brother Charles, and there were even rumors that he had taken to gambling as well. In 1819, when John Adams wrote his own will, he bequeathed no property directly to his youngest son, instead subjecting him to the humiliation of having his inheritance placed in a trust similar to the one Parson Smith had established for the family of Abigail's alcoholic brother, William. The demons that had laid siege to Uncle Smith and then to Charles were already circling around Thomas by the fall of 1818, yet he overcame them long enough to carry out each of his mother's final instructions.

Thomas's brother and father helped him comply with his mother's wishes. On November 9, less than two weeks after Abigail's death, John transferred John Quincy's $1,200 promissory note over to Louisa Smith, just as Abigail had directed. A year later, John Quincy replaced this bond with a new instrument made out to Louisa herself. No one could ever challenge his cousin's right to recover these funds, for she had never married. When Abigail's husband obeyed the provisions of her will, he transformed it into a legally valid document. In the eyes of the law, she had acted as his agent and distributed property that belonged to him.

In January 1819, when Louisa Catherine Adams learned from her brother-in-law Thomas that Abigail had left her an inheritance of $150, she told him she wanted to set aside half of the bequest to be divided equally among her three sons, who seemed to her "to have a better title to it than I could boast." By passing this money on to her boys, Louisa may have indicated disapproval of her mother-in-law's decision to exclude all of her male descendants other than her sons from her will. Yet it seems unlikely that Abigail would have considered the younger woman's gift a defeat. After all, by deciding on her own authority to present the money to her children, Louisa acknowledged what the law of the land denied and Abigail had always affirmed: that the money was hers to give.

ABBREVIATIONS USED IN NOTES

Women's married names are shown in parentheses, along with the date of their marriage.

AA–Abigail Smith (Adams, 1764)
AAS–Abigail Adams (Smith, 1786)
AEA–Adams Electronic Archive (www.masshist.org/digitaladams/aea)
AFC–Lyman H. Butterfield et al., eds., *Adams Family Correspondence* (9 vols. to date; Cambridge, Mass., 1963–)
AJL–Lester J. Cappon, *The Adams-Jefferson Letters: The Complete Correspondence Between Thomas Jefferson and Abigail and John Adams* (2 vols.; Chapel Hill, N.C. 1959)
AP–*Microfilms of the Adams Papers Owned by the Adams Manuscript Trust and Deposited in the Massachusetts Historical Society* (microfilm, 608 reels, Boston, 1954–1959). The number that follows the # symbol is the reel number.
BR–Benjamin Rush
CA–Charles Adams
CC–Conrad E. Wright et al., eds., *Colonial Collegians: Biographies of Those Who Attended American Colleges Before the War of Independence* (Boston, 2005), CD-ROM
CT–Dr. Cotton Tufts, Sr.
DAJA–Lyman H. Butterfield, ed., *Diary and Autobiography of John Adams* (5 vols.; Cambridge, Mass., 1961–1966)
ECN–Elizabeth Cranch (Norton, 1789)
ESSP–Elizabeth Smith (Shaw, 1774) (Peabody, 1795)
HW–Harriet Welsh
IS2–Isaac Smith, Jr.
JA–John Adams
JA2–John Adams (son of Louisa Catherine and John Quincy Adams)
JCC–Worthington Chauncey Ford, ed., *Journals of the Continental Congress, 1774–1789* (34 vols.; Washington, D.C., 1904–1937)
JQA–John Quincy Adams
JL–James Lovell

Journal and Correspondence of Miss Adams–[Caroline Amelia Smith de Windt], ed., *Journal and Correspondence of Miss Adams, Daughter of John Adams, Second President of the United States*...(2 vols., New York, 1841–1842)

JT–John Thaxter

LCA–Louisa Catherine (Adams, 1797)

LCG–Lucy Cranch (Greenleaf, 1795)

Letters of Mrs. Adams–Charles Francis Adams, ed., *Letters of Mrs. Adams, Wife of John Adams*, 2nd ed. (2 vols.: Boston, 1840)

MDF–Margaret A. Hogan and C. James Taylor, eds., *My Dearest Friend: Letters of Abigail and John Adams* (Cambridge, Mass., 2007)

MHS–Massachusetts Historical Society

MOW–Mercy Otis (Warren, 1754)

MSC–Mary Smith (Cranch, 1762)

NL–Stewart Mitchell, ed., *New Letters of Abigail Adams, 1788–1801* (Boston, 1947)

OFL–*Old Family Letters: Copied from the Originals for Alexander Biddle* (Philadelphia, 1892)

RC–Richard Cranch

RT–Royall Tyler

Shaw–Shaw Family Papers, Manuscripts Division, Library of Congress, Washington, D.C. Since these documents are not arranged chronologically, frame numbers have been supplied.

TBA–Thomas Boylston Adams

TJ–Thomas Jefferson

TJP–Julian P. Boyd et al., eds., *The Papers of Thomas Jefferson* (30 vols. to date; Princeton, N.J., 1950–)

WJA–Charles Francis Adams, ed., *The Works of John Adams, Second President of the United States* . . . (10 vols.; Boston, 1850–1856)

WMQ–*William and Mary Quarterly*

Writings of JQA–Worthington Chauncey Ford, ed., *Writings of John Quincy Adams* (7 vols.; New York, 1913–1917)

WSS–William Stephens Smith

NOTES

When a paragraph straddles two pages, it is considered for citation purposes to be on the first one. The citation for a multi-paragraph dialogue is keyed to its final paragraph.

Introduction

xvii¶1 William Blackstone, *Commentaries on the Laws of England*, Vol. 1 (Oxford, 1765), 430; AA to JA, June 17, 1782, *AFC*, 4:328; Linda K. Kerber, *Women of the Republic: Intellect and Ideology in Revolutionary America* (Chapel Hill, N.C., 1980), 143; Richard H. Chused, "Married Women's Property and Inheritance by Widows in Massachusetts: A Study of Wills Probated Between 1800 and 1850," *Berkeley Women's Law Journal* 2 (1986): 43n.

xvii¶2 Recipients of AA's gifts included her sister MSC, her daughter AAS, her daughter-in-law Sally, her son TBA, her nephew William Cranch, and many others. AA to MSC, July 12, 1789, in *NL*, 16; AA to Sarah Adams, Jan. 20, 1808, Kroch Library, Cornell University, Ithaca, N.Y. JA made two exceptions to his rule of evenhanded bequests, but they were apparently intended to balance each other out: he gave his eldest son the right to buy his home and several hundred acres of his land (presumably below the market price), and (in return, it seems) he bequeathed nothing to JQA's three sons. JQA could also have his father's library if he paid TBA half its value. "Abigail Adams's Disposition of Her Property," Jan. 18, 1816, John Adams, will, Sept. 27, 1819, AP#607.

xix¶1 "Abigail Adams's Disposition of Her Property," Jan. 18, 1816, AP#607.

xx¶1 AA to JA, April 25, 1782, AA to CT, [April 26–May 10, 1785], AA to MSC, July 12, 1789, *AFC*, 4:315, 6:108, 8:389; AA to TBA, Feb. 28, 1802, AP#401.

xxi¶2 JA to AA, Nov. 4, 1775, *AFC*, 1:320.

xxii¶2 AA to JA, Dec. 27, 1783, *AFC*, 5:286; AA to LCA, Jan. 12, 1810, AP#409; AA to Elbridge Gerry, Dec. 31, 1796, MHS *Proceedings*, 3rd ser., 57 (May 1924): 499.

xxiii¶1 MSC to AA, June 27, 1797, AP#384.

xxiii¶2 ESSP to AA, July 22–Aug. 21, 1787, AA to ESSP, March 4, 1786, *AFC*, 8:136, 7:81; AA to JA, Nov. 29, 1798, *MDF*, 451. A half century after AA saw Shakespeare's play, her son JQA expressed a similar attitude toward the interracial romance at the heart of *Othello*, calling it "disgusting." JQA, quoted in William Jerry MacLean, "Othello Scorned: The Racial Thought of John Quincy Adams," *Journal of the Early Republic* 4 (Summer 1984): 148–49.

xxiii¶3 JA Diary, [summer 1759], *DAJA*, 1:109.

Note on Names

xxv¶1 WSS to AA, June 4, 1787, *AFC*, 8:75.

Chapter 1: "A Tender Twig," 1744–1761

1¶1 JA Diary, Oct. 24, 1762, *DAJA*, 1:229–30; JA to AA, Christmas Day 1794, *MDF*, 380.

2¶1 The south parish of Weymouth was still contesting the north parish's right to sell the parsonage to Smith (and to retain all of the proceeds of the sale) in 1761. *AFC*, 1:9n.

2¶2 AA, paraphrased in JA Diary, Dec. 23, 1772, *DAJA*, 2:72.

3¶1 AA to AAS, quoted in *Letters of Mrs. Adams*, 1:xxvii; AA to Caroline Smith, Feb. 2, 1809, *Journal and Correspondence of Miss Adams*, 1:216; AA to JQA, Dec. 30, 1804, AP#403; AA to JQA, Dec. 26, 1790, *AFC*, 9:165.

4¶2 Gilbert Nash, *Historical Sketch of the Town of Weymouth, Massachusetts from 1622 to 1884* (Weymouth, 1885), 51–52n.

5¶3 JA Diary, Dec. 23, 1772, *DAJA*, 2:72.

6¶1 JA Diary, [summer 1759], *DAJA*, 1:108-9.

6¶2 JA Diary, [summer 1759], *DAJA*, 1:109; AA to MSC, Oct. [ante 18], 1787, *AFC*, 8:192.

7¶3 AA to AAS, quoted in Adams, ed., *Letters of Mrs. Adams*, 1:xxvii; Charles W. Akers, *Abigail Adams: An American Woman* (Boston, 1980), 22–23; Laurel Thatcher Ulrich, *A Midwife's Tale: The Life of Martha Ballard, Based on Her Diary,* 1785–1812 (New York, 1990), 61.

8¶1 AA to Mrs. H. Lincoln, Oct. 5, 1761, *Letters of Mrs. Adams*, 1:4–5; Esther 7:2.

9¶1 AA to Mrs. H. Lincoln, Oct. 5, 1761, *Letters of Mrs. Adams*, 1:4–5.

9¶2 AA to IS2, Feb. 7, 1762, Smith Carter Collection, MHS, quoted in Phyllis Lee Levin, *Abigail Adams: A Biography* (New York, 1987), 6.

9¶3 AA to IS2, March 16, 1763, *AFC*, 1:4; C. Alice Baker, *True Stories of New England Captives Carried to Canada during the Old French and Indian Wars*, vol. 1 (Cambridge, [Mass.], 1897), 47–68; Emma Lewis Coleman, *New England Captives Carried to Canada Between 1677 and 1760, During the French and Indian Wars* (Portland, Maine, 1925), 425–35; Daniel K. Richter, "War and Culture: The Iroquois Experience," *WMQ*, 3rd ser., 40 (October 1983): 528–59; Richter, *The Ordeal of the Longhouse: The Peoples of the Iroquois League in the Era of European Colonization* (Chapel Hill, N.C., 1992); John Demos, *The Unredeemed Captive: A Family Story from Early America* (New York, 1994); Ann M. Little, "The Life of Mother Esther de L'Enfant Jesus, or, How a Little English Girl from Wells Became a Big French Politician," *Maine History* 40 (2002): 278–308; William Henry Foster, *The Captors' Nar-*

rative: *Catholic Women and Their Puritan Men on the Early American Frontier* (Ithaca, N.Y., 2003), 57; Little, *Abraham in Arms*: *War and Gender in Colonial New England* (Philadelphia, 2007), 127–65.

9¶4 AA to IS2, March 16, 1763, *AFC*, 1:4. One scholar conjectures that perhaps Wheelwright actually closed the letter, which does not survive, using the abbreviation "Sr." (for *soeur,* sister) and Abigail assumed that it stood for *serviteur.* Ann M. Little, personal communication to the author, Jan. 30, 2009.

10¶1 AA to IS2, March 16, 1763, *AFC*, 1:3–4.

10¶2 AA, quoted in Akers, *Abigail Adams* (1980 edition), 9; JA Diary, Dec. 28, 1762, *DAJA*, 1:232.

11¶1 JA Diary, Dec. 28, 1762, *DAJA*, 1:232.

11¶3 AA to Mrs. H. Lincoln, Oct. 5, 1761, *Letters of Mrs. Adams*, 1:6.

12¶2 RC and JA to [MSC], Dec. 30, 1761, *AFC*, 1:1.

12¶3 RC and JA to [MSC], Dec. 30, 1761, *AFC*, 1:1.

Chapter 2: "Miss Adorable," 1761–1764

13¶1 JA Diary, [summer 1759], *DAJA*, 1:108; AA to JA, April 30, 1764, *AFC*, 1:42.

13¶2 AA to MSC, March 15, 1786, Thomas Brand Hollis, quoted in AA to Hollis, Sept. 6, 1790, *AFC*, 7:89, 9:100; JA Diary, Feb. 1, 1763, *DAJA*, 1:234.

13¶3 JA Diary, [Dec. 30], 1758, *DAJA*, 1:65.

14¶1 JA Diary, [Dec. 30], 1758, *DAJA*, 1:65–66.

14¶3 "Richard Cranch, Harvard, 1744," *CC;* JA Diary, Nov. 30, 1762, *DAJA*, 1:231–32. The expression about not turning back after putting one's hand to the plow comes from Luke 9:62.

15¶1 AA to ESSP, Feb. 12, 1796, Shaw#1, frame 269.

15¶2 JA to AA, "Saturday morning," August 1763, *AFC*, 1:8.

16¶1 JA to AA, [April 7–9, 1764], *AFC*, 1:18.

16¶2 JA to AA, Oct. 4, 1762, April 20, 1763, *AFC*, 1:2, 5.

16¶3 JA to AA, Feb. 14, April 20, 1763, *AFC*, 1:3, 5–6.

16¶4 JA to AA, Oct. 4, 1762, AA to JA, Aug. 11, 1763, *AFC*, 1:2, 6–7.

17¶1 AA to JA, April 12, 1764, *AFC*, 1:26.

17¶2 AA to JA, Aug. 11, 1763, *AFC*, 1:7. On Paulina, see H. W. Kamp, "Seneca's Marriage," *Classical Journal* 32 (June 1937): 531. On sensibility, see Norman S. Fiering, "Irresistible Compassion: An Aspect of Eighteenth-Century Sympathy and Humanitarianism," *Journal of the History of Ideas* 37 (April-June, 1976): 195; James Rodgers, "Sensibility, Sympathy, Benevolence: Physiology and Moral Philosophy in *Tristram Shandy,*" in L. J. Jordanova, ed., *Languages of Nature*: *Critical Essays on Science and Literature* (New Brunswick, N.J., 1986), 126–33; Sarah Knott, *Sensibility and the American Revolution* (Chapel Hill, N.C., 2008).

17¶3 AA, quoted in Akers, *Abigail Adams* (1980 edition), 10–11; Adam Smith, *The Theory of Moral Sentiments . . .* , 6th ed. (2 vols.; London, 1790).

18¶1 Ecclesiastes 4:14; AA to JA, Aug. 11, 1763, JA to AA, April 11, 1764, *AFC*, 1:6, 23.

18¶2 AA to JA, Sept. 12, 1763, *AFC*, 1:8; Kenneth MacLean, "Imagination and Sympathy: Sterne and Adam Smith," *Journal of the History of Ideas* 10 (June 1949): 403; G. J. Barker-Benfield, *The Culture of Sensibility: Sex and Society in Eighteenth-Century Britain* (Chicago, 1992), xvii, 1, 23, 28, 117, 144.

19¶1 Carl N. Degler, *Out of Our Past: The Forces That Shaped Modern America*, 3rd ed. (New York, 1984), 9–22. The conjecture that the couple's destination was Worcester comes from Lynne Withey, *Dearest Friend: A Life of Abigail Adams* (New York, 1981), 16.

19¶2 Hannah Storer Green to AA, Nov. 23, 1763, quoted in *AFC*, 1:10n.

20¶1 Hannah Storer Green to JA, Feb. 20, 1764, *AFC*, 1:11.

20¶2 Hannah Storer Green to JA, Feb. 20, 1764, *AFC*, 1:11.

Chapter 3: "For Saucyness No Mortal Can Match Him," 1764

21¶1 Elizabeth A. Fenn, *Pox Americana: The Great Smallpox Epidemic of 1775–82* (New York, 2001), 31–34.

21¶3 JA to AA, [April 7, 1764], AA to CT, April 9, 1764, *AFC*, 1:16, 21.

22¶1 AA to JA, April 12–13, 1764, *AFC*, 1:27.

22¶2 AA to CT, April 2, 1764, *AFC*, 1:13. In this and all other quotations containing words in italics, the emphasis is in the original.

23¶1 AA to CT, April 9, 1764, CT to AA, [April 19, 1764?], *AFC*, 1:21, 38–39.

23¶2 JA to AA, [April 13, 1764], *AFC*, 1:28.

23¶3 AA to JA, April 7, 15, 1764, *AFC*, 1:15, 31.

24¶2 AA to JA, April 15, 1764, *AFC*, 1:31.

24¶3 AA to JA, April 19–20, 1764, *AFC*, 1:38.

25¶1 AA to JA, April 16, 19–20, 1764, *AFC*, 1:32, 36.

25¶3 AA to JA, April 19–20, 1764, *AFC*, 1:37; JA Diary, Aug. 15, 1762, *DAJA*, 1:227.

26¶2 AA to JA, April 16, 19–20, 1764, *AFC*, 1:32, 37.

26¶3 JA to AA, April 26, 1764, *AFC*, 1:39–40; JA Diary, [summer 1759], *DAJA*, 1:108.

27¶4 AA to JA, April 30, 1764, *AFC*, 1:41.

27¶5 AA to JA, April 30, 1764, *AFC*, 1:41–42; Alaric Miller, "Serious Jesting: A Close Inspection of the Smith-Adams Epistolary Courtship Based on Their Early Love-Letters, 1762–1764" (M.A. thesis, University of Montana, 1997), 85–89.

28¶1 AA to JA, April 30, 1764, *AFC*, 1:42.

29¶1 JA to AA, May 7, 1764, *AFC*, 1:44–45; JA Diary, Aug. 15, 1762, *DAJA*, 1:227.

29¶2 AA to JA, May 9, 1764, *AFC*, 1:47.

29¶3 JA to AA, Sept. 30, 1764, *AFC*, 1:48–49.

30¶1 JA to AA, Sept. 30, 1764, *AFC*, 1:49.

30¶2 JA to AA, Sept. 30, 1764, AA to JA, Oct. 4, 1764, *AFC*, 1:49, 50–51.

31¶1 AA to JA, Oct. 4, 1764, *AFC*, 1:50–51.

31¶2 JA to AA, Sept. 30, 1764, *AFC*, 1:48.

32¶1 JA to AA, Sept. 30, 1764, AA to JA, Oct. 4, 1764, *AFC*, 1:50.

Chapter 4: "Mrs. Adams," 1764–1770

33¶2 *Letters of Mrs. Adams*, xxxii.

34¶1 JA to BR, Aug. 25, 1811, *OFL*, 349; JA Diary, [summer 1759], Dec. 23, 1772, *DAJA*, 1:108, 2:72.

34¶2 JA to BR, Aug. 25, 1811, *OFL*, 349.

35¶1 AA to JA, July 29, 1776, MOW to AA, March 1, 1777, *AFC*, 2:66, 267.

35¶2 In AA's October 1766 letter to MSC, the word *there* was replaced by "at Germantown." AA to MSC, July 15, Oct. 6, 1766, MSC to AA, Jan. 15, 1767, *AFC*, 1:54, 55, 59.

36¶1 *AFC*, 9:36n; Ulrich, *Midwife's Tale*, 155–58.

36¶2 AA to Hannah Storer Green, [after July 14, 1765], AA to MSC, July 15, Oct. 6, 1766, *AFC*, 1:51, 54, 55.

36¶3 AA to MSC, Oct. 13, 1766, AA and JA to MSC, Jan. 12, 1767, *AFC*, 1:57–58.

37¶1 JA to RC, Sept. 23, 1767, *AFC*, 1:63; JQA to Skelton Jones, April 17, 1809, *Writings of JQA*, 3:296; AA to William Allen, [ca. 1812], AP#414.

37¶2 AA to MSC, Oct. 6, 1766, *AFC*, 1:55–56.

37¶3 JA to RC, June 29, 1766, *AFC*, 1:52.

38¶1 AA and JA to MSC, Jan. 12, 1767, *AFC*, 1:58.

38¶2 AA to MSC, July 15, 1766, *AFC*, 1:54.

39¶1 AA to MSC, July 15, 1766, *AFC*, 1:54.

39¶2 AA to MSC, July 15, 1766, *AFC*, 1:54.

39¶3 AA to MSC, Oct. 6, 1766, AA to JA, Oct. 21, 1775, *AFC*, 1:56, 308.

40¶1 AA to JA, Sept. [13], 1767, *AFC*, 1:62.

40¶2 Laurel Thatcher Ulrich, *Good Wives: Image and Reality in the Lives of Women in Northern New England, 1650–1750* (New York, 1982), 35–50; JA to AA, May 1772, June [29], [1769], *AFC*, 183,66.

40¶3 AA to MSC, Jan. 31, 1767, *AFC*, 1:60–61.

41¶3 AA to MSC, Jan. 31, 1767, *AFC*, 1:61. For a strikingly similar account, in this case a southern planter's description of how excited his slaves were to see him after a long absence, see Jack McLaughlin, *Jefferson and Monticello: The Biography of a Builder* (New York, 1988), 239–40.

41¶4 ESSP to IS2, April 13–18, 1768, *AFC*, 1:65.

41¶5 Benjamin L. Carp, *Rebels Rising: Cities and the American Revolution* (New York, 2007), 25.

42¶1 AA to JA, July 25, 1775, Aug. 5, 1776, *AFC*, 1:263, 2:79.

42¶3 Hiller R. Zobel, *The Boston Massacre* (New York, 1970), 182.

43¶2 JA to AA, June [29], [1769], *AFC*, 1:66.

43¶3 ESSP to AA, March 14, 1812 (misfiled at March 14, 1811), AP#411.

44¶1 Thomas Preston, account of the Boston Massacre, in Merrill Jensen, ed., *English Historical Documents*, vol. 9 (London, 1964), 750–53 (first quotation); Zobel, *Boston Massacre*, 182 (second quotation); Robert Middlekauf, *The Glorious Cause: The American Revolution, 1763–1789* (New York, 1982), 203–6.

44¶2 Peter Linebaugh and Marcus Rediker, *The Many-Headed Hydra: Sailors, Slaves, Commoners, and the Hidden History of the Revolutionary Atlantic* (Boston, 2000), 232; Zobel, *Boston Massacre*, 220–21.

CHAPTER 5: "I SHOULD CERTAINLY HAVE BEEN A ROVER," 1770–1774

45¶1 Jon Butler, *Awash in a Sea of Faith: Christianizing the American People* (Cambridge, Mass., 1990), 164–93; Patricia U. Bonomi, *Under the Cope of Heaven: Religion, Society, and Politics in Colonial America*, updated edition (New York, 2003), 131–60; Douglas L. Winiarski, *Darkness Falls on the Land of Light: The Travail of New England Congregationalism, 1680–1770* (forthcoming). My thanks to Peter H. Wood for the rock-star analogy.

45¶2 Gilbert Tennent, *The Danger of an Unconverted Ministry, Consider'd in a Sermon on Mark 6:34 . . .* (Philadelphia, 1740); Albert D. Belden, *George Whitefield—The Awakener: A Modern Study of the Evangelical Revival* (Nashville, Tenn., 1930), 222–24; Frank Lambert, *"Pedlar in Divinity": George Whitefield and the Transatlantic Revivals, 1737–1770* (Princeton, N.J., 1994), 224; Phillis Wheatley, *Poems on Various Subjects, Religious and Moral . . .* (London, 1773), 22; Henry Louis Gates, Jr., *The Trials of Phillis Wheatley: America's First Black Poet and Her Encounters with the Founding Fathers* (New York, 2003).

46¶1 AA to IS2, April 20, 1771, *AFC*, 1:76–77.

46¶2 Zobel, *Boston Massacre*, 265, 294, 298.

47¶2 AA to IS2, April 20, 1771, *AFC*, 1:76.

48¶1 AA to IS2, April 20, 1771, *AFC*, 1:76.

48¶2 IS2 to JA, Feb. 21, 1771, AA to IS2, April 20, 1771, *AFC*, 1:72, 77.

48¶3 AA to JA, April 16, 19, 1764, AA to IS2, April 20, 1771, IS2 to JA, Sept. 3, [1771], *AFC*, 1:32, 36, 76, 78.

50¶1 Rosemarie Zagarri, *A Woman's Dilemma: Mercy Otis Warren and the American Revolution* (Wheeling, Ill., 1995), 56–59.

50¶2 MOW to AA, July 25, 1773, *AFC*, 1:86.

50¶3 MOW to AA, July 25, 1773, *AFC*, 1:86.

50¶4 MOW to AA, July 25, 1773, *AFC*, 1:87; Juliana-Susannah Seymour, *On the Management and Education of Children: A Series of Letters Written to a Niece* (London, 1754); Levin, *Abigail Adams*, 44–45.

51¶1 AA to MOW, Dec. 5–11, 1773, [ante Feb. 27, 1774], *AFC*, 1:89, 97.

52¶1 MOW to AA, Jan. 19, 1774, *AFC*, 1:92–93.

52¶2 MOW to AA, July 25, 1773, Feb. 27, 1774, *AFC*, 1:86, 99.

52¶4 AA to MOW, Dec. 5–11, 1773, *AFC*, 1:88.

53¶1 Benjamin Woods Labaree, *The Boston Tea Party* (London, 1964), vii, 143–45.

53¶2 AA to JA, Dec. 30, 1773, *AFC*, 1:90.

54¶1 AA to MSC, [1774?], ESSP to AA, Feb. 8, 1774, *AFC*, 1:176, 96; "Isaac Smith, Jr., Harvard, 1767," *CC*.

54¶2 AA to MSC, [1774?], *AFC*, 1:176.

55¶1 AA's letter to ESSP does not survive, but much of its contents can be inferred from her sister's detailed rebuttal. ESSP to AA, March 7, 1774, *AFC*, 1:104.

55¶2 ESSP to AA, March 7, 1774, *AFC*, 1:105.

Chapter 6: "Mrs. Delegate," 1774

56¶1 ESSP to AA, March 7, 1774, *AFC*, 1:104–5.
56¶2 ESSP to AA, March 7, 1774, *AFC*, 1:106.
56¶3 Middlekauf, *Glorious Cause*, 226.
57¶1 Middlekauf, *Glorious Cause*, 229–30.
57¶2 Middlekauf, *Glorious Cause*, 231.
58¶1 Francis D. Cogliano, *Revolutionary America, 1763–1815: A Political History* (London, 2000), 47; Woody Holton, *Forced Founders: Indians, Debtors, Slaves, and the Making of the American Revolution in Virginia* (Chapel Hill, 1999), 33, 35–36.
58¶2 Middlekauf, *Glorious Cause*, 232–35.
58¶3 AA to JA, Oct. 21, 1775, *AFC*, 1:308. On the chaos in the courts in the summer of 1774, see Ray Raphael, *The First American Revolution: Before Lexington and Concord* (New York, 2002).
59¶1 JA to AA, June 23, July 6, 1774, June 30, 1774, July 1, 1774, *AFC*, 1:108–9, 129, 117, 119.
59¶2 Edmund S. Morgan, "The Puritan Ethic and the American Revolution," *WMQ*, 3rd ser., 24 (January 1967), 3–43; Ann Fairfax Withington, *Toward a More Perfect Union: Virtue and the Formation of American Republics* (Oxford, 1991); T.H. Breen, *The Marketplace of Revolution: How Consumer Politics Shaped American Independence* (Oxford, 2004), ch. 6–8.
59¶3 JA to AA, July 7, June 30, 1774, *AFC*, 1:131, 117.
60¶1 JA to AA, July 1, 1774, *AFC*, 1:118.
60¶2 JA to AA, June 29, 1774, *AFC*, 1:113–14.
60¶3 JA to AA, May 12, 1774, *AFC*, 1:107.
61¶1 MSC to AA, Aug. 20, 1774, *AFC*, 1:143–44.
61¶2 MSC to AA, Aug. 20, 1774, *AFC*, 1:143–44.
62¶1 AA to JA, Aug. 15, 1774, *AFC*, 1:141.
62¶2 AA to JA, Aug. 19, 1774, *AFC*, 1:142–43.
62¶3 AA to JA, Aug. 19, Sept. 2, 1774, *AFC*, 1:142, 147–48.
63¶1 AA to JA, Sept. 14–16, 1774, *AFC*, 1:151.
63¶2 AA to MOW, Dec. 5–11, 1773, *AFC*, 1:88.
63¶2 AA to JA, Sept. 14–16, 1774, *AFC*, 1:152.
64¶1 AA to JA, Sept. 14–16, 1774, *AFC*, 1:152.
64¶2 AA to JA, Sept. 14–16, 1774, *AFC*, 1:152.
65¶1 Braintree town meeting, Oct. 3, 1774, quoted in *AFC*, 1:154n.
65¶2 MSC to IS2, Oct. 15, 1774, AA to IS2, April 20, 1771, *AFC*, 1:171, 76–77.
65¶3 MSC to IS2, Oct. 15, 1774, *AFC*, 1:171–72.
66¶1 MSC to IS2, Oct. 15, 1774, *AFC*, 1:171–72.
66¶2 MSC to IS2, Oct. 15, 1774, *AFC*, 1:171.
67¶1 AA to JA, Sept. 14–16, 1774, *AFC*, 1:152.
67¶2 AA, quoted in Akers, *Abigail Adams* (1980 edition), 37.

Chapter 7: "Portia," 1774–1775

68¶1 JA to AA, Sept. 8, 29, Oct. 7, 1774, *AFC*, 1:151, 164, 165.
68¶2 AA to JA, Oct. 16, 1774, *AFC*, 1:173.
69¶1 AA to JA, Oct. 16, 1774, *AFC*, 1:173.
69¶3 AA to JA, Sept. 14–16, 1774, *AFC*, 1:153.
70¶1 AA to JA, Sept. 14–16, 1774, *AFC*, 1:153.
70¶2 AA to JA, Sept. 22, 1774, *AFC*, 1:161–62.
70¶3 Madison to William Bradford, [Jr.], Nov. 26, 1774, in William T. Hutchinson et al., eds., *The Papers of James Madison* (17 vols. to date; Chicago and Charlottesville, 1962–), 1:130; Peter H. Wood, "'Liberty is Sweet': African-American Freedom Struggles in the Years before White Independence," in Alfred F. Young, ed., *Beyond the American Revolution: Explorations in the History of American Radicalism* (DeKalb, Ill., 1993), 160–61.
71¶1 AA to JA, Sept. 22, 1774, *AFC*, 1:161–62.
71¶2 AA to JA, Oct. 16, 1774, *AFC*, 1:173.
71¶3 AA to JA, Oct. 16, 1774, *AFC*, 1:173.
72¶1 AA to JA, Oct. 16, 1774, *AFC*, 1:173.
72¶2 AA to William Tudor, Oct. 15, 1774, AA to JA, Oct. 16, 1774, *AFC*, 1:170, 174.
72¶3 AA to Catharine Sawbridge Macaulay, [1774], *AFC*, 1:177–78; Middlekauf, *Glorious Cause*, 244–49.
73¶1 AA to JA, Aug. 11, 1763, AA to Catharine Sawbridge Macaulay, [1774], *AFC*, 1:6, 179.
73¶2 MOW to AA, Jan. 19, 1774, MOW to JA and AA, May 17, 1774, *AFC*, 1:92, 108.
73¶3 MOW to AA, Jan. 28, 1775, *AFC*, 1:182.
74¶1 MOW to AA, Jan. 28, 1775, *AFC*, 1:182.
74¶2 MOW to AA, Jan. 28, 1775, *AFC*, 1:182.
75¶1 MOW to JA, Jan. 30, 1775, *Warren-Adams Letters: Being Chiefly a Correspondence Among John Adams, Sam Adams, and James Warren* (2 vols.; [Boston], 1917–1925), 1:37; MOW to AA, Feb. 27, 1774, AA to MOW, [Feb. 3, 1775?], *AFC*, 1:99, 185–86.
75¶4 "Isaac Smith, Jr., Harvard, 1767," CC.
76¶1 David Hackett Fischer, *Paul Revere's Ride* (New York, 1994), 189–201.
76¶3 AA to MOW, May 2, 1775, *AFC*, 1:190.
77¶1 Peter Stone, *1776: A Musical Play*, libretto by Sherman Edwards (New York, 1976), 8–9; David McCullough, *John Adams* (New York, 2001), 21; AA to JA, June 16, 1775, *AFC*, 1:219.

Chapter 8: "My Pen Is Always Freer than My Tongue," 1775

78¶1 AA to JA, June 16, 1775, *AFC*, 1:219.
78¶2 JA to AA, July 7, 30, 1775, AA to JA, July 16, 1775, *AFC*, 1:243, 268, 249.
78¶3 AA to JA, June 18, 1775, *AFC*, 1:222.
79¶1 Cogliano, *Revolutionary America*, 57.

79¶2 Cogliano, *Revolutionary America*, 57–58.
79¶3 JQA to Joseph Sturge, March 1846, quoted in *AFC*, 1:224n; AA to JA, June 18–[20], 1775, *AFC*, 1:223n.
80¶1 JQA to Joseph Sturge, March 1846, cited in *AFC*, 1:224n; AA to JA, July 25, 1775, *AFC*, 1:261.
81¶1 AA to JA, July 16, 1775, RC to JA, July 24, 1775, *AFC*, 1:248, 259.
82¶1 McCullough, *John Adams*, 20.
82¶2 AA to JA, July 16, 1775, *AFC*, 1:246–47.
82¶3 AA to JA, July 16, 1775, *AFC*, 1:248–51n.
83¶1 AA to JA, July 16, 1775, *AFC*, 1:249.
83¶2 AA to JA, July 5, 16, 1775, *AFC*, 1:239, 247.
84¶1 AA to JA, July 16, 1775, *AFC*, 1:250.
84¶2 AA to JA, July 25, 1775, *AFC*, 1:263.
84¶3 AA to JA, July 25, 1775, *AFC*, 1:263.
85¶1 AA to JA, July 31–Aug. 2, 1775, Mary Palmer to JA, June 15, 1776, *AFC*, 1:270–71, 2:12–13.
85¶2 AA to JA, July 31–Aug. 2, 1775, *AFC*, 1:271.
85¶3 AA to JA, July 31–Aug. 2, 1775, *AFC*, 1:271.
86¶1 AA to JA, June 25, July 25, 1775, *AFC*, 1:231, 263.
86¶2 JA to AA, July 30, 1775, *AFC*, 1:268; July 29, 1775, *JCC*, 2:224.
86¶3 AA to JA, Aug. 10–11, 1775, *AFC*, 1:272.
87¶2 AA to JA, Sept. 8–10, 1775, *AFC*, 1:276–77.
88¶1 AA to JA, Sept. 8–10, [17], 1775, *AFC*, 1:277, 278.
88¶2 AA to JA, Sept. [17], 25, 1775, *AFC*, 1:278, 284. On death by disease during the American Revolution, see Cogliano, *Revolutionary America*, 204–5.
89¶1 Elizabeth Quincy Smith obituary, Oct. 6, 1775, *AFC*, 1:294.
89¶2 AA to JA, Sept. 25, 29, Oct. 9, 25, 1775, *AFC*, 1:284, 288, 297, 313.
89¶3 AA to JA, Sept. 29, Oct. 22, 1775, *AFC*, 1:287–88, 309–10.
90¶1 AA to JA, Sept. 25, 1775, JA to AA, July 24, Oct. 1, 7, 1775, *AFC*, 1:284, 256, 289, 295.
90¶2 The previous spring, there had also been a ten-day pause between John's departure for Congress and Abigail's first letter to him. But back then the news in her possession was not nearly as significant.
90¶3 JA to AA, Oct. 7, 1775, AA to JA, Oct. 22, 1775, *AFC*, 1:295, 309–10.
91¶2 It is true that John observed to Abigail that "The ways of Heaven are dark and intricate," but this was precisely the sort of offhand religious reference he and Abigail had exchanged from the early days of their courtship. AA to JA, Sept. 25, Oct. 1, 9, 1775, JA to AA, Oct. 7, 13, 1775, *AFC*, 1:284, 288–89, 296–97, 295, 300; Job 10:2.
92¶1 JA to TBA, Oct. 20, 1775, *AFC*, 1:305.
92¶2 AA to JA, Oct. 21, 25, 1775, *AFC*, 1:308, 313.
92¶3 AA to JA, Oct. 25, Nov. 12, 1775, *AFC*, 1:314, 325.
92¶4 AA to JA, Oct. 21, Nov. 8, 1775, *AFC*, 1:307–8, 322.
93¶1 JA to AA, Oct. 29, 1775, *AFC*, 1:316–17.
93¶2 JA to AA, Oct. 29, Sept. 26, 1775, *AFC*, 1:317, 285–86.
94¶1 JA to AA, Oct. 23, Nov. 4, 1775, AA to JA, Nov. 27, 1775, *AFC*, 1:312, 320, 328–29.

94¶2 JA to James Warren, July 24, 1775, in *Warren-Adams Letters*, 1:88–89; AA to JA, Nov. 12, 1775, *AFC*, 1:324.

Chapter 9: "Remember the Ladies," 1776

96¶1 AA to JA, Dec. 10, 1775, *AFC*, 1:335; William Finnie, advertisement, Purdie's *Virginia Gazette* (supplement), March 7, 1777; John Richard Alden, *General Charles Lee, Traitor or Patriot?* (Baton Rouge, La., [1951]), 82–83. My thanks to Kylie Horney for researching Spado/Spada/Sparder's breed.

96¶2 JA Diary, 1776, *DAJA*, 2:333; JA to AA, March 19, 1776, *AFC*, 1:363; Middlekauf, *Glorious Cause*, 317–19.

97¶1 JA to AA, March 19, 1776, AA to JA, Feb. 21, April 7–11, May 9, 1776, *AFC*, 1:363, 350, 376, 404. On JA's "Thoughts on Government," see McCullough, *John Adams*, 101–3; Edith B. Gelles, *Abigail and John: Portrait of a Marriage* (New York, 2009), 75.

97¶2 AA to JA, March 2–10, 1776, *AFC*, 1:353.

98¶1 AA to JA, March 2–10, 1776, *AFC*, 1:354; Middlekauf, *Glorious Cause*, 309–10.

98¶2 AA to JA, March 16–18, March 31–April 5, 1776, *AFC*, 1:357, 370; Middlekauf, *Glorious Cause*, 310–11.

99¶1 AA to JA, March 31–April 5, 1776, *AFC*, 1:370; Sarah Knott, "Benjamin Rush's Ferment: Enlightenment Medicine and Female Citizenship in Revolutionary America," in Knott and Barbara Taylor, eds., *Women, Gender, and Enlightenment* (Houndmills, Basingstoke, Hampshire, England, 2005), 656 (and the scholarship cited there); Mary Beth Norton, *Liberty's Daughters: The Revolutionary Experience of American Women, 1750–1820* (Boston, 1980), 40–41; Joan R. Gundersen, *To Be Useful to the World: Women in Revolutionary America, 1740–1790* (New York, 1996), 40–41; Carole Shammas, "Anglo-American Household Government in Comparative Perspective," *WMQ*, 3rd ser., 52 (January 1995): 104–44. On William Smith, Jr.'s mistreatment of his wife, see Catharine Louisa Salmon Smith to AA, April 27, 1785, *AFC*, 6:111–12.

99¶2 AA to JA, March 31–April 5, 1776, *AFC*, 1:370; Elaine Forman Crane, "Political Dialogue and the Spring of Abigail's Discontent," *WMQ*, 3rd ser., 56 (October 1999): 752–53, 763.

100¶1 AA to JA, March 31–April 5, 1776, *AFC*, 1:370.

100¶2 AA to JA, March 31–April 5, 1776, *AFC*, 1:370.

101¶1 AA to JA, March 31–April 5, 1776, *AFC*, 1:369–70.

101¶2 AA to JA, Dec. 10, 1775, *AFC*, 1:336.

102¶1 AA to JA, March 31–April 5, 1776, *AFC*, 1:369.

102¶2 JA to AA, April 14, 1776, *AFC*, 1:382–83.

102¶3 JA to AA, April 14, 1776, *AFC*, 1:382.

103¶1 JA to AA, April 14, 1776, *AFC*, 1:382.

103¶2 JA to AA, Feb. [13], April 14, 1776, AA to JA, March 16–18, 1776, *AFC*, 1:347, 382, 359.

104¶1 JA to AA, April 15, 1776, JA to AAS, April 18, 1776, AA to JA, March 31–April 5, 1776, *AFC*, 1:384, 388, 370.
104¶2 AA to JA, March 16–18, April 21, 1776, JA to AA, April 12, 1776, *AFC*, 1:359, 389, 376.
105¶1 AA to JA, May 7, 1776, *AFC*, 1:402–3.
105¶2 AA to MOW, April 27, 1776, *AFC*, 1:397–98.
105¶3 AA to JA, April 7–11, 1776, JA to AA, April 28, 1776, *AFC*, 1:375, 398–99.
105¶4 AA to MOW, April 13, 1776, AA to JA, April 7–11, 1776, *AFC*, 1:377, 375.
106¶1 AA to JA, Oct. 16, 1774, March 31–April 5, 1776, AA to MOW, April 13, 1776, *AFC*, 1:173, 371, 377.
106¶2 AA to JA, July 5, 1775, April 2, Aug. 12–13, 1777, MOW to AA, March 1, July 7, [ante Aug. 14], 1777, AA to MOW, Aug. 14–16, 1777, JA to AA, Aug. 25, 1777, *AFC*, 1:240, 2:194, 309, 166–67, 275–76, 312–14, 329.

Chapter 10: "This Suspence Is Painfull," 1776

108¶1 *AFC*, 2:47–48n.
108¶2 AA to JA, June 3, 1776, JA to AA, June 16, 1776, *AFC*, 2:4, 13.
109¶1 AA to JA, June 3, 1776, *AFC*, 2:5.
109¶2 AA to JA, June 3, 1776, JA to AA, June 16, 1776, *AFC*, 2:5, 13.
109¶3 Fenn, *Pox Americana*, 52.
109¶4 AA to JA, July 13–14, Aug. 1, 1776, *AFC*, 2:45, 72; Watertown dateline, *Boston Gazette*, July 15, 1776; chapters 6, 7, *Acts and Laws Passed by The Great and General Court or Assembly of the Colony of the Massachusetts-Bay . . .* (Watertown, Mass., 1776), 66–69; Charles W. Akers, *Abigail Adams: A Revolutionary American Woman* (New York, 2007), 53. The legislature's decision to turn the town over to the inoculators and their patients—placing the burden on people who did not want to be inoculated to stay out of their way—explains a mystery that has surrounded the summer 1776 inoculation. Several of those who received inoculation that summer, including AA, appear to have acted irresponsibly by going out in public at the height of their contagiousness. Fenn, *Pox Americana*, 37–39. The reality was that Adams and other inoculees could roam the streets of Boston without fear of spreading the disease, because vulnerable Bostonians had been warned to keep clear.
110¶1 AA to JA, July 13–14, 1776, *AFC*, 2:45.
110¶2 AA to JA, July 13–14, 29, 1776, *AFC*, 2:45, 66.
110¶3 AA to JT, July 7, 1776, AA to JA, July 13–14, 1776, *AFC*, 2:37, 45–47; Fenn, *Pox Americana*, 35–36.
111¶1 AA to JA, July 21–22, 1776, *AFC*, 2:56.
111¶2 AA to JA, July 13–14, 1776, *AFC*, 2:46; Akers, *Abigail Adams* (2007 edition), 52.
112¶1 AA to JA, July 21–22, 29, 30–31, 1776, JA to AA, Aug. 20, 1776, *AFC*, 2:57n, 65, 69–70, 102.
112¶2 AA to JA, July 29, 30, Aug. 1, 14, 1776, *AFC*, 2:66, 69, 72, 93; Psalm 91:6.
113¶1 AA to JA, Aug. 1, 5, 17, 1776, JA to AA, Aug. 30, 1776, MOW to AA, Sept. 4, 1776, *AFC*, 2:72, 79, 98, 115, 118.

113¶2 JA to AA, Aug. 25, 1776, *AFC*, 2:109.
114¶1 AA to JA, Aug. 1, 5, 1776, *AFC*, 2:72, 78.
114¶2 AA to JA, Aug. 5, 1776, *AFC*, 2:79.
114¶3 AA to JA, Aug. 5, 1776, *AFC*, 2:79.
115¶1 JA to AA, Aug. 3–4, 1776, *AFC*, 2:75.
115¶2 AA to JA, Aug. 29, 1776, *AFC*, 2:112; Edith B. Gelles, *Abigail Adams: A Writing Life* (New York, 2002), 176; Gelles, *Abigail and John*, 92; Elaine Forman Crane, "Abigail Adams, Gender Politics, and *The History of Emily Montague*: A Postscript," *WMQ*, 3rd ser., 64 (October 2007): 844.
115¶3 JA to AA, Aug. 3–4, 1776, AA to JA, Aug. 14, 1776, *AFC*, 2:76, 94.
115¶4 AA to JA, Aug. 14, 1776, *AFC*, 2:94; Kerber, *Women of the Republic*, 199–200, 228–31; Gundersen, *To Be Useful to the World*, 87–88.
116¶1 AA to JA, Aug. 18 [i.e., 19], Sept. 7, 1776, *AFC*, 2:101, 122–23.
117¶1 Nor was Abigail able to discern what had happened, since John, following her lead, had used language that was as obfuscatory as hers. JA to AA, July 29, Aug. 27, 28, 1776, AA to JA, July 13–14, Sept. 7, 1776, *AFC*, 2:68, 111, 47, 122–23.
117¶2 AA to JA, [May 27], Aug. 5, 1776, AA to JT, Aug. 20, 1776, *AFC*, 1:417, 2:80, 101.
117¶4 AA to JA, [May 27], 1776, *AFC*, 1:417.
117¶5 JA to AA, July 23, Aug. 6, 12, 1776, AA to JA, Aug. 5, [ca. 12], 22, 25, 1776, *AFC*, 2:60, 80, 89, 79, 87, 105–7. My thanks to Bridget Westhoven for this insight.
118¶3 AA to JA, Aug. 31–Sept. 2, 1776, *AFC*, 2:117.
118¶4 JA to AA, Aug. 27, 30, 1776, JA to CA, March 17, 1777, *AFC*, 2:110, 114, 179.
119¶1 AA to JA, Aug. 22, 1776, JA to AA, Aug. 30, 1776, *AFC*, 2:106, 115.
119¶2 JA to AA, Aug. 28, Sept. 5, 1776, AA to JA, Sept. 7, 29, 1776, *AFC*, 2:111, 119, 122–23, 136.
119¶3 JA to AA, Sept. 4, 1776, AA to JA, Sept. 20, 177[6], *AFC*, 2:117, 127–29; Middlekauf, *Glorious Cause*, 343–46.
119¶4 AA to JA, Sept. 21, 1776, *AFC*, 2:129–30.
120¶1 AA to JA, April 17, 1777, *AFC*, 2:212; Norton, *Liberty's Daughters*, 232–33.
120¶2 The evidence that Abigail told John she wanted a girl before he left Braintree is indirect. John indicated that he knew his wife's preference, though she had not expressed it in any of the letters she wrote him after his departure. JA to AA, July 10, 20, 1777, AA to JA, July 16, 1777 *AFC*, 2:278, 285, 282.

Chapter 11: "To Bear What I Cannot Fly From," 1777

121¶1 David Hackett Fischer, *Washington's Crossing* (New York, 2004).
121¶3 JA to AA, Feb. 10, 15, 1777, *AFC*, 2:159, 162.
122¶1 AA to JA, March 8–10, 1777, *AFC*, 2:173. On New England women's age at first marriage, see Zagarri, *Woman's Dilemma*, 17.
122¶2 AA to JA, March 8–10, 1777, *AFC*, 2:173; William Finnie, advertisement, Purdie's *Virginia Gazette* (supplement), March 7, 1777.

123¶1 AA to JA, March 8–10, April 17, 1777, *AFC*, 2:173, 212.

123¶2 AA to JA, June 1, 8, [15], 1777, *AFC*, 2:250, 258, 266. On Howe's departure from New York, see Middlekauf, *Glorious Cause*, 384–85.

123¶3 JA to AA, June 4, July 1–2, 10, 1777, *AFC*, 2:255, 271–72, 278.

124¶1 AA to JA, July 9, 10–11, 1777, *AFC*, 2:277, 279.

124¶2 AA to JA, July 10–11, 1777, *AFC*, 2:279–80.

124¶3 AA to JA, July 16, 1777, *AFC*, 2:282.

125¶1 AA to JA, July 16, Aug. 12–13, 1777, *AFC*, 2:282, 308.

125¶2 AA to JA, May 6, 1777; Kenneth Scott, *Counterfeiting in Colonial America* (New York, 1957), 256–60.

125¶3 JA to AA, Feb. 2, 1777, *AFC*, 2:152. On privateers, see Nov. 25, 1775, *JCC*, 3:374; William M. Fowler, Jr., *Rebels Under Sail: The American Navy During the Revolution* (New York, 1976), 281–82; James M. Volo, *Blue Water Patriots: The American Revolution Afloat* (Westport, Conn., 2007), 44–49. On decreased production, see MOW to AA, March 1, 1777, *AFC*, 2:167.

126¶1 AA to JA, June 1, 1777, *AFC*, 2:252.

126¶2 AA to JA, March 26, 1777, *AFC*, 2:187; Oct. 3, 1776, Feb. 26, 1777, *JCC*, 5:845–46, 7:158; E. James Ferguson, *The Power of the Purse: A History of American Public Finance, 1776–1790* (Chapel Hill, N.C., 1961), 35–40.

126¶3 AA to JA, June 1, 1777, *AFC*, 2:251–52.

127¶1 JA to AA, June 16, 1777, *AFC*, 2:267.

127¶2 AA to JA, July 30–31, 1777, *AFC*, 2:295; John Scollay to Samuel Phillips Savage, July 25, 1777, S. P. Savage Papers, MHS, quoted in *AFC*, 2:296n.

127¶3 AA to JA, July 30–31, 1777, *AFC*, 2:295; Barbara Clark Smith, "Food Rioters and the American Revolution," *WMQ*, 3rd ser., 51 (January 1994): 3–38; Gundersen, *To Be Useful to the World*, 158.

128¶1 John Scollay to Samuel Phillips Savage, July 25, 1777, S. P. Savage Papers, MHS, quoted in *AFC*, 2:296n.

128¶2 AA to JA, Aug. 22, 1777, *AFC*, 2:323.

128¶3 JA to AA, Aug. 11, 1777, *AFC*, 2:304; John Turner, advertisement, *Boston Gazette*, Sept. 8, 1777.

129¶1 CT to JA, Sept. 18, 1777, *AFC*, 2:346.

129¶2 AA to JA, Sept. 17, [1777], *AFC*, 2:343.

Chapter 12: "An Army of Women," 1777–1778

130¶1 AA to JA, Sept. 17, [1777], *AFC*, 2:343.

130¶2 JL to AA, Aug. 29, 1777, AA to JA, Sept. 17, [1777], *AFC*, 2:333, 343.

130¶3 Middlekauf, *Glorious Cause*, 385–89.

131¶1 AA to JA, Sept. 20, 177[6], Sept. 21–24, [1777], *AFC*, 2:129, 348.

131¶2 Middlekauf, *Glorious Cause*, 380–84.

131¶3 AA to IS2, [Oct. 30, 1777], *AFC*, 2:363; Anthony Galasso, Jr., "The Two-Fold Cord: Abigail Adams's Conception of the Relationship between Politics and Religion," seminar paper, University of Richmond, spring 2007 (in author's possession).

132¶1 AA to IS2, Oct. 30, 1777, *AFC*, 2:363.

132¶2 AA to JA, Nov. 16–18, 1777, *AFC*, 2:368n.
132¶3 Sept. 9, 1777, *JCC*, 8:724–25; Ferguson, *Power of the Purse*, 35–40; Richard Buel, Jr., *In Irons: Britain's Naval Supremacy and the American Revolutionary Economy* (New Haven, Conn., 1998), 45–46.
133¶2 AA to JL, [ca. Dec. 15, 1777], *AFC*, 2:370–71.
133¶3 MOW to AA, Jan. 2, 1778, *AFC*, 2:376.
134¶1 AA to Daniel Roberdeau, [ca. Dec. 15, 1777], Daniel Roberdeau to AA, Jan. 19, 1778, *AFC*, 2:373, 384.
134¶2 *AFC*, 2:375n.
134¶3 AA to JL, March 1, 1778, *AFC*, 2:396.
135¶1 AA to JL, March 1, 1778, *AFC*, 2:396.
135¶2 JL to AA, April 1, 1778, *AFC*, 3:1.
137¶1 JT to AA, Jan. 20, 1778, *AFC*, 2:385, 393n.
137¶2 London *Public Ledger*, quoted in *AFC*, 2:393n; AA to JT, Feb. 15, 1778, *AFC*, 2:391.
137¶3 AA to JT, Feb. 15, 1778, *AFC*, 2:391–92.
138¶1 AA to JT, Feb. 15, 1778, *AFC*, 2:392.
138¶3 AA to JT, May 21–26, 1778, Oct. 26, 1782, AA to JQA, June [10?], 1778, *AFC*, 3:26, 5:26–27, 3:37.
138¶4 JA to AA, April 25, 1778, AA to JA, June 18, 1778, *AFC*, 3:17, 46. AA later learned that the British had not actually taken the *Boston* at all; they had merely recaptured one of their own vessels previously seized by the *Boston* and dispatched under guard to an American port. AFC, 3:53n.
139¶1 AA to JA, June 30, [1778], *AFC*, 3:52.
139¶2 AA to JA, June 30, [1778], *AFC*, 3:52; [John Shebbeare], *Letters on the English Nation: By Batista Angeloni, A Jesuit, Who Resided Many Years in London, Translated from the Original Italian, By the Author of The Marriage Act, a Novel*, vol. 1 (London, 1755), 169.
140¶1 [Shebbeare], *Letters on the English Nation*, 168–69; Crane, "Political Dialogue and the Spring of Abigail's Discontent," 761.
140¶2 AA to JA, June 30, [1778], *AFC*, 3:52–53.
141¶1 [Shebbeare], *Letters on the English Nation*, 168–69.
141¶2 AA to JA, June 30, [1778], *AFC*, 3:52.
141¶3 AA to JA, Aug. 22, 1777, [ca. July 15, 1778], AA to JT, April 9, 1778, *AFC*, 2:323, 3:61, 6.
142¶1 AA to JA, [ca. July 15, 1778], *AFC*, 3:61.
142¶2 AA to ESSP, [March 1778], AA to JT, April 9, 1778, AA to JA, [ca. July 15, 1778], *AFC*, 2:407–8, 3:6, 61.
143¶1 JA to AA, July 26, 1778, *AFC*, 3:66.

Chapter 13: "I Should be a Gainer," 1778–1780

144¶1 AA to JA, [ca. July 15, 1778], *AFC*, 3:61.
144¶2 JA to AA, Nov. 6, 1778, *AFC*, 3:115.
144¶3 AA to JA, Dec. 13, [1778], March 20–April 23, [1779], RC to JA, April 26, 1780, *AFC*, 3:136, 192, 326–27; Buel, *In Irons*, 37–44.

145¶1 AA to JA, [ca. July 15], Dec. 13, [1778], *AFC*, 3:61, 136.
145¶2 AA to JA, Sept. 29, 1778, *AFC*, 3:95.
145¶3 AA to JA, Oct. [21, 25, 1778], *AFC*, 3:109, 110.
145¶4 AA to JA, Jan. 2, 1779, *AFC*, 3:147.
146¶1 AA to JA, [Oct. 25, 1778], *AFC*, 3:110–11.
146¶2 AA to JA, Dec. 27, 1778, *AFC*, 3:140.
146¶3 JQA's final phrase was crossed out but still visible. JA to AA, Dec. 18, 1778, JQA to AA, Feb. 20, 1779, *AFC*, 3:138, 176n.
147¶1 AA to JA, Feb. 13, 1779, *AFC*, 3:167.
147¶3 AA to JA, Dec. 10, 1779, *AFC*, 3:242, 229n.
148¶1 AA to JA, Nov. 13–24, JA to AA, Feb. 23, 1780, *AFC*, 4:13, 3:280.
148¶2 AA to JA, Nov. 14, Dec. 10, 1779, *AFC*, 3:233, 242.
148¶3 AA to JA, March 1, 1780, JA to AA, March 16, 1780, JT to AA, Sept. 19, 1780, *AFC*, 3:292, 305, 418.
149¶1 JA to AA, Feb. 16, 1780, *AFC*, 3:275; JA Diary, Jan. 15, 1780, *DAJA*, 4:230; Benjamin Waterhouse, *A Journal, of a Young Man of Massachusetts, Late a Surgeon on Board an American Privateer, Who Was Captured at Sea by the British* . . . (Boston, 1816), 10; Gardoqui & Sons, "Invoice of Sundries shipp'd Per the Phenix James Babson master for Newburyport on Acct. of the Honble. John Adams Esq. . . . 31 Jany. 1780," *AFC*, 3:facing page 117; 6 Anne, 1708, c. 37, in *Addenda to the Third Volume of the Statutes at Large, Beginning with the Fourth Year of the Reign of Queen Anne, and Continued to the End of the Last Session of Parliament, April 1, 1708* . . . (London, 1708), 2607; *Narrative of the Adventures of an American Navy Officer, Who Served During Part of the American Revolution* . . . (New York, 1806), 14; J. K. Laughton, "Privateers and Privateering in the Eighteenth Century," *Fraser's Magazine*, New Series, 24 (October 1881): 465.
149¶2 JA to AA, [ante March 15], June 17, 1780, *AFC*, 3:301, 366. AA readily adopted her husband's practice of referring to these small shipments as "presents," and literal readings of the Adamses' language has contributed to historians' failure to recognize the extent of their commercial operations. AA to JA, May 1, July 24, Sept. 3, 1780, *AFC*, 3:335, 381, 406.
150¶1 AA to JA, [ca. July 15, 1778], *AFC*, 3:xiv, 62; Thomas Bumstead, advertisement, *Independent Chronicle*, Aug. 30, 1781.
150¶2 AA to JA, April 15, May 1, 1780, JA to AA, June 17, 1780, *AFC*, 3: 321, 335, 366.
150¶3 RC to JA, Jan. 18, 1780, *AFC*, 3:264.
151¶1 RC to JA, April 26, 1780, *AFC*, 3:326–27.
152¶1 AA to JA, May 1, 1780, *AFC*, 3:335.
152¶2 JA to AA, Feb. 16, 1780, AA to JA, May 1, 1780, *AFC*, 3:275, 335.
152¶3 AA to JA, May 1, 1780, July 24, Sept. 3, 1780, *AFC*, 3:335, 381, 406.
153¶2 John Bishop to AA, Oct. 16, 1780, MOW to AA, Dec. 21, 1780, AA to MOW, Jan. 8, 1781, *AFC*, 4:8, 42, 60.
153¶3 AA to JA, April 15, May 1, July 5, Nov. 13, 1780, Dec. 9, 1781, John Bishop to AA, Oct. 16, 1780, MOW to AA, Dec. 21, 1780, AA to MOW, Jan. 8, 1781, *AFC*, 3:321, 335, 372, 4:17, 258, 8, 42, 60.

153¶4 AA to JA, Sept. 3, 1780, JA to AA, March 15, 24, 1780, Sept. 17, 1782, *AFC*, 3:406, 302, 317, 4:381.

154¶1 AA to JA, Nov. 13–24, 1780, Jean de Neufville & Son to AA, May 25, 1781, *AFC*, 4:16, 132.

154¶2 AA to JA, July 5, Nov. 13–24, 1780, Jan. 15, April 23, Sept. 29, Dec. 9, 1781, *AFC*, 3:371, 4:15, 64, 106, 221, 258.

155¶1 JL to AA, Sept. 3, 1780, AA to JL, Sept. 17, 1780, *AFC*, 3:409, 415; Edith B. Gelles, *Portia: The World of Abigail Adams* (Bloomington, Ind., 1992), 62–63.

155¶2 JL to AA, May 14, 1780, *AFC*, 3:343; Pelatiah Webster, *Political Essays on the Nature and Operation of Money, Public Finances, and Other Subjects . . .* (Philadelphia, 1791), 501–2; Ferguson, *Power of the Purse*, 32; Gelles, *Portia*, 63–64.

Chapter 14: "A Queer Being," 1780–1781

156¶1 JL to AA, Sept. 1, 1778, Jan. 19, 1779, Jan. 13, 1780, AA to JL, [February–March 1779], *AFC*, 3:83, 150, 258, 184.

157¶1 AA to JL, March 1, [June 24], [Aug. 19], 1778, JL to AA, Jan. 13, 1780, *AFC*, 2:397, 3:48, 76, 257; *AFC*, 2:xxxiv; Akers, *Abigail Adams* (1980 edition), 64–65; Gelles, *Portia*, 59. For another correspondent who called AA "Portia," see JT to AA, Nov. 19, 1782, *AFC*, 5:41.

157¶2 Middlekauf, *Glorious Cause*, 448–49.

158¶1 AA to JT, July 21, [1780], *AFC*, 3:378; L. H. Butterfield, "General Washington's Sewing Circle," *American Heritage*, N.S. 2 (summer 1951): 380; Norton, *Liberty's Daughters*, 178–88.

158¶2 AA to JA, July 5, 1780, *AFC*, 3:372; Rosemarie Zagarri, *Revolutionary Backlash: Women and Politics in the Early American Republic* (Philadelphia, 2007), 75.

158¶3 AA to JA, July 5, 1780, *AFC*, 3:372.

159¶2 AA to JA, March 16–18, April 21, 1776, JA to AA, April 12, 1776, AA to MOW, Feb. 28, 1780, *AFC*, 1:359, 389, 376, 3:289; *Letters Written by the Late Right Honourable Philip Dormer Stanhope, Earl of Chesterfield, To His Son, Philip Stanhope . . .*, vol. 1 (Dublin, 1774), 303.

159¶3 AA to MOW, Feb. 28, 1780, *AFC*, 3:289.

159¶4 *Independent Chronicle*, Jan. 18, 1781; AA to JA, Jan. 21, 1781, *AFC*, 4:67.

160¶1 AA to MOW, Jan. 8, 1781, AAS to ECN, Feb. 13, 1779, *AFC*, 4:61, 3:169, 4:78n.

160¶2 AA to JQA, Jan. 21, 1781, AA to JQA and CA, Feb. 8, 1781, *AFC*, 4:68, 77.

161¶1 AA to IS2, April 20, 1771, AA to JT, Feb. 5, 1781, *AFC*, 1:76, 4:75.

161¶2 AA to JT, Feb. 5, 1781, *AFC*, 4:75.

162¶1 Alice Lee Shippen to Elizabeth Welles Adams, June 17, [1781], *AFC*, 4:154–55n.

162¶2 Alice Lee Shippen to Elizabeth Welles Adams, June 17, [1781], *AFC*, 4:154–55n; Edmund S. Morgan, *Benjamin Franklin* (New Haven, Conn., 2002), 281–83.

162¶3 AA to Elbridge Gerry, July 20, 1781, AA to JL, [July 20–August 6, 1781], Sept. 12, 1781, *AFC*, 4:183, 185, 210.

163¶2 JL to AA, Feb. 27, 1781, *AFC*, 4:82.

164¶10 AA to JL, [June 23, 1781], *AFC*, 4:160–62n. JL suspected that AA had made the whole thing up, but she insisted that the conversation was "no fiction." "There realy existed the Dialogue I related, and nearly in the same words as I could recollect," she told him. AA to JL, Sept. [20?], [1781], *AFC*, 4:216.

164¶11 JL to AA, June 16, 1781, *AFC*, 4:149.

165¶1 JL to AA, June 16, 1781, *AFC*, 4:149.

165¶2 In JL's 1779 letter discussing the danger of his wife becoming pregnant, his language was so opaque that AA apparently missed the hint. JL to AA, Jan. 19, 1779, July 13, 1781, *AFC*, 3:150, 4:173.

165¶3 AA to JA, July 16, 1777, AA to JL, Sept. 12, 1781, *AFC*, 2:282, 4:209.

166¶1 AA to JL, [Sept. 20, 1781?], *AFC*, 4:215.

166¶3 JA to AA, July 11, Dec. 2, 1781, *AFC*, 4:170, 249; JA, "Second Autobiography," quoted in *AFC*, 4:170n.

166¶4 AA to JA, Oct. 21, 1781, *AFC*, 4:229–31.

167¶1 AA to JL, Nov. 15, 1781, JL to AA, Dec. 4, 1781, AA to JL, [Jan. 8?, 1782], *AFC*, 4:244–45n, 254, 274.

167¶2 AA to JA, Dec. 9, 1781, *AFC*, 4:256.

167¶3 William Jackson to JA, Oct. 26, 1781, *AFC*, 4:235.

168¶1 AA to JA, Jan. 15, Sept. 29, 1781, *AFC*, 4:64, 221; Whitney K. Bates, "The State Finances of Massachusetts, 1780–1789" (master's thesis, University of Wisconsin, 1948); Van Beck Hall, *Politics without Parties: Massachusetts, 1780–1791* ([Pittsburgh], 1972), 107–9.

168¶2 JA to AA, Dec. 2, 1781, *AFC*, 4:250.

168¶3 AA to JA, April 25, 1782, *AFC*, 4:315. The basis for my assertion that Tufts was the unnamed "Friend" to whom AA referred is that, twenty years later, when she mentioned her private funds to her son Thomas, she explained that she had amassed this cache of money over the course of "many years" and "placed it in the Hands of our good Friend Dr. Tufts." Furthermore, she stated in 1815 that "Dr Tufts has always been my trustee." AA to TBA, Feb. 28, 1802, AP#401; AA to JQA, Dec. 24, 1815, AP#428.

169¶1 JA to AA, July 1, 1782, *AFC*, 4:337.

169¶2 Elbridge Gerry to AA, Nov. 24, 1783, *AFC*, 5:275.

169¶3 RC to JA, Jan. 31, 1782, *AFC*, 4:281.

170¶1 RC to JA, Nov. 3, 1781, Jan. 31, 1782, AA to JA, Dec. 9, 1781, March 17–25, 1782, *AFC*, 4:241, 282, 258, 296.

170¶2 AA to JA, July 17–18, 1782, *AFC*, 4:346. As a lawyer who frequently represented creditors who sued debtors, JA also benefited from his neighbors' extravagance, and years earlier he had betrayed a consciousness of this irony that was similar to AA's. "The hourly Arrival of Ships from England deeply loaden with dry Goods, and the extravagant Credit that is dayly given to Country Traders," he wrote, "opens a Prospect very melancholly to the public, tho profitable to Us, of a speedy revival of the suing Spirit." JA to AA, Sept. 17, 1771, *AFC*, 1:81.

CHAPTER 15: "NOTHING VENTURE NOTHING HAVE," 1781–1782

171¶1 AA to JA, April 25, 1782, *AFC*, 4:315; Withey, *Dearest Friend*, 134–35, 215; Gelles, *Portia*, 45; Michael A. Bellesiles, *Revolutionary Outlaws: Ethan Allen and the Struggle for Independence on the Early American Frontier* (Charlottesville, Va., 1993).

171¶2 AA to JA, April 25, 1782, *AFC*, 4:315; Jan. 28, 1782, *JCC*, 22:58–60.

171¶3 JA to AA, March 22, 1782, *AFC*, 4:300.

172¶1 It is true that in 1776, AA had, on behalf of other American women, threatened to rebel against a set of laws that women had had no role in devising—but only in jest. AA to JA, March 31–April 5, 1776, June 17, 1782, *AFC*, 1:370, 4:328.

172¶2 AA to JA, June 17, 1782, *AFC*, 4:328; Frank Smith, "The Authorship of 'An Occasional Letter on the Female Sex,'" *American Literature* 2 (November 1930): 277–80; Crane, "Political Dialgoue and the Spring of Abigail's Discontent," 766–68. Five of the verbs AA used in her 1776 appeal were in the imperative form; in her June 17, 1782, statement none was. In New Jersey, a few women who owned and controlled property (which excluded those who were married) had begun voting, but if AA had learned about this remarkable development by 1782—and there is no indication that she had—she probably would have surmised, correctly, that this was an anomaly that was not destined to last. Sophie H. Drinker, "Votes for Women in 18th-Century New Jersey," *New Jersey History* 80 (January 1962): 31–45; Judith Apter Klinghoffer and Lois Elkis, " 'The Petticoat Electors': Women's Suffrage in New Jersey, 1776–1807," *Journal of the Early Republic* 12 (Summer 1992): 159–93.

173¶1 AA to JA, March 31–April 5, 1776, June 17, 1782, *AFC*, 1:370, 4:328.

173¶2 AA to JA, March 31–April 5, 1776, June 17, 1782, *AFC*, 1:370, 4:328.

173¶3 AA to JA, July 17–18, Aug. 5, 1782, *AFC*, 4:344, 357.

174¶1 AA to JA, July 17–18, 1782, *AFC*, 4:344.

174¶2 AA to JA, May 1, 1780, April 23, 1781, July 17–18, 1782, *AFC*, 3:335, 4:106, 347.

175¶1 JA to AAS, Sept. 26, 1782, JA to AA, Oct. 12, 1782, *AFC*, 4:383–84, 5:15. Neither JA nor his son JQA, who followed in his footsteps as an American diplomat, was ever granted the rank of ambassador, but friends and relatives of both men frequently referred to them as such in informal correspondence, a usage that is also adopted here.

175¶2 AA to JA, Oct. 8, 1782, *AFC*, 5:7.

175¶3 AAS to ECN, [April], [ca. Dec. 22], [1782], *AFC*, 4:318–19, 5:52.

176¶1 AAS to JA, May 10, 1783, *AFC*, 5:156.

177¶1 AAS to ECN, [April 1782], *AFC*, 4:318.

177¶2 AAS to ECN, June [1782], *AFC*, 4:335. On fears for RC's health, see AA to JA, June 17, July 17–18, 1782, *AFC*, 4: 326–27, 344.

177¶3 AA to JA, March 17–25, July 17–18, 1782, *AFC*, 4:295, 345; Jan. 28, 1782, *JCC*, 22:58–60; *AFC*, 4:316n; Gelles, *Abigail and John*, 138.

178¶1 AA to JA, April 23, 1781, April 25, July 17–18, Oct. 25, 1782, *AFC*, 4:106, 315, 345, 5:23.

178¶2 JA to AA, Nov. 6, 1778, AA to JA, Sept. 5, Oct. 25, 1782, *AFC*, 3:115, 4:377, 5:23.

178¶3 AA to JA, July 17–18, 1782, JA to AA, Oct. 12, 1782, *AFC*, 4:345, 5:15.

179¶1 AA had actually enclosed a request for "a set of china blew and white for a dining table consisting of Dishes and plates" in an order she had placed with her husband the previous spring, but at the time she had not mentioned that the china was meant for her own use rather than resale. One reason she repeated the order in August was her concern that JA might not "know what a set is." AA to JA, March 17–25, Aug. 5, 1782, May 7, 1783, AFC, 4:297, 357, 5:153.

179¶2 AA to JA, Aug. 5, Sept. 3, 5, 1782, *AFC*, 4:357, 372, 376.

179¶3 Mackenzie, *The Man of Feeling* (London, 1771); Mackenzie, *The Man of the World* (2 vols.; London, 1773), 1:68; AA to JA, Nov. 13–25, 1782, *AFC*, 5:35–36.

180¶1 AA to JA, Sept. 3, 1782, *AFC*, 4:372.

180¶2 AA to JA, [Oct. 25, 1778], AA to JQA, Nov. 13, 1782, *AFC*, 3:111, 5:xlii, 37–38.

180¶3 AA to JA, Dec. 23, 1782, *AFC*, 5:56.

180¶4 AA to JA, Dec. 23, 1782, RT to AA, [1782], quoted in AA to JA, Dec. 23, 1782, *AFC*, 5:56, 57; G. Thomas Tanselle, *Royall Tyler* (Cambridge, Mass., 1967), 8, 225–26n.

181¶1 AA to JA, Dec. 23, 1782, *AFC*, 5:56.

181¶2 AA to JA, Dec. 23, 1782, *AFC*, 5:57–58.

181¶3 AA to JA, Dec. 23, 1782, *AFC*, 5:56.

Chapter 16: "I Will Run You in Debt," 1783–1784

182¶1 JA to AA, Jan. 22, Feb. 4, 1783, *AFC*, 5:74–75, 88.

182¶2 JA to AA, Jan. 22, 29, 1783, *AFC*, 5:75, 83; Withey, *Dearest Friend*, 145.

183¶1 JA to AA, Jan. 22, 1783, *AFC*, 5:75.

183¶2 JA to AA, Jan. 22, 29, Feb. 4, 1783, *AFC*, 5:75, 83, 88.

183¶3 AA to JA, April 7, 28–29, June 20, 1783, *AFC*, 5:118, 143–44, 181.

184¶1 William Jackson to JA, Oct. 26, 1781, AA to JA, April 7, 1783, ESSP to AA and MSC, March 15, [1783], *AFC*, 4:235, 5:118, 105.

184¶2 AA to JA, April 7, 1783, AA to Charles Storer, April 28, 1783, *AFC*, 5:118, 146.

185¶1 AA to JA, May 7, 1783, *AFC*, 5:152–53. David P. Szatmary places the market glut much later than AA did. He notes that the importation of British goods into Massachusetts increased in 1783 and boomed in 1784. See his *Shays' Rebellion: The Making of an Agrarian Insurrection* (Amherst, Mass., 1980), 21–22, 26–29; Richard B. Morris, *The Peacemakers: The Great Powers and American Independence* (New York, 1965), 409.

185¶2 AA to JA, April 28–29, 1783, *AFC*, 5:141. My thanks to Anthony Galasso for this insight.

185¶3 AA to JT, Oct. 20, 1783, *AFC*, 5:261, 305n.

185¶4 William Smith, Sr., last will and testament, Sept. 12, 1783, *AFC*, 5:247.

186¶1 AA to JA, Jan. 3, 1784, *AFC*, 5:292.

186¶2 AA to JA, Nov. 11, 1783, CA to AA, [post Dec. 5, 1792], *AFC*, 5:269, 9:336; CA to James Whitelaw, Feb. 25, 1798, James Whitelaw Papers, doc. 326, folder 10, Vermont Historical Society, Montpelier; JQA to TBA, Oct. 2, 1798, "Memorandum—For My Dear Wife, Louisa C. Adams" (enclosed in JQA to LCA, May 7, 1814), AP#131, 418; Gelles, *Abigail and John*, 138; Carole Shammas, "English Inheritance Law and Its Transfer to the Colonies," *American Journal of Legal History* 31 (April 1987), 147.

187¶1 ESSP to MSC, April 6, 1781, William Smith, Sr., last will and testament, Sept. 12, 1783, AA to MSC, Sept. 11, 1785, *AFC*, 4:98, 5:247, 6:357.

187¶2 William Smith, Sr., last will and testament, Sept. 12, 1783, *AFC*, 5:247.

188¶1 AA to JA, May 7, Aug. 14, Nov. 20, Dec. 27, 1783, *AFC*, 5:153, 222, 271, 285–86.

188¶2 AA to JA, Dec. 27, 1783, *AFC*, 5:286; Withey, *Dearest Friend*, 135; Gelles, *Abigail and John*, 138.

188¶3 AA to JA, Dec. 27, 1783, *AFC*, 5:286.

189¶1 AA to JA, Jan. 3, 1784, *AFC*, 5:292; Hall, *Politics Without Parties*, 109.

189¶2 AA to JA, April 25, 1782, Jan. 3, 1784, *AFC*, 4:315, 5:292.

189¶3 Wilhem & Jan Willink to JA, July 5, 1791, JQA to Wilhem and Jan Willink, Nov. 14, 1801, AP#375, 135.

190¶2 AA to JA, Dec. 27, 1783, *AFC*, 5:285.

190¶3 AA to JA, Dec. 27, 1783, *AFC*, 5:285.

190¶4 AA to JA, Nov. 11, 1783, Feb. 11, 1784, *AFC*, 5:267, 303. The editors of *AFC* conjecture (5:305n) that Phoebe's marriage to Bristol was called off at the last minute, but it seems likelier that he had died after marrying Phoebe.

191¶1 Akers, *Abigail Adams* (1980 edition), 77.

191¶2 AAS to AA, Jan. 6, 1784, AA to JA, May 25, 1784, *AFC*, 5:296–97, 331.

191¶3 JA to AA, Jan. 25, 1784, JA to RT, April 3, 1784, AA to MSC, Aug. 2, 1784, *AFC*, 5:301–2n, 317, 417.

192¶1 AA to CT, June 18, 1784, AA to JA, April 12, 1784, *AFC*, 5:346, 318.

192¶2 AA, journal, June 20, 1784, in *DAJA*, 3:154; *AFC*, 3:322n.

Chapter 17: "A Lady at Sea," 1784

193¶1 AA, journal, June 20–[July 20], 1784, *DAJA*, 3:154–66; AA to IS2, April 20, 1771, AA to MSC, July 6–[30], 1784, *AFC*, 1:76, 5:361.

193¶2 AA to MSC, July 6–[30], 1784, *AFC*, 5:358.

194¶1 AA, journal, June 20, [23], 1784, *DAJA*, 3:155, 157; AA to MSC, July 6–[30], 1784, *AFC*, 5:358–59.

194¶2 AA to MSC, July 6–[30], 1784, *AFC*, 5:359.

194¶3 AA to MSC, July 6–[30], 1784, *AFC*, 5:360–62.

195¶1 AA to RT, July 10, 1784, *AFC*, 5:392.

195¶2 AA to CT, June 18, 1784, *AFC*, 5:346.

195¶3 AA to JA, Aug. 22, 1777, AA to MSC, July 6–[30], 1784, AA to ESSP, [July 11, 1784], *AFC*, 2:323, 5:364, 395. AA's biographers seldom fail to quote the disparaging remarks she made about the cook, but they frequently omit the fact that she was careful to note that he was a "Negro." Withey, *Dearest Friend*, 156; Natalie S. Bober, *Abigail Adams: Witness to a Revolution* (New York, 1995), 124; Gelles, *Abigail and John*, 158.

196¶1 AA, journal, July 2, 1784, *DAJA*, 3:161; AA to MSC, July 6–[30], 1784, *AFC*, 5:365, 368–69.
196¶2 AA to MSC, July 6–[30], 1784, *AFC*, 5:369.
197¶1 AA to MSC, July 6–[30], *AFC*, 5:369–70.
197¶2 AA to MSC, July 6–[30], 1784, *AFC*, 5:370–71.
197¶3 AA to MSC, July 6–[30], Aug. 2, 1784, AA to JA, July 23, 1784, *AFC*, 5:376, 417, 397; AA, journal, July 9, 1784, *DAJA*, 3:165.
198¶1 AA to MSC, July 6–[30], 1784, AA to ESSP, July 28, 1784, *AFC*, 5:373, 378, 402.
199¶1 AA to MSC, July 6–[30], 1784, AA to LCG, Sept. 5, 1784, *AFC*, 5:372–73, 383, 436.
199¶2 AA to MSC, July 6–[30], 1784, *AFC*, 5:373, 381; Anne Buck, *Dress in Eighteenth-Century England* (New York, 1979), 52–54.
200¶1 AA to MSC, July 6–[30], 1784, *AFC*, 5:374, 380.
200¶7 AA to MSC, July 6–[30], 1784, *AFC*, 5:382.
200¶9 AA to MSC, July 6–[30], 1784, *AFC*, 5:382. The Smith sisters' dispute over the word *feelings* unfortunately left no other traces in the written record.
201¶6 AAS, quoted in *Journal and Correspondence of Miss Adams*, 1:viii.
201¶7 Ibid.
201¶8 JA to JQA, Aug. 1, 1784, *AFC*, 5:416; AAS, quoted in *Journal and Correspondence of Miss Adams*, 1:viii.
201¶9 AA to LCG, Sept. 5, 1784, *AFC*, 5:436.
202¶1 AA to JA, Aug. 29, 1776, AA to ECN, Sept. 5, 1784, AA to MSC, [Sept. 5, 1784], *AFC*, 2:112, 5:433–35, 444.
203¶1 AA to MSC, [Sept. 5, 1784], AA to CT, Sept. 8, 1784, *AFC*, 5:441, 456–57.
203¶2 AA to MSC, [Sept. 5, 1784], *AFC*, 5:439–45n.
204¶1 AA to MSC, [Sept. 5, 1784], *AFC*, 5:440–42.
204¶2 AA to MSC, [Sept. 5, 1784], *AFC*, 5:443. Other upper-class observers shared Adams's astonishment that Parisian workers, especially women, had somehow managed to procure fancy accessories like fur muffs and fingerless lace mittens. Madeleine Delpierre, *Dress in France in the Eighteenth Century*, trans. Caroline Beamish (New Haven, 1997), 42–43; Jennifer M. Jones, *Sexing La Mode: Gender, Fashion, and Commercial Culture in Old Regime France* (Oxford, 2004), 74.
204¶3 AA to MOW, Sept. 5, 1784, *AFC*, 5:447.
205¶1 AA to MOW, Sept. 5, 1784, *AFC*, 5:447. Interestingly, AAS used the recently married Madame Grand as evidence of French *im*morality, since she had spoken openly about her pregnancy with two men to whom she was not related, one of whom was JQA. AAS to ECN, Sept. 30, 1784, *AFC*, 5:465.
205¶2 AA to MOW, Sept. 5, 1784, *AFC*, 5:447–48.
206¶1 AAS to LCG, Sept. 4, 1784, AA to LCG, Sept. 5, 1784, AA to RT, [Sept. 5, 1784], *AFC*, 5:431, 436–38, 445. Emily Martha Silkaitis points out that Madame Helvetius probably cleaned up the mess not with her chemise (an undergarment) but with her gown, which was designed to look like a chemise. A chemise dress had a "low round neckline gathered in with a drawstring." Silkaitis, personal communication to the author, June 25, 2009; Joan Nunn, *Fashion in Costume, 1200–1980* (New York, 1984), 93.

206¶2 AA wasted no time in telling RT about her exchange with Pauline. AAS to ECN, Sept. 4, 30, 1784, AA to MSC, Sept. 5, 1784, AA to RT, [Sept. 5, 1784], *AFC*, 5:428, 465, 434, 446 (my translation).

207¶1 AAS to ECN, Sept. 4, 1784, AAS to LCG, Sept. 4, 1784, *AFC*, 5:429, 431. On corsets (which were actually getting somewhat looser by the mid-1780s), and elaborate headdresses, see Delpierre, *Dress in France in the Eighteenth Century*, 21, 40.

Chapter 18: "This Money Which I Call Mine," 1784–1785

208¶1 JA to AA, Jan. 25, 1784, AA to MSC, Aug. 2, 1784, *AFC*, 5:301–2n, 417.

208¶2 It is possible that Elizabeth was being sarcastic. ESSP to MSC, Aug. 24, 1784, ESSP to AA, Dec. 5, 1784, *AFC*, 5:424, 6:11.

208¶3 MSC to AA, April 25, 1785, *AFC*, 6:93; AAS, journal, Nov. 7, 28, 1784, *Journal and Correspondence of Miss Adams*, 1:32, 34.

209¶1 ESSP to AA, Oct. [ca. 15], 1784, AA to ECN, Dec. 3, 1784, AA to MSC, May 8 [*sic;* actually ante 5], 1785, *AFC*, 5:472–73, 6:5, 119. The historian Jon Kukla makes an intriguing case that AA shared some of her feminist views with TJ. Kukla notes that after the Adamses left France, TJ, who remained behind, told AA, "I do love this people with all my heart. I pray you to observe, that I have used the term *people* and that this is a noun of the masculine as well as feminine gender." This statement, Kukla observes, "represents the only time in all of his voluminous writings that Jefferson used gender-inclusive language." *Mr. Jefferson's Women* (New York, 2007), 145.

209¶2 MSC to AA, Oct. 3, 10, 1784, April 25, 1785, *AFC*, 5:468, 470, 6:95.

210¶1 AA to MSC, Dec. 9–12, 1784, Sept. 11, 1785, AA to CT, Sept. 16, 1785, MSC to AA, April 25, 1785, *AFC*, 6:20, 359, 364, 95–96.

210¶2 AA to CT, Sept. 8, 1784, Jan. 3, 1785, CT to AA, Dec. 1, 1784, AA to MSC, Dec. 9–12, 1784, *AFC*, 5:459, 6:44, 2, 20.

210¶3 MSC to AA, Aug. 7, 1784, July 19–Aug. 7, 1785, AA to MSC, Sept. 11, 1785, CT to AA, April 19–May 1, 1785, *AFC*, 5:420, 6:234, 359, 87.

211¶1 ESSP to AA, April 25, 1785, AA to ESSP, Jan. 11, 1785, *AFC*, 6:101–2, 56.

211¶2 ESSP to AA, March 26, 1784, MSC to AA, April 25, 1785, Catharine Louisa Salmon Smith to AA, April 27, 1785, *AFC*, 5:313, 6:96, 111–12 (AA's letter to her sister-in-law does not survive, and its contents must be inferred from Catharine's reply). "Lords of the Creation," a sarcastic appellation for men that was in surprisingly common use, was reportedly derived from Genesis 1:28, though it is not a direct quotation. Ivor H. Evans, ed., *Brewer's Dictionary of Phrase and Fable*, Centenary edn. (London, 1970), 659; Elizabeth Knowles, ed., *The Oxford Dictionary of Phrase and Fable* (Oxford, 2000), 619.

212¶1 JA to CT, Sept. 5, 1784, April 24, 178[5], AA to CT, Sept. 8, 1784, *AFC*, 5:455, 6:88–90, 5:458.

212¶2 AA to CT, [April 26]–May 10, 1785, CT to AA, Dec. 1, 1784, CT to JA, Oct. 6, 1785, *AFC*, 6:108, 2, 411.

213¶1 AA to JA, April 25, 1782, AA to CT, [April 26]–May 10, 1785, CT to AA, Jan. 5, 1786, *AFC*, 4:315, 6:108, 7:5–6. On married women's effective control of personal property despite legal prohibitions, see Joan R. Gundersen and Gwen Victor Gampel, "Married Women's Legal Status in Eighteenth-Century New York and Virginia," *WMQ*, 3rd ser., 39 (January 1982): 131–33; Elaine Forman Crane, *Ebb Tide in New England: Women, Seaports, and Social Change, 1630–1800* (Boston, 1998), 165–66; Mary Beth Norton, "'Either Married or to Bee Married': Women's Legal Inequality in Early America," in Carla Gardina Pestana and Sharon V. Salinger, eds., *Inequality in Early America* (Hanover, N.H., 1999), 30.

213¶2 AA to CT, Jan. 3, 1785, *AFC*, 6:41–42.

213¶3 AA to CT, Jan. 3, 1785, March 8, 1785, JA to CT, March 5, 1785, *AFC*, 6:41–42, 76–77, 71.

214¶1 JA to CT, March 5, 1785, *AFC*, 6:71.

214¶2 AA to CT, March 8, 1785, *AFC*, 6:77.

215¶1 AA to CT, March 8, 1785, *AFC*, 6:76–77.

215¶2 AA to RT, [Jan. 4, 1785], AA to ESSP, Dec. 14, 1784, *AFC*, 6:46, 29.

215¶3 AA to MSC, Dec. 9–12, 1784, AA to Hannah Quincy Lincoln Storer, Jan. 20, 1785, *AFC*, 6:14, 65–66. On Boston's lack of theaters until the 1790s, see JQA to AAS, Oct. 1, 1785, *AFC*, 6:399; Kenneth Silverman, *A Cultural History of the American Revolution: Painting, Music, Literature, and the Theatre in the Colonies and the United States from the Treaty of Paris to the Inauguration of George Washington, 1763–1789* (New York, 1987), 557.

216¶1 AA to MSC, Feb. 20–March 13, 1785, *AFC*, 6:67.

216¶2 AA to MSC, Feb. 20–March 13, 1785, *AFC*, 6:67–69.

217¶1 AA to MSC, Dec. 9–12, 1784, Feb. 20–March 13, 1785, AA to CT, [April 26]–May 10, 1785, AA to MOW, May 10, 1785, *AFC*, 6:15–16, 67, 106, 139.

217¶2 AA to TJ, June 6, 1785, *AFC*, 6:169–70.

Chapter 19: "Honour, Honour, Is at Stake," 1785–1786

218¶1 AA to TJ, June 6, 1785, AA to ECN, Sept. 2, 1785, *AFC*, 6:171, 330.

219¶1 AA to MSC, June [22? appears at 24]–28, 1785, *AFC*, 6:190.

219¶2 AA to MSC, June [22? appears at 24]–28, 1785, AA to JQA, June 26–27, [1785], *AFC*, 6:189–90, 192, 196; Buck, *Dress in Eighteenth-Century England*, 28.

219¶3 AA to CT, Aug. 18, 1785, *AFC*, 6:283.

219¶4 JA to JQA, June 26, 1785, AAS to JQA, July 4–Aug. 11, 1785, AA to MSC[?], [ca. July/Aug. 1785], AA to JQA, Aug. 11, 1785, ECN to AA, Sept. 5–18, 1785, *AFC*, 6:198, 212, 242, 260, 337.

220¶1 AA to MSC, Sept. 11, 1785, *AFC*, 6:358–59.

220¶2 AA to MSC, Sept. 11, 1785, *AFC*, 6:358–59.

221¶2 AA to MSC, Aug. 15, 1785, July 4–23, 1786, *AFC*, 6:276, 7:236.

222¶1 AA to MSC, Aug. 15, 1785, *AFC*, 6:276.

222¶2 JA, quoted in AA to MSC, Aug. 15, 1785, AAS to RT, [ca. Aug. 11, 1785], *AFC*, 6:277, 262.

222¶3 AA to MOW, May 10, 1785, AA to JQA, June 26, [1785], AAS to JQA, Dec. 5–9, 1785, *AFC*, 6:139–40, 196, 480. For opposition to the Cincinnati, see "Cassius" [Aedanus Burke], *Considerations on the Society or Order of Cincinnati* . . . (Charleston, S.C., 1783).

223¶1 AAS to JQA, July 4–Aug. 11, 1785, *AFC*, 6:207.

223¶2 AA to CT, Jan. 10, 1786, AA to JQA, Feb. 16, 1786, AA to MSC, Feb. 26, 1786, AA to Charles Storer, March 23, 1786, *AFC*, 7:8, 64, 77, 114.

224¶1 AA to WSS, [Sept. 18, 1785], AA to MSC, Jan. 26, 178[6], *AFC*, 6:366, 7:30.

224¶2 AA to MSC, July 4–23, 1786, AA to JQA, Feb. 16, 1786, AAS to JQA, Aug. 26–Sept. 13, 1785, *AFC*, 7:236–37, 64, 6:302.

225¶1 AA to ESSP, March 4, 1786, *AFC*, 7:81.

225¶2 William Shakespeare, *Othello*, I.iii; AA to ESSP, March 4, 1786, AA to WSS, [Sept. 18, 1785], *AFC*, 7:81; 6:366–68.

226¶1 MSC to AA, Nov. 8, [1785], Dec. 10, 1785, *AFC*, 6:454–55, 486.

227¶1 AAS to JQA, Jan. 22–[Feb. 8], 1786, *AFC*, 7:12.

227¶2 AA to TJ, Aug. 12, 1785, MSC to AA, Aug. 14–[Sept. 16], 1785, AA to CT, Aug. 18, 1785, TJ to AA, Sept. 25, 1785, *AFC*, 6:264, 273–74, 285, 391.

227¶3 AAS to JQA, Feb. 9–27, [1786], *AFC*, 7:33–36.

228¶1 AA to MSC, April 6, 1786, *AFC*, 7:133.

228¶2 AA to LCG, April 2, 1786, AA to TJ, Aug. 12, 1785, AA to ESSP, [Aug. 15, 1785], *AFC*, 7:126–27, 6:263, 281.

229¶1 AA to ECN, Sept. 2, 1785, JQA to AAS, March 15–28, 1786, ESSP to AA, March 18, 1786, JQA to AAS, April 2, 1786, AAS to JQA, April 25–29, 1786, AA to MSC, July 4–23, 1786, AA to ESSP, July 19, 1786, AA to JQA, July 21, 1786, *AFC*, 6:330, 7:90, 93, 130, 151, 239, 263, 274.

Chapter 20: "The Grieved Mind Loves the Soother," 1786–1787

230¶1 MSC to AA, March 22–April 9, Feb. 9, 1786, *AFC*, 7:107, 48. MSC was all too aware that RT suspected her of being his chief critic. He "abus'd me and charg'd me with things which were false," she told AA. In accusing her of poisoning AAS against him, RT was "endeavouring to rob me of the affection of my dear Niece," MSC wrote, "for this I know not how to forgive him." MSC to AA, May [21], 1786, *AFC*, 7:184.

230¶2 ECN to AA, May 20, 1786, Charles Storer to AA, Aug. 15, 1786, *AFC*, 7:171–72, 321.

231¶1 Charles Storer to AA, Aug. 15, 1786, *AFC*, 7:321.

231¶2 AA to CT, Feb. 21, 1786, MSC to AA, March 22–April 9, July 2, 1786, *AFC*, 7:73, 105, 232.

231¶3 AA to MSC, June 13, July 4–23, 1786, JA to RC, July 4, 1786, *AFC*, 7:218, 235, 241.

231¶4 AA to MSC, June 13, 1786, July 4–23, 1786, *AFC*, 7:218–20, 235 (quotation mark misplaced in the original).

232¶1 AA to MSC, June 13, July 4–23, 1786, *AFC*, 7:217, 235–36. On the common practice of newlyweds not immediately establishing their own households, see Ulrich, *Midwife's Tale*, 140–42.

232¶4 AA to MSC, July 4–23, 1786, *AFC*, 7:236.
232¶5 AA to MSC, July 4–23, 1786, *AFC*, 7:239.
233¶1 AA to ECN, July 18, 1786, MSC to AA, July 19–Aug. 7, 1785, *AFC*, 7:258–59, 6:232.
233¶2 AA to MSC, May 21, 1786, MSC to AA, July 10–11, 1786, *AFC*, 7:178, 248.
233¶3 AA to CT, Sept. 16, 1785, Thomas Welsh to AA, May 24, 1786, *AFC*, 6:363, 7:195.
234¶1 MSC to AA, Sept. 28, Oct. 8, 1786, *AFC*, 7:350, 354–55.
235¶1 MSC to AA, Sept. 24, Oct. 9, 1786, *AFC*, 7:343, 358.
235¶2 MSC to AA, Sept. 24, 1786, *AFC*, 7:343–44n.
235¶3 ECN to AA, May 20, 1786, MSC to AA, July 14–26, 1786, Nov. 26–Dec. 8, 1786, Oct. 9, 1786, *AFC*, 7:170–71, 253–54, 400, 359.
236¶1 MSC to AA, Oct. 9, 1786, *AFC*, 7:359.
236¶2 [William Whiting], "Some Remarks on the Conduct of the Inhabitants of the Commonwealth of Massachusetts in Interupting The Siting of the Judicial Courts . . . " (December 1786), in Stephen T. Riley, ed., "Dr. William Whiting and Shays' Rebellion," AAS *Proceedings* 66 (1957): 152.
237¶1 ESSP to AA, May 20, 1787, AA to ESSP, Oct. 15, 1786 (draft), AA to TJ, Jan. 29, 1787, *AFC*, 8:53, 7:375n, 455.
237¶2 MSC to AA, Sept. 24, Oct. 22, 1786, *AFC*, 7:342, 381.
238¶1 CT to AA, Jan. 2, 1787, *AFC*, 7:424.
238¶2 AA to CT, Jan. 24, March 10, 1787, *AFC*, 7:454, 8:7.
238¶3 *AFC*, 8:xxii.
239¶1 MSC to AA, June 29, 1787, *AFC*, 8:95.

Chapter 21: "Wisdom Says Soloman Maketh the Face to Shine," 1787

240¶1 AA to CT, Jan. 24, July 1, 1787, MSC to AA, April 22–May 20, June 29, 1787, CT to AA, May 21, June 30, 1787, *AFC*, 7:455, 8:104, 20–21, 95, 56–57, 100.
240¶2 AA to LCG, April 26–May 6, 1787, *AFC*, 8:25–27n; Proverbs 31:26–27.
241¶1 AA to LCG, April 26–May 6, 1787, *AFC*, 8:26.
241¶2 AA to LCG, April 26–May 6, 1787, AA to ESSP, May 2–6, 1787, AA to MSC, July 16, 1787, *AFC*, 8:24, 37, 119.
242¶1 AA to TJ, July 6, 1787, *AFC*, 8:108. TJ's youngest daughter, who had also remained in Virginia, died shortly after her father's departure for France. Annette Gordon-Reed, *The Hemingses of Monticello: An American Family* (New York, 2008), 163, 191.
242¶2 AA to TJ, June 26, 27, 1787, *AFC*, 8:92–94.
242¶3 AA to TJ, June 27, July 6, 1787, *AFC*, 8:92–94, 107; Gordon-Reed, *Hemingses of Monticello,* 194–95.
243¶1 AA to TJ, July 6, 10, 1787, *AFC*, 8:108, 109.
243¶2 MSC to AA, Nov. 26–[Dec. 8], 1786, April 22–May 20, *AFC*, 7:401, 8:18–19.
244¶1 MSC to AA, Nov. 26–[Dec. 8], 1786, July 16, 1787, *AFC*, 7:401, 8:122.
245¶1 AA to MSC, April 28, 1787, RC to JA, May 24, 1787, MSC to AA July 16, [1787], *AFC*, 8:32, 60, 122–23; *Massachusetts Centinel*, July 21, 1787.

245¶2 MSC to AA, July 21, [1787], ESSP to AA, July 22–Aug. 21, 1787, *AFC*, 8:132–33, 136.
246¶1 *Massachusetts Centinel*, July 21, 1787; JQA to AA, Aug. 1, 1787, *AFC*, 8:139.
246¶2 ESSP to AA, July 22–Aug. 21, 1787, *AFC*, 8:138.
247¶6 MSC to AA, Aug. 19–Sept. 1, 1787, *AFC*, 8:144.
247¶7 MSC to AA, Aug. 19–Sept. 1, 1787, *AFC*, 8:144.
247¶8 AA to CT, July 4, 1787, AP#370; AA to CT, July 1, Nov. 6, 1787, *AFC*, 8:104–5, 203.
248¶1 JA to CT, Aug. 27, 1787, MSC to AA, Sept. 30, 1787, CT to JA, Feb. 28, 1788, CT to JQA, March 5, 1788, *AFC*, 8:149, 174, 239, 241.
248¶2 CT to AA, Sept. 20–24, 1787, AA to MSC, Oct. 8, [ante 18], 1787, *AFC*, 8:162, 186, 193.
249¶1 AA to CT, July 4, 1787, AP#370; CT to AA, Oct. 31, 1787, *AFC*, 8:201.
249¶2 MSC placed her brother's death on September 10; ESSP heard that he had died on September 3. AA to MSC, Oct. 20, 1787, MSC to AA, Oct. 21, 1787, ESSP to AA, Nov. 17, 1787, *AFC*, 8:195, 197, 206.
249¶3 AA to MSC, Feb. 10, 1788, ESSP to AA, Nov. 17, 1787, *AFC*, 8:225, 206.
250¶1 ESSP to AA, Nov. 17, 1787, CT to AA, Dec. 18–27, 1787, *AFC*, 8:204, 210.
251¶2 JQA to CT, Feb. 16, 1788, CT to JQA, March 5, 1788, *AFC*, 8:231, 241.
252¶1 AA to CT, Jan. 17, 1790, *AFC*, 9:5–6.
252¶2 CT to AA, Dec. 18–27, 1787, *AFC*, 8:211.

Chapter 22: "I Design to Be Vastly Prudent," 1787–1789

254¶1 JQA to William Cranch, Dec. 8, 1787, in Merrill Jensen et al., eds., *The Documentary History of the Ratification of the Constitution* (18 vols. to date; Madison, Wisc., 1976), 4:401; MSC to AA, Dec. 22–26, 1787, *AFC*, 8:212–13.
255¶1 AA to CT, Jan. 1, 1788, *AFC*, 8:217.
255¶2 AA to MSC, Feb. 10, 1788, ESSP to MSC, May 8, 1788, *AFC*, 8:226, 260.
255¶3 AA to Margaret Smith, [March?] 22, [1788], *AFC*, 8:246.
256¶1 AAS to JQA, Feb. 10, 1788, *AFC*, 8:228.
257¶1 AA to AAS, July 7, [Aug. 6], 1788, *AFC*, 8:277–78, 284; AA to Elbridge Gerry, Dec. 31, 1796, MHS *Proceedings*, 3rd ser., 57 (May 1924): 499.
258¶1 JA to RC, June 29, 1766, AA to JA, Nov. 16, 1788, *AFC*, 1:52, 8:306.
259¶1 AA to JA, Nov. 16, 1788, *AFC*, 8:307.
259¶2 AA to MSC, Nov. 24, 1788, *AFC*, 8:308.
259¶3 AA to JA, Dec. 15, 1788, *AFC*, 8:318–19.
260¶1 AA to JQA, May 5–6, 1789, AA to JA, May 7, [1789], *AFC*, 8:347, 350.
260¶2 AA to JA, May 26, 1789, *AFC*, 8:359. On Phoebe, see AA, directions regarding houses and farms, [ca. June 17, 1789], *AFC*, 8:372–73.
261¶1 JQA to William Cranch, May 27, 1789, AA to JQA, May 30, 1789, *AFC*, 8:361, 363. On CA, see *AFC*, 8:xxviii.
261¶2 AA to JA, April 26, May 1, 7, 1789, AA to JQA, May 5–6, 1789, *AFC*, 8:337–39, 349, 346.

262¶1 JA to AA, May 24, 1789, Dec. 19, 1793, *AFC*, 8:357, 9:477; Act of Sept. 24, 1789, ch. 19, 1 *Stat.* 72; Holton, *Unruly Americans and the Origins of the Constitution*, 80.
262¶2 AA to Thomas Brand Hollis, Sept. 6, 1790, AA to MSC, June 28, 1789, *AFC*, 9:99, 8:379.
263¶1 AA to MSC, July 12, 1789, *AFC*, 8:388.
263¶2 AA to MSC, July 12, 1789, *AFC*, 8:388.
264¶2 JL to AA, April 12, 1789, AA to JL, April 22, 1789, *AFC*, 8:331–32n, 335 (quotation).
264¶3 MOW to JA, May 7, 1789, *Warren-Adams Letters*, 2:310; AA to MSC, July 12, 1789, *AFC*, 8:390.
265¶1 Akers, *Abigail Adams* (1980 edition), 9.

Chapter 23: "Much More Productive," 1789–1792

266¶1 AA to MSC, July 12, 1789, Aug. 29, 1790, *AFC*, 8:389, 9:95.
266¶2 AA to MSC, July 12, 1789, *AFC*, 8:389.
267¶1 MSC to AA, July 30, 1789, [post Sept. 22, 1790], *AFC*, 8:394, 9:121.
267¶2 AA to MSC, Aug. 9, Oct. 4, 11, 1789, April 28, 1790, *AFC*, 8:399, 414, 421, 9:51.
267¶3 AA to MSC, Aug. 9, 1789, *AFC*, 8:397.
268¶1 AA to MSC, Jan. 5–10, 1790, *AFC*, 9:1.
268¶2 AA to MSC, Jan. 5–10, 1790, *AFC*, 9:2.
268¶3 Hamilton, Report on Public Credit, Jan. 9, 1790, in *The Papers of Alexander Hamilton*, ed. Harold C. Syrett et al. (27 vols.; New York, 1961–1987), 6:51–168; Joseph Stancliffe Davis, *Essays in the Earlier History of American Corporations* (2 vols.; London, 1917), 1:187.
269¶1 AA to MSC, Sept. 1, 1789, Feb. 20, 1790, *AFC*, 8:402, 9:18.
270¶1 AA to MSC, Feb. 20, 1790, *AFC*, 9:17; *Annals of Congress*, 1st Cong., 2d sess., Feb. 22, 1790, 2:1344.
270¶2 AA to MSC, Nov. 1, 1789, *AFC*, 8:431; AA to MSC, March 15, 1790, *NL*, 154.
270¶3 AA to MSC, March 15, 1790, *AFC*, 9:26; Norton, *Liberty's Daughters*, 232–33.
271¶1 AA to MSC, May 30, 1790, *AFC*, 9:62.
271¶2 AA to MSC, Aug. 9, Oct. 4, 1789, July 4, 1790, *AFC*, 8:400, 413–14, 9:74.
272¶1 AA to MSC, Aug. 8, 1790, *AFC*, 9:85; Claudio Saunt, *A New Order of Things: Property, Power, and the Transformation of the Creek Indians, 1733–1816* (Cambridge, 1999), 80.
272¶2 *AFC*, 9:145n; Ferguson, *Power of the Purse*, 329.
273¶1 AA to CT, Aug. 2, Oct. 3, 1790 (excerpt), *AFC*, 9:84, 84n. Tufts also took delivery of JA's new federal bonds, but in doing so he did not designate himself as JA's trustee. CT to AA, Jan. 7, 1791, *AFC*, 9:176; CT ("Trustee to Mrs. Abigl. Adams"), receipt for U.S. Treasury bonds, Aug. 21, 1792, in Jeremiah Colburn autograph collection, 7:243, property of the Bostonian Society, on deposit with MHS; Tufts ("for John Adams Esq"), receipt for U.S. Treasury bonds, Dec. 23, 1790, in ibid., 7:241.

273¶2 AA to CT, Oct. 3, 1790, quoted in *AFC*, 9:84n. AA indicated JA's approval of the will she drew up in 1816 using language that resembled the formula often employed by female testators who had separate estates. The will affirmed that AA had acted "by and with his consent." Years earlier, a New Yorker named Elizabeth Sands, who had a separate estate, wrote that she had formulated her will "by and with the advise and consent of my husband." The similar wording may indicate that AA thought of herself as having an unofficial separate estate. "Abigail Adam's Disposition of Her Property," Jan. 18, 1816, AP#607; Sands, quoted in Gundersen and Gampel, "Married Women's Legal Status in Eighteenth-Century New York and Virginia," 117. On separate estates in colonial New England, see Marylynn Salmon, *Women and the Law of Property in Early America* (Chapel Hill, N.C., 1986), 120–40.

273¶3 AA to MSC, Oct. 3, 1790, *AFC*, 9:127; Michael I. Meyerson, *Liberty's Blueprint: How Madison and Hamilton Wrote the Federalist Papers, Defined the Constitution, and Made Democracy Safe for the World* (New York, 2008), 117.

275¶1 AA to MSC, Oct. 10, 1790, *AFC*, 9:130–31; Withey, *Dearest Friend*, 215; McCullough, *John Adams*, 428–29.

275¶2 JA to TJ, June 6, 1786, *AJL*, 1:134; JA to AA, March 11, 1794, *MDF*, 364. On AA's lottery tickets, see CT to AA, Feb. 23, 1791, AA to JQA, Feb. 5, 1792, *AFC*, 9:195, 259.

276¶1 JA to TJ, July 16, 1786, *AJL*, 1:144–45.

276¶2 AA to MSC, Oct. 10, 1790, *AFC*, 9:131. This discussion of AA's sense at entitlement is heavily indebted to the author's discussions with Margaret Hogan.

277¶2 AA to MSC, Oct. 25, 1790, *AFC*, 9:140–41n; Withey, *Dearest Friend*, 220–21n. In support of Withey's claim that AA contracted malaria at this time, this was apparently her first-ever reference to having "intermitting Fever" (though in previous years she had frequently reported having a "slow fever"). Kylie Horney, personal communication with the author, June 15, 2009.

277¶3 AA to AAS, Nov. 21, 1790, AA to ESSP, March 20, 1791, Oct. 3, 1790, *AFC*, 9:149, 208, 127.

278¶1 AA to JQA, Sept. 12, 1790, *AFC*, 9:109; Palmer, quoted in MSC to AA, Oct. 8, 1786, *AFC*, 7:355.

278¶3 AA to JQA, Nov. 7, 1790, JQA to AA, Dec. 14, 1790, *AFC*, 9:142, 161, 43–44n; Samuel Flagg Bemis, *John Quincy Adams and the Foundations of American Foreign Policy* (New York, 1969), 24; Robert V. Remini, *John Quincy Adams* (New York, 2002), 20–22.

279¶1 JQA to AA, Dec. 14, 1790, *AFC*, 9:162.

279¶2 JQA to AA, Oct. 17, 1790, *AFC*, 9:132–33.

280¶1 AA to JQA, Sept. 9, 1790, *AFC*, 9:107.

280¶2 AA to CT, Dec. 18, 1791, *AFC*, 9:247–48.

280¶3 CT to AA, Sept. 28, 1790, Feb. 23, 1791, *AFC*, 9:125, 195.

281¶1 AA to MSC, Dec. 18, 1791, AA to ESSP, March 20, 1791, *AFC*, 9:244, 208.

281¶2 AA to MSC, Aug. 9, 1789, April 28, 1790, Jan. 9, March 12, Dec. 18, 1791, *AFC*, 8:399, 9:51, 180, 201, 244. Pennsylvania had decreed that everyone born after 1780 would be free; New York passed an even more gradual emancipation law in 1799.

281¶3 CT to AA, July 20, 1789, MSC to AA, Jan. 25, 1791, AA to MSC, March 12, 1791, *AFC*, 8:392, 9:183, 201.

282¶1 AA to MSC, Oct. 30, Dec. 18, 1791, *AFC*, 9:237, 245. AA's son CA also questioned the U.S. government's expeditions against the Indians, albeit for more pragmatic reasons. "Would it not be infinitely more to our advantage, and a saving of treasure to purchase peace?" he asked his mother. "Most certainly it would." CA to AA, April 22, [17]92, *AFC*, 9:280.

282¶2 AA to MSC, March 25–29, April 20, 1792, *NL*, 81–83.

283¶1 AAS's third child, Thomas Hollis Smith, was born in August 1790 but died the following year. Introduction, AAS to AA, Dec. 10, 1791, *AFC*, 9:x, xxxi, 240–41.

Chapter 24: "With All the Ardour of Youth," 1792–1795

284¶1 AA to MSC, April 20, 1792, *AFC*, 9:278.

284¶2 JA to AA, Dec. 28, 1792, Feb. 17, 1793, *AFC*, 9:359, 406; Withey, *Dearest Friend*, 224.

285¶2 AA to MSC, April 20, 1792, *AFC*, 9:279.

285¶3 AA to JA, Dec. 4, 1792, *AFC*, 9:333.

286¶1 Doctors believed African Americans were immune to yellow fever, and a group of blacks, led by the ministers Absalom Jones and Richard Allen, stayed behind to care for the sick. The reality, however, was that Africans were only slightly less susceptible to the fever than Europeans, and many of the black caregivers died along with their patients. Gary B. Nash, *Forging Freedom: The Formation of Philadelphia's Black Community, 1720–1840* (Cambridge, Mass., 1988), 121–24. Among the white fatalities in the 1793 epidemic was attorney John Todd. A year later, his widow, Dolley Payne Todd, married James Madison, the future president.

286¶2 JA to AA, Dec. 1, 1793, *AFC*, 9:460.

286¶3 JA to AA, Dec. 28, 1792, Feb. 3, 1793, AA to JA, Jan. 18, 1794, AEA; JA to AA, Dec. 22, 1793, *AFC*, 9:481–82.

287¶1 AA to JA, Dec. 31, 1793, *AFC*, 9:494; AA to JA, Feb. 26, 1794, *MDF*, 362.

287¶2 AA to JA, Jan. 12, [25]–26, 1794, AEA.

288¶1 JA to AA, Jan. 21, 1794, *MDF*, 350; AAS to JQA, Oct. 26, [1795], AP#380.

288¶2 JA to AA, March 2, 1793, *AFC*, 9:415–16n.

289¶2 JA to AA, Dec. 28, 1792, Jan. 27, 1793, AA to JA, Jan. 7, 1793, *AFC*, 9:360, 382, 373; AA to JA, March 2, 1796, JA to AA, March 11, 1796, AEA.

289¶3 AA to JA, Nov. 10, 1794, Feb. 13, 1795, JA to AA, Nov. 17, 18, 1794, AEA; Withey, *Dearest Friend*, 225.

290¶1 AA to MSC, May 24, 1797, *NL*, 91.

290¶2 AA to JA, May 23, Feb. 2, 1794, March 5, 1796, JA to AA, Feb. 23, 1796, AEA; John Taylor, *An Examination of the Late Proceedings in Congress, Respecting the Official Conduct of the Secretary of the Treasury* ([Richmond], [1793]), 10, 12.

291¶1 AA to JA, May 10, 1794, *MDF*, 369.

291¶2 AA to JA, Dec. 31, 1796, AEA; AA to AAS, March 10, 1794, *Letters of Mrs. Adams*, 2:229.

291¶3 Samuel Adams, speech to the Massachusetts Senate and House of Representatives, *Salem Gazette*, Jan. 21, 1794; AA to JA, Jan. 18, 1794, Jan. 3, 1796, AEA.

292¶1 CA to AA, [February?] 1795, "Issabella"[AA] to George Cabot, [January 1794; the Adams Papers office notes that this letter had to have been written after Jan. 17], AP#379, 377; AA to JA, July 5, 1780, *AFC*, 3:372; Zagarri, *Revolutionary Backlash*.

292¶2 JA to AA, Dec. 18, 1794, AA to JA, Jan. 4, 1795, AEA; [John Bennett], *Strictures on Female Education; Chiefly as it Relates to the Culture of the Heart, In Four Essays. By A Clergyman Of The Church Of England* (London, [1787]).

293¶1 AA to ESSP, Feb. 12, 1796, Shaw#1, frame 269; AA to JA, Dec. 11, 1794 (Elizabeth Lady Craven), AEA; AA to JA, Dec. 20, 1795 (de Staël), *MDF*, 393; MOW to AA, Oct. 1, 1796, AP#382 (Williams, Roland).

293¶2 AA to JA, Feb. 26, 1794, *MDF*, 362; AA to JQA, May 20, 1796, AP#381; *Universal Magazine of Knowledge and Pleasure* 62 (April 1778), 174–75 (my thanks to Margaret A. Hogan for this reference).

293¶3 JA to AA, Jan. 24, 1793, AA to JA, Feb. 9, [1793], *AFC*, 9:381, 394.

294¶1 ESSP to AA, Dec. 29, 1793, *AFC*, 9:488; JA to AA, Jan. 22, 1794, *MDF*, 351; AA to JA, Feb. 2, 1794, AEA (AA's emphasis).

294¶2 ESSP to AA, Jan. 12, 1795, Shaw#1, frame 622.

294¶4 ESSP to AA, Jan. 12, 1795, Dec. 21, 1794, Shaw#1, frames 622, 617; ESSP to AA and MSC, [Sept. 24, 1795], AP#380.

295¶1 Katharine Metcalf Roof, *Colonel William Smith and Lady: The Romance of Washington's Aide and Young Abigail Adams* (Boston, 1929), 226–27; "The New York Presidential Trivia Quiz," *New York Times*, April 28, 1989.

295¶2 JQA to CA, Nov. 20, 1794, May 17, 1795, July 29, Dec. 29, 1796, JQA to TBA, Oct. 2, 1798, AP#126, 128, 131; *AFC*, 9:133n, 412–13n.

296¶1 ESSP to [AA and MSC], Sept. 24, 1795, ESSP to AA, Feb. 28, 1796, AP#380–81; "Stephen Peabody, Harvard, 1769," *CC*.

296¶2 ESSP to AA, Oct. 31, 1795, AP#380; Salmon, *Women and the Law of Property*, xv, 120–40.

297¶1 ESSP to AA, Oct. 31, 1795, Jan. 9, 1796, AP#380–81; AA to Abigail Adams Shaw, April 29, 1815, Shaw#1, frame 214.

Chapter 25: "Presidante," 1796–1797

298¶1 Bernard Bailyn, *The Ideological Origins of the American Revolution* (enlarged edition, Cambridge, Mass., 1992).

298¶2 Garry Wills, *Cincinnatus: George Washington and the Enlightenment* (Garden City, N.Y., 1984).

299¶1 Fred Anderson, *Crucible of War: The Seven Years' War and the Fate of Empire in British North America, 1754–1766* (New York, 2000).

299¶2 Holton, *Forced Founders*, 3–5, 11, 37–38; Bernhard Knollenberg, *George Washington, the Virginia Period, 1732–1775* (Durham, N.C., 1964).

301¶1 Wills, *Cincinnatus*, 3, 87–89.

301¶2 TJ to James Madison, Jan. 8, 1797, in Hutchinson et al., eds., *Papers of James Madison*, 16:448.

302¶1 JA to AA, Dec. 7, 1796, *MDF*, 417–18.

302¶2 AA to JA, Feb. 20, 1796, JA to AA, Dec. 16, 1796, *MDF*, 406, 419; AA to JA, Jan. 15, 29, Feb. 19, 1797, JA to AA, March 1, 1796, AEA.

302¶3 AA to JA, Feb. 20, 1796, *MDF*, 405.

303¶1 AA to JA, Dec. 31, 1796, AEA; AA to JA, Jan. 28, 1797, *MDF*, 432.

303¶2 AA to JA, April 10, 1796, AEA; CA to AA, Sept. 11, 1796, private collection; AA to TBA, Aug. 16, 1796, AA to JQA, Nov. 28, 1796, AP#382. On St. Hilaire, see his letters to Secretary of War James McHenry in "The Papers of the War Department 1784–1800" (http://wardepartmentpapers.org), his advertisement in the *York (Pennsylvania) Recorder*, Jan. 29, 1800, and Marcius D. Raymond, "Colonel William Stephens Smith," *New York Genealogical and Biographical Record* 25 (October 1894): 154.

304¶1 AA to JA, Jan. 1, 1797, AEA.

304¶2 AA to ESSP, March 4, 1786, *AFC*, 7:81.

305¶9 AA to JA, Feb. 13, 1797, *MDF*, 439; AA to MSC, March 12, 1791, *AFC*, 9:201–2n.

305¶10 AA to ESSP, March 4, 1786, *AFC*, 7:81; Thomas Jefferson, *Notes on the State of Virginia* (excerpt), in Woody Holton, *Black Americans in the Revolutionary Era: A Brief History With Documents* (Boston, 2009), 104.

306¶1 AA to ESSP, Feb. 13, 1798, Shaw#1, frame 279.

306¶2 JA to AA, March 17, April 19, 1797, Oct. 25, 27, 1799, AEA; JA to AA, March 27, April 22, 1797, *MDF*, 443, 445.

307¶1 AA to JA, Dec. 4, 1796, AEA.

307¶2 AA to MSC, Dec. 12, 1797, *NL*, 117.

307¶3 JA to AA, March 17, 1797, Dec. 30, 1796, AA to JA, March 12, Feb. 6, 1797, AEA; JA to AA, March 22, 1797, *MDF*, 442.

308¶1 JA to AA, March 27, 1797, AA to JA, April 6, 1797, *MDF*, 443–44; JA to AA, April 7, 11, 1797, AA to JA, April 9, 1797, AEA.

Chapter 26: "I Did Get an Alteration in It," 1797–1798

309¶1 MSC to AA, May 4, 1797, AP#384.

309¶2 AA to MSC, May 16, 1797, *NL*, 89; JA to AA, Dec. 14, 1796, AEA; MSC to AA, May 29, 1797, ESSP to AA, July 3, 1797, AP#384–85; Allen C. Clark, *Greenleaf and Law in the Federal City* (Washington, D.C., 1901), 49–52.

310¶1 AA to MSC, May 16, 1797, *NL*, 89.

310¶2 JA to AA, Jan. 1, 1797, AEA; Withey, *Dearest Friend*, 252–53.

310¶3 AA to MSC, May 16, 24, June 23, 1797, *NL*, 89, 91, 98–99.

311¶1 AA to MSC, Feb. 6, 1798, *NL*, 130–31; AA to ESSP, Aug. 12, 1797, Shaw#1, frame 273; AA to JQA, Nov. 3, 1797, WSS to JA, Feb. 23, 1798, JA, quoted in AA to JQA, June 12, 1798, AP#386, 387, 389.

312¶1 ESSP to AA, Oct. 6, Dec. 19, 1797, MSC to AA, Dec. 17, 1797, AP#386; AA to MSC, Dec. 26, 1797, *NL*, 120.

312¶2 JQA to CA, June 9, 1796, AP#128; Bemis, *John Quincy Adams* 79–80; Remini, *John Quincy Adams*, 26–30.

313¶1 AA to MSC, June 1, 1798, *NL*, 183–84; JQA to CA, May 17, 1795, JQA to WSS, Jan. 18, 1802, CA to JQA, April 24, 1796, AA to JQA, Dec. 2, 1798, AP#128, 135, 381, 392.

314¶2 AA to JQA, Nov. 3, 1797, AP#386; AA to William Smith [no relation to WSS], Dec. 26, 1798, Smith-Townsend Family Papers and Papers II, MHS; JQA to CA, Aug. 1, 1797, Feb. 14, Aug. 1, 1798, AA to JQA, Dec. 2, 1798, AP#130, 133, 392. Although plausible at the time, AA's prediction that JQA would not recover any of his money eventually proved overly pessimistic. A decade after the debt was contracted, Justus Smith finally began making payments, and he continued to do so until his death on Mach 13, 1816. The $950 payment that JQA received from Smith's executors in 1818 apparently paid off the debt. JQA to Justus Bosch Smith, Jan. 8, 1805, JQA to TBA, Nov. 22, 1818, AP#135, 445.

314¶3 Bemis, *John Quincy Adams*, 88–90.

315¶2 "Plain Truth," *Independent Chronicle*, Feb. 15, 1798; "A Correspondent," *Columbian Centinel*, Feb. 17, 1798; AA to MSC, February 1798, AA to William Smith, Feb. 6, 1798, Smith-Carter Papers, MHS.

316¶1 AA to MSC, April 4, 7, 1798, May 26, 1798, *NL*, 152, 154, 179; "Toasts Drank by the Volunteer Troop of Horse, Commanded by Col. Giles, at the Celebration of the 4th of July," (New York) *Spectator*, July 7, 1798; AA to JQA, July 14, 1798, AP#390.

316¶2 AA to MSC, May 26, 1798, *NL*, 181.

317¶1 AA to MSC, May 10, 26, 1798, *NL*, 172, 179; AA to JQA, Dec. 2, 1798, AP#392.

317¶2 AA, quoted in Stanley Elkins and Eric McKitrick, *The Age of Federalism* (New York, 1993), 597.

317¶3 AA to ESSP, July 19, 1799, Shaw#1, frame 312; AA to JA, March 12, 1797, AEA.

318¶1 AA to MSC, Nov. 15, 1797, *NL*, 112.

318¶2 MSC to AA, Dec. 17, 24, 1797, Jan. 14–15, 1798, AP#386–87.

318¶3 AA to MSC, Jan. 5, 20, 1798, *NL*, 122, 125; MSC to AA, Jan. 2, 7, March 2, 1798, AP#387.

319¶1 MSC to AA, March 2, Feb. 23, 1798, AP#387.

Chapter 27: "They Wisht the Old Woman Had Been There," 1798–1800

320¶1 AA to MSC, Feb. [1–5], 6, 1798, *NL*, 129–30; MSC to AA, Feb. 23, 1798, AP#387.

320¶2 AA to MSC, June 1, Feb. 21, 1798, *NL*, 183–84, 135–36.

321¶1 AA to CT, Oct. 17, 1797, CT to AA, Nov. 24, 1797, AP#386; AA to MSC, Nov. 15, 1797, March 14, 1798, *NL*, 110–11, 145.

321¶2 AA to MSC, July 3, 1798, *NL*, 199.

321¶3 AA to MSC, July 29, 179[8], *NL*, 106; AA to JQA, Nov. 15, 1798, AP#392; JA to AA, Dec. 25, 1798, Jan. 2, 1799, AA to JA, Jan. [4], 1799, AEA.

322¶1 AA to JA, Dec. 23, 1798, AEA.

322¶2 In a Dec. 30, 1799, letter to AA, CT reported that he had purchased a security in the amount of $1,100. By 1809, when these bonds were redeemed, AA had increased her investment to $1,700. CT to AA, Dec. 30, 1799, AP#396; AA to CT, Jan. 17, 1809, Americana Room, National Society, Daughters of the American Revolution, Washington, D.C.; Albert Gallatin, announcement, April 28, 1807, *Washington Expositor*, March 12, 1809.

323¶1 JA to AA, Nov. 15, 1798, AA to JA, Jan. 20, 1799, AEA; AA to JA, Nov. 29, 1798, *MDF*, 451.

323¶2 AA to JA, Feb. 27, 1799, *MDF*, 465–66; AA to JA, Jan. 20, Feb. 1, 1799, JA to AA, Feb. [9?], 18, 1799, AEA.

324¶1 AA to JA, Jan. 12, 1799, *MDF*, 459; Richard N. Rosenfeld, *American Aurora: A Democratic-Republican Returns; The Suppressed History of Our Nation's Beginnings and the Heroic Newspaper That Tried to Report It* (New York, 1997), 32–33.

324¶2 AA to JA, Jan. 13, 1799, AEA; AA to JA, Jan. 12, 1799, JA to AA, Jan. 9, 1797, *MDF*, 459, 424.

324¶3 JA to AA, Dec. 31, 1798, AEA; JA to AA, Jan. 5, 1799, AA to JA, Jan. 12, 1799, *MDF*, 458–59; Akers, *Abigail Adams* (1980 edition), 163.

325¶1 "Address from the Legislature of Maryland to the President of the United States as Amended and Agreed to Tuesday Last," *New York Gazette*, Dec. 4, 1798; "The President's Answer to the General Assembly of the State of Maryland," *Gazette of the United States*, Jan. 10, 1799; AA to JA, Jan. 20, 1799, JA to AA, Jan. 25, 28, 1799, AEA.

325¶2 AA to MSC, Nov. 26, 1799, *NL*, 216; JA to AA, Feb. 25, 1799, *MDF*, 463.

326¶1 AA to JA, Feb. 27, 1799, JA to AA, Feb. 25, 1799, *MDF*, 464. On the other hand, a member of the U.S. Senate reportedly speculated that the whole idea of sending a second deputation to France must have come from the first lady, since "the president would not *dare* to make a nomination or appointment without *her* approbation." Baltimore dateline, *Charleston City Gazette*, March 5, 1800.

326¶2 AA to JA, Feb. 27, 1799, *MDF*, 464; AA to JA, March 9, 1799, AEA.

327¶1 Withey, *Dearest Friend*, 270.

327¶2 JA to AA, Oct. 12, 1799, *MDF*, 466; AA to MSC, Oct. 31, 1799, *NL*, 211.

327¶3 MSC to AA, March 24, 1800, AA to CT, March 15, 1800, AP#397.

328¶1 Elkins and McKitrick, *Age of Federalism*, 734–38.

Chapter 28: "A Day of Darkness," 1800–1804

329¶1 AA to MSC, Nov. 10, 1800, *NL*, 255.

329¶2 AA to MSC, Nov. 21, 1800, *NL*, 256–57.

330¶2 AA, quoted in Akers, *Abigail Adams* (1980 edition), 171; JA to AA, Aug. 18, 27, 1776, AA to JA, Aug. 5, 1776, Dec. 10, 1779, JT to AA, Sept. 19, 1780, *AFC*, 2:99, 110, 80, 3:242, 418; JA to AA, March 9, 1797, AEA.

331¶2 AA to TBA, [Dec.] 13, 1800, *Letters of Mrs. Adams*, 2:238 (the staff of the Adams Papers has shown that AA probably erred in dating this letter Nov. 13, 1800); AA to MSC, Feb. 7, 1801, *NL*, 266.

332¶2 AA to CT, Jan. 15, 1801, AP#400; Elkins and McKitrick, *Age of Federalism*, 741.

332¶3 AA to MSC, Feb. 7, 1801, *NL*, 266; AA to CT, Jan. 15, 1801, AP#400; Knott, *Sensibility and the American Revolution*, 265–322.

333¶1 AA to MSC, Dec. 21–27, 1800, private collection; Henry Wiencek, *An Imperfect God: George Washington, His Slaves, and the Creation of America* (New York, 2003), 81–82, 353–58.

333¶2 AA to JA, Feb. 19, 1801, AEA.

334¶1 JA to AA, Feb. 16, 1801, *MDF*, 474; JA to RC, June 29, 1766, *AFC*, 1:52.

334¶2 AA to JA, [Feb. 21, 1801], *MDF*, 476.

335¶1 ESSP to AA, July 13, Dec. 8–10, 1801, AP#401.

336¶1 AA to TBA, July 12, 1801, AP#401; AA to MSC, Jan. 28, 1800, *NL*, 228–29.

336¶2 JQA to TBA, June 9, 1801, HMS Misc., Harvard Medical Library in the Francis A. Countway Library of Medicine, Boston, Mass.; Stefan Riedel, "Edward Jenner and the History of Smallpox and Vaccination," *Baylor University Medical Center Proceedings* 18 (January 2005): 21–25.

338¶1 AA to TBA, Dec. 27, 1801, AP#401; LCA, quoted in Withey, *Dearest Friend*, 285; Levin, *Abigail Adams*, 397–99.

338¶2 LCA, quoted in Levin, *Abigail Adams*, 398; AA to TBA, Feb. 28, 1802, AP#401; Bemis, *John Quincy Adams*, 112.

338¶3 AA to CT, [April 26–May 10, 1785], *AFC*, 6:108; AA to TBA, Feb. 28, Dec. 13, 1802, AP#401.

339¶1 Bemis, *John Quincy Adams*, 113–14.

339¶2 Richard and Mary Cranch, deed to JA, March 29, 1802, Stephen and Elizabeth Peabody, deed to JA, Aug. 7, 1802, Quincy, Wendell, Holmes, and Upham Family Papers, reel 35, MHS.

339¶3 ESSP to AA, April 31[sic], 1802, AP#401; AA to Abigail Adams Shaw, April 29, 1815, Shaw#1, frame 214. In December 1815, AA would declare that "Dr Tufts has always been my trustee." AA to JQA, Dec. 24, 1815, AP#428. MSC had become the beneficiary of a trust by the time of her death in 1811. Since no significant amount of property came to her between 1802 and 1811, it seems safe to conclude that the trust had been created in 1802. AA to ESSP, Nov. [?], 1811, Shaw#1, frame 402. No marriage settlement has been found for JA and AA, and there are reasons to believe that none will be. AA occasionally referred to her savings as her "pocket money" or "pin money," which she almost certainly would not have done if they had been secured to her in a separate estate. AA to MSC, July 12, 1789, *AFC*, 8:389; AA to TBA, Feb. 28, 1802, AP#401; "Abigail Adams's Disposition of Her Property," Jan, 18, 1816, AP#607.

340¶1 JQA to WSS, April 4, 1803, AA to TBA, April 26, 1803, AP#135, 402; Cotton Tufts, Jr., deed to JA, April 1, 1803, Quincy, Wendell, Holmes, and Upham Family Papers, reel 35; S. R. Cope, "Bird, Savage & Bird of London: Merchants and Bankers, 1782 to 1803," *Guildhall Studies in London History* 4 (1981): 202–17.

340¶2 AA to TBA, April 26, May 8, 1803, AP#402; AA to Sarah Adams, Feb. 23, 1806, Kroch Library, Cornell University; JA, power of attorney to CT, March 15, 1803, Colburn Collection, 7:189. JA did not even have the option of canceling the purchase of Tufts's land, because he had already drawn a bill of exchange to pay for it. Rufus King (who was then the American minister in London) and two associates covered the bill when Bird, Savage, & Bird was unable to do so (saving JQA from a hefty penalty), but this unsolicited emergency loan had to be repaid instantly.

341¶1 AA to TBA, April 18, 1802, AP#401.

341¶2 JQA to AA, Nov. 7, 1803, AA to JQA, Dec. 3, 1803, AP#402.

341¶3 AA to TBA, April 26, 1803, AP#402. The Adamses were eventually able to recover most of the money they lost in the bankruptcy of Bird, Savage, & Bird, but the last of the money did not come in until long after JA's death in 1826. Bemis, *John Quincy Adams*, 114–15.

341¶4 AA to TJ, May 20, 1804, *AJL*, 1:268–69.

342¶1 TJ to AA, June 13, 1804 *AJL*, 1:270.

342¶2 AA to TJ, July 1, 1804, *AJL*, 1:273–74; Proverbs 27:6.

343¶1 AA to TJ, Oct. 25, 1804, JA, note dated Nov. 19, 1804, at the foot of AA to TJ, Oct. 25, 1804, *AJL*, 1:282.

Chapter 29: "Your Mothers Legacy," 1805–1809

344¶1 WSS to JQA, Nov. 28, 1805, AP#404; Karen Racine, *Francisco de Miranda: A Transatlantic Life in the Age of Revolution* (Wilmington, Del., 2003).

344¶2 AA to JQA, March 5, 1806, AA to JQA and LCA, Nov. 29, 1805, AP#404.

345¶2 JQA to LCA, July 13, 1806, AP#404.

345¶3 JQA to LCA, July 13, 1806, WSS to JQA, March 24, 1807, AP#404, 405; Raymond, "Colonel William Stephens Smith," 158.

346¶1 MOW, quoted in Levin, *Abigail Adams*, 424–25.

346¶2 MOW to AA, Dec. 28, [1806], AP#404; AA to MOW, March 9, 1807, in *Warren-Adams Letters*, 2:352–54; MOW, quoted in Levin, *Abigail Adams*, 424–25; JA, quoted in Jeffrey H. Richards, *Mercy Otis Warren* (New York, 1995), 22; JA, quoted in Levin, *Abigail Adams*, 424.

347¶1 MOW, quoted in Zagarri, *Woman's Dilemma*, 152; MOW, quoted in Levin, *Abigail Adams*, 426; JA, quoted in Richards, *Mercy Otis Warren*, 147. For a different view of the patronage issue, see Zagarri, *Woman's Dilemma*, 154.

348¶2 AA to Sarah Adams, Jan. 20, 1808, Kroch Library, Cornell University.

348¶3 Bemis, *John Quincy Adams*, 143.

349¶1 AA to JQA, Feb. 15, 18[0]8, AP#405.

350¶1 JQA to AA, Feb. 24, 1808, JA to JQA, Feb. 19, 1808, AP#405.

350¶2 AA to AAS, Aug. 29, 1808, in Allyn B. Forbes, ed., "Abigail Adams, Commentator," MHS *Proceedings*, 3rd ser., 66 (October 1936–May 1941), 144.

350¶3 Elizabeth Quincy Smith, quoted in ESSP to AA, Aug. 11, 1806, AP#404; AA to AAS, June 19, Dec. 8, 1808, in Forbes, ed., "Abigail Adams, Commentator," 140, 151.

351¶2 Investors were not required to redeem their bonds on December 31, 1808, but they received no interest after that date. Albert Gallatin, announcement, April 28, 1807, *Washington Expositor*, March 12, 1809.

352¶1 LCA to JQA, Feb. 12, 16, 1809, AP#407.

352¶3 William Steuben Smith to JQA, July 1, 1809, AP#407.

352¶4 [AA], note, [July 31, 1809], JQA to AA, Aug. 9, 1809, AA to Caroline Smith, Aug. 12, 1809, AP#407–8.

Chapter 30: "Rather Positive," 1810–1811

354¶1 JA, quoted in Levin, *Abigail Adams*, 479; AA to ESSP, Dec. 29, 1811, Shaw#1, frame 407; AA to JQA, Oct. 23, 1815, AP#427. For the view that the aging AA mellowed, see Withey, *Dearest Friend*, 299.

354¶2 LCA to AA, Jan. 7, 1810, JQA to AA, Feb. 8, 1810, AP#409.

356¶1 James Madison to AA, Aug. 15, 1810, AA to James Madison, Aug. 1, 1810, enclosed in AA to JQA, Feb, 22, 1811, JQA to AA, June 30, 1811, AP#410–11; Withey, *Dearest Friend*, 300–1; Levin, *Abigail Adams*, 437.

356¶2 "Extract of a Letter from Mr. Adams, Minister from the U.S. at the Court of St. Petersburgh to a Friend," Boston *Independent Chronicle*, Feb. 14, 1811; AA to [Catherine Johnson], May 9, [1810], JQA to AA, Oct. 25, 1810, AA to JQA, Feb. 22, 1811, AA to Adelaide Johnson, Feb. 26, 1812, AP#409–11, 413.

357¶1 JQA to AA, June 30, 1811, AP#410; JQA to JA, June 25, 1811, *Writings of JQA*, 4:117–19.

357¶2 Ann Adams to AA and JA, June 30, 1810, AA to JQA, July 11, 25, 1810, AP#409–10.

358¶1 JQA to AA, Sept. 17, 1810, AP#410; Smith, *Theory of Moral Sentiments*, 2:74.

358¶2 JQA to AA, Sept. 17, 1810, AP#410; JQA to TBA, Sept. 8, 1810, *Writings of JQA*, 3:497–98.

359¶1 AA to JQA, Feb. 15, April 8, 1811, AP#411.

359¶2 AA to LCA, May 15, 1810, Ann Adams to AA, June 20, 1810, AA to Catherine Johnson, Aug. 18, 1810, AA to JQA, April 8, 1811, AP#409–11.

360¶1 JQA to AA, Dec. 17, 1810, MSC to [LCA], Jan. 21, 1811, AP#410–11; Withey, *Dearest Friend*, 301.

360¶2 Unsigned review of *The Works of James Barry Esq., Historical Painter, With Some Account of His Life and Writings*, *Edinburgh Review* 32 (August 1810): 296–97; JQA to AA, Oct. 2, 1811, *Writings of JQA*, 4:226–27.

361¶1 AA to JQA, Feb. 15, April 8, 1811, TBA to JQA, April 7–8, 1811, AP#411.

361¶2 LCA to AA, Oct. 23, 1810, AP#410.

361¶3 LCA to AA, May 13, Oct. 23, 1810, AA to LCA, Jan. 21, 1811, AP#409–11; Akers, *Abigail Adams* (2007 edition), 203.

362¶2 AA to LCA, Jan. 21, 1811, AP#411.

362¶3 AA to JQA, Feb. 15, 1811, AP#411.

363¶1 [AA] to [ESSP], Feb. 28, 1811, ESSP to AA, March 8, 1811, AA to LCA, March 27, 1816, AP#411, 430.

363¶2 AA to [?], [ca. 1812], [AA] to [ESSP], Feb. 28, 1811, AP#414, 411.

364¶1 AA to Julia Rush, [July?] 1813, AP#416.

364¶2 JQA to AA, June 11, 1811, LCA to AA, June 10, 1811, AP#411.

365¶1 AA to Catherine Johnson, Sept. 22, 1811, AP#412.

365¶2 AA to JQA, March 4, April 24, 1811, AA to Catherine Johnson, March 6, 1811, LCA to AA, June 10, 1811, AP#411.

CHAPTER 31: "THE 'THREEFOLD SILKEN CORD IS BROKEN,'" 1811–1812

366¶1 AAS to BR, [early September 1811], quoted in Gelles, *Portia*, 161; WSS to AA, June 29, 1811, AA to AAS, [March 1811], AP#411.
366¶2 AA to LCA, April 28, 1811, Hannah Cushing to AA, June 20, 1811, AP#411.
367¶1 WSS to AA, Aug. 12, 1811, AAS to BR [early September 1811], quoted in Gelles, *Portia*, 160–62; AA to Catherine Johnson, July 31, 1811, ESSP to AA, Aug. 3–7, 1811, Hannah Cushing to AA, Sept. 11, 1811, AP#412.
367¶2 WSS to AA, Aug. 12, 1811, AP#412.
367¶3 AA to WSS, Aug. 28, 1811, in Forbes, ed., "Abigail Adams, Commentator," 152; WSS to AA, Sept. 15, 1811, AP#412.
368¶1 AA to JQA, June 21, 1811, William Cranch to AA, July 7, 1811, AA to Catherine Johnson, July 31, 1811, AP#411–12.
368¶2 Hannah Cushing to AA, Sept. 11, 1811, AA to JQA, Sept. 24, 1811, AP#412.
368¶3 AAS to BR [early September 1811], quoted in Gelles, *Portia*, 161–62; BR to JA, Sept. 20, 1811, in L.H. Butterfield, ed., *Letters of Benjamin Rush* (2 vols.; London, 1951), 2:1104.
369¶1 AA to JQA, Nov. 17, 1811, AP#412; JA to BR, Oct. 13, 1811, *OFL*, 363–64.
369¶2 AA to ESSP, Oct. 22, 1811, AP#412.
370¶4 AA to ESSP, Oct. 22, 1811, AP#412.
370¶5 AA to JQA, Nov. 17, 1811, ESSP to JQA, Feb. 26, 1812, AA to ESSP, Oct. 22, 1811, AP#412–13.
370¶6 JA to BR, Oct. 13, 1811, *OFL*, 363; AA to JQA, Nov. 17, 1811, AP#412.
371¶1 ESSP to AA, Oct. 19, 1811, AA to ESSP, Oct. 22, 1811, Hannah Cushing to AA, Nov. 14, 1811, AA to JQA, Nov. 17, 1811, AP#412.
371¶2 ESSP to AA, Oct. 21, 1811, Hannah Cushing to AA, Nov. 14, 1811, AA to JQA, Nov. 17, 1811, AP#412.
371¶3 AA to ESSP, Oct. 22, 1811, AA to JQA, Nov. 17, Dec. 8, 1811, JQA to AA, Feb. 8, 1812, AP#412–13.
372¶4 AA to JA2, Dec. 8, 1811, AP#412.
372¶5 AA to JA2, Dec. 8, 1811, ESSP to AA, Dec. 18, 1811, AP#412.
372¶6 AA to JA2, Jan. 5, 1812, AP#413.
373¶1 AA to ESSP, Oct. 22, 1811, AA to JQA, Nov. 17, Dec. 8, 1811, AP#412.
373¶2 JQA to AA, Sept. 10, 1811, AP#412.
373¶3 BR to JA, July 20, 1811, in Butterfield, ed., *Letters of Benjamin Rush*, 2:1090.
374¶1 JA to BR, Aug. 25, 1811, *OFL*, 348–51.
374¶2 JA to BR, Aug. 25, 1811, *OFL*, 350.
375¶1 JA to BR, Sept. 12, 1811, *OFL*, 362.

CHAPTER 32: "GOD LOVES A CHEERFULL CHRISTIAN," 1812–1814

376¶1 BR to JA, Dec. 16, 1811 and to TJ, Dec. 17, 1811, in Butterfield, ed., *Letters of Benjamin Rush*, 2:1110–12.
376¶2 LCA to AA, June 13, 1812, JQA to George Washington Adams, June 18, 1812, AP#413.

377¶1 LCA to AA, June 13, 1812, AA to JQA, May 10, 1812, ESSP to AA, May 5, 1812, AP#413.
377¶2 AA to LCA, Feb. 24, 1812, LCA to AA, June 13, 1812, AP#413.
377¶3 [AA] to [ESSP], Feb. 28, 1811, ESSP to AA, Jan. 20, 1812, AP#411–13; JA to BR, Jan. 27, 1812, *OFL*, 295.
378¶1 AA to JQA, March 12, April 12, 1812, [TBA] to JQA, March 18, 1812, AP#413.
379¶1 (Lexington, Kentucky) *Reporter*, quoted in Cogliano, *Revolutionary America*, 176; Richter, "War and Culture: The Iroquois Experience," 528–59; Gregory Evans Dowd, *A Spirited Resistance: The North American Indian Struggle for Unity, 1745–1815* (Baltimore, 1992), 123–47, 183–84.
379¶2 AA's letter was apparently addressed either to William Eustis or to Elbridge Gerry. AA to [?], Aug. 5, 1812, AP#414.
380¶1 AA to JQA, Jan. 5, March 12, 1812, AP#413; Cogliano, *Revolutionary America*, 175.
380¶2 ESSP to AA, June 13, 1812, AA to MOW, Aug. 9, 1812, MOW to AA, Sept. 1, 1812, enclosed in MOW to AA, Oct. 13, 1812, MOW to AA, Jan. 26, 1813, AP#413–15.
380¶3 AA to ESSP, July 17, Sept. 11, 1812, Shaw#1, frames 415–16, 421–22.
381¶1 ESSP to AA, July 22–Aug. 21, 1787, *AFC*, 8:136; ESSP to AA, July 14, 1812, AP#416; AA to ESSP, July 17, Sept. 11, 1812, Shaw#1, frames 416, 421.
381¶2 AA to Ann Adams, Sept. 20, 1812, AP#414.
382¶2 JQA to AA, Nov. 30, 1811, Sept. 21, 1812, AA to Thomas B. Johnson, April 3, 1813, AP#412, 414–15.
382¶3 JQA to AA, Sept. 21, Oct. 24–25, 1812, AP#414.
383¶1 LCA to AA, April 4, 1813; AA to MSC, April 7, 1798, *NL*, 155.
383¶2 JQA to AA, Feb. 8, 1812, AA to JQA, Dec. 30, 1812, ESSP to AA, Dec. 31, 1812, AP#413–14.
384¶1 AA to JQA, Jan. 25, Feb. 1, 1813, AA to George Washington Adams and JA2, Jan. 15, 1813, LCA to AA, April 4, 1813, AA to LCA, July 24, 1813, AP#415.
384¶2 AA to George Washington Adams, Jan. 9, 1813, AP#415.
385¶1 AA to Mrs. Black, Jan. 24, [1813?], AA to JQA, Feb. 25, April 23, 1813, ESSP to AA, April 7, 1813, JQA to AA, July 19, 1813, JQA, "Memorandum—for my dear wife, Louisa C. Adams," May 7, 1814, enclosed in JQA to LCA, May 7, 1814, AP#415–18; *House Journal*, 13th Cong., 1st sess., May 24, 1813, 3.
385¶2 ESSP to AA, April 7, 1813, AP#415.
385¶3 AA to JQA, April 5, July 1, Aug. 30, Sept. 24, 1813, WSS to AA, June 19, 1813, ESSP to AA, July 12, 1813, MOW to AA, [July 1813?], AP#415–16.
386¶1 AA to HW, July 7, 1813, AA to Julia Rush, [July?] 1813, AP#416.
386¶2 JQA to AA, Jan. 30, 1813, AP#415.
387¶1 AA to LCA, Jan. 12, March 6, June 2, 1810, AA to Thomas B. Johnson, Oct. 3, 1813, AP#409, 416.
387¶2 WSS to AA, June 10, 1813, AA to JQA, Aug. 30, 1813 with enclosures (AAS obituary, hymn "Longing for Heaven"), AP#415–16.
387¶3 AA to George Washington Adams and JA2, Aug. 14, 1813, AA to LCA, Oct. 24, 1813, AP#416; JA to TJ, Aug. [14?]–16, 1813, *AJL*, 2:366.

388¶1 ESSP to AA, Aug. 19, 1813, AA to LCA, Dec. 6–19, 1813, AP#416. In a letter to his mother the following summer, JQA staked out a similar position. He described his continuing anguish at the loss of his infant daughter two years earlier and then added, "If such are my feelings for a child, cut off before the day-star of intelligence could have arisen to announce the dawn of Reason in her Soul; what must be those of a *mother*, for one in whom the mind was at its highest noon . . . ?" JQA to AA, June 30, 1814, AP#418.

388¶2 AA to François Adriaan Van der Kemp, Feb. 23, 1814, AP#417.

389¶1 AA's description of Caroline as "not handsome" appears only in the draft copy of her letter to LCA, not in the copy that was actually sent. AA to LCA, Dec. 6 (draft), 6–19, 1813, AA to HW, March 18, 1814, AA to JQA, Sept. 24, 1811, May 1, June 12, 1814, AP#412, 416–18.

389¶2 HW to AA, March 18, 1814, AA to WSS, March 22, 1814, AA to HW, March 18, 1814, AP#417.

390¶1 AA to WSS, March 22, 1814, AA to HW, March 22, 1814, WSS to AA, April 2, 1814, AP#417.

390¶2 AA to ESSP, Sept. 13, 1814, AP#419.

390¶3 AA to ESSP, Nov. 20, 1814, AP#420. The Bible speaks of a "time to dance" but not of a "time to sing." Ecclesiastes 3:4.

Chapter 33: "I Was Thunder Struck," 1814–1815

391¶1 AA to HW, Oct. 30, 1814, AA to ESSP, Nov. 20, 1814, AP#420; *Bennington News-Letter*, Nov. 7, 1814.

391¶2 AA to ESSP, Nov. 20, 1814, AA to JQA, Nov. 29–Dec. 1, 1814, AP#420; AA to AAS, May 20, 1808, in Forbes, ed., "Abigail Adams, Commentator," 137; AA to AAS, July 31–Aug. 8, 1808, Abigail Smith Adams Papers, Schlesinger Library, Radcliffe Institute, Harvard University; Alexander B. Johnson, *An Inquiry into the Nature of Value and of Capital, and into the Operation of Government Loans, Banking Institutions, and Private Credit* (New York, 1813).

392¶1 AA to HW, Oct. 30, 1814, AP#420.

392¶2 AA to HW, Nov. 3, 1814, AP#420.

393¶1 ESSP to AA, Jan. 17, March 15, 26, 1814, Feb. 13, 1815, AP#417, 421–22.

394¶1 ESSP to AA, March 15, 26, 1814, Feb. 13, 1815, AP#417, 422.

395¶1 AA to JQA, Sept. 7, 1814, AP#419.

395¶2 AA to François Adriaan van der Kemp, Feb. 23, 1814, Van der Kemp to AA, March 15, 1814, AP#417.

396¶1 AA to JQA, Nov. 29–Dec. 1, 1814, AP#420.

396¶2 AA to ESSP, May 12, 1814, Shaw#1, frame 441; ESSP to AA, Jan. 17, 1814, AP#417.

397¶1 AA to HW, Dec. 8, 1814, AP#421.

397¶2 AA to HW, Dec. 23, 1814, AP#421. An inventory of JA's estate conducted after his death in 1826 showed that he owned $5,463 worth of federal bonds issued in 1814 and 1815, but it is not clear when the bonds were purchased, and there is no indication that he bought them at his wife's behest. AP#607.

398¶1 AA to JQA, Feb. 27, 1814, Henry Warren to AA, Oct. 19, 1814, AP#417, 420.
398¶2 JQA to AA, March 30, 1814, April 22, 1815, AP#417, 423.
399¶1 AA to Julia Rush, March 23, 1815, AA to JQA, April 1, 1815, LCA to AA, June 12, 1815, AP#422–24.
399¶2 AA to George Washington Adams and JA2, July 12, 1815, AA to JA2, Aug. 31, 1815, May 21, 1816, AP#425–26, 431.
399¶3 "Memorandum—for my dear wife, Louisa C. Adams," enclosed in JQA to LCA, May 7, 1814, AP#418; LCA to JQA, Nov. 15, 1814, ibid., reel 420.
400¶1 Richard Rush to AA, June 3, 1815, JQA to AA, June 30, 1815, AA to JQA, Oct. 23, 1815, AP#424, 427; AA to Dolley Madison, May 14, 1815, Dolley Madison Digital Edition (http://rotunda.upress.virginia.edu:8080/dmde/).
400¶2 AA to LCA, [ante May 20], 1815, LCA to AA, April 8, 1816, AP#423, 430.
401¶1 AA to Richard Rush, April 24, 1816, AP#430.
402¶1 AA to François Adriaan van der Kemp, April 1, 1816, AA to LCA, [March?] 1816, AP#430.
402¶2 Adelaide Hellen to AA, Dec. 1, 1815, Jan. 3, 1816, AA to LCA, March 20, 1816, AP#428–30.
403¶1 ESSP to AA, Feb. 13, 1815, AA to ESSP, Feb. 28, 1815, AP#422; AA to Abigail Adams Shaw, April 29, 1815, Shaw#1, frame 214.
403¶2 AA to JQA, May 20, 1815, Sept. 11, 1815, May 4–9, 1816, JQA to AA, Nov. 7, 1815, AA to HW, May 5, 1816, AP#423, 426–27, 431; Conrad Wright, *The Unitarian Controversy: Essays on American Unitarian History* (Boston, 1994). In time John Quincy would also become a Unitarian.
404¶1 AA to Abigail Adams Shaw, April 15, 1815, AA to HW, March 15, 1816, AP#423, 430.

Chapter 34: "Dr Tufts Has Always Been My Trustee," 1815–1818

405¶1 AA to LCA, April 14, 1815, AA to JQA, April 11, 1815, AA to HW, April 13, 1815, AP#423.
405¶2 AA to Abigail Adams Shaw, April 29, 1815, Shaw#1, frames 214–15; Abigail Adams Shaw to AA, April 28, 1815, AP#423.
406¶1 AA to JQA, Dec. 24, 1815, AP#428.
407¶1 "Abigail Adams's Disposition of Her Property," Jan, 18, 1816, AP#607; AA and JA, deed to JQA, Aug. 18, 1803, Quincy, Wendell, Holmes, and Upham Family Papers, reel 35.
407¶2 "Abigail Adams's Disposition of Her Property," Jan. 18, 1816, AP#607. JA omitted JQA's three sons from his list of heirs, apparently to balance out their father's privilege of purchasing Peacefield and the surrounding acreage from JA's estate well below the market price.
408¶1 Ibid.
408¶2 Ibid. AA was by no means unique among women testators in favoring her female heirs, though she took that preference to an unusual extreme. Gundersen, *To Be Useful to the World*, 141.
409¶1 "Abigail Adams's Disposition of Her Property," Jan. 18, 1816, AP#607.
409¶2 AA, quoted in Withey, *Dearest Friend*, 311.

409¶3 JQA, promissory note, Aug. 25, 1817, filed with AA to JQA, Jan. 18, 1816, AP#429; AA, quoted in Levin, *Abigail Adams*, 483.

410¶1 JQA to JA, Nov. 2, 1818, *MDF*, 478.

410¶2 JA to JQA, Nov. 10, 1818, *MDF*, 479; JA to TJ, Oct. 20, 181[8], *AJL*, 2:529; HW to [Caroline Smith de Windt], November 1818, AP#445.

411¶1 HW to [Caroline Smith de Windt], November 1818, AP#445.

411¶2 HW to [Caroline Smith de Windt], November 1818, AP#445.

411¶3 HW to LCA, Nov. 18–20, 1818, HW to Caroline Smith de Windt, November 1818, AP#445.

411¶4 JA to JQA, Nov. 10, 1818, *MDF*, 479.

411¶5 LCA to TBA, Jan. 7, March 14, 1819, Ann Adams to JA, Feb. 8, 1819, AP#446.

412¶1 In an August 1817 effort to strengthen his cousin's legal position, JQA had replaced his promissory note to AA with one made out to JA "on account of Mrs Abigail Adams." JQA, promissory note to JA, Aug. 25, 1817, with notes by JA dated Nov. 9, 1818 and by JQA dated Sept. 25, 1819, filed with AA to JQA, Jan. 18, 1816, AP#429; Salmon, *Women and the Law of Property*, 15, 113.

412¶2 LCA to TBA, Jan. 7, March 14, 1819, AP#446.

ACKNOWLEDGMENTS

Abigail Adams understood as well as any of her contemporaries that all seriously ill people needed "watchers" to monitor and nurse them during the critical hours between dusk and dawn. She knew, too, that with rare exceptions, this was women's work, and that no one could do it alone. While it might not be prudent to compare my book to a dying person, I cannot think of a more appropriate way to affirm the extent to which *Abigail Adams* has been a team effort. And I want to thank the book's watchers.

Bridget Westhoven volunteered her time and insight on several crucial projects, and Emily Martha Silkaitis kept exceeding my expectations. I am especially grateful to Kylie Horney, for whom no challenge—not even diplomatically pointing out my numerous errors in the text—was too great. My colleagues in the History Department at the University of Richmond provided helpful suggestions on the short essay that became this book and also covered for me in numerous ways (again). I am especially grateful to Hugh West and Debbie Govoruhk. While I was working on this book, Hugh allowed me to teach several courses based on the life of Abigail Adams, and I benefited from my students' sharp insights. I have acknowledged some of my debts to students in the footnotes, but they actually made many more contributions the paternity or maternity of which I was not able to stop and record amid the chaos of classroom discussion. I am no less grateful for them.

Other University of Richmond colleagues also played critical roles in the production of this book, especially the members of the professional staff at Boatwright Library. It sometimes seemed that Betty Tobias, the interlibrary loan guru, was working full-time on this project, and my friend Jim Gwin, the director of acquisitions, contributed not only numerous books but a babysitter. To the generosity of Ed Snead I owe my ability to read the same newspapers Abigail Adams read in the online America's Historical Newspapers (formerly Early American Newspapers) collection. I received help from numerous other librarians as well, especially Susan M. Anderson at the American Antiquarian Society, Jeffrey Flannery at the Library of Congress, and Tammy Kiter at the New-York Historical Society.

Abigail Adams had two editors and, in effect, two agents. Bruce Nichols provided support when it was most needed. The book benefited not only from Leslie Meredith's remarkable ability to polish prose but her extensive knowledge of a wide range of relevant topics. My unofficial agent, Andy Lewis, found me the official one, Jim Hornfischer (who explained what I was trying to say much better than I ever could), but he did more than that: the whole book was his idea. I also want to thank Donna Loffredo and the sharp-eyed Tom Pitoniak at Free Press for their numerous contributions to the book.

No project I have ever undertaken has depended so heavily upon a single institution—the Massachusetts Historical Society—and I am fortunate that the MHS is a place where extraordinary generosity is an ordinary virtue. Librarian Peter Drummey not only helped me make discoveries but made one of the biggest ones himself. I also received invaluable assistance and instruction from Peter's colleagues Jeremy Dibbell, Megan Milford, and Rakashi Chand, and when the book needed a miracle, Reference Librarian Elaine Grublin nonchalantly produced one. Conrad Wright, director of research, not only supervised the amazing *Colonial Collegians* project (upon which I heavily relied) but went out of his way on numerous occasions to help make this a better book. The entire staff of the Adams Papers has put me deep in their debt, but no one so much as Margaret A. Hogan, the editor of the gold-standard *Adams Family Correspondence*. Without her kind offer to share a large chunk of her team's forthcoming work with me, I could not have made my publisher's strict deadline. Moreover, she shared her vast knowledge of the Adams family with me, again and again setting aside her own work to help me with mine. Thank you, Maggie. I also want to thank the MHS for its public offerings, especially *Adams Family Correspondence* (on which I trust the staff will resist calls for undue haste) and its two amazing online collections: the Adams Electronic Archive and Founding Families.

Catherine Allgor, Linda Kerber, Sandra Van Burkleo, Cynthia Dayton, and Carole Shammas guided me through the arcane world of coverture and, in the process, helped me discover one of the book's primary themes. I am grateful to everyone who provided comments on earlier versions of portions of the book, especially T. H. Breen, Richard Drake, Ann Glick Joseph, Marjoleine Kars, Allan Kulikoff, Jan Lewis, Anne M. Little, Kenneth A. Lockridge, Greg Nobles, and Alfred F. Young.

Generous funding for the book and time to work on it came from the Guggenheim Foundation and the Faculty Research Committee of the School of Arts and Sciences at the University of Richmond. The University and the Society of the Cincinnati in the State of Virginia also provided funding for two meticulous research assistants, and Kylie and Emily join me in saying thanks. The Holton family pulled through for me once again, in a variety of ways; I am especially grateful to my sister, Anne, and father, Linwood, for offering comments on the entire manuscript. And I also want to express my gratitude to our caregivers, Shirley Sylva foremost among them. Finally I want to thank Gretchen Ferris Schoel, who somehow managed to help both the book and me in a host of ways while also taking the lead in raising two virtuoso laughers.

INDEX

Page numbers in italics refer to illustrations.

ABOUT THE AUTHOR

Abner Linwood "Woody" Holton, III, Ph.D. is an associate professor of history at the University of Richmond in Virginia. He has published two award-winning books: *Unruly Americans and the Origins of the Constitution* (2007), a finalist for the National Book Award; and *Forced Founders: Indians, Debtors, Slaves and the Making of the American Revolution in Virginia* (1999). Holton received his B.A. in English from the University of Virginia and his Ph.D. in History from Duke, and is currently an associate professor at the University of Richmond. Holton has received numerous awards, including three from the Organization of American Historians (OAH). His first book, *Forced Founders* (in which he argued that Jefferson, Washington, and other Virginia gentlemen rebelled against Britain partly in order to regain control of Native Americans, slaves, and small farmers), received the OAH's prestigious Merle Curti Award for social history. In 2006, the OAH named Holton one of its Distinguished Lecturers. Holton's article " 'Divide et Impera': The Tenth *Federalist* in a Wider Sphere," was selected by a panel of distinguished scholars for publication in the OAH's *Best American History Essays 2006*. Holton received a Guggenheim Fellowship for the 2008–2009 academic year to write *Abigail Adams* and today lives in Richmond with his wife, Gretchen Schoel, daughter, Beverly, and son, Henry.